D1569571

The Letters of
William Cullen Bryant

IV

Bryant, *c*1862,
by an unknown photographer.

The Letters of
WILLIAM CULLEN BRYANT

Volume IV
1858–1864

Edited by

WILLIAM CULLEN BRYANT II
and
THOMAS G. VOSS

New York
FORDHAM UNIVERSITY PRESS
1984

Printed in the United States of America

Contents

Key to Manuscript Sources   vi

Acknowledgments   vii

Bryant Chronology, 1858–1864   1

Bryant's Correspondents, 1858–1864   3

XIX · Life's Dim Border: 1858   5
     (LETTERS 1007 TO 1054)

XX · The Impending Crisis: 1858–1859   78
     (LETTERS 1055 TO 1122)

XXI · The Cloud on the Way: 1860   133
     (LETTERS 1123 TO 1189)

XXII · Not Yet!: 1861   192
     (LETTERS 1190 TO 1253)

XXIII · From Roanoke Island to Chattanooga: 1862–1863   241
     (LETTERS 1254 TO 1387)

XXIV · His Noblest Strain: 1864   339
     (LETTERS 1388 TO 1509)

Abbreviations and Short Titles   433

Index of Recipients, Volume IV   435

Index   439

Illustrations   between pages 232 and 233

Key to Manuscript Sources Often Cited in Footnotes

BCHS   Bryant Family Association Papers, Bureau County Historical Society, Princeton, Illinois.

BLR   Bryant Library, Roslyn, New York.

ConnHS   Connecticut Historical Society.

CU   Columbia University Libraries.

DuU   Duke University Library.

HCL   Harvard College Library.

HEHL   Henry E. Huntington Library and Art Gallery.

Homestead Collection   The William Cullen Bryant Homestead Collection of the Trustees of Reservations, Cummington, Massachusetts.

HSPa   Historical Society of Pennsylvania.

JHUL   The Johns Hopkins University Library.

LC   Library of Congress.

LH   Longfellow House, Cambridge, Massachusetts.

MHS   Massachusetts Historical Society.

NYHS   New-York Historical Society.

NYPL–Berg   Henry W. and Albert A. Berg Collection, The New York Public Library, Astor, Lenox and Tilden Foundations.

NYPL–BFP   Bryant Family Papers, Manuscript Division, The New York Public Library, Astor, Lenox and Tilden Foundations.

NYPL–BG   Bryant–Godwin Collection, Manuscript Division, The New York Public Library, Astor, Lenox and Tilden Foundations.

NYPL–Bigelow   John Bigelow Papers, Manuscript Division, The New York Public Library, Astor, Lenox and Tilden Foundations.

NYPL–Bryant–Moulton Letters   Letters of William Cullen Bryant to Leonice M. S. Moulton, Manuscript Division, The New York Public Library, Astor, Lenox and Tilden Foundations.

NYPL–GR   Goddard–Roslyn Collection, Manuscript Division, The New York Public Library, Astor, Lenox and Tilden Foundations.

NYSL   New York State Library.

PML   Pierpont Morgan Library.

QPL   Queensborough Public Library.

Ridgely Family Collection   Letters of William Cullen Bryant to Leonice M. S. Moulton, Hampton, home of the Ridgelys, Baltimore County, Maryland.

UTex   Humanities Research Center Library, The University of Texas at Austin.

UVa   The Clifton Waller Barrett Library of the University of Virginia Library.

WCL   Williams College Library.

Weston Family Papers   Letters in the possession of the descendants of the late Byron Weston.

YCAL   Collection of American Literature, Yale University Library.

ACKNOWLEDGMENTS

In addition to the seventy-five institutions and private collections represented in earlier volumes of this edition, Bryant letters from twenty-two further sources appear in this one. Acknowledgment is made, in appreciation of their cooperation, to the libraries of Berea College, Catholic University of America, University of Chicago, Claremont College, Dartmouth College, University of Iowa, Knox College, Lehigh University, Mills College, Princeton University, Scripps College, and Stanford University, and to the American Antiquarian Society, Archives of American Art, British Library, Long Island Historical Society, Maryland Historical Society, Minneapolis Public Library, New Haven Colony Historical Society, Newberry Library, Queensborough Public Library, Redwood Library and Athenaeum, and Western Reserve Historical Society. Other letters have been drawn from four private collections and seventeen printed sources.

The staff members of several institutions have been helpful in other ways in the preparation of this volume: the Alice and Hamilton Fish Library of Garrison, New York; Long Island Historical Society; Mason Library of Great Barrington, Massachusetts; Metropolitan Museum of Art; Nassau County Museum; Nassau County Museum of Fine Art; Nassau County Office of Cultural Development; New York Public Library; Union Theological Seminary; United States Departments of the Army and of State; United States Military Academy Library; and the University of Wisconsin.

Individuals who have offered generous help are George Arms, Edward F. Clark Jr., Leigh Clark, Susan Davis, Marlene L. Drew, Evan M. Duncan, Michael A. Esposito, Susan Forson, Andrew Hilen, Seth Kasten, Betsy Kornhauser, Eric Larrabee, Geraldine Mahoney, Marcia E. O'Brien, Holly Joan Pinto, Clare Ruckel, Constance Schwartz, Edward J. Smits, Robert M. Waggoner, Doris M. Wallsch, and Dorothy Weidner.

For their unstinting help and encouragement, special thanks are due to James T. Callow, Kathleen Luhrs, Andrew B. Myers, Egon Weiss, and the literary heirs of William Cullen Bryant.

Bryant Chronology
1858–1864

1858. January 22–April 30, Frances Bryant ill at Naples. cApril 1, William C. Bryant and Co. publish Frederick Law Olmsted's and Calvert Vaux's *Greensward Plan* for New York's Central Park; 25, is baptized a Unitarian. May–June, sees Nathaniel Hawthorne and Elizabeth and Robert Browning in Rome and Florence. July 21–August 21, travels and visits friends in England. September 2, arrives at New York. cOctober, George Cline becomes Bryant's steward at Cedarmere. November 13, the Bigelows sail for Europe.

1859. February, Parke Godwin rejoins *Evening Post*. April, *Letters of a Traveller. Second Series*; sees Richard Cobden in New York. July, first verse contribution to *New York Ledger*. October 6, death of Charles M. Leupp. November 11, addresses Schiller Festival at Cooper Union; 28, death of Washington Irving. December 2, execution of John Brown. December, death of Theodore Sedgwick III.

1860. February c15, death of Alfred Godwin; 20, death of James P. Cronkhite; 27, introduces Abraham Lincoln at Cooper Union. April 3, gives discourse on Irving. May 16, Republicans nominate Lincoln for presidency. June 10, Bigelows return from Europe; 23, Democrats nominate Stephen A. Douglas for presidency. July, William S. Thayer leaves *EP*. September 24–October 2, visits Boston. October c10–24, visits Mount Savage, Maryland. November 6, election of Lincoln. December 3–5, visits Albany as Lincoln elector; 20, secession of South Carolina.

1861. January, advises Lincoln on Cabinet appointments; 16, Bigelow sells interest in *EP* to Godwin. February?, Charles Nordhoff joins *EP* as managing editor. March 4, inauguration of Lincoln. April c3–17, visits Boston and Cambridge; 12–14, bombardment of Fort Sumter. May 21–cJune 1, visits Illinois. June 21, First Battle of Bull Run. August 14, Bigelow appointed consul general at Paris. September 10–17, visits Sheffield and Great Barrington.

1862. August 7–8, confers with Lincoln in Washington. October?, elected president of New York Medical College.

1863. Elected president of American Free-Trade League. cJune 15–October 5, summers in Bigelow's country house near West Point. July 1–3, Battle of Gettysburg; 13–16, New York draft riots. August 4–5, is restored to Williams College Class of 1813. October 21, speaks at laying of cornerstone for new building of National Academy of Design. December, *Thirty Poems*.

1864. March 9, Ulysses S. Grant becomes Union army commander-in-chief; 25, death of Owen Lovejoy. May 26–June 9, visits Illinois. June 8, renomination of Lincoln; c25, arrest of Isaac Henderson. August c30, *Hymns*. September 2, Fall of Atlanta. October 10, injury of Fanny Godwin in railway accident. November 5, "Bryant Festival" at Century Club; 8, re-election of Lincoln.

Bryant's Correspondents
1858–1864

DURING THIS SEVEN-YEAR PERIOD Bryant addressed at least 619 letters to 187 correspondents. Of these, 503 appear herein. The remaining 116 are mostly unrecovered, but a score or more of those which have reappeared are of little interest and have been omitted.

Though Bryant was in Italy when this volume opens, and remained abroad for nine months thereafter, he did no more extended traveling during the years which followed; the four letters he sent the *Evening Post* in the spring and summer of 1858 were the only ones he wrote for his newspaper, save for one in the fall of 1860. Correspondence with his wife was limited, until the last year of the period, to occasional notes sent from his New York office to Roslyn, or to Great Barrington or Buttermilk Falls on the Hudson River while Frances vacationed there. In the spring of 1864, during his visit to Illinois, and that summer, while Frances traveled with friends through the Adirondack Mountains, Bryant wrote fully half the sixty-six letters addressed to his wife, sixty-two of which have been recovered. There are twenty-two known letters to his daughters Fanny and Julia, and twenty-seven to his brother John, all of which are printed. Correspondence with other members of his Illinois family, several of whom visited the East during the period, was infrequent.

With such old friends as George Bancroft, Richard Dana, and Orville Dewey he kept up a periodic correspondence, sending them a total of forty-one letters, of which thirty-seven have been recovered. Twenty-four went to Robert Waterston, with whom he became intimate at Naples early in 1858; twenty-two of these are included. Other literary acquaintances, such as Emerson, Longfellow, Lowell, Verplanck, Julia Howe, Caroline Kirkland, and Harriet Beecher Stowe, are each addressed in one or two letters. Bryant continued a lively, if occasional, correspondence with women friends of long standing; seven letters to Christiana Gibson and twelve to Leonice Moulton have been recovered. There are ten to artist friends, among whom were Albert Bierstadt, John G. Chapman, George Harvey, John Kensett, Hiram Powers, and Cephas Thompson. Twenty-eight went to publishers, fifteen of them to Robert Bonner and James T. Fields, editors, respectively, of the *New York Ledger* and the *Atlantic Monthly*, wherein Bryant's verses had begun to appear during this period.

Because the presidential election of 1860 and the war years which followed found Bryant more directly involved in politics apart from editorial writing than ever before, many letters of this period were addressed to statesmen—congressmen, senators, cabinet members, and the President himself. Indeed, between 1860 and 1864 he wrote Lincoln more often than anyone else save his wife; of thirty-five known letters, twenty-eight are printed. Eighty went to other political or military leaders, including seven to treasury secretary Salmon P. Chase, five to Secretary of the Navy Gideon Welles, and three to Secretary of War Edwin L. Stanton. Senators William P. Fessenden, Edwin D. Morgan, and Charles Sumner were addressed in a total of fourteen letters.

Bryant's concern over the administration of the national government and its conduct of the war was reflected as well in his personal correspondence. After John Bigelow took a responsible diplomatic post at Paris in 1861, his observations on European reaction to the war in America drew incisive comment from his former editorial partner. Of nineteen known letters to Bigelow, eighteen have been recovered. To Dana, Dewey, Waterston, and other intimate friends, as well as to leading Republican laymen such as John Murray Forbes, Bryant confided his views of politics and the war. And throughout the crucial summer of 1864, while the outcome of battle seemed still in doubt and public figures anguished over whether to replace Lincoln as President, frequent letters to his vacationing wife reflected his doubts and fears, and then his resolution of these in renewed confidence in the administration on whose formation he had exerted a significant influence.

XIX

Life's Dim Border
1858
(LETTERS 1007 TO 1054)

ON THE EVENING OF JANUARY 2, 1858, with his wife, Frances, and her niece Estelle Ives recovering from grippe contracted at Marseilles, Bryant escorted them and his daughter Julia aboard the steamer *Capri* for a three-day passage down the Italian coast to Naples, where, after a vain search for more suitable lodgings, he settled them at the Hôtel des Isles Britanniques on the bay shore. With American minister Robert Dale Owen and his wife in hospitable attendance, the visitors met a sociable group which included the retiring American minister to Constantinople, Carroll Spence, and his wife; the Brazilian minister to Naples and his wife, a Russian princess; the Turkish ambassador; and the British scientific writer Dionysius Lardner, who had lectured on the steam engine in New York in 1842; and they began sightseeing in and around the city.

But within two weeks of reaching Naples, Frances suffered a violent attack of chills and fever, and her husband hurriedly called in a homoeopathic physician suggested by Owen, a Dr. Rocco Rubini. For three months thereafter, as Bryant repeatedly postponed their departure for Rome, Frances kept to her bed with a nervous fever and in almost constant pain, while her husband and Julia relieved each other in anxious attendance night and day. Bryant began gradually to despair of her recovery. Becoming convinced that the location of their hotel on the shore near the exhalations from open sewers, despite its striking vistas of the Bay of Naples, was a major cause of Frances' debility, he managed, toward the close of March, to find a *pensione* on a back street farther from the water, to which he moved his family. From that time until late April, when at the doctor's suggestion Cullen took Frances for a change of air to Castellamare, a resort south of Naples, she gradually recovered.

During the worst of Frances' illness, especially after a frightening relapse in late February, Bryant turned for solace to verse composition. His sense of depression was intensified by cold and rainy weather, and by his learning that the city's mortality rate had been greatly increased by many cases of smallpox and of catahrral, or rheumatic, fever. In the first of his poems written at this time, "The Night-Journey of a River," the gloomy theme is generalized. In the second, "A Sick-Bed," the voice is personalized as that of Frances; the tone, one of pathetic resignation:

> Long hast thou watched my bed,
> And smoothed the pillow oft
> For this poor, aching head,
> With touches kind and soft.

> Oh! smooth it yet again,
>   As softly as before;
> Once—only once—and then
>   I need thy hand no more.
>
> . . . And think of me as one
>   For whom thou shouldst not grieve;
>
> Who, when the kind release
>   From sin and suffering came,
> Passed to the appointed peace
>   In murmuring thy name.

At Castellamare, in May, after Frances' recovery seemed at last assured, Bryant spoke a grateful apostrophe to his wife, in "The Life That Is":

> Thou, who so long hast pressed the couch of pain
>   Oh welcome, welcome back to life's free breath—
> To life's free breath and day's sweet light again,
>   From the chill shadows of the gate of death!
>
> . . . And well I deem that, from the brighter side
>   Of life's dim border, some o'erflowing rays
> Streamed from the inner glory, shall abide
>   Upon thy spirit through the coming days.

On April 23, with Frances gaining daily, the Robert Waterstons, from whom the Bryants had parted at Heidelberg the previous July, arrived with their seventeen-year-old daughter, Helen, from Rome. Bryant at once sought out the Unitarian minister, and they walked together in the Villa Reale, or Royal Park, overlooking the Bay of Naples. Waterston later recalled, "anxiously watching, as he [Bryant] had been doing, in that twilight boundary between this world and another, over one more precious to him than life itself, the divine truths and promises had come home to his mind with new power," and Bryant, confessing that he had never formally joined the church, asked his friend to perform for him, on the following Sunday, the rite of baptism. This Waterston did, in the Bryants' rooms, and afterward the two families took communion together.

During intervals between vigils at his wife's bedside, Bryant had seen much of Robert Dale Owen, reading an early draft of Owen's book on spiritualism, *Footfalls on the Boundary of Another World*, and advising the author "not to seem to bring in question the truth of the Christian miracles." He exchanged calls with American novelist John Pendleton Kennedy, and with former New York governor and United States senator Hamilton Fish, who was then touring Europe with his wife and seven children in two carriages, with a retinue of servants. The Hartford sculptor Edward Bartholomew, living in the Bryants' Naples hotel, died during their week at Castellamare, and Bryant wrote of this sympathetically to the *Evening Post*. Mrs. Robert Sedgwick, widow of an old New York friend, came from Rome with a daughter and two nieces, and Bryant helped them get settled in Naples.

Bryant found a congenial acquaintance in the British art historian Anna Brownell Jameson, once a friend of Fanny Kemble, Ottilie von Goethe, and Lady Byron. She solicited a copy of his poems, and he read with much approval her *Memoirs of Early Italian Painters*. At her urging, he made several efforts to bring her together with the notorious Scottish spiritualist medium Daniel Dunglas Home, long a resident of the United States before returning to Britain to conduct seances attended among others by Sir Edward Bulwer and the Robert Brownings. At length Home appeared suddenly one evening with Owen at the Bryants' lodgings and startled Frances out of slumber.

The Bryants' itinerary after leaving Naples on May 11 follows:

May 11–16: en route Rome via Capua, Tusculum, Terracina, Velletri; 17–28: Rome; May 29–June 3: en route Florence via Città Castellana, Terni, Foligno, Perugia, Arrezzo.

June 4–8: Florence; 9–13: en route Venice via Bologna, Ferrara, Rovigo, Padua; 14–23: Venice; 24–26: en route Turin via Verona, Milan; 27–28: Turin; June 29–July 3: en route Paris via Susa, Lanslebourg, Chambéry, Aix-les-Bains, Mâcon.

July 4–20: Paris; 21–30: London; July 31–August 8: Evesham (excursion to Oxford).

August 9–11: Stratford-upon-Avon; 12–13: Leam; 14–18: Edgbaston (Birmingham); 19–20: Liverpool; August 21–September 2: en route New York.

The Bryant party made a leisurely journey to Rome, first by train to Capua and then in the comfortable carriage of a Neapolitan *vetturino*, Giuseppe Fontana, who had gone ahead to meet them there. Bryant had secured from Dr. Rubini, as a precaution, the names of homoeopathic physicians in Rome and Florence, but, with the exception of a brief upset at Tusculum, the second night out, where the travelers stopped at a little hotel near the ruins of Cicero's villa, Frances continued to gain in comfort. They stopped for two nights on the seacoast at Terracina, resort of the early Roman aristocracy, and leaving there on a lovely morning they listened to the songs of nightingales in elm trees along the way. On the sixth day, passing the lakes of Nemi and Albano, they entered on the newly uncovered Appian Way, and passed rapidly along it to enter Rome, where they settled in pleasant rooms at the Hôtel d'Europe engaged for them by their friend the American painter John Gadsby Chapman.

Bryant was welcomed warmly by the many American artists resident in Rome, visiting their studios and being entertained in their lodgings. Joseph Mozier showed him his statue inspired by Bryant's poem "The Indian Girl's Lament." From Cephas Thompson Bryant bought his copy of Raphael's *Madonna of the Staffa*. He visited a remarkable collection of ancient Roman statuary which had been gathered by the Marquis of Campagna through funds embezzled from a charitable trust of which he was a director, and in repeated letters to his newspaper and to friends expressed a wish it might be brought to the United States.

At Rome Bryant saw Nathaniel and Sophia Hawthorne twice, calling on them one evening, and meeting them at breakfast two days later in the home of sculptor William Wetmore Story. This meeting between poet and novelist was their first, save for a momentary encounter at Lenox, Massachusetts, a decade earlier, when, Hawthorne recalled, Bryant had sat in a wagon, "merely exchanging a greeting with me from under the brim of his straw hat, and driving on." (Earlier than that, Bryant had repeatedly given favorable notices in the *Evening Post* to Hawthorne's writings as they appeared in *The Token*, *The Democratic Review*, and *Twice-Told Tales*.) Now, as Hawthorne's family gathered about the "patriarchal" poet to hear him tell of his travels, Bryant's fellow-author thought "He uttered neither passion nor poetry, but excellent good sense," wearing a "weary look in his face, as if he were tired of seeing things and doing things." Bryant seems to have expressed no impression of Hawthorne, either in diary or in letters, beyond the simple fact of meeting him.

When the young women in Bryant's party had seen enough of Rome, he hired another *vetturino*, and they set out one morning for Florence in a comfortable three-horse carriage, after an evening during which, Bryant noted, "a great number of our friends . . . came in."

Settled in the New York Hotel on the Lung' Arno, Bryant again found old friends, in the sculptor Hiram Powers and his family, and new ones in a Lady Herbert and her lively young ladies, at whose home he met the Irish novelist Charles Lever, "in high spirits and infinitely amusing." Passing an evening with Elizabeth and Robert Browning at their Casa Guidi, Bryant noted, "The talk was of spiritualism, which *he* does not believe in and she does." The Hawthornes, who had preceded the Bryants to Florence, were among the guests. Again, the novelist recorded impressions of his fellow-Yankee, supposing him one who, though probably facing the early death of his wife, yet "cannot get closely home to his sorrow, . . . not having sufficiently cultivated his emotional nature." It seems unlikely that Bryant gave this habitual prober into the secrets of the heart any account of the months of deep concern through which he had lately passed at Naples.

After five days in Florence, the Bryants went on to Venice. Along the way Bryant had a new invalid on his hands, for Estelle Ives had suffered a series of crippling boils, and had to be carried in and out of hotels and restaurants. On her account, the party spent an extra day at Bologna, visiting the university, new municipal library, and art galleries. At Ferrara they saw the house built by the poet Ariosto, and the madhouse where the poet Tasso had been confined in the sixteenth century. Leaving Rovigo, they overtook a carriage containing the historical painter Peter Rothermel and another American artist, young Henry Loop, who would be attentive to the young ladies of Bryant's party in Venice. At Padua they left their carriage and took a train to Venice. Here, while Estelle's disability held them and the other ladies were distressed by the heat, Bryant read Dante and revisited earlier scenes—the Arsenal, celebrated in *The Inferno*, where he found the signs, disappointingly, "Germanized"; the Armenian Convent, in whose visitors' register he saw remarks he had written twenty-three years before; the cathedral; the Doges' Palace; the Academy of Arts; several of the most striking churches—and escorted his companions along canals and across lagoons, where the gondolas' motions caused in Frances "nervous spasms."

Toward the end of June Bryant checked out of the Hotel Danielli after settling a "most extortionate bill" which was "swelled to an enormous size, by charges for ice and lunches of bread and butter, at rates never heard of before," and his party went by rail to Verona, accompanied by Henry Loop. They passed from here quickly through Milan, which Bryant thought depressing under Austrian rule, and, crossing into the Sardinian kingdom, found at Turin a sense of freedom and tolerance which led them to linger for five days. Bryant was pleasantly surprised at the freedom of worship enjoyed by the long-proscribed Waldensian Protestant sect, and, visiting an industrial exhibition, impressed by "the success with which human ingenuity exerts itself when not encumbered with either the restraints or the patronage of the government." He enjoyed long conversations with his guide at the exposition, Lorenzo Valerio, a journalist and liberal member of parliament to whom he had been given a letter.

From Turin to Paris the journey was uneventful. On his arrival there, a letter from John Bigelow told Bryant he had been chosen by the legislature a Regent of the University of the State of New York. But he declined at once, on the grounds, he wrote Bigelow, of his preoccupation with business, and an "aversion to any form of public life now, by long habit made, I fear, invincible." He found Senator Charles Sumner back in Paris, suffering from painful cauterization treatments of his injured spine, and Anna Jameson, lately arrived from Naples. The three saw much of each other, while Frances was distracted by a round of shopping and dressmaking she had set for herself. In Paris Bryant was pleased to find as next-door neighbors the Brownings, whom he saw several times, and Robert gave him a list of convenient small hotels in central London. Bryant looked up several American artist friends, among them the painters Christopher Cranch and Edwin White, whose studios he visited, as he did that of Horatio Greenough's younger brother, and he wrote of their work to the *Evening Post*. He was gratified to learn, in a letter from Isaac Henderson, that the newspaper's May dividend had been the largest ever.

Before leaving France, Bryant put the still-crippled Estelle Ives on the steamer *Vanderbilt* for home, in company with Henry Loop and the Sedgwick girls, booking passage as well for his family on the *Africa* from Liverpool on August 21. On July 20 they crossed the Channel from Boulogne to Dover, and the next morning were lodged in London with a Mrs. Effingham at 41 Jermyn Street, in one of the small hotels recommended by Robert Browning.

On the evening after his arrival Bryant was entertained by his London banker, American-born George Peabody, at a "great dinner party" in the famous Star and Garter Inn at Richmond, celebrated by Dickens, Thackeray, and other writers. The next night he watched the actress Ristori perform as Queen Elizabeth in a poor play with "prodigious spirit." At Edwin Field's home in Hampstead he met a group of unusually interesting Englishmen which included the watercolorist Walter Goodall; Richard Doyle, caricaturist, and illustrator for Ruskin and Thackeray; Henry Cookson, Wordsworth's godson and Master of Peterhouse College, Cambridge; Dr. William Carpenter, a physiologist; and two of the late Samuel Rogers' nephews, one of whom, Samuel Sharpe, was a distinguished Egyptologist. On Sunday he went with Field to hear Hampstead's Unitarian preacher, Thomas Sadler, later the editor of Henry Crabb Robinson's diaries. As was so often the case, he was entertained by resident American artists—in this case, Paul Duggan, Daniel Huntington, and Jaspar Cropsey. At the Cropseys' he heard the British genre-painter William Mulready characterize Pre-Raphaelite painters as "absurd people." Before leaving London Bryant walked several miles out to 5 Great Cheyne Row to "look up Mr. Carlyle," only to learn that that friend of Emerson's was then visiting his native Scotland.

From London the party went on to visit Bryant's old New York hiking companion of years past, Ferdinand Field, who had lately left to his younger brother Alfred the family export hardware business in Birmingham, and moved to Evesham in Worcestershire. A bachelor of forty-nine who would marry the following year, Ferdinand had an attractive house overlooking the Vale of Evesham, with its extensive orchards and market gardens, where he himself was a grower of choice plants under glass. (A decade later Bryant secured publication in New York of Field's horticultural manual, *The Green-House as a Winter Garden.*) Here, for nine days, while Frances rested and slowly gained strength, Bryant walked with Ferdinand and his dog Jack over the hills and along the banks of the Avon, viewed the ruins of the old abbey, with its Norman gateway, splendid sixteenth-century bell tower, and two medieval churches, and visited the battlefield where Simon de Montfort, Earl of Leicester, had been slain by the forces of Prince Edward (later King Edward I) in 1265.

The visitors met and were entertained by a number of Field's neighbors; for the first time, Bryant found himself domiciled in a representative English village. Although he later wrote his host discreetly, "We are certainly much obliged to you for the glimpse it gave us of English social life in the middle class—the most virtuous, I suppose, and therefore the most estimable," he was less guarded in an account to Orville Dewey of his visit: "I cannot say that I much liked the peep into English life which this brief residence gave me. So many sets and classes of people, each jealous of intrusion from below, and anxious to get admission into the class above."

During their stay in Evesham, Bryant and his daughter paid a day's visit to Oxford, where they hired a guide and fly to tour the colleges and visit the botanic garden and the Bodleian Library. They ran across a "blue-stocking" student who talked of American authors, and their guide, whose Shropshire dialect gave Bryant trouble, declared that after thirty years' service to college fellows, he found them now "much better behaved and more studious—more sober and moral."

While at Evesham Bryant heard, in a letter from Robert Waterston, that his daughter, Helen, had died of heart disease at Naples on July 25. He immediately sent a touching notice of her death, given greater poignancy by Frances Bryant's near escape from a similar fate three months earlier, to the *Evening Post.*

Before leaving Ferdinand, the Bryants received an invitation prompted by Edwin Field to visit Mr. and Mrs. Edward Flower at their home, "The Hill," in Stratford-upon Avon, and went there by stage on August 9. Flower, a prosperous brewer and horse fancier, who had spent a part of his youth in Illinois, welcomed American visitors. A few years after the Bryants' visit, as mayor of Stratford, he organized a Shakespeare tercentenary; in 1879 his son Charles Edward Flower, who had also entertained the Bryants, founded the Shakespeare Memorial Theatre. Bryant passed two days with the Flowers "very pleasantly," he wrote Dewey—who had also been their guest and was "freshly remembered in the family"—although his host seemed one of those "who grow more conservative as they grow older, a common case, as Mr. Flower had the good fortune to become rich, which is another makeweight in favor of conservatism."

From Stratford the Bryants moved on to visit other members of the large Field family at Leam. They toured Warwick Castle; the ruins of Kenilworth Castle, immortalized by Walter Scott; and Leicester Hospital, refuge of twelve old soldiers and their wives, where a "plump beery-looking person" tired them with rambling talks about "coats of arms and other nonsense." Bryant walked along the River Leam, observing that it was "polluted with the sewers of Leamington and stinks terribly."

Although Alfred Field had written Bryant regretting that business was taking him to the United States just at the time of their visit, the Bryants were entertained, first at Leam and then in his home in Edgbaston, near Birmingham, by his wife Charlotte, whom they had known intimately in New York since her childhood. Bryant went with Charlotte and others to Leasowes, picturesque eighteenth-century estate of poet William Shenstone; to Aston Hall, supposed model for Washington Irving's "Bracebridge Hall"; and to Lichfield, where he remembered native sons David Garrick and Samuel Johnson, and thought a new statue of Dr. Johnson in the market square "heavy and ungainly."

On August 19 they traveled by rail through the "black country" of the Midlands, past thousands of chimneys pouring smoke and spilling cinders on the open fields and killing shrubs and trees, to Liverpool. Here, after a night at the Adelphi Hotel and a morning shopping in Lord Street, they boarded the *Africa* for the homeward voyage. Among fellow-passengers were Hiram Barney, in 1860 a collaborator of Bryant's in securing the nomination of Abraham Lincoln; Wesley Harper, once a publisher of Bryant's books; and the banker Junius Morgan of Peabody and Company, with his family. The trip was uneventful. On September 2 the Bryants debarked at Jersey City, to be greeted at the dock by Fanny Godwin and her nine-year-old son Willy, as well as by Bryant's partners Bigelow and Henderson. After a night at the Brevoort House in Manhattan, the party went out to Fanny's home in Roslyn.

1007. *To* Buckingham Smith[1]

Naples   January 7th   1858.

My dear sir.

I have this day received your letter of the 14th of December[2] which arrived at Malaga it seems after my departure—I left on the 15th— and was sent by the Consul to this place. Since that time I have at Venturi's desire, asked you to pay him eighteen dollars more—or rather to pay that sum to his wife.[3] I enclose you a draft on Messrs. John Munroe & Co of Paris, who are still my bankers—my friends in America finding it most convenient to place my funds with them, for 196 francs (one hundred and ninety six)— which I think will cover the amount paid at both times, at least according to the calculation given me. Please inform me by letter addressed to the care of these bankers, of its arrival to your hands.

I shall print something about my visit to Granada but not much,—one letter to the E. P. about Malaga and that place,[4] and will send it to you.

I have visited also Oran and Algiers on my way from Malaga to Marseilles. My wife and Miss Ives were half killed by the *grippe* at Marseilles, but are now much better. I had to wait at Marseilles more than a week of cold damp dreary weather, for my wife to recover strength enough to go on board the steamer.

Yours very truly,

WM C BRYANT.

P.S. The ladies, hearing that I am writing this, desire to be very kindly remembered. W C B.

MANUSCRIPT: DuU ADDRESS: To Buckingham Smith Esqre. ENDORSED: Mem / Sold the draft of X 196 to / O'Shea & Co for 753 [vn?] or / $38, less 35/100.

1. Buckingham Smith (1810–1871, Harvard Law 1836), historian, and United States secretary of legation at Madrid, 1855–1858, had been helpful to the Bryant party during their visit to the Spanish capital in October–November 1857. See Letters 987–994.
2. Unrecovered.
3. At Madrid Bryant had hired Carlo Venturi, a former Brazilian artillery captain, to serve as valet to his party on their further travels through Spain and Italy. Bryant, "Diary, 1857–1858," November 3, 1857.
4. See Letters 1001, 1002.

1008. *To* John Bigelow

Naples   January 22, 1858

My dear Mr. Bigelow.

I got your letter of the 28th of December[1] two days since and thank you for the information it contains. The game of politics as it has been played for a few years past is as interesting as a game of whist. It is like some of those games which I used to play when a boy, in this respect, that the principal players form new associations—take new partners and discard old ones, so often that you have not time to get tired of those you act with. I really thought after the success of the democratic party—the Buchanan party, I mean— in New York and in some of the western states, that Republicanism was on the decline; but the enthusiasm with which Douglas's championship of the cause of Kansas has been seconded all over the northwest shows that the heart of the northern people is with those who resist the entrance of slavery into the territories.[2]

What you tell me of Buchanan's unpopularity does not surprize me. The man who could sign the Ostend Manifesto might commit almost any act of folly, or a series of them.[3] When he did that, I thought he had finished himself; I thought he would never be President of the United States. Marcy[4] I have no doubt thought so too, but the intrigues of a set of men who wanted a subservient man in the Executive chair, prevailed, and got him the nomination. He is President, but he is no wiser than when he signed the Ostend Manifesto, and he is in a post where folly has more spectators and a false step leads to more important consequences, and in which a man is at every moment called upon to do some act that gives proof of his real character.

The Evening Post, I think, deserves the good fortune you say it meets with. I see in it, now and then, as I did when I was at home, an article which I say to myself has crept in somehow, that is to say an article which does not quite harmonize with the character of the journal—but it is with journals as with men—*nemo omnibus horis sapit* [no man is wise at all times]. It is conducted with great courage, independence, honesty, and ability—and these qualities deserve and ought to command success. These, however, are not enough, as we have seen, without the latest news, and that it seems to have. I do not know that I have mentioned in any of my letters to you that Mr. Gourlie[5] writes to me that it is "certainly the best paper in New York": an opinion which I cannot but hope will more exclusively prevail.

We have a cold winter here in Naples—snow on Vesuvius; while people in the neighboring region of Calabria, who have been left shelterless by the earthquake, are perishing by cold and famine. About some of the towns, the stench of the dead bodies buried in the ruins infects the air.[6]

I send you a letter about Algeria and shall have another.[7] My wife and daughter desire their kindest regards to you and Mrs. Bigelow—Julia is specially grateful to you—My wife I am sorry to say is still suffering from the *grippe*. Remember me kindly to your wife.

Yours very truly
W. C. Bryant.

P.S. Mrs. Spence, wife of the late minister to Constantinople,[8] now here, desires to be particularly remembered to Mrs. Bigelow.

MANUSCRIPT: NYPL–GR PUBLISHED (in part): *Life*, II, 104–105.

1. MS in NYPL–BG.

2. On December 18, 1857, Illinois senator Stephen Douglas had introduced in Congress an act which proposed to give Kansas settlers the option to decide whether their territory should permit slavery or not. Nevins, *Emergence of Lincoln*, I, 263.

3. In October 1854 James Buchanan, later (1857–1861) President of the United States, but then minister to Great Britain, had met in Belgium with American ministers to France John Young Mason and to Spain Pierre Soulé to discuss American relations with Spain. Here they drew up a recommendation that the United States either buy Cuba from Spain or seize it forcibly. Nevins, *Ordeal*, II, 360–361. In his annual message on December 8, 1857, Buchanan, anxious to placate a strong southern faction in his cabinet and in the Congress, supported the blatantly pro-slavery Lecompton Constitution, which had been adopted for Kansas in November by sixty delegates to a convention, "forty-eight of them from slave states, . . . chosen by a small minority of voters in a rigged election." Nevins, *Emergence of Lincoln*, I, 229. Buchanan's action antagonized the Free Soil wing of his own Democratic party, one leader calling him "just the d----dest old fool that has ever occupied the Presidential chair." *Ibid.*, 239. The *EP* and other Republican papers welcomed an expected "bitter contest between the two wings of Democracy." *Ibid.*, 247.

4. William L. Marcy (873.1).

5. John H. Gourlie (1807–1891). See 653.1. His letter is unrecovered.

6. The earthquake of December 16, 1857—the third most severe of all those recorded in Europe until that time—was of only slight intensity in Naples, but had caused more than ten thousand deaths throughout the Neapolitan kingdom, largely in the southern provinces. Robert Mallet, *The Great Neapolitan Earthquake of December 1857* . . . , 2 vols. (London, 1862), I, vii, 208–210; II, 162–164.

7. See Letters 1003–1004, 1006.

8. Carroll Spence (1818–1896), a Maryland lawyer and legislator, served as United States minister to Turkey from 1853 to 1857, leaving Constantinople in December 1857.

1009.   *To* John H. Gourlie

Naples, January 22, 1858

My dear Gourlie,

I was very glad to get a letter from you some days since, but my pleasure was greatly damped by the bad news you give me of the state of your eyes. I hope it will not be necessary for you to submit to the operation of couching for the malady; or that if it should be, the process, will be attended with as little pain as possible and crouned [sic] with entire success. Leupp writes to me[1] that the cloud which has come over your sight has thrown no shade over your spirits; and this I am very glad to hear;—for serenity and cheerfulness of mind are better than the brightest daylight.

If you have escaped the bad effects of the late panic, and the failures in business, you are, I suspect, an exception to the common fate of Wall Street.[2] There is now and then an example of a soldier who has been in a dozen bloody battles and come off without a wound. You are one of the unharmed veterans of Wall Street, who, instead of boasting of your scars, can utter the prouder boast of having no scars to show. In that warfare, he fights best who brings himself off unhurt.

Of course, I shall, as you suggest, see Chapman[3] at Rome. Since my arrival at Naples I have written to him, but have not yet received an answer. In about a fortnight I expect to go thither, and then I shall learn what he and his brethren of the pencil and chisel are about. I am afraid it has been unsufferably cold at Rome; for here, at Naples, we had snow two or three days ago, and snow lay for some time on the summits and sides of Vesuvius. The houses here are so little fitted to keep out the cold that nobody bears a cold day well. For two or three days the cold here cleared the streets of beggars.

What your friend Mr. Lawrence[4] says is very true, that no part of Europe is more interesting to the traveller than Spain. To what degree I have found it so, you will have seen in the letters I have written for the Evening Post, if you take the trouble to make yourself acquainted with their contents. I have sometimes feared that they would be found too long and minute; but to me, the novelty of the circumstances was such, that I could not help relating them somewhat at large. I ought to have taken more time to see Spain, and should have done so, but for my family who had to make their visit to Italy before our return. So I missed Toledo, and Cadiz and Seville and Cordova, and many other cities of Spain, as well as some entire provinces with which I should be glad to have formed an aquaintance. After all, what is the use of trying to see everything? There will always remain some remarkable spot unvisited; some curious neighborhood unexplored. It is enough to see what [one?] can see conveniently, and to read about the rest. I am content to have seen just a corner or two of Spain; for the rest of it I shall refer to the guide-books and the travellers.

It is for this reason that I am satisfied with the mere glimpse I have had of Algeria. It would have been very well if I could have seen Constantina; it would have been well if I could have seen something of the interior, which is quite accessible by the excellent roads which the French have made, but I had not time, and to repine because I did not see more, would be as foolish as to fret because I do not know Sanscrit.

I have been today at the Bourbon Museum here, and have seen, among the other things recently added to its collection of statuary, a bust of a very handsome Roman woman, which they call a portrait of Faustina, the consort of the Emperor Antoninus.[5] It is manifestly a portrait—the features, however, have a certain degree of regularity, and the mouth and chin are beautifully formed; the expression is at once sweet and dignified; I was much struck with it.

The hotel keepers here, say that they have seen but few American guests this winter; and I do not believe that as many English as usual have visited Italy. A great many Americans, as you know, hurried home, on the news of trouble in the money market. They will come out I suppose next year. St. Peter's won't run away, and Vesuvius stands yet, and so does Naples, though I passed yesterday through a street where the houses had been so shaken and cracked by the late earthquake, that they had been obliged to prop them with beams and posts. There was a great deal of mischief done by the earthquake in Calabria. The number of lives lost by the falling of the houses, is variously stated, and no exact information can possibly be had concerning it under such a government as this; but the American minister here,[6] says that he thinks the probable number is about fourteen thousand. They talk of a hundred and fifty thousand persons left without a shelter in this bitter season; of people perishing by famine, and of dogs feeding on the bodies of the dead.

I am glad you keep up the meetings of the Sketch Club so regularly in these hard times. If I had a pair of seven league boots I think I should come as often as any of you. When you see Leupp, tell him that I am much obliged to him for his letter, and shall answer it soon. I got yours first and therefore answer it first. I am grieved for Durand's loss. John Durand, I perceive, goes on with the Crayon—I hope prosperously.[7]

My wife and daughter desire their best regards. Remember them and me most kindly to your mother and sisters. My wife, in particular, desires me to say to you how much she is concerned for the malady that affects your eyes. Her own health, just now, is not good, in consequence of an epidemic grippe which she was attacked with at Marseilles, but I hope she is mending.

I am, dear Gourlie,
Most truly yours,
W. C. BRYANT.

MANUSCRIPT: Edith C. Gourlie PUBLISHED (*in part*): *Life*, II, 103–104.

1. Charles M. Leupp. See 487.1, 615.5. His letter is unrecovered.

2. The financial panic of October 1857; see 989.3. Gourlie was a New York stockbroker.

3. The American artist John G. Chapman, resident in Rome since 1848. See Letter 526.

4. Unidentified.

5. Faustina the Elder (*c*104–141), wife of Antoninus Pius, Roman emperor, 138–161. This bust, by an unidentified artist, is in the Museo Nazionale, Naples.

6. Robert Dale Owen (1801–1877), social reformer and former Democratic congressman from Indiana. He and his wife were constantly helpful to the Bryants during Frances' long illness in Naples between January and May 1858. Bryant, "Diary, 1857–1858," *passim*.

7. Mary Frank Durand, second wife of Asher B. Durand (214.1; Letter 660), died in 1857. *A. B. Durand, 1796–1886* (Montclair, New Jersey: Montclair Art Museum [1971]), p. 27. Durand's son John (812.1) was joint editor of *The Crayon*, pioneering art magazine.

1010.   *To* Rocco Rubini[1]

Naples   le 26 Janvier 1858.

Mon cher Monsieur

Je me rendit chez vous hier à trois heures, et aujourdhui à deux heures et demie, sans avoir le plaisir de vous trouver chez vous. J'ai voulu vous donner le récit des symptomes de la maladie de ma femme, comme ils sont à present. Les voici.

À douze heures du matin elle commence à avoir froid aux pieds.

Elle a presque toujours des douleurs entre les épaules, et dans le dos, pas piquantes, mais sourdes. —Quelques douleurs aussi dans la poitrine.

Dans l'après midi elle parait avoir, tous les jours, un leger accès de fièvre. L'[urination?] est très frequente et en très petite quantité.

Point d'appetit, point de gout naturel, mauvais haleine.

Mon domestique prendra votre prescription.

J'ai l'honneur d'être &c.[2]

W. C. BRYANT

MANUSCRIPT: NYPL–GR (draft).

1. Since January 22, when Frances Bryant had suffered an attack of chills and fever, Rocco Rubini, a prominent Italian homoeopathic physician, had attended her daily. Bryant, "Diary, 1857–1858," January 22–26, 1858, *passim.*

2. "My dear sir. I went to your home yesterday at three o'clock, and today at two-thirty, without having the pleasure of finding you at home. I wished to give you an account of the symptoms of my wife's illness, as they are at present. Here they are.

"At midnight she begins to have cold feet.

"She nearly always has pains between the shoulders, and in the back, not sharp, but dull. —Some pains also in the chest.

"In the afternoon she seems to have, every day, a slight attack of fever. Urination is very frequent and in very small quantity.

"No appetite, no genuine taste, bad breath.

"My servant will receive your prescription. I have the honor to be, &c."

1011.   *To* Cephas G. Thompson[1]

Naples   January 29, 1858

My dear Sir.

Sometime since—it was I think three weeks I wrote to Mr. Chapman at Rome, saying that I was about to come to that city and asking him various questions to which I have as yet received no answer.[2] I suppose that either he has not received my letter or is sick or absent.

I asked him at what hotel he would counsel me to stop—whether Mrs. Robert Sedgwick[3] and her daughter and nieces were in Rome—and whether he knew of any good suite of rooms that I could have for myself and my wife and two young ladies. I supposed that his long residence in Rome might enable him to answer this later question as well perhaps as any body there. —As I do not get an answer from him will you do me the favor to answer these inquiries—

Since I wrote I have been obliged to change my plans in some degree. Mrs. Bryant who was not well then has been worse since being attacked with a rheumatic fever, which has weakened her very much. Instead therefore of leaving Naples as I expected on the 6th of February I may be obliged to delay my departure for a week longer, perhaps to a still later period.

In regard to the rooms therefore, I do not wish you to give yourself any particular trouble. I would however take it very kind of you if you would take the trouble to see Mr. Chapman and inquire whether he has done any thing in the matter—for I believe I desired him to engage the rooms if they came in his way— As things now stand I cannot afford to leave my pleasant lodgings which are sunny and warm except for rooms in Rome which like these . . .

MANUSCRIPT: NYPL–GR (draft fragment) ADDRESS: To ⟨Giovanni⟩ C. G. Thompson Esqre / painter—Rome ENDORSED (by Bryant): (not sent).

1. An American artist who had worked in Italy since 1852. See 833.9.
2. This letter (unrecovered) was written at Naples on January 15. Bryant, "Diary, 1857–1858," January 15, 1858.
3. Elizabeth Ellery Sedgwick (1790–1862), widow of Bryant's early friend, a New York lawyer, who had died in 1841. See 100.6; Vol. I, 14.

1012.　*To* Isaac Henderson[1]

Naples　　February 1st　　1858.

My dear sir.

I received a few days since your letter of the 4th of January. With respect to the money deposited for my use you have made the best arrangements that the case would admit of. Messrs Munroe & Co. have behaved in the most honorable manner, and have kept me supplied with money, so that I am nearly as well off as if I had a letter of credit. I had rather submit to such trifling inconveniences as arise from not having a letter of credit than to change my banker.

I send enclosed what was at first intended as a letter for the Evening Post, but it turned out so long that I concluded to make two of it. The division—the beginning of the second letter—will be found on the eleventh page. —If I have not made the dates and headings clear I will give them here.

The first letter beginning on the first page is headed "Oran.—Algiers," and dated "Steamer Normandie, off Majorca December 22d 1857." The second, beginning at the 11th page towards the bottom is headed "Algiers—Algeria," and dated "Marseilles December 29 1857."[2] I hope they will be printed with fewer mistakes than my two last, the sense of which was in two or three places perverted by errors of the press.—

I received with your letter *two* copies of a pamphlet entitled "State Bonds." The expense of postage in their coming to Naples was considerable and I beg you will see if you can help me escape being taxed in this way hereafter. One copy is enough—and that I could have done without till I got back to New York. . . .

MANUSCRIPT: NYPL–GR (draft fragment) ADDRESS: To Isaac Henderson Esq.

1. Business manager and third proprietor of the *EP*. See 806.1, 882.3.
2. Letters 1004 and 1006.

1013.   *To* John G. Chapman

Naples   February 22nd   1858.

Dear Mr. Chapman.

My wife, I am sorry to say, is no better, and it may be some time yet before we are able to leave Naples. Her complaint was a rheumatic fever, and now that the fever has abated she is extremely weak—so weak in fact as to occasion me great anxiety. Her recovery of her former strength must be very slow, and I shall fear a relapse as something like a relapse has already taken place. Will you do me the favor to go to the post office, or send and have all the letters and papers which may come to Rome, addressed to me or to Miss Estelle Ives[1] who is of my family sent to me under cover to his Excellency Robert Dale Owen, Minister of the United States at Naples. He suggested himself that I should do this, and then if any of them should come into his possession, after I leave Naples they will be sure to be forwarded to me. I enclose a little note addressed to the post master at Rome,[2] which I hope will be sufficient. When I am ready to come to Rome I will stop them two or three days beforehand.

I have heard nothing in particular from our friends in America since I wrote to you. . . .

MANUSCRIPT: NYPL–GR (draft fragment).

1. Julia Bryant's Great Barrington cousin and companion on this journey; see Vol. III, 313.
2. This letter (draft in NYPL–GR) asked that mail for the Bryants and Estelle Ives be forwarded to Naples in care of Robert Dale Owen.

1014.   *To* Elizabeth Ellery Sedgwick

Naples   February 26, 1858.

My dear Mrs. Sedgwick.

Your letter of the 23d came to my hands yesterday.[1] I thank you for the interest you express in regard to my wife's health and so does she. Since the letter which Mr. Rogers read to you[2] she has been worse; the rheumatic or catarrhal fever suddenly changed to a nervous fever—with stupor, and extreme weakness and we were quite alarmed, but this form of the disease was soon overcome, and she is now gradually getting better. It is impossible to say yet when we shall begin our journey to Rome, though the Doctor, a homoeopathist of course, thinks she may be well enough to travel in the course of a week. She will be much disappointed if she should not forgather as the Scotch say with you and your daughter somewhere in Italy. She has talked a great deal about meeting you. We heard from New York that you were to pass the winter in Naples, and the first thing we did on arriving here was to set on foot inquiries concerning your whereabouts.

Now as to the inquiries you made concerning Naples. There has been no earthquake here since we arrived, which was on the 5th of January; and nobody entertains the apprehension that any is likely to occur. Indeed there is no more apparent reason to dread an earthquake now than there was last year at this time. There is no typhus fever in Naples. The gastro-rheumatic or catarrhal fevers which prevail do it is true sometimes run into the typhoid type—but my physician assures me that of what is properly called typhus there is none. The fever which prevails, has, however, been exceedingly destructive, principally among the poorer class who have no comfortable habitations in cold weather. Two or three weeks since I was told by Dr. Bishop an English physician who has lived with his family for some years past at Naples that the deaths amounted to two hundred daily; while the usual average number was seventy. But last night Dr. Rubini told me that the deaths were now from three to four hundred daily, while he made the average ordinary number eighty. These are not all by fevers; bronchitis carries off a great many, as well as other diseases that arise from exposure to extreme cold weather—and the cold has been such as nobody in Naples will own having experienced before. At one time since my arrival it drove the beggars from the streets, and the lazzaroni crept into unknown corners and chinks—many of them into their graves. I miss some beggars that were troublesome when I first arrived. It was dry cold weather, such as we might call wholesome in New York, but it swept off the people in shoals to the Campo Santo; the Italians rejoiced when the south wind and showers came again, yet the streets are still full of funerals. Then as to the small pox; your letter was the first intimation that I had of its existence here; but on inquiring of Dr. Rubini I find that it has been here and has been very fatal attacking even those who have been vaccinated—but it no longer exists in Naples proper, though there are yet cases of it in Posilipo and the country surrounding it. It was brought here by Swiss soldiers re-cruited for the Neopolitan service.

To sum up—there is nothing in the *earthquake* to keep you away and nothing in the typhus fever; and as to the catarrhal fevers and the bronchitis, Dr. Rubini thinks there is no occasion for dreading them at this moment. The temperature has been softening from day to day and is now comparatively vernal; the apricot trees are in bloom, and we have no fire in our rooms except on rainy days, which are esteemed the wholesomest winter weather in Naples. But as to the small pox Dr. Rubini hesitates— although homoeopathy has its preventions, he thinks it better to be where it is not.

Should you come you must judge for yourself whether it is best to take lodgings on any of the streets along the shore of Naples—which are the pleasantest parts of the city—but which have a bad reputation—so the American Minister tells me—for their effect on persons of susceptible nerves—so much so that some owners of houses and palaces on the Chiatamone Vittoria and Chiaia do not reside in them, but find it necessary to go a little back. Some think this effect arises from the proximity to the sea but I should ascribe it— if it really exists to the mouths of the sewers which here empty themselves into the bay.

I hope that we shall get to Rome before you leave, but if we do not that we shall not miss you by being on the road at the same time with you. The only question about your coming here at present is identical with the question whether you are afraid of the small pox in a neighborhood in which it must be acknowledged to exist though its ravages have become circumscribed.[3] It has been made more fatal, I am told by the error of the allopathic physicians, who mistook it for catarrhal fever and sought to relieve the patients by bleeding.

My wife desires her best love to you and your daughter as do I.

W   C   Bryant

MANUSCRIPT: NYPL–GR (draft) ADDRESS: To Mrs. Elizabeth Sedgwick — Rome.

1. Letter unrecovered.
2. On February 4 Bryant had sent a letter (unrecovered) to John G. Chapman by Charles H. Rogers of New York, who left Naples that day with his family for Rome. Bryant, "Diary, 1857–1858," February 4, 1858.
3. Mrs. Sedgwick, a daughter, and two nieces, reached Naples the day after this letter was written, not having received it before they left Rome. Bryant, "Diary, 1857–1858," February 27–28, 1858. It is uncertain which of Mrs. Sedgwick's four daughters was with her.

1015.   *To* Robert Dale Owen[1]

Naples   March 13th. 1858

My dear sir.

After I went home yesterday I found in a New York paper of the 17th. of February which I borrowed of Governor Fish[2] the paragraph which I have copied on the other half of this sheet, and which furnishes me with the name of the mental epidemic which once prevailed in Kentucky. It was called "The Jerks"—and appears to be now revived.[3]

Yours truly

WM C. BRYANT

MANUSCRIPT: Redwood Library and Athenaeum.

1. Much interested in spiritualism, Owen had asked Bryant to read early chapters of what was to be his *Footfalls on the Boundary of Another World* (London, 1860). Returning the manuscript, Bryant had cautioned Owen "not to seem to bring in question the truth of the Christian miracles." Bryant, "Diary, 1857–1858," March 11, 12, 1858.

2. Former New York governor Hamilton Fish (Letters 774, 776) spent the winter of 1857–1858 traveling with his family in Europe. Nevins, *Fish*, I, 68–69. On February 23, 1858, Fish, then staying at the Vittoria Hotel, called on Bryant, and thereafter the two, who had been acquainted in New York, saw each other from time to time as long as the Fish family remained in Naples. Bryant, "Diary, 1857–1858," February 23–24, March 4, 13, 1858, and *passim*.

3. This description of "The Jerks" is unrecovered.

1016.   *To* John G. Chapman

Naples   April 8th   1858.

My dear Mr. Chapman.

I write to request you not to give yourself any more trouble in regard to my letters and papers which you have been so obliging as to forward to me hitherto. Mrs. Bryant is now so well that she takes a drive every day and I hope in a few days to set out for Rome. We shall of course make easy journeys.

I removed her a fortnight since from the Chiaja which is proverbially unwholesome for rheumatic and nervous patients to a back street—but still in a very sunny situation and this effect I think has been very beneficial.[1] There is nothing of the disease now left but debility.

As to lodgings I do not wish you to give yourself any trouble on my account. We shall probably go to the Hotel d'Amerique at first— and as I shall not stay at Rome so long as we at first intended we shall probably pass all our time in an hotel.

My regards to Mrs. Chapman and the younger branches of your household—

Very truly

W   C   B

MANUSCRIPT: NYPL–GR (draft).

1. Reaching Naples on January 5, the Bryants took lodgings on the 7th in the Hôtel des Isles Britanniques on the Via Vittoria, near the Riviera di Chiaja. On March 24 they moved to the Pension d'Europe on the Strada Santa Teresa, several blocks farther from the water. Bryant, "Diary, 1857–1858," January 7, March 24, 1858.

1017. *To* Alfred and Charlotte Field[1]

Naples   April 18th   1858

My dear friends.

My wife not being able to write I am employed as her deputy. She bids me say that she received your very kind and friendly letters[2] in due season and that they should have been answered long ere this but for a long illness, from which she is slowly recovering. She was attacked with the catarrhal fever of last winter at Marseilles, where it was epidemic towards the end of December last. Being a little better we brought her to this city where we thought she would recover rapidly and she really seemed in the way of getting well for a few days, but it happened that we arrived at the beginning of an extremely cold interval severe beyond almost what any body remembers in Naples and accompanied by fatal complaints which have swept off the Neapolitans like the cholera—sometimes four hundred a day. Here she got the Naples epidemic, which after a time put on typhoid symptoms and kept her low for a long time. We intended to pass no more than a month in this place and then go to Rome, but we have already been here four and so slowly does my wife regain her strength that we cannot yet fix upon the day of our going. We should have been halfway to England by this time, if our original plan could have been put in execution. When we shall get there we do not pretend to guess. We must travel slowly; we must stop long enough at the most northern cities of Italy to let Julia and Miss Ives see what they contain most worth looking at, and we must get home some time towards the end of summer. It still is our hope to be able to avail ourselves of your kind invitation to pass a few days with you at Birmingham. My wife desires it very earnestly; it was one of the inducements with her to cross the Atlantic, and if by any possibility she should miss that pleasure she will return to America very much disappointed.[3]

The weather has now become very fine; the spring is always a glorious season in Naples, and this is the time when the orange trees are not only full of ripe fruit but fragrant with blossoms; the blossoms I assure you are much sweeter than the fruit. The fields are full of leaves and blossoms, for they are every where planted with fruit trees among which the crops of pulse and grain are already ripening. Naples, however, has long been a dull place to us, so earnestly have we desired to leave it. The girls have seen almost every thing worth seeing in the city and its neighbourhood, and have enjoyed themselves as well as the sharp weather and a sick friend to look after would allow them. We have had a homoeopathic physician Dr. Rubini, who has a great reputation here and who I believe has treated Mrs. Bryants case judiciously.

So much for ourselves. We were distressed to hear the bad news which your letter gave us.[4] My wife's eyes filled with tears when she read it. It is the thing which we most dread in parting from those we love to go even for a short time into another country that some of them we may perhaps never see again. I hope the time will arrive when you both may see that a residence in America is safe for your health and that of your children and that we shall see all your household settled there. But whether it is to be or not we shall always cherish in our hearts a warm esteem for you all. Your little girl by this time is I suppose almost grown up—I forget her age but I know that these little things grow in beauty and wisdom while we are rapidly growing old.

My wife desires her best love to you both and Gods blessing upon you and your children— My daughter sends her love and Miss Ives thanks you with all her heart for your hospitable invitation.

When we come to Birmingham we shall expect to see your brother Ferdinand[5] also, and I shall write to him to let him know that we mean to inflict a visit on him. . . .

MANUSCRIPT: NYPL–GR (draft) ADDRESS: To Mr & Mrs Alfred Field. PUBLISHED (in part): Life, II, 105–106.

1. After long residence in New York, the Fields (406.5) had returned to England in 1854 and settled at Edgbaston, a suburb of Birmingham. See Charlotte Field to Frances Bryant, October 13, 1854, William Cullen Bryant II.
2. Charlotte Field to Frances Bryant, December 7 [1857]; Alfred Field to Frances Bryant, December 9, 1857, William Cullen Bryant II.
3. The following August the Bryants visited the Fields at Edgbaston. Bryant, "Diary, 1857–1858," August 14–19, 1858; Letter 1055.
4. In her letter of December 7 Charlotte had reported the recent death of her youngest child.
5. Ferdinand E. Field (209.10, 545.22) was now living at Evesham, Worcestershire.

1018.   To Robert C. Waterston[1]

Naples   April 23, 1858.
Friday morning.

My dear Mr. Waterston.

I wish to speak with you this morning before you go out. At what hour shall I call?

My wife, I am glad to be able to say, is a little better this morning. She is much obliged to Mrs. Waterston for the beautiful flowers sent her, and bids me thank her for them.

We hope your daughter is well enough to see some of the sights of Naples this fine day.

Very truly yours
W. C. BRYANT

P.S.—A verbal answer will *answer*
W. C. B.

MANUSCRIPT: UVa.

1. On April 23 Robert and Anna Waterston (425.1), with their daughter, Helen, from whom the Bryants had parted at Heidelberg the preceding July, arrived in Naples from Rome. Bryant, "Diary, 1857–1858," July 20, 1857; April 23, 1858.

1019.   *To* Robert C. Waterston

Naples   April 29th. 1858

Dear Mr. Waterston.

My wife is not able to write a note yet, and therefore employs my hand. She bids me beg that you will do her the favor to accept the little View of Naples which you will receive with this, as a sort of memorial of the pleasant Sunday of the 25th. which we passed in company with your family.[1] The view is painted on silk by an artist of this city, Signor Romano,[2] and the silk is afterwards attached, by a wash gum arabic, to the underside of a convex plate of glass, through which it is viewed. She would have sent it before, but the artist has only finished it today, and she now sends with it her love to you all.

With kindest regards to the ladies, who, we hope, have by this time seen Pompeii, and are none the worse for the fatigue,

I am, dear sir,
very truly yours,
W. C. BRYANT.

MANUSCRIPT: UVa.

1. On that day the Waterstons came to the Bryants' lodgings where, at Bryant's request, Rev. Waterston baptized him, his daughter Julia, and Estelle Ives, and afterward, Bryant recorded, "all, my wife included, partook of communion." "Diary, 1857–1858," April 25, 1858. Twenty years later Waterston recalled that on the Saturday before, as they walked together in the Villa Reale overlooking the Bay of Naples, Bryant said "he had never united himself with the Church, which with his present feelings he would most gladly do. He then asked if it would be agreeable to me to come to his room on the morrow and administer the Communion, adding that, as he had not been baptized, he desired that ordinance at the same time." *Tribute to William Cullen Bryant at the Meeting of the Massachusetts Historical Society, June 13, 1878* (Boston: John Wilson & Son, 1878), pp. 8–9.
2. Not further identified.

1020.   *To* Robert C. Waterston

Castellamare   April 30. 1858.

Dear Mr. Waterston.

I write this between four and five o'clock in the afternoon. The train left Naples at a quarter past eleven and brought us to Castellamare in an hour—one hour of pleasant railway travelling—all of us the better for the excursion, with famous appetites which we satisfied with an early dinner.

My wife bore the journey exceedingly well—better than we feared she would. The fatigue passed away with a short nap and she is even better than she was yesterday. We are at the Albergo Reale or Hotel Royal on the hill among the gardens, and not far from the palace of Quisisana, the grounds of which are said to be very fine. I have just returned with the girls from a walk in the fields adjoining the house—the path is pretty and winds by the side of grassy ravines and the shore and mountain views are wonderfully fine. I wish with all my heart you and Mrs. Waterston and Helen were here to enjoy them—and well enough to take the same walk without fatigue. There are yet several vacant rooms in the house—pleasant but not well furnished— There are no carpets but my wife has a drugget for the parlour and another by her bed. Two days since there was almost nobody at the house—yesterday several guests came and took all the first floor; today others have arrived, and today has come the Prince of Syracuse, the Kings brother,[1] who is lodged beside us on the third floor. We hope to hear better news of your daughter's health, and of the entire restoration of Mrs. Waterston from the indisposition of the beginning of the week and nothing could delight us more than to hear the tidings from your own lips in this very place.

My best regards to the ladies— My wife and the girls desire their love to you all.

Very truly and sincerely
yours
W. C. BRYANT

MANUSCRIPT: UVa ADDRESS: Al Signore / Il Signor R. C. Waterston / Albergo Vittoria / Napoli.

1. Ferdinand II (1810–1859) was king of the Two Sicilies, which included Naples, from 1830 to 1859.

1021.   To Robert C. Waterston

Castellamare[1] May 2d   1858. (Sunday Evening)

Dear Mr. Waterston.

My wife thinks it would be well that you should know how comfortably we made the journey from Naples to this place. The most fatiguing part of it to her was that from the hotel to the railway station, and the whole of it from the time we parted with you was performed in about two hours. The first class cars on the railway we found are exceedingly comfortable; they are quite spacious, and furnished with cushioned seats against the wall on each side and at each end, leaving a large clear space in the midst and affording every faculty for reclining. My wife lay down after we had proceeded about half the distance and very nearly had a nap.

It may be useful to you to know that the waiting room for first class passengers at the Naples station is beyond all the others, and furthest from the entrance. It is well furnished with seats. My wife dwells upon the convenience which she found in being able to step from the platform at Castellamare, without any climbing directly into the carriage that brought us to the hotel.

We like Castellamare the better as we see more of it. Yesterday the girls took a long donkey ride to the summit of Monte Coppola, through the chestnut woods, among the rocks and glens gay with wild flowers, and I walked. The top of the summit overlooks the broad rich plain, studded with cities and villages, between this place and Vesuvius. My wife is constantly gaining strength and seems to derive essential benefit from the change of air, though today is rainy and damp and the house is not so warm as the one we left at Naples. The rest of us are all well and my wife's recovery puts us in good spirits.

We are all anxious to hear how your daughter gets on and regret that you could not have passed the day with us here. The want of quiet rest Friday night we trust was amply made up to Helen by the repose of the night following. If you do not come to us very soon we shall rely upon you to write. My wife and the girls desire their kind love to you all. My regards to Mrs. Waterston and the patient who I hope begins to doubt her right to that name.

Faithfully yours
W. C. BRYANT.

MANUSCRIPT: UVa.

1. Bryant mistakenly dated this letter at Naples.

1022.   *To* Robert C. Waterston

Castellamare   May 5, 1858.

Dear Mr. Waterston.

The day is so fine that we have not been without hope of seeing you this morning; but your failure to come is an unpleasant symptom, and we fear that your daughter's recovery is so slow, that the moment you find her well enough to go any where, you will go on board the steamer that is to take you to Leghorn.

My wife continues to improve, not exactly with rapidity, but faster than when she was at Naples. It is *now* our intention to leave this place for Naples on Friday morning—the day after tomorrow—that is to say, if my wife continues to improve as she has done. At Naples, we shall look out for a vetturino with a comfortable carriage, and if we find one, and my wife is strong enough, we shall set out on Tuesday for Rome. This is our plan, which circumstances may compel us to vary.

The girls have had a fine time here; they are off this afternoon on a little excursion on horseback. My wife has taken several drives—this morning we took her to a village three or four miles off, where we all witnessed the manufacture of macaroni, in which my wife was much interested. The village is close by the mountains, on the way from this place to Salerno, though not on the main road; the people look healthy and comfortable for this region. We found the principal streets spread with great canvas sheets covered with wheat drying and hardening in the sun, and on each side, along the walls of the houses, hung quantities of macaroni drying also.

We shall be much disappointed to miss your visit to this place. You would have been pleased with it—you and Mrs. Waterston—and I am sure the air would have done Helen good, if you could have got her here. We shall, however, see you at Naples, if you are not on your journey when we arrive. Whether you have set out or not, we hope it will not be on account of any thing discouraging in the symptoms of your daughter's complaint, that you remain.

My wife sends her love—and the girls would theirs if they were in—to you all. "A thousand expressions," as the Spanish say, to Mrs. Waterston and Helen, "on my part"—and believe me,

Very faithfully yours
W. C. BRYANT

MANUSCRIPT: UVa ADDRESS: Al Signor / Il Signor R. C. Waterston / Hotel Vittoria / Napoli.

1023. *To* Mary Jane Robinson Owen[1]

Rome   May 17th   1858.

My dear Mrs. Owen.

I write to you as women have the credit of being most sympathetic. You will be glad to hear that we are safely arrived at Rome, Mrs. Bryant being stronger at the end of the journey by a great deal than when she set out. At Terracina Julia had an attack a little like cholera morbus in consequence of which we lay by one day— Yesterday we reached Rome after one of the easiest and pleasantest journeys that I can imagine, and today is to be devoted to seeing the wonders of the place.[2]

We shall always remember with pleasure the kindness shown to us by yourself and Mr. Owen—my wife in particular cherishes a loving recollection of your sympathy —The girls are well and join her in kindest regards to you both. Excuse the brevity of this letter—I have little leisure to write, as our stay here will not be long, and we have a flood of letters from America to answer. Remember us kindly to Mrs. Marsden. Tell Miss Brewster that we miss her sweet voice greatly,[3] although on our way we have had in places a perfect chorus of nightingales.[4]

Yours very truly
W C BRYANT.

P.S. If you should see Dr. Rubini remember us to him.

MANUSCRIPT: NYPL–GR (draft).

1. First wife of Robert Dale Owen (1009.6). They were married in 1832, and she died in 1871.

2. On May 16 the Bryant party had settled at the Hôtel d'Europe in Rome, after a five-day journey by hired carriage from Capua, to which they had gone by rail from Naples on May 11. Bryant, "Diary, 1857–1858," May 11–16, 1858, *passim*.

3. While at Naples the Bryants had met through the Owens a Mrs. Marsden, and a Miss Brewster who sang, Bryant noted, "with feeling and a fine voice." She set to music his poem "The Wind and Stream" (1857) and his "Song" from the Spanish of José Iglesias de la Casa (1835). Bryant, "Diary, 1857–1858," January 8, March 24, May 10, 1858; *Poems* (1876), pp. 338–339, 214–216.

4. When leaving Terracina, on the seashore about seventy-five miles south of Rome. Bryant, "Diary, 1857–1858," May 15, 1858.

1024. [*To* Whom It May Concern]

[Rome, *c*May 17, 1858]

. . . I have employed Giuseppe Fontana to convey myself and my family from Naples to Rome. He served me generally speaking to my satisfaction having good horses a clean spacious and easy carriage, and being a careful driver, and performing the journey in the time specified.[1]

MANUSCRIPT: NYPL–GR (draft).

1. This journey cost Bryant fifty dollars and the hotel expenses of his party. Bryant, "Diary, 1857–1858," May 10, 1858.

1025. *To* John Howard Bryant

Rome   May 18, 1858

Dear Brother.

I have just arrived at Rome, where I found your letter,[1] and I answer it immediately though my answer will not leave this place for a few days yet, it being now Tuesday, and Saturday being the day for mailing letters for America. I got a letter from Mr. Bigelow sometime since at Naples in regard to this very matter—or perhaps this letter was from Mr. Henderson, and I answered it in such season that he must have heard from me by this time. I consent that the money should be lent to you, if the firm of W. C. Bryant & Co. has it to spare, and I will stand security to the firm for its repayment. The only thing which made Mr. Bigelow and Mr. Henderson hesitate to lend it, I presume, was that they knew me to be well acquainted with the state of your affairs and desired my responsibility for the repayment. This I have given them, and I hope you will have got the money before you get this.[2]

We have had an unfortunate winter of it. My wife was confined with a long sickness by which we were detained in Naples more than four months. She had the grippe at Marseilles the last week in December. It was at that time very prevalent in France and very severe. As soon as she seemed a little better and able to bear the voyage we took her to Naples by the steamer. Here, for a few days we thought her getting well, but Naples was at that time very unhealthy, a sort of catarrhal or rheumatic fever prevailing, and while she was yet weak with the attack she had suffered at Marseilles, she was seized with the Naples fever. We were obliged to call in a physician, a homoeopathic one, of course. She was brought quite low, and at one time we feared for her life, but happily she turned the corner, and began to recover, but so slowly that the Doctor said that hers was the slowest convalescence that he had ever known in homoeopathic practice. As soon as she could be moved we had her taken in a sedan chair to other lodgings, for those we were in were situated, though in the pleasantest and apparently most desirable, yet in the most unwholesome part of Naples. At length she was well enough to take short drives, and we went with her to Castellamare, a pleasant and healthy place on the mountain side by the seashore south of Vesuvius, where we passed a week much to her advantage. Our next move was to Rome which we have reached by easy journeys that have seemed to do Frances a great deal of good. We cannot stay here long as the weather is becoming warm, and we want to go to England, whence we shall in all probability sail for the United States sometime in August. We regret much not to have been able to pass more time in Rome—as it was our original intention to do.

You have read I suppose the account of our journeys in Spain, as I gave it in letters written for the Evening Post. They contain about all I could say concerning the country. Our visit to Spain was an exceedingly interesting one, though the facilities for travelling are not much better than they are between Illinois and Oregon. Since I left Spain I have been very much occupied with taking care of Frances. I am inclined to think that if she had had an allopathic physician I should not have brought her alive out of Naples and that for her recovery I have to thank the gentle methods of the new system.

Naples is the same noisy place, full of beggars and blackguards that it was twenty three years ago, when I first saw it,[3] and it is just as badly governed. There is no salvation that I can see for the people of the Two Sicilies, as the kingdom is called, but in the chance of having a good king. The people seem to me too demoralized and ignorant—all classes being ignorant of what would be most important for them to know, to be better governed under a freer form of government than they now are—perhaps, however, it would not be worse.

Rome certainly *looks* better with every visit I pay to it. The streets are cleaner and there is always some new public work completed for the embellishment of the city or the convenience of those who inhabit it. Mr. Chapman, the artist, also tells me that the police is better than it was, and he thinks the people are growing more intelligent. It does not appear to me however that much is gained by the increase of intelligence unless the people are admitted to some share in the administration of public affairs. If they are not the increase of intelligence makes them discontented restless and unhappy.

I have been watching with interest the proceedings of Congress in the Kansas affair, but the moment the House agreed to a Committee of Conference with the Senate I took it for granted that a majority for the Lecompton constitution had been bought over.[4] The question is settled before this time, but as my newspapers from New York are only to the 24th of April, they leave the matter yet in the hands of the Committee. Whatever Congress may do, the free state party are destined eventually to triumph.

Frances desires me to say that the only reason she has not written to you is that she is not well enough. She sends a great deal of love to you and your family and to all our friends in Princeton. Julia also desires her love. We regret that we cannot be of service to Julian[5] in New York, as we should be if we were at home. Remember me kindly to your wife and Elijah.[6] I shall be very glad to hear from you again, with every particular about our friends in Illinois which you think proper to communicate.

Yours affectionately
& truly
W. C. BRYANT

MANUSCRIPT: NYPL–GR PUBLISHED (in part): Life, II, 109–110.

1. Unrecovered.

2. John had written John Bigelow in mid-March asking for a two-year loan of three or four thousand dollars from *EP* funds. Bigelow felt that the paper could afford this without inconvenience. Bigelow to Bryant, March 22, 1858, NYPL–BG.

3. Cullen and Frances had spent three weeks at Naples in May 1835. Vol. I, 7; Letter 302.

4. After the House of Representatives had defeated the Lecompton Constitution (1008.3) on April 1, 1858, the pro-slavery Senate majority requested a conference committee, and "the Administration whips in Congress had to use *every* conceivable form of magic—more offices, more contracts, more army commissions, more money—to gain over the three or four anti-Lecomptonites they needed to save the President from utter humiliation." Nevins, *Emergence of Lincoln*, I, 297.

5. Julian Edward Bryant (1836–1865), second son of Arthur Bryant.

6. John Bryant's son Elijah (1835?–1892).

1026.   *To* the EVENING POST

Rome, May 21, 1858.

I have one or two things to say of Rome which may furnish matter for a short letter.

Rome has its rich collections of ancient art in the Vatican, but there is a still richer museum in the earth below. The spade can scarcely be thrust into the ground without turning up some work of art or striking upon some monument of the olden time. Most of the fine statues in the public galleries have, I believe, been discovered in digging to lay the foundations of buildings; and who can tell what masterpieces of Greek sculpture are yet concealed under that thick layer of rubbish which overlies the ancient level of the city—what representations of

"The fair humanities of old religion"[1]

are waiting the hour when they shall be restored to daylight and the admiration of the world—prostrate Jupiters, nymphs with their placid features and taper limbs imbedded in the mould, and merry fauns that have smiled for a thousand years in the darkness of the ground!

The present government of Rome is turning its attention to the excavation of those spots which promise most. As I was passing, the other day, in a street leading towards the Colosseum, in company with an American artist residing here, he said, pointing to certain ancient columns, the lower part of which stood deep in the earth: "The Pope[2] wants to dig about these columns, but the spot is leased, and he cannot. If it were but in the possession of those who own the fee he might take it, but he cannot interfere with a lease. At the foot of those fine old columns he would probably find something worth his trouble."

This passion for excavation has been fortunately gratified elsewhere. If you look at Sir William Gell's Map of the Environs of Rome,[3] you will see traced, from near the gate of St. John towards Monte Cavo, beyond the Alban lake, an ancient road bearing the name of *Via Latina*. If you look for it on the Campagna, you will find it covered with grass, and cattle grazing over it. On the line of this buried street, and not far from the city walls, workmen employed by the Pope are breaking the green turf and trenching the ground to a considerable depth. They have laid bare several solid masses of Roman masonry, and the foundations of an ancient Christian church, a basilica, over which were scattered, in the soil, many marble columns with Corinthian capitals and bases on which is carved the figure of the cross, indicating beyond a question the purpose of the building. But the most remarkable of these discoveries are two places of sepulture, consisting of vaulted rooms in the earth, to which you descend by staircases of stone. The earth had fallen into the entrances and closed them, but had not filled the space within, so that the stucco medallions and paintings overhead were found in as perfect preservation as when they came from the hands of the artist. In one of these tombs, which consisted of a single vaulted chamber with a pure white surface, I found an artist perched upon a high seat over two huge stone coffins, copying the spirited and fanciful figures of men and animals, in stucco, with which the arched ceiling was studded. The other tomb is larger and deeper in the ground, and consists of two vaulted chambers, communicating with each other, against the walls of which stood marble sarcophagi, rough with figures in high relief. On the ceiling of one of the rooms, among the stucco medallions, were arabesques in vivid colors, and landscapes in fresco, which show a far more advanced stage of this branch of the art than any thing which has been found at Pompeii. They are painted in what seemed to me a kind of neutral tint. Here are trees with gnarled branches, and foliage drawn with a free and graceful touch, and buildings rising among the trees, and figures of people engaged in rural employments; and all is given with a decided and skilful aerial perspective, the objects becoming less distinct and sharp in outline as they are supposed to recede from the eye. "Ten years hence," said the artist who accompanied us on this excursion, "you may see all these figures engraved and published in a book. Here at Rome we never do any thing in a hurry."

It is not unlikely that the admission of the external air will cause the stucco to peel from these vaults, or at least will cause the paintings to fade. "I think," said our friend, the artist, "that the landscapes are less distinct now than they were ten days since." In the mean time, all Rome is talking of this discovery; it is the great topic of the time. Numbers of people are constantly passing out of Rome to visit the excavations on the *Via Latina*. As we approached the city the other day, by the magnificent paved road called the New Appian Way, we wondered why all Rome should be rushing into the Campagna; so many people did we meet walking, and so many carriages rattling out of the gate of San Giovanni. When at length we visited the excavations, this was all explained. There was quite a throng about the principal tomb, where a man in uniform stood at the entrance, admitting only a certain number of visitors at a time, in order that they might not be in each others' way. A few strangers were among them, but the greater number were Romans of different classes—portly men of a slightly bluish complexion, who came in carriages accompanied by well-dressed ladies—and persons of an humbler condition who came on foot, the women sometimes bringing with them their infants—quiet creatures, asleep on their mothers' shoulders. There was a great deal of animated and eager discussion under the stucco figures and arabesques, for in Rome art is one of the few subjects on which people are allowed to speak freely.

As we left the spot and entered the New Appian Way to return to the city, we met two portly ecclesiastics, whose plump legs were encased in purple stockings, while a little way behind them marched three servants in livery, and at a still further distance, followed two carriages with purple cushions and trimmings. "They are cardinals, poor fellows," said our friend; "they are not allowed to walk in the streets of Rome; the dignity of their office forbids it. So, whenever they are inclined to fetch a walk, they are obliged to order their carriages and drive out to this solitary Campagna, where they can alight and stretch their legs without reprehension. A cardinal, who lives near the church of Trinita del Monte, was desirous to walk to the church, and asked to be so far indulged, but his application was denied." Their Eminences, I supposed, were going to take a look at the newly-discovered sepulchres.

Besides what he is doing on the *Via Latina*, the Pope is digging away vigorously at Ostia on the sea-shore. Here the foundations of several villas of vast dimensions, with the lower part of their walls, have been uncovered, and a large number of statues have been found.

It has been an infinite relief to us to come away from the noisy and dirty city of Naples, swarming with blackguards and beggars, and pass a few days in this quiet place. I remember when Rome was as dirty as Naples; it has now become a city of clean, well-swept streets—a city from which New York might, in this respect, take example. There is here no ostentatious display of rags and disgusting deformities by those who ask alms, such as you encounter at every step that you take in Naples. There are beggars here, it is true—quite enough of them—but not so many as formerly. Every time I come to Rome I see some external change for the better; I perceive that something has been done for the embellishment of the city or for the public convenience. Since I was here last, five years since, the New Appian Way, a broad, well-paved road, with causeys over the hollows, leading from Rome to Gensano, has been completed, crossing the beautiful woody glen of Lariccia and the deep ravine of Gensano with stupendous bridges, which, if they make the road less pretty, shorten it greatly and keep it at a convenient level. Within a few years past the small round stones with which the streets of Rome were formerly paved, and which were the torture and the terror of all tender-footed people, have been taken up, and the city is now paved throughout with small cubic blocks of stone, which present a much smoother and more even surface. The streets in the night were, not very long ago, bewilderingly dark; they are now well lighted with gas. New houses have been built, and those who have employed their money in this way, I am told, find their advantage in it. Studios for painters are erected on the tops of old houses, the lower rooms of which are let to sculptors; yet I hear that last winter, notwithstanding the number of new studios which have been built, there was not a vacant one to be had at any price.

The increase in the number of houses implies an increase in the population. There is certainly an increase in the number of artists residing here, and Rome is now more the great general school of art than ever. When I first came to this place, in 1835, there was not an American artist at Rome, that I could hear of; now the painters and sculptors from our country are numerous enough to form a little community; they amount, every winter, to thirty or more. The veterans of art from different parts of the European continent sometimes come, in a quiet way, to pass a winter at Rome. Cornelius,[4] whose frescoes are seen on the walls and ceilings of the finest public buildings of Munich, was here last winter, and occupied the same rooms which formed his studio when, more than thirty years since, he was here to study the grand frescoes of Michael Angelo, Raphael, and Guido. I perceive that in the New York journals very full accounts have been given of what the American artists here are doing, so that with regard to them I have nothing to tell which would be news. It is remarkable that they find Rome a better place for obtaining orders from their own countrymen than any of the American cities. Men who would never have thought of buying a picture or a statue at home, are infected by the contagion of the place the moment they arrive. No talk of the money market here; no discussion of any public measure; no conversation respecting new enterprises, and the ebb and flow of trade; no price current, except of marble and canvas; all the talk is of art and artists. The rich man who, at home, is contented with mirrors and rosewood, is here initiated into a new set of ideas, gets a taste, and orders a bust, a little statue of Eve, a Ruth, or a Rebecca, and half a dozen pictures, for his luxurious rooms in the United States.

You have heard of the death of poor Bartholomew, the sculptor.[5] He came to the hotel at Naples, where I was, the evening before I went with my family to Castellamare; I was absent a week, and when I came back he was dead and in his grave. He had fought a hard battle with poverty, and had just won it; orders were beginning to come in upon him from all quarters, and his great grief, when he breathed his last, was, that he could not place his mother in that state of comfort which he would easily have secured to her if a brief respite from death had been allowed him. I have been to his studio since my arrival in Rome, and there I saw the last work of his hand—a fine statue, justifying the reputation he has lately acquired— Eve, after the Fall, in an attitude of dejection, and wearing an expression of profound sorrow. I could scarcely help fancying that the marble figure mourned the death of the artist to whom it owed its being.

The French hold Rome yet—for the Pope. Every morning the streets resound with the tramp of Gallic cavalry. Troops of heavy Norman horses drink from troughs filled by the waters of the Claudian aqueduct, and in the massive Baths of Diocletian are locked up the thunders which at a moment's notice may batter down the city. The stranger who strolls near them with a segar is warned away by the French guards. There is a French police here, to which the Italian police is subsidiary, and it is said to be much the better of the two.

MANUSCRIPT: Unrecovered TEXT: *LT* II, 253–260; first published in *EP* for June 11, 1858.

    1. Samuel Taylor Coleridge, "Piccolomini," II, iv.
    2. Pius IX (1792–1878), Pope, 1846–1878.
    3. *The Topography of Rome and its Vicinity* (London, 1834).
    4. The German painter Peter von Cornelius (1783–1867).
    5. The American sculptor Edward Sheffield Bartholomew (1822–1858) had been working in Rome since 1850. *DAA*. He had died at the Pension d'Europe in Naples during the first week in May. Bryant, "Diary, 1857–1858," May 7, 1858.

1027.   *To* Richard S. Willis[1]

Rome   May 21, 1858

My dear Mr. Willis.

It is with great grief that we have heard of the calamity which has befallen you. The bad news was awaiting us here on our arrival from Naples.
We regard the death of your wife as not your loss only, but ours also, inasmuch as it deprives us of a most dear and cherished friend.[2]

I write therefore in behalf of my wife and daughter and Miss Ives, as
well as for myself, to express our deep sympathy with you in this affliction.
When a few weeks since we received the pleasant letter jointly written by
you and her who is gone,[3] my wife and I little thought as we read the kind
words she addressed us that we should never again press the friendly hand
that penned them. We have had however the consolation, which to you
must have been a great one, to know that her departure was worthy of the
innocent and beneficent life which she had led, and that she met death not
only with submission but serenity, beholding in it, what must have been
to her the birth to a better and happier life.

She had in her character all that guilelessness and was largely endowed
with that affectionate docility, which belongs to those of whom, it is said,
that of such is the kingdom of Heaven. My wife after having been very low
with illness and in great danger, is now happily recovering, and after long
imprisonment at Naples, we have begun our journey, northward. She and
the girls send their affectionate regards, and many kisses to the poor little
Annie and Blanche.

I am, dear sir,
faithfully and truly yours
W. C. BRYANT

MANUSCRIPT (copy, not in Bryant's hand): BLR.

1. See 791.1.
2. Willis' young wife Jessie (919.4), already the mother of two daughters, had died
on April 9 giving birth to a third. The news reached the Bryants in a letter from Fanny
Godwin dated April 13. Bryant, "Diary, 1857–1858," May 17, 1858. See Letter 1064.
3. Letter dated March 1 [1858], Homestead Collection.

1028.   *To* Orville Dewey[1]

Rome   May 25, 1858.

Dear Mr. Dewey,

It is a long time since I got your letter[2]—kindly and genial as your letters always are— I should have answered it before—perhaps—for it is not
best to be too positive in such a case, but for my wife's long and dangerous
illness at Naples, during which I wrote to almost nobody. She is now recovering from the complaint and is getting back her former strength— In

size she is reduced I think about a third— but her heart is as large as ever. As soon as she was able to travel we set out for Rome, and she bore the journey wonderfully well—seeming to gain more rapidly than before. I believe from what I hear of Naples that it is not a good climate for our people generally speaking—at least that they are apt to be attacked by nervous fevers on going there— The neighbourhood of Chiaja, along the sea-shore is proverbially unwholesome at Naples—many of the Neapolitans themselves cannot live there—and yet being the pleasantest part of the city it is the place chosen by strangers as their residence. All the best hotels are on the street facing the shore south of the town—near which are the mouths of the sewers and a sewer in front of the houses with frequent openings sends up constantly offensive exhalations.

On arriving here my wife got three letters from your family—one from your wife another from Mary and a third from Jerusha—which made our welcome to this quiet place still more sunshiny than it otherwise would have been—glad as we were to get here. Our pleasure was dashed by one sad piece of news which Julia took greatly to heart and which we did not communicate to Frances till the next morning—the distressing death of Mrs. Willis—the wife of Richard—tidings which we little thought to hear.

It is very interesting to me to see how differently the cities of Europe look after a few years absence from them. If the world is not growing better it is at least growing more comfortable. Rome is a much nicer place than it was when I first saw it[3]—and has grown more comfortable looking and clean, every time I have seen it and this is the fourth time. All over Europe the roads are better the facilities for travel are greater the hotels better— the arrangements for the convenience of travellers and residents better in almost every respect—travelling is easier safer speedier, more healthful. They squeeze you a little harder doubtless—but they give you more for what they take from you. To look at Rome now and *compare it with what* I have seen [of] it before, the material prosperity of the place would seem as undeniable as that of one of our own towns— One would say that Rome must be flourishing— I have not the opportunity, it is true of going deeper than the surface.

One of the most interesting things to be seen here is the collection of antique statues and busts made by the Marquis of Campagna with the money of the Monte di Pietà [Christian loan bank] of which he was the director, and which he was allowed to manage. It is as rich almost as that of the Vatican. How he could have got together so many in so short a time for he is still young seems a mystery. He is now in prison for embezzlement —defalcation it would be in our country—and instead of digging after antiques is digging rhymes—writing sonnets, and his collection—partly got together by purchase and partly by judicious excavation, for he is an accomplished archaeologist is to be sold. Among some of the most extraordinary things here are the portrait statues—Socrates Seneca, Demosthenes

—the sensible head of Pompey the great—the frowning countenance of Caius Marius; Julius Caesar his bald head crowned with laurels and his face furrowed with deeper wrinkles than in any likeness of him which I have seen— Some of the ideal statues are also fine— It is immense and ought to form a public collection open to the world.—

Since we left America—the world on your side of the Atlantic has passed through two great changes—the financial world shaken with a more violent earthquake than that of Calabria—and then this present rattling among the dry bones of religion. A religious revival I confess makes me a little uncomfortable—I respect all attention to religion, but it is so often mixed up with so much that is disagreeable and injudicious persons run it into such absurdities and pervert it so greatly—that I feel like one who finds a spoonful of salt in his strawberries.[4]

[unsigned]

MANUSCRIPT: NYPL–GR (draft).

1. See 307.4, 608.4.
2. December 28, 1857, NYPL–BG.
3. In March–April 1835. See Vol. I, 7; Letters 300, 301.
4. For a brief discussion of the religious revival movement following the financial panic of 1857 in America, see Gilbert Seldes, *The Stammering Century* (New York: Harper & Row [1965]), pp. 133–135.

1029.   *To* Caroline M. S. Kirkland[1]

Rome   May 25   1858

My dear Mrs. Kirkland.

A letter s[o] welcome as yours[2] should have [been] acknowledged long since; but during my wife's long illness which made us all very anxious I scarce wrote to any body. She is now getting back her strength as fast as could be reasonably expected. The grippe in Marseilles and the rheumatic fever at Naples attacked her in turn and reduced her to such weakness that she could not for a long time turn in her bed. At one time her complaint took the typhoid type, and then it was that we were most alarmed for her safety. We had a homoeopathic physician Dr Rubini, who has a good deal of reputation in Italy,—and who, I think treated her judiciously. Of course the recovery has been slow, but it is a comfort to see that she makes progress from day to day.

I suppose you think that you in the United States enjoy almost a monopoly of excitements, with your panics and commercial smashes, and your revivals of religion, and your elections, and your Kansas question, and your Mormon question,[3] and your public lectures freely discussing all manner of subjects and your controversies carried on by means of the press. I can assure you that here too we have causes that disturb the calm surface of life and keep the mind from stagnating even when there is no revolution on foot. Yesterday I was obliged to pay an exorbitant price for a carriage because it was the festival of the *durno amere* and every body was driving out to a church in Campagna to pay their devotions, and to see every body else. A Roman who has saved a few pounds does not spend it at a pot house, but he hires a four wheeled vehicle and filling it with his family drives Jehu like, on the next holiday, on some of the smooth Macadamized roads that lead from Rome into the Campagna. Driving out stands him instead of politics and instead of drink. Then we have pompous ceremonies in the churches, gorgeous processions & Corpus Domini on the fourth of June equal to any thing in the Holy Week, and St. Peter's day a little later when the most superb illuminations and fireworks are given in all the year and the populace is beside itself with joy. Then we have other matters of in-terest—there are the excavations going on in the Campagna and at Ostia —old tombs open near the gate of San Giovanni adorned with stucco medal-lions as sharp and white as when executed, fresco arabesques of brilliant colors, and landscapes much finer and more artist-like than any uncovered at Pompeii. All Rome flocks to the spot to look at them. At Ostia they are digging up statue after statue, once the ornament of the villas of the op-ulent Romans, on the sea shore.

There is another matter also which now engages the attention of the public. The Marquis of Campana, a director of the Monte di Pietà has been spending the money of the institution in collecting a superb gallery of antiques by purchase and excavation. He is now arrested and waiting his condemnation, and his collection is to be sold. I went the other day to see it—an army of statues of Roman statesmen, warriors, orators, emperors— portrait statues—and a host of Greek divinities—with a perfect mob of busts. I wondered where he picked them up but he is a skilful digger for antiques,—and the Roman soil is full of them—it is a great grave of statues and busts. A pity the collection which some say is equal to that of the Vati-can could not be purchased for America.

Rome is very pleasant now—the weather is delightful and we make excursions with comfort—but we must leave it in a day or two. We go to Florence—to Venice perhaps—then to Milan Turin Paris and England, coming home in August. It gives us great pleasure to hear that you are so pleasantly established at Eagleswood.[4] We wish you healthful summers and winters pleasantly divided between solitude and society—just a little of town life now and then as the sauce to the more solid banquet before you.

Thank your brother for his letter[5] which was full of interesting matter and informed me of many things which I was anxious to know. You seem to take no interest in politics, and yet politics bear a close relation to morals and to social happiness. There is always, I know great danger that one by taking a strong interest in politics may become a prejudiced partisan—just as people become intolerant by taking a strong interest in religious sub-jects—but we must not reason you know from the abuse of a thing.—

Remember us all most kindly to all the members of your family—including those of your brothers. Remember us also to our friends Mr & Mrs Spring—[6] My wife and daughter desire their best love—

> Yours truly,
>
> [unsigned]

MANUSCRIPT: NYPL–GR (draft).

1. See 517.2; Letter 991.
2. Unrecovered.
3. The threat of armed conflict between the Mormon settlers of Utah Territory and United States troops in the winter of 1857–1858 was relieved by mediation in the spring of 1858. Nevins, *Emergence of Lincoln*, I, 318–325.
4. See 921.2.
5. Edward Stansbury (Letter 540). His letter is unrecovered.
6. Marcus and Rebecca Spring; Letter 921; 583.2.

1030.   *To* William Leach Giro[1]

Rome   May 25   1858

My dear sir.

The kindness which you manifested towards me and my family during our stay in Alicante induces me to suppose that you might perhaps like to hear what became of us after we left your city. I have also another reason for writing at present—which is, that I desire especially to thank you for the civilities which you and your mother and sisters showed to my wife and the young ladies after my departure for Cartagena without them. Of the good offices they received at your hands they cannot say too much.

The ladies had a pleasant passage to Cartagena, and a somewhat stormy one from that place to Malaga. At Malaga we were delighted with the climate and made a most interesting excursion to Granada. Our time we found would not allow us to proceed to Cadiz and Seville—so we took passage for Marseilles, by way of Oran and Algiers at both of which places we made a short stay and were much interested in what we saw there. On going out, however, our steamer ran against another and caused it to sink but happily not before it got to shore—so that no lives were lost. We had another accident between Majorca and Minorca, the breaking of an air pump by which we were detained fifteen hours. Of course when we arrived at Marseilles my wife—rendered somewhat nervous by these accidents was a fair mark for the grippe which then prevailed there. As soon as she was a little better of this we took her to Naples where she seemed to mend—but suddenly she was attacked with a fever prevalent at Naples and brought very low. For four months she was ill and it is only within a fortnight that she has been able to travel. She is now gaining strength every day, and we shall soon proceed to Florence.

In no place that we have been in since we were at Alicante have we found fruit half so fine or so abundant as with you— This is a distinction which makes a strong impression on our memory as we are all great lovers of fruit. Alicante therefore hold[s] a high place in our recollections—for two reasons—the excellence of its fruits and the kindness of the friends we met there.

Be pleased to present our best regards to your mother and sisters. Do us the favor also to remember us kindly to Mr. De Landa[2] should you see him. My wife and daughter and Miss Ives desire to be remembered to you.

W C B.

MANUSCRIPT: NYPL–GR (draft) ADDRESS: To Mr. Leach Am. / Consul at Alicante.

1. See 998.1.
2. Don Juan Trabado de Landa, a gentleman of Alicante to whom Bryant had apparently been recommended by one of his Madrid acquaintances. Bryant, "Diary, 1857–1858," November 21–22, 24, 1857.

1031. *To* Robert C. Waterston

Rome   May 27th   1858.

Dear Mr. Waterston.

I wrote you immediately on our arrival at Rome, informing you of my wife's improved health, and our fortunate journey, and acknowledging your letter, which gave us the good news of your daughters progress towards a happy recovery. Mrs. Bryant continues to gain strength with every day, though she is not equal yet to sight seeing, which, you know, is one of the most laborious of occupations.

Meantime we greatly desire to hear how you [are] getting on, and in particular how Helen is. You will do us a great favor by writing, as soon as you receive this, and letting us know. If you write within a few days from this date, please direct your letter to me at Florence, where we expect soon to be. If you should not write within a week from this date, it would be better to address your letter to the care of John Munroe & Co. bankers at Paris—for we are not certain whether we shall go to Venice.

We have very comfortable lodgings at the Hotel de l'Europe, and the girls are making the best use of their time in looking at Rome. We have seen Mr. and Mrs. Hawthorne; but they have since set out for Florence.[1] At Mrs. Story's I have breakfasted, and met there Miss Hosmer, and several of our countrymen.[2] The artists and their families here have been very attentive to us, and we have so many acquaintances, that the formality of taking leave, I am afraid, will have to be performed as compendiously as civility will allow.

The weather, for the most part, has been most delightful since we have been here; the country is all verdure and flowers. Yesterday we went to Tivoli, where the streaming green drapery of the *Cascatelle* look almost like cataracts of verdure beside those of the white water.

Do not fail to write. My wife and the girls send their best love to you all. Make my kind regards to Mrs. Waterston and the young lady who has given you so much trouble, and who now, I hope, is as strong and well as either of you.

I am, dear sir,

very faithfully yours

W. C. BRYANT.

MANUSCRIPT: UVa ADDRESS: Monsieur / Monsieur R. C. Waterston / aux soins de Messrs Iggulden et Cie. / Napoli. POSTMARK: ROMA / 27 / MAG. / 58.

1. See Bryant, "Diary, 1857–1858," May 21, 1858. On that occasion Nathaniel Hawthorne recorded some impressions of his fellow-American:

May 22d.—Yesterday, while we were at dinner, Mr. [Bryant] called. I never saw him but once before, and that was at the door of our little red cottage in Lenox; he sitting in a wagon with one or two of the Sedgwicks, merely exchanging a greeting with me from under the brim of his straw hat, and driving on. He presented himself now with a long white beard, such as a palmer might have worn as the growth of his long pilgrimages, a brow almost entirely bald, and what hair he has quite hoary; a forehead impending, yet not massive; dark, bushy eyebrows and keen eyes, without much softness in them; a dark and sallow complexion; a slender figure, bent a little with age; but at once alert and infirm. It surprised me to see him so venerable; for, as poets are Apollo's kinsmen, we are inclined to attribute to them his enviable quality of never growing old. There was a weary look in his face, as if he were tired of seeing things and doing things, though with certainly enough still to see and do, if need were. My family gathered about him, and he conversed with great readiness and simplicity about his travels, and whatever other subject came up; telling us that he had been abroad five times, and was now getting a little home-sick, and had no more eagerness for sights, though his "gals" (as he called his daughter and another young lady) dragged him out to see the wonders of Rome again. His manners and whole aspect are very particularly plain, though not affectedly so; but it seems as if in the decline of life, and the security of his position, he had put off whatever artificial polish he may have heretofore had, and resumed the simpler habits and deportment of his early New England breeding. Not but what you discover, nevertheless, that he is a man of refinement, who has seen the world, and is well aware of his own place in it. He spoke with great pleasure of his recent visit to Spain. I introduced the subject of Kansas, and methought his face forthwith assumed something of the bitter keenness of the editor of a political newspaper, while speaking of the triumph of the administration over the free-soil opposition. I inquired whether he had seen S[umner], and he gave a very sad account of him as he appeared at their last meeting, which was in Paris. S[umner], he thought, had suffered terribly, and would never again be the man he was; he was getting fat; he talked continually of himself, and of trifles concerning himself, and seemed to have no interest for other matters; and Mr. [Bryant] feared that the shock upon his nerves had extended to his intellect, and was irremediable. He said that S[umner] ought to retire from public life, but had no friend true enough to tell him so. . . .

[Bryant] was not in the least degree excited about this or any other subject. He uttered neither passion nor poetry, but excellent good sense, and accurate information on whatever subject transpired; a very pleasant man to associate with, but rather cold, I should imagine, if one should seek to touch his heart with one's own. He shook hands kindly all round, but not with any warmth of gripe; although the ease of his deportment had put us all on sociable terms with him [*Passages from the French and Italian Note-Books*, 2 vols. (Boston, 1872), I, 223–225].

2. The Bryants were invited to this breakfast at the Palazzo Barberini on September 23 by the American sculptor William Wetmore Story (1819–1895) and his wife "to meet Mr. & Mrs. Hawthorne." Story to Bryant, May 21, 1858, NYPL–GR. Bryant had met Harriet Goodhue Hosmer (1830–1908) a few days earlier at the studio of the English sculptor John Gibson (537.3), under whom she was studying, and had found her a "bright resolute looking woman." "Diary, 1857–1858," May 20, 1858. At the Storys' apartments Hawthorne noticed that Bryant was "very quiet," making "no conversation audible to the general table." *Passages from the French and Italian Note-Books*, I, 230.

1032. *To* Charles M. Leupp

Rome   May 28, 1858.

Dear Mr   Leupp.

I got your letter the other day on my arrival at Rome and thank you for it.[1] I was very glad to hear that the late panic and confusion in money affairs had done you so little mischief. I hope the case will be the same with all except those who deserve to lose. Should that be always so, the fluctuations of credit would be a pleasant thing to think of and to watch. As the world goes however, honest men in active life, are as much sufferers by them as the rogues.

We are here, on our journey to the North, very comfortably lodged in the Hotel de l'Europe. The weather is genial; the public gardens and grounds of the villas, and the country generally, are in full bloom; there are few strangers here to be in one's way, and my wife is getting better every day, so that I have every reason to be in good spirits. All the town is now talking of the defalcations of a certain Marquis de Campana, a distinguished Archaeologist, who was one of the Directors of the Monte di Pietà here, and who applied the funds of the institution to the amount, it is said of a million of dollars, to the purchase of statues and other works of ancient [sculpture?][2] a great many of which, however, he obtained by directing and superintending excavations. His father had managed the concerns of the institution before him with great probity and exactness and on his death, the son, though then very young was put in his place. The Marquis is now arrested and thrown into prison where he awaits the decision of the Courts, and consoles himself by writing sonnets to his friends.

I went the other day with Mr. Terry[3] to see the collection of statuary made by him which is large and most valuable, rivalling that of the Vatican, and which is now exposed to the inspection of the public in expectation of a sale. One of the most remarkable characteristics of the gallery is the number of portrait statues. Here is the statue of Seneca that of Demosthenes, sitting, that of Seneca, that of Julius Cesar and various of the Roman Emperors and the females of their families. There are also some fine statues of the heathen divinities and a remarkably rich collection of busts of distinguished personages. I could not help wishing as I went through this magnificent gallery that we had it in the United States; it is a richer one than that in the Glyptothek at Munich; but it would cost a good deal of money to buy it; half a million Mr. Terry thought, and where is half a million to come from for Greek and Roman marbles?

Chapman I find in excellent health and hard work, completing the pictures for which he has orders. His bad health has hitherto occasioned some delay, and now that he is well again, he is determined, he says to clear off every order he has received, with as much expedition as possible. It costs more labor he says to paint a picture here, than it did in America. The artist here, he says finds it more difficult to please himself, and is surrounded by others who are no more easily pleased than he.

Chapman's sons are both artists, and both show inclination and talent for painting. They begin to render very useful assistance to their father, and I always find them with the brush in their hands. He says he would like to go back for a little while to the United States, and he wants his boys to be American artists, able to treat American subjects. Terry is as much a general favorite here as ever; he is painting diligently. Gibson[4] is a little older than he was, but they say betrays no sign of old age in his works or conversation. He is modelling a very fine statue without drapery—a Michael, I think he calls it—intended to represent the perfection of the human form. I went with Chapman the other day to an exhibition of the works of artists at Rome, near the Porta del Popolo. There was not much to interest the spectator; among the landscapes were two by George L. Brown,[5] with much of his peculiar manner, and yet I could not help acknowledging that in some respects his treatment of his subjects was impressive—a sort of [picture?] treatment. They were landscapes.

We have been rejoiced to hear of the perfectly safe arrival of Mrs Lee[6] and the young ladies in America; it is not every steamer that crosses the ocean without accident, in these days. It was our own lot in that very Mediterranean which as they boast in Marseilles, is free from steamboat accidents, to be in a steamer which struck and sunk another steamer, and a few days afterwards ruptured an air pump and kept us tumbling about on the water for fifteen hours without making any progress. Remember us all very cordially to the fair ladies. My wife and the girls desire to be kindly remembered to you also. I see Durand's Crayon here at Rome and am glad to meet it as an old friend. At Naples I got Appleton's illustrated edition of my poems. Chapman says that the portrait of me in it is the only one of me he ever saw which bore no resemblance to me.[7]

Yours ever

W. C. BRYANT

MANUSCRIPT: Leupp Family Papers, Rutgers University Library ENDORSED: Wm. C. Bryant   May 28/58.

1. Letter unrecovered.
2. Word omitted.

3. Luther Terry (834.5).

4. John Gibson; see 1031.2.

5. See 561.6.

6. Probably Mrs. Gideon Lee, Leupp's mother-in-law, and widow of his former business partner. See 487.1.

7. This portrait, by the English painter Samuel Laurence (see 859.3), was engraved for the London edition of Bryant's *Poems* published in 1857 by Appleton. Receiving a copy at Naples in March, Bryant had noted, "Laurence's crayon portrait of me is spoiled by the engraver on wood so as to leave little resemblance." "Diary, 1857–1858," March 17, 1858. Of the portrait itself, Parke Godwin remarked that Laurence "give to Mr. Bryant a look that none of his friends ever recognized." *Life*, II, 78.

1033.   *To* Leonice M. S. Moulton[1]

Rome   May 28th   1858.

My dear Mrs. Moulton.

I write this from the Eternal City, in which there are many things much older than even your letter[2] which I take shame to myself for not having answered earlier. Yet I have been more prompt than some whose example is on record. It is in the *Spectator* I believe that a history is given of a correspondence between two persons who lived before the flood. The gentleman wrote the lady a moving letter which had such an effect upon her that in less than a twelvemonth she returned an answer. And lo! I have answered your very pleasant and welcome epistle, if my computation is right, within half that space of time.

To tell the truth, I was pretty busy, while I was in Spain in writing letters for the Evening Post, and had little time to be spared from that, and the occupation of travelling and observing, for private correspondence. I flattered myself that when I got to Italy, which is old ground and has been written over almost as much as it has been travelled over, that I should have ample time to pay up all my old debts of that sort. But it was ordered that I should bring my wife to Italy in the beginning of a long, serious, and even dangerous illness, which held her from January to May—four months in a state of great weakness. I was almost constantly at her bedside and wrote no letters except such as some apparent necessity or obligation called on me to write. She is now daily gaining strength. I brought her to Rome as soon as she was able to travel; the journey seemed to do her good; and we shall soon proceed to the northern cities of Italy, making our way towards Paris, and thence to England, whence we may take passage for the United States about the end of summer.

I hope you will let these circumstances extenuate my apparent neglect. I assure you I have been hard at work since I came to Rome in balancing old scores of correspondence.

Our stay at Naples was not particularly pleasant. We did not find the climate what we expected; the winter was a remarkably inclement one for that region; the streets were full of funerals, processions of men in white frocks covering the head and face, with two holes for the eyes, bearing torches and following gilded hearses. My wife's illness kept us in constant anxiety and sometime in great alarm. Once or twice an old acquaintance found the way to Naples and brightened our sojourn with the smile of a familiar face, and talked with us of things in America. If you could only have happened in one of those dull days, with your bright face and some pleasant news from Roslyn!

With Rome, our party are much pleased. There are many Americans residing here, artists, some of them our old acquaintances. This season is the most agreeable and beautiful of the year at Rome; the breezes which sweep over the Campagna, that region which a little later is so unhealthy seem as pure and untainted as if they blew from the gates of Paradise. The Campagna is now a broad expanse of green and the fields are bright with their new leaves; flocks and herds are grazing all over it, and the tracts of grain, some of which comprise thousands of acres begin in some places to show a faint twinge of yellow. You would have been delighted to have accompanied us on an excursion we made, the day before yesterday to Tivoli. The country was in its greatest glory of verdure and wild flowers and the Anio [River Aniene], somewhat full from recent showers, dashed magnificently through his grottos and down his precipices.

Rome looks flourishing compared with what it did when I first saw it; and the priesthood seems to flourish here as much as the city in which they dwell. I do not know that the number of priests and monks has increased, but they are making converts from educated Protestants; G. L. Brown our countryman, the painter has professed the faith of the Latin church, and Jacob Barker's[3] daughter, Mrs. Ward, once so handsome and attractive, but now an invalid and beset with nervous complaints, has found consolation in the same quarter. Perhaps you may have seen all this in the newspapers. The Pope has expended a great deal of money in repairing and restoring old churches which a few years since had a dilapidated appearance. Dr. Berrian's son is here Chandler Berrian.[4] I have looked for him without success; for he often goes out of town; but I hear that he is passing an easy life with the ecclesiastics. "He is a gentle-hearted creature," said Mr. Chapman the artist speaking of him the other day, "just like his father."

Now in return for this religious intelligence from Rome, do be so kind as to give me some account of the revival at Roslyn; for it must I think have reached Roslyn, and tell me what your ministers have been doing in regard to it. I shall then be sure that you have kindly overlooked my failure to answer your letter before.

Remember us all in your prayers. My regards to your wedded lord, and to Mr. Ordronaux,[5] if still an inmate of your dwelling.

Faithfully yours
W. C. Bryant

MANUSCRIPT: NYPL–Bryant–Moulton Letters.

1. See 648.1.

2. Probably her letter dated Roslyn, August 25, 1857 (William Cullen Bryant II), which had reached Bryant at Pau. Bryant, "Diary, 1857–1858," September 22, 1857.

3. For Jacob Barker, see 155.8.

4. A son of the Rev. William Berrian (1787–1862, Columbia 1808), rector of Trinity Church, New York, from 1830 until his death. See Bryant, "Diary, 1857–1858," May 27–28, 1858.

5. Dr. John Ordronaux (1830–1908; Dartmouth 1850, Harvard Law 1852, M.D. Columbian College—later George Washington University—1859), an orphan of French extraction who had been adopted by Joseph Moulton (Letter 435). Ordronaux would later distinguish himself in both law and medicine, publishing many studies in each discipline, and teaching for many years at Columbia, Dartmouth, Boston University, and the University of Vermont. In addition, he was a successful translator of Horace.

1034. *To* Christiana Gibson[1]

Civita Castellana   May 29, 1858.

My dear Miss Gibson.

We were delighted to get your letter[2] which reached my wife at Rome —or rather, which she found on her arrival there. Your letters are so much like yourself, they are written so much in the manner you talk that to read them is almost the same thing as listening to your spirited and cheerful conversation.

We are at Città Castellana in the Roman states, just one day's journey from Rome, as the vetturini compute a day's journey. The city stands enclosed by ravines, three of them, each with its little stream, deep gulfs with perpendicular walls of rock, the projections of which are green with shrubs: the privet and elder bush now in bloom spot the green with white. I have just been out upon a lofty bridge which spans one of these ravines; on one side of it I looked down upon women washing who seemed like puppets in motion; on the other I saw a herd of black swine feeding below which looked no larger than mice. We are in rooms under a covered gallery from which we have a view of the Sabine mountains and Magliano a Sabine town on the upper part of the Tiber. On the other side of the house, only hidden from our eyes by the roof towers Soracte. My wife has made the journey today with little fatigue.

My wife supposes you may have heard all about her illness. The *grippe* at Marseilles, the rheumatic fever at Naples degenerating into a nervous fever, a sickness of four months with a slow convalescence, form the summary of its history. We were at an hotel in the Chiatamone, that neighbourhood which strangers most affect but which is most unwholesome, and as soon as we could possibly remove her, we had her put into a sedan chair, and taken to a street back from the shore a little up the hill. Then when she could bear to go so far, we took her to pass a week among the green trees and wildflowers and birds at Castellamare, and a pleasant week it was. It strengthened her for the journey which shortly afterwards we made happily and pleasantly to Rome. We have passed thirteen days at Rome and are all sorry to leave it; the only drawback to our satisfaction has been that we found so many friends there that the formality of calls abridged a little the time which the girls had for seeing the wonders of the place. But the weather was delightful; the gardens and the surrounding country in bloom, and the place had put on its brightest and most attractive aspect.

There is a remarkable collection of antique marbles now open for exhibition at Rome. It was got together by the Marquis of Campana, who was a director of the Monte di Pietà, and who took funds of the institution and spent them in digging for antiques and buying them. He is a skilful archaeologist and knew where to search for them. His collection is one of the very finest in the world, and as it is to be sold for the benefit of the Monte di Pietà, I wish we had it in America. But who will buy it! There is a vast number of busts, a great many statues of the great men of antiquity and some very beautiful ones of the Greek and Roman divinities. Campana is now under arrest and it is supposed will be condemned to a long imprisonment.

We are now on our way to Florence, whence we shall make our way to Paris and so to England, intending to come home about the close of summer. If we should go to Scotland, as is likely, it will be a great pleasure to us to meet your mother and sister there though we greatly regret the cause which has made another visit to Europe necessary. It distressed us greatly to hear of the death of Mrs. Willis, cut off in the midst of a happy and cheerful life.

My wife bids me say that we are under the greatest obligations to you for the kind interest you take in Fanny and her children. There is this in the unmarried state that it leaves the affections more at liberty to expatiate and extend themselves than the matrimonial condition, and you avail yourself of this advantage in the fullest manner. We hope that Miss Leclerc[3] will lose nothing by the late commercial troubles. It would be truly hard if what she has earned with so much toil should be lost by the indiscreet speculations of another, of which she had no knowledge.

My wife would have answered your charming letter with her own hand had she been able, but it makes her head ache to write to any body except Fanny and even that is an effort. Remember us most kindly and cordially to your mother if she be yet with you and to the sisters who are of your household, and to Mr. and Mrs. Rankin and to Mr. Tuckerman[4] when you see him. My wife gives you a thousand thanks for the warm sympathy you express, for the condition in which she was when you had the last news from her. The girls send their best love to all. Julia also desires to be remembered to Mr. Tuckerman and hopes that you will at some time find leisure to answer her letter. . . .

[unsigned]

MANUSCRIPT: NYPL–GR (draft) PUBLISHED (*in part*): *Life*, II, 111.

1. See 502.3.
2. Probably Christiana Gibson to Cullen and Frances, December 7, 1857. William Cullen Bryant II.
3. See 798.2.
4. Probably the writer Henry Theodore Tuckerman (944.1), who was apparently a friend and admirer of Julia Bryant's. The Rankins were Glasgow friends of the Gibson family; see Letter 549.

1035.   *To* John Franklin Gray[1]

Foligno   May 31, 1858.

My dear sir.

Your letter at the same time with Mrs. Gray's reached my wife at Rome, and very glad was she to get them. She employs me to give you both thanks for them and for the kind expressions of your sympathy which they contain.[2] During her illness she often spoke of you and wished that she could have the benefit of your skill. She had the most eminent homoeopathic physician in Naples Dr Rubini, and twice we called in an old physician with a Greek name Dr Sinopoli as a consulting physician—once when rheumatic fever took the typhoid type the typhus stupidus—a state which was almost immediately dispersed by arsenic— Before we got your letter she was recovering—slowly to be sure, the doctor said it was the slowest recovery he had known in homoeopathic practice—but still it was a most happy recovery, and we had taken her to pass a week at Castellamare fifteen miles from Naples a pleasant week in fresh country air among verdure and birds—and we had taken her back to Naples and then by easy journeys to Rome, growing stronger every day. We were thirteen days at Rome, but my wife did not trust herself to see many things it has to show the traveller. She went to St. Peter's once, and visited the Lateran Museum, and drove to Monte Testaccio where she took a cool draught of Frascati wine from the cellars in that curious mount of potsherds and she seemed all the better for it.

I am concerned that the air of Naples, at least during the greater part of her illness was prejudicial to her. The best hotels are contained in streets facing the water of the bay, and near them are the mouths of several sewers, and through them and under the windows of the houses run sewers in which are numerous openings that send up offensive exhalations. This is the pleasantest part of the city and strangers prefer it to any other, but the Neopolitans call it unwholesome and say that it disagrees particularly with persons who have a tendency to nervous complaints. Some who own fine winter-palaces as they are called in this part of the town cannot live in them. So fully was I convinced that the air in this part of the city where we then were had a bad effect on my wife's health that as soon as she could possibly be moved I had her put into a sedan chair and taken to the Pension d'Europe, in the street of Santa Teresa a little back from the shore, and on the hill side on which Naples is built. I thought the change of air favorable. Dr Rubini I believe treated the case judiciously for the most part—but my wife was always wishing for you—and yet believes that you would have procured her an earlier recovery. Dr Rubini closed his prescriptions with a course of sulphur which seemed to have a good effect.

I write this from a town seated among the rich meadows of the river Clitumnus. The white herds which of old furnished victims for the sacrifices have disappeared, but we have today seen the peasants ploughing with white oxen. What were once pastures are now fields of grain, wheat and oats planted with trees in rows which are kept small and low, each tree supporting a vine. Rocky Hills covered with olive groves of a hoary green bound them on the east, and at the foot of these hills lie the villages and cities in which live the cultivators of the soil and the merchants who exchange its produce. On the edges of the meadows close by the road is the source of the river, several little streams called *Le Vene* or the veins, which gush out of the ground close to each other and uniting form the clear streams of the Clitumnus which sweeps through the fields to join the Tiber. The country is now in its greatest beauty and freshness.—

[unsigned]

MANUSCRIPT: NYPL–GR (draft) ADDRESS: Dr. John F. Gray ENDORSED: My Letter to D J. F. Gray / Foligno.

1. The Bryants' family physician; see 405.4, 444.1.
2. Bryant had written Dr. Gray from Naples in March describing his wife's illness. In reply, Gray wrote Frances words of consolation, but added, "of course [I] am unable to make even a safe suggestion." MS dated April 19, 1858, William Cullen Bryant II.

1036.   To Robert C. Waterston

Florence   June 5th. 1858

My dear Mr. Waterston.

Yesterday, the day after our arrival here your letter[1] was sent us from your banker's. I thank you very much for writing and yet confess that I was sorry to see your letter. It would have been a great satisfaction to us if we had been able to conclude that soon after your previous letter, expressing the most favorable hopes, was written, your daughter had so far recovered that you could leave Naples for the north, and this conclusion we should have drawn, if you had not written to us.

But the contents of your letter distressed us much more than the misgivings occasioned by the sight of it—so different were the tidings from what your previous letter had led us to expect. My wife speaks of the subject again and again, and last night her sleep was broken by the painful thought of the anxiety which you and Mrs. Waterston must continually feel. When I mentioned to Mr. Maqua[y?] this morning the fact of your daughter's illness, he said that he hoped you would soon be enabled to leave Naples, for it had the most relaxing of all climates. Whether one part of the city be better or worse than another in this respect I will not undertake to say, but I have no doubt of the general fact. In Helen's case one most remarkable symptom from the very first has been debility. My wife while languishing at the Hotel des Isles Britanniques, was quite the weakest person I ever saw who was alive; we had to turn her in the bed as she was unable to shift her position in the least degree without help, and even the change of position when effected by the strength of others wearied while it somewhat relieved her. Yet she by God's good Providence was raised up, as we all earnestly hope your daughter Helen will be. It is a fearful thing to have the doctor say as he did to me after a consultation with another physician—"The issue is somewhat doubtful; there is one remedy to be administered and only one, and we hope much from it." I considered that as a gentle way of telling me that her chance of life was small. Yet in spite of the enervating influence of the climate her strength gradually returned. Your daughter has the advantage of a constitution possessing yet all its early vigor—a nature of yet unexhausted energy to fall back upon, which when it once begins to rally will act more powerfully than Mrs. Bryant's could be expected to do. The next letter from you I hope will inform us that this happy reaction has already begun.

In the mean time it must be a great consolation, both to her parents and to her, to reflect upon the innocent, affectionate and dutiful life she has led, a life fitting her so well either for this world or the next. There are few parents, I suppose who under the same circumstances are allowed that consolation in so eminent a degree—so that in all your sorrow there is some reason for congratulation.

I do not know whether it will be of any use to mention a little method of alleviating the pain occasioned by lying too long in one position which was practised in my wife's case with remarkably good effect. A few drops of tincture of arnica, ten or twelve—in a small quantity of alcohol and water were rubbed on the part affected and brought immediate ease.

In looking over what I have written, I can only feel how impotent are words in the presence of so dark an apprehension as that which now hangs over your little household. We have nothing to give but a barren sympathy. My wife wishes a thousand times a day that she were near you.

We came from Rome by the usual journeys; the last day only was fatiguing to Mrs. Bryant, and from the fatigue she is now recovered. We had the finest possible weather and found the country very beautiful—it was the season of vegetable luxuriance in Italy. At present the weather is quite warm; Florence is hot, but healthy in summer. In a very few days we shall set out for Venice where, also, our stay must be short, as we are in some haste to get to Paris and thence to England. At Rome we found sad news awaiting us. One of our friends, a young married woman, long our neigh-

bour in the country, most happily married and for a little time past a great
favorite in New York society, the mother of two little children whom she
devotedly loved, had we learned died, after a very short illness, of puerperal
fever, leaving a third child behind her.[2] She was one of the last persons of
whom we took leave in America, and we had provided some little presents
for her on our return.

If you can find time to write on receiving this, do us the very great
favor to address a line to us at Venice, letting us know how Helen is. As
the letter may possibly miss us, would it be too much trouble for you to
write also, either then or later, to Paris, directing your letter to the care of
John Munroe & Co. Bankers no 5 Rue de la Paix?

In coming from Rome poor Estelle suffered with a malignant boil,
which made its appearance just above her left ancle, giving her great pain
and disabling her from walking so that we had to carry her up and down
stairs. It is now better but she is still unable to walk out.

You have all of you the love and sympathies and prayers of us all. May
God grant a happy issue out of this affliction.

Faithfully yours
W. C. BRYANT

Postscript. I saw Mrs. Powers after I wrote the accompanying letter and
learned from her that her husband was subject to violent coughs,[3] and that
he invariably and speedily cured them by the inhalation of the fumes of
nitric acid from a phial. I saw Mr Powers and obtained from him a description of his method and a diagram of the contrivance used for inhalation. He says that his cough is always cured in two or three days, and that
he has communicated the method to forty persons or more, all of whom had
been cured by it with but one exception, which was that of a lady who had
lost one lung and was very far gone in consumption. He found the recipe
in an old almanac and was induced to try it.

I send you the diagram and directions drawn by his own hand[4] that
you may try it in Helen's case if you think it expedient. The contrivance
is merely a phial with a teaspoonful of nitric acid in it and a glass tube inserted a little way into the mouth of the phial and prevented from touching
the acid by a little circle of wax. He says that one should not be alarmed
if it makes the patient cough a little, but in that case the nitric acid should
be diluted with water so as to make the fumes milder, and then the
strength of the fumes increased as the patient is able to bear them.

W. C. B.

MANUSCRIPTS: UVa (final); NYPL-GR (partial draft dated June 8th).

1. Waterston had written on May 29 that his daughter Helen had had a relapse
and was now bedridden again. Letter in NYPL–BG.
2. These children of Richard and Jessie Willis (1027.2) were Annie (b. 1854), later
Mrs. Aaron Ward; Blanche (1856–1935), Mrs. William Hemsley Emory, Jr.; and Jessie

(b. 1858), Mrs. John Brodhead. Cairns Family Genealogical Chart, prepared by Helen Marlatt, BLR.

    3. The American sculptor Hiram Powers (542.3).

    4. Unrecovered.

1037.   *To* Ellen S. Mitchell[1]

                                            Florence, Italy, June 6th   1858

My dear Niece.

By this time you may perhaps have some curiosity to know what has become of us, inasmuch as it is now more than a year since we left America. In that time we have had some good fortune and some bad. We had a pleasant journey through Holland and up the Rhine, and to various remarkable places in Switzerland, and to several beautiful spots among the Pyrenees in the South of France. We made an interesting visit to Spain which, however, was attended with some hardship to Mrs. Bryant, and we saw a sample of Oriental life and manners in Oran and Algiers on the Barbary coast. But at Marseilles Mrs. Bryant was taken ill, and not long afterwards before she had quite recovered was seized with the rheumatic fever at Naples and brought very low. After a time the disorder took the nervous form, and we were in great alarm lest it should prove fatal. We were kept at Naples four months in consequence. At length the malady happily took a favorable turn and your aunt began slowly to recover.

About fifteen miles from Naples lies Castellamare in a pleasant situation, with a healthy air. We took Mrs. Bryant thither and passed a week among the new leaved trees, the grass and the flowers, and she gained strength every day; we next came more expeditiously to Florence.[2] The weather has been delightful for the last six weeks and the country is in all its beauty. It is now beginning to be warm and by and by the country will become very dusty and brown. We shall however, in a few days be moving northward where the hot weather is later in coming. We may perhaps see some of the northern cities of Italy, whence we shall make our way to Paris and from Paris to England expecting to depart for America about the end of the summer.

So you see we have had both good and bad in our lot since we left home. It was a melancholy time with us during several weeks at Naples, but we are thankful to come away from the place alive, and not only alive but in comfortable health and cheerful spirits. Julia and Miss Ives have proved very good nurses for the sick lady during our stay in Naples. At present while we are in Italy Julia seems scarcely astonished at any thing, it seems to her as if she had seen it before. So she has in fact; she saw Italy when a child and though she remembered nothing of it distinctly, she doubtless sees something familiar in the features of the country and the looks of its cities.

Remember us all kindly to your husband and your children, particularly says Mrs. Bryant to little Frances, and give our regards to your father Mitchell[3] when you see him. We often talk of you, and wonder how you are pleased with Dalton, and whether your father in law is with you. Write and let us know all about it. We should be glad to hear whether your father has recovered from the accident he met with on the road to your house.[4] Your aunt and cousin desire their best love to you.

Yours truly,
W. C. BRYANT.

MANUSCRIPTS: Weston Family Papers (final); NYPL–GR (partial draft).

1. See 738.1; Letter 972.

2. During a six-day visit to Florence Bryant renewed his acquaintance with Hiram Powers, and met several British residents of the city, including Irish novelist Charles James Lever (1806–1872), whom he thought "infinitely amusing." Bryant, "Diary, 1857–1858," June 5–7, 1858. The English poets Robert Browning (1812–1889) and his wife Elizabeth Barrett Browning (1806–1861) entertained the Bryants at the Casa Guidi, where they again met the Hawthornes. The principal topic of conversation, Hawthorne noted, was "that disagreeable and now wearisome one of spiritual communications, as regards which Mrs. Browning is a believer, and her husband an infidel." He thought Bryant "appeared not to have made up his mind on the matter, but told a story of a successful communication between Cooper the novelist and his sister, who had been dead fifty years."

As he had after their evening together in Rome, Hawthorne recorded impressions of Bryant. "If any old age can be cheerful," he wrote, "I should think his might be; so good a man, so cool, so calm, so bright, too, we may say. His life has been like the days that end in pleasant sunsets. He has a great loss,—soon to be encountered in the death of his wife, who, I think, can hardly live to reach America. He is not eminently an affectionate man. I take him to be one who cannot get closely home to his sorrow, nor feel it so sensibly as he gladly would; and, in consequence of that deficiency, the world lacks substance to him. It is partly the result, perhaps, of his not having sufficiently cultivated his emotional nature. His poetry shows it, and his personal intercourse, though kindly, does not stir one's blood in the least."

Of the meeting between the American poet and his British hosts, Hawthorne remarked, "Mr. [Bryant], as usual, was homely and plain of manner, with an old-fashioned dignity, nevertheless, and a remarkable deference and gentleness of tone in addressing Mrs. Browning. I doubt, however, whether he has any high appreciation either of her poetry or her husband's, and it is my impression that they care as little about his [tea and strawberries]." *Passages from the French and Italian Note-Books*, 2 vols. (Boston, 1872), II, 11–13.

3. Elisha Mitchell (1790–1871), of Cummington. See William W. Streeter and Daphne H. Morris, *The Vital Records of Cummington, Massachusetts: 1762–1900* (Hartford, Connecticut, 1979), pp. 47, 210, and *passim*.

4. In September 1854 Dr. Samuel Shaw (Vol. I, 12) was thrown from his carriage and badly injured. Clara E. Hudson, *Plain Tales from Plainfield* . . . (Northampton, Mass.: Metcalf, 1962), p. 53.

1038.   *To* James P. Cronkhite[1]

Bologna— June 11th, 1858

My dear sir.

I got your letter[2] on my arrival at Rome about the middle of May— It was handed me by Mr. Rogers the sculptor.[3] You did not expect when you wrote it that it would be so long in coming to my hands. While you were writing your letter on the 9th of January my wife was suffering under the beginnings of a malady which finally brought her to a state of great weakness, and kept us prisoners at Naples for more than four months. All the while Mr Rogers was expecting us every week at Rome—for I never lost hope—though I was now and then extremely alarmed and uneasy. The complaint under which my wife was laboring, beginning with the grippe at Marseilles, followed by an attack of rheumatic fever at Naples, and then degenerating into a nervous fever, was an extremely obstinate one, attended at one time with the last degree of weakness, and subject in the period of convalescence to little backsets, which sometimes alarmed us and were always discouraging. She is now I am happy to say getting a little stronger every day, and, if she continues to go on at this rate for three months to come, as I hope she will I shall have her back to America twice as strong and hale as when she left it— I only hope the progress she is making will not stop when it reaches the point from which she declined at the beginning of her illness.

Of the intelligence in your letter some part had been anticipated but I was glad to be informed under your own hand that the late commercial disasters had not seriously affected you. You stood like a house in one of the towns of Calabria, when all the rest had been shaken down by the late earthquake. My own affairs cannot be said to have been unaffected by the commercial troubles, but fortunately, a daily newspaper if well managed is only somewhat less productive in bad times, and does not merely depend on the state of the markets for its prosperity—

Our stay at Rome has been short; we meant to have passed the winter there, and our visit was only thirteen days long. Mr. Terry we saw of course—he was kind and friendly—the Chapman family are my old friends, and with a large number of the artists in Rome I had a previous acquaintance. Mr. Mozier went to Florence two days after my arrival.[4] Miss Stebbins had already departed,[5] and many persons of my aquaintance who passed the winter at Rome had left it before we reached it. If our stay at Rome was necessarily short, so was our stay at Florence where we had some kind friends whose courtesies would have made a sojourn pleasant in a less agreeable place. . . .

[unsigned]

MANUSCRIPT: NYPL–GR (draft) ADDRESS: To Mr. Cronkhite.

1. See 812.3.
2. Unrecovered.
3. Randolph Rogers; see 834.2.
4. The American sculptor Joseph Mozier (834.2).
5. The sculptor Emma Stebbins (1815–1882), from New York, worked in Rome from 1857 to 1870. *DAA*. See also Vol. III, 118.

1039.   *To* Fanny Bryant Godwin

Venice, June 21, 1858.

Dear Fanny.

Enclosed is a little poem which I wish you would dispose of,[1] and with what you get for it make a little *Ausfliess* [excursion] into the interior this summer when you are tired of staying at home. I am, for my part, tired of staying abroad. We are here waiting for Miss Ives to get well enough to go on with us; she is laid up in dock, as Julia has doubtless told you with boils. We shall of course make a shorter visit to England than we intended. The weather here has been smothering hot for the last ten days—very different from the agreeable temperature we had here twenty three years ago in the same month. The other day I saw in the books of the Armenian convent—the Register of Visitors I mean—the memorandum I made of our visit to their little island on the 22d of June 1835. We have plenty of cherries here and very nice ones; by this time yours are, I suppose in their perfection and I hope you have plenty of them.

Your mother is still making progress in strength, though she finds the weather somewhat enervating. This morning, it is fortunately a little cooler. After the mercury in Fa[h]renheit's thermometer has marked 80 degrees all night, and stood higher in the middle of the day for a week together we have now a temperature of 76.

We hear little from America, nothing in fact except what we see in the foreign papers—Galignani[2] and the French journals. We have directed our banker at Paris to keep all the letters and newspapers addressed to us till we arrive, hoping, as we did, to proceed immediately to Paris. So far as your mother and myself are concerned the plan of our travels hitherto has been devised rather more for the gratification of the younger members of our party than our own, and the plan itself was most unfortunately disarranged by her long illness at Naples. The visit to Spain, I must acknowledge, however, was a whim of my own. The visit to Naples—instead of proceeding from Marseilles to Rome—and the later visits to Florence and this place, were made to please the girls. If we had known what was before us, we should of course have arranged our tour somewhat differently—certainly we should not have taken so wide a circuit.

Love to all — Affectionately yours

W. C. BRYANT

MANUSCRIPT: NYPL–GR.

1. This was "The Life That Is" (MS unrecovered), written at Castellamare early in May 1858 and reflecting Bryant's relief at his wife's gradual recovery from her critical illness in Naples during the preceding months:

> . . . Twice wert thou given me; once in thy fair prime,
>   Fresh from the fields of youth, when first we met,
> And all the blossoms of that hopeful time
>   Clustered and glowed where'er thy steps were set.
>
> And now, in thy ripe autumn, once again
>   Given back to fervent prayers and yearnings strong,
> From the drear realm of sickness and of pain
>   When we had watched, and feared, and trembled long. . . .

See *Poems* (1876), p. 346; Bryant. "Diary, 1857–1858," June 21, 1858. Evidently Fanny did not secure periodical publication of the poem; it seems to have made its first appearance in Bryant's *Thirty Poems* (1864), pp. 49–52. See 1370.1.

2. *Gagliani's Messenger*, an English-language newspaper, published in Paris, for which Bryant had little respect; see Letter 310.

1040. *To* the EVENING POST

Aix les Bains, Savoy, July 1, 1858.

While we are stopping for a day at the ancient watering-place of Aix les Bains, I employ an hour or two in writing of some things I have observed in the journey through Italy, northward.

This place has the reputation of a remarkably healthy air, and it is certainly the abode of a healthy-looking, fresh-colored population. They boast that its harsh, saline springs, strongly impregnated with sulphur, attract to it in summer a crowd of strangers, who, at that season, swell its population of four thousand to twice the number. Yet it is a very unattractive watering-place, compared with the German ones near the Rhine, and the French ones among the Pyrenees. Its hotels are well kept, but no pains have been taken in opening and embellishing grounds and laying out walks for those who frequent Aix for the benefit of its waters and its air. Its only walks are along dusty carriage-roads, and mostly in the glare of the sun; and in this respect it is disadvantageously contrasted with the places I have mentioned. A spacious and massive building for the baths is now, however, going up, the cost of which is partly defrayed out of the Sardinian treasury, and it is very likely that commodious paths will be planned along the shady border of the clear stream that winds through the valley, and out to where the blue waters of Lake Bourget, near at hand, sleep at the foot of overhanging precipices.

In the city of Florence, which we saw in the early part of June, I found that some changes had taken place. The street called Lung' Arno, so pleasant in winter, formerly ended in the west at the bridge which bears the name of Carraia, and beyond, the foundations of the houses stood in the waters of the river. These buildings have now been pulled down, and the whole bank of the Arno, as far as that spacious public promenade, the *Cascine,* has been opened to the winter sunshine, and is overlooked on the north side by a stately row of new houses. Troops of stonecutters and masons are busy in repairing and restoring the public buildings; the fine old church of Santa Croce, which has stood for centuries, with a ghastly and ragged mass of dark brickwork forming its front wall above the portal, is to be finished according to the magnificent original design, and other churches in the same state, I was told, are to be finished in their turn.

At Bologna we found workmen employed by the papal government in finishing the ancient church of San Petronio, in which Charles V. received the crown of the Roman empire.[1] Those were the prosperous days of Bologna, now in decay, and held in a sullen quiet by rulers whom it hates. The only other symptom of enterprise I observed, was the late enlargement and adornment of their public burial-place. I thought of the silk-worm spinning its own beautiful shroud just before it goes into its winter sleep. The Campo Santo of Bologna provides the most sumptuous repository for the bodies of the dead which I ever saw. We drove out to it on a hot June day over a dusty road, on each side of which the blue-flowered clematis twined over a row of young locust trees—for this tree of our North American forests, introduced into Europe under the name of acacia, has within the last twenty years taken possession of the continent from the latitude of Paris, and even further north, to the extremity of the Italian peninsula. As we entered the cemetery, we found ourselves among the beautiful cloisters of an old Carthusian convent, built some four hundred years since, the church of which is now the chapel of the burial-place. Here, under the long galleries, are several tombs of the middle ages, dark with time, which had stood for centuries in the open air, and had been removed hither for shelter; and hither also had been brought from the churches many monuments of distinguished men—mural tablets, sculptures in relief, busts and statues, among which I observed several from the chisels of Canova and Tenerani.[2] In the open space within the cloisters, where once the Carthusians had their nameless graves, are buried those whose fortunes do not allow a more costly sepulture. As the cemetery has grown populous, new ranges of cloisters have been built around other enclosures, the patrician dead sleeping under the arches in the thick walls, and the poor finding a humbler resting-place in the enclosed squares. At one time a fashion of painting fresco monuments on the walls prevailed, but this has been interdicted; the painter has been thrust out, and no memorial is allowed to be put up except it be of metal or stone. Besides these far-stretching galleries, open on one side, several sepulchral halls have been built opening into them—long vaulted passages of massive masonry, which made me think of the tomb of Apis, in Egypt, but not like that, lying in darkness, for here the light of day shines in through a lofty iron grate at each extremity. I looked along these apartments of the dead, and saw the white statues on either hand keeping watch in the silence, while at the end where the light came in, the branches of trees and shrubs, touched by the sunshine, were seen swaying in the wind. In one or two of them stood monumental figures at the intersection of the passages, like mute sentinels of the place. A gigantic Bolognese, one of the keepers, who was dignified by the title of *dimostratore* ["guide"], opened and shut the iron-grated doors with a clash, which sounded strangely in that stillness.

"You will go back, of course, by the arcades," said our coachman; and accordingly we were taken by the side of a new arcade for foot passengers, of nearly a mile in length, joining the cemetery to the row of ancient arcades which, beginning at the city gate, extend for the distance of three miles to the church of Madonna di San Luca, on the hill, where they show you an ancient picture of the Virgin from the pencil of St. Luke. "This new row of arcades," said our guide, "has been built by free contributions—wholly by free contributions. There, on the wall, between the columns, you see the names of the givers—wealthy families of Bologna, charitable women, rich men, who remembered the cemetery in their wills—the company of cordwainers have built one of the arches, the workers in brass another, the company of grocers have given several, and so have the tailors. A funeral procession can now walk dry-shod in rainy weather, from the city to the burial-place."

So sleep the dead at Bologna. Their city is built with arcades on the streets; they walk all their lives under arcades; they are carried under arcades to their graves, and are laid under arcades in death.

At Ferrara, I found the living engaged in beating down the old houses of the city to make room for gardens, and several people were busy in the street before the house of Ariosto[3] and in other places, picking out the grass that grew between the paving stones. In Venice I was told of one new house going up, but it was on an old foundation. But though the buildings of Venice remain the same, in other respects its aspect has strangely altered within a few years past. A new northern invasion has descended upon these islets of the lagoons from the banks of the Danube, bringing with it Vienna beer, sausages, and sourcrout. You meet, at every other step, people with flaxen hair and white eyebrows; listen, and you perceive that they are talking German; they are an importation from Austria. German beer-gardens are opened; German restaurants abound where a few years since it was not easy to find an eating-house; men in military uniform, speaking the harsh dialect of Southern Germany, are strolling about everywhere. At the principal hotels you are served by German waiters and chambermaids; at the Hotel Danielli, which I would advise all travellers to avoid,[4] there is an Austrian director. All travellers who come to Venice visit the Arsenal, which has been regarded as one of the great curiosities of the place; but since the revolution of 1848, it has been placed under regulations which deprive it of much of its interest. You are no longer allowed to see the ancient arches under which the fleets of Venice, in the days of her power, were built, the old Navy Yard of the Republic. The hall containing ancient weapons and armor you are permitted to enter, but your Venetian guide is obliged to wait without, and you find the collection newly arranged. The massive helmet of Attila, which you were formerly allowed to take in your hands, and put on your head if you pleased, is hung up against the wall; and every object particularly worthy of note is now provided with its long German inscription, as if to intimate that they are Italian no longer, but are to be numbered among the tokens of Austrian dominion, like the cannon in the fortresses, and the muskets borne by the soldiery.

Milan is not Germanized to the same degree as Venice, but I doubt whether the people are better satisfied with the rule under which they live. "The revolution," said one of them to me, "took place ten years ago, and yet they treat us as if it were an event of yesterday. At every hour of the day we are made to feel that we are a conquered race. The military chief under the Austrian government, General Giulay, the successor of Radetzky, is the harsher master of the two."[5]

It was saddening to remain among a people submitting gloomily to their condition of slavery, and it was with a sense of relief that I entered the Sardinian dominions, and passing first through a tract of yellow-green rice-fields, and then through a region of fertile meadows between the grim, rocky steeps of the Alps on one side, and a range of cultivated hills on the other, reached the city of Turin. I seemed to breathe more freely in a freer country. In Turin you are surrounded with the tokens of cheerful activity, and see marks of prosperity for which you look vainly in any of the Italian cities under the governments to the east and south of it. A representative government, freedom of the press, and freedom of trade, have brought back to this part of Italy the impulses to enterprise, the energy and steadiness of action, which centuries ago made the Italian republics so great and powerful.

While at Turin I had the satisfaction of seeing another remarkable example of the success with which human ingenuity exerts itself when not encumbered with either the restraints or the patronage of the government. It happened that an exhibition of the products of Sardinian industry was open in the palace called the "Valentino," built two hundred years ago, by Catherine of France, in the pleasant environs of the city. These exhibitions are held once in five years, and they bring together samples of whatever is produced in the workshops, the looms, the furnaces, and the alembics of all the provinces and isles of Sardinia.

I was taken to see the exhibition by a very enlightened and agreeable member of the Sardinian Parliament, Signor Lorenzo Valerio,[6] to whom I was fortunate enough to have a letter of introduction. As we passed through the crowded streets, I could not help remarking that the people seemed well formed for active pursuits—thin, spare men, but with well-knit frames and a healthy look. The first thing I observed, on entering the lower galleries of the Valentino, was a long case of shelves, filled with models of the different varieties of cultivated fruits, executed with such skill as fairly to deceive the eye. I took them for real fruit, till I was told better. Here were the finest varieties of the pear, the Bon Chretien, the Duchesse d'Angouleme, the Chaumontel, and a hundred others; here glistened the green gage, the magnum bonum, and tribe after tribe of the plum family; here were apples and quinces of all sorts, so well imitated that you almost seemed to inhale their fragrance; here were the different varieties of the fig, the pomegranate, and the grape, with every tint and stain and peculiarity of shape, so perfectly copied, that any variety of fruit might at once be referred to its true appellation by comparing it with the model in the case. In this lower part of the palace, were rows of ploughs, corn-shellers, fanning-machines, and other agricultural implements, making it look like one of the departments of an agricultural fair in the United States. A machine for feeding silk-worms and keeping them clean, was among them. Here also were steam-engines, which the people of Sardinia have now learned to make for themselves, and iron stoves, and church-bells cast in the foundries of Savoy. I do not recollect whether it was in these lower galleries that my Italian friend showed me an ingenious improvement of the electric telegraph, by which a message is delivered in the very handwriting of the person sending it—a perfect *fac simile* being produced. I could perceive, at first, no practical use of this invention, except to put a new weapon into the hands of those who persecute distinguished persons for their autographs, but it might serve in certain cases to authenticate a message.

The display of silks in the upper galleries of the Valentino was absolutely dazzling. The silk-worm of Piedmont spins a beautiful fibre, regular, firm and glossy, and samples of raw silk in the exhibition were strikingly fine; some of the most so were from the mulberry orchards of Ferigliano. Of this material, quantities amounting in value to four millions of francs are annually sent to foreign countries. The silk fabrics were no less remarkable for excellence. From the vaulted roofs of the chambers, rough with figures in relief, and blazing with gold, the walls were tapestried with silk tissues of the greatest beauty, rivalling the products of the French looms. "This branch of industry," said Signor Valerio, "has grown up amidst complete liberty of trade, and within a few years past has made rapid progress." I looked round upon the long stripes of brocade descending from the ceiling to the floor; on the silk velvets, blue, red, and green, wrought by the work-people of Genoa; on the brilliant scarfs woven at Chambery; on the beautiful *moires* and *foulards*, the damasks and ribbons, and the glittering cloths of gold and silver from the looms of Turin—and felt a certain pleasure in reflecting that all this was the fruit of the simplest and earliest method of dealing with the industry of a nation—the policy of leaving it to itself.

The woollens of Sardinia are superior to those of Switzerland, though by no means of the first class. I saw samples of delicate flannels woven on the streams of the Valle Mosso, in the province of Biella. "The cotton goods of our country," said my Turinese companion, showing me several samples, "are equal in quality to those of France, and considerably cheaper." In another part of the exhibition I saw several cases filled with watches and time-pieces. "These before you," said he, "are from Cluses in Savoy; these others are from Bonneville, and these, again, are made at Sallenches. The manufacture of watches has at length crossed our frontier from Geneva, and, of late years, we make chronometers which rival those of Switzerland." Some light and graceful articles of porcelain attracted my attention. The porcelain of Sardinia is superior to that of Switzerland; but the glass from the furnaces of Savoy is hardly as good—it bears a tinge of smoke.

I shall be tedious—perhaps I am so already—if I go on to speak of the various other objects which attracted my attention—the musical instruments of wood and metal, which made one department of the exhibition look like a huge orchestra abandoned by the musicians; the massive slate of the country chiselled into tables and other articles of furniture; the tiles of a delicate grain, like marble, yet resisting heat like our fire-bricks; the products of the laboratory, piles of blue vitriol, pyramids of alum, stacks of sal-ammoniac, and the like; the delicate filigree work in silver; the gloves of Turin, just inferior to those of Paris, and as cheap again; and a hundred other things, all testifying to the vast variety of ways in which the industry of the country, under a system of freedom, voluntarily unfolds and extends itself.

I was struck with the beauty of some lithographic engravings in the exhibition. "They are line engravings, surely," said I to the gentleman who was with me. "By no means," was his answer, "they are lithographs; they are placed in that department, and cannot be any thing else." I examined them again, and such was the fineness and sharpness of the lines that I could hardly avoid shaking my head in sign of doubt. Some specimens of cabinet work, with inlaid pictorial designs, were scarcely less remarkable. They were executed with a kind of wood full of dark veins and spots, and with a skill and effect which were really astonishing. In several instances the designs were borrowed from the works of eminent masters, and in one instance the artisan had been daring enough to put the Transfiguration of Raphael on the doors of a writing-desk.

One of the days which I passed in Turin was Sunday, and I looked in upon the Waldenses, who, under the new system of religious freedom in Sardinia, are allowed to worship openly in the cities.[7] Their church in Turin is a handsome building, in the Romanesque style, with an ample semicircular recess for the communion at one end, and a pulpit built against one of the graceful pillars on the left side of the nave, as you enter. In the morning an elderly minister gave a sensible discourse in French, in which he did not spare either Nicodemus, who came to Jesus by night, nor his timorous imitators of the present day. He insisted on a frank, fearless, and sincere expression of opinion on religious subjects, with the admonition that it be uttered in all kindness and gentleness. The afternoon service was for the Italian part of the congregation, and was conducted by a young man, who gave a common-place sermon, but who had the merit of a very distinct elocution, so that I lost not a word. The prayers were mostly read by the minister from a book, but otherwise there was nothing in the services to distinguish them from those of a Presbyterian church in New York, if I except the language—and really it seemed strange to hear religious services of this sort in the tongue of Catholic Italy. Neither in the morning nor the afternoon was the congregation large, but its manner was attentive and devout. It was composed of persons manifestly of different conditions in life, the opulent and the laboring; the women sitting apart from the men; and scattered among the men were several persons in the uniform of the Sardinian army, both officers and soldiers.

MANUSCRIPT (partial draft): UVa TEXT: *LT II*, pp. 261–272; first published in *EP* for August 5, 1858.

1. Charles V (1500–1558), king of Spain, 1516–1556, was the Holy Roman Emperor from 1519 until his death.
2. Antonio Canova (1757–1822), Italian sculptor; Pietro Tenerani (c1789–1869), his pupil.
3. Ludovico Ariosto (1474–1533), Italian poet best remembered for his *Orlando Furioso* (1532), an epic tale of Roland.
4. Bryant's experience of this hotel was an unhappy one. He disliked the lodgings provided, and, leaving after a ten days' residence, paid a "most extortionate bill . . . which was swelled to an enormous size, by charges for ice and lunches of bread and butter, at rates never heard of before." "Diary, 1857–1858," June 14, 24, 1858.
5. The Austrian field marshal Joseph Radetzky (1766–1858), conqueror of Sardinia in 1848–1849, governed Upper Italy from 1849 to 1857. General Giulay has not been further identified. It seems likely that his name was garbled in the *EP* press room.
6. Lorenzo Valerio (1810–1865), Italian politician and liberal editor.
7. The Waldenses, members of a lay Protestant sect which had been persecuted as heretics since the twelfth century, were granted full civil and religious rights by King Charles Albert of Savoy in 1848. They were the subject of John Milton's sonnet "On the Late Massacre in Piemont" (1655). In 1824 Bryant recalled their sufferings in his "Hymn of the Waldenses." See *Poems* (1876), p. 88.

1041. *To* Messrs. John Munroe & Co.[1]

Paris   July 4th   1858.
Gentlemen.

I arrived in Paris yesterday afternoon, but unfortunately after your office was closed for the day. We are exceedingly anxious to hear from our friends in America and if it would not be too much trouble to you to let me have them by the bearer I shall be much obliged.

I am gentlemen
very truly yours
W. C. BRYANT

MANUSCRIPT: NYPL–GR (draft) ADDRESS: To Messrs. Munroe & Co.

1. Bryant's European bankers, with an office in New York City. See Letters 988, 996.

1042.   *To* John Bigelow

Paris, July 9, 1858.

My dear sir—

I learn through the newspapers that I have been elected by the New York Legislature, a Regent of the University.[1] I will not affect to undervalue the favorable opinion of so respectable a public body, manifested in so spontaneous a manner, without the least solicitation on the part of my friends, and I beg that this letter may be used as an expression of my best thanks.

There are, however, many motives which make it necessary for me to decline the appointment, and among these are my absence from the country, the inconvenience of combining the duties of the place with the pursuits in which I am engaged when at home, and my aversion to any form of public life now, by long habit made, I fear, invincible. I therefore desire, by this letter, to return the appointment to the kind hands which have sought to confer it upon me, confident that some worthier person will easily be found, who will bring the necessary alacrity to the performance of its duties.

I am, dear sir,
very truly yours,
W. C. BRYANT.

MANUSCRIPT: NYPL–GR (draft) TEXT: *EP*, August 9, 1858 ADDRESS: To John Bigelow, Esq.

1. It had been reported in the *Long Island Farmer* for April 20, 1858—and probably in other journals—that Bryant had been elected by the legislature a regent of the University of the State of New York. This letter declining the appointment was forwarded by Bigelow to the secretary of state. Gideon J. Tucker to Bigelow, August 7, 1858, NYPL–GR.

1043.   *To* Charles Sumner[1]

Paris   July 9th   1858.

Dear Mr   Sumner.

Mrs. Jameson is at No. 138 Avenue des Champs Elysees.[2] The Omnibus marked C. in the Rue Rivoli, sets one down at her door, and that

marked B, or the Chaillot Omnibus, sets you down at the corner of the Rue
de Berry, about a hundred yards from her door.

Yours truly
WM. C. BRYANT

MANUSCRIPT: HCL.

1. See 751.1, 976.7. When Bryant had seen Sumner in Paris the previous summer,
the senator had seemed to have recovered substantially from the brutal attack he had
suffered on the Senate floor in 1856. Now Bryant found him "very sore" from cauteri-
zations applied to his injured spine. Bryant, "Diary, 1857–1858," July 7, 1858.

2. At Naples, after his wife had begun to mend, Bryant had become acquainted
with Anna Brownell Jameson (1794–1860), versatile British art historian, seeing her
often, and reading with admiration her *Memoirs of Early Italian Painters* (1845) and
Sacred and Legendary Art (1848–1852). Meeting her again in Paris in July, he and
Frances renewed their acquaintance with this engaging friend of Lady Byron and Fanny
Kemble. A few days after this letter was written Bryant and Sumner spent an evening
together at Mrs. Jameson's apartments. Bryant, "Diary, 1857–1858," March 18–April 11,
July 8–15, 1858, *passim*.

1044. *To* John Bigelow

Paris   July 15th. 1858.

Dear Mr. Bigelow

I got your letter[1] on arriving at this place some days since and thank
you for the information it contains in respect to matters not cleared up in
the newspapers. The more I have thought of the Regency of the University
the more I am disinclined to accept it and I therefore enclose a letter
which, as there does not seem to be any body else to write to about it you
will oblige me by using as a formal refusal of the honor and the trouble.[2]

With regard to the right of ascertaining the real character of a vessel
which runs up the American flag, I do not well see how there can be much
difference of opinion among sensible and honest men, and the Evening
Post has taken precisely the course in regard to it which I should have done.
The doctrine that a pirate has a right to exemption from arrest if he will
only run up the American flag is an absurd, monstrous, and impudent assertion of impunity for crime, and always, whether put forth by Cass
Stevenson or Webster filled me with the intensest disgust. Reduced to plain
English this was the purport of Stevenson's demand on the British government in a correspondence which he had with it. That the British fleet have
not the right to stop a vessel which is known to be an American trader is
true enough, but the running up of an American flag gives no authentic
information on that point. If the British or Spanish slave trader can escape
so, he will always run up the American flag, and the British fleet can never
capture a British vessel engaged in any sort of piracy. But these are matters
so clear as to be truisms.[3]

I got letters from Mr. Henderson at the same time with yours and I wish you to say to him that I am glad he is able to give so good an account of his department of the paper. My best way, I am inclined to think is not to go near a concern which is so much the more prosperous without me.[4]

With this I send you another letter for the Evening Post.[5] I cannot say I wrote it with perfect good will to the task, and therefore it may be somewhat heavy.

My wife improves, but more slowly than I could wish. She is not equal to the task of sight seeing yet. We shall go in a few days to England where I hope a new climate and air may do her good.

The weather here for a fortnight past has been very cool—sometimes miserably cold—before that the people were parboiled with the heat. Yesterday was the first rather warm day that we have had since I came here.

My wife and daughter desire their regards. Remember us all most kindly to Mrs. Bigelow.

Yours truly
W. C. BRYANT

MANUSCRIPT: NYPL–GR ENDORSED: W^m. C. Bryant. / July 15th 1858 PUBLISHED (*in part*): *Life*, II, 115–116.

1. Probably that dated June 12, 1858, NYPL–BG.
2. Letter 1042.
3. Since 1841, when Andrew Stevenson (1784–1857) was the United States minister to Great Britain, the practice of British warships charged with suppressing a clandestine African slave trade of visiting American flag vessels suspected of complicity had met strong diplomatic opposition from Washington. By 1858 the trade had become so flagrant, with slave ships fitted out in American ports, and southern juries unwilling to convict their crews, that British naval forces were accused by Secretary of State Lewis Cass (232.6, 554.2) of harassing American commerce in the Caribbean. In a series of *EP* editorials in May 1858 Bigelow charged the Buchanan administration with seeking an excuse to enlarge the American navy, and to draw attention away from the troubles in Kansas. *EP*, May 21, 22, 27, 28, 1858; Nevins, *Emergence of Lincoln*, I, 433–440; Thomas A. Bailey, *A Diplomatic History of the American People*, 6th ed. (New York: Appleton-Century-Crofts [1958]), pp. 210–211, 215–216, 283.
4. Writing Bryant on June 8, 1858, Isaac Henderson reported Bryant's semi-annual dividend as $22,500, the largest ever declared. Homestead Collection.
5. Possibly Letter 1047.

1045.   *To* Cephas G. Thompson

Paris   July 16. 1858.
My dear sir.

Yesterday my bankers here, Messrs. John Munroe & Co engaged to pay you, through Packenham & Hooker of Rome, one hundred and fifty Roman crowns or dollars, which I suppose you have only to call and receive, sending me your copy of Raphael's beautiful little Madonna when you find the opportunity.[1]

We had a pleasant journey thus far; a slow one to be sure, but not the less agreeable for that. My wife bore travelling very well, better than she bears the fatigue of getting ready for America, with so many things to buy and get made up. Next week we go to England. Miss Ives has suffered much by a sprain of her ancle followed by several painful boils just above it, ending in a kind of neuralgia. Since she was been here she has employed a physician, is better and next week will go to America.[2]

Remember me kindly to Mrs. Thompson. My wife and the girls desire their regards to you both, not forgetting your daughter and the others. . . .[3]

P.S. Please acknowledge the receipt of the money. W. C. B.

MANUSCRIPT: DuU ENDORSED: I am sorry that sometime/passed I have cut of[f] the signature for/some one—who I dont remember / But there is no doubt of this writing being / Wᵐ Cullen Bryant's / Cephas G. Thompson.

1. While at Rome in May, Bryant had bought from Thompson that artist's copy of Raphael's *Madonna of the Staffa*. See Bryant, "Diary, 1857–1858," May 28, 1857. Acknowledging this letter, and receipt of payment, from Rome on July 29 (NYPL–BG), Thompson reported that this picture had been shipped to New York in the care of Green and Nelson, who were probably customs brokers.

2. The Bryant party had been several times delayed during their journey through northern Italy by the incapacity of Estelle Ives, who had to be carried on occasion from carriage to hotel. On July 20 she left the party at Paris to return to America on the steamship *Vanderbilt* with Mrs. Robert Sedgwick's nieces, Grace Ashburner Sedgwick (1833–1897) and Jane Sedgwick (1821–1889), and the young American artist Henry Augustus Loop (1831–1895), whom the Bryants had met first at Venice, and again at Paris. Bryant, "Diary, 1857–1858," May 30–July 20, 1858, *passim*.

3. Conclusion and signature clipped; see descriptive note.

1046. *To* Robert C. Waterston

Paris, July 16th [1858].[1]

[My dear friend]

I cannot leave Paris without writing to you again. My last was written to you from Florence [the 7th of June],[2] expressing the hope that we might get a line from you at Venice or at this place, since which time we have only heard from you indirectly. We have very, very often talked of you, and wondered what was the condition of your dear child, and at one time consoled ourselves with the hope that your daughter was better, and that you had left Naples with her; but this hope was overthrown by hearing, since we came here, that a letter from you had been received dated the 29th of June, and that Helen was very low. My wife bids me say that she was ill at Naples a longer time than your daughter has been, and that she did not think she should recover, and yet she was raised up. I know that you cannot often write with so much anxiety pressing upon you; but if at any time you would communicate to us in the briefest manner, or desire any of your friends to whom you write to communicate to us any intelligence respecting your daughter's case, there are none who would receive it with a deeper sympathy.

Next week we all leave France for England. From England, we expect to go home the latter part of August, perhaps the twenty-first.

MANUSCRIPT: NYPL–GR (draft fragment) TEXT: *Life*, II, 116 ADDRESS: [To Rev R. C. Waterston].

    1. Matter within brackets is added from the draft MS in NYPL–GR.
    2. Actually dated June 5 (Letter 1036).

1047. *To* the EVENING POST?[1]

Paris July 19th 1858.

The journals on your side of the water have frequent accounts of what the American artists are doing at Rome and Florence, but scarce any thing is said of the works they are producing in Paris. Our countrymen who visit Paris are too much occupied with other matters, the sights and amusements and institutions of this gay and animated capital to find leisure for visiting the studios of the few American artists settled here. I confess that I had fallen into the common practice in this respect—but the other day I went to see some of the American artists in their rooms and was glad that I had done so.

Cranch[2] has fixed himself near the Barrière de Neuilly at the western extremity of the city—the barrier out of which every fine afternoon on summer holidays pour the vast crowds that fill the shady alleys of the Bois de Boulogne. But the Bois de Boulogne is quite too trim a place notwithstanding the extent of its forest grounds for a landscape painter, and Cranch accordingly goes further. He betakes himself to Fontainebleau—a place where he finds wild nature—rocks and declivities and majestic trees—many of them named after the old French monarchs of three or four hundred years since, and perhaps as old as their time. Cranch has made great progress in his oil during the few years he has been in Europe. He has studied assiduously, and in the best of schools, that of nature; has acquired a freer touch and a more vigorous and confident rendering of the forms of natural beauty. His rooms are full of very interesting studies, the materials of landscapes yet to be finished. I can only wish for his productions a chance of being seen by his countrymen which they would be if he lived either at Rome or New York.[3]

White is here engaged in painting his picture of General Washington's Resignation of his Military Command into the hands of Congress.[4] It is for the state of Maryland and will be hung in their Senate Chamber. The decision was one of great moral interest, yet a very difficult one for the painter. In its unfinished state, one cannot judge of the merit of the painting, yet I was struck with the skill with which the assemblage is grouped and arranged, and the variety given to the attitudes and expressions. The figures are of course all patriots, and this is so far [a constraint?] upon the . . .

MANUSCRIPT: NYPL–GR (incomplete draft).

1. The full text of this letter, not printed in *LT II*, has not been found in the *EP*.
2. The American artist Christopher Pearse Cranch (1813–1892) was also a Unitarian clergyman and a minor poet. A friend of Ralph Waldo Emerson's, he is best remembered for some verses called "Gnosis," which seem to epitomize American Transcendentalist thought. The Bryants saw Mr. and Mrs. Cranch several times during their Paris visit. Bryant, "Diary, 1857–1858," July 12–14, 1858.
3. In 1859 Cranch exhibited at the National Academy a "Study in Fontainble[a]u Forest." *NAD Exhibition Record*, I, 98.
4. Bryant had called with the Cranches at the studio of the American painter Edwin White (1817–1877) to see this picture. Bryant, "Diary, 1857–1858," July 13, 1858.

1048. *To* Robert Dale Owen

London   July 23d   1858.

My dear Mr. Owen.

I am much obliged to you for the information you communicate respecting Miss Waterston.[1] I got a letter from her father, dated the 13th of July — yours was four days later, so that it was a kind of supplement to his, and a most welcome one it was, since it assured us that the hopes of her recovery expressed in his letter were likely to be fulfilled.

I do not exactly see why Mr. Buchanan has put Mr. Chandler in your place, provided you were willing to stay. He is an amiable man, but will be, I think, quite out of his place at Naples.[2] It is very much like sending a deaf man to report the proceedings of a public meeting. The same mistake, I believe, has been made in some of the other late diplomatic appointments.

You perceive, from the date of this, that we are at London, so that I must not expect the pleasure of seeing you again, till you arrive in America. Miss Ives left us at Paris and has gone home in the steamer Vanderbilt from Havre. Our own passage is taken in one of the Cunard steamers, the Africa, for the 21st of August, and we have sent a cartload of luggage forward to Liverpool, to be kept in the Cunard warehouse till we go.

The English air seems to do my wife good. At Paris the dressmakers and other trades people pestered her so with their failure to keep their word and their excuses and their chatter, that she became nervous and discouraged, but she has now recovered her spirits. I think of giving her the benefit of a few days of country air in Worcestershire and Warwickshire, before we set out for America.

If my wife and daughter were with me while I am writing this they would of course send their kindest regards— Remember me to Mrs. Marsden and believe me

Ever faithfully yours
W. C. BRYANT

MANUSCRIPT: HSPa.

1. On July 17 Owen had written Bryant (NYPL–GR) that Helen Waterston continued to improve, and that, although a Dr. Roskilly had given her up, Dr. Rubini hoped to save her.

2. Joseph Ripley Chandler (1792–1880), whom President Buchanan had appointed to replace Owen, was a former journalist and Whig congressman from Pennsylvania. He was the American minister to Naples from 1858 to 1861.

1049.   *To* Robert C. Waterston

London   July 23.   1858.

Dear Mr. Waterston—

Yesterday was a great day with us. We got from our bankers Messrs   Peabody & Co your letter of the 13th[1] giving us news of the favorable progress of Helen's case, and with it a letter from Mr. Owen of the 17th informing us that she still continued to improve, and there was, I assure you, great rejoicing in our household. Perhaps our exultation was a little selfish—considering what had happened as a triumph of *our* cause, homoeopathy—inasmuch as we were informed that under the care of her first physician Helen remained apparently in the same state, and that under the charge of Dr   Rubini she immediately began to mend. It was a relief too to know from some authority that you had neither been overwhelmed in the late eruption, nor dissolved by the heat— I hope you did not suffer by it so much at Naples as people did further north. We had almost begun to fear from your long silence that you had suffered the fate of Pliny, and had gone a little too near the great phenomenon—[2]

I had the pleasure of reading some parts of your letter and Mr   Owen's supplement to Mr   Morgan of the house of Peabody & Co[3] whe . . .

MANUSCRIPT: NYPL–GR (partial draft).

1. July 13, 1858, NYPL–BG.
2. The Roman naturalist Caius Plinius Secundus (Pliny the Elder, *c*23–79) suffocated while investigating the eruption of Mt. Vesuvius.
3. Since 1854 Junius Spencer Morgan (1813–1890) had been a partner in the London international banking firm of George Peabody & Co. He and his wife and daughter were fellow-passengers of the Bryants' on their return voyage to New York aboard the *Africa* in August 1858. Bryant, "Diary, 1857–1858," August 21, 1858.

1050.   *To* Fanny Bryant Godwin

London   July 28th   1858.

Dear Fanny.

After you receive this it will not be worth while for you or any body else to write any more letters to us for we shall probably be on the water before we could receive them. We have taken passage in the steamer Africa which will leave Liverpool on the 21st of August, and in all probability bring us,—if we do not change to a steamer which departs later—to New York in the first week of September. Your mother does not recover so fast as I could wish; still she gains a little constantly, and is now stronger than she was when at Paris. You will find her, unless English air should plump her up to her old dimensions, considerably fallen away in size.

We are here among Americans, Mr. Gorham D. Abbott[1] close by us on one side, and Mr Tefft an architect from Providence[2] on the other, all of us in Jermyn Street within three or four doors of each other.[3] Huntington[4] is here, homesick—Cropsey[5] is here flourishing and satisfied, and his wife a very popular person. They live in a nice house and give little entertainments; I met Mulready the painter[6] there the other night—and after I came away Julia told me that the Reverend Mr. Hulbert the Christian Socialist[7] was among the company. I thought we should not see him again after he left America. The other day we went to pass the Sunday at Mr Edwin Field's at Hampstead, and in the afternoon came over Mrs Cropsey with all her babies and her husband and Paul Duggan.[8] Mr. Duggan has recovered his health he says, though he is quite thin yet; he despises the English, he says, and will have nothing to do with them associating with Americans, and I suppose the Irish, but he likes the climate and the country.

In a day or two we go to Evesham in Worcestorshire, where Ferdinand Field lives, "retired," he says, "from the turmoil of life, hoping to end his days in peace."[9] It is a very pleasant country town they say, not far from Stratford upon Avon.

Love to all—your mother sends *hers* to all.

Affectionately yours
W C BRYANT

P.S. Please send over the enclosed to Mr Cline.[10]

W. C. B.

MANUSCRIPT: NYPL–GR.

1. Gorham Dummer Abbot (1807–1874), a Presbyterian minister, directed the Spingler Institute for young women in New York City. An art patron, he had bought for the institute in 1849 Thomas Cole's celebrated four-painting series, "The Voyage of Life." See Howard S. Merritt, *Thomas Cole: Introduction and Catalogue*, Exhibition of the Memorial Art Gallery of the University of Rochester [Rochester: Memorial Art Gallery, 1969], pp. 35–56; Letter 1051.
2. Thomas Alexander Tefft (1829–1859, Brown 1851), architect and monetary reformer, wrote on architecture for *The Crayon*. ACAB.
3. In Paris the Bryants had lodged next door to Robert and Elizabeth Browning. Several times the couples had exchanged calls, and Browning had given Bryant a list of convenient hotels. One of these was that run by a Mrs. Effingham at 41 Jermyn Street, where the Bryants stayed from July 21 to 31. Bryant, "Diary, 1857–1858," July 8, 9, 13, 21, 31, 1858; *Dearest Isa: Robert Browning's Letters to Isabella Blagden*, ed. Edward C. McAleer (Austin: University of Texas Press, 1951), p. 11. But there seems scant evidence of so close a relationship as that suggested by Parke Godwin, who wrote that "Bryant conceived a strong personal attachment for both Mr. and Mrs. Browning," and

that Browning "always" spoke of their "intercourse" thereafter "with great pleasure."
See *Life*, II, 115.

4. The painter Daniel Huntington (499.3).

5. The American architect and landscape painter Jaspar Francis Cropsey (1823–1900), who worked in London from 1857 to 1863. *DAA*.

6. The British genre painter William Mulready (1786–1863) had designed the first penny-postage envelope in 1840.

7. Probably Charles Augustus Hulbert (1805–1888; M.A. Cambridge 1837), incumbent of Slaithwaite, Yorkshire, 1839–1867.

8. The Irish-born American portrait artist and medalist Paul Peter Duggan (?–1861) exhibited at the American Art-Union and the National Academy between 1844 and 1856. *DAA*. At some time before about 1855 he had drawn the crayon likeness of Bryant owned by the Century Association.

9. Ferdinand Field to Bryant, June 16, 1858, William Cullen Bryant II.

10. Bryant's Roslyn steward, George B. Cline (1005.1).

1051.   *To* Edwin W. Field[1]

[London, *c*July 29, 1858]

My dear sir

The bearer of this is the Reverend Gorham D. Abbott of New York who is at the head of one of our institutions of education and enjoys the general respect of our community— He takes great interest in the promotion of the fine arts, and is anxious to procure an introduction to Mr. Taylor of whom you spoke to me the other day—who writes criticisms on works of art for the Times.[2]

He applied to me hoping that I knew Mr Taylor but as I do not it occurred to me that the introduction might be obtained through you. If you will have the kindness to aid Mr. Abbott in the accomplishment of his wish I shall add it to the obligations I already owe you— I shall join him in thanking you for this act of kindness—

[unsigned]

MANUSCRIPT: NYPL–GR (draft) ADDRESS: Edwin W. Field Esqre.

1. See 540.7. Field had just entertained the Bryants for several days in his home on suburban Hampstead Heath, which Bryant had visited on earlier trips to London. Here, for the first time, Mrs. Bryant met this influential London lawyer and amateur artist, his wife, and their four sons and daughters. Other guests included the Egyptologist Samuel Sharpe (1799–1881); artists Richard Doyle (1824–1883) and Walter Goodall (1830–1889); Henry Wilkinson Cookson (1810–1876, M.A. Cambridge 1835), master of Peterhouse College and godson of William Wordsworth; and the naturalist and physician William Benjamin Carpenter (1813–1885) of the University of London. Bryant, "Diary, 1857–1858," July 24, 25, 1858.

2. Tom Taylor (1817–1880, M.A. Cambridge 1843), dramatist and writer for several London newspapers, who later (1874–1880) edited *Punch*. It was Taylor's comedy, *Our American Cousin*, which Abraham Lincoln was watching in Ford's Theatre, Washington, on the evening of his assassination, April 14, 1865. Nevins, *War for the Union*, IV, 325.

1052. *To* Samuel Carter Hall[1]

London   July 30   1858.

Dear Sir

I thank you and Mrs. Hall,[2] and my wife joins in these acknowledgments for the hospitable intent of your very kind note which reached me yesterday evening.[3] The position you both hold in the world of letters makes the compliment more valuable and more grateful. You offer a strong temptation in the promise to make me aquainted with some of the artists of your country, for I have ever taken great pleasure in the society of that class of men.

I am obliged, however, to leave London tomorrow. My wife is yet an invalid, recovering from a nervous fever which held her a prisoner four months at Naples, and needs the quiet of the country, and the benefit of country air. We have taken passage on the 21st of August from Liverpool to New York, but we may possibly, though I do not think it likely, change our passage to some steamer departing on a later day. If I should make this change I shall have leisure to return to London in which case I will do myself the honor to report myself to you.

I am, dear sir,
very truly and faithfully
yours
W   C   BRYANT

MANUSCRIPT: NYPL–GR (draft) ADDRESS: To Mr. S. C. Hall.

1. Author Samuel Carter Hall (1800–1889) edited the *Art Union Monthly Journal* and its successor, the London *Art Journal*, from 1839 to 1880.
2. The novelist and playwright Anna Maria Fielding Hall (1800–1881).
3. Unrecovered.

1053. *To* the EVENING POST

Evesham, England, August 9, 1858.

I had not thought of writing again to the Evening Post before leaving Europe, but I am prompted to it by a letter containing the following sad announcement, which I beg may also be placed among the deaths in the Evening Post:

"At Naples, Sunday, July 25, departed this life, after an illness of three months, Helen Ruthven Waterston, aged 17 years, the beloved and only daughter of Robert and Anna Waterston, of Boston, U. S. A."[1]

Some of the pleasantest as well as some of the saddest recollections of my present visit to Europe, relate to this charming young person and her premature death. I must say a word of her, and of the dangers which, in some cases at least, attend a residence in Naples.

It was at Heidelberg, a little more than a year since, that I met the Reverend R. C. Waterston, of Boston, with his wife and their daughter, an only child. I confess that I felt a certain pride in so magnificent a specimen of my countrywomen as this young lady presented—uncommonly beautiful in person, with a dignity of presence and manner much beyond her years, and a sweetness no less remarkable than the dignity. Wherever she went, it was easy to see that she was followed by looks of admiration. A further acquaintance with her showed that her intellectual and moral qualities were equal to her personal graces. Her mind was surprisingly mature for her time of life. She was kind, true, sympathetic, religious, and overflowing with filial affection—the most dutiful as well as most beloved of daughters. After we left Heidelberg, we saw no more of her, until her parents, in April last, after a winter's residence in Rome, brought her, apparently in full health, to Naples, where we then were, and took lodgings at the Vittoria Hotel, in the street of that name, looking out on the beautiful bay.

The streets of Chiatamone, Vittoria and the Chiaja contain the best hotels in Naples, and their situation is highly attractive to the stranger. The public garden called the Villa Reale, extends in front of them, the only promenade for pedestrians in Naples; and a pleasant one it is; the grand peninsula of Posilipo, studded with stately country seats, and overhanging the sea with its tall gray precipices, bounds the sight to the west; to the east you have in view Castellamare and Sorrento with their background of airy mountain summits; in front rises the rocky isle of Capri, and close at hand the waters of the Mediterranean dash and murmur all day and all night on the shingly beach in front of the houses. The glorious prospect, the broad open streets, full of Neapolitan bustle, and the warm winter sunshine, allure travellers to fix themselves in this part of Naples in preference to any other. Yet this beautiful quarter has a bad reputation for health among the Neapolitans. A friend of mine, who had resided for some years at Naples, said to me; "I know a lady who has a palace on the Chiatamone, and who declares that as soon as she makes trial of living in it, she suffers with disordered nerves. So she is obliged to let it, and to live a little way back from the shore; a short distance will answer. The same thing happens to many others. They abandon their desirable mansions to those who are willing to live in them." From other quarters I heard, not long after my arrival, that people living in this spot were subject to low nervous fevers. What may be the cause I do not pretend to say. The sewers of the city have their mouths here in the edge of the bay, and under the very windows of the houses there runs one of these foul conduits, with frequent small openings, which send up offensive exhalations. Possibly this is the main occasion of the mischief.

It was in an hotel in this part of Naples that Mr. Waterston took rooms for his family. They had scarcely occupied them three days, when Miss Waterston was seized with the malady which ended her life. It was attended from the first with great weakness—so great, that before it became clear to her parents that it was desirable to remove her, a removal was impossible. Once or twice the disorder put on a favorable appearance, and they were flattered with the hope of her recovery; but at length it became manifest that it was a disease of the heart, and must prove fatal. Whether she might have escaped the attack in a more healthful atmosphere, I will not presume to conjecture, nor whether in a different climate the medical remedies applied would have had a better chance of success; but it is at least highly probable that she would have escaped the deplorable weakness, which almost at once made her removal to a more friendly atmosphere, impossible.

When I mentioned to my banker at Florence that we had left Miss Waterston very ill at Naples, he exclaimed with great energy, "Her father must get her away as soon as he can; it is certain death for her to stay; the climate of Naples is the most relaxing in the world." But whether a removal would have been beneficial or not, it had long been an impossibility. She grew weaker and weaker, bearing her sufferings with a patience and resignation so sweet and saint-like, that even the physicians, familiar as they were with the experiences of the sick-room and the death-bed, were melted to tears. At length, a little before her end, her mind began to wander, but in such a manner that it seemed as if she was admitted to a glimpse of the brighter world to which she was going, and she passed away in what might almost be taken for a beatific vision—a happy life closed by a happy death—leaving her parents broken-hearted, but for the strong religious trust which supported them.

I heard many persons, while I was in Italy, speak of the unfavorable influences of a residence in Naples on persons subject to nervous complaints, and many instances of it were related to me. Perhaps the cases were confined to this quarter so much dreaded by the Neapolitans themselves. So convinced was I of the prejudicial effect of its atmosphere in such cases, that I caused the one of our party whose illness—a nervous fever—detained us so long at Naples, to be removed from the street called Vittoria to the *Pension d'Europe*, away from the shore, on higher ground, and among the gardens; and the removal, I thought, was attended with immediate and manifest advantage. The profound sorrow in which I pen these lines would be without its proper fruit, did I neglect to caution those who are liable to nervous complaints, and who fear to be reduced by them to a state of extreme bodily weakness, against the climate of Naples, and particularly against a residence in that quarter which I have described.

MANUSCRIPT: UVa TEXT: *LT II*, pp. 273–277; first published in *EP* for August 26, 1858.

1. Sending Bryant this obituary paragraph in a letter from Naples on July 27, 1858, Robert Waterston had added, "The slightest tribute from you would be of inexpressible value whatever form it should take—but if it pleased Heaven that that Blessed Spirit which has so often inspired you—should prompt such words as you do at times write—better—far better would it be than costliest monument of chiseled marble." Homestead Collection.

1054. *To* Robert C. Waterson

Stratford-on-Avon, August 11th.   1858

Dear Mr. Waterston.

Your letter[1] did not reach me so soon as it ought to have done, by several days, having been sent by mistake, from my banker's to my late lodgings in Jermyn Street, London. The sorrowful and unexpected news it brought afflicted us all—and in a particular manner my wife, who with Julia desires me to say, for them as well as myself, how largely we share in the grief which this calamity has brought upon you and Mrs. Waterston. Yet, knowing your daughter as we did, and being made acquainted with the manner in which she bore the sufferings of a sick bed, and her admirable behavior throughout her long illness, we share also in the consolation, so dear to you both, that she was prepared in the eminent degree for that great transfiguration which awaits the good in another life. For the wound inflicted on your spirits, by so great a calamity, there can be no balm like this.

I followed the suggestion you made; I wrote a letter to be printed in the Evening Post, and gave the proper directions for sending the copies of it to Boston. After I had despatched it, I had misgivings as to the caution I gave in it respecting the climate of Naples. What I meant to say was, not that the climate caused the malady by which your daughter was attacked, nor that it hindered its cure, but that its enervating influence probably prevented her removal at a time when it seemed desirable to seek to place her in some more friendly and invigorating atmosphere. I hope the words I used will seem to imply no more than this.

I was at Evesham when your letter reached me. There is a society of Unitarians in that place, and the same day several of them spoke to me of what had happened, the news of which they had read in the Illustrated News and in the London Inquirer, and expressed their great sympathy. I am now at the house of your friend Mr. Flower,[2] all whose family I found greatly distressed at the sad tidings, having learned to love your daughter during your visit to this place last summer.

I would gladly say more, if I knew how to deal with so great a sorrow. You have referred to all the topics of consolation in your letter, and they are all summed up in the goodness of your dear child—the very goodness which makes the loss so great. Perhaps the early unfolding of her mental powers and the early ripeness of her moral and religious nature were presages that she was soon to be called to a better world, and indications that the discipline of life, for her, had accomplished its end, and was no more needed.

We shall be very anxious to learn how Mrs. Waterston continues to support this calamity. We expect to leave England for home in the steamer

Africa next week, on the 21st of this month. May we not hear from you in America?

My wife has gained somewhat since her arrival in England but the return of her strength is a very slow process and she can bear but little exertion yet. She is now suffering with an attack of influenza. Julia after a like attack and a very severe one is now quite well. They desire the expression of their warmest love and sympathy to you and Mrs. Waterston, to whom as well as yourself you will please consider this letter as addressed.

I am, my dear friends

faithfully yours

W. C. BRYANT

MANUSCRIPTS: UVa (final); NYPL–GR (draft) ENDORSED: From W. C. Bryant. PUBLISHED (*in part*): *Life*, II, 116–117.

1. Of July 27; see 1053.1.

2. Edward Fordham Flower (1805–1883) was a prosperous brewer and sheep breeder at Stratford-upon-Avon who was four times mayor of that town, and who often entertained American visitors. While at Evesham visiting Ferdinand Field, before coming to Stratford, the Bryants had received an invitation from Mrs. Flower to stay in her home while in the town. Bryant, "Diary, 1857–1858," August 6, 1858.

XX

The Impending Crisis
1858–1859
(LETTERS 1055 TO 1122)

ON THE DAY BRYANT RETURNED to New York from Europe, the *Evening Post* carried a report from its correspondent at the scene of the second Lincoln–Douglas debate, on August 27 at Freeport, Illinois. Abraham Lincoln was, he wrote, "awkward" and "ugly," but "stir him up and the fire of his genius plays on every feature; [he is] a man of rare power and strong magnetic influence." While the seven debates continued, attracting ever-widening interest throughout the country, Bryant gave no editorial opinion of them, but soon after the final one, at Alton, Illinois, on October 15, he remarked, "No man of this generation has grown more rapidly before the country than Mr. Lincoln in this canvas." Though Lincoln failed to unseat Douglas in their senatorial race, he established himself as a leading national figure.

Throughout the ensuing year Bryant remained noncommittal on his choice of a candidate for the Republican nomination for the presidency in 1860. When, in January 1859, Senator Preston King of New York tried to pin him down, he "had no candidate or at least he named none." Bryant would, he said, support his party's choice, but he had serious "apprehensions" of Senator William H. Seward of New York, King's as well as John Bigelow's favorite for the nomination. Three months later King reported to Bigelow at Paris, "I have not seen any thing in the *Post* indicating a disposition to discuss the question of Candidacy." To his brother John, however, Bryant confided that he considered Governor Salmon P. Chase of Ohio the man best qualified for the presidency, but feared Chase could not win the Republican nomination.

If he was not yet ready to propose a future President, Bryant was outspoken time and again against the present one, Democrat James Buchanan. Let the President at least try to leave the office "with credit," he wrote, "a matter of which he seems hitherto to have taken no thought." But, he added, this was a difficult task for a man "whose conscience has become callous with wrong doing." Buchanan's was a "spendthrift" administration, he charged; it was trying stealthily to enact protective tariffs on the pretext of needing revenue. Its scheme to buy Cuba from Spain was a "childish" fraud—simply a "convenient pretext . . . for invading it and attempting to possess it by force." Cuba was essential to Spain, its "West," and Europe was right to cry "hands off!" In seizing Cuba, we should "do precisely what we were warned against by the voice of Washington in his Farewell Address"—entangle ourselves in European politics.

Buchanan's greatest sin, however, was a "blind devotion to the interests of the slaveholders," whose votes he counted on to win him re-election, while holding the North through political patronage.

Two months after Bryant's return John Bigelow took his family for an extended visit to Europe, where he followed Bryant's practice of writing to the newspaper accounts of events and personalities as he traveled about France and Italy. For several months Bryant busied himself with the daily conduct of their journal. Then, in February 1859, he took his son-in-law, Parke Godwin, back into the office, and at about the same time made William S. Thayer, a former Washington correspondent, managing editor of the *Evening Post*, which had become, in the words of Isaac Henderson, "prosperous—very prosperous." With the newspaper "staggering under the burden of advertisements," Bryant confessed wryly to Bigelow in April, "The Evening Post has not been edited from the time you went away till within a few days, except by the advertisers." In recourse, an additional column was added to each of four pages in the already unwieldly folio sheet, for subscribers had begun to "complain bitterly of the encroachment of the advertisements upon the space allotted to news."

Relieved of the tedium of management, and now able to leave to others the writing of routine copy, save for leading editorials, Bryant put together a second volume of his travel correspondence, covering his most recent European visit, which Appleton published in March 1859. The next month he was asked to contribute to Robert Bonner's widely popular weekly, the *New York Ledger*, a few poems "only when you feel the inspiration to write them." For these, the editor would be pleased "at any time" to hand him a $1,000 check. His first verses, "The Lost Bird," a translation from the Spanish of Carolina Coronado's *El Pajaro Perdido*, appeared in June. During the ensuing years Bonner published a dozen of Bryant's poems, as well as his translation of Coronado's romantic novel, *Jarilla*.

A great source of satisfaction to Bryant in the spring of 1859 was the progress being made in the development of New York's Central Park. Fifteen years earlier he had proposed its establishment in the *Evening Post*, and had often since repeated his suggestion. In April he visited the park with his brother-in-law Egbert Fairchild, an engineer busy building the new Croton Reservoir within its boundaries, and afterward likened the scene of prodigious labor to "Dido and her people building Carthage."

Beyond his contribution of the park idea, Bryant had taken practical steps to bring it to fruition. He was one of those who endorsed Frederick Law Olmsted's application for the superintendency of construction, and both the annual reports of the park commissioners and the successful *Greensward Plan* for the park's development prepared by Olmsted and Calvert Vaux appeared under the impress of William C. Bryant and Company.

Bryant's admiration of Olmsted's abilities led him early in 1859 to the conclusion that the park's superintendent, "who is a man of great administrative capacity, who selects all his subordinates and agents with an instinctive wisdom, and who does not allow a dollar of the public money to be paid out except for value received, would be an infinitely better President than we have had since Van Buren, but nobody will think of nominating him, and few would know whom they were voting for when they gave him their suffrage."

Returning from abroad, Bryant had resumed an active association with fellow-members of the Sketch Club and at the Century, which was prospering in a new home on Fifteenth Street, its membership having grown to two-hundred-fifty. His popularity with the artists, both as subject and inspiration, was as great as ever. He sat for portraits to Thomas Hicks, Sanford Gifford, Alonzo Chappel, Anthon Henry Wenzler, William T. Mathews, and Charles Cromwell Ingham. John Durand caused his father's likeness of Bryant—that for which Mrs. Bryant had given the artist "a thousand thanks for making something pleasing of a face which so many have caricatured"—to be engraved for popular subscription. Matthew Brady again photographed Bryant, as he had in 1845. Several landscape painters borrowed the themes of Bryant's "The Death of the Flowers," "Green River," and "Thanatopsis."

Renewing old friendships, Bryant could only have been pleased with Richard Dana's comment on his new volume of letters, "It calmed me like a sunlight, gentle and with no glare, . . . the style beautifully pure and simple," and with Orville Dewey's tribute to the *Evening Post*, "the best paper I think in America." Dewey and George Bancroft vied for his presence at their country homes. Boston financier and an influential Republican, John Murray Forbes, who considered Bryant "the leader of the only really Democratic party which ever existed," reminded the editor of a long-standing "half-promise" to visit him at his island home, Naushon, off Cape Cod, offering to send his forty-ton yacht to meet the Bryants at New Bedford. Forbes had "set his heart" on Bryant's company, he told Catharine Sedgwick. An earlier international friendship was enhanced when the English parliamentary leader Richard Cobden visited New York in March 1859; Bryant dined with him several times, in company with Bancroft, William H. Osborn, and Charles Leupp.

In October 1859, in the death of his intimate friend Leupp, Bryant bore a loss comparable only to that occasioned by the death of Thomas Cole a decade earlier. The two had worked closely together nearly twenty years before to form the American Art-Union; they had traveled in company abroad four times; they had been active in making the Sketch Club and the Century Association primary forces in molding the city's cultural life; each had been among the most staunch friends and patrons of American artists. The shock of Leupp's death was the heavier because a growing despondency had led him to suicide. Before serving as a pallbearer at his funeral, Bryant wrote for the *Evening Post* an obituary which was read into the minutes of the Sketch Club. His "dearly cherished friend" had been, he said, "one of those whom the maxims and habits of trade had never corrupted; a man of open and generous temper, who abhorred every form of deceit and every unfair advantage, sensitive to blame, almost to excess, yet never to be driven by blame from any course which he thought right."

Less than two months later Bryant lost an older, if not so intimate a friend, Washington Irving. Soon afterward, he was asked to deliver the eulogy at a memorial meeting of the New-York Historical Society, of which Irving had been one of its earliest, most beloved members. And Bryant experienced still another bereavement that fateful autumn with the passing of Theodore Sedgwick III, son of his early mentor in economic theory, and himself Bryant's collaborator for many years in the *Evening Post*'s editorial columns, as well as in a collection of William Leggett's *Political Writings*.

That the autumn of 1859 would be remembered as fateful was made evident in a political event which quickly polarized public opinion in both North and South on the issue of slavery. On the night of October 16 John Brown of Osawatomie led a little band of radical Abolitionists in an abortive raid on the government arsenal at Harper's Ferry, Virginia. The raiders were quickly killed or captured by federal forces under Brevet Colonel Robert E. Lee, and six weeks later Brown was hanged by Virginia authorities, as newspaper readers across the land were given accounts of his final words and acts. On the day Brown was captured, Bryant, though deploring his attempt to start a slave insurrection, reminded his readers, North and South, that the brutal persecution by slaveholders of free-state Kansas settlers, and of Brown and his family, had taught him to use violence; the advocates of extending the slave trade, Bryant charged, were "as great fanatics as Brown."

Brown's execution drew from Bryant an editorial in which he called attention to its profound significance. "It is an event in our national history," he wrote, "which warrants every thoughtful man amongst us in pondering over it deeply." Brown's "heroism," his "fortitude," his "hatred of oppression," Bryant predicted, would lead a "large part of the civilized public" to "lay on his tomb the honors of martyrdom." His memory would be "more terrible to slaveholders than his living presence could ever be," for it would "bring recruits to his cause who would never have served under his banner while he was wielding carnal weapons." History, "forgetting the errors of his judgment in the contemplation of his unfaltering courage, of his dignified and manly deportment in the face of death, and of the nobleness of his aims," would "record his name among those of its martyrs and heroes."

A week after Brown's execution the national House of Representatives exploded in bitter contention, lasting nearly two months, over the election of a Speaker. The Republican candidate, John Sherman of Ohio, had—with sixty-eight other northern congressmen and many prominent citizens—signed an appeal for money to print 100,000 condensed copies of Hinton Rowan Helper's 1857 indictment of slavery, *The Impending Crisis of the South*, as a campaign document. This powerful, if intemperate, attack on the "peculiar institution" as an insurmountable obstacle to southern growth, by a North Carolinian, urged the great majority of southerners, who were without slaves, to get rid of the system, either by the ballot, or, if necessary, by violence. Extremist southern congressmen fought for a resolution declaring that no man who had signed such an instrument was fit to be elected Speaker. As the parliamentary struggle went on with ever-more-reckless language on both sides, and virtually every member of the House armed with a gun, it seemed that the as yet unorganized body might become an uncontrolled mob, and a sectional conflict erupt within the walls of the nation's Capitol.

At the time of its first publication Helper's book had been praised in the *Evening Post*. Now, as it found notoriety far beyond its popular appeal, Bryant urged each southern reader of his newspaper to examine Helper's arguments, and to "ask himself seriously whether he does not think that slavery is an evil to which an early remedy ought to be applied by the slave states themselves."

1055. *To* Orville Dewey

New York, September 9th [1858]

... I brought back Mrs. Bryant nearly as well as she was when I carried her off to Europe, and gaining strength so steadily that I have great hopes of soon seeing her even better than she was there. Julia came home in fine health and spirits. The voyage was one of the smoothest ever made; soft airs and a quiet sea, and the passengers pleased with the weather, the ship, and each other.[1] We passed a month in England, where we heard a good many inquiries about you, and answered them, I think, to the general satisfaction.

Mr. Edwin Field wrote on our account to Mr. Flower, of Stratford, and the result was an invitation to "The Hill," the name of his place. We went, and passed two days there very pleasantly. You were freshly remembered in the family, who have been noted for their hospitality to Americans.[2] Both Mr. Field and Mr. Flower are of those who grow more conservative as they grow older, a common case, as Mr. Flower had the good fortune to become rich, which is another makeweight in favor of conservatism. He is thinking of going into Parliament.

Nine days we were at Mr. Ferdinand Field's, near Evesham, a little town in a pleasant agricultural district of Worcestershire, where cucumbers flourish in the open air, and the grape ripens on the south side of walls. Here my wife gained strength every day, and I took walks with our agreeable host, for very agreeable I found him, on the neighboring hills. But I cannot say that I much liked the peep into English life which this brief residence gave me. So many sets and classes of people, each jealous of intrusion from below, and anxious to get admission into the class above.[3] At Birmingham, we were the guests of Mrs. Alfred Field; her husband at this moment is in the United States.[4] They live in a nice little village called Edgbaston, just out of the smoke and jar of the town, and from this place Julia and I made an excursion to Lichfield and Aston Hall[5] with Mrs. Field for our cicerone. Near to Edgbaston is Shenstone's famous place, the Leasowes,[6] now in possession of [an ironmaster][7] Mr. Mathews, who has put it in neat order again, bringing back the rivulets that were stagnating into marshes to their ancient channels, and opening the old paths in the dark woods by their side. I walked over it with a Birmingham[8] gentleman and the proprietor. But I did not mean when I began this letter to give you a history of our travels. They are over for the present.

[My best regards to Mrs. Dewey, and to your daughter if they are with you. My wife and daughter would send their love if they knew I was writing.

Yours faithfully
W   C   BRYANT]

MANUSCRIPT: NYPL–GR (draft fragment) TEXT: *Life*, II, 117–118 ADDRESS: [Dr. O. Dewey].

1. Leaving Liverpool on the steamship *Africa* on August 21, the Bryants reached New York on September 2.
2. As a boy of twelve, Edward Flower had been taken by his father Richard (1761–1829) to Illinois. Returning to England seven years later, he settled at Stratford, where he prospered as a brewer and horse fancier. In 1864, as mayor, he organized a Shakespeare tercentenary. His eldest son, by whom the Bryants were also entertained during their short visit, founded the Shakespeare Memorial Theatre in 1879.
3. For an account of Bryant's visit to Evesham, see his "Diary, 1857–1858," July 31–August 9, 1858.
4. Alfred Field had written Bryant on July 16 (MS William Cullen Bryant II) that he was unexpectedly required to sail for the United States on July 24 for a "business arrangement of importance."
5. Lichfield, fifteen miles north of Birmingham, and a cathedral town, had been the home of Dr. Samuel Johnson (1709–1784), son of a local bookseller. Aston Hall, Birmingham, built by Sir Thomas Holte (1571–1654), sheriff of Warwickshire, is thought to be the original of Washington Irving's *Bracebridge Hall* (1822). The printed text mistakenly reads "Litchfield."
6. The poet William Shenstone (1714–1763) was born and lived for most of his life at Leasowes, an estate near Halesowen, nine miles west of Birmingham, which he beautified in the picturesque manner.
7. Matter in brackets is taken from the manuscript.
8. The printed text mistakenly has "Brummagen"!

1056. *To* Frederick Swartwout Cozzens[1]

New York   September 10th   1858.

My dear sir.

You ask my opinion concerning the errand on which you go to Europe.[2] I certainly hope most earnestly that it will have a result favorable to the great object of protecting the property of authors and artists from pillage. Holding as I do that this kind of property rests on as just a foundation as any other, I have ever been of opinion that it is as churlish an act to refuse to protect it when belonging to a foreigner, as it would be . . .[3]

MANUSCRIPT: NYPL–GR (partial draft) ADDRESS: To Frederick Swartwout Cozzens Esq.

1. Cozzens (1818–1869), a New York wine merchant and humorous writer, is best remembered for his *The Sparrowgrass Papers* (1856).
2. Cozzens had written Bryant on September 7 (NYPL–BG) that he would attend a literary and art congress in Brussels to discuss international copyright, and wished to be certain that an equitable law protecting authors' rights would meet with Bryant's approval.
3. Bryant's long advocacy of an international copyright law is discussed in 471.2.

1057.   *To* Ferdinand E. Field

[Roslyn? September 18? 1858]

My dear Mr. Field

You may feel some interest to hear how we got on in our way to America. After we left you my wife found herself attacked with an influenza which made her cough violently and weakened her considerably. In this state she went on board the steamer Africa at Liverpool but the seasickness and sea air soon cured the cough and she gained strength during the whole voyage which lasted twelve days. It was the smoothest passage I ever made across the Atlantic—and it was the tenth. I found some acquaintances on board, and on the whole they were a pleasant set of people[1]—all apparently on good—certainly on pacific—terms with each other. It almost seemed as if the sea had been smoothed for our special advantage—for within three days of us followed the steamer Pacific which was tossed about by violent gales nearly all the way. We found Mrs. Godwin and several of our friends on the wharf waiting for us as we landed. Instead of the heat we expected to meet—for the Captain declared it was the warmest passage he had ever made in his life—we found the weather of a pleasant temperature—and no weather could be more delightful than the fortnight that has passed since. Julia is quite well, and has just left us on an excursion to the west—Chicago &c. Mrs. Bryant is still on the mending hand.

We often talk over the pleasant time we had at your house. We are certainly much obliged to you for the glimpse it gave us of English social life in the middle class—the most virtuous, I suppose, and therefore the most estimable. I feel that I know England much better for the brief residence at Evesham, and much better than I could have known it from a much longer residence in a large capital, commercial or manufacturing town.

Meantime we are curious to know how things go in your pleasant neighbourhood. Your friend Mr. Kaye[2] must by this time have established his quarters at Greenhill[3] and you are taking long smokes and long walks together. Long walks imply long talks of course—since a walk as I have found by experience is the surest and most unfailing provocative of conversation. The wasps I suppose long ago ate the last of your excellent apricots—the grass on your lawn has thickened under the autumn showers, and the leaves of the trees growing thinner as the year wanes open new views through the branches. Jack, I hope is well, and not yet eaten up by any of the beggar dogs. My wife is anxious to know how you have disposed of Beatrice. Write and tell us all about these things—Give our kind regards to the pleasant acquaintances we made at Evesham.

Yrs truly
[unsigned]

MANUSCRIPT: NYPL–GR (draft) ADDRESS: To F   E. Field Esq.

1. Besides the Junius Morgans, these included Hiram Barney (1811–1895, Union 1833), law partner of Bryant's friend Benjamin F. Butler (374.1); New York publisher Joseph Wesley Harper (1801–1870); and William David Lewis (1792–1881), a Brooklyn merchant and Russian scholar. Bryant, "Diary, 1857–1858," August 21, 23, 1858.

2. Not further identified.

3. Field's home at Evesham.

1058.   To Christiana Gibson

[New York? cSeptember 20, 1858]

My dear Miss Gibson,

Julia has eloped with Wm. B. Ogden and Miss Sands and Mr. Tilden— gone to parts unknown—somewhere in the wide west.—[1] She cannot possibly answer your letter inasmuch as she has not seen it. I write to say that my wife is quite *chirk* as they say in New England and none the worse—but a little better for getting back to Roslyn. She has at present her sister an invalid also passing a little time with her—and having no housekeeping to trouble her, finds ample leisure to get well.— She desires me to say that she will depend on your monthly holiday.

Her brother Mr. Fairchild[2] has written to her that he will bring his daughter Sarah down immediately in order to place her at your school. He will be in New York as early as the beginning of next week, and will place her with you I suppose as soon as convenient. . . .

MANUSCRIPT: NYPL–GR (draft fragment).

1. William B. Ogden (581.2); Julia M. Sands (203.10); Samuel J. Tilden (389.3). A developer of Chicago, and its first mayor in 1837, Ogden subsequently organized and directed several railroads centering in that city. An early friend of the Bryants', he wrote Frances soon after her return from Europe urging that Julia be permitted to join his party in an excursion to the westward, for which, he assured Frances, "I have a free pass for myself and party over the Rail Ways." Ogden to Frances Bryant, September 14, 1858, William Cullen Bryant II.

2. Egbert N. Fairchild (134.2).

1059.   To Julia S. Bryant

New York   Sept. 21   1858

Dear Julia.

We got news yesterday of your safe arrival in Chicago, which was the first news we had of you since you ran away.

Your mother is getting on. Yesterday she walked to Mr. Willis's cottage and back, and next week she intends to come to town for a few days. The weather is heavenly and I think agrees with her. I am at work in town; Mr. Bigelow is building a barn. I have just got Miss Ives's account from Munroe & Co. and have enclosed it to her in a letter.

Your mother bid me, this morning when I left her, say to you and the rest of your party that she wished them the pleasantest possible time. If the weather is as fine with you as we have it here it cannot be otherwise. My regards to all of them whom I know. Don't let Mr. Tilden make you a Buchanan man, with his glozing speeches.[1]

Yours affectionately
W   C   BRYANT

MANUSCRIPT: NYPL–GR.

1. Tilden, long associated with Bryant in the radical wing of the Democratic Party, had not switched with his friend in 1856 to the new Republican Party. Although their political paths diverged thereafter, their friendship persisted throughout the rest of Bryant's life.

1060.   *To* John Bigelow

Office of the Evening Post
Wednesday   September 29   1858

Dear Mr. Bigelow

I could not answer your kind note[1] yesterday, as I got it that morning and was obliged to wait till I could see my wife. She is now in town, partly that she may be with me, and partly to consult Dr. Gray, and I am engaged with my dentist. She would be very glad to see Mrs. Bigelow, but the very thought of making journeys and visits fatigues her.[2] I was obliged to use the conjugal authority—marital I should say—to get her into town. If she can go any where she thinks she ought to visit her sisters in Berkshire, whom her conscience pricks her for neglecting, but she is putting of[f] that journey and perhaps will not make it this autumn.

You will perceive, therefore, that she has some reason for declining, as she does your obliging invitation. She desires her best love to Mrs. Bigelow whom she longs to see, were it only for the brightness of her cheerful countenance. Make my regards also.

Yrs truly
W. C. BRYANT

MANUSCRIPT: NYPL–GR.

1. Unrecovered.
2. In 1857 Bigelow had built a summer home on the Hudson River at Buttermilk Falls (later Highland Falls), near West Point, about sixty miles north of New York City. Bigelow, *Retrospections*, I, 163.

1061.   *To* Julia S. Bryant

New York   October 2   1858.

Dear Julia.

We got your letter from Fond du Lac[1] yesterday and are glad to hear that you have had so pleasant an excursion. The weather here has been delightful up to the present moment, with the exception of one wet chilly day, and we take for granted that it must have been equally fine where you are—as the quantity of rain being generally less there than here. Your mother is gaining strength gradually notwithstanding she has seen the doctor every day since she came to town. We are at the Everett House—which is quite crowded and too bustling a place for an invalid. Today we return to Roslyn, where I have been cutting away trees and lopping boughs in a manner which gives the place a new aspect.

Make our best regards to the Chief of your expedition and to all the others whether officers or privates. Say to Mr. Ogden that he must not let you get out of money, and that he must give you a memorandum of all that he advances for you or to you, that I may return it as soon as I get knowledge of the amount.

Yours affectionately
W. C. Bryant.

Manuscript: NYPL–GR.

1. Unrecovered.

1062. *To* John Howard Bryant

Roslyn   October 4   1858.

Dear Brother.

I was very glad to get your letter[1] as it gave me the knowledge of what the Bryants in Princeton are doing and how they all are. With regard to what it says of the crops, the information was so important that I had it put in the Evening Post. We were sorry to hear both of Austins illness[2] and that of your wife. You must bring Harriet to the East again, to recruit and go back with a new stock of health.

Frances is gradually gaining strength, but is hardly as strong now as when I took her abroad. She was ill as I believe you have been informed for four months at Naples, and when she was well enough to travel, we set out by easy journeys. . . .

Manuscript: NYPL–GR (partial draft) Address: To John H. Bryant.

1. Unrecovered.
2. Bryant's elder brother Austin had been ill for more than eighteen months; see Letter 970.

1063. *To* George Bancroft[1]

New York   October 11, 1858.

Dear Mr. Bancroft.

I am amazed at myself when I think how long I have left your kind and cordial note[2] unanswered. I thought that I should be able, long ere this, to say to you that I had provided myself with some occasional lair in town so that I could dine now and then with a friend—but the only nights, except the first, that I have passed in New York since I came from beyond sea, have been while I was under the hands of a dentist, and the tooth-ache and the state of my masticators generally prevented me from making any calls. My daughter is now at the west and I do not like to leave Mrs. Bryant alone at our country place; but when Julia returns the case will be otherwise, and I shall seize the opportunity to have a good talk with you, and to get my share of those brilliant thoughts of which you have far more than enough for the great work you are writing.[3]

I am, dear sir,

with true regard &c

W. C. Bryant

Manuscript: MHS.

1. Bryant's long-time friend, historian and diplomat George Bancroft (Vol. I, 15), now living in New York, and an active member of the Sketch Club.

2. On September 15 Bancroft had written Bryant (NYPL–BG), "I long to see you," and asking Bryant to share his "hermit's mead" that afternoon.

3. By 1858 Bancroft had published seven volumes of his *History of the United States from the Discovery of the American Continent*; the eighth appeared in 1860. Nye, *Bancroft*, p. 198.

1064.   To Richard S. Willis

Roslyn, October 11th, 1858

My dear Mr. Willis:—

I am glad that you think of doing honor to the memory of your late excellent wife,[1] by putting into a volume the testimonials to her worth, in the hope that they may hereafter awaken in her children and other descendants a desire to imitate her example. It appears to me, that I have scarce ever known a character, the elements of which were so happily proportioned and combined, as a preparation for ingrafting on it the graces and virtues of a highly cultivated moral and religious nature. An instinctive benevolence, which embraced all her fellow-creatures, strong domestic affections, freedom from all taint of hatred or envy, a great unwillingness to believe ill or speak ill of others, the most amiable docility, an earnest desire to obey all the calls of duty, the most cheerful contentment in the ordinary condition of life, and the sweetest patience under adverse circumstances, were always remarkable in her daily life; and it seemed to me that, with the advance of years, these qualities acquired consistency and strength, and ripened into a more beautiful and harmonious whole.

I was, as you know, in a foreign land when I was startled with the news of her premature death, the circumstances of which were fully related to me. It then occurred to me, that if such a calamity could admit of consolation, her friends must have found it in the calm religious resignation with which she gave up a life which had been so happy, meeting death as an event of which she had no fear, and making for it the most wise, thoughtful, and affectionate dispositions.

It seems, therefore, in the highest degree proper, that, cherishing her memory as you do, you should seek to give it some more permanent repository than mere personal recollection, which must pass away with the lives of those who were so fortunate as to have known her. As one of that number, I shall be happy if my testimony to her virtues shall be thought worthy to be included in the memorial you are preparing.[2]

I am dear sir,

With great regard and esteem,

WM. C. BRYANT

MANUSCRIPT: Unrecovered TEXT: *Memorial of Jessie Willis: Prepared for Her Little Daughters, Annie, Blanche and Jessie, by Their Father* (New York, April 1858 [for private circulation]), pp. 14–15 ADDRESS: R. Storrs Willis, Esq.

1. See Letter 1027.
2. See descriptive note.

1065.   *To* Richard H. Dana[1]

New York   October 13, 1858.

Dear Dana.

I acknowledge that I got your letter written to me in Europe[2]—but I remember it was received at a time when I had not much time to answer it, and, as often happens, the thing which should have been done at the moment, by being put off was not done at all. I have no other excuse to make, and acknowledge that this is a very weak one.

Frances, I am glad to say is gradually improving in health and with her health she is regaining her cheerfulness. Perhaps she is hardly as strong yet, as when I took her abroad, but if she makes the same progress as she has done since she began to recover, I am sure she will be better than she has been at any time for more than three years past. I suppose you know that she was ill with a nervous fever at Naples—ill for four months and at death's door. Her physician here tells her that if she finds herself entirely recovered from the effect of that sickness at the end of a year it will be as much as she has a right to expect.

I am glad to hear so good an account of Charlotte's[3] health, though I should have had more satisfaction in hearing that her accident had eventually restored her health, as has happened in some instances of which I have lately heard—two for example in which an inveterate dispepsia was cured by the patients being thrown out of a waggon and severely hurt. Give her my kind regards—my wife I am sure would send hers if she were here, but she is in the country. Of your own health, and what it has been for a long time past you say nothing. Do not forget it the next time you write. For my own part, I have nothing to complain of on that score. What a silly sentence is this last—as if I had a right to *complain* of ill health in any other than a medical sense.

You speak of the beauty of your autumn woods. I wish I were with you a day or two by the side of the dashing sea and in sight of the gay groves of your coast. On Long Island the leaves have just begun to put on a sallow look and do not yet show much of the crimson and yellow. In two or three days however, the change must come.

They have been engraving Durand's likeness of me. Durand himself put the finishing touches to the work, and from his hands it comes, so some of my friends say, a better likeness than the original painting.[4]

I long to see your face again. How shall this be managed?

Truly yours
W. C. BRYANT.

MANUSCRIPT: NYPL–GR ENDORSED: W^m. C. Bryant, Oct   /13/5[8]   Answered.

1. Richard Henry Dana, Sr. (See Vol. I, 13).
2. Unrecovered.
3. Dana's unmarried daughter; see 282.5; Letter 1145.
4. See 867.2.

1066.   *To* John Bigelow

New York   Oct   20, 1858

Dear Mr. Bigelow

My wife wants to see Mrs Bigelow, before she goes to Europe.[1] Why can you not bring her out to Roslyn[?] If it were only for a night she could send you up to the Branch at noon.

She bid me ask you this question this morning but I forgot it till the moment you were gone.—

Any day will be all the same to her and to me.

Yrs truly
W   C   BRYANT

MANUSCRIPT: NYPL–Bigelow.

1. On November 13, 1858, the Bigelows sailed for Europe, to be gone until June 11, 1860. Bigelow, *Retrospections*, I, 181, 289.

1067.   *To* an Unidentified Correspondent

New York, October 20, 1858.

I approve in the highest degree of the plan to improve the condition of the New York females, by furnishing them with the means of obtaining a more useful education, and providing for them a reading room and library.[1]

WM. C. BRYANT

MANUSCRIPT: Unrecovered TEXT: Undated newspaper clipping, probably from *EP*.

1. Bryant was one of a number of prominent New Yorkers, among them Henry Ward Beecher, Peter Cooper, and Horace Greeley, who supported a proposal for a "first-class Female Library" which was to be discussed at a meeting on October 26, the topic of which was "The Necessity of Mental Culture in Women." See descriptive note.

1068.   *To* John G. Chapman

New York   Nov   8, 1858.

My dear sir

I have received the photographs which I left with you together with one for Miss Ives and thank you for the attention. Mr. Young to whom they were forwarded with some other things sent them to me three weeks since.

There were some engravings purchased at the Government Office, which I supposed would be sent me at the same time and as I do not get them, I fear that some mischance may have happened to them on the way. They were bought under your advice as you may remember—and consisted of Raphael's Spasimo di Sicilia, the Madonna della Seggiola, a Madonna del' Pesce, a Teologia and Michael and the Dragon. I think there was another—bought afterwards—but I do not recollect what. Miss Ives had several which were to come with mine—and among them was Titians Assumption of the Virgin and Guido's Aurora. Please write me about them and let me know whether they have been sent.

My wife has been getting better ever since you saw her. She finds her native air healing, but the process of recovering strength is very slow— Dr. Gray, her physician tells her that a year is not too long to repair the mischief done by such an illness. Julia is very well and has just returned from a visit to Berkshire, but this has been the shortest of her wanderings since her return. A few days after we got to our home in the country—our little place at Roslyn—she set out with a party of nine on an expedition to parts which when you lived in the country were unknown—to Oshkosh and such places which a few years ago were without a name, and are now flourishing towns and villages. Miss Ives I hear has been very well since her return.

The Century is prosperous and plethoric—it consists of 250 members now and the new place in Fifteenth Street is very convenient and very popular. For me there are quite too many strange figures among them. I begin to find myself a little homesick when I visit it and pine for "the old familiar faces."[1] Mr. Verplanck however is as faithful as ever in his attendance and I believe makes aquaintance with all the new people as they come in.[2] Leupp was very well when I saw him last. Gourlie is cheerfully waiting for the time when his eyes are to be couched, and John Durand is going on perseveringly with the Crayon which he says is on the gaining hand. His father's picture of me has been admirably engraved by Jones[3] with some help I believe from the painter himself. . . .

MANUSCRIPT: NYPL–GR (draft).

    1. Charles Lamb, *The Old Familiar Faces*.

    2. In 1857 Bryant's old friend and literary collaborator Gulian C. Verplanck (Vol. I, 15) had been elected president of the Century Association. Robert W. July, *The Essential New Yorker: Gulian Crommelin Verplanck* (Durham, North Carolina: Duke University Press, 1951), p. 252.

    3. Alfred Jones (867.2).

1069. *To* Robert C. Waterston

New York   November 11, 1858.

Dear Mr. Waterston.

    We have seen an account of your arrival in Boston, but can learn nothing more. Both my wife and myself and Julia besides, would be very glad to hear that you and Mrs. Waterston had reached home in health, from that sojourn in foreign countries, in part so pleasant and cheerful, and in part overshadowed with so dark a cloud of sorrow. For a single line, letting us know what sort of passage you had, and how you both are now, we should thank you with all our hearts.

    We were greatly distressed the other morning at the news we heard, of an accident, threatening to be fatal, which happened to Mr. Quincy;[1] and we immediately thought how it must afflict Mrs. Waterston and yourself, but the next intelligence from Boston relieved us.

    Mrs. Bryant, I am happy to be able to say, continues to gain strength, though very slowly. Julia is very well; and both unite with me in desiring every expression of kind regards to Mrs. Waterston and yourself.

I am, dear sir,
faithfully yours
WM C. BRYANT

MANUSCRIPT: UVa.

    1. Mrs. Waterston's father, Josiah Quincy (425.1) survived this accident, dying in 1864 at the age of ninety-two.

1070. *To* Victor Mercier[1]

New York   12 Novembre   1858.

Mon cher Monsieur.

    Monsieur J. Bigelow mon associé dans le redaction de l'Evening Post vous remettra cette lettre. Il voyage en Europe avec sa femme, charmante personne, et leurs enfan[t]s. Je sollicite pour lui cet accueil bienveillant que vous m'avez accordé. . . .[2]

MANUSCRIPT: NYPL–GR (draft fragment) ADDRESS: A Monsieur Mercier.

    1. See Letter 540.

    2. "My dear sir. Mr. J. Bigelow, my associate in editing the Evening Post, will hand you this letter. He travels in Europe with his wife, a charming person, and their children. I beg for him that kind welcome which you have granted me. . . ."

1071. *To* an Unidentified Correspondent

Office of the Evening Post
December 10th   1858.

The bearer of this Manton Marble Esqre. has been employed for nine months in the editorial department of the Evening Post, during three of which I have been actively concerned in the conduct of the paper. I have found him exceedingly serviceable,—well educated well informed, punctual, diligent, and with the capacity of bringing his information to bear upon any given subject with readiness and despatch. So far as I know and believe his habits of life are without reproach. I consider him as well qualified to take charge of any province of the political or literary department of a newspaper. He writes with fluency, clearness, correctness, and occasionally elegance; he is well acquainted with the politics of the day and makes up a newspaper judiciously and with despatch.[1]

WM C. BRYANT

MANUSCRIPT: LC ENDORSED: From / Wᵐ Cullen Bryant, / (Evening Post).

1. Manton Malone Marble (1835–1917) had apparently been engaged by John Bigelow in March 1858 during Bryant's absence abroad. This generous estimate of Marble's journalistic abilities is silent on a point which must have been crucial in the severance from the *EP*'s editorial desk of this young assistant whose Democratic political bias later made him an outspoken critic of Lincoln's conduct of the Civil War, from the day in 1862 when he took control of the heretofore Republican New York *World*. Isaac Henderson to Bryant, June 8, 1858, Homestead Collection; John Bigelow to Henderson, December 27, 1858, NYPL–BG; Nevins, *Evening Post*, p. 302; Mott, *American Journalism*, p. 351.

1072. *To* Daniel Coit Gilman

Office of the Evening Post,
New York, Decr. 11ᵗʰ   1858.

Dr. sir

We have no doubt that articles such as these your letter of the 10ᵗʰ inst refers to might be made occasionally instructive & entertaining & we should like to print such, if on being received they should be approved by our Editors.[1] The compensation which we have been in the habit of allowing for correspondence of the sort has been varied in the nature & importance of the subjects. If you should send us anything we will if we can meet your wishes

We have the honour to be
Your obdt servts.
W   C   BRYANT Co.[2]

MANUSCRIPT: JHUL ADDRESS: Danl. C. Gilman / Yale College Liby.

1. It has not been determined whether any contributions from Gilman (840.1), then librarian of Yale College, appeared in the *EP*. His letter is unrecovered.
2. This letter is not in Bryant's handwriting.

1073.   To Julia S. Bryant

Office of the Evening Post
New York, Dec   21   1858

Dear Julia.

I send with this a basket on which is attached a coat of mine, and the basket contains some things put up by your mother which she does not want opened till she comes. All are well at Roslyn. I shall go out this afternoon again. The boy will bring any message or letter that you wish sent out.

Yours affectionately
W   C   Bryant

Manuscript: NYPL–GR.

1074.   To W. C. Manning[1]

New York   January 12, 1859.

Sir.

I have not leisure to write to you at any length on the subject of your letter, but I can say that I do not agree with Schlegel.[2] All subjects that affect the heart and the imagination are proper subjects for poetry, and Christianity among the rest.

I am, sir,
respectfully yours
W. C. Bryant

Manuscript: NYPL–Thomas F. Madigan Collection.

1. Unidentified.
2. Probably Friedrich von Schlegel (1772–1829), German philosopher and literary critic. Manning's letter is unrecovered.

1075.   To William Henry Appleton[1]

New York   January 22, 1859.

My dear sir.

I agree that the percentage I am to receive on the sale of my poems[2]— 1500 copies to the Common School Libraries of Ohio may be calculated upon a 75 cts. book.

Yours truly
W. C. Bryant

Manuscript: Indiana University Library Address: Wm H   Appleton Esqre. Endorsed: I agree to a like / arrangement in reference / to my book / Fitz-Greene Halleck / New York   Jany 22, '59; W. C. Bryant / and / Fitz Greene Halleck / agreement for / percentage on / Poems to Ohio / Library— / Jany 22nd / 59.

1. William Henry Appleton (1814–1899) was then head of D. Appleton & Co., publishers since 1854 of Bryant's collected poems. See 868.4.

2. The 1854 edition of the *Poems*, which had been reprinted annually since that year. See *The Poetical Works of William Cullen Bryant*, Roslyn ed. (New York: D. Appleton, 1907), p. lxxxix.

1076.   *To* Samuel A. Allibone

New York   February 1, 1859.

Dear sir.

I either overlooked or quite too soon forgot the request at the close of your note accompanying the first volume of your excellent Dictionary of English Literature,[1] that I should inform you of its coming to my hands, and I write to apologize for a neglect of which I am now made sensible on reading the note again.

The opinion I formed of your work on looking over some of the first sheets I have found no cause to modify, except as it has risen in my esteem. I regard it as one of the best books of reference ever compiled, and have no fear that the public will fail properly to acknowledge its merit.

I am, sir,
very truly yours
W. C. BRYANT

MANUSCRIPT: HEHL ADDRESS: S. Austin Allibone Esq. DOCKETED: W. C. Bryant.

1. See 916.1. Allibone's note is unrecovered.

1077.   *To* John Bigelow

New York   February 15, 1859.

My dear Mr. Bigelow.

I take it for granted that you wonder I have not written to you before. The plain truth is that I have been so much taken up with looking to the Evening Post, that I have conceived an absolute disgust for other tasks, but being at Roslyn for a day—though my letter is dated at New York, and having a spare hour on my hands I employ it to do what I own I ought to have done before.

Mr. Henderson has written to you I understand concerning the financial condition of the Evening Post and concerning some arrangements made for carrying on the paper during your absence, but there is yet something to be said. Since the November dividend was made the weekly and semi-weekly papers have been gradually increasing circulation. The daily paper holds its own but does not increase. One reason of this may be that the [New York] Commercial [Advertiser] is every day brought to the street before our door and sold for a penny. A great effort is made to get it out a little earlier than the Evening Post, and so to anticipate us on the market. The effect of this maneuver is visible in the sales of the Commercial which take place under our eyes, but though it may obstruct the increase of our circulation it does not lessen it.[1] The collections—the receipts of the paper, are rather better than they were before the dividend. As for the advertising it has become a perfect nuisance. The trouble began about the end of November and ever since that time there has been a continual war between the composing room and the editor's room. After the holidays we fancied that the press of advertisements would be over, but we were mistaken; the advertisers have not relented a whit. At present Mr. Henderson is engaged in introducing a method of putting printed superscriptions on all the papers sent by mail, by means of a machine which sticks the printed slip on the wrapper as fast as a nail machine turns out cut nails, and effects a great saving in clerk hire. As soon as this arrangement is effected, we are to take up the question of enlarging the paper which I fear is unavoidable.

I am sorry that I did not know earlier what opinion you had of Hanscom. As soon as I saw your letters relating to him I was for dismissing him immediately as a man who had imposed upon us by a false statement. There were but four of five weeks remaining however of the session, and Mr. Henderson seemed quite averse to having a quarrel with the man, so I yielded. I should not have employed him if Mr. Thayer[2] had not been very confident that he had been promised employment as a correspondent for the Evening Post at this session of Congress.[3]

As for Dr. Wilder I have given him the preference as a correspondent at Albany partly because I found that he was personally acquainted with almost every member of both houses of the legislature, and many of the public officers and partly on account of his great industry. He has done an infinite deal of work for us while at Albany, sending us, besides his letters, the substance of reports and abstracts of bills, which require a great deal of time to make out and which in the crowded state of our columns are invaluable to us.[4]

As to politics, the Republican party is in excellent spirits and full of hope. Buchanan is more feebly supported and more generally despised than when you were here. Douglas has been gravitating about as fast, and now that he has got back to his old allegiance the Southern politicians give themselves very little trouble about him and the general opinion seems to be that he will have to stay in the ranks.

The thirty million dollars which it is proposed to give Buchanan,[5] he will not get; the Douglas democrats understand that it will be used against their leader in the next election—at all events that he can have no good of it— The *Times* at last has come out against it on the ground that it is to be spent here at home. There will be many southern votes against it. The tariff it is thought is safe for this session also. On the whole less mischief will be done than there was reason a few weeks since to fear.

Meanwhile people talk of Seward and Banks as competitors for the Republican nomination for the Presidency,[6] and nearly as little is said about Fremont[7] as you were in the habit of saying before you went away.

For the rest you will find it all in the Evening Post. I have had the honor of a visit from Mrs. Cunningham, who came to ask the name of her libeller in the E. P. that she might prosecute him.[8]

Kind regards to Mrs. Bigelow and congratulations that she has not to endure such a villa[i]nous winter as we have here. Take your own time to see the Old World—our part of the New Prospect.

Yrs truly
W   C   BRYANT

MANUSCRIPT: NYPL–GR DOCKETED: W. C. Bryant & Co / Feby 1859.

1. The combined circulation of the *EP*'s three editions in June 1858 was 12,334 copies. Bigelow to Bryant, June 12, 1858, NYPL–BG.

2. William S. Thayer (924.4), then managing editor of the *EP*.

3. Hanscom has not been further identified.

4. Alexander Wilder (1823–1908, M.D. Syracuse Medical College 1850) was employed by the *EP* for thirteen years. As its correspondent at Albany he was, Bryant commented (Letter 1087), "a perfect Hercules of a lobby member." Wilder was later on the faculties of several medical colleges, and the author of books with such whimsical titles as *New Platonism and Alchemy* (1869) and *Vaccination, a Medical Fallacy* (1875).

5. To negotiate the purchase of Cuba from Spain; see Nevins, *Emergence of Lincoln*, I, 445–449. Of Buchanan's proposal, Bryant wrote, "A bill appropriating thirty million to buy the moon would not be a more brainless project." *EP*, January 17, 1859.

6. William H. Seward (753.3); Nathaniel Prentiss Banks (1816–1894), former Democratic congressman, and in 1859 Republican governor of Massachusetts.

7. John C. Frémont (Letter 958).

8. On the night of January 30, 1857, a Dr. Harvey Burdell had been murdered at 21 Bond Street, New York. One Emma Augustus Cunningham, then known as Mrs. Cunningham–Burdell, was tried and acquitted of the crime. Subsequently, the New York surrogate found her not to be Burdell's wife, and denied her the right to his estate; she then dropped from public notice. Meanwhile, two writers for the *EP*, city editor Alfred C. Hills and Alfred J. Marsh, wrote a series of investigative articles for the paper entitled "Matrimonial Brokerage in the Metropolis," and in February 1859 devoted three of these to the suspicious and probably criminal activities of Mrs. Cunningham at the house of a marriage broker, Jessie Willis, at 18 West 43rd Stret. *EP*, February 11, 12, 14, 1859. On March 3, perhaps as a result of Mrs. Cunningham's call on Bryant and threat to prosecute the writers, the *EP* printed sworn affidavits by Hills and Marsh attesting the truth of their charges.

1078.   *To* Cyrus Bryant

New York   Feb. 17th. 1859.

Dear Brother.

Yesterday I mailed to your address the Regulations of the Military Academy which I obtained by writing to Professor Weir of West Point. When Cullen comes to the Academy you must send him down to see us, and if you were to come with him so much the better.[1]

Of my own visit to Illinois in the Spring I can say nothing at present, although I think it not improbable that I may come. I am now considerably occupied with the paper, but I do not mean to be so much confined to business as I have been since I returned from Europe. When the spring comes on, however, I shall probably be much engaged with my place. I am looking about for a regular gardener to employ along with the farmer whom I have had for several years.

With regard to Pike's Peak, and the gold mines, it is probably true that gold is to be found there, but I never knew much good to come from hunting for gold yet. It is too much like gambling; the pursuit is apt to unsettle men for any thing else, and the instances of those who have enriched themselves by it are very few. I have known a great many instances of persons to whom the pursuit turned out a real misfortune. For my part I should as soon think of making my fortune by angling in Bureau River.[2]

We are all now in town. I have bought a house for Fanny and we are all with her.[3] My wife I think is slowly getting a little strength, but is not in very good health yet. Her principal difficulties are debility and weak nerves. Noise, loud talking, bustle, hurry, and many things to think of at once, always distress her. Julia is very well, and all the rest are in comfortable health.

Our winter here has been I think much like yours—rather mild on the whole, with some intensely cold days and a perpetual shifting from rain and thaw to hard frost. It is not often that we have a season so changeable. The *Evening Post* is pretty successful. Mr. Bigelow as I suppose you know has gone to Europe, and I believe is now in Rome, with his family. Godwin has come into the office to help me.[4]

My regards to your wife and the young folks.

Yours affectionately
W. C. BRYANT

MANUSCRIPT: Andrew B. Myers ADDRESS: C. Bryant Esqre.

1. Failing of an appointment to West Point in 1859, because of "political evasions from Washington," Cyrus Bryant's third son, Cullen (1839–1909), entered the United States Military Academy in June 1860, graduating in 1864 as a second lieutenant in ordnance. Having served in various arsenals from Maine to California, he retired from the army in 1894. Cyrus to Cullen Bryant, April 14, 1859, and June 4, 1860, NYPL–GR; *Forty-First Annual Reunion of the Association of the Graduates of the United States Military Academy at West Point, New York, June 14th 1910* (Saginaw, Michigan, 1910), pp. 91–92. For Robert W. Weir, see 203.12; Letter 279.

2. A small tributary of the Illinois River running through Princeton, Illinois. For a description of the "irrational and irresistible stampede" to Pike's Peak, Colorado, in 1858–1859, see Nevins, *Emergence of Lincoln*, I, 305–308. Bryant's scorn for such a pursuit anticipates that of Henry David Thoreau in "Life Without Principle" (1863): "The ways by which you may get money almost without exception lead downward. . . . The gold-digger in the ravines of the mountains is as much a gambler as his fellow in the saloons of San Francisco."

3. At 82 East Sixteenth Street, New York. Frances Bryant to Ferdinand Field, January 21, 1859, NYPL–GR; Letter 1210.

4. Parke Godwin had left the employ of the *EP* in 1846; see 559.4.

1079.   *To* John Howard Bryant

[New York? *c*February   1859][1]

. . . to take charge of my garden, and if he were with a good practical gardener for a year I think he would be nearly his equal. Mr. Cline remains on the place; he goes into the cottage close to our house, and will continue to occupy his leisure moments on the place. He is a very industrious man, conscientious almost to an excess, and very fond of the culture of flowers and choice plants. He acts as a kind of steward to me, is very serviceable particularly when I am absent and saves me a great deal of trouble.

You speak of coming to New York when the spring opens. If you do you will probably find us already in the country, but the house in town will be open, and Fanny and her children will probably be there. It may be that I shall run out to Illinois next season whether you come or not, but I have formed no certain plan of that sort.

Seeing the head of Fremont on your letter reminds me of politics and the next President. Buchanan, weakest of men as he is, has done more to break up his party than I could possibly have expected, and the chances look very promising for a Republican President after the next election. Douglas has been, it seems to me his own executioner; he has pulled down the guillotine upon his own neck. He has gone back to his old allegiance, but will always be distrusted by those from whom he separated for a time. Such a man as Hammond[2] would be much better supported at the South than Douglas, and equally well at the North. It seems to me that the popularity of Douglas is wholly at an end in every part of the Union, except it be among his friends in Illinois. He is looked upon as a man without either convictions or party fidelity—and one of these a man must have to be the leader that Douglas aspires to be.

With regard to Fremont there is a disposition in this quarter to leave him where he is. I have heard some things about him since my return which have gone far to reconcile me to his ill success in the election of 1856. Many of those who were his warmest friends are cool towards him. Chase[3] would be the best man; but I am afraid that he cannot be nominated. Seward and his friends are exceedingly anxious to get the nomination for him. His unconscientious prodigality in dispensing the public money is the greatest objection to him. There are many who talk of Banks, against whom the sin of having been a Native American will prejudice many.[4] I hope we shall get a wise and good man. Frederick Law Olmsted,[5] the Superintendant of the Central Park in our city, who is a man of great administrative capacity, who selects all his subordinates and agents with an instinctive wisdom, and who does not allow a dollar of the public money to be paid out except for value received, would be an infinitely better President than we have had since Van Buren,[6] but nobody will think of nominating him, and few would know whom they were voting for when they gave him their suffrage.

Remember me kindly to Harriet and Elijah. We expected to see Sarah
Olds on her return from Boston and were disappointed that she did not
take New York [in?] her way—all of us— Will you say this to Louisa?[7]

Yours affectionately
WM C. BRYANT

MANUSCRIPT: Knox College Library ADDRESS: Jno H Bryant Esqre.

1. The first part of this letter is seemingly lost. It is dated conjecturally.
2. James Henry Hammond (1807–1864, South Carolina College 1825), a planter
and southern nationalist, was a United States senator from South Carolina, 1857–1860.
3. Salmon P. Chase of Ohio (Letter 753).
4. The resurgence of anti-foreign and anti-Catholic feeling in the early 1850s had
found political expression in a Native American, or "Know-Nothing," Party which in
1856 chose Millard Fillmore (753.4) as its candidate for President. Banks, earlier a
Democrat, but by 1856 a Republican, had for a time shown Know-Nothing leanings.
Nevins, *Emergence of Lincoln*, II, 237; *Ordeal*, II, 323–332, 414, 467.
5. See 406.4.
6. Martin Van Buren served one term as President, from 1837 to 1841.
7. Sarah Snell Olds was the nineteen-year-old daughter of Bryant's sister Charity
Louisa (Mrs. Justin H. Olds).

1080.   To George Harvey[1]

New York   March 2, 1859.

My dear sir.

I very much regret that I did not take more pains to find you out
when I was in London, and I regret it all the more since I have received
your obliging letter[2] in which you speak of the unsuccessful attempt you
made to find my lodgings. I was much occupied in attending to the comfort and entertainment of my wife who was recovering from a nervous fever
which had held her a prisoner during four months at Naples, and had
brought her to the brink of the grave. I was required to be much with her,
and was not without frequent apprehensions of a relapse, a danger which
constantly menaced her during her convalescence. She is not even yet well,
though so long a time has elapsed; and yet I think she mends slowly. All
the benefit to which I am entitled from this apology, I hope you will gen-
erously allow me. I certainly do not deserve to be regarded as guilty of
premeditated neglect of one who has shown himself so deserving of my
respect and esteem.

You allude in your letter to your system of measuring values and super-
seding the present monetary system of the world. I agree with you fully
that if the scheme you propose be ever so practicable, it is one which must
make slow progress in the world. You have done your part in presenting to
the world the essential idea on which it is founded, and if it is ever adopted
hereafter you will receive the credit of being its discoverer, inventor, or
author,—whichever title may be best applied to him in [whose][3] mind it had
its birth. In the mean time it seems to me that the abstract nature of the

propositions in which your system is expressed is one of the reasons why the public give it no more attention. There are many minds to whom all ideas, more particularly new ideas enunciated in this manner are mere Sanscrit; they only understand them when they see them in the concrete; when they are illustrated to their senses by some actual example. If you could show them a community ever so small transacting their business according to your system, and employing with convenience and advantage the tokens by which, according to that system, values are expressed they would for the first time form a rational idea of its nature and perhaps be willing seriously to consider its merits.[4]

I am glad in the mean time to learn that you are engaged in a business which as it gives you constant occupation, must I infer bring its pecuniary rewards. You have labored in a noble cause, that of peace and good will between two great nations, and have fairly earned a title to bestow some attention on your private affairs. I assure you that you will always have my kindest wishes, and that I shall always rejoice to hear of your prosperity.

Public affairs have got into what seems to me a bad way in this country. The man who is now our President has less of the respect of his fellow citizens than any Chief Magistrate who has preceded him and less apparent regard for right and justice either in his domestic administration or in the management of our relations with other governments.

My wife desires her kind regards to you.

I am, dear sir,
very truly yours
WM. C. BRYANT

MANUSCRIPTS: DuU (final); NYPL–GR (draft) ADDRESS: Geo. Harvey Esqre.

1. An English artist and economist who spent many years painting in the United States. See 553.2.
2. Unrecovered.
3. Bryant mistakenly wrote "its."
4. Harvey seems not to have presented his theories of monetary reform in a separate publication, but may have developed them in periodical form.

1081. *To* E. B. Seevoss and Others[1]

New York   March 10, 1859.
Gentlemen.

When I got your polite invitation to be present at the delivery of Mr. Everett's Oration this evening[2] I was uncertain whether I might not be then out of town; and afterwards it escaped my recollection that you desired an early reply. If it be not too late I shall be happy to avail myself of the opportunity you offer.

I am, gentlemen,
very respectfully yours
W. C. BRYANT

MANUSCRIPT: Andrew B. Myers ADDRESS: Messrs E. B. Seevoss / C. E. K. Sherman / W. H. Wickham.

1. The addressees were apparently members of the program committee of the Mercantile Library Association of New York. They have not been further identified individually.

2. On March 9 the *EP* announced that Edward Everett (540.9) would deliver an oration that evening on Benjamin Franklin, under the auspices of the Mercantile Library Association, at the Academy of Music. Bryant seems to have misdated his letter.

1082. *To* Leonice M. S. Moulton

New York   March 17, 1859

. . . I cannot affect to misunderstand the riddle in your note[1]—its flattering solution is so obvious. The engraving of which you speak is not to be had in any of the shops. The Century Club is the publisher and the person who has the charge of it is Mr. John Durand a son of the artist and editor of the Crayon, whose office is 373 Broadway. . . .[2]

MANUSCRIPT: Ridgely Family Collection TEXT: Hoyt, "Bryant Correspondence (I)," 69.

1. Unrecovered.
2. This was the engraving of Durand's portrait of Bryant referred to in Letter 1065.

1083. *To* an Unidentified Correspondent

New York   March 26, 1859.

Sir

Absence from town has prevented me from answering your letter before this evening. I have no objection to the use of my name in an invitation to the Rev^d. Mr. Lord to give a course of Historical Lectures in this city.[1]

I am, sir,
respectfully yours
W. C. BRYANT

MANUSCRIPT: Dartmouth College Library.

1. Probably John Lord (1810–1894, Dartmouth 1833), a historical lecturer who, in 1884–1896, published a series of books entitled *Beacon Lights of History*. No report of lectures by Lord in New York has been found.

1084. *To* Henry Lillie Pierce and Others[1]

New York   April 1st   1859

Gentlemen.

I thank you for inviting me to the festival you are about to hold in honor of the memory of Jefferson.[2] You do well to observe the birth day of that great man, one of the wisest political philosophers of his time,—wiser, I think, than any who lived in the times before him—one who saw deeper into the principles of government than his contemporaries knew. I should be most happy to unite with you in this commemoration, but am withheld by my various occupations.

> I am gentlemen
> with great regard &c.
> W. C. BRYANT

MANUSCRIPT: UVa ADDRESS: Messrs Henry L. Pierce / and others—members / of the Committee. PUBLISHED: Herman L. Spivey, "William Cullen Bryant Changes His Mind: An Unpublished Letter about Thomas Jefferson," *New England Quarterly*, 22 (December 1949), 528–529.

1. Henry Lillie Pierce (1825–1896), a cocoa manufacturer and liberal Republican Massachusetts legislator, served as mayor of Boston in 1872 and 1879. He and his committee were apparently members of the Thomas Jefferson Memorial Foundation.
2. Pierce's letter of invitation is unrecovered.

1085. *To* Frances D. Stabler

> Office of the Evening Post
> New York, April 1st 1859.

Madam.

The verses enclosed in your note are above the ordinary character of newspaper poetry and are inserted in the Evening Post with pleasure.[1] We are not in the habit of paying for literary matter but I have directed the paper to be sent to your address and any thing from the same source will be always welcome.

> Respectfully &c.
> W. C. BRYANT

MANUSCRIPT: LC ADDRESS: Miss Frances D. Stabler / Sandy Spring / Montgomery County / Maryland POSTMARK: [illegible].

1. These verses have not been located in the *EP*. Their author has not been further identified.

1086. *To* Julia S. Bryant

> Roslyn April 4th. 1859.

Dear Julia.

I did not recollect till I was on my way to Roslyn that I had left the shrubs which I brought from Roslyn heeled up, in the border of the backyard in Sixteenth Street. Will you see that they are planted?
The magnolia of Soulange[ana] is just ready to open its flowers.

> Yrs affectionately
> W. C. BRYANT

MANUSCRIPT: NYPL–GR.

1087.   *To* John Bigelow

Roslyn   Long Island   April 11th   1859.

Dear Mr. Bigelow

I take it for granted that you would like to hear from me again by this time respecting the condition of the Evening Post. A single circumstance will perhaps enable you to form as good an idea of how we stand as a sheet-full of statistics. Mr. Henderson puts on a serene look in which satisfaction is mingled with resignation and looking into the air says quietly "The Evening Post is prosperous—very prosperous."

From the beginning of December our paper has been staggering under the burden of advertisements. "After the holidays," said Mr. Dithmar,[1] "the advertisements will begin to fall off," but the holidays went over and the advertisers showed no symptoms of relenting. Then came the advertisements of the incorporated companies,—insurance companies and others and the longer we went on the greater was the press of advertising. The Evening Post has not been edited from the time you went away till within a few days, except by the advertisers. For reading matter we gave only what they left us room for and that was very little. At last the necessity of enlarging the paper pressed so hard upon us, that we had no alternative, and we took the instant resolution to enlarge.

But first we had a careful investigation made, the different methods of enlargement discussed and the cost estimated. We had an experienced man from Hoe's[2] several days in our press room. We ascertained that to give our paper the form of the Tribune and Times would involve a cost of three thousand dollars, new turtles in that case being necessary. To lengthen the columns of the paper, merely, would not give us additional room enough. We chose the cheapest method of enlargement, that of giving an additional column to each page, and last week the change went into effect. The paper may now be said to be edited, yet we have not an inch too much room and before you get back I shall not be surprized if we have to lengthen the columns to the utmost capacity of the frames that contain them.

Until Congress rose I was constant in my attendance at the office, working hard and as steadily as I ever did. At present I am hiding. The suit of Forrest against N. P. Willis for a libel is in court and Forrest wants me for a witness; so I find it convenient to be out of the way as I do not want to be questioned about the old difficulties between Forrest and his wife.[3] The part taken by the[4] Evening Post in regard to the assassination of Key by Sickles has been, thus far at least, a fortunate thing for the Evening Post. The other journals were silent, or spoke in favor of the act, and all of them admitted the one-sided accounts of the friends of Sickles in Washington. To me it seemed imperative that something should be said of a decided character and instantly. I thought of obeying my conscience in the matter but it happens that what was said struck a vein in the public mind and the waters gushed up, a perfect flood. It happened to be the very thing that the best, and I verily[5] believe, by much the largest part of the community was waiting for.[6]

You will have seen that the bill to increase the compensation for legal advertisements has been lost in the Senate after passing the Assembly of the State. It was not lost for want of pushing. Wilder according to all accounts is a perfect Hercules of a lobby member—the most popular man about the capital, sleeping by turns with the different members, and Thayer was there a considerable part of the time to help him. Yet I was uncomfortable all the while at the idea of having a bill before the legislature from which if it passed I was to derive a personal advantage, and I was quite relieved when I saw that it was defeated.

Every thing else is going on well at the office. Your letters are read with interest and much enquired for. There is a disposition very general among readers to find fault with the author for not giving more of them.[7]

After a sour winter we have had a March like May, but rather severe influenzas have prevailed. Julia I heard a day or two since was quite ill with that complaint. My wife gradually improves in health. I do not hear that any of your many friends are ill. In politics I can tell you of nothing which is not in the newspapers. Sensible men are congratulating each other that there was no Post Office Appropriation Act—which puts the department upon a course of some economy. Kindest greetings to Mrs. Bigelow, who I doubt not enjoys herself much in Rome. My wife and daughter would send their best love if with me.

Very truly &c &c
W   C   BRYANT

P.S. New York   April 12.— The advertisement bill, I find has been fished up and passed. The fates would have it so.[8]

MANUSCRIPT: NYPL–GR.

1. The German Henry Dithmar was foreman of the *EP*'s composing room. Nevins, *Evening Post*, pp. 342–343, 422.

2. Robert Hoe & Co., makers of printing presses. See 705.5.

3. The actor Edwin Forrest and his former wife, Catherine Sinclair Forrest (see 665.5).

4. Bryant mistakenly wrote "its."

5. Bryant mistakenly wrote "very."

6. On February 27, 1859, United States district attorney Philip Barton Key (1819?–1859) was shot to death in Lafayette Square, Washington, by New York congressman Daniel Edgar Sickles (1819–1914), to whose wife Key had paid open attention. Sickles was later acquitted on the ground of temporary insanity. Nevins, *Emergence of Lincoln*, I, 432. Bryant urged editorially that even the admitted unfaithfulness of Sickles' young wife was no excuse for coldblooded murder by this "profligate" who, "to the discredit of this city, is one of its representatives in Congress," and who "has in his career reached the stage of assassination, and dipped his hands in human blood." *EP*, February 28 and March 1, 1859.

7. Letters from Bigelow, signed "J. B.," were printed often in the *EP* during 1859 and early 1860, and were helpful to Bryant in writing on European affairs.

8. However, no such bill was made into law during the eighty-second session of the New York State Legislature, which was adjourned on April 19, 1859. Information from the Reference Services of the New York State Library.

1088.   To Richard H. Dana

Office of the Evening Post
New York, April 15th, 1859

Dear Dana,

I have this moment got your letter[1] on my return from the country, and before I go to work, I answer it on the first piece of paper that comes to hand. You ask what can be done to place a statue to Cooper in New York. Nothing. We had you may remember, some years since a great public meeting in the city at which Webster presided. I delivered a sort of address and distinguished men made speeches, and contributions were obtained and a treasurer appointed.[2] Dr. Griswold was the principal getter up of the affair. A few hundred dollars were subscribed and we thought we should have a monument—but there the matter ended. A few weeks since Mr. Stevens the treasurer,[3] with the assent of the principal subscribers, and with my concurrence, paid over the money to the persons concerned in getting up the monument at Cooperstown. That seemed to be a live undertaking, while this at New York was dead beyond hope of revival for the present at least. Sometime hereafter, I have no doubt the people of this city will think it is time to do something of the kind but I think that we must wait a few years yet, and in the mean time it seems to me that it is well to have a monument at Cooperstown. I agree with you that there is a good deal of danger that the project of a statue of Leatherstocking will not be executed in the right manner.[4]

The troublous spirit you speak of, is, I suppose, one of the devils called blue. Turn him out. If he wont go, leave him at Boston and come and see the flowers open with me on Long Island—Do.—Kindest regards to Charlotte.

Truly and kindly yours
W. C. BRYANT

P.S. What Dr. Dewey told you of my wife is exact. She is slowly recovering—and is more like what she was six or seven years since than when I took her to Europe

W. C. B.

MANUSCRIPT: NYPL–GR ADDRESS: R. H. Dana Esqre DOCKETED: Bryant PUBLISHED (*in part*): *Life*, II, 124.

1. Unrecovered.
2. See 783.3, 6.
3. Probably John Austin Stevens (1795–1874), president of the Bank of Commerce, and an officer of the New York Chamber of Commerce. For Rufus Griswold, see 390.1; Letter 768.

4. The monument at Cooperstown, New York, erected in 1857 by a committee of which Washington Irving was the chairman, consists of a marble shaft topped by the figure of Cooper's most memorable character, frontiersman Natty Bumpo, or "Leatherstocking." It is located in Lakewood Cemetery. Rufus Rockwell Wilson and Otilie Erickson Wilson, *New York in Literature* . . . (Elmira, New York: Primavera Press, 1947), p. 328. The project for a memorial to Cooper in New York City was never consummated.

1089. *To* Robert C. Waterston

New York   April 18, 1859.

Dear Mr. Waterston.

By the Express of Adams & Company, I have this day sent you a copy of my Letters from Spain and other countries, recently published[1] which I pray you to accept as some sort of memorial of the pleasant days we passed together in Europe. I have ventured to add Mrs. Waterston's name to yours in the manuscript inscription on the flyleaf.

Your friend Mr. J. G. Clarke has been to our home several times, but I happened always to be out of town. My wife saw him once. I called since at his hotel but *he* is out of town in his turn. I suppose he wants letters for Spain, and I may be able to give him one or two.[2]

Mrs. Bryant is gradually improving in health and strength. Julia has had a severe attack of influenza, and my eldest daughter is now confined with a still severer one.

The season is opening pleasantly, and I wish I could have you and Mrs. Waterston here to show you the first verdure and early flowers at our place on Long Island beside the little lakelets and the salt sea.

Remember me most kindly and affectionately to Mrs. Waterston. If I were at home instead of writing this at the office of the Evening Post, I should have a whole budget of love from my family for you both.

I am, dear sir,
very truly yours
W. C. BRYANT.

MANUSCRIPT: PML

1. *Letters of a Traveller. Second Series* Half title, *Letters from Spain and Other Countries* (New York: D. Appleton, 1859). This comprised twenty-five letters written to the *EP* between June 11, 1857, and August 9, 1858.
2. This was probably Jonas Gilman Clark (1815–1900), a merchant who founded Clark University at Worcester, Massachusetts, in 1887.

1090. *To* Christiana Gibson

New York, April 19, 1859

. . . To-day Mr. Fairchild took my wife, Julia, and myself to see the new park, in which thousands of men are at work blasting rocks, making roads, excavating, rearing embankments, planting trees—a sight that reminded me of Virgil's description of Dido and her people building Carthage. The park is to be enlarged so as to take in all the precipices and intervening hollows as far as the plain of Harlem. The new reservoir is to be a great lake with curved, winding shores, and on the highest point of the grounds an Astronomical Observatory is to be erected.[1]

Mr. Cobden has been a good deal in the city since you left us. I have seen him twice, and found him very agreeable.[2] On Thursday morning I am to meet him again at Mr. Bancroft's. When asked about Mr. Cobden's conversational powers, Mr. Bancroft said they were "unequalled, unequalled." Mr. Cobden dined last week at Mr. Leupp's, and talked much of Peel[3] and other English statesmen. I hear, however, that he complains of being "dined to death." . . .[4]

MANUSCRIPT: Unrecovered PUBLISHED (in part): Life, II, 125.

1. Frances Bryant's brother Egbert N. Fairchild (134.2) was an engineer engaged in the construction of the reservoir in New York's Central Park, on which work had commenced in 1857. The park's superintendent was Frederick Law Olmsted, who in June 1859 married his brother John's widow, Frances Bryant's godchild, the former Mary Cleveland Bryant Perkins. See 406.4; Virgil, Aeneid, I.420–440; Laura Wood Roper, FLO: A Biography of Frederick Law Olmsted (Baltimore and London: The Johns Hopkins University Press [1973]), p. 142.

2. Bryant had first met Richard Cobden (545.2) at London in 1845. Now, as the British parliamentary leader visited Washington and New York early in 1859, he and Bryant renewed their acquaintance. The following year Cobden informed the American editor of his confidential negotiations for a commercial treaty with France. Cobden to Bryant, January 12, 1860, Life, II [131]–132; John Bigelow to Bryant, January 18, 1860, NYPL–BG.

3. Sir Robert Peel (544.3), earlier British prime minister.

4. For Cobden's account of these social engagements see The American Diaries of Richard Cobden, ed. Elizabeth Hoon Cawley (Princeton: Princeton University Press, 1952), pp. 143–148, 171.

1091. *To* Orville Dewey

New York, May 6, 1859

. . . I wish you could take a look at our little place in the country this beautiful weather. The sunshine is pure gold, and there are floods of it, poured over a wilderness of blossoms, like cream over strawberries. I have been planting and transplanting, and removing fences, and putting in stone sluiceways for water instead of plank ones; but whether the place looks better for what I have done is more than I can tell. But I have a gardener who was brought up, he boasts, under Loudon and Lindley;[1] and, if what he produces bears any proportion to what he has made me pay for garden-seeds and garden-tools, I shall have flowers enough to overwhelm Mrs. Dewey with bouquets, and all manner of choice vegetables for your dinner, and all manner of garden-fruits for your dessert, if I should be able to draw you two to Roslyn to pass with us

"One long summer day of indolence and mirth."[2]

I do not know how it may be with you, but for my part I feel an antipathy to hard work growing upon me. This morning I have been laboriously employed on the "Evening Post," and do not like it. Did you never feel a sense of satiety—a feeling like that of an uncomfortably over-loaded stomach, a rising of the gorge—at the prospect of too much to do? Does the love of ease take possession of us as we approach the period when we must bid the world good-night—just as we are predisposed to rest when the evening comes on? . . .

MANUSCRIPT: Unrecovered TEXT: *Life*, II, 125–126.

1. The English horticulturalists John Claudius Loudon (1788–1843) and John Lindley (1799–1865), whose writings were widely influential in this country in the nineteenth century.
2. This quotation has not been identified.

1092. *To* John Brown Paton[1]

[New York, May 6, 1859][2]

My dear sir,

I was glad to hear from you a few days since[3] though I confess some words in your letter were in a chirography that still puzzles me. Last evening I heard an anecdote of Dr. Chalmers—[4] He used to write his father, who on receiving one of his letters, used to say— "Ah a letter from Tom; well, put it by he shall read it to us when he comes.["]

Our friends address for which you inquire is "Edward Buck No. 11 Court Street Boston." I have not seen him since we parted in Switzerland,[5] but he writes to my daughter occasionally and I hear that he preserves his good humor and that his wife is all the better for her travels.—

The other brunt of your letter relates to what I may write. I shall have no objection to the arrangement you suggest if it can be brought about. I have a kind of engagement to send what I write in the way of verse to a periodical here, and if its proprieter consents. . . .[6] Of prose I write nothing except for my journal—a political and commercial paper.

My wife and daughter thank you for your kind recollection of them. Our companion who was Miss Ives and is now Mrs. Mackie is in town and Julia has taken your letter to show her. . . .

MANUSCRIPT: NYPL–GR (draft) ADDRESS: To Mr. John Brown Paton / Sheffield England.

1. Rev. John Brown Paton (1830–1911, B.A. London 1849, M.A. 1854) was a Congregational minister in Sheffield, England. *Who Was Who, 1897–1916* (London: Adam and Charles Black, 1920), pp. 549–550. The Bryants met him during their travels through Switzerland in the summer of 1857. Bryant, "Diary, 1857–1858," July 28, 1857.
2. The date is supplied from the source named in Note 6 below.

3. Paton, who edited the *Eclectic Review*, had asked Bryant to contribute poetry to his periodical. Paton to Bryant, n.d., 1859, NYPL–GR.

4. Probably Thomas Chalmers (1780–1847, D.D. Glasgow 1816), professor of divinity at Edinburgh University, 1828–1843, and a founder of the Free Church of Scotland. See 547.4.

5. In 1857 the Bryants had traveled for several days in Switzerland in 1857 with a Dr. and Mrs. Edward Buck of Boston, not further identified. Bryant, "Diary, 1857–1858," July 23–August 3, *passim*.

6. Sentence incomplete in this draft letter. However, in an excerpt from the final manuscript, offered for sale in 1983 in a catalogue, *Literary Letters, Manuscripts, & Documents*, by the Rendells Inc., of Newton, Massachusetts, it seems to have been completed by the words "I will see whether there is no objection to my sending it to England to appear at the same time."

1093.   *To* Hector Orr[1]

New York   May 16th, 1859

Sir.

I thank you for the honor you have done my lines entitled "October." You have associated them with others which are really beautiful and which I never had the pleasure of seeing before.[2]

I am, sir,
respectfully yours
W. C. BRYANT.

MANUSCRIPT: UVa ADDRESS: Hector Orr Esqre. / No. 310 Chestnut Street / Philadelphia.

1. A Philadelphia printer from 1837 to 1859, Hector Orr was listed thereafter in the city directory as a wood engraver.

2. See *Poems* (1876), p. 142. No publication of this sonnet by Orr has been located.

1094.   *To* John Bigelow

New York   May 24. 1859.

My dear Mr. Bigelow.

You inquire whether I make any objection to your remaining abroad another winter. I supposed when you went away that one winter would hardly satisfy you; indeed I do not see how it should. Short of two years would not give you time enough to see half what you went out to look at, unless in a miserably hurried way. I would therefore have you take your own time. Our journal is more prosperous than ever; the circulation of all three editions is growing; the advertisers are pressing and utterly remorseless; the profits as you will have seen are beyond what they ever were before. We have abundance of aid in the different departments of the paper, at present, and the public seem well satisfied with the manner in which they are edited. So you see, there is no pressing necessity for your return. When the Evening Post begins to decline, hold yourself in reserve to hurry back and prop it up.

The Enlargement of our sheet is not likely to lose us money as you seem to imagine. On the contrary, we should have lost money if we had not enlarged the paper. People began to complain bitterly of the encroachment of the advertisements upon the space allotted to news. Intelligence, the news of the day, abridged to the baldest summary had to be left out day after day, and I was convinced that unless we gave more reading matter the circulation would suffer. The shape of the sheet is not improved by the change; but we had a choice of evils before us. If we merely lengthened the columns we should not have had room enough; if we widened and lengthened the sheet at the same time we should have had too much. If we made our journal a quarto the expense of altering the turtles would have been three thousand dollars. Besides, Mr. Henderson was very confident that by giving our journal the form of the Tribune and Times, we should lose the advertisements of the importers and wholesale dealers.[1]

You speak of a letter of yours which has not appeared in the Evening Post. All your letters intended for the paper have been duly published. The direction to send the Evening Post to the Paris *Constitutional* I remember, and thought it had been attended to.

As to Foreign Correspondence, you have probably seen that we have had here Signora Jessie White Mario. She came here with her husband, who is a Venetian, and a Republican, and an exile of course. She is well-informed, lively, and an enthusiast and has lectured in our principal cities on the subject of Italy to large audiences. She has just sailed for Europe, with a design to return to Italy and before she went I made an arrangement with her to write weekly letters for the Evening Post when there was any thing to write about, for ten dollars a letter. This was before I got your letter respecting Mr. Strutt.[2] Madame Mario, I should mention was formerly a correspondent of the London Daily News.

What shall we do? Mr. Strutt's letters will certainly be wanted until Signora Mario begins to write, which may be some time yet. Besides she will write from Northern Italy, and he from Southern. May it not be desirable to retain both[?] They will probably write either about somewhat different matters or at least about matters seen from different points of view.

I congratulate you on being back at Paris, though May is almost heaven in Italy. You are beyond the reach of inconvenience from the war[3] —or rather Mrs. Bigelow is—as for you, you would be able to shift for yourself. My best regards to Mrs. Bigelow. My wife and daughter send theirs to you both. They are both pretty well—Mrs. Bryant has been gradually though slowly improving in health.

Yours truly &c
W. C. BRYANT.

MANUSCRIPTS: NYPL–GR (final and draft) DOCKETED: W. C. Bryant / May 24, 1859.

1. On April 4 the four-page folio sheet of the *EP* was widened from nine columns to ten. The smaller *Tribune* and *Times* carried five and six columns, respectively.

2. The "remarkable English woman" Jessie White Mario was on one occasion "stolen" from the *EP* by the *Tribune*, but resumed writing thereafter for the *EP* until her death. Nevins, *Evening Post*, pp. 342, 559. Bigelow's letter is unrecovered; Strutt was probably Edward Strutt, first Baron Belper (1801–1880, M.A. Cambridge 1826), an authority on legal reform and free trade.

3. The war of 1859 between Austria and Sardinia.

1095.   *To* Anna Q. Waterston

New York   May 24. 1859.

My dear Mrs. Waterston.

We all—my wife, Julia and I—thank you a thousand times for the memorial you have sent us of your daughter,[1] loved so tenderly and lost so early. It seems to us an admirable likeness, preserving the dignity the sweetness and the spirituality of her expression, if not in the fullest degree, yet in as great a measure as we could hope in any such shadow of the beautiful original. It will serve to remind us not merely of her, but of the pleasant days we all passed together before she was removed from a world of which she was the ornament.

If you and Mr. Waterston go away from home this summer, it would give us infinite pleasure to welcome you to our place at Roslyn. If you can do us that favor, choose your own time, only let us know in season, that we may not by any chance be absent.

My best regards to Mr. Waterston. My wife and daughter unite in love to you both.

I am, dear Madam,
truly and faithfully yours
W. C. BRYANT

P.S. The English papers perceive that Dr. Lardner is dead.[2] When I first came to Naples, he was at the same hotel in which I took rooms—the Hotel des Isles Britanniques. He was then and some time afterwards in florid health. When I left Naples, he and his wife were quite low with a nervous fever caught on the Chiaja where they then lived. Julia says she heard some time since that they were still ill—and now comes the news of his death. I have little doubt of the fact that his death was owing to the climate.

W. C. B.

MANUSCRIPTS: UVa (final); NYPL–GR (draft) PUBLISHED (*in part*): *Life*, II, 126.

1. This memorial, apparently a photograph, has not been recovered.

2. Rev. Dionysius Lardner (420.10). See Bryant, "Diary, 1857–1858" January 19, February 9, April 3, 1858.

1096.   *To* Israel K. Tefft[1]

Roslyn   May 26, 1859.

Dear Mr. Tefft.

Finding myself at Roslyn and having an hour of leisure, I employ myself in copying the poem mentioned in your note,[2] and destined to have
the honor of a place in your rich and vast collection of autographs.

I am glad you were pleased with Miss Gibson. She on her part cannot
say too much of the kindnesses she received from you and Mrs. Tefft.

We are all well, and all at our country place in this holiday of the year.
Kind regards to Mrs. Tefft. My wife and daughters desire a place in the
friendly remembrance of you both.

I am, dear sir,
your much obliged
W. C. BRYANT

MANUSCRIPT: PML ADDRESS: I. K. Tefft Esqre.

1. A Savannah autograph collector; see 454.1.
2. The poem is unidentified; Tefft's note is unrecovered.

1097.   *To* [the President of Brown University?]

Office of the Evening Post,
New York. June 15   1859.

Dear Sir:

The proprietors of the New York Evening Post take this means of offering to send, if agreeable to you, regularly, and with no charge for subscription, a copy of their Semi-Weekly or Weekly Journal to the Institution
of which you are the President. Before doing this, however, they would
require to be assured that the proffered gratuity would be acceptable, and
that their journal would be preserved in some place where the students
could have free opportunity to peruse it. They would also like, in case
their offer be accepted, to know the address to which the paper should be
directed.[1]

Respectfully Yours,
WM. C. BRYANT CO.

☞ See Circular on Opposite Page

MANUSCRIPT: Brown University Library.

1. This printed letter was apparently sent to a number of college and university
presidents. It was accompanied by a prospectus of the *EP*—the "Circular on Opposite
Page"—for its "Fifty-Eighth Year."

1098.   *To* Orville Dewey

[Roslyn? c June 24   1859]

Dear Doctor.

I do not know why I did not answer your letter[1] immediately—the day I got it—which is always the best way in such cases. I read it to my wife and we agreed that I should say that we would come as you suggest to pass the 4th of July with you, and now when I look again at your letter I find that you desired to know what time we would come so that you might arrange for others—and my business was to have answered you on the instant. So we go in this world sinning and regretting—swinging backwards and forwards between wrongdoing and penitence—The mischief is that the penitence makes no amends for the transgression.

[unsigned]

MANUSCRIPT: NYPL–GR (draft).

1. Dewey had written Bryant on June 2 (NYPL–BG) renewing his subscription to the *EP*, "the best paper I think in America," and inviting the Bryants to visit Sheffield before the "Great Fourth."

1099.   *To* Orville Dewey

Roslyn   June 25   1859.

Dear Mr. Dewey,

We are thinking—my wife and Julia an[d] I—a whole family of us—of coming to Sheffield on Friday by the first train from New York. If you are not prepared to receive us then we will go on to Barrington; if you are [we] think of inflicting ourselves upon you till Tuesday. So you may put yourselves in training and lay in a stock of patience to be practised after our arrival. Kind regards to all—My wife and daughter desire their love.

Yours very truly

W. C. BRYANT

MANUSCRIPT: NYPL–GR ADDRESS: Rev^d. O. Dewey.

1100.   *To* George Bancroft

Roslyn   June 26. 1859.

Dear Mr. Bancroft.

Je suis au desespoir,[1] and my wife is tearing her hair. Of all the days of the year, the 4th of July is the one which my wife and Julia and I have promised to pass with our friends the Deweys in Sheffield, and we are to go up on Friday. You see therefore that we cannot accept your most obliging invitation.[2] *Compatitemi*[3] as they say in Italy, only I say it with more intensity of meaning. My kind regards and my thanks—a thousand of them to Mrs. Bancroft whose invitation has a force with me that would make me break through any impossibilities but moral ones to make me comply with it.

I am, dear sir,
very truly yours
W. C. Bryant.

P.S. I enclose a note from my wife to Mrs. Bancroft which I beg you to hand her.

W. C. B.

MANUSCRIPT: LC ADDRESS: Hon   Geo   Bancroft.

1. "I am in despair."
2. Bancroft had written on June [25] "entreating" the Bryants to accompany him and Mrs. Bancroft to their summer home at Newport, Rhode Island, on July 2, "by the new land and water route, which is a charming one." Bancroft to Bryant, NYPL–BG.
3. "Sympathize with me!"

1101.   *To* Julia S. Bryant

New York   July 15, 1859.

Dear Julia.

Your mother is exceedingly anxious that you should be written to—though there is nothing to be said. We found Roslyn in good order to all outward appearance, and took a pleasant sail in getting to it. Since that we have been sweltered with the heat till last evening—we hope you have not enjoyed the same blessing.

But among the servants there was civil war, and we thought at one time they would all leave us on account of a quarrel between Ann and Stasia on one side and Charley and his wife on the other. A truce has been established for the time—but perhaps your help in looking up a handmaid may be wanted when you come to town.

Regards to Mr. & Mrs. Mackie and Mrs. Ives and all friends.[1]

Yrs affectionately
W. C. B.

MANUSCRIPT: NYPL–GR.

1. Julia was apparently then visiting at Great Barrington her late traveling companion Estelle Ives (1832–*post* 1899), who had been married on January 27, 1859, to John Milton Mackie (1813–1894, Brown 1834), author and retired professor of rhetoric at his alma mater, and more recently a dairy farmer. *Biographical Review, Containing Life Sketches of Leading Citizens of Berkshire County, Massachusetts* (Boston, 1899), XXXI, 379–380.

1102.   *To* Hector Orr

New York   July 15, 1859.

Dear sir.

Your letter[1] reached the office of my paper while I was absent in Massachusetts for several days.

Since my return I have inquired concerning the "Currency Association" of which you speak. The club or society bearing that name is composed of several intelligent men who take an interest in that subject. Among them are Messrs. George Opdyke and Wilson G. Hunt,[2] both well-known men in our community.

I am, sir,
respectfully yours
W. C. BRYANT.

P.S. I see that I have not answered all your inquiries. I doubt whether the "Currency Association["] has any corresponding officer—at least I cannot hear of any. The object of the Association is to check the tendency of the expansion of the currency in this country, and to introduce safe and solid principles of banking. Mr. Opdyke, I have no doubt or Mr. Hunt would with pleasure give you minuter information than I possess respecting its proceedings

W. C. B.

MANUSCRIPT: UVa ADDRESS: H. Orr Esqre.

1. Unrecovered.

2. George Opdyke (1805–1880), a clothing merchant and currency reformer, became mayor of New York in 1863. For Hunt, see 944.1.

1103.   *To* Julia S. Bryant

Roslyn   July 18, 1859

Dear Julia,

You will find the key of the store room or dining room closet in Godwin's library table drawer.

The sheets and pillow cases are partly in the middle drawer of your mother's bureau and partly in the middle drawer at the bottom of the wardrobe.

The cook has left us suddenly but with free permission. If you should be passing the Bible House and have time perhaps it would be well to speak to Mrs. Myers about a cook—but do not put yourself to any inconvenience as I shall come into town in a day or two and will attend to it myself.

Yours affectionately
W. C. BRYANT

MANUSCRIPT: NYPL–GR.

1104. *To* Calvin Durfee[1]

Roslyn, Long Island, July 19, 1859.

My Dear Sir:—

I regret that I can contribute so little from my own recollection in aid of your undertaking. I will endeavor, however, to answer your inquiries.

I entered Williams College in the autumn of the year 1810,—almost half a century since,—having prepared myself in such a manner that I was admitted into the Sophomore Class.

At that time Dr. Fitch was President of the College, and instructor of the Senior Class.[2] I have a vivid recollection of his personal appearance,— a square-built man, of a dark complexion, and black, arched eyebrows. To me his manner was kind and courteous, and I remember it with pleasure. He often preached to us on Sundays, but his style of sermonizing was not such as to compel our attention. We listened with more interest to Professor Chester Dewey,[3] then in his early manhood, the teacher of the Junior Class, who was the most popular of those who were called the Faculty of the College. Two young men, recent graduates of the College, acted as tutors, superintended the recitations of the two lower classes, and made their periodical visits to the College rooms, to see that everything was in order. These four were at that time the only instructors in Williams College.

Before my admission, it had been the practice for the members of the Sophomore Class, in the first term of their year, to seize upon the persons of some of the Freshmen, bring them before an assembly of the Sophomores, and compel them to go through a series of burlesque ceremonies, and receive certain mock injunctions with regard to their future behavior. This was called *gamutizing* the Freshmen. It was a brutal and rather riotous proceeding, which I can, at this time, hardly suppose that those who had the government of the College could have tolerated; yet the tradition ran, that, if it was not connived at, at least no pains were taken to suppress it. There were strong manifestations of a disposition to enforce the custom after I became a member of the Sophomore Class, but the Freshmen showed so resolute a determination to resist it, that the design was dropped; and this, if I am rightly informed, was the last of the practice.

The College buildings consisted of two large, plain brick structures, called the East and the West College, and the College grounds consisted of an open green, between the two, and surrounding them both. From one College to the other you passed by a straight avenue of Lombardy poplars, which formed the sole embellishment of the grounds. There was a smaller building or two of wood, forming the only dependencies of the main edifices, and every two or three years the students made a bonfire of one of these. I remember being startled one night by the alarm of fire, and going out, found one of these buildings in a blaze, and the students dancing and shouting round it.

Concerning my fellow-students I have little of importance to communicate. My stay in College was hardly long enough to form those close and life-long intimacies of which college life is generally the parent. Orton and Jenkins—I am not sure of their Christian names, and have not the catalogue of graduates at hand—were among our best scholars, and Northrop and C. F. Sedgwick among our best elocutionists. When either of these two spoke, every ear was open. I recollect, too, the eloquent Larned, and the amiable Morris.[4]

The library of the College was then small, but I recollect was pretty well supplied with the classics. The library of the two literary societies into which the students were divided was a little collection, scarcely, I think, exceeding a thousand in number. I availed myself of it, however, to read several books which I had not seen elsewhere.

Where the number of teachers was so small, it could hardly be expected that the course of studies should be very extensive or complete. The standard of scholarship in Williams College, at that time, was so far below what it now is, that I think many graduates of those days would be no more than prepared for admission as Freshmen now. There were some, however, who found too much exacted from their diligence, and left my class on that account. I heard that one or two of them had been afterwards admitted at Union College. There were others who were not satisfied with the degree of scholarship attained at Williams College, and desired to belong to some institution where the sphere of instruction was more extended. One of these was my room-mate, John Avery,[5] of Conway, in Massachusetts, a most worthy man and a good scholar, who afterwards became a minister of the Episcopal Church, and settled in Maryland. At the end of his Sophomore year he obtained a dismission, and was matriculated at Yale College, New Haven. I also, perhaps somewhat influenced by his example, sought and obtained, near the end of my Sophomore year, an honorable dismission from Williams College, with the same intention.[6] I passed some time afterwards in preparing myself for admission at Yale, but the pecuniary circumstances of my father prevented me from carrying my design into effect.

Such is the sum of my recollections of Williams College, so far as they can have any interest for one who is writing its history, which I am very glad to learn that you have undertaken, and which I hope you will find ample encouragement to complete and put to press.

I am, sir, yours with great regard,
WM. C. BRYANT.

MANUSCRIPT: Unrecovered TEXT: Calvin Durfee, *A History of Williams College* (Boston, 1860), pp. 106–109 ADDRESS: To Rev. Calvin Durfee.

1. Historian of Williams College; see descriptive note.

2. Rev. Ebenezer Fitch (1756–1833) was the first president of Williams College, serving from 1793 to 1815.

3. See 95.3.

4. Azariah Giles Orton (1789–1865) was later a distinguished theologian; Charles Jenkins (1786–1831) became a Congregational minister; William Northrop (1795–1819); Charles Frederick Sedgwick, Jr. (1795–1882) practiced law in Connecticut; Sylvester Larned (1796–1820) went into the Congregational ministry; Philip Van Ness Morris (1795–1864) first was a prosperous merchant, then late in life took a medical degree. George Tremaine McDowell, "The Youth of Bryant: An Account of the Life and Poetry of William Cullen Bryant from 1794 to 1821" (Unpublished Ph.D. diss., Yale University, 1928), pp. 101–103; *Catalogus Collegii Gulielmensis MDCCCLXXIV* (Williamstown, 1874), pp. 18–19.

5. See Letters 4, 5.

6. Although at Williams for only eight months in 1810–1811, Bryant was awarded an honorary Master of Arts degree by the college in 1819, was restored to his undergraduate class on its fiftieth anniversary in 1863, and the following year was elected to the Williams Phi Beta Kappa chapter. McDowell, "Youth," pp. 113–114, and *passim*.

1105.   *To* George Bancroft

New York   July 27th   1859.

My dear Bancroft.

Your hospitality is like the rain of heaven falling on the just and the unjust. I am glad you forgave my refusal of your first invitation—an enforced refusal—so easily—

As you leave *me* a liberal margin I will come, if you please on Wednesday next—the 3d of August—to remain perhaps, till Monday following.[1] If my wife continues as well as she is at present, she and Julia will accompany me.

I have both your notes—and keep them as a testimony to the heartiness of the hospitality which could lead you to take so much trouble.

My kind regards to Mrs. Bancroft and believe me as ever

Yours truly

W. C. BRYANT

MANUSCRIPT: NYHS DOCKETED: W. C. Bryant / July 27./59.

1. The invitation was to visit the Bancrofts at Newport, with or without Mrs. Bryant, this week, next week, or "*any part*" of the first weeks of August. Bancroft to Bryant, July 21, 1859, NYPL–BG.

1106.   *To* Elizabeth D. Bancroft[1]

Roslyn   July 31, 1859.

My dear Mrs. Bancroft.

My wife has your very kind note, and commissions me to answer it. It is our intention to leave New York by the eight o'clock train on Wednesday morning,—which will inflict us upon you in the afternoon of that day.

I send this to New York to be mailed there and write also by the Roslyn mail not knowing which letter may reach you soonest. My wife and daughter desire their love. I lay myself, *à l'Espagnole*,[2] at your feet.

W. C. BRYANT

MANUSCRIPT: LC.

1. Mrs. George Bancroft (d. 1886).
2. "In the Spanish manner."

1107.   *To* Richard H. Dana

Roslyn, Long Island, August 1st.   1859.

Dear Dana.

I have never written to you to say what I think of your son's book on Cuba[1]—though I have carried about two letters of yours[2] in my side pocket for weeks, as a memorandum of my duty in that respect.

I like it exceedingly. Few books of travels in which any information is conveyed are so little dull. Just now there is a good deal of curiosity about Cuba and its inhabitants, and this book gratifies it in regard to many important particulars, at the same time that it is a book which cannot fail to detain the reader who simply takes it up for entertainment. It is the lively talk of an intelligent traveller at a dinner table, listened to with profit and without fatigue. It seems to me that the author has just hit the true point between too much and too little description. Many travellers tire you to death with overdescribing. In this book a few touches give the picture, but they are the characteristic essential touches of a master. He must have made a remarkably good use of his time to have picked up during his short visit so many things worth knowing.

I hope your son will find in the visit he is making to Europe the restorative to perfect health he is in search of. He is one of the over-worked ones. We kill ourselves here, in various ways—some by dissipation—some by denying themselves all amusement—some by too sedentary habits—some by too great activity.

Remember me kindly to Charlotte. My wife and daughter desire their love to you both.

Yours ever
W. C. BRYANT.

MANUSCRIPT: NYPL–GR ENDORSED: Wm C. Bryant, / Aug. 1/59. Ans. / Feb. 23/60—.

1. Richard Henry Dana, Jr., *To Cuba and Back; A Vacation Voyage* (Boston, 1859).
2. One of these was probably Dana's letter of May 10, 1859 (*Life*, II, 126); the other is unrecovered.

1108. *To* Elizabeth D. Bancroft

New York   August 11th   1859.

My dear Mrs. Bancroft.

You were so kind as to ask a promise from me to let you know how we got home. We had a pleasant night after leaving your beautiful seat by the shore, and were at the wharf on the Hudson before seven the next morning. My wife experienced no inconvenience from the voyage except that she slept a little less than usual. In the afternoon we had a delightful passage in another steamer to Roslyn. My wife and daughter both desire me to say how pleasant are their recollections of your charming place and its hospitable inmates by whom also they wish to be most kindly remembered. My best regards to Mr. Bancroft and your son.

I am, dear Madam,
very truly yours
W. C. Bryant.

P.S. The storm which fell upon Newport on Friday afternoon was quite as violent at Roslyn. Nobody ever saw so much rain fall in so short a time— so they say—and the thunder was terrible and incessant.

W. C. B.

MANUSCRIPT: LC.

1109. *To* James P. Walker[1]

Garrison's Landing   N. Y.[2] August 27th   1859.

Sir.

The past experience of the proprietors of the Evening Post has decided them not to employ a Boston Correspondent. We have already given this answer to several clever writers who have made the same application that you have done.

I am, sir,
very respectfully yours,
W. C. Bryant

MANUSCRIPT: Princeton University Library ADDRESS: Jas   P. Walker Esqre.

1. Unidentified.
2. The Bryants were then visiting William Henry Osborn (1820–1894), president of the Illinois Central Railroad, in his summer home at Garrison's Landing on the Hudson River. Osborn was a son-in-law of Jonathan Sturges (421.1). See Frances Bryant to Christiana Gibson, July 29?, 1859, NYPL–GR.

1110. *To* Messrs. Richard Griffin & Co.

New York, September 6, 1859.

Gentlemen.

I return to you the manuscript which was enclosed in yours of last month, having corrected two inaccuracies. In New England young men are not articled to attorneys—they pursue their legal studies in the office of some counsellor, and the professions of attorney and counsellor are not distinct as with you.[1]

I am, gentlemen,
respectfully yours
W. C. BRYANT

MANUSCRIPT: British Library ADDRESS: R. Griffin & Co.

1. The letter and accompanying manuscript referred to are unrecovered. They apparently concerned a biographical sketch of Bryant to be printed by these London publishers in *The Comprehensive Dictionary of Biography* . . . (London and Glasgow, 1860). But the brief account of Bryant, on p. 11 of a "Directory of Contemporary Biography" which follows the main text in that work, simply states, "William Cullen Bryant was born at Cummington, Massachusetts, 3d Nov. 1797 [*sic*]. At an early age he decided to make the law his profession. He has written a great deal of poetry, showing a considerable amount of talent. He has also been long connected with one of the leading American newspapers."

1111.   *To* D. W. Lee

New York   Oct. 6, 1859.

My dear sir.

I have your note and will attend the funeral as pall-bearer.[1]

I am sir
yours truly
W. C. BRYANT

MANUSCRIPT: Leupp Family Papers, Rutgers University Library ADDRESS: D. W. Lee Esqre.

1. On the day this letter was written, Charles M. Leupp (421.1, 487.1), with whom Bryant had been intimately associated in managing the American Art-Union, and with whom he had traveled abroad four times, died at New York by his own hand, in his fifty-second year. In an *EP* obituary Bryant wrote that day of his friend, "He was one of those whom the maxims and habits of trade had never corrupted; a man of open and generous temper, who abhorred every form of deceit and every unfair advantage." D. W. Lee was evidently Leupp's brother-in-law.

1112.   *To* John Howard Bryant

Office of the Evening Post
New York, October 8, 1859

Dear Brother

We have received a letter from Justin H. Olds[1] enclosing the three notes for which I wrote. In exchange I send you the present note of four thousand dollars. Please acknowledge its receipt. All well. In haste.

Truly yours,
W. C. BRYANT

MANUSCRIPT: Unrecovered TEXT: "Bryant and Illinois," 643 ADDRESS: Jn. H. Bryant Esq.

1. Bryant's brother-in-law (520.1). Olds's letter is unrecovered.

1113.   To Messrs. Derby & Jackson[1]

New York   October 11th   1859.

Gentlemen.

I understand that Professor Adler has offered you his translation of Raynouards History of Provençal Poetry,[2] and I called this morning to speak with you concerning its publication, but was not so fortunate as to find you in.

The work, you know, is a standard book on the continent, and with scholars every where. It has been the source from which lecturers on the literature of different countries and periods have drawn the materials for their accounts of the poetry of the Troubadours. It is therefore a book of solid pretensions, likely always to be in a certain demand,—a book which those who are interested in such works as Sismondi's History of the Literature of the South of Europe,[3]—Bouterweck's[4] and Ticknor's[5] works.[6] Its publication would be respectable and creditable to any publisher in our country. A very considerable class of persons—those whose tastes in reading resemble my own—of whom I suppose the number cannot be small—would like to have it in their libraries.

Professor Adler is a scholar and a man of great industry. I cannot doubt of the exactness and fidelity with which he has executed his task.

With this memorandum of what I desired to say to you I have only to commend the enterprise of Professor Adler to your friendly consideration.

I am gentlemen

very truly yours

W. C. BRYANT

MANUSCRIPT: Brown University Library ADDRESS: To Messrs Derby & Jackson.

1. The firm of J. C. Derby and Edwin Jackson were New York book publishers from 1855 to 1861. Derby was the author of *Fifty Years Among Authors, Books and Publishers* (New York, 1884).

2. George J. Adler (1821–1868), a German-born philologist, was professor of modern languages at New York University from 1846 to 1853. Among his publications was a translation of Claude Charles Fauriel's *History of Provençal Poetry* . . . (New York: Derby & Jackson, 1860).

3. J. C. L. Sismonde de Sismondi, *De la littérature du midi de l'Europe* (1813). Bryant reviewed Thomas Roscoe's English translation of this work in the *United States Review and Literary Gazette*, 2 (September 1827), 467–468.

4. Friedrich Bouterwek, *Geschichte der Poesie und Beredsamkeit* (1801–1819).

5. George Ticknor, *History of Spanish Literature* (1849).

6. Bryant failed to complete this sentence.

1114.   *To* Daniel Coit Gilman

New York   October 31, 1859.

Dear sir.

I enclose you five dollars—the Annual Assessment for the Oriental Society, together with a stamp. May I ask the favor of a receipt.

Yours respectfully

W. C. BRYANT

MANUSCRIPT: JHUL ADDRESS: D. C. Gilman Esqre, / Treasurer &c.

1115.   *To* Frances F. Bryant

Office of the Evening Post

New York, Nov. 11th. 1859.

Dear Frances.

I have found Mr. Gourlie in. He says [John G.] Chapman has been pulled about by all manner of calls and little affairs—but that he will try to bring him to see you today, going early from his office and looking him up.

He thinks the American shawl as acceptable a present as you could make. They have nothing of the sort there, and Chapman might wear it over, and there would be no duty on it, and it would be the very thing to wear to Tivoli in the winter—that is the season for going there.

If you could send it to 26 West 17th St. Mr. Gourlies house, he would see that Chapman had it.—

Dr. Gray is in 20th Street, No   18 next door to Broadway on this side. I went there.

Cannon[1] will come out on Monday Evening for certain—

Yours ever

W. C. B.

MANUSCRIPT: NYPL–GR.

1. A furnace repairman; see Letter 1121.

1116.   *To* Alfred Field

New York   November 15, 1859.

My dear sir

I send you a few books and pamphlets relating to American politics. The book of Hildreth[1] I am not sure that you will find many facts in bearing upon the questions you ask, but there may be something in it of which use may be made. The Political History of New York[2] is a work full I think of instruction though not well written—

It will be seen that in New York there was once a property qualification for voters, and that it has been abolished. I am not aware that any mischief has arisen from the change. Political men are not less virtuous than they formerly were, I think. I am not sure that there is more corruption and I am almost sure there is less tyranny. In Massachusetts the property qualification has been changed for universal suffrage—nor am I certain that any thing has been lost by it.

Of acts of tyranny exercised by the majority over the minority—the law which once existed in Massachusetts, compelling all denominations, Baptists Methodists Epis. to contribute to the support of the regular Congregational churches was an example. The democrats got the power in Massachusetts and repealed it in part—and finally it was repealed altogether. Of a like nature was the law compelling every man to attend some *place* of religious worship under penalty of a fine. If he did not make his appearance once in three months, in a church or meeting house he was mulcted. This law has been done away.

But there are examples of the tyranny of the minority. The owners of manufacturing establishments are a minority in the United States—a minority even in Massachusetts. Include all their work people they are still a minority in every one of the states. Yet they are wealthy active and powerful—powerful through concert of action, and they have influenced even the politics of the federal government. Members of Congress and statesmen of every class have paid court to them—they have even influenced the conduct of those whose interests are not at all the same with theirs. They have tyrannized over the majority with a protective tariff.

You ask whether any thing has been done to make the rights of the minority safe, against the legislation of those who represent the majority. Nothing that I hear of. If you mean by the minority the rich, they do not need it. Every body here expects to belong to that minority some day or other. If you mean those who have some substance they are a majority. There is one experiment, however, which is now making, that of an elective judiciary, in regard to which there are differences of opinion—and in regard to the election of judges of the criminal interests, the opinion of sensible men seems to preponderate in favor of a return to the old practice of Executive appointment. It strikes me, however, that if the practice of electing the judges prove mischievous the old system will be restored. In Vermont at one time the judges were elected; the practice was then changed and they were appointed by the Governor, and since I believe they have changed again to the elective system.

In all these cases it is not easy [to] compare the past and present—we can always see what changes are made in laws and constitutions, but not always whether the change is for the better. There are no statistics of corruption, of venality, of the hypocritical adoption of popular opinions. Men who are not easily satisfied see the inconveniences and evils of present regulations, but they have not the past regulations with their evils before their eyes—so that they can make an impartial comparison.

What you say of the habit of public men "going it blind," as the saying is, for party ends, and the withdrawing of men of lofty virtue and intellect from connexion with politics certainly does not apply to the present time in America. There are very great differences of opinion and they are freely indulged. We have almost as many shades of political opinion as of religion. We have conservatives who hold the constitution to be a wicked compact—we have abolitionists we have free soilers—we have Republicans agreeing only in their enmity to slavery—we have three or four distinct sects in the democratic party—we have Native Americans, and these are divided into North & South, and these again into those who would exclude from office only the foreign born and those who would also exclude Catholics. Party ties are loosely worn, and party fidelity at a discount. I think, moreover, that the proportion of those who take an interest in political questions is larger than formerly— There will always be some who are so absorbed in other matters as to pay no attention to politics—but there are few who give politics up in disgust.—

You will be apt to infer therefore that I for my own part, am not dissatisfied with the result of the political experiment we are making—thus far at least. I have reached that age when men begin to compare the present unfavorably with the past, and I cannot see for my part, that the American people in the more than a third of a century that I have been a journalist are going back in any important respect.

Mr. Godwin tells me that the country is full of letters written from England of a tenor similar to yours.[3] I hope the answers will convey information that will be of use—

You do not say any thing of Mrs. Fields health. Pray give our best regards to her and your sister and their children—and remember us to . . . [conclusion illegible]

MANUSCRIPT: NYPL–GR (draft) ADDRESS: To Alfd. Field.

1. Richard Hildreth, *The History of the United States of America . . . 1497–1789* (1849–1852); or *Theory of Politics* (New York, 1853).
2. Probably Jabez D. Hammond, *The History of Political Parties in the State of New York* (1842).
3. Field's letter is unrecovered.

1117.   *To* Theodore Sedgwick III[1]

New York   November 18, 1859.

My dear Mr. Sedgwick.

I hear you have a saddle-horse in this city for sale. My daughter Julia wishes me to inquire of you if the animal be perfectly gentle, and of an easy gait, and such a horse as you would purchase for your own daughters.

Do you remember that you once gave me the heads of a warranty of a horse? I have the paper on file yet. Would the description it contains apply to the horse you have for sale?

I am sorry to hear of your continued ill-health. By this time I hope you are on the mending hand ere this, and that this application will occasion you no annoyance or trouble. We miss you very much here, for though I did not see you very often, yet the knowledge that you were among us made New York seem to me more homelike than it does when you have withdrawn yourself from it.[2]

Vivite et valete,[3]
Your old friend
W. C. BRYANT.

MANUSCRIPT: NYPL–BG ADDRESS: Theo. Sedgwick Esqre.

1. See 209.8, 475.1.
2. Having been appointed United States Attorney for the Southern District of New York in 1858, Sedgwick had retired soon after to his family home at Stockbridge, Massachusetts, where he died the month following this letter.
3. "May you live and be well."

1118. *To* Lorenzo Nelson

Roslyn   Dec. 1, 1859.

Sir.

Mr. Cline has shown me a letter which you wrote to him concerning an arrangement he desired to make with you in regard to your assistance in taking care of my place here. For the year beginning with April next, Mr. Cline is to have the principal charge of the place, and the responsibility for keeping it in order. With regard to your personal character I entertain no doubts from Mr. Cline's account of its respectability. What I desire to know particularly regards your industry and expertness. There are some questions, your own answer to which would be entirely satisfactory to me. I wish to know whether you are well acquainted with the care of horses, of which there will be three on the place, whether you have been accustomed to tend to their feeding—whether you can drive a pair in a vehicle of any sort with dexterity and fearlessness. I suppose, that you are acquainted with the culture of the usual four crops, that you know how to mow and cradle and the like. Is this so?— Do you understand the culture of flowers; are you acquainted with the management of a cold vinery, are you practised in the transplantation of trees and shrubs; can you graft and bud? Expertness in these branches would make your services the more valuable.

Then as to your habits of activity and industry what I would like to have is the attestation of some of your conscientious neighbors known to Mr. Cline. Would you procure one or two of these and send on to me or him?

You will excuse this particularity— Since the compensation you require is considerably beyond what is commonly given here, I wish to be sure that I am to get something near the worth of the money paid. That you are a postmaster and held a commission of the peace, certainly implies that you are a man in whom confidence is placed, but not that you are a good farmer. I wish to have a person on the place on whom I may confidently call for any proper service to be done on the place. Mr. Cline I have found a very valuable man in these respects.—

I have been in the habit of giving the farmer on my place a quart of milk a day, and such as he needed of the roots and greens, cabbages, lettuce and so forth as are raised on the place, including potatoes for the year. In regard to matters of this sort we should have no variance I am sure.—

When your answer to this arrives I will give it an immediate consideration, and Mr. Cline will write to you without delay. —When the arrangement is once concluded I should like to have it regarded as fixed and certain, since to be disappointed in your coming after the bargain is made would put me to very great inconvenience.[1]

I am sir
respectfully yours
[unsigned]

MANUSCRIPT: NYPL–BG (draft) ADDRESS: Lorenzo Nelson Esqre / Blandford   Mass.

1. Nelson's letter to George B. Cline is unrecovered. It is evident from Letter 1167, however, that Bryant engaged his services.

1119.   *To* L. M. Gardner[1]

New York   December 12th   1859.
Sir.

I am sorry I have no manuscript from the hand of Washington Irving to send you.[2] Although we were on excellent terms whenever we met, and although I was under some personal obligations to his kindness, it happened somehow that there was never any thing like an interchange of letters between us.

I am, sir,
very respectfully yours
WM. C. BRYANT

MANUSCRIPT: Carl H. Pforzheimer Library ADDRESS: L. M. Gardner Esqre.

1. Unidentified.
2. Irving had died at Tarrytown, New York, on November 28, at the age of seventy-eight.

1120.   *To* John Bigelow

New York   December 14th   1859.

Dear Mr. Bigelow,

I am quite ashamed not to have written to you in so long a time, but if you knew how lazy I feel when there is a letter to be written I am sure you would forgive me.

In one of your late letters you say that you do not think Bartlett the exactly proper man for a Washington correspondent.[1] He is the best man we can find, so we must be content; besides he has improved lately, and writes letters that are read with a good deal of interest.

Probably Mr. Seward stays[2] in Europe till the first flurry occasioned by the Harper's Ferry affair is over, but I do not think his prospects for being the next candidate for the Presidency are brightening. This iteration of the misconstruction put on his phrase of "the irrepressible conflict between freedom and slavery["], has I think damaged him a good deal,[3] and in this city there is one thing which has damaged him still more. I mean the project of Thurlow Weed to give charters for a set of city railways, for which those who receive them are to furnish a fund of from four to six hundred thousand dollars, to be expended for the Republican cause in the next Presidential election. This scheme was avowed by Mr. Weed to our candidate for Mayor Mr. Opdyke and others and shocked the honest old democrats of our party not a little. Besides the democrats of our party, there is a bitter enmity to this railway scheme cherished by many of the old whigs of our party. They are very indignant at Weed's meddling with the affair, and between Weed and Seward they make no distinction, assuming that if Seward becomes President, Weed will be "Viceroy over him."[4] Notwithstanding, I suppose it is settled that Seward is to be presented by the New York delegation to the Convention as their man. Frank Blair the younger talks of Wade of Ohio,[5] and it will not surprise me if the names which have been long before the public are put aside for some one against which fewer objections can be made

Our election for Mayor is over. We wished earnestly to unite the Republicans on Havemeyer,[6] and should have done so, if he had not absolutely refused to stand when a number of Republicans waited on him to beg that he would consent to stand as a candidate. Just as the Republicans had made every arrangement to nominate Opdyke, he consented to accept the Tammany nomination, and then it was too late to bring the Republicans over. They had become so much offended and disgusted with the misconduct of the Tammany supervisors in appointing Registrars, and the abuse showered upon the Republicans by the Tammany speakers, and by the shilly shallying of Havemeyer that they were like so many unbroke colts—there was no managing them. So we had to go into a tripartite battle and Wood[7] as we told them beforehand carried off what we were quarreling for. Havemeyer has since written a letter to put the Republicans in the right. "He is too old for the office," said many persons to me when he was nominated. After I saw that letter I was forced to admit that this was true.

Your letters are much read. I was particularly, and so were others interested with the one—a rather long one on the policy of Napoleon,[8] but I could not subscribe to the censure you passed on England for not consenting to become a party to the Congress unless some assurance was given her that the liberties of Central Italy would be secured. By going into the Congress she would become answerable for its decisions and bound to sustain them, as she was in the arrangements made by her and the other Great Powers after the fall of Napoleon—arrangements the infamy of which has stuck to her ever since. I cannot wonder that she is shy of becoming a party to another Congress for the settlement of the affairs of Europe, and I thought that her reluctance did her honor.[9] I should have commented on your letter in this spirit if it had been written by any body but yourself.

I hope you are satisfied with the income of the paper. It is acknowledged by many, most I believe to be the most entertaining of the dailies. Williams, the dullest looking of men is turning out a trump and is to be relied on for any quantity of matter that is wanted, and the quality is sometimes, to my surprize first rate.[10] I worked very hard in the paper until last May, but since that [time][11] I have given myself rather an easy time. I am now coming into town again, and shall probably resume my old habits. The Union savers, who include a pretty large body of commercial men, begin to look on our paper with a less friendly eye than they did a year ago. The southern trade is good just now, and the western rather unprofitable. Appleton says there is not a dollar in any bodys pocket west of Buffalo.

My wife is in the country yet—essentially improved, and just ready to come in. Julia is getting strong by riding on horseback. My kind regards to Mrs. Bigelow, who I doubt not enjoys the gayeties of Paris greatly.

I am dear sir

truly yours

W. C. BRYANT.

MANUSCRIPT: NYPL–GR PUBLISHED (in part): Life, II, 127–128.

1. Possibly William O. Bartlett, after 1868 an assistant editor of the New York Sun under Charles A. Dana. Mott, American Journalism, p. 376.

2. Bryant mistakenly wrote "Seward's stay."

3. On October 25, 1858 Senator Seward of New York declared at Rochester that there were two incompatible political systems in the United States, one resting on slave, the other on free labor, and that their increasingly close contact would produce an "irrepressible conflict." His speech, an attack on the Democratic Party, was widely misinterpreted as urging the suppression of slavery by the federal government. Six months later, urged by political friends to escape from a controversy which seemed likely to hurt his chances for the presidency, Seward sailed for Europe, to be gone until the end of 1859. Thus, he was abroad during John Brown's raid on Harper's Ferry in

October, for which he was charged with complicity by southern opponents. Van Deusen, *Seward*, pp. 193–194, 211, 213–214.

4. In 1859 Thurlow Weed (1797–1882), journalist, powerful political boss, and Seward supporter, "built up a war chest by soliciting contributions from New York City business men, and by shaking down Republican office holders in the state. He obtained the promise of large contributions to the campaign fund from the promoters of New York City street railways whose franchises he guided through the state legislature." *Ibid.*, p. 215. "Weed had damaged the Senator fearfully," Allan Nevins concluded, "by helping engineer the corrupt passage of six street-railway bills which gridironed half a hundred New York streets without conditions as to compensation, tenure, or fares." *Emergence of Lincoln*, II, 235.

5. Francis Preston Blair (1821–1875, Princeton 1841), Free Soil congressman from Missouri, 1856–1858, was, from 1860 to 1862, a Republican congressman, and later a Union general in the Civil War. Senator Benjamin Franklin Wade (1800–1878), of Ohio, was an anti-slavery leader in Congress.

6. William Frederick Havemeyer (1804–1874, Columbia 1823), a wealthy merchant and banker, had been Democratic mayor of New York in 1845 and 1848.

7. Fernando Wood (1812–1881), a Tammany Hall leader, had been elected mayor of New York in 1854 and again in 1856, and once more in 1859.

8. Louis Napoleon Bonaparte (1808–1873), Emperor Napoleon III of France, 1852–1870.

9. Bryant's judgment was sound. English support in 1859–1861 of Sardinian premier Camillo Cavour's efforts to unify an independent Italy was an important factor in the establishment of the Kingdom of Italy under Victor Emmanuel II. George Macaulay Trevelyan, *History of England* (London: Longmans, Green, 1926), pp. 654–655.

10. This was evidently Walter Francis Williams, who sent the *EP* "admirable letters from the field" during the Civil War. Nevins, *Evening Post*, p. 318. See Letter 1162.

11. Word omitted.

1121. *To* Frances F. Bryant

[New York] Wednesday evening   December 14th   1859.

Dear Frances

I wrote to you yesterday morning and this morning—you probably got my first letter today and will get my second soon after this. I have had two letters from Julia.[1] I called on Mr. Cannon today—he doubts whether the boiler of our furnace leaks—if it did it would make mud in the cellar. He says we need be under no concern about the safety of the boiler as long as it is half full—not the tank but the boiler.

Since I wrote you I have been to McKibbin's in the Fourth Avenue, Mrs. Kirkland's man, and he has given me the number and street of several places where I can have furnished rooms and a private table. I called at one of them in the 4th Avenue, a block or two above Blancard's and just such a house. An Englishwoman who keeps the house, showed me precisely the same rooms as Blancard did, and after some calculation asked me precisely the same price. She however, did not insist so much on my keeping them till May, intimated that she might take less, and would charge but half price without board or when we were absent. I shall go to look at the other ones tomorrow after the dentist has done with me. I think now I shall come to Roslyn on Sunday morning, but I must come back to the dentists on Monday.

I found a little note from Miss Sedgwick when I came in, and answered it.[2] I send you a letter from Miss J. Dewey.

Yours ever
W. C. B.

MANUSCRIPT: NYPL–GR.

1. None of these four letters has been recovered.
2. Neither Miss Sedgwick's note nor Bryant's reply has been recovered.

1122.   To F. S. Perkins[1]

New York   December 22nd   1859.

My dear sir.

The house in Cummington in which I was born has been pulled down. That in which I passed my childhood and early youth and which was the family homestead for many years afterwards is still standing with much the same external appearance that it had when I lived there—the only alteration made I think is that my father's office—he was a physician—is taken away. The house and farm are now owned by a man named Tilson— I think that is his name.[2] The out buildings have been somewhat changed —new ones built and on new sites.

I am, sir,
very truly yours
W. C. BRYANT

MANUSCRIPT: NYPL–Berg ADDRESS: F. S. Perkins Esqre.

1. Perkins is unidentified. No letter of inquiry from him has been located.
2. The Bryant homestead had been sold in 1835 by Austin Bryant to Welcome Tillson (1800–1877), a Cummington farmer. In 1865 Cullen Bryant bought the property back from the purchaser. William W. Streeter and Daphne H. Morris, *The Vital Records of Cummington, Massachusetts: 1762–1900* (Hartford, Connecticut, 1979), pp. xlv, 234; Helen H. Foster and William W. Streeter, *Only One Cummington: A Book in Two Parts* (Cummington, Massachusetts: Cummington Historical Commission, 1974), p. 354.

XXI

The Cloud on the Way
1860
(LETTERS 1123 TO 1189)

See, before us, in our journey, broods a mist upon the ground;
Thither leads the path we walk in, blending with that gloomy bound.
... One by one we miss the voices which we loved so well to hear;
One by one the kindly faces in that shadow disappear....
—"The Cloud on the Way," January 1860.

WITH BUT ONE EXCEPTION, the few poems Bryant wrote in 1860 sounded an elegiac tone: "The Cloud on the Way," "The Tides," and "Waiting by the Gate." This reflected in part sorrow at the recent loss of his friends Charles Leupp, Theodore Sedgwick III, and Washington Irving, and that in February of his little grandson Alfred Godwin, the first death in his immediate family since that of his mother fourteen years earlier. But he shared as well a national sense of foreboding at the execution of John Brown, and at the near chaos in Congress as the bitter sectional struggle over the choice of a Speaker dragged on. Although that issue at last reached a compromise acceptable to the North, there were constant rumblings in both House and Senate prefiguring southern secessions, and southern threats that the election of a Republican President would shatter the Union.

The choice of a Republican candidate was as yet uncertain when in February Bryant and other leading New York Republicans including Hamilton Fish, David Dudley Field, and John Jay—all advisers to the Young Men's Central Republican Union and firmly opposed to the nomination of Senator William H. Seward—raised funds to bring Abraham Lincoln of Illinois before an audience of fifteen hundred of the city's influential citizens at Manhattan's new Cooper Union. This was Lincoln's first appearance in the Northeast. Bryant, chosen by the meeting to preside, called him a "gallant soldier of the political campaign of 1856" who would have gone to the Senate in 1858 had it not been for an "unjust apportionment law," concluding, "I need only to pronounce the name of Abraham Lincoln of Illinois . . . to secure your profoundest attention."

Lincoln addressed his audience with a carefully reasoned eloquence which brought his dignified audience, termed by the New York *Tribune* the largest "assemblage of the city's brains and character . . . since the days of Clay and Webster," to their feet in a shouting ovation. This speech, called by Allan Nevins "a landmark in the thought of the period," contributed largely to Lincoln's nomination three months later. He was reported afterward to have been eager to learn what Bryant had written of his address in the *Evening Post*, and to have remarked, "It is worth a visit from Springfield Illinois to New York to make the acquaintance of such a man" as Bryant. The *Evening Post*'s edi-

torial comment the next day, though not so hyperbolic as that of the *Tribune*—
"No man ever before made such an impression on his first appeal to a New
York audience"—was more to the point: "It is wonderful how much a truth
gains by a certain mastery of clear and impressive statement."

Until Lincoln's selection in May to lead the Republican ticket, Bryant
wrote little editorially of his candidacy, but left no doubt thereafter of his support. "The Convention could have made no choice," he wrote, "which, along
with so many demonstrations of ardent approval, would have been met with
so few expressions of dissent. . . . Whatever is peculiar in the history and development of America, whatever is foremost in its civilization, whatever is good
in its social and political structure, finds its best expression in the career of such
men as Abraham Lincoln. . . . It is written on the tablet of destiny that Lincoln
is to be the next President of the United States."

During the first half of the year, until John Bigelow returned from Europe
in June, Bryant was again the sole responsible editor of the newspaper, for William S .Thayer had become ill in January and failed to return to the office. But
the *Evening Post*'s influence grew steadily as the organ of Republican resistance
to the spread of slavery. In January Senator King remarked that it was "doing
its whole duty as it did in 55 and 56" by the party. Years later George Haven
Putnam, who had been present at the Cooper Union address, regretted that
Bryant's "fame as a poet has possibly eclipsed the importance of his service as
an editorial teacher . . . and as a wise and patriotic leader of public opinion."

Bryant's concern with politics in this crucial year spared him little leisure
for creative writing. Although the handful of poems he did produce drew praise
from friends, particularly for "The Cloud on the Way," which Bigelow called
"one of the most impressive poems I ever read," it was his commemorative appreciation of Washington Irving before the New-York Historical Society which
drew the widest acclaim. This response reflected in part a universal affection
for the genial essayist and creator of a native mythology who had been the first
American author to gain wide respect abroad. It was equally a tribute to its
author's felicitous treatment of such a subject, which had been evidenced earlier
in his orations on Thomas Cole and Fenimore Cooper, and which, with the
Irving speech, established him as the memorialist of his literary generation.
Dana found in the Irving address "that completeness which shows a man to have
full possession of his subject." Bigelow called it "the model of an eloge." Even
Seward, though smarting under the *Evening Post*'s denials of his fitness for the
presidency, had the grace to salute this "most wonderful elogium, . . . a monument of American literature." During Bryant's visit to Boston in October, Longfellow made a strenuous effort to persuade him to dine with the exclusive
Saturday Club of New England authors. President Robert Winthrop of the
Massachusetts Historical Society "cherished" an inscribed copy of the address,
and notified Bryant of his unanimous election to the honorary membership in
that organization lately held by Irving.

Though Bryant did not visit his brothers in Illinois that year, he continued to buy through his brother John farms and farmland in and near Princeton, adding over three hundred acres to his considerable holdings there. An
item of family interest was the appointment of Cyrus Bryant's son Cullen as a
West Point cadet.

Because scarcely any of John Bryant's letters to Cullen during 1859–1860 seems to have survived, it remains uncertain to what degree John may have encouraged his brother's advocacy of Lincoln as presidential nominee. John had been an associate of Lincoln's in the Illinois legislature as well as a founder of the state's Republican party, and there is no doubt of his enthusiasm in supporting Lincoln's candidacy. The day after the November election, he wired the winner, "Bureau Co. sends greetings with twenty three hundred majority for Lincoln Lovejoy and Liberty."

Whatever impelled him toward support of Lincoln, Cullen Bryant made it his chief political concern during the second half of the year, gradually assuming the role of confidential admonitor. Assuring the candidate in a June letter that the country was to be congratulated on his nomination, achieved without "pledges or engagements," and that the people "are satisfied with you as you are, and they want you to do nothing at present but allow yourself to be elected," he warned, they "want you to make no speeches write no letters as a candidate, enter into no pledges, make no promises, nor even give any of those kind words which men are apt to interpret into promises." He was confident of Lincoln's coming election, and wanted him to take office with "every advantage for making the most judicious and worthy appointments and lending [his] aid to the wisest and most beneficial measures." Lincoln returned thanks for "the additional strength your words give me."

In August Bryant sent a trusted reporter to Springfield, ostensibly for an interview, but equally to feel out the extent to which Lincoln might have made commitments of the kind Bryant had warned against. Shortly before the election he became alarmed at an effort by New York politicians close to Seward as well as to "Wall Street" to persuade the candidate to make a "soothing speech" to "quiet the public mind" by temporizing with the South on the issues of slavery and secession, and he urged Lincoln to stand firm against their pressure. A few days after Lincoln's election on November 6 Bryant tried to prevent a rumored choice of Seward to the first position in his cabinet by urging on the President-elect the appointment of Salmon P. Chase of Ohio as Secretary of State. And on Christmas day—five days after South Carolina had seceded from the Union—he warned again that any concession to the slave interests would "disgust and discourage the large majority of Republicans in this state and cool their interest in the incoming administration down to the freezing point." That month John Murray Forbes hailed Bryant's "wise and steady advice to the Republican party to keep firm and quiet."

1123.   *To* Edwin D. Morgan¹

New York   January 27, 1860.

My dear sir.

The bearer of this is Mr. John Cockle of Brooklyn,² an old free soil democrat, a thorough Republican, a man of sense, integrity and high respectability, whom I have known for many years. I give him this letter, and state these things in his favor, that you may know what credit to give to such communications as he may make to you in your official capacity.

I am, dear sir,
very truly yours
WM. C. BRYANT.

MANUSCRIPT: NYSL ADDRESS: To Governor Edwin D. Morgan.

1. See 943.1.
2. Not further identified.

1124.   *To* John Jay¹

New York   January 28, 1860.

My dear sir.

I have just found your article in reply to the two Episcopalians, and if it had been of reasonable length would have put it in type immediately. Just now we begin to be pressed for advertisements—and we cannot leave out the proceedings of Congress, nor the fires, nor the doings of the legislature, and we have a dozen columns or less already in type—matter pressing for admission and getting stale— Can you not in mercy condense your reply? I send it that you may see if this can be done. Twice as many would read it if it were twice as short. Do this and I will state the cause of delay as fully as you please.²

Yours truly
W C BRYANT.

MANUSCRIPT: CU ADDRESS: J. Jay Esqre.

1. See 640.2.
2. Early in 1860 a New York Episcopal Church convention had refused to entertain resolutions offered by Jay deploring the slave trade, bringing upon its members condemnation by the New York *Tribune* and other journals. On January 18 and 19 the *EP* printed letters from "Rector" and "A High Church Abolitionist," calling Jay a "pertinacious and persistent friend of the Negro" who had always been "good-humouredly treated," but was the sort "who are never satisfied that they can do anything unless they can do it on the platform." No reply from Jay has been found in the *EP* for the month following these criticisms.

1125.   *To* Brantz Mayer[1]

New York   January 29th, 1860.

My dear sir.

Miss Eveneline J. Kinne, the daughter of Judge Kinne of this state, lately deceased, has desired of me a letter to some person in Baltimore whose advice would be valuable to her in regard to the disposition of the law books of which her father was the author.[2]

I hope you will not disapprove of the liberty I have taken in giving her this note to you, and that you will kindly counsel her in what manner she should proceed. With the reputation of her father's works the fruit of *vigenti annorum lucubrationes*,[3] you are already familiar.

I am sir
very truly yours
W. C. BRYANT.

MANUSCRIPT: UVa ADDRESS: Mr. Brantz Mayer.

1. Brantz Mayer (1809–1879), a Baltimore lawyer and a founder of the Maryland Historical Society, wrote books on Mexican and Maryland history.
2. Asa Kinne (d. 1859?) edited *Kinne's Quarterly Law Compendium*, and selections from Blackstone's and Kent's *Commentaries*.
3. "Twenty years of night study."

1126.   *To* John Bigelow

New York   February 6   1860

Mr dear Mr. Bigelow

I have just got your letters of the 12th and 18th of January and another of a still later date. That from Montpelier was a most interesting one and I immediately put it in type and the letter respecting the Treaty of Commerce between France and England was a perfect piece of luck.[1] I shall send off copies of the paper as you desire, and a copy of the semiweekly regularly to No 4 Rue de Berri.

Your letters respecting the policy of the Emperor are eagerly read and much talked of. Those on literary subjects, I am afraid frighten people by their length. The first sell the paper; the others I cannot find have caused the sale of a single one. That of M. Ste Beuve, caused no remark whatever, except that the subject of Beranger had been exhausted in your own letters written previously. I read both what related to Beranger and what related to Buffon with much interest,[2] and so did a few others, but I cannot learn that they attracted much attention from the public. For a daily paper they were rather long, but perhaps that was not the main difficulty. The public at large here knows very little of the history or personal character of either of these personages, and what is old relating to them, has in the eyes of the mass of readers here as much novelty as what is just brought to light; but they are not familiar enough with their works to have that craving for anecdotes of their lives conversation and correspondence which they have in the case of men distinguished in English literature. You will pardon me for speaking so frankly but it is just what you would say if you were here.

You refer to something which Mr. Thayer wrote you about my differing with you in the view you took of the rumored refusal of Great Britain to take part in the European Congress without some assurance that the independence of Central Italy should be maintained. My objection was stated in a letter to yourself—[3]but circumstances have since occurred which put another face on the matter, and it would serve no purpose to discuss the question now. I should never have thought, however, of keeping your letter out of the paper. It was read with general interest, and many persons concurred in its views, Mr. Pell for example,[4] who is a great Napoleonist. I have no [set?] objection to Napoleon's doing as much good as he can, whether in the cause of commercial or personal liberty notwithstanding his crimes.

We are in a bad plight here in the office. Mr. Thayer has been confined for six weeks or more with an inflammation of the lungs. He is better but has a bad cough yet, and I am afraid the doctor will kill him with iron. Godwin's mother has been very ill with an ulcerated leg; it was amputated, she sank away, and died in a few days;[5] this kept him away from the office a while; and now he is kept at home by a rheumatic fever—though he is doing better at last. For my own part I have for several days had one eye blocked up by a very bad stye, but I now see daylight again. I have attended, however, at the office constantly and kept the battle going. I am afraid we shall have no such good luck as to see Governor Wise nominated for President by the democratic party. The northern democrats it is certain do not expect it, and profess to be quite ashamed of him. In fact he has made so ridiculous a figure in the eyes of the whole country that he would be the easiest candidate to beat that I can possibly think of.[6]

This is a very unhealthy winter. Violent colds, fevers, bronchitis, scarlet fever, the malignant sore throat, or dip[h]theria, rheumatisms, &c prevail. My wife is confined with the worst cold she ever had. Fanny's youngest child but one has that fatal distemper the diphtheria. Mr. Tweedy[7] was made childless by that disease last winter at Albany. It is perhaps well that you have your little ones at such a distance from the spot where it rages.

My kind regards to Mrs. Bigelow. Please make my particular acknowledgments to Mr. Cobden.[8] I shall write to him when I get time.

I am sir
very faithfully yours
W C BRYANT.

MANUSCRIPT: NYPL–GR DOCKETED: M.ʳ *Bryant*. PUBLISHED (*in part*): *Life*, II, 133.

1. Bigelow's letter dated at Paris on January 18, 1860 (NYPL–BG), enclosed two letters for the *EP*; that dated at Montpelier, January 11, 1860, was printed on February 6; the second was evidently that from Richard Cobden to Bryant of January 12, 1860, quoted in *Life*, II, 131–132. See Bigelow to Bryant, February 28, 1860, NYPL–BG.

2. An unsigned letter from the French literary historian Charles Augustin Sainte-Beuve (1804–1869) appeared in the *EP* on January 26 under the caption "Literary Matters in France."

3. Letter 1119.

4. Alfred Pell; see 329.7, 920.3.

5. Martha Parke Godwin, Mrs. Abraham Godwin (d. 1859).

6. As Democratic governor of Virginia, Henry Alexander Wise (1806–1876) had greatly exaggerated the threat to the South from John Brown's raid of October 16, 1859, on Harper's Ferry, contributing to national hysteria over Brown's execution. He had further compromised his credibility by attacking the national administration and other elements of his own party. Nevins, *Emergence of Lincoln*, II, 42, 92, 105, and *passim*.

7. Possibly Edmund Tweedy of Albany, New York, and Newport, Rhode Island, whose wife Mary Temple Tweedy was the novelist Henry James's "Aunt Mary." See *Henry James: Letters*, ed. Leon Edel (Cambridge: The Belknap Press of Harvard University Press, 1974), I, 21, and *passim*.

8. Cobden's letter (Note 1) reported on his negotiations for a commercial treaty between England and France. In writing Bryant on January 18, Bigelow had said that Cobden wished his letter to be considered confidential.

1127.   *To* John Bigelow

New York, Feb. 20, 1860.

Dear Mr. Bigelow:

I am not much disappointed by the loss of M. Ste. Beuve's letters.[1] He is a brilliant writer, but much of French brilliancy disappears in translation, and I am not certain that a Frenchman can write good letters for an American newspaper.

It does not seem to me that the outlay of the correspondence you have planned will ever be returned to us, but if you think differently I would have you try it. The letters I am sure will not be read with the interest that your own have been. A clever man might gather, it appears to me, both literary and scientific matter from the French publications, matter as interesting as a Frenchman in Paris could possibly furnish, and put it into a shape better proportioned to our space and more attractive for general readers. Do not, however, let me stand in the way of any project of the kind which appears to you to promise well. The trial will shew.

As to the candidate for the Presidency, I do not recollect that I gave an opinion as to who would not get the nomination. I find that Bates is more and more talked of for the Republican Candidate.[2] He is said, for example, to be the man who can carry Illinois against Douglas by bringing out a large number of old whigs living in the middle of the state—originally from the slave states. The probability—rather let me say the chance that Douglas will be nominated by his party seems to increase. The great reason for believing that he will be nominated is that he is their strongest candidate, and to that idea their minds are opening. There is not the slightest prospect of the nomination of Wise. Nine tenths of the democratic party regard the idea as absolutely ludicrous.

Mr. Seward is not without his chances of a nomination, though some of your friends here affirm that he has none. He is himself, I hear, very confident of getting it. While the John Brown excitement continued, his prospects improved, for he was the best abused man of his party. Now that he is let alone his stock declines again and people talk of other men. For my part I do not see that he is more of a representative man than a score of others of our party. The great difficulty which I have in regard to him is this, that by the election of a Republican President the slavery question is settled, and that with Seward for President, it will be the greatest good-luck, a special and undeserved favor of Providence, if every honest democrat of the Republican party be not driven into the opposition within a twelve-month after he enters the White House. There are bitter execrations of Weed and his friends passing from mouth to mouth among the old radical democrats of the Republican party here. I suppose Weed never behaved worse than now—and his conduct alarms the best men here—they think it an omen of what we may expect from Seward's administration. We have a shamefully corrupt legislature.

Captain Schultz[3] is very anxious that you should return and electioneer for Seward's nomination. I must say frankly that I would prefer that the question should be left to the convention.

. . . My wife and daughter desire to be cordially remembered to you both.

Yrs truly
[signature not printed]

MANUSCRIPT: Unrecovered TEXT: Bigelow, *Retrospections*, I, 252–253.

1. Bigelow's attempts to engage Sainte-Beuve as a regular literary contributor to the EP had failed; the French critic thought himself too old and infirm to write for the press on such a basis. Bigelow to Bryant, London, February 3, 1860, NYPL–BG.
2. Edward Bates (1793–1869), Missouri lawyer and former congressman, was favored in the Border States as a Republican presidential candidate. Later, in 1861–1864, he was Attorney General in the Lincoln cabinet.
3. Possibly Jackson S. Schultz, a New York leather merchant who became president of the Union League Club in 1870.

1128.   *To* John W. Edmonds[1]

New York   Feb. 22   1860.
My dear sir.

I hesitate about publishing your letter[2] for this reason. Mr. [Robert Dale] Owen—who is a spiritualist—informs me that Harris has aspersed the

American spiritualists in grossest manner and in the most wholesale terms, and Mr. Owen is recently from England where he became acquainted with what Harris is doing. The charges Harris makes I understand are of the foulest nature.³

I think he had better be let alone, unless he is to be shown up as a slanderer.

I am sir
respectfully yours
W   C   BRYANT

MANUSCRIPT: Indiana University Library ADDRESS: Hon. J. W. Edmonds.

    1. See 492.4.
    2. Unrecovered.
    3. Thomas Lake Harris (1823–1906), eccentric English-born Universalist clergyman, aspiring poet, and founder of a socialist colony, first in New York and later in California, was notorious a few years after this for having made a "spiritual slave" of the English travel writer and mystic Lawrence Oliphant (1829–1888). Near the end of his life, Oliphant married a daughter of Robert Dale Owen. In 1859–1860 Harris, then editor of the spiritualistic journal *The Herald of Light*, made a lecture tour of England, in response to a divine call to preach "the Breath of God in Man and Humane Society." His collected writings, published thirty years later, did not include this "wonderful series of sermons," since he felt their use was "over and done with." See Arthur A. Cuthbert, *The Life and World-Work of Thomas Lake Harris* (Glasgow: C. W. Pierce, 1908), pp. 182–183.

1129.   *To* G[eorge?] W. Porter¹

New York   February 23d   1860.

My dear sir.

I thank you for the very kind expression of sympathy in your letter,² which has just been put into my hands. Mrs. Bryant and my daughter also desire to make their grateful acknowledgments.

We all pray that you and Mrs. Porter, who have young children growing up around you, may be spared an affliction like that which has befallen us.³

I am, dear sir,
very truly yours,
WM. C. BRYANT.

MANUSCRIPT: YCAL ADDRESS: Revd. G. W. Porter.

    1. Presbyterian minister in Manhasset, Long Island. See Letters 1440, 1475.
    2. Unrecovered.
    3. The death of Bryant's second grandson, Alfred Godwin, born in 1855. See Letters 1126 and 1146.

1130.   *To* Christiana Gibson

New York   Feb. 25. 1860.

My dear Miss Gibson.

My wife and I are alone this evening, and she bids me say, that if you are sure that you have no better way to employ yourself, you would do her, and me also, the greatest favor in the world by coming and sitting an hour with us. Margarita[1] will wait and come with you, and I will see you home.

Very truly yours

W. C. BRYANT.

MANUSCRIPT: DuU ADDRESS: Miss Christiana Gibson.

1. Apparently a servant of the Godwins'.

1131.   *To* John Howard Bryant

New York   March 2d   1860.

Dear Brother.

Mr. Henderson has answered the business part of your letter.[1] The seven thousand dollars we are willing to take; the other three we prefer to leave to somebody else, not liking to make a loan for so long a time.

My wife and daughter strongly advise your wife and sister to have the silk dresses made up for Harriet and her sister. They do not think the flounces at all gay. Flounces are not thought so here. Women twice as old as your wife and her sister wear them; nor do I think Mrs. Grundy will make much noise about them in Princeton. If she should, let her. Who cares for Mrs. Grundy?[2]

We are all pretty well. My wife is quite smart again, and goes out every day. She walked with me to church last Sunday. Fanny and her children are well. Godwin has just begun to go to the office again.

Abraham Lincoln made quite a stir here the other evening. The audience was crowded listened attentively and applauded vehemently.[3]

For a few days past the weather has been close and foggy melting all the ice and making the roads deep with mud. Today is a bright springlike day, and we think the winter is over and that the roads will be settled and firm in a short time.

Remember me kindly to your family. My wife and daughter desire their best regards to you all—

Yours affectionately

W   C   BRYANT.

MANUSCRIPT: Wellesley College Library ADDRESS: Jno H   Bryant Esqre.

1. Their letters are unrecovered, but see Letter 1025.
2. The symbol of conventional English propriety in the comedy *Speed the Plough* (1798) by Thomas Morton (1764?–1838). This play was often performed in New York,

following its first production there in 1800. George C. D. Odell, *Annals of the New York Stage*, 15 vols. (New York: Columbia University Press, 1931), *passim*.

3. Bryant's terse comment gives no hint of his part in bringing Lincoln, for the first time, before an influential eastern audience, thus giving him the chance to deliver one of the most telling speeches in his 1860 campaign for the Republican nomination for the presidency. Engaged at first to lecture at Henry Ward Beecher's Plymouth Church in Brooklyn, the Illinois lawyer found himself scheduled instead by the Young Men's Central Republican Union—of which Bryant was an "Advisor"—to make a major political statement in New York's new Cooper Union. An audience of 1,500 political and civic leaders chose Bryant to preside over the meeting on February 27. His introductory remarks were printed the next day in the *EP*:

It is a grateful office that I perform in introducing to you an eminent citizen of the West, hitherto known to you only by reputation, who has consented to address a New York assembly this evening. A powerful auxiliary, my friends, is the great West in that battle which we are fighting in behalf of freedom against slavery and in behalf of civilization against barbarism, for the occupation of some of the fairest regions of our continent now first opened to colonization. [applause.] I recognize an agency higher and wiser than that of man, in causing the broad and fertile region which forms the northern part of the valley of the Mississippi to be rapidly filled with a population of hardy freemen, who till their own acres with their own hands, and who would be ashamed to subsist by the labor of slaves. [applause.] These children of the West form a living bulwark against the advance of slavery, and from them is recruited the vanguard of the mighty armies of liberty. [Loud applause.] One of them I present to you this evening, a gallant soldier of the political campaign of 1856, [applause] in which he rendered good service to the Republican cause, and the great champion of that cause in Illinois two years later, when he and his friends would have won the victory but for the unjust apportionment law, by which a minority of the population are allowed to elect a majority of the legislature. I need only to pronounce the name of Abraham Lincoln of Illinois—[loud cheers]—I have only to pronounce his name, to secure your profoundest attention.

Lincoln's address was a closely reasoned constitutional argument for the restriction of slavery. The next day the New York *Tribune* remarked, "No man ever before made such an impression on his first appeal to a New York audience," and Bryant commented in a leading *EP* editorial, "It is wonderful how much a truth gains by a certain mastery of clear and impressive statement." *EP*, February 28, 1860; Nevins, *Emergence of Lincoln*, II, 183–188; James A. Briggs, *An Account of Hon. Abraham Lincoln Being Invited to Give an Address in Cooper Institute, N. Y. February 27, 1860, Together with Mr. Bryant's Introduction and Mr. Lincoln's Speech* (Putnam, Connecticut, 1915), pp. 1–5. Briggs's version of Bryant's remarks often departs from the *EP* text, which is presumably the more authentic.

One member of Lincoln's Cooper Union audience credits Bryant with the initiative which brought the Illinois lawyer into national prominence as an alternative to the leading candidate for the Republican nomination for the presidency, William H. Seward. George Haven Putnam (1844–1930), son and successor of publisher George P. Putnam, recalled many years later that Bryant, "a patriotic and unselfish leader of public opinion," brought together a group of influential New York political leaders to invite Lincoln to speak in the metropolis and persuaded them to finance his trip to the East. "It is well," Putnam wrote, "that Americans should remember the valuable service rendered by William C. Bryant in helping to bring about the selection as the leader, not only of the new party, but of all Americans who fought and worked to save the republic, the great Captain, Abraham Lincoln." Rufus Rockwell Wilson, *Intimate Memories of Lincoln* (Elmira, New York: Primavera Press, 1945), pp. 256–260.

1132.   *To* John Bigelow

New York   March 22d   1860.

Dear Mr. Bigelow.

Both Mr. Henderson and myself are sorry that you should have been disappointed in regard to the office occupied by Mr. Eckel.[1] We both supposed that you desired merely a place to deposite the articles which might arrive for you from France, and we drew this conclusion from something you said in one of your letters about storing some boxes there which were to be sent on before you. If you had intimated the purpose for which you wanted the room it would have been kept for you. But inasmuch as it was no place for goods, and as moreover, we could not deposite in it the boxes which should first arrive, and finally as Mr. Eckel when he heard it was encouraged to believe that he might have it another year and would have been much disappointed if he did not get it, I concurred with Mr. Henderson in letting him have it. Yet the understanding with Mr. Eckel did not amount to an engagement and we should have obliged him to evacuate, if we had not imagined that the room was not suitable for the purpose you had in view and therefore you must be under some misapprehension in regard to it.

You have this to console you in the meantime, that, if you have been disappointed, another person has been saved from disappointment, which is the next best thing to being saved from disappointment yourself, and if looked at from a Christian point of view quite equal to it.

We have had an unhealthy winter. Several persons of note have gone. Stephen Whitney is not only dead but forgotten.[2] The clergy trooped to his funeral like crows to a dead horse; but he gave them not a penny by his will—neither to them nor their institutions. George Wood, you see, has followed him.[3] All the old people will, I suppose, have died off by and by, and only young men be left in the world, and then the day of great reforms will arrive. They are wanted—that is the reforms. The present legislature has the reputation of being the most corrupt that we have had for a long time. People begin to grumble about your friend Governor Morgan and say that he is trying to manage with a view of being made United States Senator.

The attempt to put forward Bates as the Republican candidate for President causes some discussion and some feeling. It seems to me, as at present advised, that his friends will hardly be able to make him enough a Republican to induce our party to take him up. The Blairs you know are zealous in his favor—but we have been beaten already by a candidate nominated by the Blairs.

At the office we are getting on as well as we could expect. The old trouble of too many advertisements and too little reading matter has returned upon us. There is a fight every day between the editorial room and the composing room, with Dithmar the sturdy friend of the advertisers parrying all attempts to displace advertisements by reading matter. We are lately getting out a third edition, to occupy the ground taken by the third edition of the *Express* which many persons have been till now obliged to read against their will.[4] Our third edition is only a day or two old so that we can give no guess as to its success.

My best regards to Mrs. Bigelow. My wife and daughter send her their love and desire me to remember them most kindly to you.

Yours faithfully
W. C. Bryant.

P.S. Julia thanks Mrs. Bigelow for her pleasant letter and asks me to enclose the copy of a poem for which Mrs. Bigelow has enquired.[5]

W. C. B.

manuscript: NYPL–GR docketed: Wm. C. Bryant & Co.

1. Bigelow had asked Bryant and Isaac Henderson whether, on his return from abroad in June 1860, he might occupy an office in the *EP* building formerly rented to a Dr. Robinson. Bigelow to Henderson, cDecember 10, 1859; Bigelow to Bryant, February 6 and 28, 1860, NYPL–BG. Christian G. Eckel, a lawyer, had offices at 53 Liberty Street during the period 1859–1861. *Trow's New York City Directory* for 1859, 1860, 1861 (New York: Trow [1858, 1859, 1860]).

2. Stephen Whitney, who died on February 16, 1860, at the age of 84, was a wealthy New York merchant who was the last to keep a home facing Bowling Green, at the foot of Broadway.

3. George Wood (1789–1860, College of New Jersey [Princeton] 1808) had been a leading New York attorney and legal scholar.

4. The New York *Express*, started in 1836 as a Whig morning paper, had become an evening paper in 1858 with Democratic politics. Mott, *American Journalism*, pp. 261–262, 446.

5. Mrs. Bigelow's letter is unrecovered; the poem is unidentified.

1133.   *To* Elizabeth D. Bancroft

New York   April 2d   1860

Dear Mrs. Bancroft.

Mrs. Bryant is to have a box for tomorrow night in the Academy of Music, and as you like as little as she does the idea of waiting an hour and a half for the proceedings to begin I write this in her behalf to offer you a seat with her.[1] If you do her the favor to accept it, you might either go with her from this place at a quarter past seven—or come directly to the box which is on the left hand as you go into the theatre from the front entrance —the first box you come to on the 2d tier.—

I am, dear madam,
faithfully yours
W. C. Bryant.

P.S. My wife tells me to say that she hopes you will come here and go with
her and Miss Sands—   W. C. B.

MANUSCRIPT: LC ADDRESS: Mrs. E. Bancroft.

1. On November 28, 1859, Washington Irving had died—in Longfellow's words, "In
the bright Indian Summer of his fame." A few days later the New-York Historical Society, of which Irving had been one of the "earliest, most distinguished, and most
cherished members," planned a memorial meeting to be held at the Academy of Music
on April 3, 1860, his seventy-sixth birthday. There Bryant gave the principal eulogy
(see Bryant, "Irving," pp. [95]–154). John Bigelow called this "the model of an eloge,"
and even Bryant's long-time political opponent William H. Seward saw it as " 'a monument of American literature.' " Longfellow, "In the Churchyard at Tarrytown" (1876);
Vail, *Knickerbocker Birthday*, pp. 395–398; Bigelow to Bryant, May 8, 1860, NYPL–BG;
Seward to Bryant, quoted in *Life*, II, 134.

1134.   *To* Edwin D. Morgan

                                      New York   April 11th   1860
My dear sir.

     You will not I am confident take it ill if I speak to you frankly in re-
gard to what the people of New York expect from one to whom they have
been proud to point as a man who would do his duty without flinching.

     Those whose good opinion is worth having most earnestly hope that
you will put your veto on the City Railroad bills which have just passed
the legislature.[1] It is not easy to conceive how intense is the disgust and how
vehement is the indignation which these corrupt measures have awakened
among that class of men with whom you agree in their views of the proper
duty of legislators. They look upon the legislature as governed and managed by rogues, and in this I am fully of their opinion. I doubt, for my
part, if we ever had so corrupt a legislature as we have at present and the
imprecation

                    "A plague on both your houses"[2]

is in almost every man's mouth. The franchises given away by the railroad
bills are the most outrageous misappropriation of public property that has
ever been known in the annals of legislation on this continent—such I assure you is the general sentiment. On the prospects of the Republican party
its effect is likely to be most disastrous. If the bills become a law the Republican party is annihilated in this city, and the action of public opinion
here on the country cannot fail of being extremely unfavorable. On the
prospects of Mr. Seward, the effect here has already been as bad as it well
could be and nothing but the refusal of the Governors signature to these
bills can prevent some of those who have been his best friends from giving
way to an "irrepressible" desire to throw him overboard.

     But party considerations are not the proper ones for deciding this ques-
tion. The bills are unrighteous, against the interest and rights of the city;

public opinion here is vehemently adverse to their passage—these are the true reasons for rejecting them. What good men here desire with all their hearts is an opportunity to celebrate another noble rebuke of legislative corruption by Executive integrity and firmness.[3]

I am dear sir

faithfully yours

W. C. BRYANT

MANUSCRIPT: NYSL ADDRESS: To Governor Edwin D. Morgan DOCKETED: 1860 / Wm C. Bryant / Apl 11.

1. See 1119.4.
2. *Romeo and Juliet* III.i.103.
3. These franchise bills passed the legislature over Governor Morgan's opposition and veto. Nevins, *Emergence of Lincoln*, II, 235; Van Deusen, *Seward*, p. 215.

1135.   *To* George P. Morris[1]

New York   April 12th   1860.

Sir.

The publication of *Thanatopsis* in the North American Review of which you speak, was the original one. My father found the fragment among some manuscripts which I had written several years before and left at Cummington, and took them with him to Boston where they were handed to those who then conducted the North American Review. The lines of which you speak, as being in a different metre, were another fragment, and were I suppose printed by mistake as part of Thanatopsis. The opening and concluding lines of Thanatopsis were written afterwards in 1821.[2]

I am sir

respectfully yours

W. C. BRYANT.

MANUSCRIPT: HEHL ADDRESS: Gen   Geo. P. Morris / Office of the *Home Journal* POSTAL ANNOTATION: [private].

1. From 1846 until shortly before his death in 1864, Morris (194.6) shared the editorship of the *Home Journal* with Nathaniel Parker Willis.
2. See 46.2, 73.2.

1136.   *To* John Bigelow

New York   April 13th   1860.

Dear Mr. Bigelow.

I wrote my last letter in such haste, that I omitted to do what was in my mind when I began it—that is to say to desire you to return my best thanks to M. le Chevalier de Chatelain for the honor he has done my verses. To be translated into French by the translator of Chaucer is an honor indeed. Please to thank him in my name for the new graces he has given to the *Burial of Love,* and to several others of my poems. Among these the version of *The Strange Lady* seems to me executed with particular skill.[1]

The two letters concerning which you inquire came to hand but they reached us at a time when [we] were puzzled to find room for the news of the day and for matters which the readers of the Evening Post *must* see. We are keeping them till the Spring flood shall have subsided, and when the muddy waters disappear we shall turn them in to make music in the regular channel.[2]

I admit that you have made your reasons for nominating Mr. Seward clearer by your explanation—[3] but I do not care to enter into the argument now. His friends I have reason to believe are not dissatisfied with the course of the Evening Post, and whether he be nominated or not depends on causes of another kind. If you were here I think you would understand some parts of the question better than you can at a distance.

I hear that Mr. Thayer is a great deal better and he writes that he thinks of coming back to the office in May. This however, I do not think certain; for his cough it seems continues. Meantime he has made himself exceedingly disagreeable to Mr. Henderson by the manner in which he has talked to him—so that though I think very highly of Mr. Thayer's capacity as a purveyor of intelligence and other matters for a newspaper, I do not feel certain that it will be a pleasant thing for Mr. Henderson to see him in the office again. One of Thayer's offences though probably not the principal is his ambition to be regarded as the manager and director of the paper.[4]

We have your article on the paper duties which is timely and excellent and shall use it editorially—as I suppose you designed it to be used, or at least as I inferred that you were willing it should be used.

My regards to Mrs. Bigelow.

I am dear sir
faithfully yours,
W. C. BRYANT.

P.S. The Irving meeting was a great affair—so far at least as the concourse which attended was concerned—an immense audience and very attentive. Professor Greene's speech—the latter part at least was not heard—the audience was impatient for Everett, who delivered his remarks with more vehemence than usual.[5]   W. C. B.

MANUSCRIPT: NYPL–GR DOCKETED: W. C. Bryant & Co / April 1860.

1. Bigelow had forwarded from London French translations of several Bryant poems by the naturalized British journalist Jean-Baptiste François Ernest de Chatelain (1801–1881). Bigelow to Bryant, February 28, 1860, NYPL–BG. Enclosed also was a letter from Chatelain to Fitz-Greene Halleck, accompanied by a translation of that poet's "Alnwick Castle." Bryant delivered this letter and its enclosure to Halleck, who was at home ill, and who remarked later, "I wish you had been present when he read the

translation. His appreciation of the fun of the thing was visible in his eyes. They sparkled like stars in a frosty sky in the absence of moon and cloud: a study for an artist." Halleck to Bigelow, May 24, 1860, quoted in Bigelow, *Retrospections*, I, 265–267. Chatelain also rendered several of Longfellow's poems into French. Nelson Frederick Adkins, *Fitz-Greene Halleck: An Early Knickerbocker Wit and Poet* (New Haven: Yale University Press, 1930), pp. 146–147; Longfellow, *Letters*, III, 482; IV, 17, 63. Chatelain's translation of Chaucer was *Contes de Cantorbéry* (London, 1857).

2. Not yet having received Bryant's letter of February 6 (Letter 1126) when he wrote on the 28th, Bigelow had asked what his partner thought of his long letters for the *EP* on the writings of Buffon and Beranger.

3. Apparently not yet fully aware of the growing interest in Lincoln in the East, after his Cooper Union address and subsequent speaking tour through New England, Bigelow wrote repeatedly of his conviction that Seward was the only reasonable choice for the Republican nomination for the presidency. The *EP* had, in truth, made little or no mention of Lincoln throughout March, and Bryant was equally noncommittal in his correspondence—though his distaste for Seward was quite evident. An unfortunate misreading, or oversight, caused Allan Nevins to write (*Evening Post*, p. 262) that Bigelow "had no use for Seward," and "saw in Lincoln the only hope of the party," while in fact, in the very letter Nevins cites, Bigelow said nothing of Lincoln, but insisted that Seward was the only acceptable candidate and would be nominated. Bigelow to Bryant, March 20, 1860, NYPL–BG.

4. Bigelow and Bryant seem to have agreed that William S. Thayer (924.4), who had served briefly as managing editor, was of more use to the *EP* as a reporter. See Bigelow to Bryant, May 8, 1860, NYPL–BG.

5. Bryant's address at the Irving commemoration had been followed by several shorter ones, including those of Edward Everett and George Washington Greene (1811–1883), later the first professor of history at Cornell University. Vail, *Knickerbocker Birthday*, p. 398.

1137.   *To* Robert Bonner[1]

New York   April 16   1860

Dear sir

I am sorry I cannot give you the man's name at this moment. He is a person whose face I often see in the office—but whose name—though he gave it and I meant to remember it has wholly escaped my memory. Mr. Godwin knew him and spoke with him yesterday—and he is in the country. He *may* be in this morning—I will see him as soon as he comes in and find you the name.[2]

Yours truly

W   C   Bryant

Manuscript: QPL Address: R   Bonner Esq. Docketed: Apl 16/60 / Wm Cullen Bryant.

1. Robert Bonner (1824–1899) came to the United States from Ireland in 1839, and, after learning the printing trade on the Hartford *Courant*, moved to New York in 1844 to open a print shop. In 1851 he established the *New York Ledger*, a phenomenally successful weekly story-newspaper to which Bryant contributed a number of poems between 1859 and 1872, as well as a translation from the Spanish of Carolina Coronado's romantic novel, *Jarilla*.

2. The subject of Bryant's remarks is unidentified.

1138.   *To* Edwin D. Morgan

New York   April 26,   1860

My dear sir.

I take pleasure in bearing my testimony to the merits of Mr. D. T. Marshall whose name, I understand has been suggested to you as that of a proper person to fill the vacancy in the Board of Police Commissioners.[1]

Mr. Marshall, I think, has eminent qualifications for that post. He is honest, just, quick-sighted, clear-headed, active and resolute. Without being contentious, he has a determined manner in all questions involving his integrity as a private or as a public man, which inclines less scrupulous persons to give way to him.

I am, dear sir,

very truly yours,

WM. C. BRYANT.

MANUSCRIPT: NYSL ADDRESS: To Governor E. D. Morgan. DOCKETED: W. C. Bryant / Apl 26th.

1. Marshall has not been further identified, and he seems to have failed of appointment.

1139.   *To* John Howard Bryant

New York   Apl. 27. 1860

Dear Brother.

I am willing that you should do almost any way with your debt to me —except that I do not like to own mortgaged land. If you want to keep the land would it not be better that you should give me a note at seven per cent interest, secured by a mortgage, for all that you would owe me? I will think however further of the matter—and I wish you would.

Your letter came to hand this morning. With regard to the Republican Manual, we decided not to publish it, the very hour that we [received?][1] your letter and that of your friend. We have always lost on such publications.[2] But I put the letters into the hands of a person employed about our office, who promised to see the people in the office of the Tribune and ask if they would undertake it. They referred him to Greeley. Greeley could not be seen for some time, and only this moment have I been able to get his answer. He declines—observing that if the production had been offered gratuitously he might perhaps undertake it—but not otherwise. If your friend desires further communication with Greeley, he may address him directly.

As to the verses—I have been waiting for Mr. Godwin to return that I might ask him to do something with them. He has just returned this morning. I think them good and he has promised to see the Harpers Magazine men concerning them. I will write to you again about them.[3]

We are all passably well here, except Frances who is half dead with a severe influenza—or has been—and is fortunately coming to life again. The season is backward cold, sleety, and rheumatic. My kind regards to your wife and Elijah.

Yours truly
W C BRYANT

MANUSCRIPT: NYPL–BFP ADDRESS: JNº H Bryant Esq.

1. Word omitted.
2. For several years, at least—between 1839 and 1842—the *EP* had published an annual *Democrat's Almanac*. See *EP*, April 24, 1840, and June–July 1841, *passim*; Letter 388. Neither John's letter nor that of his friend, unidentified, has been recovered.
3. *Harper's New Monthly Magazine*, founded in 1850, carried literary contributions by many prominent English and American authors. Though Parke Godwin apparently had no direct connection with the periodical, he was an intimate friend of George William Curtis (915.1), one of its principal contributors, with whom he had been associated in editing *Putnam's Magazine*. Godwin, "George William Curtis," in *Commemorative Addresses* . . . (New York, 1895), pp. 3, 17–18. The verses referred to are unidentified.

1140. *To* Orville Dewey

New York, April 30, 1860

. . . If we will have you? Doctor,

"what words have passed thy lips unweighed!"

If the earth will have the spring—if the sunflower will have the sunshine—if the flock will have the grass. You might as well put an *if* between a hungry man and his dinner. You shall come to Roslyn, you and your Sultana, and shall be welcome, and treated *en rois* [like kings].[1] If I were writing for the press I should not say *en rois*, for in public I hold it my duty to maintain on all occasions the supremacy and sufficiency of the English language: but I have said *en rois* because it came into my head. Come on, and we will make the most of you both, and anybody else you choose to bring with you—that our poor means allow. You shall not be walked out more than you absolutely choose, nor asked to look at anything. You shall have full leave to bury yourself in books, or write, or think, or smoke away your time, and I will make a provision of segars for your idle hours, with the prudent toleration which the innocent have for the necessary vices of others. I have a coachman, and he shall take you about the country whenever you and Mrs. Dewey take a fancy for a ride. And having done this, I will neglect you, for I am afraid that is what you like, to your heart's content. And then, if—for I, too, must have my if—if you will only stay over

Sunday, you shall be asked to preach by our orthodox Presbyterian minister, who inquires when Dr. Dewey is expected, for he wants to ask him to preach. Come, then, prepared for a ten days' sojourn, with a stock of patience in your heart, and a sermon or two in your pocket, of your second or third quality, for we are quite plain people here, and anything very fine is wasted upon us.

For any imperfections in my eulogy on Irving I beg you to consider the Historical Society as responsible; they put it upon me without consulting me; and at first I flatly refused, but I was afterward talked into consent. Besides the excuses of incapacity, unworthiness, and all that, I did not want the labor of writing the discourse. There has been no end of work with me the past winter. . . . Among other symptoms of age, I find a disposition growing up within me to regard the world as belonging to a new race of men, who have somehow or other got into it, and taken possession of it, and among whom I am a superfluity. What have I to do with their quarrels and controversies? I, who am already proposed as a member of the same club with Daniel Defoe and Sir Roger L'Estrange.[2] Is it fitting that, just as I have taken my hat to go out and join the Ptolemies, I should be plucked by the elbow and asked to read a copy of silly verses, and say whether they are fit to be printed? Besides, it seems to be agreed by everybody who is about my own age, or older, that the world is nowadays much wickeder than when they were young; and it is no more than it deserves to leave it to take care of itself as it can. But we will talk over these things when you come. . . .[3]

MANUSCRIPT: Unrecovered TEXT (partial): Life, II, 134–136.

1. Dewey had written Bryant on April 28 (NYPL–BG) that he and Mrs. Dewey would visit Roslyn in the summer, provided Mrs. Bryant were well and they were wanted. The quotation is unidentified.
2. Daniel Defoe (1661?–1731) and Sir Roger L'Estrange (1616–1704) were controversial political journalists.
3. The Deweys apparently paid their visit about the middle of July. See Letter 1156; Dewey to Bryant, July 5, 1860, NYPL–BG.

1141.   To Cassius Marcellus Clay[1]

New York   May 4th. 1860.

My dear sir.

I thank you for what you are so kind as to say concerning my discourse on Washington Irving.[2]

That your own life has not been allowed to pass in the same peaceful tenor as his ought not to excite in you any repinings. You have been placed by Providence in circumstances, for dealing with which you have shown a peculiar fitness. The great work of bringing a community prejudiced in favor of slavery to see their error, and to permit its evils to be freely discussed has been laid upon you and you have shown yourself fully equal to it.[3] He may be esteemed a fortunate man who does not fall below the occasion to which he is summoned.

I am dear sir,
truly yours
W   C   BRYANT.

MANUSCRIPT: New York University Library ADDRESS: C. M. Clay Esqre.

1. Cassius Marcellus Clay (1810–1903, Yale 1832) was a Kentucky journalist and Abolitionist.
2. Clay's comment on the discourse has not been found.
3. In 1855 Clay had founded an anti-slavery community at Berea, Kentucky, where white and black children were educated together. In 1859 its residents were driven from the state by a mob, but Clay refused to be intimidated by his slaveholding neighbors. Nevins, *Emergence of Lincoln*, II, 109, 115.

1142.   *To* James Grant Wilson[1]

New York   May 4th.   1860.

Dear sir.

As I promised some days since, I have sent you by the mail of today, a copy of my discourse before the Historical Society.

I am, sir,
very truly yours,
W. C. BRYANT.

MANUSCRIPT: Andrew B. Myers ADDRESS: Grant Wilson Esqre.

1. This is the earliest known evidence of an acquaintance between Bryant and James Grant Wilson (1832–1914), Scottish-born journalist whose chief claim to fame was a self-stated intimacy with the aging Bryant. To Wilson's sycophancy and ultimate negligence some of Bryant's friends attributed the poet's death in 1878. See, for example, John Gourlie to John Bigelow, July 1, 1878, Union College Library. See also Wilson's own account of Bryant's fatal injury in his "Memoir of William Cullen Bryant," *The Family Library of Poetry and Song, . . .* ed. William Cullen Bryant (New York: Fords, Howard, & Hulbert [1880]), pp. 29–31.

1143.   *To* Frances F. Bryant

Wednesday Morning.
New York   May 9, 1860

Dear Frances.

I find the Bixby bill and money and have attended to paying the shoemaker. The Diary I do not see but I shall look further.

Last evening I went to look for Miss [Catharine] Sedgwick. I went to Harry's, his door plate was gone and nobody would answer the bell. I then went to Rackemann's. He had moved and with his family they said was at the Clarendon Hotel. In going to the Clarendon Hotel I stopped at Dr.

Bellows's—he knew nothing about Miss Sedgwick's place of sojourn and had been looking for it in vain. At the Clarendon, they told me that Mrs. Rackemann was in Berkshire and he was out. I stopped at Mr. Valerios door. The girl said Miss Sedgwick was at Mrs. Carpenters No 58 in the same street. I went thither, it was Mrs. Faulkener's and Mrs. Robert Sedgwick came forward. Miss Sedgwick she told me was at Mr. Dudley Field's. I did not go further.

Soon after my return Mr. Charles Butler called and we arranged to go to his place on Friday if the weather be good. If I return in season I will come out to Roslyn on Friday afternoon.[1]

Yours ever
W C BRYANT.

MANUSCRIPT: NYPL–GR.

1. In addition to the novelist Catharine Sedgwick and her nephew Harry, Henry Dwight Sedgwick (1824–1903), the persons named above who have been identified were Henry W. Bellows (734.3), Elizabeth Ellery Sedgwick (100.6; Letter 1014), David Dudley Field (492.4), and Charles Butler (946.2).

1144.   *To* John Howard Bryant

New York, May 14, 1860

Dear Brother

It has struck me that if it would be profitable to cultivate the land of mine which is now grazed by those who have farms contiguous to it, it would answer for me to try my luck with your help. You say that you haven't the money at command which would be necessary for the cost of fencing and tillage. What do you say to my sending you all the money necessary and your taking charge of the matter and paying yourself out of the crop. Is there no rule of partnership applicable to such cases? If there is I am willing that you should go on under it and I will send all the funds which are necessary. Will you write to me on the subject as soon as you receive this letter?

We have had the same drought here which you have had in the west, only it came later. The grass suffers for want of rain—and some of the other crops. The season, however, is now rather forward.

We are all well and are again established in the country which is in all of its beauty.

As to your paying me for the money you owe me I am content that you should do it in your own way and time.

And regards to all.

Yours affectionately
W. C. BRYANT.

MANUSCRIPT: BCHS TEXT: "Bryant and Illinois," 643–44.

1145. *To* Charlotte Dana

New York   June 12   1860

My dear Miss Dana.

I came into town this morning thinking that I should stay overnight and meaning to call on you at 19 University Place. But matters are so arranged that I must return tonight and come in on Thursday morning, and I have been busy all the day till near the time of my departure.

It would give us great pleasure if you could come down to Roslyn if only for a night. There is a steamer, the Long Island which makes daily trips to Roslyn leaving James Slip at four o'clock in the afternoon, and coming back to town in the morning. You would have a pleasant sail at least and if Mrs. Ripley[1] would come with you we should be all very glad to see her. James Slip lies a little above Peck Slip—between that and Catherine Street Ferry.

I wish very much to see you. I have a great many inquiries to make about your father and the rest of you. If you do not come out I shall look for you when I come to town again. My wife and Julia when I showed them your letter were very sorry that you could not find time to come and see them, and would send lots of love if they were with me. When you see your father please tell him that he should have come and made his abode with me till you should return. What is he doing that should keep him so close at home?

Yours truly
W. C. BRYANT.

MANUSCRIPT: LH ADDRESS: Miss Charlotte Dana. DOCKETED: From W^m C   Bryant / June 1860.

1. Probably Mrs. George Ripley (726.4).

1146. *To* Richard H. Dana

New York   June 14th. 1860.

Dear Dana.

I hardly thought you would speak so well of my Eulogy on Irving as you have done. On such occasions we are apt to over praise and I was not sure that I had avoided that fault. The eulogy was well received, but Irving was a universal favorite and what I said was commended to men's kindness by the subject. But when you praise I know you mean it.[1]

With regard to giving letters to persons in England, I have always been embarrassed when asked to do it. The English are sometimes capricious in the matter of introductions and I am afraid of them. My literary aquaintances there are few. I have sought no man's aquaintance among them. I shall, however, rummage in my memory and see what I can do for your friend Mr. Dix.[2]

I have not written to you since the death of my little grandson. He was about three years old; quite a favorite in the family, waggish, playful, and of quick sensibilities. His loss was a great grief to all of us. I see that you too have had your losses by death. At our time of life we find the world becoming empty of those we love and filling up with strangers.

I have just called at No. 19 University Place to see Charlotte, and have found that she went to Boston yesterday morning. I have been in town but one day before since I learned she was here, and then I had to go back the same day, nor had I time to go up town to see her. I thought that I might persuade her to take a trip to our place on Long Island which at this season is pretty.

Your son Richard I suppose, when he returns, as I think he must, for after the hair breadth escapes he has made I account him pretty safe, for this journey at least, will make another book of travels. If it only contains personal adventures with nothing about the people and countries he has seen it will be interesting. But if he goes to Japan, he will be certain to give us a book which every body will read. I am quite curious to know how the Japanese will look seen through such eyes as his.[3]

My partner, Mr. Bigelow, who has been absent in Europe for a year and a half has just returned and I expect to have more leisure hereafter— though perhaps, for the last eight or nine months I have had as much as I ought to have. I sometimes think of visiting Boston again, but somehow I have a dread of Boston. To go to any country place is an entertainment to me; to go to a large town I find myself, for what reason, I can scarcely say reluctant. I shall not find Boston what it was when I knew it, and the change I am sure will not strike me pleasantly. In one respect it will affect me with sadness. Most of my old friends there and in its neighborhood are gone.

As you are mentioned in my Eulogy on Irving, I shall ask you to accept a copy of an edition got out by Putnam[4] which I will send you by express.

Kind regards to Charlotte, and say to her, if you please, that I did not by any means intend to let her get out of town without seeing her.

I am, dear sir,

faithfully yours

W. C. BRYANT.

MANUSCRIPT: NYPL–GR ADDRESS: R. H. Dana Esq. ENDORSED: Wm C. Bryant, June 14 / 60 / Ans. June 19 PUBLISHED (*in part*): *Life*, II, 137–138.

1. After reading the address, Dana commented on Bryant's "naturalness, simplicity, and beauty of expression, tender thoughtfulness with all due praise, yet nothing in excess." Dana to Bryant, May 19, 1860, quoted in *Life*, II, 136.

2. Possibly John Homer Dix (1811–1884), a Boston ophthalmologist. No Bryant letter of introduction for Dix has been found.

3. Between July 1859 and September 1860 Richard Dana, Jr., traveled around the

world, visiting Japan. Robert L. Gale, *Richard Henry Dana Jr.* (New York: Twayne [1969]), p. 85. Dana apparently published no account of this voyage.

4. *A Discourse on the Life, Character and Genius of Washington Irving* (New York, 1860).

1147. *To* Samuel A. Allibone

New York   June 15th   1860.

My dear sir.

My opinion of the bad effect of composing at night upon the health, is founded principally on my personal experience. I find that it excites the nerves; that I cannot sleep after it, or that if I sleep I wake too early, and that after a short time it brings on weakness of body. I have heard many others complain that writing in the evening had the effect of making them sleepless afterwards. The early hours of the night I believe it is generally admitted are those in which we have the most refreshing and restoring slumbers.

Authors, it seems to me should have plenty of sleep, else the brain which is the organ brought into activity by their occupation will become over-worked. It should have ample time to rest and repair its vigor. Besides, it is in the latter part of the day that we generally make our most liberal meals, and to put the stomach and the brain to their hardest tasks at the same time is an indiscretion by which one or the other must suffer.

With regard to your own case I think you give too large a portion of time to your studies, and reserve too little for exercise society, your meals and your sleep. Nearly twelve hours a day are devoted, I believe, if I understand your letter, to your literary tasks. If Mr. Irving sometimes wrote fifteen hours a day I have the authority of his nephew that he suffered for it afterwards by languor listlessness and depression of spirits. Taking his literary life altogether he must have given much less time to the task of writing than you are doing for he sometimes did not touch his pen for many weeks together.[1]

You are familiar with the case of Southey who must have been as constantly at work as you are, who made change of subject stand him in the stead of recreation occupying himself with one kind of study in the morning, another at mid-day and a third at night, and yet who became prematurely superannuated.[2] I remember that John C. Spencer an eminent lawyer of the New York bar, and at one time Secretary of the Treasury[3] once told me that he was at work nearly all the time he was awake, busy in his professional or official labors. He was a remarkable example of energy and industry; he allowed himself no time for recreation or exercise, and always boasted of his excellent health, yet he suddenly became a mere wreck shattered both in mind and body and died I think not far from the age of sixty.

You have now arrived at a time of life in which it seems to me that one should make some provision for a decline of the power of endurance. To refer to my own case, I have found great benefit from a regular system of chest exercises. I take them in the morning continuing them for about an hour. They favor a healthy arterial action, which you know accompanies the natural temperament of youth and cheerfulness.

Excuse this rather dogmatic letter which I might have made longer if I had been willing to bore you.

I am, sir,
faithfully yours
W. C. BRYANT.

MANUSCRIPT: HEHL ADDRESS: S. A. Allibone Esqre.

1. Toward the end of his address on April 3, Bryant remarked of Washington Irving, "In the evening he wrote but rarely, knowing—so at least, I infer—that no habit makes severer demands upon the nervous system than this." Bryant, "Irving," p. 150. On May 23 Allibone had written Bryant (NYPL–BG) asking that he justify this statement.

2. The English Poet Laureate Robert Southey (1774–1843), whose literary output was prodigious, is said to have died from softening of the brain.

3. John Canfield Spencer (1788–1855, Union 1806), was also Secretary of War, 1841–1843.

1148.   To John Howard Bryant

Office of The Evening Post,
New York, June 16   1860

Dear Brother

If I have not acknowledged having received your note of $4.480— so promptly as you might have expected, it has been because I wished to inform you of my having seen the $250 endorsed on the note which Fanny holds against you. I paid it to her when she was in town, and the note in the country. Since that time she has been in town most of the time, and when I have been in town she has been in the country. She has also been quite ill which delayed her going to the country. I shall attend to it immediately as she is at Roslyn and I go in an hour or two.

I enclose the note given by you & Mr. Dee[1] for $4.480, with a $200 note which has been paid. Let me know when you receive them.

Do you know of a good opportunity of investing a few thousand dollars—say from five to ten thousand? Please answer soon.

Yours truly
W   C   BRYANT

MANUSCRIPT: NYPL–BFP.

1. Unidentified.

1149. *To* Abraham Lincoln

New York   June 16, 1860.

My dear sir.

I was about to begin this letter by saying that I congratulate you on your nomination,[1] but when I consider the importunities which will beset you as a candidate and the cares, responsibilities and vexations which your success will throw upon you, I do not congratulate you. It is the country that is to be congratulated. I was not without apprehensions that the nomination might fall upon some person encumbered with bad associates, and it was with a sense of relief and infinite satisfaction that I with thousands of others in this quarter heard that it was conferred upon you.

It is fortunate that you have never gathered about you a knot of political confederates who have their own interests to look after. You will excuse the frankness of an old campaigner who has been engaged in political controversies for more than a third of a century, if I say that I hope you will allow none to be formed around you while you are before the country as a candidate for the Presidency. I have observed that those candidates who are most cautious of making pledges, stating opinions or entering into arrangements of any sort for the future save themselves and their friends a great deal of trouble and have the best chance of success. The people have nominated you without any pledges or engagements of any sort; they are satisfied with you as you are, and they want you to do nothing at present but allow yourself to be elected. I am sure that I but express the wish of the vast majority of your friends when I say that they want you to make no speeches write no letters as a candidate, enter into no pledges, make no promises, nor even give any of those kind words which men are apt to interpret into promises. Several of our Presidents have had a great deal of trouble from this cause, and I suspect that Fremont if he had been elected would have had quite as much as any of them.

I trust that what I have said is no impertinence. I feel the strongest interest in your success, but it is only the interest of a citizen of our common country. What you do and say, concerns not yourself alone, but the people of the United States. I think you will be elected and I am anxious that you should go into the Executive chair with every advantage for making the most judicious and worthy appointments and lending your aid to the wisest and most beneficial measures.[2]

I am, dear sir,
faithfully yours
WM. C. BRYANT.

MANUSCRIPT: LC ADDRESS: Hon. Abraham Lincoln. PUBLISHED: *The Lincoln Papers,* ed. David C. Mearns (Garden City, New York: Garden City Publishing Co., 1948), I, 257–258.

1. In Chicago on May 16 the Republican Party had chosen Lincoln over Seward

as its presidential candidate. Three days later Bryant wrote, "It is written on the tablet of destiny that Lincoln is to be the next President," and, two days after that, "Whatever is peculiar in the history and development of America, whatever is foremost in its civilization, whatever is grand in its social and political structure finds its best expression in the career of such men as Abraham Lincoln." *EP*, May 19, 21, 1860.

2. In reply, Lincoln wrote Bryant on June 28 (NYPL–GR), "I appreciate the danger against which you would guard me; nor am I wanting in the *purpose* to avoid it. I thank you for the additional strength your words give me to maintain that purpose."

1150.   *To* George P. Putnam[1]

New York   June 18   1860

My dear sir.

Will you be so kind as to send me six copies of my discourse on Irving —the smaller size?

Yours truly
W. C. BRYANT.

MANUSCRIPT: UVa ADDRESS: Geo   P   Putnam.

1. Publisher of Bryant's discourse on Irving; see 433.1, 1146.4.

1151.   *To* Orville Dewey

New York   June 19, 1860.

Dear Doctor.

Last evening I called at Dr. Bellows's house with the hope that I might see you but you had flitted.

When you and Mrs. Dewey shall have fixed the day for coming to visit us, you will of course let us know, that we may not have any engagement in the way. Our Presbyterian pastor, if pastor he may be called, who never holds a sheep-shearing, nor ever accepts the small clippings of a donation party, and yet who objects not to receive any handsome lock of wool that comes off in the brambles, is ready to resign his crook to you for one Sunday and trust you to lead his flock to

"fresh fields and pastures new,"[1]

and guide them to untasted springs. I hope they will

"bless their stars and think it luxury."[2]

If they do not they will be sheep indeed, and deserve for the rest of their lives to be compelled to browse upon

"Darnells and all the idle weeds that grow,"[3]

and quench their thirst at puddles where the pigs cool themselves.

The sky over our heads is not brass quite—nor the earth under our feet ashes, but Roslyn suffers for want of rain, and if the showers do not fall soon the country will lose much of its beauty. The rains which are with-held from the region east of the Rocky Mountains have been poured down on the Pacific coast in California where the rainy season has lingered for weeks beyond its usual period.

Kind regards to the Doctorin as the Germans call the Doctors wife, and believe me

Yours ever
W. C. BRYANT.

MANUSCRIPT: NYPL–GR ADDRESS: Revd Dr   O. Dewey. PUBLISHED (*in part*): *Life*, II, 138.

1. *Cf.* Milton, *Lycidas* 193: "To morrow, to fresh Woods, and Pastures new."
2. Addison, *Cato* I.iv.70.
3. *King Lear* IV.iv.5.

1152.   *To* Richard H. Dana

New York   June 22d   1860.

Dear Dana.

The letter to which you refer, written soon after the death of my little grandson, came duly to hand and if I have not thanked you for it already I do so now.[1]

With regard to my coming to Boston, I did not mean to say that I thought of it very seriously—if by *seriously* is meant that I regarded it as a thing *very* likely to take place this season. I am not much given to making little journeys, except from Roslyn to New York and back again. And yet I feel a certain yearning to see Boston and some of my old friends once more. It seemed to me possible that when my wife went to see her friends in Berkshire, I might make a deviation from the direct route and go or come by your good old town—but there are a great many things that strike us as pleasant to do and yet are never done, for somehow the fitting occasion never comes.

I should like I confess to see your place on the sea shore but whether I shall get there is a different matter— As for getting you to Roslyn I have almost given it up. There is room enough for you, chambers without guests, that would rejoice in your presence, and my wife and I find that we have fewer friends every year. I find it impossible to do what Dr. Johnson advised to keep my friendships in repair.[2] I can set out a young tree where an old one died last year, but I cannot make a new friend fill the place of an old one.

I am glad to hear that your sister is doing so well. Say to all your family that I desire a place in their kind remembrance.

I am dear sir
faithfully yours
W. C. BRYANT.

MANUSCRIPT: NYPL–GR ADDRESS: R. H. Dana Esqre. DOCKETED: Bryant / 22 June 60.

1. See Dana to Bryant, February 25, 1860, *Life*, II, 133–134.
2. Bryant was fond of this advice of Samuel Johnson's; see Letter 481.

1153. *To* Robert Bonner

New York   June 27th   1860

My dear sir.

I enclose you another poem for the Ledger.[1] You will of course give me an opportunity of correcting the proof.

Yours faithfully
W. C. BRYANT.

MANUSCRIPT: QPL ADDRESS: R   Bonner Esqre. DOCKETED: June 27/60 / W. C. Bryant.

1. The poem was probably "The Tides," printed in the *New York Ledger*, 15 (July 28, 1860), 1. See *Poems* (1876), pp. 365–366.

1154. *To* Gulian C. Verplanck[1]

New York   July 3d   1860

My dear sir.

As your name is several times mentioned in the accompanying address I have thought that you might be not unwilling to do me the favor of accepting a copy of it.[2]

I am dear sir
truly yours
W. C. BRYANT.

MANUSCRIPT: NYPL–Berg ADDRESS: Hon   G. C. Verplanck,

1. Though Bryant and Verplanck were no longer intimate, they met at meetings of the Sketch and Century Clubs quite often.
2. In discussing Irving, Bryant had reminded his listeners that Verplanck was one of the New Yorkers of Dutch descent who were at first irritated by the humorist's broad caricatures of their ancestors in *A History of New York* (1809). He referred also to biographical articles Verplanck had written for the *Analectic Magazine* while Irving was its editor in 1813–1814, and to Verplanck's intercession with Irving in 1832 to secure publication of Bryant's *Poems* at London. See Bryant, "Irving," pp. 114–116, 135.

1155. *To* John Howard Bryant

Roslyn   July 9th   1860

Dear Brother

Your letter of the 3d instant reached me here on Saturday evening, and I [answer][1] by the first mail that leaves this place—that is, on Monday. In regard to the purchases of which you speak, it seems to me that they offer all the advantages I could expect.[2] The employment of an attorney to ascertain the goodness of the title is indispensable. I do it always, when I make a purchase of land here. You may draw on me for any amount within the sum I mentioned in my last —giving me information at the same moment, by letter, of what you have done.[3]

I am glad your crops are likely to come in so well. Here also they are good with the exception of hay—and that on my farm, though generally light elsewhere is more than an average crop.

Yours affectionately
W. C. BRYANT

P.S. As to fences I should of course be ready to bear any reasonable expense for putting them in order—though it is to be considered that bad fences abate something from the value of the land purchased.

W. C. B.

MANUSCRIPT: BCHS TEXT: "Bryant and Illinois," 644.

1. The printed text mistakenly has "answered."
2. In his letter dated Tuesday, July 3 (NYPL–BG), John reported finding several small farms of eighty acres each near Princeton, with buildings in fair shape for tenantry, at twenty dollars an acre. See Letter 1148.
3. Cullen Bryant's purchases of land in Bureau County, Illinois, in 1860, all presumably managed by John, totaled 729 acres costing $17,725. "Bryant: Illinois Landowner," 12–13.

1156. *To* Orville Dewey

Roslyn   July 9th, 1860

My dear Doctor.

I have your note appointing next week for your visit to Roslyn.[1] No time could suit us better. After a long drought the earth has been saturated with rain. The burning of gunpowder—such is Espy's theory[2]—on the fourth brought down the showers and the earth can hardly lose the reinforcement of freshness it has gained before you come. We should have been glad to have you in the season of cherries and roses which are just going out—the roses especially, but you shall be welcome to the raspberries gooseberries and verbenas with I hope a carnation or two. The church has been got ready for you—renovated as the Italians say—the ceiling as a country newspaper described it the other day, "painted in water colors"—that is to say, endued with a fresh coat of white-wash, the walls neatly papered, the pulpit and pews painted, and the floor neatly carpeted—and the segars are bought and ready for your smoking. I am told they smell of tropical sunshine and the Vuelta Abajo, but I know not, though I have been in San Antonio[3]— you shall judge. Have no apprehensions concerning the second sermon; the custom of the place tolerates but one on the Sunday.

If you do not like the word superfine applied to your sermons, exchange it for philosophical. Here in Roslyn we cannot all of us read, and yet we wear beards as long as any body. I wished merely to caution you against being misled by those external symbols of wisdom. What we require is milk for babes—the simplest rudiments of that *divinarum rerum notitia* [notion of divine things] of which you speak. And then our congregation is small, so that a great discourse will not be necessary. Our pastor will not run away you may be assured, but will sit beside you, both for his own edification, and to give his flock the assurance that what you shall set before them is good and wholesome.[4]

As for the visit you and your spouse must come as early and stay as long as you can. It will be time enough to think of a migration when you see the bottom of the segar box and no prospect of an immediate supply.

I sent you the other day a copy of my Discourse on Washington Irving, which as you were kind enough to commend,[5] I thought you might consent to accept.

We are all as well as usual—in the *patois* of Berkshire, they say I believe usually well. My wife and daughter desire their love to you all—and when you are delivering that message please to add that I also desire a place in their kind remembrance.

I am, dear sir,
very truly yours
W. C. BRYANT.

MANUSCRIPT: NYPL–GR ADDRESS: Rev^d. Dr. O. Dewey. PUBLISHED *(in part)*: *Life*, II, 138–139.

1. Dewey to Bryant, July 5, 1860, NYPL–BG.

2. James Pollard Espy (1785–1860), American meteorologist, *Philosophy of Storms* (1841).

3. San Antonio de los Baños, Cuba. Bryant visited there in 1849; see Letter 675. The Vuelta Abajo is a region in western Cuba famous for the production of tobacco.

4. Replying to Bryant's suggestion that he take the pulpit at the Presbyterian Church during his coming visit to Roslyn (Letter 1151), Dewey had written on July 5 (NYPL–BG), "I understand you, Monsieur, about the preaching, 'Don't bring any of your superfine sermons here!' Bah! I don't bring such any where. Your good pastor must not expect me to preach twin—making a convenience of me, to run away & visit his father-in-law, or something—for I will do no such thing. I preach but once a day, in my own pulpit, you know."

5. In a letter dated April 28, 1860 (NYPL–BG) Dewey had remarked of the discourse, "Catharine Sedgwick says it is the best thing of the kind you have ever done. So do I."

1157. *To* George Bancroft

Roslyn   August 1st   1860.

Dear Bancroft,

I have been thinking ever since I read the eighth volume of your history that I would write to thank you for the pleasure I had derived from it. My wife who has been dipping into it insists that I shall do this morning what I have delayed so long.

It is a great thing for a man to surpass himself; and this is what you have done. You have given us an Iliad with John Adams for the Achilles.

"Impiger, iracundus, inexorabilis, acer."[1]

It had never struck me that this period of our history was susceptible of such an epic interest—but it was the part of genius to bring it out. The narrative parts and the delineation of characters are alike admirable.

I am dear sir truly yours
W   C   BRYANT

MANUSCRIPT: MHS ADDRESS: Geo   Bancroft Esqr.

1. "Diligent, irascible, inexorable, vehement." Horace, *Ars Poetica* 121.

1158. *To* John Howard Bryant

New York   Aug   2, 1860

Dear Brother.—

I have this moment received your letter of the 30th of July.[1]

As to the place in which the farms you purchase are situated I meant merely to say what I preferred—other things being equal, or nearly so. I, however intended to leave the matter to your judgement, expecting that you would do for me just as you would for yourself. The reasons you give for purchasing at some little distance from Princeton seem to me perfectly sound and convince me that what you have done is more for my interest than if you had purchased the high priced farms lying nearer.—[2]

I hope therefore that you will go on as you have begun, and carry out the plans you have formed.

I am yours truly,
W. C. BRYANT

MANUSCRIPT: Mrs. Mildred Bryant Kussmaul, Brockton, Massachusetts ADDRESS: John H. Bryant Esq.

1. Unrecovered.
2. These purchases of July 18, 21, and 31, 1860, totaling 304 acres at a cost of $9,755, are detailed in "Bryant: Illinois Landowner," 12.

1159. *To* Christiana Gibson

New York, August 16, 1860

. . . Your summer must have been very agreeable if the season there has been like ours—temperate days, cool nights, almost perpetual sunshine, yet mild as the sunshine of early June. I desire nothing pleasanter in the way of weather than this summer has been on Long Island. Then the fruits have been so fine—plenty of strawberries, cherries of the finest, lingering into the latter half of July, till we became impatient to have them gone. Now the plums are coming in abundantly, almost for the first time, and basketfuls of juicy pears.

I was in town lately for two or three days, leaving Mr. William B. Ogden at Roslyn. When I returned, I found he had taken off Fanny and her husband, Julia and Bryant,[1] to Mauch Chunk and Bethlehem. They were particularly delighted with Bethlehem and the Moravians, as you would be, for they are the most musical of all the little communities in the United States, and their litanies, which are addressed to the Supreme Being in choral harmonies peculiar to themselves, are very impressive. Fanny came back much improved in health. The Great Eastern has come and gone, but neither my wife nor I have seen it, so we shall have no cause to boast over you. I would not go where there was such a crowd, and the Great Eastern remains what my imagination pleases to make it. Those who have seen it have not that advantage. To them it is a circumscribed idea.[2] Knowledge—particularly knowledge of the works of the human hand—is the great destroyer of the sublime. . . .

MANUSCRIPT: Unrecovered TEXT (partial): Life, II, 139–140.

1. Fanny's eldest son, William Bryant Godwin.
2. The Great Eastern, largest steamship of the day, was causing a sensation in New York after its first trans-Atlantic voyage. It was even the subject of a comedy at Wallack's Theatre. In 1866 the Great Eastern was employed by Cyrus W. Field in laying the first transoceanic cable. See George C. D. Odell, Annals of the New York Stage (New York: Columbia University Press, 1931), VII, 208.

1160.   To Robert C. Waterston

Roslyn   August 16   1860.

Dear Mr. Waterston

My wife and I give many thanks for the beautiful little book in which you have embalmed the memory of your beloved daughter.[1] We prize it not only as a memorial of the virtues and graces which we had learned to admire and to love, but also as something which brings back and makes more vivid the recollection of pleasant days passed in the society of yourself and your family. You allude to them in a touching manner, but you can hardly know [how] much good your sympathy did us when on coming to Naples, you found us after an anxious winter, still anxious and uncertain as to the issue of the long illness with which my wife had suffered. You can hardly recollect that Sunday of which we speak with more emotion than we.

It seems to me that the collection of tributes to your daughter's memory is very happily made up— What you have said yourself is said in so becoming a manner; what your friends have said is said with so much feeling![2] Even those who are strangers to you all cannot but be interested in reading it. I have no doubt that you and Mrs. Waterston frequently recur to its pages, and find in them a certain consolation.

It is a satisfaction to me to know that you think so kindly of my eulogy on Irving.[3] I undertook it most unwillingly. The Historical Society of which I was not then a member—they have made me an honorary member since—almost forced it upon me. They passed a resolution appointing me as the eulogist—and it was in all the newspapers, before I had any suspicion of what they were about. It is some comfort if you think that I did not commit an act of foll[y] in reversing my first determination which was to decline the task altogether.

I fear that we shall not be able to come to Boston this summer. I am busy with some little improvements on my place which must be executed while the season allows it. Otherwise I have leisure enough, and I should really like to see Boston again. So would my wife and as for Julia she is always ready for a journey.

But you if I rightly interpret your letter might find time to come to Roslyn, and nothing would give us all greater delight than to welcome you and Mrs. Waterston to our roof. The country is charming this summer fruitful and verdant, and we live in a rather pretty part of the country, among woods and waters and hills—not mountains—among winding roads and quaker houses. You and Mrs. Waterston would like the neighborhood I know. Our friends, Dr. Dewey and his wife, made us a visit lately. The Doctor preached at the invitation of the Presbyterian pastor and nobody discovered that he was not as good a Christian as the most orthodox. Only let us know at what time you will come and we will give you the whole season to choose from. Write as soon as you receive this and say that you and your better half will come, and if I might advise you will come soon. The season is remarkably cool, and comfortable for travelling, the nights never hot and the days charmingly temperate. Come while the hours between sunrise and sunset are still many, and the arrangements for travelling conveniently made. What do you say to the end of next week, or some time in the week following?

Julia is not here at this moment or she would join as my wife does in this entreaty and would desire her special love. She has made a little excursion to the Moravian town Bethlehem and its pleasant neighborhood. We expect her tonight and I wish I was able to gratify her with the news that you and Mrs. Waterston were soon coming to see us. My wife is well at present; a fall down some stone steps about four weeks since obliged her to keep her a bed a little while and her room for some days, but she is now wholly recovered. She sends much love to you both.

I am greatly pleased to hear of the token of reverence paid to Mr. Quincy on the occasion of which you speak. It was well deserved and I hope he will live to receive many more such.

A day or two since we were pained to hear of a calamity which has over-taken Mrs. Mackie whom you remember as Miss Ives when in our family at Naples. She has lost her first born, a fine little boy on whom she and her mother doted.

Kindest regards to Mrs. Waterston—and believe me

ever and truly yours
W. C. BRYANT

MANUSCRIPT: Stanford University Library ADDRESS: Rev^d R C Waterston.

1. Robert C. Waterston, *Helen Ruthven Waterston* (Boston, 1860).

2. These tributes included a poem by Whittier, "Naples." See *The Complete Poetical Works of John Greenleaf Whittier*, Household edition (Boston and New York: Houghton, Mifflin, 1904), pp. 247–248.

3. Writing Bryant on July 26 (NYPL–BG) after receiving a copy of his *Discourse on Irving*, Waterston had called it "as discriminating and felicitous as any thing which ever came from his own pen."

1161. *To* John Howard Bryant

[Roslyn?] August 20, 1860

Dear Brother

I wrote you not long since that I wish to invest only $20,000 at the West—repairs and fencing included. I have since received your letter[1] relating to that matter.

In the $20,000 I do not mean to include the fencing of the lands which I already owned, and which you thought of taking to raise wheat upon. But all the new purchases with the incidental expenses I wish brought within that sum.[2] Having that amount to invest, I wish to be understood literally that I desire literally to stop when it is exhausted, and make no subsequent additions at least till I am in funds to do so.

With regard to the letting of the farms which have been purchased or may be so I should like to know what percent on their value they generally bring when rented to good tenants in your part of the country. You think with me that the value of these lands will rise in the market—but what I wish to know is what income I may expect from them if they keep only their present value.

Yours affectionately
W. C. BRYANT

P.S. On considering again what I have written, I wish to say that I do not wish you to decline making an advantageous purchase because it may oblige you to expend a few hundred dollars over the sum I have mentioned. Perhaps, even it may in the course of a few months become convenient for me to go as far as you mention—but it is not so now.

W. C. B.

MANUSCRIPT: BCHS TEXT: "Bryant and Illinois," 645.

1. Unrecovered.
2. In addition to the purchases outlined in 1158.2, on August 7 and October 7, 1860, and March 27, 1861, John bought for his brother 585 acres for $9,570. "Bryant: Illinois Landowner," 13.

1162. *To* Abraham Lincoln

New York   August 23   1860.

My dear sir.

The bearer of this note is [Walter] Francis Williams Esqre. a gentleman of worth and talent connected with the Evening Post.[1] Being on a tour to the western states he is naturally desirous to see the curiosities of the country and among others the next President of the United States. I have therefore taken the liberty of giving him this introduction to you.

I am, dear sir
truly yours
W   C   BRYANT.

MANUSCRIPT: LC ADDRESS: Hon   Abraham Lincoln / Springfield / Illinois DOCKETED: W. C. Bryant. / Aug   23/60.

1. See 1119.10.

1163.   *To* J. Dennis Harris[1]

Roslyn, Long Island, August 26, 1860

Dear Sir:—

I have looked over with attention the letters you left with me, and return them herewith. It appears to me it will be very well to publish them. Of the Spanish part of the island of Santo Domingo very little is known—much less than of the French part; and the information you give of the country and its people is valuable and interesting.

I am, sir,
Respectfully yours,
W. C. BRYANT

MANUSCRIPT: Unrecovered TEXT: J. Dennis Harris, *A Summer on the Borders of the Caribbean Sea, with an Introduction by George William Curtis* (New York, 1860), p. iv. ADDRESS: Mr. J. D. Harris.

1. A free black from North Carolina, Harris had first called on Bryant, then later written asking him to contribute a preface to his forthcoming book, intended to break down prejudices among North American Negroes against Spanish American countries as too tropical. Harris to Bryant, Cleveland, August 23, 1860, NYPL–GR. See descriptive note.

1164.   *To* A. D. Faulkner[1]

New York   August 28th   1860

Sir.

    The lines you quote were written by me, but the first line as you quote it contains a verbal error. Instead of

The crescent morn and crimson eve—

it should read

The crescent moon and crimson eve.

The lines form part of a poem entitled "The White-footed Deer."[2]

Respectfully &c

W. C. BRYANT.

MANUSCRIPT: University of Pennsylvania Library ADDRESS: A. D. Faulkner Esqre.

   1. Unidentified.
   2. *Poems* (1876), p. 303.

1165.   *To* Frances F. Bryant

New York   Sept. 6. 1860.
Thursday morning

Dear Frances.

    I got your letter of yesterday[1] for which I thank you; but I am somewhat disappointed that you stay so long. Whether I shall come after you is a matter that requires consideration. I scarce believe that I shall.[2]

    Yesterday I sent some grapes to Mrs. Smith the sick woman and the boy brought me word that she was getting better. Mrs. Nelson is ailing yet.

    The evening before last we had the closing proceedings of a Sunday School Convention. A meeting was held in Mr. Ely's church; the middle pews were filled with the Sunday Scholars and the outside pews with the audience. Addresses were made by Professor Irvin, Mr. Hart, the Brittania Ware man of Burling Slip, and Mr. McCormick, the same who once visited us in company with Mr. Frank Ballard. Irvin was sensible, Hart funny and McCormick clever. I took Julia, Miss Jenny Hopkins, Minna and Annie. When asked which she liked best Annie answered "the funny fellow." Hart has a prodigious deal of a peculiar humor, and the entertainment was as amusing as a comedy.[3]

    The same evening, a little past ten as I was going to bed, there was a pattering of rapid feet on the piazza, a pull at the bell and a thundering knock at the door. Every body got to the door as quick as possible and there were Minnie and Miss Gordon,[4] who was scarce half dressed, and they had a mysterious story to tell. Bryant was absent—out of the house—not to be found. He was last seen in the parlor about eight o'clock having been out all day or nearly all in a boat with Willie Carpenter. The bolt of one of the shutters was shoved back, probably to allow him to return through the window. Miss Gordon had gone to bed early leaving him in the house, and now being apprized of his escape had rushed over to ask what was to be done.

After a good deal of consultation it was determined to send down to Frederick's—for Frederick had been sent in the evening to bring back the boat from where the low tide had obliged the boys to leave it, and also to send to Mr. Cairns's to see if Bryant was with Willy Carpenter. But first it was suggested that it would be well to make another search for the missing boy in every room in Fannys house.

Minna and Miss Gordon went back and found Bryant fast asleep on the sofa, rolled up in a shawl as snug as a bug in a rug—he had probably been there all the evening.

A long story about nothing—Fanny I hear came to town last night.

Regards to all— Yours ever

W. C. BRYANT.

MANUSCRIPT: NYPL–GR ADDRESS: Mrs. F   F. Bryant.

1. Unrecovered.
2. Frances was then visiting her sisters in Great Barrington.
3. Rev. Samuel R. Ely, D.D. (d. 1873) was the pastor from 1854 to 1870 of the Roslyn Presbyterian Church, which the Bryants attended when in the village. Goddard, *Roslyn Harbor*, p. 106. Except for Julia, Bryant's granddaughters Minna and Annie Godwin, his Roslyn neighbor Jenny Hopkins, and Frank Ballard (Letter 1489), those persons named in this paragraph are unidentified.
4. Probably the Godwins' nursemaid.

1166. *To* Hiram Powers

New York   September 13th   1860.

My dear sir.

The bearer of this letter is Mr. William Livingston Alden of this city, a promising young member of the bar in this city[1] who is about to sail for Europe with the intention of passing some time in its southern countries. May I ask of you to bestow upon him those attentions, which you take pleasure in showing your countrymen and for which I have myself been indebted to you. Be pleased to present my regards to Mrs. Powers and the young ladies.

I am, dear sir,
truly yours
W. C. BRYANT.

MANUSCRIPT: National Collection of Fine Arts ADDRESS: Hiram Powers Esqre.

1. Alden (1837–1908), journalist and lawyer, is credited with introducing canoeing as a sport into the United States.

1167.   *To* Frances F. Bryant

Roslyn   Saturday   Sept. 14, 1860

Dear Frances.

I meant to have seen you off yesterday morning, but when I returned from the hill found to my surprize that I was too late.

Mrs. Nelson is the better for your prescription. Her complaint was dysenteric, and she finds herself relieved. Mr. Nelson, however, is not so well and does not work today. I have been to see him and have prescribed for him. I went with him to look at the well. He did not think that any thing was the matter with it nor did I. There was a little clear water at the bottom, and that was all that we could see. The smell was that of any wet place, so Mr. Nelson says. His complaint is different from that of his wife; it is a diarrhea. He complains of great weakness.

I saw Mr. Cairns yesterday. He inveighed at great length at what he called Mr. Willis's neglect of his children, saying he had just discovered that they got no whortleberries and no fish, and that he was just beginning to send them these things.[1] It is curious enough that Mr. Willis who returned to Roslyn last evening, brought a fish to our house this morning and is to come and help eat it today.

The fair at Manhasset brought one hundred and sixty dollars. The price which is to be paid for the land selected as the site of the church is four hundred dollars.[2]

Mrs. Cairns has got home from Easthampton delighted with her visit. She says that Mr. Ely was welcomed with open arms by his old parishioners.

The horse is getting better; the barn is all but done; the new cook begins well. Fanny's new cook is much commended for her respectable appearance. I have written this morning to Mr. Waterston.[3]

Remember me kindly to Mr. and Mrs. Hopkins and to Mrs. Henderson, who I hope is better and to Hannah and the rest.

Yours ever,

W. C. BRYANT

MANUSCRIPT: NYPL–GR ADDRESS: Mrs. F. F. Bryant.

1. Mr. and Mrs. William Cairns of Roslyn (565.2) were the parents of the late Mrs. Richard Willis (1027.2).

2. This was probably an Episcopal chapel, built in 1862. Goddard, *Roslyn Harbor*, p. 107.

3. Bryant's letter to Waterston is unrecovered.

1168.   *To* Cullen Bryant

New York   September 18th   1860

Dear Nephew

Sometime since I forwarded to West Point by Express addressed to you a portable writing desk, which my wife directed to be purchased for you.[1] At the same time I put into the post office a note addressed to you desiring you to inform us of its safe arrival.[2] We have heard nothing of you or the writing-desk since. Will you be kind enough to write as soon as you receive this and let us know whether it came to hand or not. Write to Roslyn Long Island.

Yrs truly
W C BRYANT

MANUSCRIPT: NYPL–BFP ADDRESS: Mr. Cullen Bryant / at the Military Academy / West Point / N. Y. POSTMARK: [illegible].

1. See Francis Bryant to Cullen Bryant at West Point, cAugust 15, 1860, NYPL–GR.
2. Bryant's earlier note is unrecovered.

1169. *To* John Howard Bryant

New York   September 22nd   1860

Dear Brother.

I enclose the receipt which you have written for.

As to the purchases I wish you to make the one for $1600 by all means if you can. If you should be able to do this it will be well I think to let that be the limit of your purchases.

In case that cannot be done I think it might be well to buy the farm for $2300 which you say is very cheap, unless some advantageous bargains for a smaller sum should come in your way. I leave that to your discretion.

We are all well. Frances has been generally better this summer than she was last year. We expect to go to Boston for a short visit next week.

The season is favorable. The grain is abundant and so is the fruit; the Indian corn good, and the potatoes fair. The political harvest is now promising. New York is for Lincoln; the other factions are discouraged.

Yours ever
W. C. BRYANT

MANUSCRIPT: Mrs. Mildred Bryant Kussmaul, Brockton, Massachusetts ADDRESS: John H. Bryant Esqr.

1170. *To* Julia S. Bryant

Roslyn   Saturday   Sept. 22   1860.

Dear Julia

We go to New York on Monday and on Tuesday to Boston by way of Springfield, arriving at our destination a little before [five?] o'clock. If you could reach Boston about the same time it might be convenient; if not you might come on Wednesday morning. Should you get this in season I wish you would write immediately to Mr. Waterston, informing him at what time you will come. I know nothing about the most convenient way to get to Boston from Newport— Mr. Gillilan[1]—though I should be glad to spare him that trouble—will add to his other obliging civilities that of finding out for you and will see you on board the right train.

You speak in your letter to your mother, of going to the Prince of Wales Ball. If you wish to go, I do not wish to prevent you, though I feel an invincible aversion to going myself, the occasion being one which is not at all to my taste. I am perfectly willing to get a ticket for you if one is to be had, and another for any person who might go with you—but I do not think it worth while to pay the prices which I learn from the newspapers are now paid for them. I am not one of the committee and if I wanted to go should be at the mercy of those who speculate in tickets. I shall inquire how the matter stands when I go to town on Monday and will tell you all I can learn when I see you. . . .[2]

MANUSCRIPT: NYPL–GR.

1. Unidentified.
2. In the summer and fall of 1860 the eighteen-year-old Prince of Wales, later King Edward VII of Great Britain, visited Canada and the United States unofficially as "Lord Renfrew." While in New York briefly, he was entertained on October 12 at the Academy of Music. Although it is uncertain whether Julia attended, her father's distaste for such an affair seems to have been justified by the account given of it afterward by the Prince himself to his mother, Queen Victoria. "The great ball took place," he wrote, "but it was not successful. 3,000 people were invited and 5000 came. . . . We arrived at 10 o'clock, and before the dancing had begun a great part of the floor gave way and it took two hours to set it right, so that dancing did not begin until 12 o'clock, and the crowd was so great that it was very difficult to move." Quoted in Sir Sidney Lee, *King Edward VII: A Biography* (New York: Macmillan, 1955), I, 103–104. Also see "The Ball to Lord Renfrew," *EP*, October 13, 1860. The complimentary close and signature to this letter are missing.

1171. *To* Robert Bonner

[New York?] Sept   24th [1860]

Dear Sir

I send you a poem for the Ledger.[1] If you have occasion to send me a proof after 2 oclock P. M   today and before next Friday—send it to me at Boston care of Rev[d] R. C   Waterston

Yrs truly
W   C   BRYANT

MANUSCRIPT: QPL ADDRESS: R   Bonner Esq.

1. Probably "Italy," *New York Ledger*, 15 (October 20, 1860), 5. See *Poems* (1876), pp. 367–369. Bonner replied the same day (NYPL–BG), promising a proof in an hour or two, and adding, "I am glad that you sent me this poem, this morning, as in the same number . . . I shall have original poems from Willis, Morris, Saxe, Alice Cary, Mrs. Sigourney; besides contributions from James Buchanan, the President of the United

States, Hon. Geo. Bancroft, Edward Everett, Henry Ward Beecher, Geo. D. Prentice, and others."

1172.   *To* Richard H. Dana

Boston   September 28th   1860.

Dear Dana.

If I must go back to New York without seeing you, I assure you I shall be as sorry as you can be.[1] At present your household is in such a state, that I could not think of adding to its inconveniences by coming to Manchester [Massachusetts], even if I had more time here—but I cannot wait for your invalids to be better, and you among the rest—for I have an appointment with a surveyor on Wednesday at my place on Long Island, when I am to adopt some plan for changing the public road from the front to the back of my house. I must therefore be off on Monday or Tuesday. However, I am determined to see you, if I live, after you come to town, and if I do not get a sight of you now, I shall be in Boston again before you get back to the sea shore. My wife who is as much grieved not to see you and Charlotte as I am, thinks she will come with me. She thanks your daughter with all her heart for her obliging letter,—but being somewhat of an invalid is withheld by still stronger reasons than I am from coming to your place in the country.

I should have come later in the season, but my wife dreaded the approach of cold weather. She is always fearful of getting chilled through which always makes her sick, and to tell the truth I hardly thought you would be out at Manchester after the middle of September.

However, I say again, it shall all be made right between us. I am getting to be a journalist *emeritus*, superannuated, I think they call it in the army—an unpleasant phrase, but one to the reality of which we must all come at last, if we do not go out of life prematurely. I had never so much leisure as now and I mean to make use of some of it to see you.

Kind regards to your daughter and sisters. My wife and Julia desire their love to you all.

Yours very truly
W. C. BRYANT.

MANUSCRIPT: NYPL–GR ADDRESS: R. H. Dana Esqre. DOCKETED: W^m. C. Bryant, Sep 28 / 60.

1. From September 24 to October 2 the Bryants visited the Waterstons at Chester Square in Boston. Bryant was kept busy. One evening Mrs. Waterston entertained a large company to meet him, and to celebrate the entrance of Giuseppe Garibaldi into Naples on September 7. Another day they visited Mrs. Waterston's father, Josiah Quincy, former president of Harvard, at his home in Quincy. *Life*, II, 140. And Longfellow is said to have made an "ineffectual effort" to induce Bryant to dine with the Saturday Club, Boston's prestigious literary rendezvous. Charles Francis Adams, *Richard Henry Dana: A Biography* (Boston and New York, 1890), II, 248.

1173.   *To* Robert C. and Anna Q. Waterston

New York, October 3, 1860,
Six o'clock in the Morning

... We had the pleasantest journey from Boston to New York that could be imagined. A beautiful Indian summer's day, with floating clouds and a golden sunshine streaming between them through a soft autumnal haze, no dust, nor any other inconvenience. We reached New York in safety, Mrs. Bryant not much tired, at half past five, full of delightful recollections of our visit to Boston, and of your hospitality and extreme kindness. ...

MANUSCRIPT: Unrecovered TEXT *(partial)*: *Life,* II, 140.

1174.   [*To* Jacob Beakley?][1]

[Roslyn? *c*October 5, 1860]
My dear sir.

I am fully sensible of the value of the compliment paid me by the Homoeopathic College in requesting me to deliver the address at the opening of their institution. I must, however decline the task. It is not often that I appear before the public in this way and when I do it is in obedience to a certain force of circumstances which almost amounts to compulsion. There is another circumstance which strengthens my aversion to such a display on this occasion— and that is that I have given sufficient attention to the homoeopathic system to be assured that I know little of it, and am quite incompetent to discuss it as it should be discussed.

Allow me in the meantime along with my thanks, to present to the Faculty of your institution my congratulations on the opening of a regularly organized place of medical instruction in the doctrines and practice of our school—a school the effect of which is not only greatly to lessen the [pain?] of human misery—but [promotive?] of the [interests?] of morality—

Yrs truly—
[unsigned]

MANUSCRIPT: NYPL–GR (draft).

1. Dr. Jacob Beakley was the first dean and professor of surgery at the New York Homoeopathic Medical College, established at Third Avenue and Twentieth Street on October 15, 1860. The college was an outgrowth of the New York Homoeopathic Society, of which Bryant had been the president in 1841. See 420.6; Letter 1508; Leonard Paul Wershub, *One Hundred Years of Medical Progress: A History of the New York Medical College Flower and Fifth Avenue Hospitals* (Springfield, Illinois: Charles C. Thomas [1967]), pp. 33–35.

1175.   *To* James T. Fields

New York, October 9, 1860

... I do not see how I can comply with the request you make.[1] The Pierian spring on my grounds runs low; it is like the Fountain of the Virgin when

I saw it at Bethlehem—only a drop oozing from the ground at a time. "Spare my age," as Pope says somewhere. . . .[2]

MANUSCRIPT: Unrecovered TEXT (partial): *Life*, II, 141.

1. Then about to succeed James Russell Lowell as editor of the *Atlantic Monthly*, lately acquired by his publishing firm, Fields (973.1) had written Bryant on October 7 (NYPL–BG) soliciting a poem for the January number.

2. Cf. 1476.3. Apparently committed for the time being to offer his verses to the *New York Ledger*, Bryant made his first contribution to the *Atlantic Monthly* with "The Planting of the Apple-Tree," which was printed in January 1864. See *Poems* (1876), pp. 320–323.

1176.   *To* Anna Q. Waterston

Mount Savage   Maryland   October 15, 1860

My dear Mrs. Waterston.

We got your letter at New York just as we were setting out for this place on a visit to an old friend of mine a New Yorker who has been here for thirteen years.[1] The "case" concerning which you express so much kind concern reached us safely in due time, but has been transported safely to this mountain region a hundred and eighty miles west of Baltimore among the Alleg[he]nies, the woods of which are now glorious with the hues of autumn. Here we are in the midst of forests of grand old trees, and grassy slopes, and deep valleys watered by shallow brawling streams and mountain summit overlooking mountain summit. We are in the Cumberland coal region, with mining villages around us and railway trains snorting and whistling as they bear their burdens to market. Today we have been on a visit to one of the coal mines, Mrs. Godwin and Julia and myself with our kind hosts; my wife I am sorry to say took cold on her journey and could not go— These mines are long black passages in the earth leading to low black chambers propped by posts where the workmen ply their sledges to break away masses of coal from the roof and walls. Out of some of these passages run little brooks yellow with alum and copperas, Stygian streams and the begrimed workmen black as Ethiopians bearing each a little crooked lamp in his cap look like horrid demons of the mine. At the end of one of these passages blazed and roared a fierce [fine?] fire of coal in a furnace reaching up through the mountain to the upper air, drawing after it a current of air from the entrance of the mine—with swarthy bare-armed workmen feeding the flames, so that the visitor might almost fancy he was going to be roasted alive—but it was only intended for ventilation.

Enough of this— It was very kind of your father and sister to think of visiting us on Chester Square, and it was our misfortune to have missed both this call and an earlier one. When you see your sister who wrote those kind words concerning us please thank her for them. We keep our visit to Chester Square among our pleasant memories— Best regards to Mr. Waterston from my wife and Julia as well as myself—they send much love to you, and with me desire to be kindly remembered by your father and his amiable and excellent family.

[unsigned]

MANUSCRIPT: NYPL–GR (draft) PUBLISHED (*in part, with changes*): *Life,* II, 141.

1. Identified in *Life,* II, 141 as John A. Graham. See Letter 1177.

1177.   *To* the EVENING POST
Mount Savage, Maryland, October [c18], 1860.

Before I say anything of this region, let me speak of what I saw at Baltimore. Our kind friend, at whose invitation we came hither, met us in that city and took us down to a point on the shore of the Patapsco, to see the new iron steamer which the Messrs. Winans have built upon a model of their own, by way of experiment, before making a trial of anything on a larger scale. Its shape has been compared to that of a segar; keel, sides and deck are round alike; and at each end it tapers to a sharp point.[1] The length is a hundred and eighty feet, with a breadth of sixteen. It is formed of two hollow iron spindles, firmly connected with each other at the broad end by strong iron plates, and between these spindles plays a wheel with screw paddles, with which the steamer is urged forward. The blows of the sea from before or behind can take no effect upon it; all that the waves can do is to slide softly over it, and when they strike it on the sides they meet with much less resistance than in vessels of ordinary shape. It can never ship a sea.

A trial trip has lately been made with this steamer. "It ran round one of the fastest steamers in our harbor," said a gentleman to me, "playing about it like a shark about a sailing packet." I do not know what may be the expectations of the Messieurs Winans in regard to its speed, but the talk at Baltimore is of making the passage to Europe in four or five days, bearing with it the mails and specie and a few passengers. As I looked on this enormous iron shuttle, the velocity of which can be scarcely more affected by storms and head winds than that of a fish, and thought of it darting through the sea with the speed which is claimed for it, it occurred to me that if a sailing vessel should come in its way it must be pierced through and through, like a pine shingle by a bullet.

The railway which brought us to Mount Savage is one of the most picturesque in the United States. For more than a hundred and fifty miles it follows the course of the Potomac, winding as the river winds, making sudden turns around lofty crags, sweeping round the base of grassy hillsides, passing under old forests, now bright with their autumnal leaves, and sometimes coming out into fair open valleys. Harper's Ferry, where the Shenandoah comes breaking through its rocky pass to pour itself into the

Potomac, would of itself be sufficient to give this railway a pre-eminence, were there nothing else worth looking [at] along its track. Here the train generally stops a few minutes, and the passengers alight to look at the majestic cliffs and to see the place which has recently acquired a new and memorable historical association by the strange adventure of John Brown. A hundred and eighty miles from Baltimore you reach Cumberland, one of the most beautiful sites for a town I ever saw. It lies on the north bank of the Potomac, amid a circle of lofty hills, clothed with forest and divided by half a dozen deep gorges. The town has one or two pleasant streets —the rest are shabby and unsightly. At Cumberland you leave the Baltimore and Ohio Railroad and enter a single passenger car at the end of a long row of empty coal wagons, which are slowly dragged up a rocky pass beside a shallow stream, into the coal region of the Alleganies [sic]. You alight among smoking furnaces and forges and vast heaps of cinders at Mount Savage, near the foot of the mountain range of that name, a village of four thousand inhabitants, gathered from various nations, mostly employed in the iron works and the mines, and living in dirty cottages. As you ascend from the village you perceive more and more of the beauty of the region. You are among deep winding valleys and broad mountain sides, forests of grand old trees and grassy fields, and at every step some new charm of the prospect opens upon you. From the mouths of coal mines on the mountains short railways descend to the village, down which rattle trains of trucks loaded with coal, the weight of which drags up the empty cars.

Our party made a visit the other day to a coal mine some three miles distant from Mount Savage. From one of the black entrances flowed a lively little stream with yellow waters, into which I dipped my finger to ascertain their flavor. It was acidulous and astringent, holding in solution both alum and copperas. Leaving this Stygian rivulet we came to another entrance, out of which a train of loaded trucks was passing, every one of which was attended by a miner, blackened from head to foot with the dust of his task, and wearing in front of his cap a small crooked lamp to light his way. As they emerged from the darkness they looked like sooty demons of the mine, with flaming horns, coming from the womb of the mountain. We now entered, each carrying a lantern, attended by a guide, whom the courteous proprietor directed to go with us. The vein of coal here is from eight to ten feet thick, and the passage is of that height, with a roof of glistening slate, propped in some places by wooden posts. Here and there, on each side of the passage, yawned chambers cut in the coal vein, and extending beyond the reach of the eye in the faint light of our lanterns. At length we heard the sound of sledges, and proceeding for some distance further came to the end of the passage, where the grimy workmen, each with a lamp in his cap, were driving wedges into the cracks and fissures of the coal, to separate it from the roof and walls. We saw several large blocks detached in this manner, the workmen jumping aside when they fell, and then we retraced our steps. Before returning to the entrance, however, our guides took us into a branch of the main passage, in which, after proceeding a little way, we heard a roar as of flames, and then saw a bright light before us. A furnace appeared, in which a fierce fire was blazing; the blackened workmen were stirring and feeding it, and a strong current of air rushing by us, went with the flames up the shaft, which reached to the surface of the ground above. This, we were told, was a contrivance to ventilate the mine. All the foul air, all the fire-damp and other noxious gases are drawn from the passages and chambers by this method, and carried up to be dispersed in the outer atmosphere.

On our way back to the entrance we perceived that the vein lay at just such an inclination as allowed the workmen to roll the loaded trucks by hand along an easy descent to the mouth, as I hear is the case with all the veins. We emerged in a pretty amphitheatre shaded by primeval trees, and saw what we had not before noticed—a proof that the approaching election of a President was as much a matter of interest to the people of this remote region as to you in New York. A flag was flying on a prodigiously tall pole near the mouth of the mine. It was a Lincoln and Hamlin[2] flag, they said, and the workmen had chalked the name Lincoln (only a little ill-spelled) on the sides of the trucks.

When I was in this region twenty-eight years since, they had not begun to work the mines of iron and coal. From the little town of Frostburg, where I then passed the night, a place lying high among the mountain ridges, where the winter comes early and lingers late, you now look down upon several mining villages. There are twenty-five of them in this coal region, and they are adding greatly to its populousness. New mines are opened from time to time, so that the mountains ere long will be pierced from side to side with these artificial caverns. A curious effect is observed in some of them; the little veins of water in the earth are collected in the *drifts*, or main passages, and issue noiselessly forth, with a current of the color of a porter bottle. Whether the soil above derives any advantage from this sort of underdraining I have not learned.

The population of the mining villages—though to this remark there may be exceptions—does not appear to me to be of the most hopeful kind. They owe little to the schoolmaster, and know so little of the advantages of education that they are not generally anxious to procure them for their children. Such of them, however, as are provident, invest their earnings in lands, and they and their children will ultimately pass into the agricultural class. The farmers whom the mining companies found here, living at great distances from each other, are ill-schooled, if schooled at all, and have fallen into habits of life only a little less rude, I should judge, than those of the miners. An increase of their numbers will have a tendency to raise the scale of civilization among them. They inhabit a region of considerable fertility; their fields yield good crops of wheat and other grains, the finest hay and a sweet pasturage for their herds. These farmers are Catholics, and almost in sight of where I write, in one of the greenest and pleasantest nooks of the hills, stands their old church and the house of their priest, surrounded by trees.

From the point at which I write many interesting excursions may be made. The visitor may follow my example in a drive to the neighboring mines, or he may pass to the Glades, as they call the country west of Cumberland on the railway, a tract of hills and dales covered with rich grass and grazed by numerous herds; or go on horseback to the pine woods of Mount Savage, and lose himself among trees with stems a hundred and fifty feet high; or proceeding a few miles further and crossing the Pennsylvania boundary, find himself among the Dunkers, a primitive and friendly people living in the Dutch Glades, who never suffer the razor to pass over their chins.

MANUSCRIPT: Unrecovered TEXT: *EP* for October 22, 1860.

1. In 1859 the engineers and inventors Ross Winans (1796–1877) and his son Thomas De Kay Winans (1820–1878) developed this cigar-shaped steamer, the prototype of later ocean liner hulls.
2. Hannibal Hamlin (1809–1891), a United States senator from Maine since 1848, was the Republican candidate for Vice President in 1860.

1178.   *To* Charles Folsom[1]

New York   October 24, 1860.

My dear sir.

I have this moment read your letter of the 17th. having returned but a few hours since from a visit of a fortnight to Maryland.

Certainly I shall be very happy to say to any of my acquaintances, or to any body else who asks me for my opinion, that I have not the least [doubt?][2] that any young girl educated in your family would be educated in the very best manner. I should hardly confine myself to what you request—namely that I should refer the inquirer to some of my friends in your quarter.

Use my name therefore in any circular or announcement that you may think fit to draw up.

Present my kind regards to Mrs. Folsom, and believe me,

dear sir,

truly yours.

W. C. BRYANT.

MANUSCRIPT: Boston Public Library ADDRESS: C. Folsom Esq.

1. Bryant's co-editor on the *United States Review* in 1826–1827; see Vol. I, 16, and

passim. Folsom, whose letter of October 17 is unrecovered, had been librarian of the Boston Athenaeum from 1846 to 1856.

2. Word omitted.

1179. *To* Townsend Ward[1]

New York   October 24. 1860.

Sir.

I am sensible how much I lose in declining the invitation of the Historical Society of Pennsylvania to be present at their dinner on the 8th of November. My engagements, however, are such that I must forego the pleasure of being one of the guests, and it only remains that I make my best acknowledgements to the Committee for the honor they have done me.

I am, sir
very respectfully yours
Wm. C. Bryant.

manuscript: HSPa address: Townsend Ward Esq. / Secretary of the / Committee &c.

1. See descriptive note.

1180. *To* Abraham Lincoln

New York   Nov   1, 1860.

My dear sir.

It has been intimated to me that it is the intention of some of your friends here, particularly certain persons concerned in commerce and the transactions of Wall Street to request you to make some statement in the newspapers, which shall as they say "quiet the public mind"—some declaration of your intentions and the policy you mean to pursue if elected President. It is too late to do this before the election, but they would be satisfied if it were done immediately afterwards.[1]

I write to say that I am confident that this is not the desire of the most discreet of your friends. Such a declaration would be regarded as a concession to our political adversaries. They would consider it as something extorted by the violence of their attacks and would be encouraged to continue them. They would not be satisfied with any thing that could be said and would clamor for something more decidedly in their favor.

This is I think the view taken by the coolest heads among the Republicans here, and you will excuse me, I hope, for stating it—since I do so with the view of preventing any mistake on your part as to the wishes of your friends here.[2]

I need not say that we are perfectly sure of New York—the state.[3]

Yours very truly
W. C. Bryant.

MANUSCRIPT: LC ADDRESS: Hon   Abraham Lincoln.

1. As the campaign of 1860 neared a close, southern warnings of national dis-union if Lincoln were elected impelled some Republican leaders to deny the proba-bility of Abolitionist action by his administration. Thurlow Weed urged Senator Seward to make a "soothing speech" suggesting that the party was "all for peace, union, and prosperity." This Seward did, before a great crowd at the Palace Garden Music Hall in New York on November 2, promising "no acts of aggression against the slave states." Van Deusen, *Seward,* p. 235; Nevins, *Emergence of Lincoln,* II, 300–301, 306–309. Pressure on Lincoln to temporize continued to build up; he was urged to deny the implications of his "House Divided" speech of 1858 and to promise no interference with slavery. Horace Greeley hinted in his New York *Tribune* that the southern states might be allowed to secede peacefully, as the Buchanan administration had implied.

2. On November 12 Republican Senator Preston King of New York (810.2) wrote John Bigelow, "I think there is no danger of Lincoln making any declaration to antici-pate the day of his inauguration, but I am glad that Mr. Bryant wrote—for we cannot be too secure upon such a point." Bigelow, *Retrospections,* I, 316.

3. On November 6 Lincoln carried New York, as well as all other free states. The next day, from Princeton, Illinois, John Bryant wired his old legislative companion, "Bureau Co. sends greetings with twenty three hundred majority for Lincoln Lovejoy and Liberty." Telegram in Lincoln Papers, LC. Owen Lovejoy (748.5) was re-elected to Congress for a third term.

1181.   *To* an Unidentified Correspondent

[New York? *c*November 1?, 1860]

I have your letter[1] informing me that I have been designated by a state Convention of the Republican party as one of their candidates for elector through whom the votes of the state are to be cast for Lincoln and Hamlin, as President and Vice President. I accept the nomination with which they have honored me and if elected shall faithfully fulfil the trust reposed in me.

I am sir
respectfully yrs
W   C   BRYANT.

MANUSCRIPT: NYPL–GR (draft).

1. Unrecovered.

1182.   *To* Abraham Lincoln

New York   November 10th   1860.
My dear sir.

You will not I hope find what I have to say unseasonable or intrusive; if you should, you will of course treat it as it ought to be treated.

I have no doubt that you are already receiving frequent suggestions respecting the formation of your Cabinet when you take the Executive chair. It is natural that your fellow-citizens who elected you to office should feel the greatest interest in the selection which you may make of the men who are to be your confidential advisers and your special assistants in the administration of public affairs. You will therefore, I am sure, readily pardon the exhibition of some zeal in regard to this subject, even if it should go somewhat beyond the limits of a well-bred reserve.

You have numerous friends in this quarter, and they include some of the most enlightened and disinterested men in the Republican party, who would be infinitely pleased if your choice of a Secretary of State should fall on Mr. Salmon P. Chase of Ohio. He is regarded as altogether one of the noblest and truest among the great leaders of that party.—as a man in all respects beyond reproach—which you know can be said of few public men. He is a man of a well-stored mind and large experience, able, wise, pure, fair-minded, practical,—as he has shown in his administration of the affairs of the state of Ohio—never the associate of bad men, nor likely to advise the employment of such men in any capacity.[1] A cabinet with such a man in its principal department, and colleagues worthy of him in the others, would command the immediate confidence of the country.

Of course, I do not expect that you will make any reply to this letter. I pray you to receive [it][2] as a proof of my desire for the success of your administration and give its suggestions such weight as you may think they deserve.

I am, sir,
sincerely yours,
W. C. BRYANT.

MANUSCRIPTS: LC (final); NYPL–GR (draft) ADDRESS: Hon. Abraham Lincoln PUBLISHED (from preliminary draft): Life, II, 150.

1. Bryant's inexorable opposition to the Seward–Weed faction in New York politics had won him a position of national leadership among those Republicans who had blocked the nomination of Seward for the presidency, and were as adamant against allowing him to dominate Lincoln's cabinet. With such former Free Soil leaders as David D. Field and Gideon Welles, the EP editor was determined to strengthen Lincoln's resolve against the temptation to compromise with southern radicals, by bringing Chase, the former anti-slavery governor of Ohio, into close proximity with the President. Hendrick, Lincoln's War Cabinet, pp. 95, 126; Nevins, Emergence of Lincoln, II, 444–446.

2. Word omitted.

1183. To Robert Bonner

New York   Nov. 15, 1860

My dear sir.

I called at the Ledger Office yesterday to speak with you concerning the enclosed manuscript, but was not so fortunate as to find you in.

You may remember that some time since I sent you a story which I had been desired by a lady to submit to your consideration, and that you paid her liberally for it. The accompanying sketch is from her pen.[1] I do not wish to trespass upon your good nature or to make that liberality an occasion for further demands upon it. If the sketch pleases you—and I think it is pretty well done—and if moreover you think it is worth any thing, I should be glad to have her paid according to the rate you pay for such contributions. If you do not want it or do not care to pay for it, I beg you to deal with it as you deal with what is sent you from other quarters and send it back to me without ceremony.

I am sir
truly yours
W. C. BRYANT

MANUSCRIPT: QPL ADDRESS: R. Bonner Esqre / Editor of the Ledger.

1. The lady and her sketch are unidentified.

1184.   *To* Robert C. Waterston

Roslyn   Long Island
November 16, 1860.

My dear Mr. Waterston.

Roslyn is so pleasant just now that I am wishing every day that you would come and see it. I am fearing, all the time, that the next week will envy the beautiful weather of this. This sweet sunshine cannot always last; the season of blustering winds and lowering skies is at hand; the roses that are now so fresh in my garden cannot flaunt there long; they will be surprized some night by a deathly frost and the green grass that I see from my window must become of a russet hue. I hope you will be here before the ground stiffens into stone.

We returned long since from our little tour to the interior of Maryland, pleased with our visit, and my wife all the better for it. Julia is now off again, for a little while, on a visit to a friend in Baltimore. When you come this way do not think of visiting Roslyn on the first Monday in December, for then you know I must be in Albany to give my vote for President and Vice President of the United States. With that exception choose your own time, only, if you happen to be very sure of it beforehand, be so kind as to let me know also.

I suppose you rejoice, equally with myself, that the cause of justice and liberty has triumphed in the late election. I am sorry, on their own account that the people of South Carolina are making so much fuss about their defeat, but I have not the least apprehension that any thing serious will result from it.[1]

Kindest remembrances to Mrs. Waterston and yourself and from me to Mrs. Waterston.

I am, dear sir,
faithfully yours
WM. C. BRYANT.

MANUSCRIPT: Brown University Library ADDRESS: Rev^d. R. C. Waterston.

1. Bryant's guess was scarcely prophetic! Within a few days of Lincoln's election a States Rights flag was flown over public buildings in Charleston, South Carolina's two United States senators resigned, and the legislature passed a bill calling a secession convention and another authorizing the governor to spend $100,000 for arms. Nevins, *Emergence of Lincoln*, II, 318–320.

1185.   *To* John Howard Bryant

Roslyn   Nov. 29th   1860.

Dear Brother.

I have your letter of the 19th and the map of Bureau County,[1] for which I thank you—as well as for the statement of the purchases made on my account. On the map are five squares colored blue to represent the new purchases—in the statement six purchases are mentioned. Are two purchases of 160 acres each comprehen[d]ed in one square—that having the name of Starkweather? There is also a purchase of 160 acres not paid for— is that in Bureau County?[2]

I shall direct your draft for fences &c to be paid. You must begin to think what compensation I shall make you for the trouble you have taken and let me know.

We are rejoicing here over the election but we are not without our anxieties lest the cabinet may not be what we could desire. As to disunion nobody but silly people expect it will happen. The course of trade however, has been greatly disturbed by a panic which somehow or other has been got up, while the country is in a condition of the greatest prosperity. The panic has occasioned great losses and embarrassments.

Our autumn has been delightful with the exception of three very cold days last week and a cutting wind that seemed to come from the very pole. As to the summer I never knew a pleasanter one in any country that I have seen. Kind regards to Harriet and Elijah, in which my wife joins— Julia is on a visit to Baltimore.

Yours affectionately
W. C. BRYANT.

MANUSCRIPT: NYPL–BFP.

1. Unrecovered.
2. See Letters 1155, 1169.

1186.   *To* Frances F. Bryant

Albany   Tuesday morning
December 4th, 1860

Dear Frances.

I came up yesterday by the Harlem railroad, leaving New York at half past ten. It is pleasanter than the Hudson railroad; the cars more roomy and not so crowded and the motion much easier.

Elias Leavenworth[1] was on board and one of the electors whom he knew got in with us at a place called Bedford. I am at Congress Hall with a comfortable room with a fire.

Today we do nothing but organize and fill vacancies. Tomorrow we vote for President &c. I shall come down to New York tomorrow if I can, and if it does not oblige me to arrive late in the evening.

Yours ever
W. C. B.

MANUSCRIPT: NYPL–GR.

1. Bryant's early law clerk; see 123.1; Letter 431.

1187.   To Robert Bonner

Office of the Evening Post
New York, Dec. 8th   1860

My dear sir.

A poem for the Ledger.[1] Can you oblige giving a proof today before one o'clock? If not please send it to me at Roslyn Long Island—

Yours truly
W. C. BRYANT.

MANUSCRIPT: QPL.

1. This was doubtless "A Day-Dream," written at Naples in May 1858, and published in the *New York Ledger*, 16 (January 5, 1861), 8. See *Poems* (1876), pp. 369–371.

1188.   To Abraham Lincoln

New York   Dec. 25, 1860

My dear Sir.

The rumor having got abroad that you have been visited by a well known politician of New York who has a good deal to do with the stock market and who took with him a plan of compromise manufactured in Wall Street, it has occurred to me that you might like to be assured of the manner in which those Republicans who have no connection with Wall Street regard a compromise of the slavery question.[1] The feeling of decided aversion to the least concession was never stronger than it is now. The people have given their verdict and they do not expect that either their representatives in Congress or their politicians out of Congress will attempt to change or modify it in any degree. The restoration of the Missouri Compromise would disband the Republican party. Any other concession recognizing the right of slavery to protection or even existence in the territories would disgust and discourage the large majority of Republicans in this state and cool their interest in the incoming administration down to the freezing point. Whatever else be done the slavery question, so far as it is a federal question must remain as it is or the Republican party is annihilated. Nor will any concession of the sort proposed satisfy the South. South Carolina cannot be hired to return to the Union by any thing short of the removal of all restraints on the African slave trade.[2] To do that would convert at once into friends of the Union, a class of the southern politicians who are doing a great deal to foment the discontents of the South and might effect what the Wall Street managers hope to bring about by restoring the Missouri line, and giving protection to slavery south of it.

You will excuse me if I say a word concerning the formation of the Cabinet. I am glad to hear that it is decided to have regard in its composition to that part of the Republican party which is derived from the old democratic party. It would be most unfortunate if the Cabinet were to be so constituted as to turn the policy of the administration into the old whig channels. To instance a single branch of that policy—the policy of restraints upon trade for the advantage of the manufacturers. We of the old democratic party who are the friends of free trade are perfectly willing that this should be regarded as an open question, but we shall be placed in immediate antagonism to the administration, the moment this is made a part of its governing policy. A bigot to protection placed at the head of the Treasury department would at once open a controversy on that question which would be carried on with zeal, perhaps with heat.[3]

You will I know excuse these suggestions. If not wise they are at least disinterested. I have not, that I know of the remotest interest in politics except that our country should be governed with wisdom and justice, and with the allowance of the largest liberty in all things consistent with good order. You will receive perhaps from me letters in favor of persons desiring some office under the federal government or see my signature to recommendations got up by them or their friends. I pray you, in all these cases to believe, that no personal favor will be conferred on me, in any possible instance by bestowing the desired office on the person whom I may recommend. What I say for them should be taken as my opinion of their fitness and nothing more.

I am, dear sir,
very truly yours
W. C. BRYANT.

P.S. In regard to the slave-trade, the zeal for its restoration arises from its profitableness. Large capitals are invested in it and it is the most lucrative of all branches of commerce.   W. C. B.—[4]

MANUSCRIPT: LC ADDRESS: Abraham Lincoln Esqre / Springfield / Illinois POSTMARK: Roslyn / N. Y. / DEC / [25?] ENDORSED: Wm C. Bryant / Compromise — protection — personal. PUBLISHED: Spivey, *Bryant Cautions and Counsels Lincoln*, pp. 4–5.

1. Thurlow Weed—the "well known politician"—having failed to beguile Lincoln into calling on his defeated rival at either Auburn, New York, or Chicago, visited the President-elect in Springfield, Illinois, with the aim of securing for Seward a dominant

role in the new administration. Weed was also determined to foreclose cabinet appointments of former Democrats Salmon Chase, Gideon Welles, and Frank Blair by proposing instead southern Whigs disposed to follow Seward in conciliating the South. And just three days before his December 20 visit, Weed had repeated in his Albany *Evening Journal* his earlier proposal to restore the Missouri Compromise line of 1820, allowing the spread of slavery into new territories. See Hendrick, *Lincoln's War Cabinet*, pp. 114–120; Nevins, *Emergence of Lincoln*, II, 393–396.

Bryant and his New York associates were the more indignant over this visit because Weed had got to Lincoln before they did. On December 2 Senator Lyman Trumbull of Illinois told Lincoln of a call Bryant and two others had paid him in New York, expressing opposition to Seward's entering the cabinet, and reporting the formation of a committee to convey their opinion to the President-elect. See draft letter, Trumbull to Lincoln, Chicago Historical Society.

2. On December 20 South Carolina had adopted an ordinance of secession from the Union.

3. It was known that Seward and Weed wished to see Simon Cameron (1190.2), Pennsylvania manufacturer and high-tariff politician, made Secretary of the Treasury. Hendrick, *Lincoln's War Cabinet*, pp. 113–114.

4. In his reply to this letter on December 29 (NYPL–GR) Lincoln assured Bryant that, in the choice of a cabinet, "I promise you that I shall, unselfishly, try to deal fairly with all men." But he was less than frank in a flat statement that the " 'well known politician' . . . did not press upon me any such compromise as you seem to suppose, or, in fact, any compromise at all." See also Nevins, *Emergence of Lincoln*, II, 396–397.

1189. *To* Robert C. Waterston

Roslyn,[1] December 26, 1860

Dear Mr. Waterston,

I do not write this to answer your most agreeable letter,[2] which I got a few days since, but to say that I have sent you by express a copy of my Discourse on Irving for the Massachusetts Historical Society, and along with it a copy of an Illustrated Edition of my Forest Hymn[3] for you and Mrs. Waterston.

With regard to the Discourse it seems to me that I promised when in Boston to send a copy to the Historical Society.[4] If I did I wholly forgot it. Could you tell me from any recollection you have whether I said I would send a copy to any other of the collections I visited in your company. If I did I shall be somewhat mortified, but the mortification may do me good.

With regard to the "Hymn" I am sure that you and Mrs. Waterston will like the illustrations. They are done by a young artist named Hows, the son of an Englishman whose name you may have seen as an elocutionist in the newspapers. The young man was born in this country—he is but a youth still—and is a diligent student of our woods, and an enthusiast in his profession.[5] The publication was got up without any agency of mine; the first I knew of it was when the bookseller brought the drawings to me, and asked my permission to publish the verses in a volume by themselves, which, as you may suppose, the beauty of the designs readily induced me to give.

I hope you and Mrs. Waterston have had a cheerful Christmas, and I wish you may enter next Tuesday upon a happy year. Looking at the date of my letter I see that I have written New York when I should have written Roslyn, for my wife and I are passing a rather solitary Christmas, in sight of the tides wrought into white caps by the northeast wind dashing at the foot of our garden, with flocks of screaming seagulls sitting on them, or wheeling in the air, and a drowsy warmth within our dwelling.

I have seen Whittiers beautiful lines and have them by me, to republish as soon as the holidays are over.[6]

The madness of the South astonishes me. Some good people in your state—several of them I know to be good people—others are a little below the average standard of goodness—have issued an address the purport of which seems to be that the Massachusetts Personal Liberty law is in fault and ought to be repealed.[7] I am astonished as much at the remedy they propose as at the audacity and wickedness of the secessionists. They care very little for the Personal Liberty laws. Nothing will purchase the acquiescence of South Carolina in the Union, short of repealing all our laws against the slave trade and allowing it to be carried on without obstruction. There is no traffic so profitable, and as I hear there are large capitals invested in it in Salem as well as New York. I do not say that the importers of slaves from Africa are the only instigators of the southern revolt, but I am sure that if this most lucrative branch of commerce could be freely pursued, some of the most active and noisy of the rebels would be among our most loyal citizens. Chief Justice Shaw's prescription is as wise as a proposal to set a broken leg by giving the patient a dose of valerian.[8]

My best regards to Mrs. Waterston. My wife, who is quite well and active desires love to you both—Julia is in town.

I am dear sir,

very truly yours

W. C. BRYANT

MANUSCRIPT: NYHS ADDRESS: Rev^d. R. C. Waterston.

1. Bryant mistakenly wrote "New York"; see letter text.
2. Waterston had written Bryant on December 19 (NYPL–BG) saying he and his wife had hoped to visit the Bryants in the fall.
3. *A Forest Hymn*. With illustrations by John A. Hows (New York: J. Gregory [1860]).
4. In thanking its author for a copy of the discourse on Irving, Robert Charles Winthrop (1809–1894, Harvard 1828), president of the Massachusetts Historical Society, wrote Bryant, "It gives me peculiar pleasure to unite in giving the unanimous vote by which you have succeeded to the place of Irving on the roll of our old Historical Society." Winthrop to Bryant, February 27, 1861, quoted in *Life*, II, 136–137.
5. John Augustus Hows (1832–1874, Columbia 1852) of New York was primarily a wood engraver and book illustrator. *DAA*.
6. See 1160.2.
7. During the 1840s and 1850s, in the face of the federal fugitive slave laws, most

northern states passed legislation "designed to prevent kidnapping and to safeguard the rights of free Negroes." Massachusetts provided defense for fugitives at public expense. Russell B. Nye, *Fettered Freedom: Civil Liberties and the Slavery Controversy, 1830–1860* ([East Lansing] Michigan State University Press [1963]), pp. 275–276.

8. Lemuel Shaw (1781–1861, Harvard 1800) was chief justice of Massachusetts, 1830–1860. Shaw held that the Massachusetts Personal Liberty Law was in conflict with the United States Constitution and federal laws, including the Fugitive Slave Law. On December 18, 1860, his name headed a petition from a number of prominent men which was published in daily newspapers, urging repeal of the Personal Liberty Law on the grounds that it violated the compact between Massachusetts and other states, and prevented federal officers from performing their duties. Frederic Hathaway Chase, *Lemuel Shaw, Chief Justice of the Supreme Judicial Court of Massachusetts, 1830–1860* (Boston and New York: Houghton, Mifflin, 1918), pp. 177–179.

XXII

Not Yet!
1861

(LETTERS 1190 TO 1253)

> O COUNTRY, marvel of the earth!
> O realm to sudden greatness grown!
> The age that gloried in thy birth,
> Shall it behold thee overthrown?
> Shall traitors lay that greatness low?
> No, land of Hope and Blessing, No!
> —"Not Yet," July 1861

AT THE BEGINNING OF JANUARY 1861, in an editorial leader captioned "The Fifty-Ninth Anniverary of the Evening Post," Bryant summarized the public measures advocated by the newspaper over the past fifteen years, "often against most discouraging adverse influences." This policy, he maintained, had "finally received its most suitable national vindication in the choice of Abraham Lincoln ... for President of the United States." And he made it immediately clear that he would employ his most forceful arguments to persuade the President-elect to implement that policy.

On January 8 Charles H. Ray, editor of the Chicago *Tribune* and an early Lincoln supporter, urged Bryant to visit the new President who, he wrote, "has profound respect for your fidelity to the cause and for your disinterestedness, and will be greatly influenced by your advice." He concluded, "I think you are greatly needed here, to make sure all will go right." Bryant himself did not travel to Springfield, Illinois, but a delegation had just left New York in his stead, and Bryant wrote Lincoln asking a "kind reception and an attentive hearing" for these men who represented, he said, "the anti-corruptionists of the Republican party in our state." It was the intent of this "Bryant faction," as it has been called, to forestall the appointment of William H. Seward as Secretary of State and Simon Cameron to the Treasury, by urging instead that Salmon P. Chase be given State and Gideon Welles either Treasury or another key post.

Even before his associates left for the West, Bryant had made Lincoln aware of his opposition to any Cabinet appointment for Cameron. There was generally, he wrote the President-elect on January 3, "an utter, ancient and deep seated distrust of his integrity—whether financial or political. The announcement of his appointment ... would diffuse a feeling almost like despair." The next day he enlarged upon his objections to Cameron, while implying his opposition to Seward by characterizing, without naming, the Weed–Seward combination in New York as "the men who last winter seduced our legislature into that shamefully corrupt course by which it was disgraced." But Cameron had been promised a Cabinet post by one of Lincoln's aides, in return for switching support of the Pennsylvania delegation from Seward to Lincoln at the Chicago nominating convention, and the Seward–Weed faction, in an attempt to bar Chase from the Cabinet, were supporting Cameron for the Treasury. As for Seward, Lincoln had long intended to appoint his defeated rival to the Secretaryship of State, and Seward had accepted his invitation before Bryant's friends left for Springfield.

As early as the beginning of December Lyman Trumbull of Illinois, after seeing Bryant and like-minded New Yorkers, had reported to Lincoln their opposition to Seward. Early in January Lincoln assured the senator that Cameron had not been offered the Treasury; that it must go to Chase, for "he alone can reconcile Mr. Bryant and his class, to the appointment of Gov. S. to the State Dept." But after Bryant's friends had seen Lincoln at Springfield, one of them wrote Bryant that though the new President considered Chase the "ablest man in America," and preferred Welles as the representative of New England, he intended to postpone further Cabinet choices until he reached Washington in mid-February. When at length he named a full Cabinet, Lincoln favored neither New York faction, for while Seward was given the State Department and Cameron that of War, Chase became Secretary of the Treasury and Welles Secretary of the Navy. With these selections Bryant had to be content.

The *Evening Post*'s editor soon found himself generally thought to be "personally and intimately acquainted with Mr. Lincoln," and thus the dispenser of political patronage in New York, although Bryant himself complained to Gideon Welles a few weeks after Inauguration day that former Democrats in the Republican party were not receiving a fair share of appointments in the new administration unless they had "made themselves speedily acceptable to Mr. Weed and Mr. Seward." Bryant's successful nomination of Hiram Barney to be the collector of customs at New York made him the inevitable target of countless applicants for work in the custom house—especially since, as George W. Curtis reported in seeking a job for one man, Barney "said he must know what you thought of it." To Orville Dewey Bryant complained on March 13 that even at home in Roslyn "I am teased with constant applications to help people to offices under the new administration. I want to run away from them," and "give these office beggars the slip." By April 1 the pressure was so great that he printed in his newspaper a card stating that he had recently found pleas of this sort "so numerous and importunate that he has been obliged to go out of town to avoid them." As late as October Frances Bryant wrote her brother-in-law Cyrus that her husband had that day been "so *be-set* by office seekers—and beggars, that he came home in quite a fever."

Bryant's escape in April took the form of a visit with old friends in Boston and Cambridge, the Danas, Deweys, Waterstons, and Willard Phillips. His relief from pressure was evident in Longfellow's comment, "Bryant has been here; very gentle and pleasant, with his benign aspect and soft blue eyes. He looks like a Prophet of Peace, amid the din of Civil War." But this interlude was brief, and he returned to pressures of a more troubling nature. Soon after joining the Cabinet, Salmon Chase had written John Bigelow, "If Mr. Bryant wd. go to Europe (say Paris), & take Mr. Godwin as Private Secretary he should have my voice." The belief that the senior editor of the *Evening Post* expected, or would be offered, an ambassadorship or other high office under the new administration was voiced so often in other journals that on April 1 there appeared in his paper, under the heading "Mr. Bryant's Case," the firm disclaimer, "Those who are acquainted with Mr. Bryant know that there is no public office from that of President of the United States downwards which he would not regard it as a misfortune to be obliged to take. They know that not only has he asked for no office, but that he has not allowed others to ask for him—that he has expected no offer of any post under the government, and would take none if offered."

Though Bryant asked no favor for himself, and was troubled by the solicitations of others, he had, as his disclaimer put it, "cheerfully borne his testimony in writing to the merits" of such claimants. Many of his suggestions were acted on favorably, not only in the custom house, but also in diplomatic appointments and elsewhere. Different from these, however, was his successful appeal to the Commissioners of Central Park early in 1861 to prevent Frederick Law Olmsted from being downgraded from the superintendency of the park to an advisory position. Once vindicated, Olmsted took a leave of absence to become secretary to the United States Sanitary Commission, under the direction of Bryant's pastor Henry W. Bellows, and left in June for Washington to inspect conditions in the military camps about Washington. From there, after the First Battle of Bull Run in July, he wrote Bryant for the *Evening Post* a letter which described the ignominious retreat of Union regiments on the capital in appalling confusion, with many officers leading the rout and drawing from private soldiers the contemptuous epithets of "cowards and fools." Olmsted's was one of many direct accounts of conditions in the field sent Bryant as the war continued, a number of them from senior military officers who, like himself, chafed at the slow progress of campaigns and the apparent incompetence of army commanders.

At the close of 1860 Bryant had faced, for the second time in two years, the prospect of having to assume the daily management of his newspaper, when John Bigelow expressed a wish to divest himself of his interest in the *Evening Post* in order to resume literary writing. The partners agreed to sell his interest to Parke Godwin, who had worked for the past two years at the city desk, and to let him pay for his share gradually from dividends. On January 16 Bigelow left the paper. But Bryant soon found a managing editor in Charles Nordhoff, a successful writer of sea tales based on his own experience before the mast, who had more recently served as an editor for the Harper Brothers. Throughout the war, and during the rest of the decade, Nordhoff proved an able adjutant to the senior proprietor.

With the advent of war, Bryant found little time or inclination to compose poetry. Of the half-dozen poems he wrote in 1861, only the meditative verses in "The Constellations" and "The Third of November, 1861" (his sixty-seventh birthday) were not explicitly concerned with the conflict. In January he was revising his Cooper oration of 1852 as a preface to the first collected edition of the novelist's works. During the year translations of his poems were made by two German scholars. He declined an invitation to deliver the annual Phi Beta Kappa oration at Harvard, where, forty years earlier, he had read his long poem, "The Ages."

In May Cullen and Frances traveled by rail to Illinois, to find their relatives well, but the state in financial confusion, with its residents rejecting local bank notes as worthless. Earlier that spring Bryant had made, through his brother John, his last purchase of farmland in the West, one-hundred-sixty acres near Princeton. Soon after their return the couple were visited by Cyrus Bryant and his wife, who had come on to see their son Cullen at West Point. Two weeks after the attack on Fort Sumter the first-year cadet had written his aunt of the great excitement at the military academy when, after most southerners had departed, the whole corps had cheered two regiments of volunteers, "wild with enthusiasm," as they steamed past on the way down the Hudson River.

Though not yet openly committed to emancipation, in late August the *Evening Post* applauded the declaration by General John C. Frémont in Missouri that the slaves of known southern sympathizers throughout that state would be freed, calling this "the most popular act of the war." When Lincoln revoked the general's order, Bryant condemned his action. In October he all but called for emancipation when, in a leader headed "Playing at War," he termed slavery a "prodigious wrong which ought to be abrogated," asking, "Shall we deal with these barbarous wretches as though they were friends? Shall we withhold our hand from the very blow which they fear the most?" He answered the question himself: "The masses will tolerate no playing at war; . . . if it becomes necessary to extinguish slavery in order to put down this most wicked and wanton rebellion, it will be swept from the board."

Though Bryant did not, during 1861, admonish the President directly on his conduct of the war, writing him only to introduce visitors to Washington, or to recommend office seekers, he began to express through his newspaper the cautions and exhortations which he would continue throughout the conflict, and which—though some called them journalistic generalship—drew from one source the comment that his editorials were worth as much to the North as an army corps, and from another that they were "of more use to the Union than some of its armies." Between Fort Sumter and Bull Run many timid northerners, especially those in finance and trade, urged that the issue of secession might be negotiated. "Grant anything that looks like compromise," he wrote on June 25, "and you only minister to the arrogance of the rebels. . . . In the present state of things, therefore, compromise is only an encouragement." In July he anticipated by eight months the appearance of John Ericsson's *Monitor* at Hampton Roads, by suggesting the construction of "half a dozen thoroughly shot-proof gunboats, of light draft," which could silence southern forts, or run past them to dominate the principal ports. After the rout at Bull Run, he urged that it would have a salutary, sobering effect on the Union; it was, Frances Bryant quoted him as saying a few days later, the "best thing that could have happened to us—that it will take the conceit out of us . . . and . . . will give the contest so serious a character that when we do settle it we shall insist on so crippling the slave interest that it will never lift its head again."

Toward the close of the year Bryant gave much space, both in letters and in editorials, to the misconceptions held by the British government and press of the nature of the rebellion and the conflicting aims of the Union and Confederate administrations. Indignant at charges in British newspapers that the national administration was under the domination of a "reckless and brutal mob, which compels the government to do its bidding," while the Confederate leadership was composed of gentlemen, and that "in the southern states all is quiet, order and respect for the law," he at first expressed his approval of the seizure from the British mail steamer *Trent* by the American naval commander Charles Wilkes, of two Confederate emissaries, Mason and Slidell, and their arbitrary imprisonment at Boston—contrary to the long-maintained American insistence on freedom of the sea. But reflection soon tempered this momentary concession to American chauvinism; before Washington had acceded in December to British demands for release of the men, Bryant printed a sober argument for impartial, binding arbitration of the case.

In August John Bigelow was appointed American consul at Paris, and by the end of the year he was sending his former partner confidential reports of European political attitudes toward the United States government and the armed conflict in this country. Another successful applicant that year for a consulship was William Dean Howells, of Ohio, who had published a campaign biography of Lincoln. In August, before going to Washington to seek a post, Howells called at the *Evening Post* office with a letter from James T. Fields, who wrote that the young writer's stories and verses already published in the *Atlantic Monthly* had given its conductors so high an opinion of his talents that "if we could keep him we would." Howells, he said, hoped to find literary employment, adding, "He chooses *The Post* of all papers in the Union." But that newspaper was not yet ready for a regular book editor, nor could a place be found on its small staff for a writer of belles-lettres; so Howells went on to Venice, where he wrote his first significant books.

1190.   *To* Abraham Lincoln

New York   January 3d   1861.

My dear sir.

I have this moment received your note.[1] Nothing could be more fair or more satisfactory than the principle you lay down in regard to the formation of your council of official advisors. I shall always be convinced that whatever selection you make it will be made conscientiously.

The community here has been somewhat startled this morning by the positiveness with which a report has been circulated, reaching this city from Washington that Mr. Simon Cameron was to be placed in the Treasury Department. Forgive me if I state to you how we all should regard such an appointment—I believe I may speak for all parties, except perhaps some of the most corrupt in our own— The objection to Mr. Cameron would not be that he does not hold such opinions as we approve, but that there is among all who have observed the course of our public men an utter, ancient and deep seated distrust of his integrity—whether financial or political. The announcement of his appointment, if made on any authority deserving of credit would diffuse a feeling almost like despair.[2] I have no prejudices against Mr. Cameron except such as arise from observing in what transactions he has been engaged and I have reason to suppose that whatever opinion has been formed respecting him in this part of the country has been formed on perfectly impartial and disinterested grounds. I pray you, again, to excuse my giving you this trouble. Do not reply to this letter— Only let us have honest rigidly upright men in the departments—whatever may be their notions of public policy.

I am, dear sir,
very truly &c
W   C   BRYANT.

MANUSCRIPT: LC ADDRESS: Hon   A. Lincoln.

1. See 1188.4.
2. Simon Cameron (1799–1889), Pennsylvania manufacturer, railroad builder, political boss, and twice a United States senator, had switched his support at the Chicago nominating convention from Seward to Lincoln, in return for a promise from one of Lincoln's aides of a position in the cabinet. Nevins, *Emergence of Lincoln*, II, 257; Hendrick, *Lincoln's War Cabinet*, pp. 73–76. Bryant's opinion of Cameron, a former Democrat, had long been shared by leaders of his own party. Andrew Jackson had called him a man "not to be trusted by anyone in any way." President Polk thought him a "managing tricky man in whom no reliance is to be placed." And his fellow-Pennsylvanian President Buchanan considered him "a scamp" and "an unprincipled rascal." Hendrick, *Lincoln's War Cabinet*, pp. 65–66.

1191.   *To* Abraham Lincoln

New York   January 4th   1861.

My dear sir.

I wrote to you yesterday concerning the rumored intention to give Mr. Simon Cameron of Pennsylvania a place in the Cabinet which you are to form. I had then scarcely spoken to any body on the subject, but since that time I have heard the matter much discussed and I assure you that the general feeling is one of consternation.

Mr. Cameron has the reputation of being concerned in some of the worst intrigues of the democratic party a few years back. His name suggests to every honest Republican in this state no other than disgusting associations, and they will expect nothing from him when in office but a repetition of such transactions. At present those who favor his appointment, in this state, are the men who last winter seduced our legislature into that shamefully corrupt course by which it was disgraced.[1] If he is to form one of the Cabinet, the Treasury Department, which rumor assigns him, is the very last of the public interests which ought to be committed to his charge.

In the late election, the Republican party, throughout the Union, struggled not only to overthrow the party that sought the extension of slavery, but also to secure a pure and virtuous administration of the government. The first of these objects we have fully attained, but if such men as Mr. Cameron are to compose the Cabinet, however pure and upright the Chief Magistrate may himself be,—and it is our pride and rejoicing that in the present instance we know him to be so,—we shall not have succeeded in the second.

There is no scarcity of able and upright men who would preside over the Treasury department with honor. I believe Mr. Gideon Welles of Hartford has been spoken of.[2] There is no more truly honest man, and he is equally wise and enlightened. We have a man here in New York whom I should rejoice to see at the head of that department, Mr. Opdyke, the late Republican candidate for Mayor of this city a man who has made finance the subject of long and profound study, and whom no possible temptation could move from his integrity. If a man from Pennsylvania is wanted, that state has sons whose probity has never been questioned—so that there will be no need to take up with a man hackneyed in those practices which make politics a sordid game played for the promotion of personal interests.

I must again ask you to pardon this freedom for the sake of its motive. It has cost me some effort to break through my usual reserve in such matters, but I feel a greater interest in the success and honor of your administration than in that of any which have preceded it.[3] I am, dear sir, truly yours,

WM C   BRYANT

MANUSCRIPTS: LC (final); NYPL–GR (partial draft) ADDRESS: Hon A Lincoln. PUB-
LISHED (from draft): *Life*, II, 152–153, under date of February 5.

1. See 1119.4; Letter 1134.

2. Like Bryant, Welles (353.1) admired Salmon P. Chase and vigorously opposed the Seward–Weed combination.

3. Without question, Bryant influenced Lincoln's choice of cabinet members, although he was not yet fully aware that the President-elect had already made some critical decisions concerning them. Dr. Charles H. Ray, an editor of the Chicago *Tribune* and an early Lincoln supporter, wrote Bryant on January 8, 1861 (NYPL–BG), "Mr. Lincoln has profound respect for your fidelity for the cause and for your disinterestedness and will be greatly interested in your advice." And on January 7 Lincoln wrote Lyman Trumbull (Chicago Historical Society), "Gen. C[ameron] has not been offered the Treasury, and, I think, will not be—It seems to me not only highly proper, but a necessity, that Gov— Chase shall take that place. His ability, firmness, and purity of character [pronounce?] the propriety; and that he alone can reconcile Mr. Bryant, and his class, to the appointment of Gov— S[eward] to the State Department produces the necessity."

1192.   *To* Abraham Lincoln

New York   Jan. 10, 1861.

My dear sir.

Two friends of mine and I may say of yours,—Mr. Opdyke, whom I have spoken of in a previous letter as one of our most sterling men, and Judge J. T. Hogeboom,[1] a gentleman of high character and plain outspoken honesty, are now on their way to Springfield. It is possible that they may be joined in Washington—which they will take in their way—by Hiram Barney Esq. who you may know was very efficient in conducting the proceedings of the Chicago Convention to its final result, and who is highly esteemed here by all to whom he is known.[2] It is their desire to confer with you on certain matters of public interest in regard to which we all feel confident that you would desire the fullest and most trust worthy information before coming to a final decision. I should have given these gentlemen a letter to you had I been at home when they left town. I write this to say who they are and whom they represent, though who they are you may possibly know already as well as I. They represent the anti-corruptionists of the Republican party in our state; they speak for that class of men who thought it unsafe to nominate Mr. Seward for the Presidency on account of his close associations with a class of men of whose want of principle our state legislature last winter gave most melancholy proof.

I am glad these gentlemen are on their way to your residence, and feel that I have no need to bespeak for them a kind reception and an attentive hearing.[3]

I am, sir,
very truly yours
W. C. BRYANT.

MANUSCRIPT: LC ADDRESS: Hon   Abraham Lincoln / Springfield / Illinois. POSTMARK: N[EW YO]RK / [JAN] / 10 / 1861 ENDORSED: needs no ans / Bryant / Introducing Opdyke a[nd] / Hogeboom.

1. John T. Hogeboom, a former county judge and state assemblyman from Columbia County, New York, was appointed an appraiser in the New York Custom House on October 3, 1861. Edgar A. Werner, *Civil List and Constitutional History of the Colony and State of New York* (Albany, 1888), pp. 440, 410, 179.

2. Barney, a former Democrat, had been instrumental in forming the Republican Party. In 1861 Lincoln appointed him Collector of the Port of New York. See Letter 1202.

3. After their meeting with the President-elect, Barney reported to Bryant from Chicago that invitations to join the cabinet had gone to Seward, Edward Bates, and Cameron, though, "In regard to the latter-named, . . . Mr. Lincoln became satisfied he had made a mistake, and wrote him requesting him to withdraw his acceptance or decline." Lincoln "wants and expects," Barney continued, to have Chase and Welles in the cabinet, but "is advised . . . not to conclude further upon the members of his Cabinet until he reaches Washington." Barney to Bryant, January 17, 1861, NYPL–BG.

1193.   *To* Frances F. Bryant

New York   Wednesday
January 16th   1861.—

Dear Frances.

I think I shall not return till Friday. I want to finish the revision of the Memoir of Cooper,[1] and this I must do from materials furnished by "Pages and Pictures from Cooper," a big book, too large to be conveniently brought out to Roslyn. The publisher Townsend the same who published the Forest Hymn is waiting for me.

All well here. The E. P. is virtually in Godwin's hands, and he begins to breakfast earlier. Only some papers are to be executed as soon as they are drawn up.[2]

Yours ever
W. C. B.

MANUSCRIPT: NYPL–GR.

1. A revision of his "Discourse on the Life and Genius of Cooper" (783.6), done as a preface to a new edition of Fenimore Cooper's novel *Precaution* (New York, 1861).

2. On this date, January 16, 1861, John Bigelow sold his one-third interest in the *EP* properties to Parke Godwin. See Letter 1223.

1194.   *To* Charlotte Dana

New York   January 21. 1861.

Dear Miss Dana.

I came to town this morning and found your note. I shall return to the country this afternoon or I should call to see you. My wife will come in on Wednesday unless prevented by very bad weather, or some other obstacle,

and will be at No. 82 East Sixteenth Street. I shall give her your address—
and perhaps I may be able to come to town with her.

Yours very truly,
W. C. BRYANT.

MANUSCRIPT: LH DOCKETED: From W. C. Bryant / Jany — 61.

1195. *To* Abraham Lincoln

New York   January 22, 1861.

My dear sir.

At the risk of being deemed somewhat troublesome, yet with the greatest respect and deference, I take the liberty of addressing you once more
on the subject of your cabinet appointments.

I believe that you do not differ with me in regard to the importance
of giving Mr. Chase a place in the Cabinet, as one whose wisdom, rigid
integrity and force of character would make him a safe counsellor and efficient coadjutor of the Chief Magistrate, not to speak of the need of his
presence as a counterpoise to another member who, to commanding talents,
joins a flexible and in[d]ulgent temper, and unsafe associations. The appointment of Mr. Chase would give a feeling of security and confidence
to the public mind which the rascalities of Mr. Buchanan's cabinet have
made exceedingly sensitive and jealous, and would, it seems to me, settle
the point in advance that the new administration will be both honored and
beloved. For some time to come, the federal government must depend
largely upon its credit for its resources, and how potent is the effect of placing an honest and economical man at the head of the Treasury Department,
is shown by an example now before our eyes. General Dix, with all his mistakes, is a man of unquestioned integrity, and his appointment as Secretary
of the Treasury has already greatly raised the credit of the government
brought so low by the misconduct of Cobb.[1]

Now, according to what I learn from Mr. Opdyke, who has just returned from Ohio, it is nearly certain that Mr. Chase would not take a
place in the Cabinet, unless it were offered him early. He is not inclined to
do it at all, preferring a seat in the Senate, but this preference he would
forego; yet there are, I am told, some personal reasons, as well as others
connected with the choice of his successor in the Senate, that will, if the
offer be delayed, induce him to remain where he is. I am not a judge of the
force of these reasons; it is enough that they exist.

The only motive for delay is the hope of pacifying Mr. Cameron and
his friends.[2] It is thought here, by some who know him to be very tenacious
of his purposes, that there is no probability of doing this effectually, whether
the offer to Mr. Chase be postponed or not. If, however, it be possible to
satisfy him, it is to be considered, whether it will not be as easily done after
Mr. Chase shall have been fixed upon as now, and whether the hope of ob-

taining better terms may not lead Mr. Cameron to affect to spurn any reconciliation, as long as the appointment which he expected is kept open. One
thing, however, is perfectly clear, that by failing to secure the services of
Mr. Chase in the Treasury Department, both the country and the Republican party will lose infinitely more than the incoming administration can
possibly suffer from the enmity of Mr. Cameron and his adherents.

I leave this subject here, that I may say a single word on another. From
Mr. Opdyke, I learn, that, in a letter written to you some weeks since, on
the subject of "protection,"[3] I did not make myself fully understood. It
seemed to me that I had clearly expressed my meaning when I said, that
those who thought with me were "willing that this should be an open question." I wished merely to express a hope that the administration would not
throw its entire influence on the side of protection. The Republican party
not being agreed among themselves on this point, the cabinet policy as it
seemed to me, should be so moderate as not to disaffect the friends of free
trade.

I am, dear sir,
truly yours.
W. C. BRYANT.

MANUSCRIPTS: LC (final); NYPL–GR (draft) ADDRESS: Hon   A. Lincoln PUBLISHED: *Life*,
II, 150–152 (from draft dated January 21).

1. Following the resignations as President Buchanan's Secretary of the Treasury of
Howell Cobb (1815–1868, Georgia 1834) of Georgia, on December 8, 1860, and his short-
lived successor Philip Francis Thomas (1810–1890), of Maryland, on January 11, 1861,
John A. Dix of New York (388.8, 519.1) succeeded to that cabinet post. Nevins, *Emergence of Lincoln*, II, 359, 380.

2. In his letter of January 17 Hiram Barney had told Bryant that Cameron had
been "greatly offended" by Lincoln's suggestion that he decline a cabinet appointment,
and that "Mr. Lincoln has thus a quarrel on his hands." See also *ibid.*, 441–443; Hendrick, *Lincoln's War Cabinet*, pp. 132–133.

3. Letter 1188.

1196.   *To* Abraham Lincoln

New York   January 24, 1861
My dear sir.

I write this to introduce to you Richard C. McCormick Esq.[1] a young
gentleman of fine talents great maturity of mind and excellent character,
who desires an interview with you as the representative of the Young Mens
Republican Union of this city, a numerous and most respectable association, which did the country good service in the late election.

Mr. McCormick wishes to express to you the desire of the Republicans
who form the Young Men's Union, to see Cassius M. Clay of Kentucky at
the Head of the War Department. It has been suggested to me that in introducing my young friend I should say a word or two as to the manner in

which such an appointment would be received here. The manly bearing of Mr. Clay in his visits to our city has prepossessed the people greatly in his favor, and throughout our part of the country his courage, disinterestedness, and generous unquenchable enthusiasm in the cause of liberty and humanity have given birth to a feeling of admiration that amounts almost to personal attachment. Whatever politicians may say his appointment would be exceedingly popular with the mass of the people, who think that his energy and spirit fit him in these perilous times in a peculiar manner for that place.

I have heard the remark made that if the War Department was not open for Mr. Clay, the mission to Mexico would afford a suitable field for the exercise of those qualities which have won him such general respect.[2]

> I am, sir,
> truly yours
> W. C. BRYANT

MANUSCRIPT: LC ADDRESS: Hon   A. Lincoln. PUBLISHED: Spivey, *Bryant Cautions and Counsels Lincoln*, p. 6.

1. Richard Cunningham McCormick (1832–1901) reported from the Crimean War, and in 1861–1862 from the Army of the Potomac, for New York newspapers. In 1863 he was made secretary of Arizona Territory, and in 1866 its governor.

2. Cassius M. Clay was United States minister to Russia in 1861–1862, and again in 1863–1869.

1197.   *To* Edward Everett

> New York   Jan   25. 1861

Dear Sir,

At the present period in our history, we feel that the life and character of the "Father of his Country" should be constantly held up for the reverence of the people. We respectfully but earnestly request you to repeat your Washington oration in this city on the approaching anniversary of his birth.[1]

> With great regard, We are,
> Truly Yours
> WM. C. BRYANT [and others][2]

MANUSCRIPT: MHS ADDRESS: To the Hon   Edward Everett.

1. This, the most popular oration by Everett (Letter 1081), had been delivered repeatedly in major cities throughout the country since he had first spoken it before the Mercantile Library Association of Boston in 1856. Apparently he did not speak in New York on Washington's birthday in 1861; he did, however, address an overflow crowd at the Academy of Music in that city on July 4, 1861, his subject "The Present State of the Country." Paul Revere Frothingham, *Edward Everett: Orator and Statesman* (Boston and New York: Houghton, Mifflin, 1925), pp. 373–385, *passim*; 422.

2. Bryant's signature was one of sixteen of prominent New Yorkers on this letter, which is not in his holograph.

1198. *To* an Unidentified Correspondent

New York   February 8th   1861.

Sir.

Freilegrath translated my little poem of the Winds into German, and it appeared in a small volume of his poems.[1] There have been various other translations in newspapers and periodicals. Prof. Leo Romer of Detroit writes me that he is translating them all into German.[2]

I am, sir

respectfully yours

WM. C. BRYANT.

MANUSCRIPT: WCL.

1. The German poet Ferdinand Freiligrath (1810–1876), long a friend and correspondent of Longfellow's, had published translations from the verses of that poet and others in his *Englische Gedichte aus neuerer Zeit* (Stuttgart, 1846). See Longfellow, *Letters*, II, 415, 417; IV, 525–526.

2. Letter unrecovered.

1199. *To* Robert Bonner

New York   February 13th   1861.

My dear sir.

The bearer of this letter is Mr. F. F. de la Figanière, the son of my friend the Portuguese Minister Plenipotentiary.[1] Mr. Figanière is a native of this country, but has resided in Portugal for some years past. He is devoted to literary pursuits, and desires to make his talents as a writer contribute in some degree to his support. I remember a well written description of a visit made by him to Portugal, printed some ten or twelve years since.

I am, sir,

truly yours

W. C. BRYANT.

MANUSCRIPT: QPL ADDRESS: R. Bonner Esq. DOCKETED: Feb 13/61 / W C Bryant.

1. Frederico Francisco de la Figanière (b. 1827) was the author, among other works, of *Memorias das rainhas de Portugal* (Lisbon, 1859). His father, Joaquin de la Figanière, was an early member of the Sketch Club. Information from James T. Callow.

1200. *To* James Russell Lowell

[New York? *c*February 13, 1861]

To the Editor of the Atlantic Monthly.[1]

The writer of the note which accompanies this is a native of this country, and yet is numbered among the authors of recent Portuguese literature.

He is the author of a work entitled Memoirs of the Queens of Portugal, and several other publications in the Portuguese language, one of which, a politico-economical tract, I have looked over, and was well pleased with its scope and the treatment of the subject.

Mr. Figanière is familiar with the modern literature of Portugal of which little is known in this country, and being a practiced writer in both languages, I have no doubt of his ability to give the American public sketches of the present state of that literature which would be read with general interest.

> I am sir
> very respectfully &c
> W. C. BRYANT.

MANUSCRIPT: HCL.

1. The poet and essayist James Russell Lowell (1819–1891) edited the *Atlantic Monthly* from 1857 until the spring of 1861, when he was succeeded by James T. Fields. See 1175.1.

1201.   *To* Abraham Lincoln

New York   February 20. 1861.

Sir,

My friend E. A. Stansbury Esq. of this city, being about to ask for the appointment of United States Consul either at Liverpool or at Paris, I take great pleasure in supporting his application.[1] I have been acquainted with Mr. Stansbury for more than twelve years, and have formed a high opinion of his personal character and his talents. He is in every way worthy of the post he solicits; his habits of business would enable him to discharge its duties with accuracy and dispatch, and his talents, accomplishments and gentlemanly manners would make him a credit to the government that appointed him.

He has been a zealous Republican from the formation of the party, and has rendered valuable service to the cause. Few persons it seems to me have equal claims in the distribution of public employments which is soon to be made.

> Very respectfully &c.
> W. C. BRYANT.

MANUSCRIPT: LC (copy, not in Bryant's hand).

1. A letter from the Office of the Historian, United States Department of State, dated July 21, 1981, reports that "A Check of the *List(s) of Diplomatic and Consular Officers of the United States* indicates that Edward A. Stansbury of New York [719.1] did not receive a consular appointment during the years 1861–1869."

1202.   *To* Abraham Lincoln

New York   Feb   25   1861.

Sir

The friends of Hiram Barney Esquire of this city are about to ask of you his appointment as Collector of Customs for this port. As one of that number I take this method of bearing my testimony to his merits and qualifications.[1] Mr. Barney seems to me uncommonly well fitted by capacity, by mental constitution and personal character for the place. As a man of business, he has established himself in the confidence of the community; his profession which is that of the law has not made him captious or too observant of technicalities; his judgement is fair and equitable, his temper kind and obliging and in the performance of all private and public duties he is strictly and deeply conscientious. I am sure that the general voice of the community if he should be appointed will applaud the selection of so fine and competent a man. As a politician [he] has been uncommonly active and efficient in the support of principles which we deem essential to the well-being of the Union. He was one of the earliest members of the Republican party and never faltered in his fidelity to its doctrines.—

[unsigned]

MANUSCRIPT: NYPL–GR (draft) ADDRESS: To the Hon   Abraham Lincoln, &c.

1. Appointed Collector of Customs at New York in March 1861, Barney served in that office until 1864. See Letters 1209, 1463.

1203.   *To* Robert C. Waterston

Roslyn   February 26. 1861.

My dear Mr. Waterston.

A day or two since I sent under cover to you, by express a copy of my Discourse on Irving for Mr. Winthrop.[1]

I am certainly much obliged to you for the interest you took in procuring my name a place on the list of honorary members of the Massachusetts Historical Society. As a general rule I am, as you may suppose, indifferent to the compliment of being made a member of any literary or learned society but the Massachusetts Historical is so sparing of its honors that it is a great matter to obtain them—it is somewhat like the French Academy, a society of the few. I hope there is no suspicion that I wished to remind them of my merits when I sent my Discourse to be put in their collection.

What an interesting occasion that was when their eldest member reached the close of his ninetieth year, and they celebrated it as they would have celebrated the centennial anniversary of the foundation of their Society! One who has lived so long as Mr. Quincy and so happily preserved his faculties, is an Historical Society in himself, a living record of the annals of more than two generations. I hope he will see the dissentions of that republic of which he saw the birth, happily composed. It would be too short a period for the life of the United States, if it should begin and end within the lifetime of even the oldest living men.

I have given a paragraph to your proposed lectures—as you may have seen, in the Evening Post.[2] I do not know any body who could treat the subject so well. Some who have talent enough for it, have not the taste and the knowledge; others who have both these are wanting in eloquence and literary skill. In your profession I know of nobody who has given these subjects the study that you have done—nor indeed in any other of the learned professions. Your review of Leslie's Autobiography I thank you for;[3] it is written as you might be expected to write such things, in a vein of unaffected enthusiasm, which carries along the reader delightfully.

I am here at Roslyn, amidst the sunshine streaming into the naked woods and lying on the russet banks of greensward while the seagulls are shrieking over our little harbor—yet I cannot shut out politics but look every day with impatience for the arrival of the mail, that I may see what the madmen of the South propose to do next, or what new folly they have already committed. I hope the time will soon arrive when I shall not care a pin whether the mail comes or not.

I lay myself as the Spaniards say, at the feet of your excellent Señora. My wife desires her love to you both.

> I am dear sir
> Most truly yours
> WM. C. BRYANT.

MANUSCRIPT: Scripps College Library ADDRESS: Revd R. C. Waterston.

1. See Letter 1189.
2. This notice has not been located in the *EP*.
3. Charles Robert Leslie (1794–1859), British-born American painter. His *Autobiographical Recollections* . . . (Boston and London, 1860) was the subject of an unsigned notice, perhaps by Waterston, in the *North American Review*, 91 (October 1866), 562–563.

1204. *To* Edward E. Richards[1]

New York March 1st, 1861.

My young friend.

I have looked among my letters, but find nothing from "great men" which I can send you. It is not often that I trouble that class with letters, and they rarely give themselves the trouble to write to me; the consequence is that I have scarcely any thing from them which I do not wish to keep, and what I can spare is taken from me immediately by autograph collectors near home.

> I am
> truly yours
> WM. C. BRYANT.

MANUSCRIPT: University of Chicago Library ADDRESS: Mr. Edwd E. Richards.

1. Unidentified.

1205. *To* Abraham Lincoln

Roslyn, Long Island
March 4th. 1861.

My dear sir.

At the desire of the Rev^d. Samuel R. Ely, who is about to visit Washington, I take the liberty of giving him this introduction to you. Mr. Ely is the pastor of the Presbyterian Church in this place, where I have my country residence. He is a highly respectable member of his profession, and much esteemed here, where he has distinguished himself by his useful and disinterested services.

I am, dear sir,
very truly yours
WM. C. BRYANT.

MANUSCRIPT: LC ADDRESS: His Ex^y. A. Lincoln.

1206. *To* Messrs. J. B. Lippincott & Co.

New York   March 4th, 1861.

Gentlemen.

I am glad to know that you are about to republish in this country, by an arrangement with the Messrs Chambers, their new Encyclopedia.[1] The reputation of these publishers, and the many excellent works, designed for popular reading, which we have had from them, would naturally lead us to expect the most careful arrangements on their part for making such a work all that it purports to be—"a dictionary of universal knowledge for the people." In looking over the first volumes with this expectation I have not been disappointed. It is just such a book of reference as every man has occasion for. The different articles have the appearance of being furnished by writers possessing the most accurate knowledge of the subjects of which they treat; they are as free from abstruseness as may be, consistently with scientific exactness, and without being meagre, they are admirably concise.

I am, gentlemen,
respectfully yours
WM. C. BRYANT.

MANUSCRIPT: HSPa ADDRESS: To Messrs J. B. Lippincott & Co.

1. *Chambers's Encyclopedia: A Dictionary of Universal Knowledge*, 10 vols. (Philadelphia: J. B. Lippincott & Co., 1860–1869).

1207.   *To* Abraham Lincoln

[New York? *c*March 5, 1861]

The name of the Hon. Bradford R   Wood of Albany will be placed
before you as that of a gentleman worthy to be appointed our Minister to
the Prussian Court. Mr. Wood has already distinguished himself in public
life, having had a seat in Congress of which he was a useful and able member. He is a man of the purest character, of the most conscientious regard
to the rights of others and of an independent judgment and as might be inferred from this, an original Republican. The appointment of Mr. Wood
to the station which is asked for him would be a creditable one to the
administration.[1]

I am, sir,
respectfully yours.—
[unsigned]

MANUSCRIPT: NYPL–GR (draft).

1. Bradford Ripley Wood (1800–1889, Union 1824), a New York lawyer and Democratic member of Congress, 1845–1847, was a founder of the Republican Party in 1856.
From 1861 to 1865 he served as United States minister to Denmark. *BDAC.*

1208.   *To* Robert C. Winthrop

New York   March 9th.   1861.

My dear sir.

I thank you for the kind terms in which you speak of my Discourse,
and I place your letter among the favorable testimonies which I most
value. Allow me, at the same time, to make my acknowledgements for the
part you took in conferring upon me the honorary membership of the
Massachusetts Historical Society.[1] I am fully aware of the value of the
distinction, and only wonder that it should have been bestowed on one
who had done so little to earn it.

I am, dear sir,
truly yours,
WM. C. BRYANT.

MANUSCRIPT: MHS ADDRESS: Hon   R. C. Winthrop.

1. See 1189.4. Winthrop had written Bryant from Boston on February 27 (NYPL–
BG) praising his *Discourse on Irving* and reporting Bryant's unanimous election to replace Irving as an honorary member of the Massachusetts Historical Society.

1209.   *To* Hiram Barney

New York   March 11, 1861.

Dear sir.

You must not let the noise made by a certain set of men dishearten
you. Take the office and it will subside immediately.[1] Your friends rely

upon you to carry out the original intention. In that there was no mistake; the mistake will be committed if you recede now. You must not back out; if you do the public service will suffer.

Yours truly
W   C   Bryant

Manuscript: HEHL address: Hiram Barney Esq endorsed: Wm Cullen Bryant / March 11/61 / — / Urging me to allow / my name to be / used for the / Collectorship.

1. See 1202.1.

1210.   *To* John H. Gourlie

New York March 12th 1861—

Dear Mr. Gourlie.

I should like to have the Sketch Club at No. 82 East 16th Street next Friday. Cannot this be done? If so will you be kind enough to let me know —and then issue the notices?[1] —It would be a real convenience for me to have my turn this week.

Yours very truly
Wm   C   Bryant.

Manuscript: University of Pennsylvania Library address: Jn° H   Gourlie Esq. docketed: W   C   Bryant / 12 March 1861.

1. This meeting was held on March 14, 1861 at Fanny Godwin's town house. Gourlie had been secretary of the Sketch Club since 1851. Information from James T. Callow.

1211.   *To* Orville Dewey

New York March 13th 1861.

My dear Doctor.

Somebody has written to a neighbor of mine at Roslyn desiring to know where to find the fastenings for window blinds which I got for you. They are the Mackeral Blind Fastenings, and I got them at the shop of A. T. Russell No. 137 Fulton Street. The purchaser must say whether they are for a wood or a brick house, for there is a little difference in their make on that account.

My wife desires me to say that it was her intention before this to have replied to Mrs. Deweys letter—that she is ashamed to have neglected it so long, and other expressions of penitence, which I hope will be accepted, as intended, instead of a letter. The *Frau* is tolerably well for her—better, I think, than she was last winter. She has passed most of the season at Roslyn, where we have been fussing with certain improvements as we call them—a change of the road, and an enlargement and embellishment of the cottage in which Mrs. Kirkland lived. The furnace which we have in the house is Leed's Water Furnace, and it brings in such a volume of new air from without, blowing a constant gale from the mouth of the register, that nobodys health suffers from foul air.

I want to come to Boston and would go this minute, but for these rascally improvements. Here in New York and even in Roslyn though there to a less degree I am teased with constant applications to help people to offices under the new administration. I want to run away from them, but the Paddies and the carpenters and masons keep me here in spite of myself. I have promised my old friends Judge Phillips[1] and Mr. Dana a visit, and it shall go hard but I give these office beggars the slip when they little think of it.[2]

Your sermon on the Times—the thanksgiving or fast day sermon was it?—I saw it in the Christian Inquirer was well thought out and nobly said.[3]

Mrs. Bryant and Julia desire their love to Mrs. Dewey and you. They and Fanny's family are well. Kind regards to your *Señora esposa*.

ever yours
WM. C. BRYANT.

P.S. I am ready to tear out my hair. The Sketch Club meets tomorrow evening—Friday—and I knew it yesterday only—and failed to write immediately.[4] It meets at Fanny's No 82 East 16th St.

W C B.

MANUSCRIPT: NYPL–GR ADDRESS: Dr. O. Dewey.—

1. Boston lawyer and former jurist Willard Phillips; see Vol. I, 13–14; 479.2. Phillips visited the Bryants at Roslyn the following summer. Phillips to Bryant, August 1, 1861, NYPL–BG.

2. Despite his apparent reluctance, Bryant recommended a considerable number of candidates for office during the early months of the Lincoln administration. His reasons for so doing are suggested in Letter 1213.

3. Dewey had left retirement in 1857 to take temporary charge of the New South Church in Boston. His pastorate there ended in 1861–1862, and the historic building, erected in 1717, was torn down in 1868.

4. Dewey replied on March 15 (NYPL–BG) that he was pleased to learn the Sketch Club was not dead—"I had given it up"— and would gladly come to New York on purpose to see "those dear old fellows."

1212. *To* Gideon Welles[1]

New York   March 16. 1861.

My dear sir.

The bearer of this is Edward Walker Esqr. of this city, one of the firm of E. Walker & Sons, bookbinders in this city.[2] He has desired of me an introduction to some persons of influence at Washington, and as my acquaintances there are far from numerous I have taken the liberty to give him this note to you. His errand to the seat of government is a business one—to obtain some portion of the government bookbinding. He is a highly respectable man both personally and in his vocation, in which he has acquired a deserved eminence.

Yours truly
W. C. BRYANT.

MANUSCRIPT: NYHS ADDRESS: Hon   Gideon Welles / Secretary of the Navy.

1. In the face of strong opposition from his choice as Secretary of State, William H. Seward, President Lincoln had nominated Welles on March 15 as Secretary of the Navy. Nevins, *Emergence of Lincoln*, II, 452–455.

2. This firm was then "notable" among several such engaged in edition binding in New York. Hellmut Lehmann-Haupt, *The Book in America: A History of the Making and Selling of Books in the United States* (New York: Bowker, 1952), p. 153.

1213.   *To* Gideon Welles

New York, March 24, 1861.

. . . I am sure that you will not take my frankness ill when I say that numbers of our political friends here are perplexed to explain on what principle of fairness to the different classes of the Republican party the appointments to office have thus far been made by the present administration. The men of democratic derivation have been excluded from office, as if by design. The exceptions to this remark seem to be of those men who have made themselves speedily acceptable to Mr. Weed and Mr. Seward. We have great apprehensions that the remaining appointments may be made in the same manner. I write to you as an old political and personal friend . . . to inform you of the feeling which has been awaked here; assured that so far as it is just, your exertions and influence will be used to allay it. I have written more fully to Mr. Chase on this subject, inasmuch as the important nominations for this city are to be made from his department.[1] I have no personal wish to be gratified in regard to any of them, desiring only to see them bestowed upon honest and competent men and with such a regard to equity in their distribution that no division of the Party will have reason to complain. It will require however, a great number of appointments to be conferred upon our wing of the Party in order to make it clear that no injustice was intended them. . . . I am as much surprised as any body at the character of the appointments and have no desire to conceal my opinion that a grievous mistake has been made. . . .

MANUSCRIPT: Unrecovered TEXT (*partial*): Paul C. Richards, Templeton, Massachusetts, Catalogue No. 73, Item 171, October 1977.

1. This letter is unrecovered, but a reply from Chase to Bryant on April 10, 1861 (NYPL–BG) indicates that in it Bryant had urged the appointment of a New Yorker named Briggs to government office.

1214. *To* Frances F. Bryant

Cambridge   Friday morning
April 12th   1861.

Dear Frances,

    I have told every body till now that I should go back to New York on Monday morning; but now I have yielded to Mr. Phillips's persuasions to remain till Tuesday morning. Mr. Parsons the law professor[1] is very desirous to have me at his house on Monday and my host almost insists that I shall stay. I have been into Boston to see the Waterstons and Danas and Deweys. The Danas I saw both yesterday and the day before. They are all well, except Mr. Dana who is suffering with the influenza. I am to go to their house today and stay till Saturday when I come back to this place. The Deweys I did not find in on Wednesday and yesterday Mr. Dewey came out here to find me out also—so I was revenged. I shall try to see them today. Yesterday Mr. Waterston, on whom I had called the day before, and found him and Mrs. Waterston both well—took me to a meeting of the Historical Society where I saw a good many of the notables of Boston.[2] I must try to get to Chester Square again today or tomorrow, or perhaps Monday. Mrs. Howe and Mrs. Ware[3] I have yet to see. The days seem inconveniently short, and I am afraid I shall not get to Batchelder and Black's or Black and Batchelder's whichever it be.[4] On Wednesday Mr. & Mrs. Sparks[5] with Mr. Pickering the Reporter of the Supreme Court[6] dined here, and yesterday Dr. Palfrey, who has just got the commission of postmaster for Boston.[7] Tomorrow we dine with Professor Gray the Botanist.[8] Last evening we went to Mr. Spark's—a little tea party— There you have the journal of what I have been about, though I believe I have not set everything down in chronological order. You may suppose it was with a little reluctance that I changed my intention to return on Monday, but when I thought of the office seekers who are waiting for me I was reconciled to the change. A great many inquiries are made about you and Julia and every body is sorry you did not come—I among the rest.

Ever &c W   C   B.

MANUSCRIPT: NYPL–GR.

    1. Theophilus Parsons; see 94.1.
    2. Among these was evidently Henry Longfellow, who wrote Henry Theodore Tuckerman on April 17, "Bryant has been here; very gentle and pleasant, with his benign aspect and soft blue eyes. He looks like a Prophet of Peace, amid the din of Civil War." Longfellow, *Letters*, IV, 235–236.
    3. Sarah Lydia Robbins Howe, widow of Bryant's early law tutor Samuel Howe (Vol. I, 19; 8.1), and Mary Waterhouse Ware, widow of Rev. William Ware (100.7).
    4. Black and Bachelder, photographers, of 173 Washington Street, Boston. See illustrations.
    5. Jared Sparks; see Vol. I, 16; 110.1, 420.10.

6. Edward Pickering (d. 1876), co-editor with Willard Phillips of a treatise on the law of partnership, and author of *Reports of Cases Argued and Determined in the Supreme Judicial Court of Massachusetts . . . by Octavius Pickering* (Boston, 1833–1862).

7. The historian of Massachusetts, John Gorham Palfrey (1796–1881, Harvard 1815), a Unitarian clergyman and Harvard professor, had also been a Whig congressman. See Longfellow, *Letters*, IV, 232–233.

8. Asa Gray (266.5) was then Fisher Professor of Natural History at Harvard.

1215.   *To* Frances F. Bryant

Boston   April 12, 1861
Friday morning.

Dear Frances.

I wrote you this morning from Cambridge where I have been staying with Judge Phillips,—giving you an account of all I have been doing since I arrived—and left the letter on the table. It will go probably tomorrow. I am to stay here at Mr. Danas till tomorrow—when I shall go back to Cambridge— They have persuaded me to stay till Tuesday morning next, when I shall set out for New York D. V.[1] Every body is well —All ask for you, and wonder why you and Julia did not come—

Yours ever
W. C. B.

MANUSCRIPT: NYPL–GR.

1. *Deo volente* ("God willing").

1216.   *To* Miss Newbold[1]

New York, April 17th. 1861.

Madam.

I have no sample of the handwriting of Washington Irving in my possession, nor can I inform you where to procure one. Perhaps Mr. L. G. Clark the editor of the Knickerbocker, if he has not given away every thing of the kind might furnish you with one.[2]

I am, madam,
respectfully yours.
WM. C. BRYANT

MANUSCRIPT: BLR ADDRESS: Miss Newbold.

1. Unidentified.

2. Lewis Gaylord Clark (392.1) had published many of Irving's writings in the *Knickerbocker,* which owed its name to one of Irving's best known characters, Diedrich Knickerbocker.

1217. *To* Hiram Barney

New York, April 18, 1861

[Dear Sir?]

T. M. Burt Esq. of Kinderhook[1] desires the place of Cashier in the New York Custom House. He is a most worthy man, laborious, exact, upright, faithful, a democrat, in better times of the Silas Wright[2] School, an original free-soiler, and a Republican of the genuine stamp. He has done good service in the warfare lately crowned with victory.

If you appoint him to the place he asks you will bestow the office on a very competent man and gratify numbers of his friends.

Yours truly
W. C. BRYANT.

MANUSCRIPT: HEHL ADDRESS: H. Barney Esqre.

    1. Burt is unidentified, except as described below.
    2. Former New York Democratic governor and United States senator. See 388.7.

1218. *To* Solomon Lincoln Jr.[1]

New York   April 18, 1861.

Dear sir.

I beg to make, through you, my best acknowledgments to the Literary Committee of the Phi Beta Kappa Society for the compliment paid me in the invitation to deliver the next annual Oration before the Society. Various reasons oblige me respectfully to decline it.[2]

I am, sir,
truly yours
WM. C. BRYANT.

MANUSCRIPT: HCL ADDRESS: Solomon Lincoln jr. Esq. / Corresponding Secretary of the / Phi Beta Kappa Society / Cambridge / Massachusetts. POSTMARK: NE[W] YO[RK] / APR / 18 / 1[861].

    1. Solomon Lincoln, Jr. (1838–1907, Harvard 1861?), was later a public orator and historian of the town of Hingham, Massachusetts.
    2. This would have marked the fortieth anniversary of Bryant's delivery of the Phi Beta Kappa poem at Harvard College in 1821. See Letters 71, 72. Lincoln's letter of invitation is unrecovered.

1219. *To* Abraham Lincoln

New York   April 20, 1861.

Sir.

The bearer of this letter is Dr. J. Wynne,[1] a most respectable gentleman of southern origin, but now resident in this city, who is going southward on an errand of peace to which he is prompted by his love of our common country. May I ask for him the kind reception which his character and purpose deserve.

> I am, sir,
>   most respectfully yours
>   WM. C. BRYANT.

MANUSCRIPT: LC ADDRESS: To Mr. Lincoln / President of the United States. ENDORSED: Having known Dr. Wynne / most favourably, I concur in / the above. W^m. Curtis Noyes.[2]

1. James Wynne (1814–1871), of Utica, New York, had practiced medicine in Baltimore before moving to New York City during the 1840s, where he had published several reports on public hygiene, the Asiatic Cholera, and legal medicine. *ACAB.*
2. William Curtis Noyes (1805–1864), a prominent New York lawyer, had been associated with David D. Field in 1857 on the codification of New York laws. See Letter 1286.

1220.   *To* Leonice M. S. Moulton

New York   April 24. 1861.

My dear Mrs. Moulton.

I got your letter yesterday morning, and when I came up town in the afternoon I showed it to Julia, who, I learned, had already received a letter from you, and had attended to your request by writing to Josephine.[1]

I wonder not that you should be concerned for your daughter and her little ones. You should, however, reflect that women and children are not in the same danger at such times as these, that men are. Their weakness and defencelessness are respected, and their safety cared for, even by the most excited and ferocious. It is very right in you to hasten her departure for the north, but I think that in any event she is much safer than her husband.

It is not improbable that Baltimore will be occupied by the government troops. It will be if the administration acts with proper energy and some reference to what the people expect of it. There is no measure which can now be taken too strong or decided for the public feeling here and all over the free states.

(I perceive that martial law has been proclaimed in Baltimore, and this will bring about a certain degree of order. Military rule is better than mob rule.[2])

In the hope that you will soon embrace your children safe in your quiet home at Roslyn

> I am, dear Madam,
>   truly yours
>   WM. C. BRYANT.

MANUSCRIPT: NYPL–Bryant–Moulton Letters ADDRESS: Mrs. L. M   S. Moulton.

1. Mrs. Moulton's daughter Josephine, Mrs. John Stewart (965.1), lived in Baltimore.
2. From April 19 to 24 pro-southern mobs rioted at Baltimore, driving hundreds of Union loyalists from the city. Nevins, *War for the Union*, I, 81–84.

1221.   *To* Robert Balmanno[1]

New York   April 29, 1861.

My dear sir

I thank you and Mrs. Balmanno for the moss roses and chestnut trees from Chatsworth. They are already in the soil of Roslyn, at my place in the country, where I hope they will not pine for the more uniform climate of Derbyshire.[2]

> I am, dear sir,
> truly yours,
> WM. C. BRYANT.

MANUSCRIPT: NYPL–Ford Collection ADDRESS: R. Balmanno Esq.

1. Robert Balmanno (d. 1861) was an employee of the New York Custom House. When he died later that year Bryant tried to secure his job for his son Alexander.
2. In June 1845 Bryant had visited Chatsworth, home of the dukes of Devonshire, in Derbyshire, England. See Letters 539, 540.

1222.   *To* Hiram Barney

New York   May 9th   1861.

My dear sir.

I cannot help thinking of the state of distress in which the Bleeckers are plunged. To be entirely without occupation and without means of subsistence is certainly a hard case, and such I understand is their situation. Mr. A. Lispenard Bleecker, the son in law of Anthony J.[1] has I understand crept into some corner where he has received his father in law, and where they are trying to support existence with scarce any means for the present and little hope from the future.

I write this in sincere compassion for their situation, and only wish I had the appointment of weigher which is what the young man asks for, at my disposal that I might get the idea of their destitution out of my mind. This not being my good luck I can only again present their case to your notice.

> Yours truly
> W. C BRYANT

MANUSCRIPT: HEHL ADDRESS: H. Barney Esq. ENDORSED: 174 / W. C. Bryant / May 9.

1. Anthony J. Bleecker (1799–1884), New York real estate auctioneer and former Democrat, was a founder of the Republican Party and in 1856 a candidate for mayor of New York City. Perhaps through Bryant's intercession, he served as an assistant in-

ternal revenue inspector during the Civil War. *EP*, January 18, 1884. His son-in-law has not been further identified.

1223.   *To* John Howard Bryant

Roslyn   May 10   1861

Dear Brother,

I was in town yesterday and got your letter[1] which Mr. Henderson after we had consulted together answered.

I am sorry not to be able to do better by you. If I had not laid out all the money I have, and made arrangement for paying out what you owe the firm I might have taken your debt to myself. But we have engaged to pay money to Mr. Bigelow of whom Mr. Godwin has bought a third part of the Evening Post[2] and cannot do without the money due from yourself and Mr. Dee.[3] It was supposed that the note would without question be paid at maturity. I hope the sixty days will answer your purpose.

As to coming out, if I were to come alone I could for a day; but Frances comes with me and it is her whole convenience I must consult. I can only say now that we mean to set out sometime in the beginning of week after next, that is probably on the 21st (Tuesday) or the 22nd or 23rd—that we shall stop at Rochester the first night, and the next night somewhere else, and get to Chicago in three days, and Princeton in four.

So if you see us on the last day or last but one of [the] week afterward, it will be as early as we can expect to be there.

Perhaps I may write again to say more precisely what day we set out.

Kind regards to all

Yours affectionately

W. C. BRYANT

MANUSCRIPT: Mrs. Mildred Bryant Kussmaul, Brockton, Massachusetts ADDRESS: John H. Bryant.

1. Unrecovered.
2. In December 1860 John Bigelow had expressed a wish to sell his share in the *EP* properties and devote himself to writing and other activities. Bryant and the third partner, Isaac Henderson, agreed to take Parke Godwin into the firm, letting him work out his debt to Bigelow from his share of the profits. The transfer of stock was effective on January 16, 1861, with the firm of William C. Bryant & Co. underwriting Godwin's debt of $111,457.06. MS Bill of Sale and Articles of Agreement in NYPL–BG; Bigelow, *Retrospections*, I, 319–325; *EP*, January 30, 1861.
3. See Letter 1148.

1224.   *To* Abraham Lincoln

New York   May 14, 1861.

To the President.

Samuel J. Wood Esqre. of Peekskill in this state is one of those who suffered the loss of every thing they had by the destruction of Greytown.

This was the act of our own government, and Mr. Wood has a fair claim for reparation on the public treasury. Hitherto, however, he has asked for justice from the government without success.[1]

While he is prosecuting his claim before Congress he must live and he desires to receive some office which shall give him a subsistence till Congress finds time to listen to his case and grant him the indemnity which the country fairly owes him. It seems to me that this is a very reasonable desire. Mr. Wood is an honest and worthy as well as an ill-used man and has a fairer claim on the patronage of the administration, than most of those who solicit it. I therefore cheerfully recommend his case and his application to the favorable notice of the Executive.

I am, sir,

very respectfully yours

WM   C   BRYANT

MANUSCRIPT: University of Rochester Library.

1. Greytown, or San Juan del Norte, Nicaragua, was in dispute between the United States and Great Britain as a center of trade, and as the potential Atlantic terminus of an isthmian canal. On July 13, 1854, after the American minister to Central America, Solon Borland, had been slightly injured by mob action, the commander of an American warship demanded reparation. When it was refused, he warned the population of Greytown to flee, and then destroyed the town by gunfire. Samuel Eliot Morison, *The Oxford History of the American People* (New York: Oxford University Press, 1965), p. 581. Wood has not been further identified.

1225.   *To* Leonice M. S. Moulton

Roslyn   May 17th 1861.

My dear Mrs. Moulton.

I thank you very much for the pretty fruit knife which you have been so kind as to send me. You have made it impossible for me to pare or slice an apple, which is what I am always doing, without thinking to whom I am indebted for the means of doing it in a becoming manner.

As I may not see you before you sail for Europe you will allow me to take this opportunity of wishing you a prosperous voyage, pleasant journeys on land and a safe and happy return to your country and home.

I am, dear Madam

truly yours

WM. C. BRYANT.

MANUSCRIPT: NYPL–Bryant–Moulton Letters ADDRESS: Mrs. L. M. S. Moulton.

1226.   *To* Fanny Bryant Godwin

Princeton   Illinois

Saturday   May 25, 1861.

Dear Fanny.

I write in some haste to say that we are here quite well, having arrived yesterday afternoon at about half past two. Your mother bore the journey remarkably well. The third day we went by rail from Cleveland to Chicago a distance of 345 miles. Mr. Ogden came with a carriage and took us to his house from the Tremont House, and the next morning carried us to the starting place of the Burlington and Quincy Railroad which brought us to Princeton. All our friends here are in their usual health, Austin better than usual and somewhat stouter than usual. Your aunts Louisa and Harriet have been for several weeks at Dr. Hays's water-cure in Cleveland, where they soak their patients comfortably in warm water, and they have come back all the better and quite portly bodies.

The money market here is in a terrible situation. Today nobody will take the notes of an Illinois bank; the people with one consent reject it, and there is nothing else yet in the state. No business can now be done. The produce of the country—such as can be taken to market—is sent to Toledo, in Ohio, where good notes can be had for it. I have talked with John about what he owes you. He must wait for the currency to improve before he can send it to you—there being now no currency whatever. Necessity must soon bring in the notes of other states. He cannot invest the money here better than by lending it at ten per cent which he can do if you wish it.

I hope Mr. Godwin is better before this. Your mother sends her love.

Affectionately yours
WM. C. BRYANT.

P.S. We get the news by telegraph here as early as you do in New York. We have just got the news of Colonel Ellsworths death.[1]

W. C. B.

MANUSCRIPT: NYPL–GR ADDRESS: Mrs. F. B. Godwin.

1. Elmer Ephraim Ellsworth (1837–1861), who had been Lincoln's law clerk briefly before organizing and commanding a New York Zouave regiment, had fallen on May 24 during the occupation of Alexandria, Virginia, by federal troops. He was the first man of note to die in the Civil War. At Lincoln's suggestion, Ellsworth's body lay in state in the East Room of the White House before burial near his birthplace in upstate New York. Nevins, *War for the Union*, I, 145–146.

1227.   *To* Julia S. Bryant

Princeton   Illinois
Saturday, May 25th, 1861.

Dear Julia

We arrived here yesterday at half past two in the afternoon safe and sound after a not unpleasant journey. The second days journey brought us in good season to Cleveland, where we found good quarters in the [Angier?] House. The next morning, rising at four oclock and setting out in the train at five, we reached Chicago, at six in the afternoon having travelled three hundred and forty five miles—the latter part of the day being unpleasantly warm and the car badly ventilated. We got a room up three flights of stairs at the Tremont House, and after tea I called on Mr. Ogden, who immediately came with his carriage and took us to his house. Your mother was a little fatigued but after a good sleep was perfectly restored, and the next morning at half past eight we were at the starting place of the Burlington and Quincy Railway on which we came by a pleasant passage through a rich country to Princeton. Here we found every body well—or as well as usual— Your uncle Austin is particularly well having left off tobacco, and increased somewhat in rotundity. Louisa and Harriet have been passing a few weeks at the water-cure establishment of Dr. Hays at Cleveland, and have returned healthier and stouter. The season is late, but the weather is now soft and warm, and the vegetation makes rapid progress. Princeton has grown a great deal since you were here and is full of shops. But the people can neither sell nor buy for there is no money here now but Illinois money, and nobody will take it—the banks are not obliged to pay specie; and are in so little credit that the people with one consent reject their notes.—

Your mother sends her love.

Yours affectionately
W. C. BRYANT.

P.S. The news by telegraph reaches us here almost as soon as it reaches you. We have just got tiding of Col. Ellsworth's death.

W. C. B.

MANUSCRIPT: NYPL–GR ADDRESS: Miss Julia Bryant.

1228.   *To* John Howard Bryant

New York   June 20, 1861.

Dear Brother.

I got your letter respecting Mr. Mather's proposal yesterday.[1] I can agree to every thing in it except sending out more money to build a house. When I put down $1500— for houses stables and so forth, and $1000— for your house I went to the furthest extent of my means.

If the house can be built out of the rents that are coming in I consent, but otherwise I shall not be able to do any thing in the matter. The times increase the circulation of the Evening Post very largely but cut off the advertisements.

All well. Kind regards to all.

Yours affectionately,
WM   C   BRYANT.

MANUSCRIPT: Chicago Historical Society ADDRESS: Jnº H   Bryant Esq.

1. Letter unrecovered.

1229.   *To* John Howard Bryant

Office of The Evening Post
New York, June 28th. 1861

Dear Brother.

I have your letter of the 24th.[1] I said nothing in my last about moving the Thompson House to higher ground, because I thought that you had concluded to do it, and I had no objection.

Your drafts will be duly honored. The difficulty of sending out money to build a house on the Clark farm I believe I fully explained in my last. If Mr. Mather insists on a house before it can be built with the rents, then I suppose that no arrangement can be made with him.

Cyrus and his wife reached here this morning and go to Roslyn this afternoon. They have been to West Point.

Yours affectionately
W. C. BRYANT.

MANUSCRIPT: WCL ADDRESS: Jn⁰ H   Bryant Esq.

1. Unrecovered.

1230.   *To* G. L. Colton[1]

Roslyn   July 4th, 1861.

Dear sir.

I re-enclose you Mr. Everett's letter which was put into my hands last evening.

It had never entered my thought that I should be asked to preside at the assembly which he was to address and I had made other arrangements for the day. You may not know of my disinclination to place myself in positions of the kind, but it is unaffected— Others preside with more presence of mind and more skill. When Mr. Everett speaks the seat of the Chairman should be filled by some person who to high distinction joins the power of presiding with a dignity worthy of the occasion. You will see therefore that want of respect for Mr. Everett and of admiration for his talents has no place in the motives which have made me decline the honor which has been offered me.[2]

I am, sir,
respectfully yours
WM   C.   BRYANT.

MANUSCRIPT: MHS ADDRESS: G L. Colton Esq.

1. Unidentified.
2. On July 4 Edward Everett spoke to "rapt attention" for two and one-half hours before a large audience at the New York Academy of Music, his topic "The Great Issues Now Before the Country." The meeting's chairman was Judge John Slosson of the New York Supreme Court. *EP*, July 5, 1861.

1231.   *To* Hiram Barney

New York   July 5, 1861.

Dear Mr. Barney.

We do not get the Import and Export Tables at half past two under your administration of the Custom House as the public did under your predecessor. Every body looks for them and nobody gets them till the next morning, they are kept back for the benefit of the morning papers.

What we want is that the old way should be preserved in that the tables should be handed out to all the evening papers as soon as they are prepared and that they should be prepared as seasonably as they were two months ago.

We do not ask for any change of clerks, we only ask that the clerk in office shall be made to know his duty.

Your truly
W. C. BRYANT.

MANUSCRIPT: HEHL ADDRESS: H. Barney Esq. ENDORSED: Enclosed is a letter / from Mr. Wm C. Bry / ant, dated July 5th / 1861 / Complaining of the / Import & Export Clerk / In neglecting to make / out his Report in / season.

1232.   *To* Hiram Barney

Office of The Evening Post,
New York, July[1] 7th   1861.

My dear sir.

Your note of the   [2] was duly received. We desire no change in the time of publishing the commercial statistics of this port. We only ask that the time of publication may be continued substantially as it has been for some years past.

The Evening Express and the Journal of Commerce in their afternoon editions, have on Friday published the statement of the Dry Goods Imports and on Saturday the General Merchandize Imports, and on Tuesday the Export Table. The figures have always been ready by 3 o'clock P. M. an hour convenient for us in the future, and which we should be glad to have continued.

The figures are not now published either in the Journal of Commerce or the Express, at three o'clock P. M. as they have been heretofore for some years. They are we have reason to believe, purposely kept back by the clerk under pretense of making them more complete by adding the later imports of the day—an evident trick to delay their publication. The custom of the desk has been to make them up in time for distribution among the newspapers by two o'clock P. M. and no material interest is promoted by adding another days figures.

You thus perceive that we ask no *change*. We ask that no *change* shall *be* made to favor a particular newspaper or class of newspapers, but that this important information heretofore obtained by the Express and by the Journal of Commerce at three o'clock in the afternoon for their later editions be now furnished at the hitherto accustomed hour to the Evening Press and the Morning Press simultaneously to be used by them in their afternoon editions which they all publish.

I am sir

very respectfully &c

WM. C. BRYANT.

MANUSCRIPT: HEHL ADDRESS: To Hiram Barney Esq. Collector of the / Port of New York.

1. Bryant mistakenly wrote "June."
2. The date is left blank: Barney's note is unrecovered.

1233. *To* Abraham Lincoln

New York   July 16, 1861.

Dear sir.

The bearer of this note is Ogden Haggerty Esqre.[1] who desires an introduction to you.

Mr. Haggerty is well known and eminent in the commercial world here. He ranks among our most intelligent and worthy citizens and I take pleasure in bearing this testimony to his personal merit.

I am, sir,

very respectfully yrs

WM. C. BRYANT.

MANUSCRIPT: LC ADDRESS: To Abraham Lincoln / President of the United States.

1. Ogden Haggerty (1810?–1875) was a New York auctioneer with offices at 279 Broadway. New York *Times* obituary, September 1, 1875; *Trow's New York City Directory* for 1861 (New York: Trow [1860]). There is no indication that Haggerty, who remained in business in New York until his retirement because of ill health in 1867, received any appointment under the Lincoln administration.

1234. *To* Leonice M. S. Moulton

New York August 8 1861.

My dear Mrs. Moulton.

Your letter was read by us all with great interest.[1] It was very kind of you to think of us when you had so many interesting objects claiming your attention. Your habit of close and attentive observation, and your tenacious memory will have made your mind, before you return to us a perfect treasury of facts and images to which you will ever after recur with pleasure. We were very glad to hear that you and your party were making your tour in so pleasant a manner, and that you in particular had been so little disappointed in what you expected from it.

If you are like the rest of the world, however the time will come when you will feel a certain satiety of interesting sights—a certain feeling somewhat akin to loathing when you come to a place in which there is a great deal to see. You will not I am sure yield to this feeling; you will faithfully see what is to be seen as a matter of duty; and you will always be glad to have done so, but at the same time, you will feel a high degree of satisfaction, as I once heard an Englishman say he did, when you happen to get to one of those charming quiet places where there is nothing at all to see.

Meantime, I suppose you are not quite indifferent to what is going on in your country and in the neighborhood of your home. The newspapers I doubt not keep you informed of public events and your husband of what does not get into the newspapers. He seems to be passing the summer pleasantly; he looks healthy and fresh and reads the newspapers as regularly as ever. With the Vandeventers he is agreeably domiciled, and reads the newspapers to the doctor's lady.[2]

At our own place there is little change. I have been going on with my changes which are now nearly completed. The public are settling down into perfect acquiescence in the alteration of the road, though one or two persons grumbled a little at first but now I believe nothing whatever is said.[3]

You will see that I have written the second page of the letter upside down, but you are too sharp to be puzzled with such a misplacement. To proceed: our island and all this neighborhood have suffered cruelly from a long continued drought. The roads have been deep with dust, the fields parched and red and many young trees newly planted have perished. This morning there has been a little rain, the first liberal shower that we have had for two months, and we hope it is the beginning of a series that will fill our cisterns again, which have been empty for weeks. I suppose you may have heard of the accident which happened to Mr. Henry Thorn, last year one of the Street Commissioners.[4] He was in a store at Lakeville when a gun which his son had loaded and placed against the door fell by accident and was discharged. The charge was received in both his legs. One was amputated and he died of lockjaw.

The war occupies every body's thoughts. The women take a special interest in it. They are our most zealous patriots; they will hear of no compromises or patchings up of the difference between the North and the South. They make [haversacks?], they make shirts for the wounded in the hospitals; they send on boxes of jellies and other little comforts for the sick. Roslyn does her part in these benevolent doings.

I have here written you a dull kind of letter. It seems to me that I have sometimes done better. Make my regards to Mr. Cairns and the rest of your party. Tell Mr. Ordronaux that I have his letter[5] and thank him for the attention he gave to my business, which was afterwards properly completed. I left Mrs. Bryant and Julia this morning in their usual health, as well as Mrs. Godwin's family, with the exception of Minna who had some temporary indisposition. You are just upon the threshhold of your travels and I suppose do not give any thought to the subject of your return. I only fear that you may find so many things to attract you from place to place that we shall not see you till another summer.

Yours very truly
WM   C   BRYANT.

MANUSCRIPT: Amherst College Library ADDRESS: à Madame / Madame L. M. S. Moulton / aux soins de Messrs John Munroe & Cie / No   5 Rue de la Paix / *Paris* / France ENDORSED: Rue Scribe / 1861.

1. Unrecovered.

2. Dr. and Mrs. Vandeventer have not been further identified, except that Bryant's frequent subsequent references to them in letters to his wife and Julia suggest that they were nearby neighbors.

3. These are the changes outlined in Letters 1172 and 1211. See also Goddard, *Roslyn Harbor*, p. 39.

4. Not further identified.

5. Unrecovered.

1235.   *To* James T. Fields

New York   August 9th   1861.

Dear Mr. Fields.

My brother, John H. Bryant, has composed some verses which if they suit your purpose, he would be glad to see in the Atlantic Monthly, and which I send you with this note.

He has desired me to offer them, and as you see I have sent you them in a copy which I have made, in order that if you reject them, I might have the original to return to him. If you do not print the lines, throw the copy among your waste paper.[1]

I am, sir,
very truly yours
WM. C. BRYANT.

MANUSCRIPT: UVa ADDRESS: James T. Fields Esqre.

1. No verses identifiable as by John Howard Bryant have been located in the *Atlantic Monthly* during this period.

1236.   *To* Salmon P. Chase

New York   August 20, 1861.

My dear sir.

At the desire of the bearer J. H. Hammond Esq.[1] I give him this letter
of introduction to you. He comes recommended to me by one of our truest
and most upright men, as a person ardently devoted to the Union and desirous of contributing his efforts to its service, for which he possesses some
peculiar advantages, having though a native of New York lived many years
at the south and having been educated at a southern literary institution.
He has left California where of late years he has resided, with a view of
taking some part in the struggle for the preservation of the Union. In this
work he is willing to act in any capacity for which he may be found best
fitted. I have no doubt you will readily give him such counsels as his case
may require and point out the best way of employing himself in the service
of his country.

I am, sir,
truly yours
WM   C   BRYANT

MANUSCRIPT: HSPa ADDRESS: Hon S. P. Chase ENDORSED: *Wm Cullen Bryant* / New
York   Aug   20   1861 / Introducing *J. H. Hammond* Esq.

1. Unidentified, except as described below.

1237.   *To* Gideon Welles

New York   Aug. 20th. 1861.

My dear sir.

Allow me to introduce to your acquaintance J. H. Hammond Esqre. a
native of this city, educated at the South, and for some time past a resident
of California. He has left San Francisco with the desire of serving his
country in this emergency which he is willing to do in almost any capacity.
I have the assurance of one of the truest men in New York, an old democrat, and a Republican of the present day that he is a patriot and a friend
to the Union, and possesses qualifications for being of service to his interests. His knowledge of the South, its people and its country seem to
give him peculiar advantages in some important respects. I commend him
to your favorable regards.

I am, dear sir,
truly yours
WM   C   BRYANT

P.S. If you have time to question Mr. Hammond I am persuaded that he
can give you some valuable information concerning matters in California
of which it might be well for the administration to be apprised.

W. C. B.

MANUSCRIPT: NYHS ADDRESS: Hon   G. Welles.

1238. *To* John M. Forbes[1]

Office of the Evening Post,
New York, August 21, 1861.

My dear Sir,

It does not seem to me at all indiscreet or imprudent to make the change in the Cabinet which you suggest.[2] Indeed, I think that Mr. Cameron's retirement would, instead of being impolitic, be the most politic thing that could be done, by way of giving firmness to public opinion and strengthening the administration with the people. The dissatisfaction here is as great as with you, and I hear that at Washington it is expressed by everybody, except Cameron's special friends and favorites, in the strongest terms. If I am rightly informed, there is nothing done by him with the promptness, energy, and decision which the times demand, without his being in a manner forced to it by the other members of the Cabinet, or the President. A man who wants to make a contract with the government for three hundred mules, provided he be a Pennsylvanian, can obtain access to him, when a citizen of East Tennessee, coming as the representative of the numerous Union population of that region, is denied. There are bitter complaints, too, of Cameron's disregard of his appointments and engagements in such cases as that I have mentioned.

Mr. Lincoln must know, I think, that Cameron is worse than nothing in the Cabinet, and a strong representation concerning his unpopularity and unacceptableness, of which he may not know, may lead him to take the important resolution of supplying his place with a better man. I do not think the newspapers are the place to discuss the matter, but I make no secret of my opinion.[3]

I am, dear sir, truly yours,

WM. C. BRYANT.

P.S. I open my letter to say another word on the subject of yours. It does not appear to me that H.[4] would be the man for the War Department, for the reason that he might give us trouble on the slavery question. Cameron has managed that part of our relations with the seceding States very badly, and I feel H. would do no better. He would do very well in the place of Smith;[5] but with the exception of making a place for him, it might not be of much consequence whether Smith were retained or not, though he adds no strength to the Cabinet. Some here talk of requiring the dismissal of Seward, but I fear this would be asking more than it is possible to get, and might endanger the success of the scheme for getting rid of Cameron.

W. C. B.

MANUSCRIPT: Unrecovered TEXT: Forbes, *Letters and Recollections*, I, 236–237.

1. In the spring of 1857, shortly before sailing for Europe, Bryant made the acquaintance of the Boston financier and railroad builder John Murray Forbes (1813–

1898). A former Whig, Forbes was a strong supporter of the Lincoln administration and the Union cause. See Forbes to Bryant, July 25, 1859, NYPL–BG.

2. Apparently this suggestion was made in an unrecovered letter.

3. Five months later, on January 14, 1862, President Lincoln finally secured the resignation of Simon Cameron as Secretary of War, and appointed in his place Edwin McMasters Stanton (1814–1869). Thomas and Hyman, *Stanton*, p. 137.

4. Joseph Holt (1807–1894), a Kentucky Democrat and Postmaster General, 1859–1861, also served as Secretary of War during the final two months of the Buchanan administration.

5. Caleb Blood Smith (1808–1864), a lawyer and former Indiana Whig congressman, 1843–1849, was Lincoln's Secretary of the Interior, 1861–1862.

1239. *To* John M. Forbes

Office of the Evening Post,
New York, August 27, 1861.

. . . I do not much like the idea of putting Sherman into the Treasury Department. He would make, I think, a better secretary of war. The great objection I have to him in the Treasury Department is that, so far as I understand the matter, he is committed, as the saying is, to that foolish Morrill tariff.[1] Yet I am very certain that it would be considered by the country an immense improvement of the Cabinet to place him in the War Department. The country has a high opinion of his energy and resolution and practical character.

Of Governor Andrew I do not know as much as you do, though I have formed a favorable judgment of his character and capacity—not a very precise one, however.[2]

They talk of H[olt] here as they do with you, but I am persuaded that the disqualification I have mentioned would breed trouble in the end. The dissatisfaction with Cameron seems to grow more and more vehement every day. His presence taints the reputation of the whole Cabinet, and I think he should be ousted at once. I am sorry to say that a good deal of censure is thrown here upon my good friend Welles, of the Navy Department. He is too deliberate for the temper of our commercial men, who cannot bear to see the pirates of the rebel government capturing our merchant ships one after another and defying the whole United States navy. The Sumter and the Jeff Davis seem to have a charmed existence.[3] Yet it seems to me that new vigor has of late been infused into the Navy department, and perhaps we underrated the difficulties of rescuing the navy from the wretched state in which that miserable creature Toucey left it.[4] There is a committee of our financial men at present at Washington, who have gone on to confer with the President, and it is possible that they may bring back a better report of the Navy Department than they expected to be able to make.

Rumor is unfavorably busy with Mr. Seward, but as a counterpoise it is confidently said that a mutual aversion has sprung up between him and Cameron. This may be so. The "Times," I see, does not spare Cameron, nor the "Herald." There is a good deal of talk here about a reconciliation between Weed and Bennett,[5] and a friendly dinner together, and the attacks which the "Herald" is making upon the War and Navy Department, are said to be the result of an understanding between them. Who knows, or who cares much?

I have emptied into this letter substantially all I have to say. There are doubtless men in private life who would fill the War Department as well as any I have mentioned, but the world knows not their merits, and might receive their names with a feeling of disappointment.

P.S.—With regard to visiting Naushon,[6] I should certainly like it, and like to bring my wife. I have another visit to make, however, in another part of Massachusetts; but I shall keep your kind invitation in mind and will write you again.

W. C. B.

MANUSCRIPT: Unrecovered TEXT: Forbes, *Letters and Recollections*, I, 242–244.

1. As one of his last official acts in 1861, outgoing President Buchanan had signed into law a tariff bill sponsored by Vermont Whig congressman Justin Smith Morrill (1810–1898), and supported by John Sherman (1823–1900) of Ohio, who was chairman of the House Ways and Means Committee. Nevertheless, this increased existing tariff rates only moderately. Nevins, *Emergence of Lincoln*, II, 304, 448–449. Forbes had written Bryant on August 24 proposing Sherman as Secretary of the Treasury and Salmon P. Chase as Secretary of War. Forbes, *Letters and Recollections*, I, 241–242.

2. John Albion Andrew (1818–1867, Bowdoin 1837), Republican governor of Massachusetts, 1860–1866, was an anti-slavery leader and strong Unionist. In his August 24 letter, Forbes had said that, though Andrew had all the essential moral qualities of a good cabinet minister, he was perhaps too openly against slavery, and found it hard to delegate authority on small matters.

3. These were two of the most effective Confederate commerce raiders, commanded, respectively, by former United States naval commander Raphael Semmes (1809–1877), and a Nova Scotian mariner, Louis Mitchell Coxetter (1818–1873). Semmes was later captain of the *Alabama* in its losing battle against the U.S.S. *Kearsage* off the coast of France in 1864.

4. Isaac Toucey (1792–1869) of Connecticut, Buchanan's Secretary of the Navy, 1857–1861, had been much criticized for his apparent southern sympathies.

5. James Gordon Bennett (1795–1872), Scottish-born editor and publisher of the New York *Herald* from 1835 to 1867.

6. One of the Elizabeth Islands, a chain running southwest from Cape Cod and dividing Buzzards Bay from Vineyard Sound. Forbes had bought this island several years earlier and made it his summer home. He had first urged the Bryants to visit there in 1857. See Forbes to Bryant, July 25, 1859, NYPL–BG.

1240.   *To* Julia S. Bryant

Roslyn   Friday   August 30, 1861.

Dear Julia.

The cook we have does not expect to stay with us, and it therefore will be necessary to get one in town. Your mother, however, thinks that it will not be possible to bring out one either on Friday or Saturday owing to some superstition which these sort of people entertain.

If your mother is well enough, she will go to Berkshire in the second week of September and I with her. At present, she is quite laid up with a very severe cold. This morning it looks like breaking up and I hope there will be an end of it before you get home. Her ailments come so frequently that she is always obliged to promise with an *if*. Perhaps too it may not be so convenient for me to go as I now think it will.

With this I send a letter which came to Roslyn three or four days since. It was not forwarded because we did not know when you might leave Berkshire.

Your mother thinks that you might as well come down on Wednesday with Mr. Mackie, and she will send in somebody on Thursday morning who will go to Fanny's and help you look up a cook who is to come out with you. She begs that you will not question the cook so closely as you did the girl at Eastman's,—since that sort of proceeding may discourage a servant.

Yours affectionately
WM. C. BRYANT.

MANUSCRIPT: NYPL–GR.

1241. *To* Bradford Kingman[1]

New York   August 30. 1861.

Dear Sir.

It is a mistake to suppose that I was born in North Bridgewater, although both my father and mother were. They left it in early life, my mother in her childhood. I have never even lived in North Bridgewater.

I am glad to learn that the history of that place is to be carefully written and shall look for its appearance with interest. My time, however, is so fully taken up with other matters that I cannot make any such contributions to it as you suggest, nor is my information respecting its history such that I could communicate any thing worthy of insertion in your work.

Inasmuch as I was not born in North Bridgewater, the dates at which my writings were published will I suppose be of less consequence—perhaps of none at all. Yet as you have asked for them I give here the principal ones,

The Embargo a Satire   1808.

Do. Second Edition and other Poems   1809.

Thanatopsis published in the North American Review.   1817.[2]

Poems   1832.

The Fountain and other Poems   1842

The Whitefooted Deer and other Poems.   1844.

Letters of a Traveller   1850

Letters from Spain   1859.

Hoping that you will receive every facility for the satisfactory execution of the task you have undertaken

> I am, sir,
> respectfully yours
> WM C. BRYANT

MANUSCRIPT: Indiana University Library ADDRESS: B. Kingman Esqre.

1. The addressee was then gathering information for his *History of North Bridgewater, With Family Registers* (Boston, 1866). No letter from Kingman to Bryant at this time has been located.
2. Bryant mistakenly wrote "1816."

1242.   *To* Orville Dewey

Roslyn   August 31st. 1861.

Dear Doctor.

I hear—or, truly and literally speaking, I read in a letter from Julia—that you are to be at home, that is in Sheffield—for one's real home is the country after all—all next week and the week after. My wife and I meditate an incursion into Berkshire week after next. We shall leave Roslyn on Monday Sept. 9th. and New York on Tuesday morning—but whether we stop at Sheffield in going or in returning, I believe is not yet decided. Will it be convenient for you and Mrs. Dewey to see us either at one time or the other? Do you pass the Sunday following the second week of September in Sheffield? I confess I did hope that you might have found your way with your better half to Roslyn this season, and there is time yet. I wanted you to look at the changes we have made here, in the principal one of which you took so kind an interest. The place has quite another look, and is greatly improved, though all the rubbish is not yet removed. It has quite an air of seclusion.

I hope you succeed in reconciling the present state of the country to your optimistic notions—not that I think it difficult to do so. Our old friend human nature, whom it is rather dangerous to praise, must I fear, bear the blame of the calamity which has come upon us. Yet I see a glorious sunshine behind this cloud and a plentiful harvest of good from these bitter showers.

My wife desires her love to all. Make [my][1] regards to the mistress and her daughters.

> I am, dear Doctor,
> most truly yours
> WM. C. BRYANT

MANUSCRIPT: NYPL–GR ADDRESS: Dr. O. Dewey.

1. Word apparently omitted.

New-York, June 16, 1860.

My dear sir:

I was about to begin this letter
by saying that I congratulate you on
your nomination; but when I consider
the importunities which will beset you
as a candidate and the cares, responsibilities and vexations which your success
will throw upon you, I do not congratulate you. It is the country that is to be
congratulated. I was not without apprehensions that the nomination might fall
upon some person encumbered with bad
associates, and it was with a sense of
relief and infinite satisfaction that I
with thousands of others in this quarter
heard that it was conferred upon you.
It is fortunate that you have never

Bryant counsels Lincoln: the opening of Letter 1149.

THE BLIGHT-SPELL.

"AND IN THOSE DAYS DIVERS EVIL-MINDED FOLKE DIDDE FOLLOW YE WATER-FOULE WIZARD OF YE EVENING POSTE AND YE FEILE WITCH OF YE TRIBUNE, AND WITH MUCH BADDE SPELLES AND WICK'D WORDS DIDDE STRIVE TO WORKE A BLYGHTE UPONNE YE GOOD GENERALLE MacCLELLAN."—*Old Tract, slightly alter'd.*)

A POET POSES FOR *VANITY FAIR*

Bobbett and Cooper's wood-engraved portrait of Bryant
for the cover of *Vanity Fair* for May 3, 1862.

Bryant and Horace Greeley "roast" General McClellan; wood engraving by Albert Bobbett and Edward
Hooper from *Vanity Fair*, March 29, 1862, facing p. 154
(see Letters 1265, 1286).

The Metropolitan Museum of Art

Thomas Cole's 1843 illustration "The Fountain, No. I" (see Letter 1399).

Bryant in 1861, in a carte de visite photograph by Black & Bachelder, Boston (see Letter 1214).

Bryant's September 1862 carte de visite; photograph by J. Gurney & Son, New York (see Letters 1293, 1330).

William Cullen Bryant II

Richard Henry Dana's autographed 1863 carte de visite; photograph by Marshall, Boston (see Letter 1065).

Cephas Giovanni Thompson's carte de visite; photograph by Matthew Brady, New York (see Letters 1011, 1045).

William Baylies, *c*1863; carte de visite photograph by P. R. Read, Taunton, Massachusetts (see Letter 1330).

George William Curtis' carte de visite; photograph by A. A. Turner for D. Appleton, New York (see Letter 1139).

James Thomas Fields in a carte de visite photograph by Black & Bachelder, Boston (see Letter 1175).

John Frederick Kensett's carte de visite; photograph by George Gardner Rockwood, New York (see Letters 1401, 1410).

The robin and the wren are flown,

   And from the shrubs the jay,

And from the wood-top calls the

      crow

   Through all the gloomy day.

Where are the flowers, the fair young flowers,

   That lately sprang and stood,

In brighter light, and softer airs,

   A beauteous sisterhood?

Illustration by John Augustus Hows for "The Death of the Flowers" in 1863 for *In the Woods* (see Letter 1318; cf. Letter 1407 on the text).

The five Bryant brothers, in Princeton, Illinois, in 1864
(see Letters 1417–1419).

1243.   *To* Julia S. Bryant

Sheffield Sept. 11th 1861.
Wednesday morning.

Dear Julia.

We got here safely at two o'clock yesterday afternoon and found Dr. Dewey at the station waiting for us. Your mother was somewhat tired but is very bright this morning. The Deweys are all well. Mary's school is in such esteem that she is obliged to refuse scholars.[1]

I found at New York a letter from Mrs. Ware. She says that she will leave home on Monday and be in New York on Tuesday morning. If she should not arrive by the early train, send down somebody to the station in the evening of Tuesday to meet her and bring up her baggage. I have written to her to tell her how to come.

Your mother will not think of leaving Berkshire until Tuesday, so that Mrs. Ware may be at Roslyn first.

Yours affectionately
W. C. BRYANT

MANUSCRIPT: NYPL–GR.

1. Orville Dewey's daughter Mary E. Dewey, then conducting a school in Sheffield, later edited her father's *Autobiography and Letters* (Boston, 1884).

1244.   *To* Robert Bonner

Office of The Evening Post
New York, Oct. 5   1861

My dear sir.

An acquaintance of mine Prof. Walchner, a German poet[1] is ambitious of seeing in your Ledger, a ballad composed by him and respectably translated into English by James Nash.[2] I send it enclosed. Can you do me the favor to look over it and say whether you will print it and if not return it to me by the bearer as I have no other copy?

Yours truly
W. C. BRYANT.

MANUSCRIPT: QPL ADDRESS: Robt. Bonner Esqre. DOCKETED: Oct 5/61 / Wm Cullen Bryant.

1. Probably Friedrich August Walchner (911.1).
2. Unidentified.

1245.   *To* Salmon P. Chase

Roslyn   Oct. 22, 1861.

My dear sir.

I have a friend who is a first rate clerk quick and accurate in accounts and a good business man; and besides a man of good sense and unimpeached integrity, and rigidly exact in his duty who would like the place of which you spoke to me in your letter. It is John Cockle Esq   of this city who was for some time, Entry Clerk in the Naval Office under Michael Hoffman and was much confided in by that most able and upright man.[1]

I have spoken with him and if the place is not bestowed I will convey to him any communication you may have to make.

With regard to a visit to Washington I find that it will not be convenient for me to make it at present, though I cannot refrain from again expressing my acknowledgments for your offered hospitality.[2]

I am dear sir
truly yours
W C BRYANT

MANUSCRIPT: NYPL–GR (draft) ADDRESS: Hon   S. P. Chase / Secry of the Treasury.

1. Michael Hoffman (1787–1848) of Saratoga, New York, a Democratic congressman from New York, 1825–1833, later occupied several state offices before serving for the last three years of his life as Naval Officer of the Port of New York. *BDAC.* John Cockle has not been further identified.

2. Chase replied that Cockle should come to Washington at once, and urged Bryant to visit him as soon as possible. "In my house," he wrote, "you will find yourself at home." There was a strong mutual respect between the two men. A few days after Lincoln's inauguration, Chase had written John Bigelow that if Bryant would consider going to Paris as the American minister, "He should have my voice." Chase to Bryant, October 23, 1861, NYPL–BG; Chase to Bigelow, March 11, 1861, quoted in Bigelow, *Retrospections,* I, 348–349.

1246.   *To* George Bancroft

Roslyn   Nov. 5. 1861.

Dear Mr. Bancroft.

I told Mr. Conway yesterday that I would come to the meeting in behalf of the North Carolina fishermen at which I am glad to learn that you are to preside, and that I might say a word or two to the assembly,—words for which you will be responsible as the instigator. But lest you might not see him again in season I write this. I shall not speak more than five or ten minutes—there is not matter for a longer speech for an intellect so unfruitful as mine and if there were I am not for tiring an audience.[1] Thanking you for the compliment you have paid me in asking me

I am, dear sir,
truly yours
WM C BRYANT

MANUSCRIPT: MHS ADDRESS: Hon. Geo   Bancroft.

1. On November 7 at the Cooper Institute, with Bancroft presiding, Bryant was one of several speakers at a meeting sponsored by New York merchants, whose purpose was to finance a shipment of food and clothing to North Carolina fishermen made destitute by their loyalty to the Union. Rev. T. W. Conway, organizer of the meeting

and a speaker, was chaplain of the Ninth New York Regiment. *EP* and New York *Times*, November 8, 1861.

1247. *To* John Howard Bryant

Roslyn   Nov. 9th. 1861.

Dear Brother.

I got your letter yesterday[1] and immediately wrote to Mr. Wm. H. Osborn late of this city, now of Chicago and President of the Illinois Central Railroad, asking him to send you a pass over the road as the correspondent of the Evening Post.

If you should not get the pass within a very few days I wish you would write to him, mentioning, that it is done at my request, and stating the necessity of having the pass as soon as may be.

We are all well. William Snell has paid us a visit. He has come east for his health's sake and for the sake of getting money to buy a bell for his church. He writes to me that uncle Thomas is not so well as usual being much enfeebled by "two serious turns of bleeding at the nose, and is subject to faint occasionally.["] His mind is somewhat affected.[2]

The season here has been wonderfully fine. The frosts held off uncommonly late, the fields are now in full verdure, and the trees retain at least half their leaves. Some of them are in full foliage.

I find that the list of apple trees I took down at Princeton does not answer for our region. The Jonathan which succeeds so well with you is apt to die at the root here and is a poor grower. By the *root* I suppose is meant the insertion of the graft which is near the root.

The feeling that it will be necessary to get rid of slavery before we can hope to obtain any very decided advantages over the rebels is greatly on the increase here and manifests itself particularly at the public meetings whenever any allusion to the subject is made.

Kind regards to . . .[3]

MANUSCRIPT: NYPL–BFP ADDRESS: Jn⁰ H. Bryant.

1. Unrecovered.
2. Rev. William Wingate Snell, then apparently settled in California, was a son of Bryant's maternal uncle, Rev. Thomas Snell (1.4), who died at North Brookfield, Massachusetts, the following year at the age of eighty-eight.
3. The conclusion and signature have been cut from the manuscript.

1248. *To* John Howard Bryant

Office of The Evening Post,
New York, Dec. 9th   1861.

Dear Brother.

Mr. Godwin has received a letter from Mr. Bigelow in Paris, in which he desired him to say to me that if the letter to you has not been forwarded, I should withhold it, and if there is yet time to countermand the order for the survey that I should countermand it, as he has no occasion for the survey.[1]

I hasten to give you the information that if it be not too late you may refrain from proceeding in the matter. If you will tell me how the thing now stands I will write to him, or if you will send me a letter for him I will forward it. All well.

Yours affectionately,
W. C. BRYANT

MANUSCRIPT: Newberry Library ADDRESS: Jn⁰ H   Bryant Esq.

1. In August Bigelow had been appointed consul general at Paris, whence he wrote Parke Godwin on November 11, 1861 (NYPL–BG) that he did not need at present the money he had apparently invested earlier in Illinois land through the agency of John Bryant.

1249.   *To* Cullen Bryant

Office of The Evening Post,
New York, December 21. 1861.

Dear Nephew.

I am sorry to say that just now we are neither in town nor out of town. I should like to see you at our house in town if we had any, but we have none, and Fanny who has just been confined entirely fills up Mr. Godwin's house with her family.[1] We had expected to be in town during the holidays and are looking up a boarding place for the purpose. My wife and daughter are now with a friend at Astoria, a little without the city and I am here for a day or two for the same purpose sleeping in a little back room at Mr. Godwins. Our house, however, is open at Roslyn, and still warmed with a furnace, and if you think you could entertain yourself there for a day or two or longer, as much longer as you please, without us, the place and the table is at your service, and it may be that we shall be down there a few days yet, before finally coming in—but we expect to pass the holidays here.—

Yours truly
WM. C. BRYANT.

MANUSCRIPT: NYPL–BFP ADDRESS: Mr. Cullen Bryant / Military Academy / West Point / N. Y.— POSTMARK: NEW-YORK / DEC 21.

1. Fanny Godwin's eighth child, Walter, was born in December 1861, and died in 1867.

1250.   *To* John Bigelow

New York, December 23rd, 1861.

Dear Mr. Bigelow:

. . . The case of Mason and Slidell makes an infinite deal of talk here and I suppose the excitement in America is quite as great as it is in England in regard to that subject. The mercantile feeling is a little timid as regards the prospect of a war with Great Britain, but even among the mercantile class, there is an undercurrent of indignation at the insolence of Great Britain in perverting into a cause of quarrel an act copied directly from her own example, and in perfect accordance with the law of nations as her own jurists have expounded it. Nothing but having another war on our hands prevents a violent outbreak of resentment. Unless the demand made by the British Government be exceedingly moderate in its nature, a feud will be created which can never be so healed as not to leave an ugly scar.[1]

With regard to our quarrel with the Southern States the general feeling is one of impatience suppressed with some difficulty at the tardy proceedings of those who have the direction of affairs. People wonder and wonder what is the reason for keeping such an immense army at Washington, an army now admirably disciplined and perfectly equipped, and ready for any expedition on which they may be sent—when it is clear that the seat of government might be defended with a quarter of the number.

My own view of the matter however leads me to be contented with these delays, and I can see that good may grow out of the encouragement which the rebels will derive from the differences into which we have got ourselves with Great Britain.

General Scott's letter was very much liked here and whether justly or not the credit of its authorship was given by many to you.[2] —Best regards to Mrs. Bigelow and believe me,

Truly yours
[signature not printed]

MANUSCRIPT: Unrecovered TEXT: Bigelow, *Retrospections*, I, 422–423.

1. On November 8, 1861, the newly appointed Confederate diplomatic commissioners to Great Britain and France, James Murray Mason (1798–1871) of Virginia, and John Slidell (1793–1871) of Louisiana, had been forceably removed from the British steamer *Trent* by United States marines from the warship *San Jacinto* and taken to Boston for imprisonment. When the news of this "Trent Affair" reached London, there were immediate British threats of war against the Union government. But before the end of December conciliatory efforts on both sides of the Atlantic brought release of the prisoners. Nevins, *War for the Union*, I, 388–393; Van Deusen, *Seward*, pp. 306–317.

2. A letter from General Winfield Scott, recently retired as general-in-chief of the United States army, to Bigelow, printed in Paris and London newspapers, as well as one from Bigelow to Secretary of State Seward on December 5, urged surrender of Mason and Slidell to ensure the preservation of freedom of the seas. Van Deusen, *Seward*, pp. 315–316. On December 2 Bigelow wrote from Paris to Isaac Henderson (NYPL–BG) that Scott's "tranquilizing" letter might extricate Washington from the affair with credit—which was, on the whole, the outcome.

1251.   *To* John Howard Bryant

Office of The Evening Post,
New York, Dec. 23, 1861

Dear Brother

I do not see that you have any reason to return any part of the money received from Mr. Bigelow, and I shall write to him that I have said the same thing to you.[1] He employed you in a matter of business and will expect to make you a fair compensation as his agent. It is not at all likely that he would consent to receive back any part of the $50.

If in consequence of your expenditures on your house you become at all embarrassed you must let me know. We have been obliged to order a new press which will throw a heavy expense on us and we expect to feel something of the pressure of the times between this time and next May, but as I urged you to make the alterations, I should be sorry to see you brought into any difficulty by it that is in my power to prevent.

I have not heard a word from Mr. Olds since he left us for the west. He promised to write and let us know how he got on, but we have not heard a syllable concerning him, even from your letters or those of Arthur[2] and know not whether he be dead or alive, better or worse.

Yours affectionately
WM. C. BRYANT

MANUSCRIPT: BCHS PUBLISHED: "Bryant and Illinois," 645–646.

1. Bryant's comment on this was probably omitted from the printed text of Letter 1250.

2. Arthur Bryant; see Vol. 1, 12.

1252.   *To* Ferdinand E. Field

New York, December, 1861

... It is some satisfaction to me to know that, if you and I took the same view of the facts, we should not differ so much in our conclusions as you suppose. The British newspaper press has not given all the facts to its readers. In all the States in which the civil war was raging, at the date of your letter to me,[1] there was an ascertained majority in favor of remaining in the Union. These States are Virginia, North Carolina, Kentucky, Tennessee, and Missouri. These States the rebellion attempted to wrest from us. You will agree that the war on behalf of the majority of their citizens was a just one on our part.

We claim, also, that there is a majority in favor of the Union in Arkansas, Louisiana, and Texas; in Alabama, Georgia, and Florida, and perhaps in Mississippi; in short, that there is no State in which the secessionists possess a clear majority, except it be South Carolina. In none of the slave States was the question whether they desired to remain in the Union submitted to the people. We of the North said to them: First show that your own citizens are in favor of separating from the Union. Make that clear, and then bring the matter before Congress, and agitate for a change of the Constitution, releasing you in a peaceful and regular way from your connection with the free States. There is no hurry; you have lived a great many years in partnership with us, and you can certainly now wait till the matter is thoroughly discussed. They refused to do anything of this nature; they had for the most part got their own creatures into the State legislatures, and into the governors' seats; they rushed the vote for separation through these legislatures; they lured troops; they stole arms from the government arsenals, and money from the Government mints; they seized upon the Government navy yards and Government forts; in short, they made war upon the Government. Taking the whole of the Southern States together, this was done by a minority of the people.

You will agree with me, I am sure, that we could not honorably abandon the friends of the Union in these States. You would not have the British government, if a minority in Scotland were to seize upon that country and set up a mock parliament at Edinburgh, give up the country to the insurgents.

As to the Star blockade, it strikes everybody here as singular that the British government and public should be so ill-informed in regard to that matter. Several rivers find their way to the ocean in the channels that lead to Charleston Harbor. Some years since, the channels being too numerous, and becoming more shallow, the Government was at the expense of filling them up, which made the others, particularly Maffit's Channel, deeper. The Government has now filled up another channel, which makes Maffit's Channel still deeper, which is an advantage to the harbor; but, in the mean time, the blockade is more easily enforced, because there is one channel the less for us to watch. If the obstructions we have placed do any mischief, they may be removed. The rebels are doing the same thing at Savannah, yet your press make no complaint. They have obstructed one of the channels leading to their city, and we have just taken them up. Set that against what we have done at Charleston.[2]

You see, then, the entire groundlessness of the unfavorable conclusions formed in England. As for the Trent affair, that will be settled, and I will not say what I might concerning it, except to remark that the preparations for war with which your government accompanied its demand have left a sense of injury and insult which, I fear, will not soon pass away. But none the less do I cling to my pleasant memories of England and the excellent people I met there. . . .

MANUSCRIPT: Unrecovered TEXT (partial): Life, II, 157–159.

1. Unrecovered.
2. A blockade of all Confederate ports proclaimed by President Lincoln on April 19, 1861, ineffectual for the first few months, had by the end of the year seriously crippled the South's foreign commerce.

1253.   *To* Abraham Lincoln

[1861?]

We the undersigned Citizens of the United States beg leave to recommend to your consideration Barent Vanderpool of Fort Hamilton[1] as a fit and proper person to be appointed a Lieutenant in the Army of the U. S. He is a young man of unblemished character and firmly attached to the Constitution and government of which your Excellency is the Head.

His grandfather was a soldier in the
Revolutionary War
and with the army at the surrender of Gen. Burgoyne. His uncle was also engaged in the War taken prisoner and died in the Prison Ship.

WM. C. BRYANT [and others][2]

MANUSCRIPT: Boston University Library ADDRESS: To His Excellency / Abraham Lincoln, / President of the United States.

1. Not further identified.
2. This petition, signed by Bryant and a dozen others, including Generals John A. Dix and Winfield Scott, is in an unidentified handwriting.

XXIII

From Roanoke Island to Chattanooga
1862–1863
(LETTERS 1254 TO 1387)

IN MID-JANUARY 1862 Secretary of War Simon Cameron, against whose appointment to the Cabinet Bryant had warned the President a year before, was dismissed from office after revelations of great waste and corruption in provisioning the army, to be succeeded by Edwin M. Stanton. Governmental finances were at that time virtually crippled through the refusal of Eastern banks to make specie payments, which caused Treasury notes to be sharply discounted. In the crisis, Treasury Secretary Chase yielded to congressional pressure by accepting a bill empowering the administration to print unsupported currency, or "Greenbacks," by designating them as legal tender.

Bryant protested strongly and repeatedly against this measure, in editorials and in letters to Lincoln and Chase. "Desperate remedies should be left for desperate circumstances," he argued in an open letter to the President; he thought no such stringency existed. "We are," he wrote, "the richest nation in the world in proportion to our population." Our great wealth could easily bear taxes to support the war. The unlimited issue of paper money would destroy government credit and force the North to "patch up an ignominious peace." Further, subject to ruthless speculation it must depreciate rapidly, with the burden of rising prices bearing most heavily on the old, the sick, and the poor. To John Murray Forbes, who begged him to intensify his struggle against "financial folly," he replied, "probably you do not know that I am covered all over with the scars received in the battle fought twenty years ago for specie payments. . . . We gained the victory and I had hoped it was a victory for my day at least. To be obliged to go into the battle again, to be forced to do all the work over a second time, fills me with intense disgust—and is exceedingly discouraging."

Nonetheless, he pressed on. We must pay as we go, he insisted, not through increased tariffs and excise taxes such as Congress had ineffectively levied, but by laying a charge on all legal and business transactions. What could not be realized from taxes should be raised through long-term bond issues, which he was sure would be patriotically subscribed. He pleaded with Charles Sumner and other members of Congress to oppose the legal tender clause, but in vain. Chase wrote him that, though the bill was as "repugnant" to him as to Bryant, "as a temporary measure, it is indispensably necessary." The law was passed, and Bryant's urgent appeal to Lincoln to veto it was fruitless. His position was soon vindicated, for the flow of Greenbacks reached nearly half a billion, with prices soaring until only thirty-nine dollars in specie bought one hundred in currency.

The year 1862 saw a marked shift in Bryant's opposition to slavery, from his earlier argument that freedom for slaves would probably result from military

exigencies, to direct advocacy of emancipation as a moral and human imperative. After Lincoln had made a futile proposal that slaves in the Border States
be freed by their masters, with compensation from federal funds, a plan which
radical Senator Thaddeus Stevens called a "diluted, milk-and-water gruel prop-
osition," Bryant assumed the presidency of a newly-formed Emancipation
League in New York. Soon after, he presided over a mass meeting at Cooper
Union, introducing as the main speaker martyred Elijah Lovejoy's brother
Owen, an Abolitionist Illinois congressman, who wrote him afterward that it
was "highly gratifying . . . that you should give the influence of your name and
fame to the cause of emancipation." On the day Lincoln first read a draft of his
proposed Emancipation Proclamation to his Cabinet, Bryant made a fervent
plea in the *Evening Post* for the abolition of slavery, and soon afterward supported the demand of Robert Dale Owen for immediate emancipation.

Many cautious anti-slavery voices suggested that freedom should be granted
only gradually, so as not to alienate loyal slaveholders or upset the economies
of Border States. To Bryant, such a plan was intolerable. Lincoln's proclamation, taking effect on January 1, 1863, freed slaves only in states then in rebellion against the national government. It was essentially a war measure which,
as Secretary Seward put it, "emancipated slaves where it could not reach them,
and left them in bondage where it could have set them free." The measure was
necessarily one of gradual application, effective only as Union forces occupied
rebel territory. And Lincoln explicitly stated his support of gradualism. But
his policy was unacceptable to anti-slavery leaders. At a meeting in support of
Missouri loyalists who had come east to protest harassment by southern sympathizers, Bryant aimed his sharpest scorn at the gradualists who controlled that
state. "Gradual emancipation!," he exclaimed; "there is no grosser delusion
ever entertained by man." Reversing an illustration Lincoln had cited to explain why gradual emancipation would be the better course in Missouri—his
story of the man who would die if a tumor on his neck were removed in a single
operation, but would live if a surgeon "tinkered it off by degrees"—Bryant
countered, "My friends, if a child of yours were to fall in the fire would you pull
him out gradually? If he were to swallow a dose of laudanum sufficient to cause
speedy death, and a stomach pump were at hand, would you draw the poison by
degrees? If your house were on fire, would you put it out gradually? . . . Slavery
is a foul and monstrous idol, a Juggernaut under which thousands are crushed
to death. . . . Must we consent that the number of the victims shall be gradually
diminished? If there are a thousand victims this year, are you willing that nine
hundred should be sacrificed next year, and eight hundred the next, and so on
until after the lapse of ten years it shall cease? No, my friends, let us hurl this
grim image from its pedestal. . . . Dash it to fragments; trample it in the dust."
A few days later Senator Sumner wrote, "Y[ou]r words for Immediate Emancipation thrilled me; there is the true ring in them. I doubt if ever the case has
been stated so strongly in so few words."

After successful naval operations against southern ports early in 1862,
Bryant was for a time confident that the Union cause was gaining ascendancy.
As the months passed, and General McClellan's inexplicable delays in maneu-
vering his Army of the Potomac in the vicinity of the South's capital culminated
in June in a series of bloody and indecisive battles, Bryant's patience, like that

of many citizens and soldiers alike, was tested beyond restraint. In April he warned against the "Dangers of Delay." A few weeks later he compared unfavorably the inaction of McClellan's massive and well-drilled forces with General Grant's decisive action in capturing Fort Donelson in Tennessee, despite the mud and his raw troops. He had no tolerance for the popular belief that the capture of Richmond would strike a heavy blow against the Confederacy. He thought McClellan's incompetence might defeat the federal cause.

Behind distrust of field generalship was his growing conviction that the administration was derelict in its direction of strategy, if not incapable of applying it wisely. Whereas in February he had told the President "You are now winning great credit by a wise direction of our armies," by July he wondered if much of the trouble was not due to Lincoln's indecision, and a "certain tone of languor and want of earnestness" in his administration, caused by his overreliance on subordinates. On August 7, at the urging of other impatient New Yorkers, Bryant went to Washington for a talk with the President, during which he warned that many of his associates felt the Union cause might be "drifting to ruin if instant and powerful means were not applied to give things a new direction." In September, on the eve of the crucial battle at Antietam, Maryland, while conceding that Lincoln was "honest, devoted, and determined," he felt that "a large part of the nation is utterly discouraged and despondent," suspicious that "treachery lurks in the highest quarters." This, he thought, had "grown out of the weakness and vacillation of the Administration, which itself has grown out of Mr. Lincoln's own want of decision and purpose." Addressing the President personally the next month, and speaking for the "friends of the administration and the country in this quarter," he reported them "distressed and alarmed at the inactivity of our armies," and uncertain "whether the administration sincerely desires the speedy annihilation of the rebel forces." If the present policy persists, he concluded, "the Union in our view is lost, and we shall resign ourselves to the melancholy conviction that the ruin of our republic is written down in the decrees of God."

Sharp as were Bryant's strictures, they were mild by comparison with those of some of his Republican friends. One of these urged him, as among "the first & best men of the nation," to make clear to Lincoln the need for firm action to save free government from the "horrible corruption and abominable stupidity in high places," which was "paralyzing the strength of the army." Another, historian George Bancroft, called the President "ignorant, self-willed," and "surrounded by men some of whom are almost as ignorant as himself."

Though Bryant's judgments on military operations were scoffed at by journalistic opponents, among them his former employee Manton Marble, now editor of the southern-sympathizing New York *World*, he had access to sources of information from the front lines which were probably better than those of any other influential editor. Besides reports from his friends Olmsted and Henry W. Bellows of the Sanitary Commission on conditions among the troops, he corresponded with or saw such high-ranking federal officers as Generals James Wadsworth, Ethan A. Hitchcock, Benjamin Butler, Dennis H. Mahan, and Daniel Butterfield, and Colonels Henry B. Carrington and his own nephew Julian E. Bryant, each of whom read the *Evening Post* and reacted to its comment. Early in 1862 Wadsworth wrote, "I repeat the conclusion intimated in my last letter. The commander in chief [McClellan] is almost inconceivably incompetent, . . . or disloyal." After the Union defeat at the Second Battle of Bull Run in August had freed Lee's army to invade Maryland, Wadsworth wrote, "We have been badly whipped in front in consequence solely of the insane adherence to McClellan. . . . The results have proved & will prove the wisdom of your suggestions." Their similar estimates of McClellan's deficiencies were vindicated two months later when he was relieved of his post.

As early as July 1862, nine months before a draft was adopted, Bryant proposed conscription as the only sure means of sustaining an army whose short-term volunteers were leaving the service faster than they could be replaced by enlistment. In January 1863 he urged that the thousands of freed and fugitive slaves streaming northward be armed for offense as well as defense, for, he cautioned Senator William P. Fessenden, "there is danger that the soldiers from the free states, sent so often upon unfortunate expeditions, which result so often in terrible and fruitless loss of life, and left so long without payment of their wages, while their families are starving at home, will become utterly disgusted with the service." After the Union defeat at Chancellorsville in May 1863 had opened the way for the Army of Virginia to move northward toward Pennsylvania to challenge General Meade at Gettysburg, Bryant's private advices enabled him to predict this move two weeks before there were visible signs of movement in Lee's army.

The *Evening Post*'s unceasing advocacy of a vigorous war effort, and its editor's constant activity at Union rallies and in organizing the Union League in New York, drew praise from many quarters. Philadelphia anti-slavery leader William H. Furness hailed the calm vision of the *Evening Post*, which, he wrote Bryant, "stands in my esteem at the head of the American press. It is cheering that there is abroad such an educator of the public mind." Professor Charles Eliot Norton of Harvard expressed his "hearty sympathy with the principles maintained by the *Evening Post* at this time," and his "admiration for the ability with which they are sustained." From Paris John Bigelow, wondering at what seemed the queer behavior of editor Horace Greeley of the New York *Tribune* in proposing compromise with the South, praised his former partner's journal as "the highest newspaper authority now in the country."

With the Union victories of the first week of July 1863 at Vicksburg and Port Hudson on the Mississippi, and especially after Lee's defeat at Gettysburg, Bryant exulted in the "three glorious days." Paying tribute to those who had "given their lives in the noblest cause in which man was ever called to suffer," he foresaw an early end to the rebellion. But the violent draft riots in New York and other cities a week later, as the first conscripts were drawn by lot, brought a sobering shock. Much of the fury of the mobs in New York fell upon blacks, of whom some one-hundred-fifty were murdered. Other targets were the draft offices, and journals such as the *Evening Post* which strongly supported the Union cause. Greeley, who failed to take protective measures at the *Tribune* office, hid in a hotel until attackers were driven off by troops. But Bryant and his staff barricaded doors and windows and turned live steam from the presses into hoses mounted at upper windows. As the violence was ended by police and troops after four days, Bryant sent to his superintendent at Roslyn revolvers and ammunition for defense against a threat overheard on a railway train that "Bryant's house would have to blaze." No such attack, however, was made.

During the winters of 1861–1862 and 1862–1863 the Bryants boarded in town on Fourth Avenue. They passed the summer of 1862 at Roslyn, but in the spring of 1863 Bigelow offered them his house at Buttermilk Falls in the Hudson Highlands near West Point. Here they spent nearly four months between June and October, with Bryant traveling down the river periodically to attend to his newspaper while Frances gained strength in the mountain air. In the city Bryant stayed in his elder daughter's house on East Thirty-Seventh Street, occasionally going by steamer out to Roslyn to advise George Cline on the care of Cedarmere. That summer several members of the Illinois family visited the East. Cyrus' son Cullen was completing his third year as a cadet at West Point, where Bryant renewed acquaintance with Robert Weir, still professor of drawing at the academy, and others on its faculty. At the annual commencement of Williams College in August Bryant was restored to the rolls of the class of 1813, of which he had been a member for only eight months in 1810–1811, and although he did not attend its reunion, his poem "Fifty Years," composed for the occasion, was read there by a classmate.

During these crucial war years such writing as Bryant did, apart from that for the newspaper and his public addresses, gave expression largely to verses of fantasy: "A Tale of Cloudland," "Castles in the Air," "Sella," and "The Little People of the Snow," and in a translation of the fifth book of Homer's *Odyssey*— which presaged the chief literary task of his late years, translations of the entire *Iliad* and *Odyssey*. But the most notable verse composition of this time was "The Poet," a distillation of the poetic creed he had developed in his *Lectures on Poetry* of 1826:

> ... Deem not the framing of a deathless lay
> The Pastime of a drowsy summer day.

> ... The secret wouldst thou know
>   To touch the heart or fire the blood at will?
> Let thine own eyes o'erflow;
>   Let thy lips quiver with the passionate thrill;
> Seize the great thought, ere yet its power be past,
> And bind, in words, the fleet emotion fast.

> Then, should thy verse appear
>   Halting and harsh, and all unaptly wrought,
> Touch the crude line with fear,
>   Save in the moment of impassioned thought;
> Then summon back the original glow, and mend
> The strain with rapture that with fire was penned.

This and other verses of the past few years were gathered in December 1863 in *Thirty Poems*, his most successful collection since *The Fountain and Other Poems* of 1842.

In October 1862 Bryant's long fidelity to the homoeopathic system of medicine won him election to the presidency of the council of the New York Homoeopathic Medical College where, in the following March, he conducted its commencement exercises and awarded its degrees. As a result of the Morrill tariff act of July 1862 an earlier and more basic tenet found recognition in his election as president of the newly formed American Free Trade League. He helped organize a National Freedmen's Relief Association, presiding over its annual meetings, as he did other efforts to ease the condition of freedmen, such as that early in 1862 to aid a large number of slaves abandoned by their owners when Port Royal, South Carolina, was taken by Union forces, and the meeting in June, referred to earlier, of the Emancipation League.

On the eve of Vicksburg and Gettysburg Bryant directed his editorial irony at the popular obsession with the rallying cry, "On to Richmond!" It was, he wrote, "our fixed idea, our enchantment, our pleasant illusion, our fatuity. . . . Nothing short of a surgical operation," he said, "will get this delusion out of the heads of our public men." It was not the political symbols of rebellion, but rather its armies and their sources of supply, which must be pursued and destroyed. More and more, he saw the successes of Grant and Sherman in the West as the best hope of Union triumph. He had gained respect for Grant since his early victories in Tennessee; with the fall of Vicksburg he felt certain that this capable, "clear-headed general," who got things done, should be the one to lead the federal forces. When John Murray Forbes questioned whether Grant's rumored drinking was not a drawback to his effectiveness, Bryant replied that he had in his desk a "batch of written testimonials" by Grant's acquaintances attesting that "he is now a temperate man." After Grant's great victory in July 1863 Bryant declared in the *Evening Post* that he had won more victories than any other man, and that "If any one after this still believes that Grant is a drunkard, we advise him to persuade the Government to place none but drunkards in important commands." When, at Chattanooga in November, Grant drove the Confederates out of Tennessee and thus opened the way for Sherman's march into Georgia, Bryant's faith had not long to await its reward; three months later the leader he sought was given command of all federal armies.

1254. *To* Leonice M. S. Moulton

The Evening Post
New York, Jany. 2d 1862

. . . I am glad to hear that your sojourn at Baltimore has been so pleasant. I suppose that in consequence you may be detained from Roslyn longer than you otherwise would have been. Mr. Moulton, being nearer the seat of war, has the satisfaction of getting the news a little earlier than he would do here, though I believe the details are given more fully in the New York than in the Baltimore papers.

My family are now in town for the winter at Blancord's on the Fourth Avenue. Until we came away the weather had been remarkably fine; there were green places here and there and the autumnal dandelions were in bloom, in spite of your absence. We left Roslyn about the 20th of December. The negociations for a site for the new chapel I understood were going on, but Mr. Skillman, asked more for his land than it was thought prudent to give, and the probability was thought to be that Valentine's lot on the opposite side of the way would be purchased.[1]

Meantime, we bear the consequences of the war in New York as well as any body could have supposed we should. There is the old bustle in the streets—there was the old hurrying to and fro on New Years day. The war has seriously interfered with some old interests; it has promoted a few and created some new ones. There is little gaiety—few parties—and some check given to luxury. . . .

MANUSCRIPT: Ridgely Family Collection TEXT: Hoyt, "Bryant Correspondence, I," 69.

1. This was the Roslyn Episcopal chapel, built in 1862. Goddard, *Roslyn Harbor,* p. 107. Francis Skillman was an early diarist–historian of Roslyn; his neighbor James Valentine owned a mill. *Ibid.,* pp. 18, 22, 125.

1255. *To* John Howard Bryant

Office of The Evening Post
New York, January 4th 1862

Dear Brother.

I did not mean to have sent out any more money to Illinois, and I begin to fear that my investments there in real estate were not quite so well-judged as they might have been—or rather that it would have been quite as well to lend the money. Be that as it may, the fault is my own and I am content to bear its consequences. I do not wish any thing more to be expended except what is derived from the rents—not even in fencing or draining.

I see the importance of your being enabled to turn your corn to some account, and I therefore authorize you to draw upon me for a thousand dollars at three days sight— The drafts should be on W^m. C. Bryant and Co. Mr. Henderson has directions to pay them. If my corn should be allowed to remain long in the cribs unsold I may want you yet to do something of the same kind for me, sometime or other.

Yours truly
WM. C. BRYANT

MANUSCRIPT: WCL ADDRESS: Jn° H Bryant Esqr.

1256.   To Frances F. Bryant

Office of The Evening Post, New York,
January 12th   1862. Monday morning.

Dear Frances.

I suppose you may possibly care, by this time, to hear from me. At the [Century] Club on Saturday night, I saw many of your friends, most of whom had heard of your accident and inquired about you with much interest.[1] Yesterday afternoon, I called, with Mr. Bancroft, on Mr. Chase, who is here at the Fifth Avenue Hotel, and not in a very cheerful mood. After that we took a long walk Mr. Bancroft and I, and called at Fanny's— Fanny and Godwin were out—but all are well there. To night I mean to call at your brother's.

Fanny is here at the office. She says that Harold[2] has got over his croup— but snorts in the morning. They had a sort of masquerade on a small scale at Mrs. Miller's on Friday night in which Mrs. Henderson was the chief performer and acted her part very well. Love to Julia.

Yours ever,
W. C. B.

MANUSCRIPT: NYPL–GR ADDRESS: Mrs. F. F. Bryant.

1. The nature of Frances' accident has not been determined, but its minor nature is suggested in the final paragraph of Letter 1259.
2. Fanny Godwin's third son, Harold (1857–1931).

1257.   To Frances F. Bryant

Office of The Evening Post,
New York, January 13, 1862

Dear Frances.

I called on Egbert [Fairchild] and his wife yesterday. A few days since he was not so well as usual, but the doctor has changed his medicine and prescribed Vichy water, the product of a French mineral spring, tasting very much like a weak solution of common soda, and he is now better. He goes down every day to his office, but comes back rather early. He is not so well as to think it perfectly safe to come out to Roslyn and his wife thinks she ought to stay with him and watch him.

I was asked last evening to Mr. Jay's in Fifth Avenue to meet Mr. Chase, and went. There I saw a good many Wall Street people, and some young ones of both sexes, Mr. Bancroft and his wife—zealous abolitionists now—and Mrs. Chapman, an abolitionist of long standing[1] whose son married Mr. Jays oldest daughter. She knew Miss Robbins[2] and her sisters very well, and informed me of what I did not know before that Mrs. Howe is dead.[3] I sneaked home before supper.

Please tell Mr. Cline that I got his letter this morning and directed the whitewood boards to be sent on board the Sloop Adeline tomorrow morning from a lumber yard in 31st. Street.

I think of coming home tomorrow. Love to Julia.

Yours ever
W. C. B.

MANUSCRIPT: NYPL–GR.

1. This was probably Maria Weston Chapman (1806–1885), early anti-slavery associate of William Lloyd Garrison, and editor and writer for several Abolitionist journals.
2. Eliza Robbins (127.6, 842.1).
3. Sarah L. R. Howe (1214.3).

1258. *To* Samuel Osgood[1]

Office of The Evening Post
New York, Jan. 29th 1862.

My dear sir

The objection to the neuter "it" I confess struck me, but not very forcibly when I was constructing the line to which you object. I have no objection to its being altered to

And bids the lisper pray to thee.

It must be *the* lisper and not that, inasmuch as a little before I have written "that dear infant" &c.[2]

I have not time to recast the stanza, just at present—but perhaps I may think of something before the proof comes.[3] It is now two o'clock in the afternoon, and it has not come—

Yrs truly
W C BRYANT

MANUSCRIPT: DuU ADDRESS: Rev Dr Osgood.

1. Rev. Samuel Osgood (1812–1880, Harvard 1832, Cambridge Divinity School 1835, D.D. Harvard 1857) had succeeded Orville Dewey in 1849 as pastor of the Unitarian Church of the Messiah.

2. From "The Mother's Hymn," third stanza. The lines in question appeared in *Thirty Poems* (1864), p. [116] as

> ... With that dear infant on her knee,
> She trains the eye to look to heaven,
> The voice to lisp a prayer to thee.

See *Poems* (1876), p. 384.

3. "The Mother's Hymn" was composed in response to a request from Osgood, who had written Bryant on January 6, 1862 (NYPL–BG), saying there were no such verses in Protestant hymnbooks, and promising that it should be sung at a vesper service in his church on the first Sunday of February. Writing again on January 17 (NYPL–BG), he said the hymn was "just what is wanted," and promised that it would be printed in "our book."

1259.   *To* Leonice M. S. Moulton

New York   January 21, 1862.

... I do not know what you may have thought of my neglect to answer your note of the other day[1] till now. I wanted to go to Roslyn before giving you an answer. I went there last week, and since that time have deferred my duty as people are apt to defer it—when it is not done the very instant it ought to be.

You do not tell me the name of the "small careful and peaceable family" of which you speak as applying for my house, but if it be the one I am thinking of, there certainly could not be better tenants.[2] The people who are in the house now are there rather because I did not like the building to remain unoccupied than for any other reason, and I have always expected them to leave it in the Spring.

As for the terms I am ready to discuss them when I know with certainty what family it is that wants the house. I dare say however we should not disagree.

My wife got your letter the other day, and we were all much interested in the account you gave of matters and things in Baltimore. Here we are in the midst of a general exultation at the defeat of the forces under Zollikofer in Kentucky, a newspaper editor formerly, then a member of Congress, next a rebel General, and now a corpse.[3] I write this at the office of the Evening Post, beleagured with a crowd eager for the news.

At Roslyn I found every thing in good order. Mr. Timothy Smith, whom you may remember as a man of large stature and mild look, for some years a Custom house officer, died while I was out there, of an inflammation of the lungs. Mrs. Stuart[4] and Mrs. Cairns had gone to Pennsylvania to place the Stuart boys at the School in Nazareth, and the girl at the School in Bethlehem.

My wife, I think is in rather better health than usual. Julia is also very well. ...

MANUSCRIPT: Ridgely Family Collection TEXT: Hoyt, "Bryant Correspondence, I," 70
ADDRESS: (from MS cover in NYPL–Bryant–Moulton Letters): Mrs. L. M. S. Moulton
/ Care of Joseph W. Moulton Esq. / Baltimore / Maryland. POSTMARK: New-York /
JAN / 22.

1. Unrecovered.
2. By 1862 Bryant had added to his Roslyn property several cottages and small
houses which he let to friends. Goddard, *Roslyn Harbor*, pp. 67–73.
3. Confederate Brigadier General Felix Kirk Zollicoffer (1812–1862), a former Ten-
essee congressman, was killed at Mill Springs, Kentucky, on January 19, 1862, by federal troops under General George H. Thomas.
4. See 951.2.

1260.   *To* William W. Snell

Office of The Evening Post
New York, January 22d   1862

My dear Cousin.

My wife got your letter yesterday in which you mention the receipt
of the seven dollars which I enclosed in a letter to you some days since. She
will answer it soon, and in the mean time your note to Mrs. Cairns shall be
duly sent to her, and I am sure she will be pleased to receive it.

I now enclose the remaining ten dollars, and shall be glad, in due time,
to know that it has come to your hands.

We are all as well as usual. My wife, I think, is in rather better health
than when you were here. She and Julia would desire to be kindly remembered if they were with me. My regards to Mrs. Snell, and believe me.

truly yours
WM. C. BRYANT.

MANUSCRIPT: Claremont College Library ADDRESS: Rev^d. W. W. Snell.

1261.   *To* Hiram Barney

The Evening Post, New York, January 24, 1862

Dear Mr. Barney,

You have not, I hope, flattered yourself that by going to Washington
you have got beyond the reach of importunities for office. Post equitem
sedet atra cura, as Horace says.[1] The office beggar pursues the bestower of
offices to the end of the world.

Mr. James Reed,[2] formerly in the Custom house, and sometime Sachem
in the Tammany Society applies to me in great distress. He voted—gave a
casting vote, in the Council of Sachems in favor of freedom in the territories, and was immediately thrust out of office. He is very poor and now,
in the prosperity of the party for which he lost his employment asks some
post the pay of which would keep his family from starving. I believe he did
his duty faithfully; he seems a capable man—writes a good hand and a well
worded letter.

He has begged me to write both to you and Mr. Opdyke while you are
at Washington which I have now done.[3] It will be a deed to be remembered
in your favor if you can do any thing for him.—

> I am dear sir
> truly yours
> W. C. BRYANT.

MANUSCRIPT: HEHL ADDRESS: H. Barney Esqr.

1. *Odes*, III.i.40. Lit., "Behind the cavalryman sits black care."
2. Reed, a city alderman in 1862 and 1863, was at the time of his death in 1868 a
member of the state Assembly. New York *Times* obituary, February 9, 1868; Edgar A.
Werner, *Civil List and Constitutional History of the Colony and State of New York*
(Albany, 1888), pp. 418–419. No record of an appointment in the custom house subsequent to Bryant's letter has been found.
3. Bryant's letter to George Opdyke is unrecovered.

1262.   *To* John M. Forbes

> Office of The Evening Post
> New York, January 25   1862.

My dear sir.

I thank you for the suggestions in your letter, and you will see that I
have made use of them. You may think, and I confess, not without reason,
that the Evening Post has been somewhat sluggish in remonstrating against
the financial folly which they are meditating at Washington, but probably
you do not know that I am covered all over with scars received in the battle
fought twenty years ago for specie payments, and against the credit system
and in behalf of an independent treasury.[1] We gained the victory and I had
hoped it was a victory for my day at least. To be obliged to go into the battle again, to be forced to do all the work over a second time, fills me with
intense disgust—and is exceedingly discouraging.[2] Besides, I have no taste
for financial speculations, in themselves considered, engaging in them only
on account of the great moral or political ends to be looked at, just as I
would bear any other hardship for the public good. I never dabbled in
stocks, never bought or held stocks of any kind, and hate to hear of stock
operations. I do not say these things for the sake of talking of myself, but to
excuse in some degree an apparent reluctance to enter into this controversy.

I find one of Mr. Grays articles in the Intelligencer and have had it
put in type[3] but cannot get hold of the others.

> I am dear sir
> truly yours
> WM. C. BRYANT.

MANUSCRIPT: HCL ADDRESS: J M Forbes Esq. DOCKETED: W. C. Bryant— / N. Y. /
January 25/62—.

1. On January 22 Forbes had written Bryant decrying the administration's recourse

to a "vicious currency," and urging that the *EP* expose its evils. Forbes, *Letters and Recollections*, I, 281.

2. By the end of 1861 Eastern banks had suspended payment in specie. As a result, Congress began consideration, on January 22, 1862, of a bill providing for the issue of $150 million in legal-tender paper currency, or "Greenbacks." Nevins, *War for the Union*, II, 211–212. Bryant had warned editorially against such a resort to unsecured paper money. He urged repeatedly that the war be financed through increased taxes and bond issues. See, for instance, *EP*, January 15 and 16, 1862. On February 4 Treasury Secretary Chase, reluctant himself to see such a debasement of government credit effected, wrote Bryant nevertheless, "Your feelings of repugnance to the legal-tender clause can hardly be greater than my own, but I am convinced that, as a temporary measure, it is indispensably necessary," and he pleaded for Bryant's support of the measure. Chase to Bryant, February 4, 1862, quoted in *Life*, II, 165.

3. An article entitled "The Poor Made Poorer," taken from the *National Intelligencer* of an unspecified date, was reprinted in the *EP* for January 25, 1862, with the introductory comment that it exposed the "mischievous effects of an irredeemable paper currency in taking from the poor the earnings laid up for a wet day."

1263.   *To* Samuel J. Tilden

New York   January 28, 1862.

Dear Mr. Tilden

The Sketch Club meets at the Century Rooms on Friday evening. Will you do me the favor to come.[1]

Yours truly

WM. C. BRYANT

MANUSCRIPT: NYPL–Samuel Jones Tilden Papers DOCKETED: W. C. Bryant / Jan 28, 1862.

1. The friendship between Bryant and Tilden withstood great political strains. Tilden had remained a Democrat when many of his close associates turned to the new Republican Party in 1856. He opposed Lincoln in 1860, and he and Bryant argued the matter in the *EP* (see *EP*, October 30 and November 7, 1860). A few days before the election, in the newspaper office, Tilden cried, "I would not have the responsibility of William Cullen Bryant and John Bigelow for all the wealth in the sub-treasury. If you have your way, civil war will divide this country, and you will see blood running like water in the streets of this city." John Bigelow, *The Life of Samuel J. Tilden*, 2 vols. (New York: Harper, 1895), I, 153–154. Although once the war had started Tilden urged that the rebellion be crushed, he remained in "loyal opposition" to what he thought the arbitrary power and unconstitutional acts of the administration. It is not known whether Tilden attended this meeting, since the Sketch Club minutes for that date have not been recovered. Information from James T. Callow.

1264.   *To* Abraham Lincoln

New York   January 31. 1862.

My dear sir.

It is said here, on what some deem good authority, that Mr. Welles is to retire from the Navy Department.[1] I sincerely hope not. I regard Mr. Welles with so profound a respect, on account of his enlightened views and rigidly upright character, that I should lament, and greatly lament the cessation of his connection with the federal administration. I do not wonder that he should be impatient at finding the integrity of his motives impeached for the first time in his life, but I hope the disgust he must feel on this account will not be the cause of his retirement.

If, however, it must be that Mr. Welles withdraws, he must have a successor, and I have been told that he will probably be taken from this state. Permit me to say a word in favor of the Hon. David Dudley Field of this city as a person well qualified for the post. In his character mesh many qualities which fit him for the present emergency in public affairs. He is familiar with business and exact and expeditious in transacting it; he is enterprising, resolute and persevering. He would insist on the rights of the government and show no indulgence to those who encroach upon them in any respect. He has been employed in the public service of this state, and has distinguished himself by the ability with which he has performed the duties entrusted to him. His integrity is unimpeached. To confer the post of which I speak, if it should become vacant, as I hope it will not, on such a man, would give a new proof of the determination of the Executive to prosecute the war with energy.[2]

I am sir

with great respect &c &c

WM. C. BRYANT.

MANUSCRIPT: LC ADDRESS: To Mr. Lincoln / President &c. ENDORSED: Wm Cullen Bryant / N. Y. / 1862 / Recommending D. D. Field / as Secy Welles successor.

1. Widespread impatience with the slow progress of the war led Lincoln in January 1862 to replace Secretary of War Simon Cameron by Edwin M. Stanton, and there were rumors of a more general cabinet reorganization to come. On February 3 Attorney-General Edward Bates noted in his *Diary*, "If we fail to do something effectual in the next twenty days, the administration will be shaken to pieces—the cabinet will be remodeled and several of its members must retire." Quoted in Hendrick, *Lincoln's War Cabinet*, p. 353. Gideon Welles recorded that he was being "furiously attacked by many of the newspapers and active partisans, as well as by disappointed speculators and contractors." Welles, *Diary*, I, 60.

2. Field was given no office in the Lincoln administration, and, in fact, in 1864 led a movement in opposition to the President's renomination. See Hendrick, *Lincoln's War Cabinet*, pp. 511, 531; Nevins, *War for the Union*, IV, 91, 107.

1265. *To* Leonice M. S. Moulton

New York   February 12, 1862.

My dear Mrs. Moulton.

Since I received your last letter I have not seen your landlady until last evening. She then informed me that she should make quick work of putting up a house for you, observing that in New York they sell houses ready made, convey them to the places where they are to be erected and put them up in a very little time. She intimated that she should do this, in building a house for you and that your desire would be consulted in the plan of it.

I suppose, therefore, that you will have no occasion for my house. You would not care to take it for a year when your own was to be ready for you so soon. I take it for granted that you would prefer to make some temporary arrangement of another kind until your house should be so far finished as to allow you to move into it.

There is great rejoicing today at the victory gained by Burnside at Roanoke Island and Elizabeth City.[1] In regard to General McClellan the feeling of impatience and distrust is increasing, and if it be true as is said, that the command-in-chief of the armies of the United States has been taken out of his hands, the majority of the people, and, I suspect, in the country too, are pretty well satisfied that it is high time.[2] His attempts to screen General Stone from blame only strengthen the general feeling that all is not right with him. . . .[3]

MANUSCRIPT: Ridgely Family Collection TEXT: Hoyt, "Bryant Correspondence (II)," 193–194.

1. On February 7, 1862 a Union amphibious force led by General Ambrose Everett Burnside (1824–1881, United States Military Academy 1847) captured Roanoke Island, off the coast of North Carolina, easily defeating its Confederate defenders under General Henry A. Wise, former governor of Virginia. Nevins, *War for the Union*, II, 90.

2. Though it was rumored in January 1862 that George Brinton McClellan (1826–1885, United States Military Academy 1846) would be replaced as general-in-chief of the Union armies by General Irvin McDowell (1818–1885, United States Military Academy 1838), his demotion did not occur until March 8, when Lincoln put the various army departments directly under Secretary of War Stanton. Nevins, *War for the Union*, I, 405–406; II, 45–46; Thomas and Hyman, *Stanton*, p. 183.

Bryant's distrust of McClellan was deepened by letters to him from the war front, such as one dated February 6, 1862, from General James Samuel Wadsworth (1807–1864), who wrote, "I repeat the conclusion intimated in my last letter. The commander in chief is almost inconceivably incompetent, or he has his own plans—widely different from those entertained by the people of the North—of putting down this rebellion." NYPL–BG.

3. On February 10, 1862, General Charles Pomeroy Stone (1824–1887, United States Military Academy 1845), a close friend of McClellan's, was imprisoned on charges of misconduct in the defeat of federal forces at the battle of Ball's Bluff on October 21, 1861. He was released after six months, although without clear exoneration, and served in later campaigns. Thomas and Hyman, *Stanton*, pp. 260–261; Nevins, *War for the Union*, I, 298; II, 314–315. The conclusion and signature of this letter were omitted from the printed text.

1266. *To* Charles Sumner

[Confidential]
New York   February 13, 1862.

Dear Mr. Sumner.

I hope you do not mean to vote for the legal tender clause, in the Treasury note bill, nor for the bill with that clause in it. It is clear to me that the framers of the constitution never meant to confer upon the federal government the right of issuing Treasury notes at all, and the reason was that they meant to tie its hands from making them a legal tender. Look at the Madison Papers—the report of the debates in the Convention on the 16th of August and you will see that this is the fact. If we do not respect their decision in the matter as it relates to the form, we should assuredly do so as regards the substance and abstain from exercising a power which it was never meant by the people or by them to grant, the power of making bills of credit a legal tender.

The idea of a necessity for the measure is the shallowest of delusions. My friend Mr. John D. Van Buren[1] now at Washington in consultation with the Ways and Means Committee on the taxation question—a better theoretical and practical political economist than any bank cashier or president in the country—can give you in ten minutes a scheme which will be sure to revive the credit of the country and furnish the means of carrying on the war.

Let me say plainly—Mr. Chase is wrecking himself in the course he is steering, and I feel some solicitude that you should not drive upon the same rock.[2]

I am dear sir
truly yours
Wm C Bryant.

MANUSCRIPT: HCL ADDRESS: Hon   C. Sumner.

1. John Dash Van Buren (1811–1885, Columbia 1829), a New York lawyer and financier, wrote many financial articles for the *EP*. Not long after this, Secretary of the Treasury Salmon P. Chase solicited Van Buren's help in scheduling taxes to raise funds for the war effort.

2. "Even Sumner was deeply troubled by the apparent necessity of incurring all the evils of an inconvertible currency." But the legal-tender bill, with Chase's reluctant support, passed both houses of Congress by substantial margins. Nevins, *War for the Union*, II, 212–213.

1267.   *To* Emma Hardinge[1]

New York, February 25th, 1862.

The undersigned have heard, with great pleasure, of a plan proposed by you for the relief of Outcast Women. That this plan may be made known to our fellow-citizens, and thus public attention called to the solution of this distressing social problem, we respectfully request you to deliver a PUBLIC ADDRESS on this subject, at your earliest convenience. It seems eminently fitting that in an effort to reclaim the sisters of shame and sorrow, a large-minded and warm-hearted woman should take the initiative.

Wm. C. Bryant [and others][2]

MANUSCRIPT: Unrecovered TEXT (*printed handbill?*): NYPL–GR ADDRESS: To Miss Emma Hardinge.

1. Mrs. Emma Hardinge Britten (d. 1899) was a prolific speaker and writer on spiritualism in the United States and Great Britain.

2. Bryant was one of twenty prominent men whose names were appended to this printed letter. In an accompanying note, Miss Hardinge announced that her "Second Address" on the subject of "Outcast Females" would be given at the Cooper Institute on the evening of March 4. See *EP*, March 4, 1862.

1268.   *To* Leonice M. S. Moulton

New York, March 4th   1862

. . . The house of which I speak I took for granted you had engaged and therefore did not write to you again. I was last week at Roslyn and saw that Mrs. Cairns had repaired, enlarged somewhat and considerably embellished the house that Lockwood lived in, so that with its projections and piazzas it is now quite pretty. Mr. [James] Losee is the architect, but as Mr. Cline and I last summer, when Cline thought he might live there took Losee over the whole building and suggested to him such alterations as we thought should be made, I do not consider him as wholly entitled to the merit of all the improvements which have been made. Besides, he borrowed the idea of some of them from what had been done on my two cottages. When your house is put up and the hut belonging to Captain Smith[1] is pulled down the aspect of the place will be wonderfully improved. The new road answers its purpose famously; it keeps in good order, and those who at first grumbled at it are now, I believe, perfectly satisfied.

The London Quarterly you know is a Methodist periodical. Leonard Scott publishes the old Tory periodical, the British Quarterly under the title of the "London Quarterly" which is a misnomer—but he does so I suppose to distinguish it from the Edinburgh. The article to which you refer was written by the Revd. William Arthur, a divine of note in the Wesleyan church. It is one of the few things published in England concerning our rebellion which show even a moderate acquaintance with the facts.[2] Mr. Arthur's dissertation has the merit of being written by one who has visited this country and learned something of its geography and its form of government, and who seems to have thought it necessary, before writing about the quarrel between the slaveholders and the government, to take a little pains to understand its nature. It is next to John Brights speech in fairness and veracity of statement.[3]

The British Quarterly, the Edinburgh and the Westminster—the last numbers of all three—have very absurd and ill natured articles about our civil war. The truth is the English generally hate our form of government, and are glad of any plausible opportunity to decry the character of our people. . . .

MANUSCRIPT: Ridgely Family Collection TEXT: Hoyt, "Bryant Correspondence (II)," 194–195.

1. Stephen Smith (513.1).

2. This article was perhaps an unsigned notice of Count Agenor de Gasparin, *The Uprising of a Great People; or, The United States in 1861*, which appeared in the *London Review*, 17, No. 33 (October 1861), 252–276. The notice was temperate and sympathetic to the federal cause, while blaming many northern businessmen for perpetuating slavery by favoring the South in trade and other business matters. Subsequently, the London Methodist clergyman William Arthur (1819–1900) published a twelve-page pamphlet entitled *The American Question. 1.—English Opinion on the American Rebellion* . . . (London, 1861).

3. Speaking at Rochdale, England, after the Trent Affair, the Lancashire parliamentary leader John Bright (545.2) declared that the British upper class attitude toward the North in the war was that "the republic is too great and powerful and that it is better for us— . . . the governing classes and the governing policy of England—that it should be broken up." Quoted in Hendrick, *Lincoln's War Cabinet*, p. 238. For comment on Bright's staunch support of the American government during the Civil War, see Nevins, *War for the Union*, II, 249, 271.

1269.   *To* Abraham Lincoln

New York   March 5. 1862

My dear Sir.

I learn that the friends of John A. C. Gray Esq.[1] of this city are interesting themselves to obtain for him the post of diplomatic representative of the United States at Rome. Allow me to bear my testimony to his qualifications and to express my hope that the application may be successful. Mr. Gray is a man of worth and intelligence, an able and successful business man, a gentleman of agreeable manners and high social standing, and though not a politician by profession, a zealous republican and an enlightened observer of public events and political movements. His appointment would be highly creditable to the administration.[2]

I am, sir,

very respectfully & truly &c

WM. C. BRYANT.

MANUSCRIPT: NYPL–GR (draft) ADDRESS: To Abraham Lincoln / President of the United States ENDORSED: My letter to President Lincoln / concerning A C Gray / March 186[2].

1. John Alexander Clinton Gray (b. 1815) was president of the Bank of New York and vice president of the Board of Commissioners of Central Park, 1857–. *The Papers of Frederick Law Olmsted. III. Creating Central Park, 1875–1861*, edd. Charles E. Beveridge and David Schuyler (Baltimore & London: The Johns Hopkins University Press [1983]), pp. 65, 93, and *passim*.

2. The records of the Office of the Historian, Department of State, Washington, indicate that Gray was not given a diplomatic or consular position during the Lincoln administration. The American minister to Italy from 1861 until his death in 1882 was

George Perkins Marsh, who had been United States minister to Turkey from 1849 to 1854. See 828.7, 831.3.

1270.   *To* Gideon Welles

New York   March 18th, 1862.

My dear sir.

I give this letter to Albert Bierstadt Esq. a very able and meritorious artist of this city who has already been a traveller in the remote west, to which he accompanied an excursion under the late General Lander, and brought back some striking delineations of the scenery of the Rocky Mountains and illustrations of the habits of the savage tribes who inhabit that region.[1]

He desires now to be appointed an Agent of the government to convey to the Shoshonee and other tribes beyond the Rocky Mountains the annuities and supplies destined for them.[2] Mr. Bierstadt is eminently worthy of the appointment and will faithfully execute the trust, which he desires principally for the opportunity it will give him to gratify the curiosity of the public with views of the extraordinary features of nature in that region.[3]

I am, dear sir,
truly yours
WM   C   BRYANT.

MANUSCRIPT: UVa ADDRESS: To the Hon   Gideon Welles. ENDORSED: Navy Dept— / Respectfully refer / to the Secretary of the / Interior, and I need not / assure him of the high / character &c of Mr. Bryant / G Welles.

1. In 1858, after four years of European study, the German-American landscape artist Albert Bierstadt (558.2) joined the government-sponsored expedition of Frederick West Lander (1821–1862) which surveyed an overland wagon road to the Pacific. Elected to the National Academy in 1860, Bierstadt showed to great acclaim at its exhibitions and others heroic canvases based on sketches made in the Far West. *DAA*; *NAD Exhibition Record*, I, 32–33; E. P. Richardson, *Painting in America: The Story of 450 Years* (New York: Crowell [1956]), pp. 229–230. See Letter 1279.

2. The several branches of the Shoshone tribe inhabited a large area from the Mountain States to California.

3. As a result of this letter Bierstadt gained an honorary appointment as a government agent. See Bierstadt to Bryant, June 5, 1862, NYPL–GR.

1271.   *To* Thomas Edgar Stillman[1]

New York   March 20, 1862.

Dear sir

A neighbor of mine Frederick S. Copley Esqre.[2] who has paid some attention to naval architecture and is ingenious in such matters, has designed an iron-plated gunboat for sea navigation. To secure the necessary buoyancy for its safety on the high seas he has made its shape such that the balls striking it will glance from the surface. He wishes to exhibit his design for the judgment of some intelligent person and at his desire I have taken the liberty of giving him this note to you.

I am, sir,

truly yours

Wm. C. Bryant.

MANUSCRIPT: NYPL–GR ADDRESS: Thomas Stillman Esq.

1. Thomas Edgar Stillman (1837–1906), a young attorney who had recently begun law practice in New York, later helped establish new principles in American maritime law.

2. Copley (d. 1905) was a Roslyn architect who later that year designed a cottage which was built for Jerusha Dewey on Bryant's Roslyn property; see Letter 1316. Copley's design for an ironclad warship was apparently not realized in its construction; in fact, the first such ship built by the Union navy, John Ericsson's *Monitor*, had been launched at the Brooklyn Navy Yard on January 30, 1862, and had fought its first, spectacular battle on March 9 in Hampton Roads, Virginia, against the Confederate ironclad, the *Merrimac*. Nevins, *War for the Union*, II, 52–53.

A versatile artist, as well as architect, Copley exhibited portrait, genre, and landscape paintings at National Academy exhibitions in New York between 1855 and 1870. *DAA*; *NAD Exhibition Record*, I, 95.

1272.   *To* an Unidentified Correspondent

New York, March 29, 1862

... Inasmuch as I wrote the poem called the Embargo,[1] I have no objection to its being quoted as mine, though perhaps it will be just by way of apology for so poor a thing to mention the age at which it was written— thirteen. . . .

MANUSCRIPT: Unrecovered TEXT (*partial*): Anderson Galleries Sales Catalogue, November 17, 1914.

1. See Vol. I, 6; Letter 1241.

1273.   *To* Frances F. Bryant

Office of The Evening Post

New York, April 10th   1862.

Dear Frances.

I cannot go to Roslyn till this afternoon. When I reached Hunters Point I took a seat in the Ladies Room and read patiently till past ten when no sign of a train about to start appearing, I began to look about me. I suspected a change of hour and looked on the walls for a time table. There was none, so I went to the Men's Room and there found one. The hour of starting from James Slip had been changed from half past nine to eight, and this is the first day that the change goes into effect.

I had now nothing to do but to go back to New York. I accordingly went to the James Slip Ferry paid my fare and took my place in the boat moored in the slip. Here I read nearly half an hour longer, and then went to the ferry master and asked what was the matter. He said that a boat from James Slip had come into the other dock and departed since I paid my fare and said that he had told Smith to tell me. I then had to wait another half hour, after which I took passage to New York again. Coming along to the steamer Island City I found that she had lain wind bound for two days at the wharf, but goes out this afternoon if possible, and I on her.

Affectionately,
W   C   B.

MANUSCRIPT: NYPL–GR.

1274.   *To* Fanny Bryant Godwin

New York   April 10, 1862
Thursday morning.

Dear Fanny

Your mother commissions me to write to you. We have received Minna's note and are glad to hear that you are so comfortably situated— You have bad weather to be sure—we wish it was better, but it is probably worse here. Tuesday was a most dreary day ending at night in a snow storm. Yesterday was a sloppy day with a melancholy east wind and this morning there [are?] several inches of snow in the streets. At your house every thing is going on well. Julia is keeping house with all her might. Annie was here yesterday, her cough is rather troublesome yet, but we prescribed for her and hope to hear that she is better. Your mother says there is no reason whatever for your being in any haste to return.

Affectionately
W. C. B.

MANUSCRIPT: NYPL–GR.

1275.   *To* Frances F. Bryant

[New York, cApril 11, 1862]

Dear Frances.

There is bad news from Charles W. Hopkins.

A telegraphic message from Mr. Sherwood informs me that he died at twelve oclock last night.[1] The disease is not mentioned.

The funeral will take place on Saturday at 3 or 4 oclock P. M.

ever yrs
W   C   B.

MANUSCRIPT: NYPL–GR.

1. Charles W. Hopkins (38.5) was Frances Bryant's brother-in-law. His obituary, presumably written by Bryant, appeared in the *EP* for April 15. For William Sherwood of Great Barrington, see 100.9.

1276. *To* Edwin D. Morgan

Office of The Evening Post
New York, April 16th   1862.

My dear sir.

I am much obliged to you for the information contained in your note of the 15th,[1] that it is now in your power to appoint a Commissioner of Deeds for this city. It will certainly be a convenience to me if Mr. Butcher should receive the appointment, and I can answer for his being worthy of it.[2]

I am, sir,
very truly yours
W<small>M</small> C   B<small>RYANT</small>.

MANUSCRIPT: UVa.

1. Unrecovered.
2. It seems unlikely that Butcher received the appointment; see Letter 1312.

1277. *To* Daniel Bogart[1]

Roslyn   May 30   1862.

Dear sir.

I am afraid that I may not be a very punctual attendant at the meetings of the Trustees of the Roslyn Presbyterian Church, but on condition that some deficiency in this respect is overlooked, I will as, I am elected, accept the office of Trustee for the present year.

I am, sir
truly yours
W<small>M</small> C   B<small>RYANT</small>

MANUSCRIPT: BLR ADDRESS: Daniel Bogart Esq.

1. Daniel Bogart (1820–1896) was apparently the chairman of the board of trustees of the Roslyn Presbyterian Church, which, in 1861, incorporated the Roslyn Cemetery. See Goddard, *Roslyn Harbor*, p. 107; Letter 1334.

1278. *To* Orville Dewey

Roslyn   June 9th   1862

Dear Dr. Dewey.

It is so cold, that I am sure you would be all the better for coming a little nearer the sun. To prove to you how much more benignant he is to us just now than to you, I will mention that when we reached this place on Saturday evening we found a large dish of large strawberries ready for us, gathered from the beds in our own garden. Yesterday at dinner we had green peas, also from our garden. If you can come down this week we can promise you an abundance of both. As for the improvements you are making in your dwelling, if you mean to get the greatest amount of enjoyment out of them, do not stay at home till they lose the charm of novelty, but wisely seek to prolong the impression of novelty by a judicious absence.

Say to Mrs. Dewey, that the roses and pinks—the sweetest of flowers, for all they have been in fashion so long—and in spite of the mob of rival flowers which the gardeners are bringing in, are beginning to bloom and will be in their prime of beauty as soon as she can get here. If you should chance to come by steamer, there is one which leaves Peck Slip for Roslyn every afternoon at a quarter before four—the Jessie Hoyt—a nice boat and fast sailer which will bring you to our place in about two hours and a half. I shall be in town on Thursday and pass the night. If you and Mrs. Dewey could come down on that day we could come to Roslyn together on Friday, and when we get here we should keep you as long as we could make you contented. When the strawberries were out you might if you pleased go back to the enlarged dining room and to Sheffield strawberries.

Make my kind regards to Mrs. Dewey and all your family. My wife and daughter send their affectionate greetings to you and yours.

very truly yours
WM. C. BRYANT

MANUSCRIPT: NYPL–GR ADDRESS: Rev^d Dr. O. Dewey.

1279. *To* Albert Bierstadt

Roslyn   Long Island   June 23d   1862.

My dear sir.

I thank you for the beautiful sketch of Conway Meadows which you were so kind as to send me. It is much admired and I am glad to possess so fine a sample of your skill in the art you have chosen.[1]

I am, sir,
truly yours
WM. C   BRYANT

MANUSCRIPT: UTex ADDRESS: A. Bierstadt Esq.

1. See Letter 1270. Bierstadt had written Bryant on June 5 (NYPL–GR) enclosing this sketch and remarking that, although his visit to the Rockies had been put off until the next year "on account of the Indian troubles," Bryant's letter to Secretary Welles had secured him the appointment he sought. An uprising of Sioux Indians in 1862 resulted in the massacre of about 800 settlers and soldiers in Minnesota, and defeat of the Indians at the battle of Wood Lake by a punitive expedition led by General Henry Hastings Sibley (1811–1891), the first governor of Minnesota, 1858–1860.

1280.   To Charles Gallup[1]

Roslyn, Long Island, June 23d.   1862.

Sir.

I can only in part comply with the request expressed in your letter. I possess nothing in the handwriting of Mr. N. P. Willis.[2]

I am, sir,

respectfully yours

WM. C. BRYANT.

MANUSCRIPT: New York University Library ADDRESS: Chas. Gallup Esqre.

1. Apart from this evidence that he collected autographs, Gallup has not been further identified.

2. Gallup's letter is unrecovered. Later that summer, however, Bryant received a letter from Nathaniel P. Willis enclosing a proof copy of his next week's leading editorial for the *Home Journal*, and commenting, "To be seen in your paper is to be known to 'Keep good company,' and therefore, when I do any thing better than (my) usual, I like to be seen there." Willis to Bryant, September 13, 1862, NYPL–GR.

1281.   To Ellen S. Mitchell

Roslyn, Long Island, July 16th, 1862

Dear Niece.

Do you never mean to come and see us again? It is now several years since we have seen your face or that of any of your children. Our house is always open to you and your husband or any other member of your family. This is the season of sea bathing, a little of which taken at the bottom of my garden might do you a great deal of good. There is no probability that either my wife or I will leave this place during the present summer, so that you can choose your own time to come, and we shall always have or make room for as many as you choose to bring. My wife joins me heartily in this invitation. She and Julia send love to all. Write.

Yours affectionately,

W. C. BRYANT

MANUSCRIPT: Weston Family Papers.

1282.   To Adolf Laun[1]

New York   July 21. 1862.

Dear sir.

I have just received your letter respecting the translations you have done me the honor to make of my poems, along with several numbers of the Breme[r?] Sonntagsblatt. I thank you for them and for the kind things you have said of me. The translations seem to me admirable both in regard to their fidelity and the possession of that grace and spirit, without which the most exact metrical version is of little value. With regard to this latter point, however, I am under that disadvantage which all must acknowledge who attempt to judge of poetry written in a foreign language.

The previous translation to which you refer I have never seen.

I shall certainly receive as an honor the dedication of your translation to me, and esteem it the more that it comes from a country which has given the world so many masterpieces of poetic literature.

I am sir,

very respectfully

W   C   Bryant.

Manuscript: NYPL–GR (draft) Address: To Dr. Adolf Laun / Oldenburg / Germany.

1. The German scholar Adolf Laun (1807–1881) had written on July 3, 1862 (NYPL–GR), asking Bryant's permission to publish a collection of his poems in German, and enclosing several specimens of his translations. These were published among others in his *Amerikanische Gedichte von William Cullen Bryant in deutscher Nachbildung nebst Einleitung von A. Laun* (Bremen and Leipzig, 1863).

1283.   *To* Abraham Lincoln

New York   July 31, 1862

Sir.

An application having been laid before you in behalf of Richard Busteed Esq. of this city asking for him a Brigadier General's Commission in the Volunteeer Army of the United States, I take pleasure in bearing my testimony in his favor.[1] Mr. Busteed is a man of great activity and energy of character and of excellent capacity—a lawyer in extensive practice yet willing to leave it for the sake of serving his country in the present civil war. He possesses in my judgment some of the most important qualities of the military character—such as courage, resolution, perseverance, presence of mind fertility in the invention and readiness in the combination of expedients. What he has yet to learn of the military art, his quick apprehension and active mind would enable him soon to acquire. He is of Irish birth, although educated in this country, and possesses great influence with our Irish population, upon which we must depend for a considerable portion of our volunteers. He would, if commissioned devote himself zealously to the very important work of gathering new recruits into our armies and I am confident with success.

In the support of the present administration, Mr. Busteed, although a member of the democratic party and although he did not vote for the Republican candidates for the Presidency and Vice Presidency took a part honorable to himself and beneficial to the country. At the very breaking out of the rebellion he ranged himself on the side of the government and zealously opposed all compromises and every concession to the rebels. His influence has been largely used among our fellow citizens of Irish birth to make them zealous and firm in their loyalty. He is for prosecuting the war with the utmost vigor and bringing it to a speedy end by the use of all the means known to civilized warfare.

I hope therefore that the application in his favor will be granted.

I am sir,

most respectfully yours,

WM C. BRYANT.

MANUSCRIPT: NYPL–Berg ADDRESS: To Mr. Lincoln, President &c. ENDORSED: There seems to be a peculiar reason why Mr. Busteed should enter the Military services; & if the Sec. of War concurs, he may be appointed a Brigadier General; and with the concurrence of the Governor of New York, may engage in raising troops there. A. Lincoln.

1. Son of a Dublin lawyer who, as a British colonel and Chief Secretary of Saint Lucia, British West Indies, in 1829 was removed from his post because of his advocacy of the emancipation of slaves there, Richard Busteed (1822–1898) was taken as a boy to London, Canada, where he learned typesetting on a newspaper run by his father. After a brief period as a reporter on the New York Commercial Advertiser, Richard returned to Ireland, where he was admitted to the bar in 1846 and practiced extradition law. Back in New York, he entered politics as a Democrat, and from 1856 to 1859 served as corporation counsel of New York. In 1860 he campaigned for Stephen Douglas, but after Fort Sumter he became a strong Unionist, enlisting in the army and distinguishing himself for bravery in the field. On August 7, 1862, a week after Bryant's letter to Lincoln, Busteed was appointed a brigadier general of volunteers. In March 1863, while commanding at Yorktown, Virginia, he resigned his commission because of criticism of his appointment by some members of the Senate. In September of that year Lincoln appointed him a United States District Judge in Alabama, a position in which he served from 1865 to 1874. Returning then to New York, he began a noteworthy criminal law practice. War of the Rebellion, Ser. I, vol. 18, pp. 482, 203.

1284. To Oliver Johnson[1]

Roslyn   August 12th   1862.

Dear Sir.

I enclose you a letter to Mr. Owen[2] who I understand left in your care a letter of his to which this is an answer. If I had known his address I would not have given you this trouble. He asked me whether I would permit Mrs. Satter[l]ee to place my name in her list of references and adds that you will act upon my answer. I have no objection certainly.[3]

May I ask you to send the enclosed to Mr. Owen if he is in town. If not please put it in an envelope returning it—if you will take the trouble to the office of the Evening Post.

Yours truly

W   C   BRYANT

MANUSCRIPT: Wellesley College Library ADDRESS: Mr. Johnson.

1. Oliver Johnson (1809–1889), a founder of the New England Anti-Slavery Society, was then editor of the *Anti-Slavery Standard*. In 1881 he published a biography of Abolitionist William Lloyd Garrison (1805–1879), his early associate.

2. Letter 1285.

3. Robert D. Owen had written Bryant on August 1 (NYPL–BG) asking him to lend his name to a circular advertising the New York boardinghouse of a Mrs. Satterlee, sister of Miss Mattie Griffith of Kentucky, who had freed her slaves unconditionally, "almost her whole property."

1285. *To* Robert Dale Owen

Roslyn   Long Island
August 12th   1862.

My dear sir.

My wife thanks you very much for the photograph of Mrs. Owen, and bids me remind you, that she has a promise, not I believe from you, but certainly from Mrs. Owen that she should have yours also. I believe the law that made the husband responsible for the wife's debts is in force yet. At least you will pay "for the honor of the drawer," as they say in commerce.

The talk "on national affairs" might best be had here in the quiet of the country. Why cannot you come to Roslyn[?] There is a nice steamboat, the Jesse Hoyt, which every day at a quarter to four in the afternoon leaves Peck Slip in New York for this place. Put yourself on board of her with the afternoon paper and you are here without any trouble, where we shall all be glad to see you, and choose your own time for coming; we shall find a corner for you.

Your letter in the newspapers is a capital thing, and is making much impression.[1]

I know of nobody at present whom I can send to Mrs. Satterlee's, but what you say of her will induce me to do all that I can for her. She is welcome to my name among her references.

I am sorry not to have seen you this summer, and regret that you should have had so much trouble in looking for me. If I had known any thing of your inquiries after me I should have tried hard to persuade you to pass a night or two here.

My wife desires her kind regards.

Yours very truly
WM C. BRYANT.

MANUSCRIPT: HSPa.

1. A letter from Owen to Secretary of War Stanton dated July 23, 1862, urging that the country was now ready for the emancipation of all slaves, was reprinted in the *EP* on August 8, 1862, under the caption "The Policy of Emancipation; Words of a True Democrat." In a leading editorial that day, the *EP* supported Owen's argument strongly.

1286. *To* Orville Dewey

New York, August 17, 1862

... I *must* answer your letter[1] a little. Neither you nor I understand war nor medicine; but of medicine we know enough not to employ a physician who regularly doses all his patients, nor one who proposes to cure an inflammation of the bowels by poulticing the little finger. *I* judge of the merits of military men in the same way. Again, I have a right to choose between the opinions of men well acquainted with the military art, and I know that officers of great merit hold that McClellan has mismanaged the campaign throughout. Pope, one of the most successful of them, does so. (I *know* this;) so does Wadsworth; so does General Hitchcock, a veteran officer personally kind toward McClellan, and disposed to judge him candidly (I speak from personal knowledge): so also, I have reason to believe, do hundreds of other officers.[2]

What the "Evening Post" has said in regard to the course taken by the Government I said in still stronger terms to Mr. Lincoln himself ten days since, when I went to Washington for the purpose.[3] With me was Mr. K——,[4] a millionaire (or millionary—which?) of this city, who said to him that unless the war was prosecuted with greater energy—far greater—and the confiscation and emancipation act carried into vigorous execution, not sixty days would elapse before the Government securities would be so depressed that the administration would not have a dollar to carry on the war.

Mr. Lincoln knows that McClellan is wanting in some of the necessary qualities of a general officer. He said to Mr. Field[5]: "McClellan is one of the most accomplished officers in all the army. No man organizes or prepares an army better, but when the time for action comes he is greatly deficient."

As to emancipation, I have none of the fears which you entertain, and the conduct of the blacks already freed—more than fifty thousand of them— convinces me that there is no ground for them. Their peaceful and docile behavior assures me that we have neither "wild disorder nor massacre to dread." The rebellion has buried its roots so firmly into the social system of the South that they must both be pulled up together.

You anticipate a bad effect upon the recruiting service from such criticisms on the conduct of the Government as the "Evening Post" had thought it necessary to make. The mischief was done before the "Evening Post" began to criticise. A gloomy and discouraged feeling prevailed, throughout this city and this State at least, which seemed to make the raising of the necessary number of volunteers hopeless. The only remedy that the case seemed to admit was the adoption by the press and by public speakers of a more vigorous style of animadversion on the conduct of the war, and the representations of disinterested persons made personally to the President. Mayor Opdyke, William Curtis Noyes, Dr. Charles King, and many others, singly or in pairs, have visited Washington for this purpose. There is not one of these men to whom such conclusions as you have reached would not be a matter of exceeding surprise. They have all regarded the cause of the Union as drifting to ruin if instant and powerful means were not applied to give things a new direction. I believe their representations, and the language held in public meetings, and to some degree also the comments of the press, have had a certain effect. I hear this morning that it was Pope who recommended Halleck to the President as a fit person to force McClellan into action, and to push on the war with vigor. Other proceedings of the administration within a few days give token that it is waking to a sense of the danger we are in from causes very much like those of which you speak.

I have written thus largely because I had some things to say which I cannot print. If I could, I would have received your rebuke without a reply. . . .

MANUSCRIPT: Unrecovered TEXT (*partial*): *Life*, II, 176–178.

1. Unrecovered.
2. General McClellan had been ordered on August 3 to move his Army of the Potomac from the James River in Virginia to the Potomac River, nearer Washington, to reinforce the Army of Virginia under Major General John Pope (1822–1892, United States Military Academy 1842). McClellan's reluctance to do so, and a resulting delay, brought sharp criticism from Bryant's *EP* and other northern journals, as well as from the Union general-in-chief, Henry Wager Halleck (1815–1872, United States Military Academy 1839). Major General Ethan Allen Hitchcock (1798–1870, United States Military Academy 1817), a veteran of the Florida and Mexican Wars, and earlier in 1862 an adviser to Secretary Stanton, had more recently been ill at New York, where, presumably, Bryant had talked with him. General Wadsworth, who would distinguish himself at the battles of Gettysburg and the Wilderness—at the second of which he was mortally wounded—was another of Bryant's military confidants. As early as February 1862, as we have noted, Wadsworth had called McClellan "almost inconceivably incompetent." See Nevins, *War for the Union*, II, 45, 142–143, 170–172; Thomas and Hyman, *Stanton*, pp. 185–187, 204.
3. See Letter 1288. According to Godwin (*Life*, II, 178), Bryant visited Lincoln "at the urgent request of many distinguished citizens of [New York] . . . to do what he could toward stimulating the activities of the Cabinet."
4. Probably Charles King (196.3); see below.
5. Probably David D. Field.

1287.   To Theodore S. Fay[1]

Office of The Evening Post
New York, Aug. 21, 1862

My dear sir

I have written at different times two notes[2] addressed to you at the Astor House, and having heard nothing from you since, I suppose you could not have recovered them. I therefore send this to the post office.

In one of these notes I invited you to my place in the country at Roslyn Long Island. Every afternoon at a quarter before 4 o'clock the steamer Jessie Hoyt leaves Peck Slip for Roslyn, and lands you near my house where we shall all—there are three of us—be glad to see you, and will show you a very pretty region, if we have no other means of entertainment.

I am little at this office, and am generally much occupied while here—but should make time to see you if you were to call—but at home I have perfect leisure. I should be sorry if you were to go back to Europe without giving me an opportunity to see you.[3]

I am, dear sir, . . .[4]

MANUSCRIPT: NYPL–GR (draft?) ENDORSED (by Bryant): My Letter to / Theo^d. S   Fay /
    —Aug   1862.–.

1. Since Bryant had seen him at the American embassy at Berlin in 1845 (see Vol. II, 291), the novelist and diplomat Theodore S. Fay (1807–1898) had served as United States Minister to Switzerland, 1853–1861.

2. Neither note has been recovered. Fay had written Bryant on August 5 (NYPL–BG) of his recent "interesting interview" with President Lincoln "which I should like to relate to you."

3. After retiring from the diplomatic service and visiting the United States briefly, Fay passed the rest of his long life in Germany.

4. Bryant's signature appears to have been clipped.

1288.   *To* Horatio N. Powers[1]

Roslyn, September 15, 1862

. . . Your letter of the 7th instant makes a very natural suggestion.[2] Lest you should suppose that the real friends of the country in this neighborhood have been remiss, I would inform you that this very method which you mention has been tried with Mr. Lincoln. Some of our best and most eminent men have visited Washington to remonstrate with him, but with only partial effect. The influence of Seward is always at work, and counteracts the good impressions made in the interviews with men of a different class. I was strongly pressed to go to Washington myself, and went somewhat reluctantly, not having any confidence in my powers of persuasion. I saw Mr. Lincoln, and had a long conversation with him on the affairs of the country, in which I expressed myself plainly and without reserve, though courteously. He bore it well, and I must say that I left him with a perfect conviction of the excellence of his intentions and the singleness of his purposes, though with sorrow for his indecision.[3] A movement is now on foot to bring the influence of our best men to bear upon him in a more concentrated manner, by a wider concert among them. Meetings have been held for that purpose and a committee raised.[4] . . .

MANUSCRIPT: Unrecovered TEXT (*partial*): *Life*, II, 178–179.

1. See Letter 627.

2. On September 7 Powers had written Bryant from Davenport, Iowa, urging him, as one of "the first & best men of the nation," to declare with others to President Lincoln the need for firm action to save free government from "horrible corruption and abominable stupidity in high places, paralyzing the strength of the army." NYPL–BG.

3. In an *EP* editorial of the same date as this letter Bryant wrote that, although Lincoln seemed "honest" and "determined," his "want of decision and purpose" was reflected in the "weakness and vacillation" of his administration, which led to suspicion in many minds that "treachery lurks in the highest quarters."

4. This was in all likelihood an exploratory group of prominent Republicans and Democrats whose consultations resulted on March 20, 1863, in a great organizing meeting at Cooper Union of the New York Union League, whose purpose was "Effective organization for the Union cause, emancipation, and a more energetic prosecution of the war." Its council included Bryant, George Bancroft, William E. Dodge, Francis Lieber, and A. T. Stewart. "Although its founders wished to keep it out of party politics, it was an arm of strength for Lincoln in most respects." See Nevins, *War for the Union*, III, 162–163.

1289.   *To* Henry Dwight Sedgwick, Jr.[1]

Roslyn   Sept. 15   1862.

Dear Mr. Sedgwick.

I got your letter only on Saturday night. We had already been startled by seeing the mention of Mrs. Sedgwick's death in the newspapers.[2] Her energy and activity both physical and intellectual had made us presage for her a longer term of life.

In the sorrow which my wife and myself feel at this intelligence, we can well understand how much her nearer friends will miss her. Her life, though not prolonged as we had hoped, was crowded with active duties and if the hour of rest came to her . . .[3] it came to one who had nobly borne the burden and heat of the day and had shrunk from no exertion or sacrifice which the circumstances of life suggested to her generous heart.

Might I ask you to make known to the immediate relatives of her whom you have lost our sympathy with them in this affliction.

I am dear sir
truly yours
W   C   B.

MANUSCRIPT: NYPL–GR (draft) ADDRESS: H. D   Sedgwick Esq.

1. Henry Dwight Sedgwick, Jr. (1824–1903), was a son of Bryant's early friend, one of the several Sedgwick brothers who sponsored his move from Great Barrington to New York in 1825. See Vol. I, 14–15; Letter 120.

2. Elizabeth Ellery Sedgwick (Mrs. Robert Sedgwick, 1011.3; Letter 1014) died at Stockbridge, Massachusetts, on September 9, 1862.

3. Several words illegible.

1290.   *To* Abraham Lincoln

Office of The Evening Post,
New York, September 23   1862

Sir.

If Mr. Clay is not to be reappointed as our minister to Russia, I most
heartily recommend Mr. Bayard Taylor the present Secretary of Legation
for that post.[1] Mr. Taylor has many important qualifications for the place
and would fill it with honor to his country

I am sir most respectfully &c
W. C BRYANT.

MANUSCRIPT: PML ADDRESS: To Abraham Lincoln / President of the United States.

1. After six months as United States minister to Russia, Cassius Clay was succeeded
in 1862 by Lincoln's first Secretary of War, Simon Cameron; the travel writer Bayard
Taylor (Letter 632) remained as secretary of legation until 1863. In the year of his
death, 1878, he was briefly United States minister to Germany. Clay served again as
minister to Russia from 1863 to 1869.

1291.   *To* Frances F. Bryant

Roslyn   Tuesday morning
September 30, 1862.

My dear Frances.

It was my purpose to write you yesterday from New York, but I had
not time in consequence of an accident, which made us arrive late. We
waited at the Bethlehem [Pennsylvania] Station a little beyond the usual
time for the train, and when it came we were surprized to see only the
engine and its tender with a few passengers on the tender among the coals.
It appeared that a bridge which needed repairs was not finished so as to be
passable, and the engine was on one side and the cars on another, so the
engine came on alone.

After three quarters of an hour longer our engine was hitched to a car
belonging to another railroad company, and took us to Easton, where we
found that the train which was to have taken us had just gone. We were
then told that we must wait till twelve o'clock for the next train. But a man
with an omnibus told us that a mixed train conveying passengers and
freight left Phillipsburg on the other side of the river at 9 o'clock for New
York. He took us over and we then had to wait two hours which Mr.
Henderson and I employed in walking over the town. We had a slow
journey to New York, reaching the city at a quarter before three o'clock.

Mrs. Henderson and myself proceeded immediately to Mrs. Williams's. She was not in and we looked at the rooms. The servant, however,
said they were taken and Mrs. Williams coming in, as we were about to go,
said that they had been engaged by a Mr. Irving. We asked whether she

could recommend any other place. She gave us the name of a Mrs. Sperry on the same block with herself, at the corner, and of Mrs. Heath opposite. We went to Mrs. Sperry's. Here were four rooms on the same floor, the second story, two large rooms and two small end bedrooms. Her price was $60— a week and $30— when the family were away. There was another room up stairs which might be had for $10— more. I had no time to stay longer, and Mrs. Henderson said she would look at Mrs. Heath's rooms on the other side of the way.

I find every thing going on well here. Fanny's children are well. The baby[1] is picking up, and quite happy. Mrs. Crawford Isaac and Annie went yesterday to town and will probably return today. The slaters are busy on the roof of the mill and will soon finish. The new cottage is handsomer than ever. The plumbers are laying down the pipes and the water will be in the reservoir before you return.

I think I have emptied my budget of news. We will endeavor to have every thing quiet here before you return. I might add that the country was slightly refreshed by a sparing shower on Saturday night and Sunday morning just as Bethelem was, and that more rain is needed yet further. I learn that William Ely called here yesterday with his wife and brought Mrs. Snow with them—the mother, I suppose. They knew, however, before coming that you were absent. Of our other neighbors I have not heard a word.

I doubt whether a better place will be found for us next winter than Blancard's—but we shall see.

Fanny has not returned. Minna had a note from her yesterday saying that she would come home in a couple of days—but does not believe she will come till the end of the week. Make yourself as comfortable as you can and amuse yourself with what offers at Bethlehem, where I fear matters of amusement do not abound. Love to Julia.

Yours ever,
W. C. B.

MANUSCRIPT: NYPL–GR ADDRESS: Mrs. F. F. Bryant.

1. Walter Godwin.

1292. *To* Frances F. Bryant

Roslyn   October 1, 1862
Wednesday morning.

My dear Frances.

I received the enclosed letter yesterday, which was intended as you see for yourself—opened and read it and send it to you as good as new.

The rooms of which I spoke in my last on the side of the street opposite to Mrs. Williams's were looked at on Monday by Mrs. Henderson, and found not to be what we wanted. There are now only Blancards rooms to depend on— If you and Julia like them, I will take them. Mrs. Henderson came out last night and found that Miss Crawford had packed up every thing to go today, and had gone off herself. It rains, however, and they defer their departure till tomorrow. The rain delays the slating of course.

I have given the little heifer that won't grow to Miss Amy Mudge.[1] I suppose you know that it has been in her pastures all summer, and as it did not seem likely to turn out well I talked of selling her. Mr. Cline suggested giving her away, to which I agreed, and gave her to Miss Amy who has pasture enough and more. Last evening in going in the boat for my paper I met the Miss Hopkins's who made me quite ashamed with their acknowledgments.

They are all well at Fanny's this morning. Minna came over and read to me this morning.

The water pipe is laid acros the pond and the road and a little way up the hill, but the rain hinders any thing from being done with it today. The filtering cistern is finished. I have had a smaller one built beside the main one. I hope you find means to entertain yourself. Love to Julia.

Yours ever
W   C   BRYANT.

MANUSCRIPT: NYPL–GR ADDRESS: Mrs. F   F. Bryant.

1. See 700.5.

1293.   To Frances F. Bryant

Roslyn   October 2d   1862
Thursday morning.

Dear Frances.

Another rainy morning. Mrs. Henderson and such of her children as had remained went by the steamer. Frederick took them down in the little waggon as the road is quite muddy. The horses and carriages went yesterday. It is now quite solitary here. Fanny's colored Quaker cook went away day before yesterday afternoon, and they have nobody now there but Maria and the seamstress.

I have [had] the grate put into the dining room fire-place and they are now busy in laying down the carpet so that you may have a fire if necessary as soon as you return. Yesterday was quite chilly here and I took out the fireboard in the library and burnt up the pile of papers in the Franklin stove, but made no fire otherwise, though I brought down the andirons. With October comes the season for fires.

I take advantage of the rainy weather to have the ice-room over what we call the fruit room cleared of rubbish, never to have ice in it again.

The Gurneys have just sent me another photograph taken last Saturday.[1] It is better than the first—in attitude at least.

I have not yet learned whether Mr. Henderson will go to Bethlehem on Saturday. If he should, I think I may stay here and meet you in New York on Monday. I shall not write again as this letter I suppose will not reach you till Saturday.

Yours ever
W C. B.

MANUSCRIPT: NYPL–GR ADDRESS: Mrs. F. F. Bryant.

1. This was a carte de visite portrait, taken by J. Gurney & Son of 707 Broadway, New York. See illustration.

1294. To Thomas Hillhouse[1]

Office of The Evening Post
New York, October 6, 1862

My dear sir.

The bearer of this letter is O. J. Downing Esqre of North Hempstead on Long Island,[2] a neighbor of mine and a young man of merit, and excellent capacity. He has been very active in raising recruits for the army, in which service he spent a great deal of time and money, obtaining more than two hundred enlistments. As an encouragement to his exertions he was commissioned supernumerary Second Lieutenant, but the moment he had taken his recruits to Washington, he with the other supernumeraries was mustered out of the service and suddenly deprived of the position he expected to hold and which by every title of usefulness and merit he ought to have held. There are now five vacancies in the regiment for which he recruited—Harris's Light Cavalry—one of which he hopes to receive. I take the liberty of commending Mr. Downing's case—which is a hard one to your attention—assured that you will be ready to aid so far as depends on you, in doing him justice[3]

I am sir very respectfully yours
WM. C. BRYANT.

MANUSCRIPT: NYHS ADDRESS: To Adjutant General Hillhouse ENDORSED: New York   Oct 6, 1862 / — / W[m] Cullen Bryant / Parke Godwin / & / — Rec[dg] Nomination of O. J. Downing / to 2nd Lieutenancy, / 7th Cav. N. Y. S. vols / — / Rec Oct 7th.

1. Thomas Hillhouse (1816–1897), a state senator from Geneva, New York, had been appointed adjutant-general of the state in July 1861.
2. Obadiah J. Downing, whose father apparently owned a small property on the Hempstead Harbor shore a mile or two north of Cedarmere (see Goddard, *Roslyn Harbor*, p. [21]), has been otherwise identified only as indicated in Note 3 below.
3. Downing was evidently reinstated in his commission; see Letter 1315. On June 9, 1863, as a captain in the Second New York Cavalry, First Brigade (Harris's Light Cavalry), he was mentioned in dispatches for gallant conduct in an action at Brandy Station, Virginia. Several times thereafter he was mentioned in dispatches for "good

conduct and gallantry," and on October 12, 1863, his brigade commander wrote, "I particularly request that the name of this officer may be forwarded to headquarters of the army with a statement of the service he rendered, that he may receive in general orders the approbation he so richly deserves." *War of the Rebellion*, Ser. I, vol. 28, pt. 1, pp. 996–997; Ser. I, vol. 29, pt. 1, pp. 123, 375–376, 388.

1295.   *To* A[lfred?] T. Goodman[1]

Roslyn, Long Island,
October 14th. 1862

Sir.

In complying, so far as I am able, with your request,[2] I have to express my regret that I can send you no autograph but my own. I correspond little with distinguished men, and soon part with such of their letters as I do not specially wish to keep.

I am, sir,
respectfully &c.
WM. C. BRYANT.

MANUSCRIPT: WCL ADDRESS: A. T. Goodman Esq.

1. Quite possibly Alfred T. Goodman (1845–1871), a precocious scholar of Cleveland, Ohio, who, although still in high school, was an "indefatigable searcher after historical books and especially Mss," and who published several works on political and military biography before his early death.

2. Goodman's request, presumably in a letter, is unrecovered.

1296.   *To* John M. Forbes

Office of the Evening Post,
New York, October 16, 1862.

My Dear Sir.—

What your friend says of Grant may be the truth, so far as he is acquainted with his history. But I have friends who profess to be acquainted with him, and who declare that he is now a temperate man, and that it is a cruel wrong to speak of him as otherwise. I have in my drawer a batch of written testimonials to that effect. He reformed when he got or was put out of the army, and went into it again with a solemn promise of abstinence. One of my acquaintance has made it his special business to inquire concerning his habits, of the officers who have recently served with him or under him. None of them have seen him drunk, or seen him drink. Their general testimony is that he is a man remarkably insensible to danger, active, and adventurous.

Whether he drinks or not, he is certainly a fighting general, and a successful fighter, which is a great thing in these days . . .[1]

MANUSCRIPT: Unrecovered TEXT: Forbes, *Letters and Recollections*, II, 335–336.

1. After exceptional bravery as a young lieutenant in the Mexican War, Ulysses Simpson Grant (1822–1885, United States Military Academy 1843) resigned from the army in 1854, having been warned that his solitary drinking would lead to a court-martial. In 1861, promising abstinence, he was commissioned a colonel of Illinois volunteers. As a brigadier general, his victory at Forts Henry and Donelson in February 1862 brought him a major general's rank and command of the Army of the Tennessee, but after his lack of preparation resulted in a costly surprise at the battle of Shiloh in April, he was bitterly criticized in the northern press, with unsupported charges of his drunkenness. Nevins, *War for the Union*, I, 166, 328; II, 78–85; III, 143.

Bryant was among the first to perceive in Grant the promise of a great commander. After Fort Donelson he called him a "capable, clear-headed general" who got things done. Following the Confederate repulse at Corinth on October 3–4, 1862, he characterized Grant as the one general "able not only to shake the tree, but to pick up the fruit." When the crucial southern bastion of Vicksburg on the Mississippi fell to Grant in July 1863 Bryant defended him against the drinking charge, declaring that he had won more battles than any other northern commander, and concluded, "If any one after this still believes that Grant is a drunkard, we advise him to persuade the Government to place none but drunkards in important commands." See *EP*, February 14 and October 8, 1862; July 8, 1863.

Several years after the war a letter to the *EP* charged that Grant and his staff had once got drunk while riding from Springfield to Cairo, Illinois, in a private car on the Illinois Central Railroad. The receipt of this letter coincided with a call upon Bryant by William H. Osborn, president of that railroad, who termed the charge "a malignant falsehood." Osborn recalled that the Grant party had indeed ridden to Cairo in the president's car. "I took them down myself," he said, "and selected that car because it had conveniences for working, eating, and sleeping on the way. We had dinner in the car, at which wine was served to such as desired it. I asked Grant what he would drink; he answered, a cup of tea, and this I made for him myself. Nobody was drunk on the car, and to my certain knowledge Grant tasted no liquid but tea and water." Nevins, *Evening Post*, p. 310.

1297. *To* Frances F. Bryant

Office of The Evening Post,
New York, October 21, 1862
Tuesday morning

Dear Frances.

I came in this morning and having received Julia's note of last evening take it for granted that you are gone. If I had not supposed that you would set out yesterday morning, I would have come to town, then.

Every thing is going on well at our place. The woods are beginning to brighten. Fanny and the children are as well as usual. Harold does not want to come to town and Bryant is sorry to be obliged to leave Roslyn,— and indeed it never seemed more charming than now in this golden sunshine. It is only a pity that the days were not longer. I get through the days very well, but the evenings are dolefully solitary. I read myself sleepy and then get up and walk the room.

Of the incidents of the farmyard, I have two to relate. The heifer which I gave to Miss Amy [Mudge] was found dead on Sunday morning in her pasture field. Mr. Godwin offered her Nelly but she declined the gift because she had nobody to take care of the animal.

Goodbye—write immediately, and tell me when you will return—and let that not be far off. I enclose some letters. Kind regards to everybody at Great Barrington.

Ever yours
W C. B.

MANUSCRIPT: NYPL–GR.

1298.   *To* Frances F. Bryant

Roslyn   Wednesday   October 22d   1862.

Dear Frances.

I send you a letter which came yesterday to this place while I was in town. Your brother seems to mend slowly, but still mends.

Minna went to town yesterday and Bryant and little Fanny[1] this morning. Harold tells me that he is not to go till the snow comes. Mrs. Cairns and the three children returned in the steamer last evening with Mr. and Mrs. Stuart also.

At West Point Mrs. Cairns fell in with Miss Rebecca Smith who used to plague me last winter. This lady told her that she was engaged to be married to a lad of fifteen, named Ledyard, the grandson of our old acquaintance, Mrs. Ledyard.[2] He is now a cadet at West Point. She also threatened to come to Roslyn to see my place. Mrs. Cairns's conclusion was that the poor woman was "cracked." I am not certain that she is any thing more than excessively silly and vain.

Nothing extraordinary has happened here, except the hoar frost of yesterday morning which was very copious and whitened every board in the neighborhood on which dew could fall. It did no harm however to vegetation. Love to Julia. Kind regards to Mrs. Hopkins and Mrs. Hendersons family.

Yours ever
W. C. B.

MANUSCRIPT: NYPL–GR.

1. Fanny Godwin (1854–1933), fourth daughter of Parke and Fanny Bryant Godwin, was later Mrs. Alfred White.
2. See Letters 145, 194.

1299.   *To* Abraham Lincoln

New York, Oct. 22d   1862

My dear sir.

Allow me to say a very few words on a subject in which the friends of the administration and the country in this quarter feel a profound interest.

We are distressed and alarmed at the inactivity of our armies in putting

down the rebellion. I have been pained to hear lately from persons zealously loyal, the expression of a doubt as to whether the administration
sincerely desires the speedy annihilation of the rebel forces. We who are
better informed acquit the administration of the intention to prolong the
war though we cannot relieve it of the responsibility. These inopportune
pauses, this strange sluggishness in military operations seem to us little
short of absolute madness. Besides their disastrous influence on the final
event of the war they will have a most unhappy effect upon the elections
here, as we fear they have had in other states.[1] The election of Mr. Seymour
as Governor of New York would be a public calamity. A victory or two
would almost annihilate his party and carry General Wadsworth triumphantly into office.[2]

If what is apparently the present military policy of those who conduct
the war be persisted in, the Union in our view is lost, and we shall resign
ourselves to the melancholy conviction that the ruin of our republic is
written down in the decrees of God.

> I am, sir,
> with high respect
> Your obt. servant,
> WM. C. BRYANT.

MANUSCRIPT: LC ADDRESS: To Abraham Lincoln / President of the United States. DOCK-
ETED: Wm C. Bryant / New York. Oct. 22. 1862. PUBLISHED: Spivey, *Bryant Cautions and Counsels Lincoln*, pp. 7–8.

1. After the great, indecisive battle of mid-September at Antietam Creek, near
Fredericksburg, Maryland, General McClellan had failed to pursue the retreating
southern forces, while offering the administration one unconvincing excuse after another for the delay. Lincoln, already impatient with his commander of the Army of the
Potomac, was "beset by Bryant, Raymond, and a hundred other editors to give the
country some progress." Finally, on November 5, 1862, he relieved McClellan of his
command, and appointed in his place Major General Ambrose Everett Burnside (1824–
1881, United States Military Academy 1847). Nevins, *War for the Union*, II, 227, 327–
330.
2. Bryant's condemnation of Horatio Seymour (1810–1886), who had already served
one term as New York's governor, in 1853–1855, may have been overly harsh. Nevertheless, the Democratic platform on which he ran and was elected to another term in 1862,
which proposed to "restore the Union as it was," and to maintain slavery south of the
Missouri Compromise line, "gave comfort to all enemies of the Administration and
most sympathizers with the South." *Ibid.*, 302. Seymour's Republican opponent in 1862
was Brigadier General James S. Wadsworth (1265.2).

1300.   *To* A. S. Wallace[1]

New York   Oct   22, 1862

Sir.

I have given your address to a medical friend who has promised to
write to you stating what course of treatment he thinks might be beneficial

in your case. But he is of the allopathic school, and I am a homoeopathist. I shall therefore say what method I think would be best.

The best way, I think, would be to employ a homoeopathic physician under whose prescriptions I think your case would be greatly improved and perhaps a comfortable measure of health attained. If such a physician is not at hand, then I would suggest in the first place, constant employment, of such a nature as to keep the thoughts always occupied; very early rising, allowing no time to be passed in bed except for necessary sleep; bathing the small of the back and loins every morning in cold water; chest exercise with ample inflation of the lungs, the avoidance of bad company and of such reading as excites the passions. Some recommend what the Germans call the sitz-bad [hip-bath] and electricity. Spiritous liquors and excess in eating should be carefully avoided. Sleep on a hard bed and cultivate hardy habits.

As for drugs—Caspari a German homoeopathist[2] recommends *Cinchona* the 24th attenuation repeated every three or four days. If this after several trials has no good effect—then alternate it with Phosphoric acid and Conium in high attenuations.

Hering[3] recommends, after *cinchona nux vomica*, and then *sulphur* and *c[a?]lcana*.

I think however that cold water and the means of which I have spoken as the first to be applied are the most to be depended on.

Yours respectfully
W   C   BRYANT.

MANUSCRIPT: NYPL–GR (draft) ADDRESS: To A S. Wallace / Newburgh Cuyahoga County   Ohio. ENDORSED (by Bryant): Letter *to* / A. S. Wallace / Oct. 1862.

1. The young inquirer whose letter apparently provoked this reply is unidentified, except as in the descriptive note.

2. Carl Gottlob Caspari (1798–1828), with whose *Homeopathic Domestic Physician*, translated from the German by W. P. Esrey (Philadelphia, 1851) Bryant was probably acquainted.

3. Constantin Hering (1800–1880), whose *The Homoeopathic Domestic Physician* (Philadelphia, 1835) was often reprinted, was mainly responsible for introducing into the United States the medical system of the German physician Samuel Hahnemann (1755–1843).

1301.   *To* Frances F. Bryant

Roslyn   Saturday morning
October 25th   1862.—

My dear Frances.

I thank you for your letter dated Wednesday evening,[1] which I got yesterday. By this time I hope the rest of your cold has followed that part of it of which you had got rid when you wrote.

Last evening I had two unexpected guests. The steamer came late to Roslyn. At nine o'clock a loud rapping was heard at the door. I opened it and there was Annie [Godwin] who had come to pass Sunday. Behind Annie advanced a gentleman, who immediately introduced himself as Mr. Kilborn of Jersey City.[2] He entered the room and laid on the table a heavy package consisting of three or four stout rolls enveloped in brown paper and well corded side by side. It was he said a manuscript which he wished to submit to me for my opinion. "I cannot look at it," I replied, ["]I must positively decline. It is poetry I suppose." "It is," said he. "It is a political poem. I have been three times to your office, to lay it before you." "I cannot and will not look at it. I have neither eyes nor time for such things. I am plagued to death with these applications. I have enough of them in town, and hoped not to be persecuted with them here." "But I went three times to your office and could not see you." "Well, there was the mail. If you had written to me, I should have answered that I could not look at the manuscript, and would thus have saved you this trouble." Mr. Kilborn then asked the way to the hotel. I told him that I should be happy to give him a bed here, which after a decent appearance of hesitation he accepted. I ordered tea for him. He begged I would not; he had had a late dinner. I knew better; the tea was brought in, and he showed that he was not sorry to see it. He talked politics and not unintelligently, but he appeared to be somewhat fanatical, and convinced me that he is a man who sees very far into mill stones.[3] This morning he came to my door, before I came down, and apologized for his intrusion, and thanked me for my hospitality. He would not let me give him breakfast, but footed it away to Glenwood, in the grey of the morning, a wiser man than he came. The lesson he got, I think, will do him more good than my criticism on his poetry could possibly have done. I think this story will amuse Mr. Sherwood.

My cough is rather better today, and with this pleasant weather I do not see much encouragement for it to stay with me.

Affectionately as ever yours
Wm. C. Bryant

P.S. I write this postscript at the postoffice, where I have just got your second letter. When I come up, I think I shall take the afternoon train—if that goes through so far. I shall see. I wish you were here, the weather is so fine and the woods so beautiful.

W. C. B.

manuscript: NYPL–GR.

1. Unrecovered.
2. Not further identified.
3. "Extraordinarily acute" (iron.).

1302.   *To* Frances F. Bryant

Roslyn, October 26th[1]   1862
Sunday evening.

Dear Frances.

Yesterday I got a letter from Sarah Olds[2] in which she says she shall set out for New York on the 14th of November, and asks what she shall do on reaching the city of which she has great dread. I will answer her after seeing you.

The mill-wrights finished their work on the machinery Saturday noon and then Mr. Cline had the lower story of the mill cleared of rubbish and swept. Charlotte[3] has scoured the inside of the new cottage and it is now locked ready for inmates. Today is stormy with a roaring east wind; there is no church in the village Mr. Ely having gone to Easthampton to attend Mrs. Roger's[4] funeral. I go about the rooms here like a cat when there is only one in the house and the doors are open. Yet the place has been rather gay lately. A few days since there was a meeting of the Mite Society for the benefit of the New Chapel at Mrs. Moulton's which Mr. Cline, who went told me was quite large, and last night there was a tea-drinking at Mrs. Cairns's to which all here were invited and Mr. Cline and Annie went. There were Mr. and Mrs. Willis[5] who had just come out with a lady friend and their two boys, and the Pollitz's[6] and the Vandeventers and the Moultons and I believe some others and there was music and card playing and segars—the lady friend smoked—and sponge cake and grapes and wine. My cough was my excuse for my absence; it is better today.

I find the afternoon train does not go through—so I infer from the advertisement. I shall therefore go up on Thursday morning and stop at Sheffield. You will of course come back with me. This place has been a wilderness long enough and you and Julia are wanted to people it again. The noise of the workmen is over; the mill has had the doors and windows put in and the carpenters who have nearly finished, work within it. I must be at home here a week from next Tuesday, for then, if I am not quite out in my reckoning is the election and I must not lose my vote. I go to town tomorrow morning and on the evening of the next day must take the chair at a political meeting here at which Mr. Geo. W. Curtis[7] is to speak. The morning after I must go to town again to be ready to take the Thursday morning's train to Sheffield.

New York   Monday   Oct. 27. I came to town with Annie this morning in the train, having got my cold under with bryonia and [cunslicum?]. It is a chilly rainy morning with a raw east wind. I hear that Godwin is better. He intended to come to the office this morning, but the weather being so bad, he sent down a leader and staid at home.

There is a Mrs. Mary J. Dentzel here who has called two or three times at this office to see me, and left her card. Can it be Miss Hepp?[8]

Yours ever
W. C. BRYANT.

MANUSCRIPT: NYPL–GR ADDRESS: Mrs. F. F. Bryant.

1. Bryant mistakenly wrote "25th."
2. Unrecovered.
3. Presumably a household servant.
4. Not further identified.
5. Probably Nathaniel P. Willis and his second wife, Cornelia Grinnell Willis (665.5), then living in New York.
6. Mr. and Mrs. O. W. Pollitz, apparently a German refugee couple, lived near the upper pond in Roslyn village. Goddard, *Roslyn Harbor*, pp. [21] [104].
7. No further information has been found regarding this meeting, which was apparently not reported in the New York papers.
8. A former Heidelberg friend, Julie Hepp; see Letter 410.

1303.   *To* Andrew Hull Foote[1]

Office of The Evening Post,
New York, October 29   1862

Sir.

The bearer of this is Mr. Amos Andrews,[2] a native of Massachusetts and for many years a resident in Missouri. He is an intelligent and ingenious man, of good connexions and good character; his vocation is that of ship carpenter. He was several months employed in the Brooklyn Navy Yard on the Adirondack and other vessels, and afterwards at Cairo in fitting out and finishing the gun-boats of the expedition which you commanded on the Mississippi. During the present season he has been engaged on the Ironclad Monitors building in Jersey City, where he became disabled in consequence of an accident the effect of which is to incapacitate him for the present and probably for a year to come from pursuing his accustomed employment.

The object of this letter is to ask for him, on the presentation of such testimonials as shall satisfy you of his fitness and capacity, some employment, among those places which you have the power to give, which in his present condition he can usefully discharge. I have no doubt that he will exert himself to the extent of his ability to make his services satisfactory, and of his ability I have a very favorable opinion.

I am, sir,
most respectfully yours
WM C. BRYANT

MANUSCRIPT: New Haven Colony Historical Society ADDRESS: To Commodore Foote ENDORSED: I concur in the foregoing recommendation / David Dudley Field.

1. Wounded during the assault on Fort Donelson, Commodore Andrew Hull Foote (1806–1863) had been made a rear admiral and placed in charge of a bureau in the Navy Department in Washington.
2. Not further identified.

1304. *To* Edwin M. Stanton

[New York?] Nov. 6, 1862

My dear sir.

My brother Arthur Bryant of Princeton Illinois has a son Julian Bryant in the army, who has served from the beginning of the War.[1] He is a Lieutenant in Company E. of the 33d Regiment of Illinois Volunteers, now much reduced in number, and has distinguished himself by his coolness and courage on various occasions in the campaigns of the Southwest. His friends now desire for him an appointment as a field officer, to which they think his services his experience and his qualifications entitle him. An appointment on the staff of General Rosecrans is suggested, if there be vacancies and if there be nothing in the way of their being filled in this manner.[2] With this I send the testimonials to his merits—asking nothing for him which he may not fairly receive as one who has done well and who is likely to render valuable services in his new position.[3]

I am Sir
very respectfully
W   C   B

MANUSCRIPT: NYPL–GR (draft).

1. Julian Bryant (1025.5), who served throughout the war and reached the rank of colonel at the age of twenty-eight, was drowned off the Texas coast in 1865.
2. Major General William Starke Rosecrans (1819–1898, United States Military Academy 1842) had recently taken command of the Army of the Cumberland at Nashville, Tennessee. Nevins, *War for the Union*, II, 289.
3. Although there is no evidence he served on General Rosecrans' staff, Lieutenant Julian E. Bryant was given honorable mention on January 13, 1863, as a member of the staff of Brigadier General Charles E. Hovey, commanding the Second Brigade, First Division, Fifteenth Army Corps, near Arkansas Post. Subsequently, in 1864–1865, he commanded several divisions of Negro cavalry and infantry in Louisiana. *War of the Rebellion*, Ser. I, vols. 32, 39, 41, 48, *passim*.

1305. *To* Hobart Berrian[1]

[New York?] Nov. 7   1862

My dear sir

At the suggestion of Mr. [Samuel R.] Ely I enclose to you a letter to the Secretary of War.[2] I am well aware that he cannot read all the letters addressed to him, and as the matter to which this relates lies very near the heart of my brother Arthur, I am anxious that he should see it. If you will do me the favor to see that it is put into his hands I shall be greatly obliged to you. I have taken another liberty which I hope you will pardon, that of desiring my brother to send to you the testimonials to his son's services and merits, which you will soon have, and which I will further request you to hand to the Secretary at the same time with my letter. Again asking you to pardon me for this demand on your time and attention

I am dear sir
W   C   B.

MANUSCRIPT: NYPL–GR (draft).

1. Probably a son of the Rev. William Berrian (1033.4).
2. Letter 1304. Berrian, former Chief Clerk of the Navy Department, was in 1862 an auditor in the Treasury Department. *War of the Rebellion*, Ser. I, vol. 51, pt. 1, p. 320; Ser. II, vol. 2, p. 204.

1306.   *To* Samuel Hanson Cox[1]

New York, November 7, 1862

... I thank you both for your kind wishes and the Latin version of my poem ("Thanatopsis"), which you have been so obliging as to send me. However slight may be the merit of the original, the thoughts seem to acquire dignity when clothed in the majestic language of Virgil; and, if they had the capacity to feel and express gratitude, would make their acknowledgments to you for the becoming dress you have given them....

MANUSCRIPT: Unrecovered TEXT (*partial*): *Life*, II, 186–187.

1. Rev. Samuel Hanson Cox (1793–1880), rector of Trinity Church in Utica, New York, had written Bryant on November 5 enclosing his Latin translation of "Thanatopsis," *Mortis Visio* ("View of Death").

1307.   *To* C[harles?] H[enry?] Hart[1]

Roslyn, Long Island,
November 11th   1862

Sir.

The proprietor of the Engraving to which you refer is Mr. John Durand of New York, the son of the painter of that name. The plate has always been in his possession. My friends esteem the likeness to be the best of all that have been engraved, though the remark has been made that it is rather a favorable one.

I am, sir,
respectfully yours
W. C. BRYANT.

MANUSCRIPT: NYPL–BG ADDRESS: C. H. Hart Esq.

1. Possibly the father of Charles Henry Hart (1847–1918) of Philadelphia, a lawyer, and an expert student of historical portraiture.

1308.   To Leonice M. S. Moulton

New York, Nov. 28   1862

Dear Mrs. Moulton.

I did not get your note of the 22d.[1] until yesterday. At the cost of losing a family of kind and obliging neighbors, I must answer its inquiry in the negative. The destination of the house you occupy was arranged sometime since, as I supposed, though I cannot exactly tell why, that you understood. I hope you are making a pleasant visit at Troy, while your husband is studying the newspapers and watching the progress of the war, if it may be so called, from Taunton. Make my respects to Mrs. Wool,[2] if you will be so kind, and to the other members of the family with whom I am acquainted. . . .[3]

MANUSCRIPT: NYPL–Bryant–Moulton Letters ADDRESS: Mrs. L. M. S. Moulton / [Care of Mrs. General Wool][4] / Troy / —N. Y. — POSTMARK: NEW-YORK / NOV / 28 / 1862 ENDORSED: William Cullen Bryant / Autograph / Solicited.

1. Unrecovered.
2. Wife of General John E. Wool (563.3), Leonice Moulton's uncle.
3. Complimentary close and signature missing.
4. The brackets are Bryant's.

1309.   To John Bigelow

New York   Dec. 3d, 1862

Dear Mr. Bigelow.

The view you take of the proposal of the French government that there should be a suspension of hostilities between the parties to our civil war, in order to give the great powers of Western Europe an opportunity to mediate between them is the one which almost universally prevails here.[1] All see that it is neither more nor less than asking us to give up all we are fighting for. The most favorable construction that can be put upon it, makes it a device to give the rebel government an opportunity to get upon its legs again, take breath, rest, recruit and take a new start. That is on the supposition that the interference would proceed no further than is implied by the terms of the letter of M. Drouyn de L'Huys which is not likely. The tip of the wedge being once inserted the rest would of course be driven in after it. An interference of the nature proposed being once allowed would be the preliminary to interference of the most domineering character and transfer to our continent the system of dictation by which three or four sovereigns give law to the nations of Europe. *Principiis obsta.*[2]

I do not think the French ministry will be much pleased with the manner in which the project is received here. The most blatant member of the peace party here would not venture upon the unpopularity of proposing a cessation of hostilities. Governor Seymour found himself absolutely forced to come out with a vehement asseveration of his earnest wish to see the war prosecuted with the utmost energy till the rebels should lay down their arms.[3]

You put the case strongly against England in your letter to the *Independence Belge*.[4] Notwithstanding the open expression given by the French emperor to his wish to intermeddle in our quarrel and the rejection of his proposal by Great Britain, the feeling of dissatisfaction here with Great Britain is much stronger than that with France. The truth is, I suppose, that we expected more sympathy from the English, or, perhaps, we are never in a mood to bear as much from them as from any other nation. The dissatisfaction with Great Britain pervades all classes. Those,—a large portion of them at least—who used to look at every thing British through a prism are reached by it and scold vehemently about their old favorites. The English have lost more ground in public opinion here, within the past year and a half than they can recover in a century. It is an unpopular thing here to be an Englishman.

We all are devoured with impatience at the slow progress made by our arms. Before the President decided to issue his proclamation declaring the slaves emancipated in the rebellious districts, delay had its compensations —our *vis inertiae* [inertia] was dragging us on towards that measure. Now, delay has no advantage that I can see, and the sooner the rebel states are overcome by our arms the sooner the rebellion will be trodden out.

We are all well. Kind regards to Mrs. Bigelow. My wife and daughters desire theirs to you both.

I am dear sir
truly yours
W. C. BRYANT.

MANUSCRIPTS: NYPL–Bigelow (final); NYPL–GR (draft) ADDRESS: Jn° Bigelow Esq. PUBLISHED (*in part*): *Life*, II, 182–183.

1. In October 1862 Napoleon III of France proposed, through his newly-appointed foreign minister Eduard Drouyn de Lhuys (1805–1881), that the major European powers intervene to effect a six-month armistice in America. But the Union army's repulse of a Confederate invasion of the North at Antietam in mid-September, followed quickly by Lincoln's Emancipation Proclamation on September 22, had already cooled the British government toward such a move, and Napoleon's proposal was rejected by London and received without enthusiasm in St. Petersburg. See Nevins, *War for the Union*, II, 267–271; Van Deusen, *Seward*, pp. 322–323. In a letter to Bryant from Paris on November 14 (NYPL–BG), Bigelow called it important that the American government reject this proposal "as an enormity and repel it as decidedly and respectfully as they can."

2. "Resist the beginnings"—Ovid, *Remedia Amoris*, line 91.

3. See Nevins, *War for the Union*, II, 394.

4. After Napoleon's truce plan had been made public in mid-November, Bigelow addressed an unsigned letter to the French-language paper *Independence Belge* de-

nouncing the proposal as unfriendly, and condemning British help to the southern cause. Margaret Clapp, *Forgotten First Citizen: John Bigelow* (Boston: Little, Brown, 1947), pp. 181–182.

1310.   To Pierre-Abraham Jônain[1]

New York, December 3, 1862

... I thank you for the translations you have sent me of three of my poems, and the kind letter with which they were accompanied.[2] My verses have gained in the dress you have given them—a grace which I could not give them in English. They are more faithful in rendering the meaning of the original than French translations of English poetry generally are; and yet, so far as a foreigner may be allowed to judge, they are as spirited and easy as if written without that constraint to which a faithful translator is obliged to submit. . . .

For your good wishes concerning my country I also thank you. This cruel war is a frightful state of things, but from it I hope will result good to our country and to mankind—the extinction of the accursed institution of slavery, and the restoration of our Union on the basis of universal liberty —a result which I look for with confidence.

In the hope that the freedom of your country may not cost so dear, I am, dear sir, yours, very truly. . . .

MANUSCRIPT: Unrecovered TEXT (*partial*): *Life*, II, 187.

1. Pierre-Abraham Jônain (1799–1884) was a French poet, lexicographer, and translator. See 1311.1.
2. Jônain's letter and translations of Bryant's verses are unrecovered. Although he may have published such translations in periodicals or newspapers, he seems not to have printed them in any of his published works.

1311.   To Adolf Laun

New York   Dec   3d   1862

My dear sir

The additional translations of my poems in the Sonntagsblatt forwarded by you have arrived,[1] and I find them equally well done—so far as a foreigner may be allowed to judge—with their predecessors—specimens of that skill in rendering the poetry of other countries into your noble language, in which your country men excel all other nations with whose literature I am acquainted. Your dedicatory verses are only too complimentary.

With regard to the publication of your version, so far as relates to this country, it is not easy for me to judge what would be its success. Notwithstanding our civil war, books are still bought and read, though the booksellers are by no means as enterprising as in time of peace, and the number of books published is much less now than it was two years since. Just at present it strikes me that it would be impossible to find a publisher for your work here for this reason—that the price of printing-paper is now twice what it was six months ago. This has a most discouraging effect on the publication of books here. What paper there is in market is taken up for the newspapers, which *must* be published to supply the demand for the news of the day. This makes in favor of books published abroad where paper is cheaper.

How long this state of things will continue I cannot say—at present I do not see any thing to change it—and in all probability it will last as long as the war does.

I hope this information may be of use to you, and in the mean time

I am dear sir

truly yours

W. C. B.

MANUSCRIPT: NYPL–GR (draft) ADDRESS: To Dr. Adolf Laun / Oldenburg–Germany PUBLISHED (*in part*): *Life*, II, 187.

1. Replying to Bryant's letter of July 21, 1862 (Letter 1282), Laun wrote on October 8 (NYPL–GR) enclosing a letter from his friend Jônain and specimens of Jônain's French translations of Bryant poems (see Letter 1310). Since German editors were then cautious about publishing because of the American war, Laun wondered whether a New York publisher might undertake to print a volume of German translations of Bryant's poems. However, after Bryant's discouraging reply, Laun did find a German publisher for them; see 1282.1.

1312. *To* Edwin D. Morgan

Office of The Evening Post,

New York, December 17   1862

My dear sir.

The Commission of John Butcher Esq. of this city as Notary Public having expired, I write in his behalf to request that it may be renewed. Mr. Butcher is a most worthy citizen, exact in the performance of his duties, and as he is employed in this office, where we have very frequent occasion for a Notary, the renewal of his appointment would be a great convenience to the proprietors of the Evening Post.[1]

I am, sir,

very respectfully yours

W. C. BRYANT.

MANUSCRIPT: NYSL ADDRESS: To His Excy. Edwin D. Morgan / Governor of the State of New York ENDORSED: Office of The Evening Post, New York, Dec   17th, 1862 / To His Excellency / Edwin D. Morgan / Governor of the State of / New York / Sir / I beg leave to enclose letter/ from W. C. Bryant Esq, which will explain / itself. My *last commission was for* / *Kings Co.* but being now a resident of / this City I wish to have a commission / for *New York County* so as to be of / use in swearing affts &c for the office / I am Sir / Yours most respectfully / John Butcher.

1. Butcher has not been further identified, except as herein and in Letter 1276.

1313.   *To* Salmon P. Chase

Office of The Evening Post,
New York, December 18th, 1862

My dear sir.

I have had your letter for several days and am somewhat embarrassed how to answer it. The article which occasioned it was written by a gentleman who has sometimes contributed articles on financial subjects to the Evening Post, and was inserted while I was absent in the country, so that I knew nothing of it, until it appeared in the paper.[1]

I am fully aware of the embarrassments and difficulties in the midst of which you find yourself and when I do not see things precisely in the light that you do, I am always free to admit your extraordinary ability and the success with which you have overcome obstacles that would have reduced others to despair and inaction. It is not my desire to increase in the slightest degree the difficulties with which you are beset in sustaining the credit of the government, and I think the course which the Evening Post will take will convince you of this.

I am, dear sir,
very truly yours
WM. C. BRYANT.

MANUSCRIPT: HSPa ADDRESS: Hon   S. P. Chase. ENDORSED: William Cullen Bryant / New York   December 18, 1862. / The article on Secy. Chase's Financial / Policy.

1. In an editorial on December 10 captioned "The Financial Ideas of Mr. Chase," the *EP* had taken issue with the Treasury Secretary's proposed plan for a uniform national banking system, drawing from Chase on December 13 a letter to Bryant justifying his position, and concluding, "My country engages all my best earthly thoughts and affections. Most willingly will I sacrifice all for her. To serve her, my labors have been incessant. Must I fail for the want of concord among her most devoted lovers?" Quoted in *Life*, II, 186.

1314.   *To* Richard H. Dana

New York   December 18th   1862

Dear Dana.

When I got your letter the other day[1] I was about to answer it immediately, but the bad news from Fredericksburg came and I had no heart to write. The battle was a dreadful piece of butchery for which I fear General Halleck is responsible. They say that the officers of Burnside's corps were all against making the attempt to carry the enemy's intrenchments.[2]

I had heard that Edmund was in ill health last summer,[3] but I had no idea of the serious nature of his malady. I do not wonder at the effect such long-continued anxiety had on your health and spirits; if I wonder at any thing it is that you should have recovered your strength to such a degree.

You find many things amiss in our people, and I cannot deny that you have reason, but I do not see that any change in our political constitution would mend matters. Every arrangement for making laws and keeping order amongst men has its better side and its worse side, and it is only a very impartial and unprejudiced mind that can strike a just balance between them and truly decide which, taking all things together, is the best. You like the British form of government but you see its operation at a distance. My attention has lately been called to the picture of the moral condition of England given in its daily journals and it seems to me that it reveals a frightful corruption of morals in their higher class. What shall we say of the prostitute Anonyma, with nearly half the peerage in her train, bowing around her carriage in public?[4] What of two men pommelling each other to death in the ring with a throng of titled personages looking on, who had put the price of admission at two guineas to keep out the rabble?[5] Highway robberies and murders have grown so frequent in London—the robberies often perpetrated at noon day—that the place is hardly more safe than Johnson described it to be in his satire.[6]

But you go on to show that the character of our people is improving in this season of adversity. I agree with you there; I see the same result. Perhaps much of what has awakened your disgust was the effect of our temporal prosperity.

But you know I hate to dispute. Let us be thankful that God is bringing so much good out of the terrible evil that has fallen on us. Kind regards to Charlotte and to your son Edmund and your sisters—not forgetting the circumnavigator.[7]

I am, dear Dana
truly yours
W. C. Bryant

MANUSCRIPT: NYPL–GR ADDRESS: R. H. Dana Esq. ENDORSED: Wm C. Bryant / Dec 18/ 62 / Ans. / Ap. 20/63. PUBLISHED (in part): Life, II, 187–188.

1. Unrecovered.
2. On December 12–13 the Army of the Potomac, under its new commander, General Burnside, suffered its worst defeat thus far in the war at Fredericksburg, Virginia. Though the plan for the battle had been made by Burnside, much of the slaughter inflicted on his troops by the Confederates under General Robert Edward Lee (1807–1870, United States Military Academy 1829) was the result of an inordinate delay, attributed to Union general-in-chief Halleck, in delivering pontoons for bridging the swollen Rappahannock River. Nevins, War for the Union, II, 343–350.
3. Dana's younger son Edmund (417.2), a lawyer, was a chronic invalid.
4. This notorious courtesan, by name Catherine Waters but widely known as "Skittles," was christened "Anonyma" in an amusing letter to the London Times of July 3, 1862. The writer noted that this handsome young woman, who had habitually driven her smart carriage drawn by matched brown ponies along the Ladies' Mile in Hyde Park, to the admiration of sporting gentlemen and the envy of fashionable ladies, had lately moved to a previously deserted road between Hyde Park Corner and Kensington. Here she attracted an entourage who paid high prices to emulate her dress and

ponies. But, the letter continued, "They can none of them sit, dress, drive, or look as well as she does; nor can any of them procure for money such ponies as Anonyma continues to get for love."

Discovering that the *Times*'s "letter" had really been written by one of the paper's own journalists, the *Daily Telegraph* commented the next day, "The plain truth of the matter is that Hyde Park...has been for a lengthened period infested by a number of lewd women, who, being well paid by wealthy profligates for selling their miserable bodies for the purpose of debauchery, are enabled to dress splendidly, and drive handsome equipages. Many of these shameful creatures are the daughters of stablemen and rough riders in the country and elsewhere; and are dexterous enough in using the whips, which, in the old Bridewell days, would have been laid about their own shoulders.... This is 'Anonyma.' She has neither wit nor sense, nor manners nor morals; but she has plenty of fine clothes and sparkling jewels, and a pretty body which she sells to the highest bidder.... This is the ingenious creature whom *The Times* is endeavouring, under a preposterous alias, to convert into a heroine." See also Virginia Spencer Cowles, *Gay Monarch: The Life and Pleasures of Edward VII* (New York: Harper & Row [1956]), pp. 75–77.

This spectacular figure of Victorian lowlife was the subject of several popular romances, one of which, *Anonyma; or, Fair but Frail. A Romance of West-End Life, Manners, and "Captivating" People* (London, 1864), appeared in a Paris version the following year as *Une Autre Biche Anglaise. Histoire Authentique d'Anonyma.*

5. On April 17, 1860, Tom Sayers (1826–1865), who had been the "Little Wonder" of British prize fighting for eleven years, fought the American "Bernica Boy," John Carmel Heenan (1835–1873), to a draw in a bloody thirty-seven–round battle at Farnborough, England.

6. Samuel Johnson, *London* (1738).

7. Richard H. Dana, Jr.

1315.   To Edwin D. Morgan

Office of The Evening Post,
New York, Dec   20, 1862.

My dear sir.

I fully agree with the accompanying letter of Governor King[1] in its recommendation of Lieutenant Downing[2] for promotion in the army.

I am sir
most respectfully
W. C BRYANT

MANUSCRIPT: NYSL ADDRESS: To Governor Morgan DOCKETED: 1862 / W. C. Bryant / Dec 20.

1. Unrecovered. John Alsop King (1788–1867), son of the Federalist statesman Rufus King (1755–1827, Harvard 1777), had been Republican governor of New York, 1857–1859.

2. See Letter 1294. That Downing's promotion was effected is evident. As an officer in the Second New York Cavalry ("Harris's Light Cavalry"), First Brigade, Captain Obadiah J. Downing was mentioned for "gallant conduct on the field" in a cavalry action at Brandy Station, Virginia on June 3, 1863. *War of the Rebellion*, Ser. I, vol. 27, pt. 1, pp. 996–997.

1316. *To* an Unidentified Correspondent

Roslyn Dec 27 1862

Frederick S. Copley Esqre. of Roslyn on Long Island has made several architectural designs for me which I have caused to be executed at my place near that village and which in my opinion do great credit to his taste and his invention.[1] Mr. Copley has given much attention to the subject and has taken great pains to inform himself of the modern improvements in building both with respect to economy in construction and the accommodation of the inmates. In his designs he has shown much skill in combining beauty and variety of proportion with convenience of arrangement. I cheerfully recommend him to be employed by those who have occasion for an architectural designer.

Wm. C Bryant

MANUSCRIPT: BLR (draft?).

1. One of these designs was that for the Victorian cottage which Bryant built on his property in 1862 for Jerusha Dewey. Goddard, *Roslyn Harbor*, p. [71] (illustration); pp. 70, 73.

1317. *To* Fanny Bryant Godwin

Office of The Evening Post,
New York, Dec. 30. 1862

Dear Fanny.

As your mother can get nothing for a Christmas present to send you, and I do not know what to get—she has suggested that I should send you the enclosed $20— and let you get what you might like.

Yours affectionately
W. C. Bryant.

P.S. Dec 31. This note was accidentally left out of the cover that contained the money.— yesterday.—

W C. B.

MANUSCRIPT: NYPL–GR.

1318. *To* Robert C. Waterston

N Y Dec. 31, 1862

My dear sir.

A young artist of this city has put together three poems by different American authors, as a convenience for hanging his own clever illustrations upon them.[1] My wife likes what he has done so much that when I left Roslyn yesterday morning she made me promise that I would get a copy and send to you and Mrs. Waterston. You will have it by Express.

Poor woman. About a fortnight since she broke her wrist—the right one which I should think the wrong one by a fall, and cannot write. She is getting on as well as could be expected—but it will be yet some days before the splints are taken off. Meantime she remains at Roslyn till the hurt is sufficiently healed for her to bear the jar of a carriage without pain.

I write briefly, having other matters on my hands this morning. My best regards to Mrs. Waterston—

Yours ever
W C BRYANT.

MANUSCRIPT: NYPL–GR (draft).

1. *In The Woods with Bryant, Longfellow, and Halleck. Illustrated from Drawings by John A. Hows....* (New York: James Gregory, 1863). Bryant's "The Death of the Flowers" appears on pp. 1–10. See illustration.

1319. *To* Edwin D. Morgan

[1862?]

My dear sir.

Robert Stuart Esqre of the Harris's Light Cavalry has desired me to ask of you in his behalf the Commission of Second Lieutenant in that Regiment or any other New York State Regiment of Cavalry. Mr. Stuart has had a regular education as an officer of the American navy in which he at one time served as Lieutenant, and resigned his commission about I think four years since. He is an active and intelligent man, and having enlisted as a private in the Cavalry regiment before mentioned has been I learn promoted to the post of orderly sergeant. This as well as his education and experience are justly in his favor, in the application he now makes, and I presume he will furnish credentials from army officers as to his military capacity and his conduct since he enlisted in the service.[1] If these should be of a satisfactory character and if there should be any vacancy to which he can be appointed, you will confer a favor on his friends by complying with his request.

I am sir
respectfully yours,
W C BRYANT

MANUSCRIPT: NYPL–GR (draft).

1. Lieutenant Robert Stuart of Roslyn, husband of Ellen Eliza Cairns Stuart, died on July 30, 1863, presumably a war casualty. Cairns Family Genealogical Chart, prepared by Helen Marlatt, BLR.

1320. *To* Frances F. Bryant

Office of The Evening Post,
New York, January 3, 1863.

Dear Frances.

All I can hear of Julia I hear from Mr. Henderson. He saw her on New Years day. She appeared very well he says, and said that she should go to Roslyn the next day and remain till you come to town. She was with Fanny Williams.[1] Godwin can tell me nothing about her. I should not at all wonder if she remained over night on account of some party or something of the sort.

While you were thinking of the Waterstons they were thinking of you. I find on my table this morning three packages which were sent by express from them—containing books—one for you and me—one for Fanny and a third for Julia, with a note to you.

I dare say Julia is with you long before you receive this. I hope I shall find you, when I come back, with the wooden shackles taken from your arm. Miss Gibson's visit will expedite that result, I shall expect, by a day or two. Tell her that Mr. Flanders the newly elected member of Congress from New Orleans[2] says that he does not believe the stories of General Butler's extortions, though he says that Butlers reputation has suffered very much from the conduct of a brother of his, a scape-grace, who resorted to New Orleans from California. Godwin says he cannot trace the stories to any authentic source. The *World* has been the principal vehicle of these charges and that is very bad authority.[3]

ever yours

W. C. B.

P.S. Just before coming away from home I observed that the damper on the tube that brings the air from without to our furnace is shut and cannot be moved. Will you ask Mr. Cline to get Henry to repair it?

W. C. B.

MANUSCRIPT: NYPL–GR.

1. Unidentified.

2. Benjamin Franklin Flanders (1816–1896, Dartmouth 1842) moved in 1843 from New Hampshire to New Orleans, where he held various city positions before and during the early part of the Civil War. In December 1862 he was elected to the Congress, and in July 1863 was mustered into the federal service as commander of a New Orleans volunteer regiment. *BDAC.*

3. General Benjamin Franklin Butler (1818–1893, Colby 1838), commanding the Department of the Gulf after the capture of New Orleans in April 1862, was relieved of his command the following November, not so much because of such unsubstantiated charges of corruption as for his authoritarian, if highly efficient, administration of the conquered city. Nevins, *War for the Union,* II, 401; Thomas and Hyman, *Stanton,* pp. 256–257. Butler's elder brother, Colonel Andrew Jackson Butler (1815?–1864), managed the commanding general's sales of supplies in order to provision New Orleans, and was the subject of a special investigation by the Treasury Department into his suspected trading of contraband material with the enemy, as well as of profiteering to the extent of more than a million dollars between the fall of New Orleans and the end of 1862. See Nevins, *War for the Union,* III, 357–359; Richard S. West, Jr., *Lincoln's Scapegoat General: A Life of Benjamin F. Butler, 1818–1893* (Boston: Houghton Mifflin, 1965), pp. 186–192; Robert S. Holzman, *Stormy Ben Butler* (New York: Macmillan, 1954), pp. 91–95.

1321.   *To* Robert C. and Anna Q. Waterston

Roslyn   January 9th   1863[1]

My dear Friends.

I wrote the other day to Mr. Waterston mentioning the accident which had happened to my wife, who is not yet able to write—the fracture being of the dexter wrist—and may not be for some weeks to come. So she has commissioned me to thank Mrs. Waterston for the welcome gift of her poems.[2] She bids me say that she is quite proud to receive a copy of a book of hers printed only for distribution among those she loves. We have both read it with great pleasure. The poems are full of feeling—there is often a vein of tender sadness in them, but a sadness brightened and glorified by hope. They are sweetly versified. My wife is delighted with them and puts the book among her favorites. We like in a particular manner the Locust Tree the Wounded Indian and the last poem in the volume.

We have our acknowledgments also to make for the beautiful volume of Sacred Poetry[3] which I found waiting for me in town when I went in on Monday. The selections seem to be well made and the illustrations beautiful. It is pleasant to know that we were in your thoughts at a season when we naturally take an account of our friends to see how many the lapse of the year has spared us.

Our sympathies have been strongly moved by the vacancies which death has lately made in your circle of friends, removing some of the dearest and most cherished. There are certain losses by death the sorrow for which can scarcely be rendered less acute by any premonition, such as the slow decline of age or long continued disease. If one of our arms were to be torn from its socket, the anguish could not be diminished by any previous warning.

The new year which has opened so gloriously with the proclamation of liberty to the enslaved in the greater part of the United States where the law of bondage has been in force, will I hope close upon a republic entirely composed of free states.[4]

Meantime accept, dear friends, for yourselves and yours, from my wife and daughter and myself our wishes that the year upon which we have entered may pass pleasantly away and see the Union reestablished on the basis of universal liberty—

[unsigned]

MANUSCRIPT: NYPL–GR (draft) ADDRESS: To Mr. and Mrs. Waterston.

1. Bryant mistakenly wrote "1862."
2. *Verses by Anna Cabot Quincy Waterston* (Boston, 1863).
3. Unidentified.
4. President Lincoln's Emancipation Proclamation of September 1862, freeing the slaves in all states and territories still in rebellion against the United States on January 1, 1863, became effective on that day.

1322. *To* Daniel Bogart

Office of The Evening Post,
New York, January 12, 1863.

Dear sir.

I have done nothing in the matter of the post-office at Roslyn, and have come to the conclusion that I had best not intermeddle in the matter. Mr. Nostrand,[1] a very respectable and competent young man called on me early to get me to write in his favor. I declined, however, for various reasons—among which was this that I did not feel certain that the place would accommodate the neighbourhood so well as it is accommodated at present. Mr. Titus,[2] another very respectable and competent person who has been for sometime assistant postmaster at Roslyn called on me also, desiring that the post-office may be kept where it is now, and bringing a letter from Mr. Eastman.[3] I did see fit to write to the Postmaster General in his behalf,[4] thinking that the wish of the inhabitants of the neighborhood ought to settle that question, and not knowing for my own part what that wish was.

You see therefore the reasons which have led me to the conclusion I have formed.

I am sir respectfully yours
W. C. BRYANT.

MANUSCRIPT: BLR ADDRESS: D. Bogart Esq.

1. C. P. Nostrand, a Roslyn storekeeper, was drafted into the Union army later that year; see Letter 1363.
2. Willet Titus (1828–1911), a tinsmith, operated a general store at the southern end of what is now Bryant Avenue, Roslyn. Goddard, *Roslyn Harbor*, p. 110.
3. Henry W. Eastman (1826–1882), an attorney, was for a time joint publisher with Augustus W. Leggett (648.2) of the Roslyn *Plaindealer. Ibid.*, p. 108.
4. Letter unrecovered.

1323. *To* William Pitt Fessenden[1]

Office of The Evening Post
New York, January 12   1863.

Sir.

A memorial was brought to me this morning for my signature, addressed to Mr. Lincoln asking him to provide himself with a better Cabinet. I understand that it was sent on from Washington by Judge White—[2] I could hardly ask the President to dismiss certain members of his cabinet, confident as I am that it would be difficult to find more able counsellors— The war, however, has been and continues to be badly conducted, and I fear the responsibility rests somewhere upon the Cabinet. A good many of us here believe that the views of the manner in which the slave-holders ought to be dealt with, entertained by Mr. Seward, are incompatible with a successful prosecution of the war.[3] We think the salvation of the country

depends on the immediate arming of the blacks for offensive as well as de-
fensive purposes—and that the advisers of Mr. Lincoln ought to insist upon
this being done. We do not expect any such advice to be given by Mr.
Seward. Meantime there is danger that the soldiers from the free states,
sent so often upon unfortunate expeditions, which result so often in terrible and fruitless loss of life, and left so long without payment of their
wages, while their families are starving at home, will become utterly disgusted with the service. At least, there will be no more voluntary additions
of whites to our army.

What evil genius orders our expeditions with so little forecast as to
expose us to the losses we have lately suffered at Fredericksburg, at Vicksburg, at Springfield in Missouri and at Galveston, nobody here pretends to
know. Improvidence and want of vigilance make our superior numbers
and our greater resources of no avail.

I should be glad to know what those of our friends at Washington who
are nearer than we to the springs that move the machine desire of us. I understand that the movement among the members of the Senate in relation
to the reconstruction of the cabinet is not at an end, but that another consultation is to be had.[4] Can you give me any hints by which our conduct
here might be guided?[5] If so I should be glad to receive them.

I am, sir,

respectfully yours

W. C. BRYANT.

MANUSCRIPT: NYHS ADDRESS: Hon   W. P. Fessenden.

1. William Pitt Fessenden (1800–1869, Bowdoin 1823), lawyer and former congressman, had been since 1854 a United States senator from Maine, and since 1857
chairman of the Senate's finance committee. In 1864 he succeeded Salmon P. Chase as
Secretary of the Treasury upon Chase's appointment to the Supreme Court.

2. Judge White has not been identified.

3. Secretary of State Seward, who opposed the Emancipation Proclamation, had
made public in December a letter, written earlier, in which he had linked northern
Abolitionists with southern secessionists as "acting in concert together to precipitate
a servile war." Hendrick, *Lincoln's War Cabinet*, pp. 384–385. Seward had tried to
persuade Lincoln to postpone freeing the slaves until after the North had won greater
successes in battle. He urged that emancipation would injure the northern cause in
European eyes; that foreign nations might "intervene to prevent abolition of slavery
for the sake of cotton." He was reported by one caller to have remarked, "You appear
to think, in common with many other foolish people, that the great business of this
administration is the destruction of slavery. Now allow me to say that you are much
mistaken." Yet, in the first version of Francis Bicknell Carpenter's painting *First Reading of the Emancipation Proclamation* (1864), which was widely circulated in an engraving, Lincoln seems to have just received from Seward's hand a paper drafted by
the dominant figure in the picture, the Secretary of State! See *ibid.*, pp. 423–430. The
revised version of this painting, which hangs in the Senate wing of the National Capitol,
shows Lincoln in the properly dominant position, proclamation in hand. See *Art in the
United States Capitol* ... (Washington: Government Printing Office, 1976), pp. 152–153.

4. The repulse, with dreadful losses, of federal forces at Fredericksburg, Virginia, in mid-December, had caused an immediate reaction among radical Republican leaders, one of them Fessenden, who had long held Seward accountable for an apparent impotence in the conduct of the war. On December 16, 1862, an almost unanimous Republican senatorial caucus passed a resolution calling for "a change in and partial reconstruction of the Cabinet." Seward offered his resignation, but the President frustrated the incipient revolt by securing the resignation of Seward's chief cabinet opponent and favorite of the radicals, Secretary Chase, then refusing to let either man go. There were, in fact, no significant cabinet changes until 1864. Hendrick, *Lincoln's War Cabinet*, pp. 390–409. Nevins, *War for the Union*, II, 352–362.

5. In reply, Fessenden wrote on January 17 (NYPL–BG) that he and like-minded senators felt that an unsuccessful effort to effect a cabinet shakeup would weaken "confidence in a government none too strong." He thought that, in any event, without speedy military successes Lincoln would soon have to reorganize the cabinet.

1324.   *To* Leonice M. S. Moulton

Office of The Evening Post
New York, January 23, 1863.

Dear Mrs. Moulton.

I was greatly pained by the news, communicated in your note, of the departure of the dear little one whom you loved so well.[1] I pray you to assure your daughter and her husband of my warm sympathy in the affliction which has overtaken them. I have a most vivid remembrance of the little creature's looks—so beautiful in feature, and with a face so full of answering smiles. Those smiles are now called forth by the objects of a world in which there are no tears and in which she will never know sin.

I am, madam,
truly yours
W. C. BRYANT.

MANUSCRIPT: Maryland Historical Society ADDRESS: Mrs. L. M. S. Moulton.

1. Sara Wool Stewart, infant daughter of Mrs. John Stewart of Baltimore (1220.1), Mrs. Moulton's daughter.

1325.   *To* John E. Wool[1]

Office of The Evening Post,
New York, February 5th. 1863.

My dear sir.

I write this note in behalf of William G. Boggs Esq. formerly for several years a proprietor of the Evening Post.[2] He is now out of employment, and understanding that your present position gives you the opportunity of appointing persons to various subordinate branches of public service, desires to be considered as a candidate for some one of them.[3] Mr. Boggs is intelligent, active and industrious, of an amiable character and obliging temper, and would strive to discharge any duty assigned him, to the satisfaction of his employer and the public. In the hope that his application will be kindly received and if possible granted

I am, dear sir,
faithfully yours
W. C. BRYANT.

MANUSCRIPT: UVa ADDRESS: Maj. General J. E. Wool DOCKETED: Wm Cullen Bryant / Feb 5/63.

1. See 563.3.
2. See 341.2, 708.1.
3. General Wool then commanded the Union army's Department of the East, with headquarters in New York. It is uncertain whether Boggs received an appointment.

1326. *To* James T. Fields

New York, February 13, 1863

. . . I am glad to see you so well employed as you are, in giving us good old English books in your handsome editions. The dedication to me of your edition of Fuller's "Good Thoughts in Bad Times"[1] I shall certainly receive as a great honor, though I have done little to earn it. . . .

MANUSCRIPT: Unrecovered TEXT (*partial*): *Life*, II, 194.

1. Thomas Fuller (1608–1661), *Good Thoughts in Bad Times* (1645), a collection of reflections on his own shortcomings and those of his times in a humorous and witty vein, was reprinted as *Good Thoughts in Bad Times, and Other Papers* (Boston: Ticknor & Fields, 1863).

1327. *To* Edwin D. Morgan

New York Feb. 16. 1863.

Dear sir.

The design of which you speak in your note is a most laudable one, and I readily consent to the use of my name which you have requested.[1]

I am, sir,
respectfully yours—
W. C. BRYANT.

MANUSCRIPT: NYSL ADDRESS: E. D. Morgan Esqre. DOCKETED: 1863 / Wm C. Bryant / Feby 16.

1. Morgan's note is unrecovered; his "design" is unidentified.

1328. *To* Charles Greely Loring[1]

New York, March 2d 1863.

Dear sir.

I thank you for the copy you have been so kind as to send me of your correspondence with my friend Mr. Field.[2] One had already come into my possession which, on account of its research and its ability in other respects, I had found of great use in discussing the public questions of the time. This, from the hand of the author I shall value still more highly.

> I am, sir,
> very respectfully yours,
> W. C. BRYANT.

MANUSCRIPT: HCL ADDRESS: Ch. G. Loring Esq. DOCKETED: W. C. Bryant.

1. Charles Greely Loring (1794–1867, Harvard 1812) was a Boston lawyer and a founder of the Boston Union Club. A firm opponent of the Fugitive Slave Law, in April 1851 he had represented the slave Thomas Sims, delivered by marshals to his master and hurried out of Boston in early morning darkness to escape a scheme of rescue. Nevins, *Ordeal*, I, 388–389.

2. *Correspondence on the Present Relations Between Great Britain and the United States of America* (Boston, 1862). These were letters exchanged between Loring and Edwin W. Field on the Trent Affair, British attitudes toward the war, and American reaction, in which Field expressed strong anti-slavery opinions, while Loring was less outspoken on that subject.

1329. *To* Daniel C. Gilman

New York   March 5, 1863.

Dear sir

The appearance of a bill for my dues to the Oriental Society sent by you with the pamphlet of the Society's Journal reminds me that I neglected the payment of last year. I send the money, enclosed, by the first mail, along with a stamp that you may return the receipt signed.

> Yours respectfully
> WM. C. BRYANT.

MANUSCRIPT: JHUL ADDRESS: D. C. Gilman[1] Esq.

1. Bryant mistakenly wrote "D. B. Gilman."

1330. *To* Joseph W. Moulton

New York, March 9th   1863.

My dear sir:

I am reminded of the request you have made that I should give you a card with my ugly mug on it. You have it enclosed.[1]

Please to thank your wife for the photograph of Mr. Baylies which she was so kind as to send me.[2] She could hardly have sent me any thing which I should value more highly. The face is not precisely in the photograph as it stands in my memory, for years have somewhat changed the outline, but there is still a resemblance, and I shall see the more of this, probably, the more I look at it. For Mr. Baylies's character I have always entertained the profoundest respect. I rarely think of him without recollecting what one of his neighbors in West Bridgewater once told me, that when he had completed his law studies, the gentleman in whose office he had prepared himself for his profession, said, "That young man has a character like General Washington's." He must have referred to his natural dignity and his greatness of mind, for Mr. Baylies had none of that occasional irritability which belonged to Washington.

I am glad to learn that you are so wide awake in the afternoons. Mrs. Moulton writes that she has not improved in any thing, which perhaps is owing to the progress she had made before she left home. After reaching a certain point, you know, advancement becomes less perceptible. My regards to her and to the ladies with whom you are domesticated for the winter, and believe me

truly yours
W. C. BRYANT.

MANUSCRIPT: Ridgely Family Collection TEXT: Hoyt, "Bryant Correspondence (II)," 195–196 ADDRESS: J. W. Moulton Esqre.

1. This was undoubtedly the carte de visite taken in September 1862. See illustration, and Letter 1293.
2. Bryant's law tutor in 1814–1815, former congressman William Baylies (Vol. I, 14; Letter 473). See illustration.

1331.   *To* [William Henry Green?][1]

[New York?] March 19th   1863.

My dear Sir.

Enclosed are the translations concerning which you were so kind as to inquire.[2]

Yours truly,
WM C. BRYANT.

MANUSCRIPT: PML ADDRESS: Professor Greene.

1. The recipient of this letter, addressed only as "Professor Greene," was perhaps William Henry Green (1825–1900, Lafayette 1840, Princeton Theological Seminary 1846), a Presbyterian clergyman who was professor of Hebrew and Oriental languages at the Princeton Seminary from 1851 to 1900.
2. No letter from Green to Bryant has been recovered, but accompanying the manuscript of Bryant's letter is a separate sheet of five lines of verse, in his holograph, headed "Iliad, Book 8th, near the conclusion." These lines are composed in English hexameter, presumably the only surviving example of Bryant's attempt to render Homer's verse in a meter approximating the Greek original. When, in 1866, he began his translation of the *Iliad*, published in 1870, he turned to blank verse, remarking in his preface to that work, "I did not adopt the hexameter verse, principally for the reason that in our language it is confessedly an imperfect form of versification, the true rhythm of which it is difficult for those whose ear is accustomed only to our ordinary metres to perceive. . . . We have so many short words in English, and so few of the connective particles which are lavishly used by Homer, that often when I reached the end

of the Greek line I found myself only in the middle of my line in English. . . . I therefore fell back upon blank-verse, which has been the vehicle of some of the noblest
poetry in our language." *The Iliad of Homer. Translated into English Blank Verse*
(Boston: Houghton, Mifflin [1870]), pp. vi–vii. Bryant's apparently unique exercise in
turning Homer's verses into English hexameter, which may be compared with the blank
verse version in *ibid.*, p. 220, lines 682–685, follows:

> As when the stars of the night, encircling the moon in her brightness,
> Glitter in heaven, and the winds of the air have sunk into silence,
> Bright are the headland heights and bright the peaks of the mountains,
> Bright are the lawns and, opening deep, the abysses of ether
> Sparkle with star after star and the heart of the shepherd rejoices.

1332. *To* Messrs. Lever & Francis

New York   April 1, 1863.

Gentlemen

I certainly cannot have any objection to your retaining my little poem
in the collection of which you speak, but shall rather esteem myself honored
by your not omitting it.[1]

I am gentlemen
respectfully yours
W. C. BRYANT.

MANUSCRIPT: Boston Public Library ADDRESS: Messrs Lever & Francis. DOCKETED: W. C.
Bryant / Apl 1/63.

1. This poem, and the collection containing it, published by the Boston firm of
Lever and Francis, have not been identified.

1333. *To* John Bigelow

New York   April 9th   1863.

Dear Mr. Bigelow.

My wife bids me return her best thanks for your obliging offer of your
house in the country for the ensuing summer,[1] and Julia, who is no less
pleased, desires me to add hers. I, who come in for a share of the obligation,
bear my part in the acknowledgments. By and by when the weather softens
a little, we shall go up to look at the place and see what arrangement we
can make with your Teuton who has taken a spouse to his bosom since my
wife was there. I suppose you will write to him, so that he may not be
surprised by our coming.

Our spring is late; the European violets are tardy in forming their
flower buds and the crocuses peep cautiously from the earth. We have had
a remarkably mild but quite unpleasant winter, with little very cold
weather, frequent rains, frequent snow storms, with little snow remaining
on the ground and oceans of mud in town and country. Of course there
has been a great deal of grumbling at the weather and the climate has been

well scolded. When I hear people abusing the weather I think of an uncle of mine a clergyman who died only last year.[2]

"We want rain, Dr. Snell," said one of his parishioners.

"We *think* we do." was his answer.

The war goes on as slowly as the season. "The winter of our discontent" is not yet "made glorious summer."[3] Public opinion, however, on the subject of the war is rectifying itself very rapidly, and the people of the North are becoming more and more emancipationists. I look for the time, and it is not far off I believe, when to be called an anti-abolitionist will be resented as an opprobrium.[4]

The Evening Post is getting on very well. We contracted its dimensions, when the dearth of paper was greatest, I am not sure wisely, for almost ever since we have been at our wits' end to find room in our columns for what we must publish, or else defraud the *readers* of our paper in favor of the advertisers. There is every day a battle with Dithmar in the editors rooms or the composing room, over matter which we are bent on getting into the paper, and he is as strenuously bent on keeping out. We have raised the price of advertisements, but this has seemingly had the effect of bringing more of them to the paper.

We were glad to hear of your being so pleasantly situated, as Mrs. Bigelow [said] you to be, with your family, in her letter to my wife. It never seemed to me that I became acquainted with a foreign country till I kept house in it. When you keep house you are a denizen, till then you are a visitor.

Mrs. Bryant and Julia are now pretty well—just recovered from severe colds—a sort of influenza which this winter takes a bronchial type and gives the patient a barking cough. They would desire kindest regards to you and Mrs. Bigelow if they were with me as I write. Say to Madame that I lay myself at her feet.

I am, sir,
faithfully yours
W. C. Bryant.

MANUSCRIPT: NYPL–Bigelow ADDRESS: Jnº Bigelow Esqre.

1. In 1856 or 1857 Bigelow had bought land at Buttermilk Falls (later Highland Falls) on the Hudson River just south of West Point, where he built a summer home, "The Squirrels." Bigelow, *Retrospections*, I, 163. His letter offering the Bryants the use of his house for the summer, dated at Paris, March 16, 1863, is in NYPL–BG.

2. Rev. Thomas Snell (1247.2).

3. *Richard III* I.i.1–2.

4. Several months later Bryant attacked those moderates who cautioned against precipitous action in the matter of slavery, urging only "gradual emancipation." At a mass reception in Cooper Union on October 2, 1863, for a delegation of Abolitionists from Kansas and Missouri, he charged that there was "no grosser delusion ever entertained by man" than gradualism. "Have we not suffered mischief enough from slavery," he cried, "without keeping it any longer? . . . My friends, if a child of yours were to fall

in the fire would you pull him out gradually? If he were to swallow a dose of laudanum sufficient to cause speedy death, and a stomach pump were at hand, would you draw the poison by degrees? If your house were on fire, would you put it out gradually? . . . Slavery is a foul and monstrous idol, a Juggernaut under which thousands are crushed to death. . . . Must we consent that the number of the victims shall be gradually diminished?" *EP*, October 3, 1863. See also Nevins, *War for the Union*, III, 160–161. A few days after Bryant's speech Massachusetts Senator Charles Sumner wrote him, "Yr words for Immediate Emancipation thrilled me. . . . I doubt if ever the case has been stated so strongly in so few words." October 5, 1863, NYPL–BG.

1334.   *To* Daniel Bogart

Office of The Evening Post
New York, April 9th   1863.

Dear sir.

In laying out the lots in the cemetery, according to the plan determined on the other evening, I think that a passage of four feet, between my lots and the lot of Mr. Ely on one side and of Capt. Kirby[1] on the other, would be sufficient, and then I can remove my entire fence a little more to the south.[2] I am not sure that this is not your understanding, but I write that there may be no mistake.

Yours truly
W. C. BRYANT.

MANUSCRIPT: BLR ADDRESS: Dan[1] Bogart Esqr.

1. J. M. Kirby, a Roslyn schooner captain (513.1).
2. In 1861 Bryant had bought the first plot sold in the new Roslyn Cemetery, established by the Roslyn Presbyterian Church at the corner of Northern Boulevard and Wellington Road. In 1865 he deeded this plot to his estate superintendent, George Cline, and bought plots Nos. 139–142, where he and most of the members of his family have been buried. Donald Canton, "Roslyn Cemetery," *The American Cemetery* (May 1975), pp. 34–36; "Roslyn Cemetery 1860," typescript prepared by the Roslyn Cemetery, Port Washington, New York. Bogart was one of five original trustees of the cemetery. Goddard, *Roslyn Harbor*, p. 107.

1335.   *To* Charlotte Dana

Office of The Evening Post
New York, April 13th. 1863.

My dear Miss Dana.

It made me smile, in reading your note,[1] to see that you set out with an apology for writing to me. I am generous enough to have overlooked the offense even though you had made no apology.

The best portrait painter of *men* in our country, I think, is Elliot. He does not succeed so well with women. He once painted a portrait of me, one of the few in which he was not very successful—but I think he would make a grand portrait of your father.[2] He would also give him less trouble than some other artists, his precision and facility are so great. We have other artists also who in the way of portrait are greatly esteemed. Hunting-ton not long since painted a very fine and dignified portrait of Verplanck.[3] Baker is a capital portrait painter.[4] Elliot's portraits are remarkable for vigor, character, and what the artists call fine modelling.—

Whether your father sits to a painter or not—I hope he will however— he must come on to New York as you say "in the Spring." You seem to for-get that it is Spring already. The crocuses and squills are in bloom and the European violets are opening at Roslyn, where we shall expect to see you and your father.

> I am, dear madam,
> truly yours
> W. C. BRYANT.

MANUSCRIPT: LH ADDRESS: Miss R   Charlotte Dana.

1. Unrecovered.
2. Charles L. Elliott (859.4) had painted Bryant in 1854. The portrait is in the Corcoran Gallery, Washington.
3. Daniel Huntington's portrait of Gulian C. Verplanck (1857) is in the National Portrait Gallery, Washington; that of Bryant (c1855) is in the Brooklyn Museum.
4. The prolific portraitist George Augustus Baker, Jr. (1821–1880) had exhibited at the National Academy since 1839, as well as at the American Art Union throughout its existence. *DAA*; *NAD Exhibition Record*, I, 17–20; Mary Bartlett Cowdrey, *American Academy of Fine Arts and American Art-Union*, 2 vols. (New York: The New-York Historical Society, 1953), II, 14–15.

1336.   *To* Benjamin Paul Blood[1]

> Office of The Evening Post,
> New York, April 27   1863.

Dear sir.

I have just got your second letter.[2]

After the commendations which your book has received from the able thinkers you mention my opinion of it can be of little consequence.[3] I will say, however, that I have read it with interest and pleasure. It is not a book to be read in a hurry and my time is so much occupied, that I have been obliged to take it up interruptedly, but at the very first opening of its pages I was struck with the independence of your way of thinking and with the original views presented on many points of your subject. Without accept-ing all your positions, I was glad to see the doctrine of optimism so ably and cogently enforced. Your book deserves to be studied by all who are out of humor with the universe, and scarcely less by those who are on good terms with it, by way of confirming them in their faith.

> I am, sir,
> respectfully yours
> W. C. BRYANT.

MANUSCRIPT: HCL ADDRESS: B. Blood Esqre.

1. Benjamin Paul Blood (1832–1919), a native of Amsterdam, New York, was a poet, philosopher, and mystic, and author of books in each of these fields.

2. Blood's letters are unrecovered.

3. *Optimism, the Lesson of Ages* (Boston, 1860).

1337.   *To* Abraham Lincoln

Office of The Evening Post,
New York, May 11th   1863.

Sir.

You will, I am sure pardon the liberty which I take in representing to you the universal desire of our German fellow citizens that General Sigel should be again placed in command of that part of the army of the Rappahannock which is composed of German soldiery and which has suffered some loss of credit in the recent battles.[1] The enthusiasm in his favor among our German population is unanimous and they are confident that with him to lead them—a man of such skill experience and bravery, of whom they are so proud, who speaks to them in words which they understand and whom they are willing to follow wherever he may point the way, they would be able to retrieve the reputation they have lost. It is impossible, sir, for you, where you are, to conceive of the strength and fervor of this wish of our German population. It is almost equally strong among such of our own people as happen to know the state of feeling among our German fellow citizens. The other day when it was said that General Sigel had been called to join the army under General Hooker it was the common exclamation that that single step "was equal to the addition of ten thousand men to the army."

I am, sir,
respectfully yours
W. C. BRYANT.[2]

MANUSCRIPT: LC ADDRESS: To Mr. Lincoln / President of the United States. ENDORSED: Wm Cullen Bryant / May 1863— / Desires Genl. Sigel to be restored to duty.

1. The former German revolutionary leader Franz Sigel (1824–1902) had come to the United States in 1852. Made a colonel in the Missouri Militia at the start of the Civil War, by early 1863 he was a major general in command of the Eleventh Corps of the Army of the Potomac, under General Joseph ("Fighting Joe") Hooker (1814–1879, United States Military Academy 1837). But, before the Union defeat at Chancellorsville, Virginia, on May 2–4, 1863, Sigel had been succeeded in his command of largely German-American troops by General Oliver Otis Howard (1830–1909, United States Military Academy 1854). After two German regiments panicked during that battle, there was strong pressure from Secretary Chase and others, as well as Bryant, to have Sigel restored to command. Nevins, *War for the Union,* II, 435, 444–446, 457.

2. In reply, Lincoln wrote on May 14 (NYPL–GR), "I kept Gen. Sigel in command for several months, he requesting to resign, or to be relieved. At length, at his request & repeated solicitation, he was relieved— Now it is inconvenient to assign him a command without relieving or dismissing some other officer, who is not asking, and perhaps would object, to being so disposed of. This is one of a class of cases; and you perceive

how embarrassing they are." By March of 1864, however, Sigel had been given command of the Department of West Virginia, where, after his defeat by a smaller Confederate force at New Market in May, he was again relieved of his command and sent to a less critical position at Harper's Ferry. Nevins, *War for the Union*, IV, 14, 51; Thomas and Hyman, *Stanton*, pp. 298, 303.

1338.   *To* Richard H. Dana

Roslyn, Long Island,
May 14th   1863.—

Dear Dana

When I saw your daughter last I inferred from something she said that you might be persuaded to visit me this season. We are now back at our home in the country, in the midst of a wilderness of flowers, with a soft temperature and the birds at their merriest. What do you say? If you are going to let some New York artist take your portrait to oblige your friends, you might make this your place of nightly retreat, for there is a steamer which goes from within a few rods of my house every morning to town, returning in the afternoon, and I would go with you if you have nobody else. Charlotte will come with you of course, and we might take turns in accompanying you to town. Take this into consideration and tell me what you think of it.

There is only one thing which might strike you as inconvenient; the hour at which the steamer leaves here in the morning—but that is never an objection to me and would not be to you after a morning or two. Who knows but that such a necessity of taking the early air might put new health and vigor into you?

How this war drags on! Yet I cannot help believing that it will end suddenly, almost unexpectedly, as the Indian war did in Florida, twenty years ago, when General Worth penetrated to the Everglades, to the wigwams where the savages had their families, and they seeing that further resistance was hopeless yielded themselves as submissively as lambs.[1] We have all along, in my opinion, conducted the war on a false principle, weakening our forces by the loosest dispersion and strengthening the rebels by keeping them in a compact body, when there was no necessity of all this. I think I see symptoms of a disposition to depart from this policy, and when we do, I shall think the war is near an end.

I have been looking over Cowper's translation of Homer lately and comparing it with the original.[2] It has astonished me that one who wrote such strong English as Cowper did in his original compositions, should have put Homer, who wrote also with simplicity and spirit, into such phraseology as he has done. For example, when Ulysses in the Fifth Book of the Odyssey asks "What will become of me?" Cowper makes him say

— — — —   "what destiny at last

Attends me?"[3]

and so on. The greater part is in such stilted phrase, and all the freedom and fire of the old poet is lost.

I am sorry to hear so bad an account of Edmund's health.

Remember me kindly to your children and your sister if she is with you.

I am, dear sir,
truly yours
W. C. Bryant.

MANUSCRIPT: NYPL–GR ADDRESS: R. H. Dana Esq. ENDORSED: Wm C. Bryant, May / 14/ 63. Ans. June 13. PUBLISHED (in part): Life, II, 192.

1. The Second Seminole War, concluded in 1842; see Letter 459.
2. William Cowper (1731–1800) published English translations of Homer's *Iliad* and *Odyssey* in 1791.
3. Bryant's version of this passage, in his translation of the *Odyssey* (Boston: Houghton, Mifflin, 1881), V.558–559, is ". . . what yet / Will happen to me?"

1339.   *To* Orville Dewey

Roslyn, May 14th [1863]

. . . My wife and I read your second "Talk with the Camp" together, and were much edified.[1] She thought you had written nothing better, and I was half inclined to agree with her. You cannot think how it consoles me and puts me in spirits when I see an old fellow at your time of life outdoing himself.[2] I read the lives of literary Englishmen, and find them nearly good for nothing after a certain age that shall be nameless, and the effect is dispiriting. I declare I think that the intellect here retains its vigor longer in this country than in theirs, with all their boasts of the healthfulness of their climate.

As to the necessity of wars, I find it somewhat difficult to go along with you. It does not seem to me that they are more necessary than religious persecutions. Henry IV of France was wise beyond his age when he contemplated a tribunal for settling the differences between nations without a resort to force.[3] But we *have* wars whether they be necessary or not, just as we have had religious persecutions, imprisonments, and burnings for heresy. And, while we have wars, we must try to extract what good from them we can. . . .

MANUSCRIPT: Unrecovered TEXT (partial): Life, II, 194–195.

1. On May 13 Bryant had reprinted in the *EP*, from the *Christian Inquirer* of May 9, 1863, a portion of "Dr. Dewey's Second Talk with the Camp," calling it "a characteristic production, and animated with the eloquence which arises from profound feeling." Though he took exception to that portion of Dewey's talk which urged the "rightfulness of war in general," he nevertheless gave his assent to its "magnificent con-

clusion," in which Dewey urged a military draft as the only means left to achieve victory, liberty, and justice.

2. Dewey was just Bryant's age.

3. Henry IV (1553–1610), king of France, 1589–1610, initiated commercial treaties with Spain, England, and Turkey. His "Grand Design" was the first significant effort to organize Europe and end wars.

1340.   *To* A. Cooke Hull[1]

Roslyn   May 14th   1863.

My dear sir.

I am sensible of the honor done me by the Long Island Historical Society in placing my name on their List of Counsellors. I suppose, however, that the acceptance of the office implies the necessity of attending the meetings of the Board.

In that case, I must decline it, in favor of some one possessed of more leisure, and to whom attendance will be more convenient. Please to regard this as declining the office, if my attendance is expected—otherwise I shall be proud to accept it.

I am, sir,
very respectfully yours
W. C. BRYANT.

MANUSCRIPT: Long Island Historical Society ADDRESS: Dr. A. C. Hull. DOCKETED: W   C Bryant / May 15/63.

1. A. Cooke Hull (1818–1868, Union, College of Physicians and Surgeons, 1840), a homoeopathic physician associated in practice at one time with Dr. John F. Gray (444.1), was a founder of the Long Island Historical Society in Brooklyn and its secretary from 1864 to 1868. Henry R. Stiles, *The Civil, Political, Professional and Ecclesiastical History and Commercial Record of the City of Brooklyn, N. Y. from 1863 to 1884* (New York, 1884), II, 906–907. Bryant served from 1863 to 1878 as one of three Counsellors on the Board of Directors of the society from Queens County. Letter to the senior editor, May 12, 1982, from Betsy Kornhauser, Curator of the society.

1341.   *To* Frances F. Bryant

New York, Wednesday
May 20, 1863.

Dear Frances.

I came in this morning, principally to look up an instrument that Mr. Willis wanted to look at, having received a note from him to that effect last evening. I thought he was a little unceremonious in asking for it, but I came notwithstanding.

Miss C. Gibson persisted in sitting in a very strong draught on the boat, and was sleepless all the night in consequence, with a severe pain in the left side and fever. In the morning I prescribed and she mended, but did not leave her room till the middle of the afternoon, and came down very languid.

I think there is something brewing between W. and the late mother in law—the mamma. He talks about an approaching crisis.— All well at Roslyn. The cook does well. The country is glorious and the shrubbery blazing with flowers, and I suppose, judging from the appearance fragrant.[1] The Dividend is large for the times.—[2] I am going back to night. In fact I was quite unwilling to come, for the stonecutters men are altering the enclosure in the cemetery. . . .[3]

MANUSCRIPT: NYPL–GR.

1. This suggests that Bryant had already suffered the olfactory impairment of which he complained eight years later: "To me, . . . nosegays are nosegays no longer. The great delight which I once took in the fragrance of flowers is with me little more than a memory, since my sense of smell, which was once acute—almost morbidly so—is now become very much deadened." Letter to Christiana Gibson, July 4 [1871], Life, II, 303–304.

2. The semi-annual EP dividend was normally declared on May 15. Although accurate figures for the Civil War years have not been located, John Bigelow noted that net income for 1860 was nearly $69,000. Retrospections, I, 320. Nevins states that, "in one year of the war," the EP earned more than $200,000. Evening Post, p. 427.

3. Conclusion and signature missing.

1342. *To* John Bigelow

Office of The Evening Post,
New York, May 23d   1863.

Dear Mr. Bigelow.

My wife bids me say to you and to Mrs. Bigelow that she will carefully observe every tittle of your wishes as communicated in your letters. She is about to proceed to West Point to reconnoitre, and see whether Kolisch is as obliging as he was last summer, and what arrangements can be made with him and his wife.[1] She will have things so ordered, so far at least as depends upon her, and her family, that you will have no occasion to wish that you had not made us the offer of your house for the summer. As for Kolisch, he seems faithful and not disposed to allow any liberties to be taken with your interests, but even if he were he shall be furnished with no pretext for it, from us.

It only remains that I should renew her thanks and mine both to you and Mrs. Bigelow, and to express my hope that the benefit my wife will receive from the change of air will be equal to the kindness of the offer you have made.

On this side of the water we do not feel so apprehensive of a war with Great Britain as you seem to do—though I infer that your apprehensions are quieted by this time.[2] There is nobody who wants a war but a few Irishmen, and they make no impression on the public mind. Inasmuch as neither nation desires war it would be an odd result if Great Britain should make war upon us, merely because she fancies that she would oblige us by doing so—

It is as hot for the last few days as in July. The season is rushing through its blossoming days with the speed of a comet.

Say to Mrs. Bigelow that I put myself at her feet. My wife and daughter would send their love if they were here.

Yours truly &c

W. C. BRYANT.

MANUSCRIPT: NYPL–Bigelow ADDRESS: Jno. Bigelow Esq.

1. Kolisch was the superintendent, or caretaker, of the Bigelows' home at Buttermilk Falls, where the Bryants summered between June and September 1863, Cullen travelling back and forth to New York, and occasionally to Roslyn.

2. Writing from Brussels on April 27 (NYPL–BG), Bigelow told Bryant he had recently been in London, where "I have been trying to do what I could to keep the peace if possible a little longer," for "it will require all the wisdom to be found on both sides of the Atlantic to prevent a war between the U. S. & Great Britain." He was distressed to hear the common opinion that the American government desired war, or the alarm of war, to stimulate the enlistment of men and money in the Union cause, and he urged that the American press speak less often of the ease of whipping Britain, and that it emphasize the "indecency" of the two great English-speaking Protestant democracies' being unable to live in peace with each other.

1343.   *To* Hiram Barney

New York   May 28th, 1863.

Dear Mr. Barney.

My time honored friend Joshua L. Pell Esqre,[1] a Clerk in your Custom House, who joined in recommending you for the office you hold, has been told that if I only say the word, you will increase his compensation, which is now but a beggarly eleven hundred a year, from which in these times of high prices he is obliged to support his family. The possession of power is so pleasant a thing, that I am going to try the experiment of saying the word.

Mr. Pell was bred a lawyer and is an experienced Custom House Clerk, a capacity in which he is entrusted with the drawing of law papers requiring great accuracy, and themselves of great importance. While his salary remains at the old rate he sees the salaries of younger men, who have had comparatively small experience advanced, from the same rate as his own, to fifteen hundred dollars. Now, if his services were worth eleven hundred dollars yearly, eight years since, it is clear that they ought to be worth a third more nominally now, when the cost of living has increased fully one third. Mr. Pell is no drone, but quick and active, diligent and faithful, and I interest myself all the more willingly in his behalf, from knowing that he has exercised these qualities in the post he occupies, for many years, and at periods when the New York Custom House was full of idlers and rogues.

I am sir

truly yours

W. C. Bryant.

MANUSCRIPT: HEHL ADDRESS: H. Barney Esq.

1. Apparently a cousin of Alfred Pell's. See Letter 1430.

1344.   To Frances F. Bryant

New York. June 3d   1863.

Dear Frances

I got here about eleven o'clock after a pleasant sail. This moment a letter has been brought me from Margarita.[1] She reached Genoa in forty days, on the 9th of May—her letter was dated the 16th. She was in bed she says only the first week of the voyage. At Sarzana she met her father and mother who were very glad to see her and she was quite happy. The country she found all in bloom and it seemed to her a paradise. Two of her sisters she found had died, one leaving a child of seven years of age. Every body she says calls her American and she answers that she likes the American ways. She is now perfectly well.

There is nothing else that I hear of. I have attended to Julia's errands, and hope they will turn out no worse than the affair of the trunk.

In haste

Yours ever

W. C. B.

MANUSCRIPT: NYPL–GR.

1. A former servant; see Letter 1130.

1345.   To Frances F. Bryant

New York. June 6, 1863.

Dear Frances.

Sarah Olds came last night about ten minutes before five, and I was at the station at that time to receive her. She looks very well, but says that the Emersons[1] are all ailing. Her father has something to do with the collection of the revenue and has removed with his family to Peoria.

Julia will go to Roslyn this afternoon, probably in the steamer, as it is my intention to do. I told her this morning, when it was raining, that I should probably go by rail, but as the weather has cleared so soon, and it is dusty, I shall go by water.

Godwin went into the country yesterday.

Yours ever
W. C. BRYANT.

MANUSCRIPT: NYPL–GR.

1. Unidentified.

1346.   *To* Henry Norman Hudson[1]

New York   June 8th   1863.

My dear sir.

I have received your letter concerning Col. Halpine[2] with the accompanying documents. It would I think be both just to the merits of that officer and wise as a step of policy to give him the commission asked for him. I have accordingly written to Mr. Lincoln strongly urging his appointment.[3] In this I have depended a good deal upon your representation, yet not on that alone, for I have heard the best account of your friend from other quarters.

I am, sir,
truly yours
W. C. BRYANT

MANUSCRIPT: HEHL ADDRESS: Revd H. N. Hudson.

1. Rev. Henry Norman Hudson (1814–1886), a distinguished Shakespearean scholar, was then an Episcopalian chaplain in the Union army.

2. During the Civil War the Irish-born Union officer Charles Graham Halpine (1829–1868) contributed to the *EP* a number of humorous poems, gathered later in *Miles O'Reilly: His Book* (1864). Nevins, *Evening Post*, p. 325. Hudson's letter is unrecovered.

3. Letter unrecovered. At this time Lieutenant Colonel Halpine was an assistant adjutant general of volunteers stationed in Washington. In May 1864 he was attached to the staff of Major General David Hunter in West Virginia, where he was cited for gallantry at the battle of Piedmont. Retiring from the army at the end of July that year because of failing eyesight, he was brevetted a brigadier general. *War of the Rebellion*, Ser. I, vol. 28, pt. 1, pp. 41, 189–190; Ser. I, vol. 37, pt. 1, p. 508.

1347.   *To* Edwin D. Morgan

Office of The Evening Post,
New York, June 15, 1863.

My dear sir.

The bearer is Horace B. Tebbetts Esq. a gentleman of respectability and of an enterprising character, who though friendly to the Union has considerable interests in the Southern states where he has resided the greater part of the time for the last five years—the last two unwillingly.[1]

He has a plan of some importance to the country on which he wishes to consult you, both as a member of the United States Senate[2] and as a man of practical sagacity and great experience in business. Allow me to ask for what he has to say your friendly attention.

> I am, sir,
> truly yours,
> W. C. BRYANT.

MANUSCRIPT: NYSL ADDRESS: Hon   E. D. Morgan. / Fifth Ave   Hotel DOCKETED: 1863 / Wm C. Bryant / June 15.

1. Horace B. Tebbitts, of Louisiana, was a pioneer in the effort to lay a transatlantic cable, which was brought to a successful conclusion, after several failures, by Cyrus W. Field and his associates in 1866.

2. Governor of New York from 1859 to 1863, Morgan had entered the United States Senate in March.

1348.   *To* Orville Dewey

Roslyn, June 19th [1863]

... I wish I had written to you as was becoming, and as my wife more than once suggested to me, the moment I received your letter, to tell you how glad we all were that Charles had come out of the battle of which you speak unhurt.[1] To be engaged in a bloody conflict like that, and to be alive at the end of it, is like going to the gate of death knocking defiantly, and being allowed after that affront to return

"To the warm precincts of the cheerful day."[2]

I hope there will not be many more such battles; but who can say? I feel that the rebel cause is on a decline that must put an end to it sooner or later, as inevitably as old age will carry off the longest liver of us all; but who shall say when the oldest of your or my neighbors will be called for? Perhaps, if he does not chew tobacco, he will live to ninety-nine. I do not expect so long a date, comparatively, for the rebellion. It is like a dying man kept alive from day to day by stimulants, to the wonder of everybody. When it goes, I expect to see it go all at once; life will not linger in some of the members after the rest are lifeless. After the head is cut off, there will be no wriggling in the limbs. . . .

MANUSCRIPT: Unrecovered TEXT (*partial*): *Life,* II, 195–196.

1. Dewey's letter is unrecovered, but on August 9, 1863, he wrote Bryant (NYPL–BG) that his son Charles, who had been engaged at the battle of Chancellorsville on May 1–4, was now at Donaldsonville, Louisiana.

2. Gray, *Elegy,* xxii.

1349.   *To* Daniel Bogart

Office of The Evening Post
New York, June 22d   1863

My dear sir.

I believe you were right in your construction of the law—notwith-standing the obscurity of the phraseology in the papers professing to explain it. If you were not I trust to have the benefit of the better interpretation. I enclose you the papers made out according to your view.[1]

I am, sir,
very respectfully yours
W   C   BRYANT.

MANUSCRIPT: BLR ADDRESS: Danl Bogart Esq.

1. Presumably concerning Bryant's cemetery plot; see Letter 1334.

1350.   *To* Alfred Field

249 Pearl St.   Saturday
June 27th   1863.

Dear Mr. Field.

My wife came down with me from West Point this morning and we both fully expected to take you out with us to Roslyn. We did not come down expressly for that purpose, but that was one of the inducements—and I am disappointed, and she will be so, at learning that you probably will not be back from Philadelphia till Monday.

Next Saturday we have an engagement at West Point—so that we cannot receive you then. If nothing better occurs can you not come down on Monday evening and pass the night and perhaps the next day, with us[?] You are shortening your visit in a most extraordinary manner. We really thought our country might keep you till towards September.[1]

It may be that we shall not leave Roslyn till Wednesday morning, which will give time for a visit from you— We certainly shall not until Tuesday afternoon. Let us see as much of you as possible. My wife is pretty well for her and in good spirits.

Yours faithfully
W. C. BRYANT.

MANUSCRIPT: NYPL–Berg.

1. This was apparently Alfred Field's second visit to the United States since the beginning of the war. See Laura Wood Roper, *FLO: A Biography of Frederick Law Olmsted* (Baltimore and London: The Johns Hopkins University Press [1973]), pp. 158, 496.

1351. *To* Edwin W. Field

New York   July 2d   1863.

My dear Mr. Field.

A friend of mine whom I and all my family value very highly, being about to become a sojourner in your immediate neighborhood, I have taken the liberty of giving her this introduction to you. Miss Christiana Gibson, although born in your island, has been for the last thirty years a resident in this country, where we had hoped to keep her for the rest of her life. How much our society loses in her departure from among us, you will at once perceive.

I take this occasion to thank you for the copy of the correspondence between you and Mr. Loring, which he sent me at your desire.[1] The letters have been widely read in this country and with great interest.

My wife and daughter desire to be kept in your kind remembrance and that of your family. Make my regards to Mrs. Field—*placens uxor* [agreeable wife]—and to your children.

> I am, dear sir,
> faithfully yours
> WM. C. BRYANT.

MANUSCRIPT: UTex ADDRESS: Edwin Field Esq.

1. See Letter 1328.

1352. *To* Frances F. Bryant

Roslyn   July 5th   1863.

Dear Frances.

We had a pleasant passage to New York on Friday morning, and I put Miss Gibson into an omnibus at the corner of Duane Street and Broadway.

In the afternoon I embarked on board of the Arrowsmith with about seven hundred passengers for different parts of Long Island, and reached Roslyn a little before eight—a tedious passage. Mr. Field came the next morning. We had rather a pleasant day of it and dined at Fanny's. In the afternoon Godwin and Mr. Field went to Glenwood on horseback. Today neither of us went to church. I attended to your directions concerning the carriage and horses to convey people to the Sunday School &c.

Mr. Field goes to Europe in the screw steamer China, of the Cunard line, which sails on the 15th. He says that you have already spoken to him concerning Miss Gibson, and that he shall make a point of looking her up as soon as he embarks.

I found the enclosed letter today on your workstand in the dining room.

Fanny and her children are as well as usual. She talks of going to West Point on Wednesday.

Enclosed is the Italian letter to answer Margarita's.[1] Love to Julia and all the rest.

Yours ever
W. C. B.

MANUSCRIPT: NYPL–GR ADDRESS: Mrs. F. F. Bryant.

1. Letter unrecovered.

1353.   *To* [Elbert Stothoff Porter?][1]

Roslyn, July 6th, 1863.

. . . It seems to me that in style we ought first, and above all things, to aim at clearness of expression. An obscure style is, of course, a bad style. In writing we should always consider not only whether we have expressed the thought in a manner which meets our own comprehension, but whether it will be understood by readers in general.

The quality of style next in importance is attractiveness. It should invite and agreeably detain the reader. To acquire such a style, I know of no other way than to contemplate good models and consider the observations of able critics. The Latin and Greek classics of which you speak are certainly important helps in forming a taste in respect to style, but to attain a good English style something more is necessary—the diligent study of good English authors. I would recur for this purpose to the elder worthies of our literature—to such writers as Jeremy Taylor, and Barrow, and Thomas Fuller—whose works are perfect treasures of the riches of our language. Many modern writers have great excellencies of style, but few are without some deficiency. . . .

I have but one more counsel to give in regard to the formation of a style in composition, and that is, to read the poets—the nobler and grander ones of our language. In this way warmth and energy are communicated to the diction, and a musical flow to the sentences. . . .

MANUSCRIPT: Unrecovered TEXT: *Life*, II, 384–385.

1. This letter, which Godwin states was printed in *The Christian Intelligencer* for July 11, 1877, has not been located in that periodical; nor was there an issue of that date. Rev. Elbert Stothoff Porter (1820–1888), minister of the First Reformed Church of Williamsburg, Long Island, was for many years editor of *The Christian Intelligencer*, official organ of the Dutch Reformed Church.

1354.   *To* Cyrus Bryant

Roslyn   July 7th   1863.

Dear Brother.

I find two notes of yours. One is the enclosed which you may wipe your pen on if you please; the other is [a] note for $95— a year later, with an endorsement of something over five dollars on it.[1]

Sarah [Olds] begins to talk of going home. My wife who is with her and Julia at Buttermilk Falls, writes that she would like to go alone this week. I shall go up thither tomorrow and will see how matters stand. I have written to Ellen [Mitchell] about her going to Dalton. All well.

Yours affectionately
W. C. BRYANT

MANUSCRIPT: NYPL–BFP ADDRESS: Cyrus Bryant Esq.

    1. The notes are unrecovered.

1355.   *To* John Howard Bryant

Buttermilk Falls   N. Y.
July 13th   1863.—

Dear Brother.

    I believe I did not answer your last letter in which you spoke of some improvements that ought to be made on some of my farms in your neighborhood.[1] I leave that entirely to your judgment. If you think there is any thing of this kind which is proper to be done, I would have it done without further question. I suppose you have or will have in your hands the means of meeting any expense of this nature.

    I am glad to learn that the prices of wheat and Indian corn in Illinois have considerably improved lately, so that the farmers are able to send the products of their lands to market. When the Mississippi is opened the prices I suppose will be still better.

    Elisha Fish wrote me not very long since, giving me some account of his family,[2] and spoke doubtfully of his ability to keep the place on which he has lived almost all his life. The farm was left to him burdened with legacies and the interest on these, or on the money borrowed to pay them has kept him poor. He is now going into the business of keeping sheep. I think his condition is somewhat improved since he wrote.

    Cyrus is in Cummington. I believe that Sarah Olds is intending to return with him about the beginning of August.

    Every body except the Copperheads is rejoicing at the good news from Pennsylvania and the Southwest.[3] My wife sends her love to you all.

Yours affectionately
W. C. BRYANT.

MANUSCRIPT: NYPL–BFP ADDRESS: John H. Bryant Esq.

    1. Letter unrecovered.

    2. Bryant's cousin in Gilsum, New Hampshire. See 465.8; Letter 472.

    3. The Union victory at Gettysburg, Pennsylvania, on July 1–3 was followed at once by the Confederate surrender of their stronghold at Vicksburg, Mississippi, on July 8. "Copperheads" were northern sympathizers with the South.

1356.   *To* Harvey Rice

Office of The Evening Post,
New York, July 14, 1863.
Dear sir.

I have received your volume and read several of the poems which it contains, in particular, the one from which the collection is named—Mount Vernon.[1] The versification is very sweet and musical, and many of the stanzas are beautiful. For the sake of that poem I thank you for sending me the volume.

I am, sir,
very truly yours,
W. C. BRYANT.

MANUSCRIPT: Western Reserve Historical Society, Cleveland, Ohio ADDRESS: Harvey Rice Esq. / Cleveland / —Ohio— POSTMARK: NEW-YORK / JUL / [18] / 1863.

1. Harvey Rice (1800–1891), *Mount Vernon and Other Poems* (Boston and Cleveland, 1858).

1357.   *To* George B. Cline

Office of the Evening Post.
New York, July 18, 1863.
Dear Sir,—

Mr. Henderson has just shown me your letter.[1] Four revolvers and ammunition will be sent down to you this evening. Mr. Godwin and Bryant[2] know how they are to be used, if you and others about you do not. You will, I hope, be discreet in what you say, and though not believing too much of what is reported, be ready for the worst. If John and Jacob are willing to aid in the defense of the house, you may remunerate them. As to Thomas, I am sure I may depend on him as one not easily frightened.[3]

MANUSCRIPT: Unrecovered TEXT: John Bigelow, *William Cullen Bryant*, "American Men of Letters" (Boston and New York: Houghton Mifflin, 1897), p. 84.

1. Unrecovered.
2. Bryant's grandson William Bryant Godwin was then barely thirteen years old.
3. A military draft, signed into law by President Lincoln on March 3, 1863, had become operative in New York on Saturday, July 11, with the first drawing of conscripts by lot. The following Monday the city exploded in a bloody riot by longshoremen and other laborers, whose venom was largely directed at Negroes, which raged almost unchecked for four days until it was suppressed by militiamen and by regular troops recalled hastily from the Pennsylvania battlefields. Other targets of the rioters were the staunchly Union, pro-Emancipation newspapers, such as the *EP*, which had been categorized by editors opposed to the war as the "Niggerhead Press." For several days the *EP*'s doors and windows were barricaded, and George Cline wrote Isaac Henderson from Roslyn that someone on the train had been heard to say that "Bryant's house would have to blaze." Nevins, *Evening Post*, pp. 304–309, and *War for the Union*, III,

119–122; *Life*, II, 191; Bigelow, *Bryant*, p. 84. Although Bryant's precautions were probably justified, no attack was made on his Roslyn home. John, Jacob, and Thomas were apparently workmen on the Cedarmere property.

1358. *To* Orville Dewey

Roslyn, July 29th [1863]

... Why were you not planted here beside me, where I could say, or would be glad to say, with Tibullus[1]:

> Me mea paupertas vitae traducat inerti,
> Dum meus asiduo luceat igne focus.
> Ipse seram teneras maturo tempore vites,
> Rusticus et facili grandia poma manu.[2]

Did Tibullus mean to say that he kept his parlor-fire burning all the year round? Let us try his lines in English:

> May my small wealth procure a life of ease,
>   Upon my hearth the fire be always bright,[3]
> The tender vines, the fruitful apple-trees,
>   To plant in their due time be my delight.

I came down to Roslyn last night, and, instead of the *grandia poma*, the big apples Tibullus speaks of, found some pears, the kind called Osband's Summer, just ripened for me on their dwarf trees, and very handsome, with their orange skin and scarlet cheek. . . .

MANUSCRIPT: Unrecovered TEXT (*partial*): *Life*, II, 196.

1. Albius Tibullus (48?–19 B.C.), Roman elegiac poet, author of "Delia" and "Nemesis," books of love elegies.

2. Tibullus, I.i.5–6, 15–16. Six minor errors in the printed transcription of the Latin text have been silently corrected.

3. Replying to this letter on August 9 (NYPL–BG), Dewey commented, "As to Tibullus, let assiduo mean what it will, he couldn't have 'kept his parlor fire burning all the year round,' since he lived—didn't he?—just about East, (& some 20 miles) from Rome."

1359. *To* Frances F. Bryant

New York   August 8th, 1863.

Dear Frances.

We had a pleasant passage down the river; the sky shaded with clouds and the breeze pretty fresh. There had been no rain however in the lower part of the town, and now, a little past one it is quite warm but not unbearable. I find Arthur [Bryant] here; he came yesterday and passed the night at No. 19 East Thirty Seventh Street. I take him down to Roslyn tonight, and wish with all my heart that you were well enough to go with us. I have

written to Ellen [Mitchell] that he will go back in the first week of September if she wishes it—otherwise he will stay till the middle of the month.
He does not contemplate making very extensive excursions, confining them
to Dalton and Cummington. He heard from Julian [Bryant] as late as the
16th of July. Julian had been attacked by the bilious fever but was recovering. The other families at Princeton were in their usual health. The prices
of produce—corn and wheat—in that region are much improved—so that
people are beginning to sell again.

I hope we shall see you in the beginning of the week. If Mr. Godwin
goes away, I shall be obliged to stay within call awhile. West Point is quite
too far off.

Yours ever,
W. C. BRYANT.

MANUSCRIPT: NYPL–GR.

1360.   To Charles F. Sedgwick Jr.

[Roslyn] Aug. 15, 1863.

My dear sir.

I thank you for the service you did me in reading my poem at the late
Commencement of Williams College.[1] I recollect that you were the crack
declaimer in our class, and I know how much good reading sets off a bad
poem, while Verses of the greatest merit if ill read cannot be appreciated—
perhaps not even understood by an audience.— I thank you for the kind invitation to visit you at your residence, and shall not forget it—though I
never go to Albany except when I am obliged which is very rarely. Meantime I have a pleasant retreat here on a little bay putting up from the Sound
where I am sure I shall be delighted to see you when any occasion shall
bring you to New York. —Make my compliments to your family whom you
mention in your kind letter—

Truly—
W   C   B.

MANUSCRIPT: NYPL–GR (draft) ADDRESS: To Hon   C. F. Sedgwick— / of Sharon   Connecticut—

1. At the college commencement of August 4–5, 1863, Bryant's name was restored
to the roll of the class of 1813, from which he had withdrawn in 1811 after only eight
months in college as a sophomore (see Vol. I, 18). For this fiftieth anniversary Bryant
composed an eighty-line blank verse tribute, "Fifty Years," which, Sedgwick wrote him
on August 11 (Life, II, 196–197), he had been "required to read . . . at the closing exercise of the public meeting of the alumni on Tuesday." For this poem, see The Poetical
Works of William Cullen Bryant, ed. Parke Godwin (New York: D. Appleton, 1883), II,
327–330.

1361.   *To* Parke Godwin

Office of The Evening Post,
New York, Sept. 2   1863.

I do not care any thing about the publication of the enclosed sketch[1] as it stands. Will you look over it and see what you have to say to it, and return the "Sketch" to Mrs. Julia Hatfield[2] &c according to Dr. [Geurulays?] direction.

W C B.

MANUSCRIPT: NYPL–GR ADDRESS: Mr. Godwin—.

1. Unidentified.
2. In 1870 one Julia Hatfield, "The Idle Scholar," published in New York a strangely and excessively laudatory tribute to Bryant entitled *The Bryant Homestead Book* in which she characterized the poet's Cummington home as "a thought shrine for the New World." She has not been otherwise identified.

1362.   *To* Julia S. Bryant

Buttermilk Falls
September 4th. 1863.

Dear Julia.

Your mother desires me to say, that she is very much better—that she came to town on Tuesday, and staid at Fanny's till Wednesday, where she saw Minna and Nora,[1] on their way home—that she came to this place on Wednesday and found Josephine at the landing, waiting for her, in good health, but somewhat disappointed at not being of your party—that your uncle Arthur came with us, and goes to Dalton tomorrow—that the weather has been delightful, and that she wonders why you have not written to her before this, but hopes you are not ill.

Our regards to all who are with you.

Yours affectionately,
W C BRYANT.

MANUSCRIPT: NYPL–GR ADDRESS: Miss Julia Bryant.

1. Fanny Godwin's fourth child, then twelve years old. See 772.5.

1363.   *To* Julia S. Bryant

Office of The Evening Post,
New York, Sept. 17th   1863.

Dear Julia.

Coming from West Point this morning I find your letter of the 15th.[1] I am very glad to know that you have had so pleasant a time. Here we have had nothing specially pleasant except the fine weather, which until today has been very agreeable indeed— Today is very hot and sultry.

Fanny has been quite ill, but is now happily recovering and gets better every day. We heard from her yesterday. Your mother made a visit of several days to Roslyn and then as many more to New York, while I took care of the paper. She is now much better than when you were with her.

At Roslyn some commotion has been occasioned by the draft which has taken for the most part those whom we could least willingly spare and passed by the drones whom we should be glad to see march off to the war. Mr. Hamilton the schoolmaster, and Weeks and Nostrand the shopkeepers are drafted.[2]

Mrs. Vandeventer's little boy died of the fever he was ill of. Last week two of the Doctor's friends, a physician and his wife, took down their little child to his house, very ill. This morning I hear it has died. The country about New York seems very unhealthy, in consequence perhaps of the extreme drought.

In other respects things go on well. Bryant had a good time in his yachting excursion and Mr. Ely says made himself quite popular. Roslyn is very beautiful. The grapes are ripening rapidly in the grape house and out of doors.

At West Point things go on much as when you were there— I hear of hops and drills and Cullen's equestrian exercises. The other day we took a drive to Long Pond a fine sheet of water among the mountains, where we found an old man in a tent which belongs, we were told, to the Professor of Languages at West Point. The excursion was a very pleasant one.

Yours affectionately
W. C. BRYANT.

MANUSCRIPT: NYPL–GR ADDRESS: Miss Julia Bryant.

1. Unrecovered.
2. For Nostrand, see 1322.1. The others named have not been further identified.

1364.   *To* Frances F. Bryant

Office of the Evening Post,
New York, September 19   1863

Dear Frances.

If I had known you were at New York and intending to come to Roslyn, I would not have come to town today. But having come, and having thought over what I am to say tomorrow,[1] and not liking the mosquitoes at number nineteen East Thirty seventh Street, I think I will go on to Buttermilk Falls. On Monday I will, if I am not prevented by something I do not think of come back and go the same day to Roslyn. I send you a letter from

Fanny, and another which I received from Julia, and a nosegay which I gathered for you this morning.

Yours, ever,
W. C. B.

Kind regards to Mrs. Hopkins.

W   C   B

MANUSCRIPT: NYPL–GR.

1. No record has been found of a speech by Bryant at this time; perhaps his reference is to an editorial he planned to write.

1365.   *To* Fanny Bryant Godwin

Office of the Evening Post,
New York, September 19, 1863.

Dear Fanny.

I got your note[1] just as I was about to start, and thinking it was for somebody else put it into my pocket. On getting to New York I looked at it and found it meant for me.

The sores of which you speak do not seem to me pure erysipelas—but to partake of the nature of boils. I had two or three of them last summer and used sulphur—I thought with benefit. Harolds I think are the same with those of the Cline children. I should try sulphur.

Yours affectionately
W. C. B.

P.S. Your mother is here with Mrs. Hopkins and I believe a Mrs. Clark. They will perhaps come to Roslyn on Monday.

W   C   B.

MANUSCRIPT: NYPL–GR.

1. Unrecovered.

1366.   *To* Orville Dewey

Roslyn, September 24, 1863

Dear Doctor of Divinity.—

There are three D's for you—three semilunar fardels, as Dr. Cox[1] called them, one more than you ordinarily get. You see what a fine thing it is to be of a munificent disposition, and to have ready a surplus of capital letters to bestow on one's friends upon proper occasions. I did not intend so soon to "trouble you with a line," as a hangman once said to an unfortunate subject of his art, but I think it my duty to warn you of what you have to expect. Yesterday I sent off to you by express a basket of grapes at Sheffield. It contained samples of five American sorts—next year I hope to have more—and a few clusters from the cold vinery. Perhaps a trial of them will persuade you and the lady of your heart to come to Roslyn, in order to have a fuller experience of those you like best. After all, however, it seems to me that there is nothing in the way of grapes so delightful to the palate as the Muscats of the Old World. Come and see. There is a fair supply of European grapes in our cold vinery, and all around the cornice of our house the Isabellas are hanging "as black as a thunder-cloud." My wife is at this moment at West Point, but she is anxious for an excuse to come down to Roslyn. Mrs. Kirkland has lately returned from the West, and I will try to have her here also. I doubt whether she will be disposed to say nay if you will come. Come and sun yourselves awhile, like venerable snakes, here at Roslyn, before you turn into your den for the winter. The line gales have blown themselves out of breath, and the sun is hurrying off as fast as he can go toward the winter solstice; but in the mean time he is pouring out a flood of golden sunshine, that we prize all the more because, on account of the shortening days, we get less and less of it every twenty-four hours. The warm sunshine is never so sweet as when a frosty air stands in close neighborhood to it. . . .

MANUSCRIPT: Unrecovered TEXT (*partial*): *Life*, II, 197.

1. Probably Samuel H. Cox (Letter 1306).

1367.   *To* Lydia H. H. Sigourney[1]

Roslyn, Long Island,
September 25, 1863.

My dear Madam.

I thank you very much for the favorable judgment of my productions expressed in your letter, and for the kind wishes with which it closes.[2] I remember the pleasure with which I read some of your very early productions, and anticipated the repu[ta]tion you would yet acquire, and this recollection adds to the satisfaction with which, after so long a period, I receive your commendations of what I myself have written.

It is said that the autumn of your life is as serene and genial as its spring time was promising; I am sure, at least, that it is rich in fruits of goodness and beneficence.

It would give me pleasure to be allowed to send you a complete edition of my poems, as far as they have been collected. If you will accept them, and writing to me at New York, let me know your address, I will forward a copy.

I am, dear Madam
cordially yours
W. C. Bryant.

MANUSCRIPT: ConnHS ADDRESS: Mrs. L. H. Sigourney.

1. Lydia Howard Huntley Sigourney (1791–1865), popular poetess, was known as the "Sweet Singer of Hartford," or the "American Hemans" (after her even more popular English counterpart, Felicia Dorothea Browne Hemans, 1793–1835). See 420.8 and 347.1.

2. Mrs. Sigourney had written Bryant on September 21 (NYPL–BG) expressing high praise for his 1842 volume, *The Fountain and Other Poems*, which she had recently seen for the first time.

1368. *To* Frances F. Bryant

New York   Friday
October 2d   1863.

My dear Frances.

I called at your brother's this morning and saw him. Dr. Clark, for he has dismissed Marcy,[1] has made a second examination, and today or tomorrow is to make a third. It is not the kidneys that are diseased, but the bladder, in which he discovers a sort of tumor. Marcy has treated him all along for a kidney complaint. Dr. Clark thinks that he can do something to diminish the patient's suffering. Egbert said that he felt a little stronger and had a little more appetite, but in other respects, his condition was unaltered.

I saw Mrs. Kirkland yesterday afternoon. When I spoke of her making a visit at West Point, she shook her head and said she was much engaged just now in getting out a book. When, however, I spoke of Dr. Dewey's possible visit to Roslyn, she seemed to relent, and said that she would try to go down at the same time, if I could let her know when he came. She is very well now, but only just recovered from a fever, which requires a year for an entire recovery. It has left its marks in her appearance.

Mrs. [Hiram?] Barney was near killing me yesterday. She rattled at me for more than an hour and a half here at the office, and when I took my hat and rose to go, she got between me and the door. I went to the dinner afterward and recovered. Regards to all.

Yours ever
W. C. BRYANT.

MANUSCRIPT: NYPL–GR ADDRESS: Mrs. F   F. Bryant.

1. The doctors to whom Bryant refers were perhaps Alonzo Clark (1807–1887, Williams 1820, College of Physicians and Surgeons 1835), a leading New York pathologist who was then president of the medical board of consulting physicians at St. Luke's Hospital; and Erastus Edgerton Marcy (b. 1815; Amherst 1831, Jefferson Medical College 1837), prominent New York physician and editor of the *North American Journal of Homoeopathy*. ACAB. Frances Bryant's brother Egbert Fairchild (134.2) died three months later. See Letter 1389.

1369. *To* Salmon P. Chase

Office of The Evening Post,
New York, Oct. 2d   1863.

My dear sir.

Mr. Reed[1] the writer of the enclosed has desired of me some testimony to his character. He is a worthy man who has endured considerable privations on account of his fidelity to his principles. I believe him to be thoroughly honest. He is in great need and has a family dependent upon him. What he says of his familiarity with Custom House business as well as what he says of his political history is strictly true.

> I am, sir,
> very truly yours,
> W. C. BRYANT.

MANUSCRIPT: HSPa ADDRESS: Hon   S. P. Chase. ENDORSED: Wm C. Bryant / Encl letter fr Jas Reed / Octo. 2d., 1863.

1. James Reed (Letter 1261). His letter is unrecovered.

1370.   *To* Caroline M. S. Kirkland

New York   October 2d   1863.

Dear Mrs. Kirkland

I send you a copy of the Cloud on the Way,[1] in which I have made some corrections of errors of the press, and supplied the omission of four lines. I hope the title is not ambiguous. I have a translation of the poem by M. Chevalier, a French author, in London, who has published more than one volume of metrical translations from the English, and who calls it, "Le Nuage qui passe."[2]

> I am, dear madam,
> truly yours
> W   C   BRYANT.

MANUSCRIPT: YCAL ADDRESS: Mrs. C. M. Kirkland.

1. Bryant's poem "The Cloud on the Way" (1860), prescient of his wife's impending death, was first collected in his *Thirty Poems*, pp. [73]–77. See *Poems* (1876), pp. 363–365.

2. Bryant probably means to refer to the Chevalier de Chatelain; see 1136.1, Letter 1393.

1371.   *To* Frances F. Bryant

New York   October 3d   1863.

Dear Frances.

Julia and Mrs. Ives went down to Roslyn this morning, and I shall go this afternoon. I was thinking of remaining in town, if Julia had not come, but perhaps this warm weather would have made me prefer the country.

I enclose some wedding cards. This moment, another card, bigger than both of these, enclosed in an envelope, has been put into my hands. It is an engraved invitation from Mrs. C. W. Field[1] for you and Julia and myself, to meet Sir Alexander Milne the British Admiral[2] and his Lady, and other British naval officers now in port. I suppose you will not care to go.

The meeting last evening was rather a curious one. After the speakers in English had ended, and the Germans began to talk, the assembly which had been quite large and enthusiastic, began to break up, and there was an immediate rush to the door, and the people kept going out till not more than a quarter of the original number remained. The leading article in the Evening Post of today is mine and refers to the proceedings, which were in some respects not quite what I could have wished.[3]

Yours ever
W. C. BRYANT.

P.S. Mr. Alden—Dr. Alden[4]—called on me yesterday. He is at Aqueckneck in New Jersey on the Passaic and on the road to Paterson, in a cottage with nine acres of ground where he has been building and planting all the season—and where his wife's health is greatly improved.

W. C. B.

MANUSCRIPT: NYPL–GR ADDRESS: Mrs. F. F. Bryant.

1. Mary Bryan Stone Field (Mrs. Cyrus West Field); see 926.1.

2. Sir Alexander Milne (1806–1896), then British naval commander in the West Indies and North American Station, and later Admiral of the Fleet. This invitation, for October 8, is in NYPL–BG.

3. A continuing controversy in Missouri between radical proponents of immediate emancipation of slaves and moderates who urged "gradualism" impelled the leaders of a "National Club" (the Union League Club?) in New York City to entertain a delegation of immediate emancipationists from Missouri at a mass meeting in the Cooper Institute on October 2, 1863. One of its principal speakers was Bryant, who attacked the position of the gradualists in the remarks quoted in 1333.4. See Nevins, *War for the Union*, III, 160–161.

4. Joseph Alden (1807–1885), long a teacher at Williams and Lafayette Colleges, and later president of Jefferson College (1857–1862) and the State Normal School at Albany (1867–1882).

1372.   *To* Orville Dewey

Roslyn, October 5, 1863

... Looking at your last a second time, it strikes me that you might, perhaps, expect that I should answer some part of it. Let me say, then, that we will give you a reasonable time to consider the question of coming to Roslyn—you and Mrs. Dewey—if you will only come at last, and before the days arrive described in the verses which you will find on the other leaf of this sheet. Mrs. Kirkland says she will come when you do.[1]

The season wears an aspect glum and glummer;
The icy north wind, an unwelcome comer,
Frighting from garden-walks each pretty hummer,
Whose murmuring music lulled the noons of summer,
Roars in the woods, with grummer voice and grummer,
And thunders in the forest like a drummer.
Dumb are the birds—they could not well be dumber;
The winter-cold, life's pitiless benumber,
Bursts water-pipes, and makes us call the plumber.
Now, by the fireside, toils the patient thumber
Of ancient books, and no less patient summer
Of long accounts, while topers fill the rummer,
The maiden thinks what furs will best become her,
And on the stage-boards shouts the gibing mummer.
Shut in by storms, the dull piano-strummer
Murders old tunes—there's nothing wearisomer.

[Observe the distinction made between *glum* and *grum*; glum applies to visible objects, and *grum* to sounds.] . . .[2]

MANUSCRIPT: Unrecovered TEXT (*partial*): *Life*, II, 198–199.

1. Dewey had written Bryant on September 27 that he and Mrs. Dewey wished they were at Roslyn; that "to meet Mrs. Kirkland if there were a chance of that would be a great temptation." NYPL–BG.
2. In reply, Dewey wrote on October 16 regretting that he and Mrs. Dewey could not visit "poet-Laureate Bryant," and adding, "But oh! Magnus Apollo! to think that you should write doggerel! I shall keep it as a curiosity!" NYPL–BG. The brackets are presumably Bryant's.

1373.   *To* Thomas C. P. Hyde[1]

Roslyn, October 5, 1863

. . . I thank you for your letter,[2] and all the kind expressions it contains. I am not certain that I had before heard from you since we parted at Williams College. I recollect you as held in esteem for your amiable qualities of character, but my memory preserves no image of your personal appearance. It gives me pleasure to know that you have been so usefully employed in the interval of more than half a century which has elapsed since I saw you. Dr. Alden, since I received your letter, has told me that you had two sons educated at the college where you went through your course of studies. For my own part, I have been what the world might call fortunate in life. I have been happily married, and my wife is spared to me. I have had two children; both are alive. I have been poor enough while poverty was best for me; I have now a competence at a time of life when it seems most desirable. My health is good—better of late years than formerly, and my activity of body scarcely diminished. I do not yet use spectacles, though next November I shall complete my sixty-ninth year. The world, for some reason, has always used me quite as well as I deserve. I hope I am not ungrateful for all these blessings to the Giver of them.

The posthumous writings of Carlos Wilcox I have read; but until now I was not aware that to my old classmate the public was indebted for selecting and arranging them for publication.[3] He was a young man of fine genius, and the task performed by you was a service to our literature. For the photographic likeness of yourself I thank you; and, though I may be charged with returning evil for good, I send my own. The beard I allowed to grow eleven years since, while traveling in Egypt and the Holy Land, and have never shaved it off. . . .

MANUSCRIPT: Unrecovered TEXT (partial): Life, II, 197–198.

1. Hyde (c1789–1865) had been a member of Bryant's class of 1813 at Williams College. See Catalogus Collegii Gulielmensis MDCCCLXXIV (Williamstown, 1874), p. 18, where he is listed as "Lavius Hyde."

2. Unrecovered.

3. Remains of the Rev. Carlos Wilcox . . . with a Memoir of His Life (Hartford, 1828). In his Selections from the American Poets in 1840 (Letter 390), Bryant had included five poems by this young Yankee romantic, his exact contemporary, who had died in 1827.

1374.   To Bradford Kingman

Roslyn   Long Island, Oct   10, 1863.

Dear Sir.

I send you with this brief notices—all I am able to collect—of the lives of my father, and of my grandfather, Dr. Philip Bryant.[1]

I have no "plate from which a likeness could be struck" either of myself or any of my Bridgewater ancestors. The only engraving of a likeness of myself which I think good, is that from Durand's portrait, and that is owned by his son, who does not allow it to be used for purposes such as you mention. For the honor you propose doing me in your work I am much obliged.[2]

Yours truly

W C. BRYANT.

MANUSCRIPT: NYPL–GR (draft) ADDRESS: Bradford Kingman Esq / North Bridgewater.

1. For inclusion in Kingman's History of North Bridgewater (Boston, 1866). See 1241.1.

2. Kingman's letter proposing an "honor" to Bryant is unrecovered; presumably it expressed an intention to dedicate his book to the poet. For Asher Durand's portrait of Bryant in 1853 and its engraving in 1858, see 867.2.

1375.   To Samuel H. Cox

New York   Oct   26   1863

My dear sir.

For your good opinion of the Evening Post expressed with your characteristic originality,[1] be pleased to accept my best acknowledgments. I thank you no less for the excellent counsels you give. Allow me to express the hope that your age is as serene and healthful as your personal appearance would indicate.

I am, sir,

with great respect and esteem

W. C. BRYANT.

MANUSCRIPT: NYPL–GR (draft) ADDRESS: Rev^d Dr. S. H. Cox.

1. No such written opinion from Cox has been found.

1376.   To Edwin D. Morgan

New York   Oct. 28, 1863.

My dear sir,

The bearer Frederick G. [Hubbard?] late of Pittsfield Massachusetts has desired of me a letter of introduction to you which I cheerfully give him. Mr. [Hubbard?][1] is a gentleman of much experience in commercial and business matters, whom his father a most worthy and excellent citizen of Massachusetts has commended to my good offices and has specially requested that I should give him a letter to you.

Of the character and capacity of the bearer of this note I have the most satisfactory assurances, and trust that it will be in your power to aid him in his wish to obtain some post under the federal government.

I am sir

very truly yours

W   C   BRYANT

MANUSCRIPT: NYSL ADDRESS: Hon   E. Morgan DOCKETED: 1863 / W. C. Bryant / Oct^o 28.

1. Bryant's apparently varied spellings of this name leave it unclear. If the subject was indeed Frederick G. Hubbard, he was perhaps a son of Bryant's early legal acquaintance Henry Hubbard (35.1).

1377.   To Elizabeth Kirkland[1]

[Roslyn, October 1863?]

Dear Lizzie.

I thank you for your pleasant letter.[2] I congratulate you on your new house, and your convenient method of getting up stairs, borrowed from the hen houses. It is said that man learned from the nautilus to use sails, and shaped boats in imitation of the body of a duck. Why should he not learn also something from the hens?

It is pleasant to know that the hymnbooks I sent you have served so good a purpose. You deserve a crown of gold for your Sunday School labors, and if you do not get it in this world, well I hope you have a crown of glory in the next. I begin this letter on Sunday and wish I were with you to see you teaching your young pupils.

So you have been reduced to chopsticks. Have you any Chinese in your neighborhood, migrating from California and teaching you that new fashion? But to cut bread with a pair of shears as you cut broadcloth—that is a touch above the Chinese.

We have passed the summer at a place close to West Point and are now back in this milder latitude, where the grapes hang black on our cornice in heaps asking to be gathered.[3] We could spare you a bushel or so of them, and I wish with all my heart you were here to help us make away with them.

[unsigned]

MANUSCRIPT: NYPL–GR (draft).

1. Elizabeth Kirkland (b. 1829), eldest of Caroline M. S. Kirkland's five children.
2. Unrecovered.
3. Cf. the similar image in Bryant's "The Third of November, 1861": "On my cornice linger the ripe black grapes ungathered." See *Poems* (1876), p. 383, third stanza.

1378.   *To* Fanny Bryant Godwin

New York   Nov. 10   1863.

Dear Fanny

I have brought a small basket of grapes for Esperanza.[1]

Enclosed are $166.70 which is your third part of the legacy left by Major C W Hopkins.

Yours affectionately
W   C   B

P.S.   Enclosed is also a memorandum from your mother—
W   C   B

MANUSCRIPT: NYPL–GR.

1. Perhaps a Godwin servant.

1379.   *To* James T. Fields

New York   November 14, 1863.

Dear Mr. Fields.

Before I got your letter I had had a talk with the Appletons about publishing my new volume,[1] which they were to bring out in such a manner, that it might make the third volume of their duodecimo edition.

After I had got the cash for the check you sent me, I saw them again and found that they were bent upon bringing out the book before the holi-days. It then occurred to me—what had not entered my head before—that my poem on the "Planting["] &c could hardly be said to appear first in the Atlantic Monthly.[2]

So I cannot keep the money with a safe conscience, and therefore re-turn you enclosed the check of W^m C Bryant & Co. for $100— with many thanks for your intended liberality.[3] You will I am sure acquiesce in the propriety of your receiving it. I may perhaps hereafter send you something which will be in no danger of making either an earlier or simultaneous appearance elsewhere than in the Atlantic.

I am, sir,

very truly yours,

W. C. BRYANT.

MANUSCRIPT: HCL ADDRESS: Jas. T. Fields Esq.

1. Fields had written Bryant on November 9 (NYPL–BG) thanking him for his "exquisite" poem, "The Planting of the Apple-tree" for the January number of the *Atlantic Monthly*, and begging Bryant to let Ticknor and Fields publish his new volume. But this was already committed to Appleton; see 1370.1.

2. "The Planting of the Apple Tree," *Thirty Poems* (1864), pp. [9]–13; see *Poems* (1876), pp. 320–323.

3. Sending $100 in payment, Fields had called it a poor recompense "for so charm-ing a lyric."

1380. *To* Frances F. Bryant

Office of The Evening Post,

New York, Nov. 19   1863

Dear Frances.

I send you two letters which came to me at Roslyn where I have been hard at work for two days. Appletons printers hurry me relentlessly. I send also a basket of grapes and flowers. The furnace is all ready to be lighted as soon as you come and the place is waiting for you to make it pleasant. I go back today.

Yours ever

W. C. B.

MANUSCRIPT: NYPL–GR.

1381. *To* L. G. Alexander[1]

Roslyn, Long Island,

November 20, 1863.

Dear Madam.

I thank you for the photographs. I had none of them before, except that of the Assumption by Titian. That of Mr. and Mrs. Powers, whom I have the pleasure of knowing, was particularly interesting to me.

On the other leaf of this sheet is the little copy of verses which you have done me the honor to ask for.[2]

I am, Madam,
respectfully yours,
W. C. BRYANT.

MANUSCRIPT: University of California at Berkeley Library ADDRESS: Mrs. L. G. Alexander.

1. Probably the wife of Francis Alexander (1800–1880), an American portrait and genre painter resident in Florence, Italy, as were Mr. and Mrs. Hiram Powers.
2. A fair copy of Bryant's sonnet "Consumption" (1824); see *Poems* (1876), p. 75. Neither Mrs. Alexander's letter nor the enclosed photographs have been recovered.

1382. *To* James T. Fields

Roslyn, Long Island,
Nov. 20th. 1863.—

Dear Mr. Fields.

I see that you intend to fatten me for another poem. Well, I keep the check on this condition,[1] that if I write another, I am to send it to you, and it is already paid for. Do not forget this stipulation.

Yours very truly
W. C. BRYANT.

MANUSCRIPT: HCL ADDRESS: Jas. T. Fields Esq.

1. Fields' letter returning the $100 check (see 1379.3) is unrecovered.

1383. *To* Henry W. Longfellow

Office of The Evening Post,
New York, November 23d   1863

My dear Mr. Longfellow.

The bearer Robert Dodge Esq.[1] of this city, has I believe some right to consider himself as your acquaintance having already met you. Inasmuch however as his modesty is such as to prevent him from claiming your acquaintance without a formal introduction, I have taken the liberty of giving him this note to you.

I am, dear sir,
truly yours
W. C. BRYANT

MANUSCRIPT: HCL.

1. Robert Dodge (1820–1899) was a New York lawyer and writer.

1384.   *To* Salmon P. Chase

New York   Nov. 24. 1863.

My dear Mr. Chase

Some years since, Congress took in hand the subject of the emoluments of the Collector's Naval Officer and Surveyor at the several ports of entry, and the members thought they had accomplished a reform. The salaries were fixed, and the public in general supposes that, since that time, their salaries are their only compensation. That Congress supposes this to be so, I have no doubt, and it has occurred to me that you might have the same impression. The proof that the fact is not so, and that each of these officers, at the port of New York, receives larger emoluments than the President of the United States, is only to be found in certain accounts which, unless there was some obvious reason for looking into them, would not be examined, either by yourself, or any of the members of Congress.

When Mr. John Cockle, an old Custom House officer under honest Michael Hoffman, and now a clerk in your department, was in New York the other day, I obtained some information of him on this subject, and if you desire to be informed in regard to the matter, I will take the liberty to refer you to him.

It happened, that when the act of Congress fixing the compensations of the three officers I have mentioned was enacted, certain portions of previous acts, one of them as old as 1799, were left unrepealed, at least as the Custom House officers choose to construe the later statute. By these acts, the "fines penalties and forfeitures" for frauds on the revenue are divided into two equal parts, one of which is received by the government, and the other is shared equally between the Collector, the Naval Officer and the Surveyor.

The amount received from this source by the Naval Officer of our port in the space of 25 months and four days from his appointment, was $44.640.67, which with his salary of $5.000 yearly for that time would make a total of $56.049.20.

The Collector has received some two thousand dollars more than this; the Surveyor some five hundred less—each of them is better paid than the President of the United States—and you will agree with me exorbitantly paid.[1]

I am, sir,
very truly yours,
W. C. BRYANT.

MANUSCRIPT: HSPa ADDRESS: Hon   S. P. Chase.

1. There is a wry irony in Bryant's exposure of these irregularities, since his partner Isaac Henderson was soon afterward charged by the government with similar acts. See Letters 1423 and 1424.

1385. *To* Frances F. Bryant

Office of The Evening Post,
New York, Nov 27th 1863.

Dear Frances.

I came by the train this morning and have been to the printer's. I am sorry that you had not waited a little longer at the office.

The Arrowsmith goes tonight only to Glenwood. I have promised to wait for my proof and take the train at half past three.

Now, if you choose to go by the train, I shall try to take as good care of you as I can. If not, and you prefer to go tomorrow morning, I will send a carriage for you to the Branch— Buy your ticket, however, for Roslyn. Or if you prefer the boat this afternoon, and will stay at Glenwood till a carriage comes, I will send one.

Please let me know.—

Yours ever,
W. C. B.

MANUSCRIPT: NYPL–GR.

1386. *To* E. D. Pease[1]

Roslyn Dec 14th 1863.

Sir.

The list of American poets from whom you propose to publish selections, appears to me so far as you have gone judiciously made, though I cannot say that you have included all who are worthy of a place in your collection. I infer, however that your aim is rather to make it unexceptionable than absolutely complete.

I do not know whether you think of including in your publication all the poems of which you have given the titles. If you should, the question may arise whether you have not taken too many from some authors whose copyright is secured. This may be the case with Mr. Longfellow. You will pardon my frankness, if I say it would be the case with me. About one fourth of what I have published is contained in the poems in your list. It is reasonable, however, to suppose that you only mention their names, as designing to select a part of them.

I am, sir,
respectfully yours
W. C. BRYANT.

MANUSCRIPT: NYPL–GR (draft) ENDORSED (by Bryant): [Answ^d] / E D Pease / Dec 12 1863. / [and answer].

1. Pease had written Bryant from French's Hotel in New York on December 12 (NYPL–GR) enclosing a list of poems which he expected to publish in a "compilation

of Select American Poetry." He asked whether it seemed a "judicious one," and whether he might use Bryant's name in finding a publisher. Pease has not been further identified, nor is he listed as an author in the *National Union Catalogue*.

1387. *To* Richard H. Dana

New York   December 15th. 1863.

Dear Dana,

I am glad of almost any thing that induces you to write to me, but really, my daughter had no suspicion that you or any of your family were neglecting her when she was in Boston. She knew very well that you were in the bustle and confusion of moving, and that several of your family, you among the rest, were not well, and she would have been unreasonable past enduring if she had expected you to take any trouble on her account. So far was that from being the case, that she was only charmed with the cordiality with which you received her.

By this time I hope you are well settled in your town abode, and that the invalids are in better health. With the return of quiet, in your household, it is reasonable to suppose that you will all be in better spirits, unless you are like some who are never so well in body or in mind as when they are in hot water—which I do not suppose is the case with you.

My book to which you refer in terms that almost make me unwilling that you should see it, will, I suppose, be out in a week or two. I shall get a copy to you notwithstanding, as soon as the bookseller has the volume ready. My family is yet in the country, where the weather for the most part is still beautiful. Julia has got there at last.

Please remember me most kindly to all of your household.

Yours ever

W. C. BRYANT.

MANUSCRIPT: NYPL–GR ADDRESS: R. H. Dana Esq. ENDORSED: Decr 16/63. Wrote / him Jany 26/64 On receiv- / ing his "Thirty Poems."

XXIV

His Noblest Strain
1864
(LETTERS 1388 TO 1509)

THE PORTENTOUS YEAR OF 1864, which presented to Bryant political problems anguishing at times in their insistence, was nonetheless marked at its inception and its conclusion by heartwarming recognition of his poetic achievement. At its beginning his new volume, *Thirty Poems*, drew high praise from fellow-writers as well as readers. Its penultimate month saw a celebration of his seventieth birthday of a kind rarely accorded an artist during his lifetime.

In January, after reading Bryant's tribute to his wife in "The Life That Is," Catharine Sedgwick wrote him, "Mrs. Bryant may now hold her head above Beatrice and Laura." Regarding "The Planting of the Apple-Tree," and "The Song of the Sower," Caroline Kirkland thought he seemed to "enjoy the mellow inward sunshine which brings such fruits to perfection." Orville Dewey was "charmed" with the lines from the *Odyssey*, in which "the blank verse is so simple, clear, and exquisite." The poems evoked in Richard Dana a "pleasing consciousness of subsistence into a perfect calm." To Henry Longfellow, mourning a wife who had died tragically more than two years before, the whole volume was "very consoling both in its music and in its meaning." In April, a committee of the Saturday Club consisting of Emerson, Holmes, and Lowell asked Bryant to Boston to celebrate Shakespeare's three-hundredth birthday, an invitation which he could not at first "well resist," but the acceptance of which he later withdrew because of pressing affairs.

One of these was the need to determine his newspaper's policy on the selection of a Republican presidential nominee for the fall election. As early as February Bryant felt that, despite the availability of other qualified candidates, if Abraham Lincoln could say at the end of the summer that the rebellion had been put down, he would be renominated "almost by acclamation." In April, while owning to no preference, he suggested that the nominating convention not be convened until September. When Lincoln was selected unanimously at Baltimore on June 8, the *Evening Post*'s approval was moderate, with high praise only for the vice-presidential nominee, Andrew Johnson of Tennessee. Bryant wrote Bigelow at Paris, "I do not, for my part, doubt of [Lincoln's] re-election, though among those who would have preferred some other candidate, there are many who profess to have their fears."

Foreseeing Lincoln's victory as probable, Bryant nonetheless questioned whether his administration was capable of so coordinating the massive war effort as to bring it victory. After Union defeats and frustrations early in the year, his doubts increased in May and June, as Union forces, under their new commander-in-chief Ulysses Grant engaged Lee in the same part of northern Virginia where McClellan had been stalemated two years before, in the thickly wooded and swampy Wilderness. At the indecisive and costly battles of Spotsylvania, North Anna River, and Cold Harbor, northern casualties of fifty thousand were three times those of the South. Though slow attrition had rendered Lee's less numerous Confederates unable to threaten another invasion of the northern states, his army was intact and could hold Grant at bay in front of Petersburg, which the North's commander put under seige.

As Grant's Army of the Potomac lay before that southern stronghold, with many loyal journalists echoing Horace Greeley's lament that "the life of the republic is still in imminent peril, and its bitterest enemies are of its own household," Bryant's objectivity toward and faith in the administration met an agonizing test. Three years earlier his business partner Isaac Henderson had taken the office of Navy Agent at New York over Bryant's strong objection. The senior editor, who seems never to have doubted his partner's fiscal integrity, was shocked to learn on June 25 that Henderson had been removed from his post and arrested, by order of Bryant's friend Secretary of the Navy Gideon Welles, after investigation had indicated that Henderson had mishandled moneys in buying naval stores. Bryant defended him in indignant editorials and in letters to both Welles and the President. He insisted upon his partner's innocence, blaming the perfidy of a Brooklyn hardware merchant who had brought the complaint, a man, Bryant protested, "utterly without character," and then in prison charged with fraud. He suggested that the real instigator was the *Evening Post*'s old antagonist Thurlow Weed, the confidant of Secretary of State Seward. In reply, both Lincoln and Welles maintained that there was prima-facie evidence against Henderson. Lincoln reminded Bryant that in the past the *Evening Post* had assailed him "for supposed too lenient dealing with persons charged of fraud & crime." Welles assured the editor that, although the reputation of his newspaper was "about as dear to me as to its proprietors," there could have been no collusion by Weed, who would not have learned the facts from Seward before the day of Henderson's arrest.

Although Henderson would eventually be acquitted by a federal jury the next spring, it is conceivable that Bryant's indignation that summer aggravated his disenchantment with the administration, just as more sharply disaffected party leaders tried to convince him that efforts should be made to persuade the President to withdraw his candidacy, and to organize a new Republican convention in September. In mid-August Bryant told his wife that it was "remarkable" how much ground Lincoln had lost since his nomination, and that many now thought the *Evening Post* had been right to urge postponement of the convention until September. At the end of the month he was furious when Hiram Barney was replaced as collector of customs at New York by Simeon Draper, protégé of Weed, and a party fund-raiser whose solicitation of contributions from postal and customs employees was so blatant that it brought angry protests from several New York papers. Learning that the President was being urged by editor Henry Raymond of the New York *Times* to sue for a peace without victory, Bryant wrote a strong leader, "No Negotiations with the Rebel Government," but declined a suggestion from John Murray Forbes that he write Lincoln reiterating that stand, for, Forbes reported him to have replied, "I am so utterly disgusted with Lincoln's behavior that I cannot muster respectful terms in which to write to him." His disgust, with perhaps an element of spleen, was evident in a letter he addressed to the President at this time on another matter; here he reported a conviction as "universally" prevailing that there was "extreme wastefulness" and "gross corruption" in the operation of the Navy Department by its assistant secretary Gustavus Fox, to the profit of enemies of the Union cause.

There can scarcely have been truth, however, in a report circulated by Detroit newspapers that Michigan senator Zacariah Chandler, visiting the *Evening Post* office about September 15, found Bryant "about to publish an editorial urging Lincoln's withdrawal, and the assembling of a convention to name a new candidate," for on the preceding day Forbes had written from New York to Massachusetts governor John Andrew that, after a "long and satisfactory talk" with Bryant, "I think the Evening Post will come out squarely for Lincoln & a vigorous policy. . . . & disappointed as Bryant was in Lincoln I do not think he would want him to withdraw at this late day even if the office holders would let him." On the 15th Bryant wrote Frances, "The Union party here is in better spirits from day to day and confident of success." On the 20th an *Evening Post* leader proclaimed its solid support of Lincoln, who "has gained wisdom by experience. . . . Every year has seen fewer errors, greater ability. . . . while Mr. Lincoln continues in power, this healthy and beneficial state of things will continue."

Bryant's change of heart derived in high degree from the nomination for President by the Democratic party, on August 30, of General McClellan, on a platform which called the war "four years of failure," and urged a cessation of hostilities, with the restoration of full states' rights, and with no mention of slavery. Other factors were a series of Union triumphs, with the Confederate army driven out of Atlanta by General Sherman on September 2, and successive victories by General Philip Sheridan in the Shenandoah Valley of Virginia which freed his forces to join Grant's army before Petersburg. When, in November, Lincoln won a clear mandate over his opponent, with McClellan carrying only three states, and New York giving the President a modest majority, Bryant was confirmed in the confidence he had expressed in September.

Bryant lost several friends in 1864. In January his wife's brother Egbert Fairchild, engineer of the new Croton Reservoir in Central Park, died, and in March the Abolitionist Illinois congressman Owen Lovejoy. He was a pallbearer at Lovejoy's funeral at Henry Ward Beecher's Plymouth Church in Brooklyn, and in June traveled to Princeton to address a meeting called to plan a monument to this champion of manumission, of whom Lincoln wrote to that meeting "he was my most generous friend." In June the Bryants declined John Bigelow's offer of his country home "The Squirrels" for a second summer, since Frances was about to set out on a three-month visit with friends to the Adirondack Mountains. At the close of August Bryant printed privately a collection of nineteen hymns, copies of which he distributed among his friends. In October Fanny Godwin was painfully, though not seriously, injured in a train wreck on the New Haven Railroad in upper Manhattan, as she and her husband were returning from a visit to Westport, Connecticut.

A seventieth birthday "Festival" honoring Bryant at the Century Club on November 5 was a unique tribute. Before five hundred members and guests, in a hall festooned with flowers and hung with twenty-five new pictures by artist members, Bryant was greeted by his friend of forty years, the club's president George Bancroft, and after a graceful response on the "barren topic" of "one's senility," listened to praise from many of the nation's leading authors. Emerson hailed this artist who had "contrived to levy on all American nature" until there was "no feature of day or night in the country" which did not, "to a contemplative mind, recall the name of Bryant." Holmes asked, "How can we praise the verse whose music flows / With solemn cadence and majestic close, / Pure as the dew that filters through the rose?" Whittier maintained, "Who weighs him from his life apart / Must do his nobler nature wrong. / ... / His life is now his noblest strain, / His manhood better than his verse." Longfellow wrote of this friend who had stimulated his youthful poetry, "He has written noble verse, and led a noble life; and we are all proud of him." But it was Lowell who signalized most directly Bryant's role in the struggle still raging: "In our dark hour he manned our guns again; / Remanned ourselves from his own manhood's store / ... / And shall we praise? God's praise was his before; / And on our futile laurels he looks down, / Himself our bravest crown." In climax, a committee of the Century's artists led by Daniel Huntington gave Bryant a morocco portfolio containing oil and water-color sketches by forty-six of the club's members. Left by Julia Bryant to the Century Club in 1908, these constitute a permanent memorial to the poet–journalist who served as its president during the last eleven years of his life.

1388.   *To* Charles Theodore Eben[1]

New York   Jan. 11th   1864.
Dear sir,

   I received your "four American poems" some days since. It seemed to me that the translation was executed with very great skill, and I said as much in the Evening Post.[2] Not that I profess to be a judge of German poetry, and consequently my opinion is of little value—but really it struck me that you had mastered the difficulties attending the peculiar metrical structure into which you had undertaken to render these poems with great dexterity. I regret to hear of your illness and hope that you are now well enough to proceed with the pursuits which you find so congenial to your tastes and your talents.

I am, sir,
respectfully yours
W. C. Bryant.

MANUSCRIPT: UVa ADDRESS: Prof. C. T. Eben.

   1. Professor Charles Theodore Eben (b. 1836) had written Bryant on May 1, 1863, from Philadelphia (NYPL–BG) saying he planned a volume of translations from American poets, from Philip Freneau to the present, and listing sixteen of Bryant's poems which he wished to include. Apparently this collection was not published, nor has a reply to that letter from Bryant been recovered.
   2. *Vier americanische Gedichte. Der Rabe. Von Edgar Allan Poe. Die Glocken. Von demselben. Lenore. Von demselben. Die Rose. Von James Russell Lowell. Metrisch in 's Deutsche übersetzt von Carl Theodor Eben* (Philadelphia, 1864).

1389.   *To* Oliver Johnson

Office [of The *Evening Post*][1]
January 11th   1864.
Dear sir.

   An unexpected event has put it out of my power to be present [at] the meeting of Wednesday evening [at] the Cooper Institute.[2] My [wife's br]other, a person very dear to me,[3] has [ju]st died and the funeral is on Wednesday [af]ternoon. I have written to Miss [Roth?] to say that I [must ask] her to [find? some?] other person to preside. As I do not know her address may I ask you [to] send her the accompanying note?[4]

I am respectfully
W. C. Bryant

MANUSCRIPT: Mills College Library ADDRESS: Oliver Johnson Esq.

   1. The manuscript of this letter is badly frayed. Conjectural matter is supplied in brackets insofar as is possible.

2. On January 13 the orator and journalist Frederick Douglass (1817?–1895), who had escaped from slavery in 1838, addressed a meeting in the Cooper Institute on the "Mission of the War." *EP*, January 13, 1864.

3. Egbert N. Fairchild.

4. Unrecovered.

1390.   *To* Committee of the Long Island Fair[1]

Roslyn, Long Island,
January 19th   1864.

I can think of nothing more pertinent to this occasion than the thought expressed in the noble lines of Longfellow.

> "Thou too, sail on oh Ship of State!
> "Sail on, oh Union! Strong and great!
> "Humanity, with all its fears,
> "With all the hopes of future years,
> "Is hanging breathless on thy fate.

*   *   *   *

> "In spite of rock and tempest's roar,
> "In spite of false lights on the shore,
> "Sail on, nor fear to breast the sea!
> "Our hearts, our hopes are all with thee,
> "Our hearts, our hopes, our prayers, our tears,
> "Our faith triumphant o'er our fears,
> "Are all with thee,—are all with thee!"[2]

This is better than anything that I can say.

I have the honor to be
very respectfully &c.
WM. C. BRYANT.

MANUSCRIPT: American Antiquarian Society ADDRESS: To the Committee of the Long Island Fair.

1. A great Metropolitan Fair, for the benefit of the United States Sanitary Commission, opened in Brooklyn on February 22, 1864. Among its exhibits was an autograph book with the signatures of twenty-eight American authors, presumably including this letter from Bryant. *EP*, January 25, 26; February 22, 23, 1864.

2. From "The Building of the Ship" (1849), lines 377–381, 392–398. Addressing a member of the fair's committee in response to a similar request, Longfellow wrote, "It is certainly a very graceful compliment which Mr. Bryant has paid me, and which you are kind enough to send me. I should like to send you a stanza from one of his poems in return, but it would look like a parody upon his idea, and parodies always take away the grace of the original." Longfellow to Sophia L. Whitwell, Longfellow, *Letters*, IV, 390.

1391.   *To* John Howard Bryant

Office of The Evening Post,
New York, January 21st. 1864.

Dear Brother.

I got your letter and the Account some time since.[1] I am glad that you employed Mr. Wiggins[2] on the business of putting my farms in order, and hope that whenever you can save yourself time or trouble by setting some responsible person at work for me under your direction I hope you will do so. Another year I suppose the expenditures on the farms will be less.

The other day I sent you by mail a copy of a book which I have been bringing out. I shall send copies to my other brothers and to Louisa.

I see that you are put into the book of "Western Poets," published by Foster,—I think at Cincinnati[3]—though he now does business in New York. The compiler did not include in his selections, one of your very best things, The Little Cloud.

All pretty well here, except Godwin, who is ailing, and keeps at home. Kind regards to Harriet and Elijah.

yours affectionately
W. C. BRYANT.

MANUSCRIPT: Lehigh University Library ADDRESS: Jnº H Bryant Esq.

1. Unrecovered.
2. Unidentified.
3. See William T. Coggeshall, *The Poets and Poetry of the West* (Columbus, 1860; New York, 1864), *passim*.

1392.   *To* Edwin M. Stanton

Office of The Evening Post,
New York, January 2[9?]   1864.

Sir.

I write in behalf of Mr. Erastus Whitney of this city a young man who has lately completed his twenty first year, and desires to obtain a clerkship in the public service. He is of a respectable family in this city, and was for some time a pupil in our excellent Free Academy, where he distinguished himself by good conduct and scholarship. Of his personal character and capacity I hear the most favorable accounts. He has been for a time employed as a clerk by the Quartermaster General of one of our Southern departments, but the climate not agreeing with his health he was obliged to return.[1] The post which he would now desire to fill is that of a clerk in the Bureau of Emancipation about to be established, and, if I am rightly informed to be connected with the War Department.

I am satisfied that Mr. Whitney would discharge the duties of that office, or of any other requiring similar qualifications, and I sincerely hope his application will meet with a favorable answer.

> I am, sir,
> respectfully yours
> W. C. BRYANT.

MANUSCRIPT: UTex ADDRESS: To the Hon. Edwin M Stanton / Secretary of War.

1. Whitney has not been further identified.

1393. To Jean-Baptiste de Chatelain

New York   February 3d   1864

My dear sir.

I received the translations which you have done me the honor to make from my poems, transferring them to your liquid vernacular, and give you many thanks for them. It is only a pity that the originals are not more worthy of the graceful dress in which you have clothed them.

I thank you also for the likeness of yourself, on the photographic card which came with the rest, and in equal safety. I am happy to be favored with the visible presentment—though in an imperfect way—of the accomplished writer to whom I owe the obligation of being allowed to address the reading world of France.

Your letter[1] would have been answered earlier, had I not waited till I could comply with your request to send you a likeness of myself, which I have only just now been enabled to do satisfactorily. I send it with this to return your call, and hope it will find you well. My own health, concerning which you kindly inquire, is excellent.

> I am, dear sir,
> faithfully yours
> W. C. BRYANT.

MANUSCRIPT: WCL ADDRESS: Le Chevalier de Chatelain.

1. Neither this letter nor its enclosures have been recovered, but see 1136.1.

1394. To Alexander Bliss[1]

New York   February 11th   1864.

Dear Mr. Bliss.

I send you a copy of a little poem of mine, which I hope you will find to be what you want. I made it, as you requested, with lithographic ink, which I found an awkward thing to manage, and did not make it with ease, so that it is not so neat a copy as it should be. I shall be curious to see the result of your Maryland Fair.[2]

> I am sir,
> very truly yours,
> W. C. BRYANT.

P.S. I have spoken with one or two [literary?] persons on the subject and will with pleasure speak with any others whom I may meet. As to my "counsel" in regard to the getting up of the album[3] it is not worth a rush.

W. C. B.

2d Postscript. I do not exactly think that I have sent you my best poem— but I have sent one of the least bad—of such dimensions as to be conveniently copied into the prescribed space.

W C. B.

MANUSCRIPT: LC ADDRESS: Alexander Bliss Esq.

1. Alexander Bliss (1827–1896, Harvard 1847) was a son of widowed Elizabeth Davis Bliss (1799?–1886), who had married George Bancroft in 1838. Longfellow, *Letters*, IV, 393; Nye, *Bancroft*, p. 120.
2. Bliss's letter asking Bryant to contribute a poem (unidentified) to an album for the benefit of a sanitary fair is unrecovered. He made a similar request of Longfellow on February 6, 1864. Longfellow, *Letters*, IV, 393.
3. Alexander Bliss and John Pendleton Kennedy, comps., *Autograph Leaves of our Country's Authors* (Baltimore, 1864).

1395.   To Sarah M. F. Webster[1]

New York   Feb. 12th. 1864.

My dear Madam.

I am sorry that I have no notes from officers of the army or in fact from any other distinguished personages to contribute to the collection which you are making for the Metropolitan Fair.[2] The autograph hunters have got away all I could spare. I send my own, since you have done me the honor to ask for it.

I am, madam,
very truly yours,
W. C. BRYANT.

MANUSCRIPT: UVa ADDRESS: Mrs. S. M. F. Webster.

1. Sarah Morris Fish Webster (1838–1923), Mrs. Sidney Webster, was the eldest of Hamilton Fish's five daughters. Nevins, *Fish*, I, 94.
2. Mrs. Webster's mother, Julia Kean Fish (1817–1887), was president of the Metropolitan Fair (see 1390.1). *Ibid.*

1396.   To Frances F. Bryant

[Roslyn] Tuesday morning
February 15—   1864.

Dear Frances.

I am glad to know that you had so pleasant an evening on Friday— Your letter I got only last evening,—and with it came four applications for autographs—two from Sanitary Fairs—asking for poetry.

I may come home tomorrow—Wednesday or perhaps Thursday or still later. I am fully occupied here—and if I were in town I should only be pestered by people who want to use me. So do not look for me till I come. When I get there I must stay a few days. I am to be in town you know Wednesday evening, the 25th when there is a meeting of the Freedmen's Relief Association at which I preside.[1]

It is very pleasant here—the roads firm and dry and the weather soft and mild for the season—a sort of pleasant November weather. Nothing extraordinary has happened. I hear that Saml. Taber's daughter[2] is slowly recovering. Dr. Vandeventer's little daughter is out every where looking quite plump and rosy. I saw the Mudge's on Sunday—all well.

It was so pleasant on Saturday and again today that I thought you might come—but you have good reasons for staying, which I did not know of. For my own part, I am so free from interruption here that I do not know on second thoughts whether I shall come in until Saturday!

Yours ever
W. C. B.

MANUSCRIPT: NYPL–GR.

1. On Friday evening, February 26, Bryant presided at an anniversary meeting of the National Freedman's Relief Association at the Cooper Institute, at which Henry Ward Beecher, William Allen Butler, and others spoke. The next morning the *Times* printed a derogatory report of the proceedings, noting Bryant's "usual style of platform oratory" and Beecher's "rollicking" address, but charging that no one in the audience could determine from the speeches what had been accomplished, or even planned, to account for the $50,000 to $100,000 which had been subscribed to the association. That evening the *EP* charged that the *Times* reporter had evidently overlooked a printed statement of aims and actions provided each seatholder, as well as previously printed statements in both the *EP* and the *Tribune*. *EP*, February 25, 27, 1864; New York *Times*, February 27, 1864.

2. Samuel T. Taber (1824–1871), of Chestnut Ridge, Dutchess County, New York, inherited land near Bryant's Roslyn property in 1856. Ten years later, having acquired more acreage from the town, he developed a farm where he bred Durham cattle which won annual prizes at the fair of the Queens County Agricultural Society. Goddard, *Roslyn Harbor*, p. 55.

1397.   *To* Mary B. S. Field[1]

[New York?] March 2d. [1864?]

Dear Mrs. Field.

I am very happy to be able to accept your kind invitation to dinner on Monday.

Very truly yours
W. C. BRYANT.

MANUSCRIPT: DuU.

1. Mrs. Cyrus Field; see 1371.1.

1398. *To* Christiana Gibson

[New York?] March 6, 1864

Dear Miss Christiana Gibson.

Your letter of the 12th of February[1] was received a few days since, after we had felt some anxiety concerning your family on account of a vague rumour which was floating about that there had been a death in your family. Your letter relieved us greatly. After we had the letter the rumour took a more definite shape and a gentleman called to me to inquire whether you were living, saying that he had heard to the contrary, and that the report was said to have been set on foot by "Miss Bryant." I assured him that it had no such source, but the next day—or next but one—I had a letter from Baltimore, signed Agnes V. Morton[2] expressing her deep sorrow for your loss and asking me for the date and circumstances of your decease. These I could not give her—and took upon myself to say that fame in this as in many other respects, was a liar.

But the story was not like other false rumours circulated at the expense of the who was the subject of it. I assure you that you were much lamented, as you will certainly be when you leave us at last—and far off may the day be. We must have you back to America first.

The great event of the day is the Brooklyn Fair—which has been very much crowded, and . . .

MANUSCRIPT: NYPL–GR (incomplete draft).

1. Unrecovered.
2. Unrecovered.

1399. *To* Francis Vinton[1]

New York   March 16th. 1864.

My dear sir.

I return you Mr. Brown's letter[2] which seems to me very satisfactory. I send back also your draft of a heading to the subscription book. It is carefully done and seems to me to contain every thing that is proper to be said. If I were to be hypercritical, perhaps I should object to the word "scenes" near the end. Would not "designs" be better?[3]

> I am, sir,
> faithfully yours,
> W. C. Bryant

MANUSCRIPT: HEHL ADDRESS: Rev^d Dr. Francis Vinton.

1. Francis Vinton (1809–1872, United States Military Academy 1830) resigned from the army in 1836 and was ordained an Episcopal clergyman in 1839. A fluent preacher, he served in several Rhode Island parishes, as well as in Brooklyn and at Trinity Church,

New York, before becoming a professor of canon law in the General Theological Seminary, New York, 1869–1872.

2. Unrecovered.

3. It seems likely that this letter was concerned with a forthcoming sale of twenty-eight pictures by as many artists, illustrating Bryant's poem "The Fountain" (1839), which were first shown at the Brooklyn Art Association in March 1863. Unsold at that time, these pictures were offered at auction in the Brooklyn Academy of Music in May 1864, to benefit a Brooklyn and Long Island Fair in aid of the United States Sanitary Commission. See Clark S. Marlor, *A History of The Brooklyn Art Association with an Index of Exhibitions* (New York: James F. Carr, n. d.?), pp. 15–16. See illustration.

1400.   *To* Messrs. Ticknor & Fields[1]

Office of The Evening Post,
New York, April 7th   1864

Gentlemen.

Mrs. G. F. de Vingut, being about to visit Boston on a literary enterprize, as I understand, has desired of me a letter of introduction to your publishing house. I need only mention that she is the daughter of the poet Fairfield[2] and the widow of Professor de Vingut late of this city, author of several works designed to facilitate the acquisition of the Spanish language, and editor of several works of elegant literature in that tongue,[3] and that she herself is not unknown to the reading world, by means of several contributions to our lighter literature.[4]

I am, gentlemen,
very respectfully yours
W. C. BRYANT.

MANUSCRIPT: University of California at Berkeley Library ADDRESS: To Messrs. Ticknor & Fields.

1. See 973.1.

2. Sumner Lincoln Fairfield (1803–1844), a teacher and poet, edited the *North American Magazine* from 1832 to 1838.

3. Francisco Javier Vingut (1823–1857), a Cuban, came to the United States in 1848 and taught modern languages at New York University, 1848–1857. Editor of several Spanish-language newspapers, and author of books for the study of Spanish, French, and English, he also published an anthology, *Gems of Spanish Poetry* (New York, 1855). Stanley T. Williams, *The Spanish Background of American Literature* (New Haven: Yale University Press, 1955), I, 201, 383.

4. Gertrude Fairfield Vingut was the author of several tales and an autobiography.

1401.   *To* Henry W. Longfellow

New York   April 8th. 1864.

My dear sir.

George G. Rockwood Esqre. of this city,[1] in whose behalf I write, is not only a respectable and intelligent citizen but one of our most skilful photographers. He is forming a series of likenesses of persons whom he calls Representative Men, and would be most happy if allowed to include yours in the number—an ambition which I hope you will be willing to gratify.[2]

I am, dear sir,
faithfully yours,
W. C. BRYANT.

MANUSCRIPT: UVa ADDRESS: H. W. Longfellow Esq.

1. George Gardner Rockwood (b. 1832), a former journalist in his native city of Troy, New York, turned to photography in 1855, and in 1858, after three years at St. Louis, opened a studio at 839 Broadway, New York, where he was the first to specialize in cartes de visite and instantaneous photography, as well as photo-sculpture and photo-engraving. Among his subjects were the artists John Frederick Kensett, Cephas Giovanni Thompson, and Worthington Whittredge. Photographs in the possession of the present senior editor.

2. Though Rockwood published such works as *The Classic Grounds of American Authors* (New York, 1863), and books on Dickens and a description of Irving's home, no volume of photographs with the title "Representative Men" has been found.

1402. *To* Mary E. [Bucky?][1]

New York   April 11th   1864.

Dear Madam.

For various reasons I cannot send you an original poem for your fair. I have copied, however, one from my last collection which I hope will answer your purpose.

The fairs in this city and Brooklyn and elsewhere have drawn upon me so largely for copies of my poems that I must be pardoned if I send no more than two or three copies of my last publication to yours. I shall as you request, write my name in them.

I am Madam,
very respectfully yours
W. C. BRYANT.

MANUSCRIPT: Berea College Library ADDRESS: Miss Mary E. [Bucky?].

1. Unidentified; her letter of request is unrecovered.

1403. *To* Ralph Waldo Emerson and Others

New York, April 12th, 1864.

Gentlemen.

I cannot well resist an invitation given in such obliging terms as those which you and your Chairman in his postscript have used,[1] and coming from men whom I hold in such esteem, and I shall, therefore, endeavor to be with you on the 23d, the birth day of Shakespeare. With every acknowledgment for the honor done me,

> I am, gentlemen,
> faithfully yours,
> W. C. BRYANT.

MANUSCRIPT: HCL ADDRESS: Messrs R. W. Emerson / J. R. Lowell, / O. W. Holmes. / Committee &c.

1. On April 6 Emerson, Holmes, and Lowell had written Bryant jointly (NYPL–GR) inviting him to a dinner at the Saturday Club in Boston to commemorate Shakespeare's three-hundredth birthday on April 23.

1404.   To Eloise E. P. Luquer[1]

New York   April 15. 1864.

My dear Mrs. Luquer.

Probably the reason why you got no answer to the letter you wrote to our Consul at Tunis, was that you addressed the wrong person.

I found, on consulting the Blue Book, that Mr. Amos Perry is our present Consul there and to him I wrote making the inquiries which you desired me to put to him. Today a very prompt answer arrived, sent me from the State Department at Washington. You will see that Mr. Perry entered very heartily into the matter, and did every thing in his power to get at the facts.[2] I shall now leave the matter on your hands. I would willingly write to the State Department as he suggests—and will if you desire it—but there are persons who would have more influence with the Secretary Mr. Seward than I, and it will be better that one of them with whom you are acquainted should write.

I send you inclosed also, all the pressed plants gathered on Howard Payne's grave which were in Mr. Perry's letter. With them I also send the copy of Mr. Perry's letter to Dr. Osgood,[3] which after reading I must beg you to reenclose to me that I may send it to Dr. Osgood who perhaps did not receive the original.

> I am, dear Madam,
> Yours faithfully,
> W. C. BRYANT.

P.S. I hope you will answer Mr. Perrys obliging letter as soon as may be.

> W. C. B.

MANUSCRIPT: CU ADDRESS: Mrs. E   P. Luquer.

1. Eloise Elizabeth Payne Luquer, a childhood friend of Julia Bryant's, was a daughter of Thatcher T. Payne (126.2), younger brother of the late playwright John Howard Payne (1791–1852). See 406.2, 3.

2. John Howard Payne had served as United States consul in Tunis, 1842–1845, and 1851–1852. After his death and burial there, many of his books were sold at auction to satisfy his creditors, and his manuscripts were dispersed. At Mrs. Luquer's request, Bryant wrote Perry on February 22, 1864 (letter unrecovered), asking him to enquire into the whereabouts of these papers. Perry's reply of March 19, and further letters dated March 26 and April 13 (all in CU), reported that a search had recovered many of the manuscripts, which he would feel justified in forwarding to Payne's heirs upon authorization from the State Department in Washington.

3. In his letter of March 19 (CU) Perry enclosed a copy of a letter he had sent the previous November to his friend the Rev. Samuel Osgood (see Letter 1258), presumably about the Payne matter.

1405.   To Ralph Waldo Emerson

New York   April 18th. 1864

My dear sir.

When I answered the letter of your Committee, saying that I would endeavor to be with the Saturday Club on the 23d, there did not occur to me several circumstances which stand in the way of my purpose. I find that there are certain things to be done from which I ought not to excuse myself, even for the sake of the pleasantest festivity.[1] Will you, therefore, do me the favor of making my excuses to the other members of the Committee, for revoking my acceptance of the invitation so kindly given, and assure them of my regret at losing the pleasure I promised myself in their society and that of the other members of the Club. . . .[2]

MANUSCRIPT: HCL ADDRESS: R. W. Emerson Esq.

1. Emerson had written on April 16 (NYPL–GR) expressing pleasure at Bryant's acceptance (in Letter 1403) of the Saturday Club's invitation.

2. Complimentary close and signature missing.

1406.   To Daniel Bogart

Roslyn   April 19   1864

My dear sir.

I enclose you my tax return. The hesitation of the Assessor in New York arose from a doubt as to the manner in which the three per cent paid on advertisements should be deducted from the five per cent tax. He applied as I understood to the Treasury Department for instructions as the proper course, and the return is made out as these instructions directed.

I am, sir,
truly yours
W. C. BRYANT.

MANUSCRIPT: BLR ADDRESS: Daniel Bogart Esqr.

1407. *To* John H. Woods[1]

New York, April 21, 1864.

Dear sir

I thank you for speaking so kindly of what I have written. I hope, at least, that my verses, if they have done no good, have been the occasion of no mischief to any of my fellow creatures.

In the "Death of the Flowers" the line to which you refer was written by me "calls the crow" &c. *Caws* would be a more striking term—but it would hardly answer for the "jay" in the previous line. In all my editions it stands "calls."[2]

In the poem entitled "Blessed are they that mourn," I agree that the word "goes" should have read "go."[3]

There is no small blue and gold edition of my "Thirty Poems," nor do I know that there will soon be. The duodecimo edition has, however, been occasionally put in blue and gold by the Appletons, who are my publishers.

I am, sir,

truly yours

WM. C. BRYANT.

MANUSCRIPT: Minneapolis Public Library ADDRESS: John H. Woods Esq.

1. Unidentified. No letter from Woods to Bryant has been recovered.
2. In the first stanza of this poem, written in 1825, the lines in question are:

"The robin and the wren are flown, and from the shrubs the jay,
And from the wood-top calls the crow through all the gloomy day."

See *Poems* (1876), p. 132.

3. Stanza 5 of this hymn (1820) reads

"Nor let the good man's trust depart,
Though life its common gifts deny,—
Though with a pierced and bleeding heart
And spurned of men, he goes to die."

Bryant did not, however, make this change; see *Poems* (1876), p. 47.

1408. *To* John Howard Bryant

New York, April 22d [1864]

... I have been making myself my own executor, in part, at least, and am paying off by anticipation, while I have the means, some little legacies to my relatives and those of my wife. As I have a few notes of yours, it has appeared to me that I might as well send some of them to you as send the money. It will, at least, stop the interest. Enclosed you have two of the smaller notes, which, with the interest due on them, will amount to about a thousand dollars. I hope you will make no difficulty about accepting them, as it will save me the trouble of giving them to you in my will. You see that I have cancelled the name in each of them, so that they cannot be good for anything to me or anybody else. The attention which you have for so many years given to my affairs in Illinois deserves some acknowledgment. . . .

MANUSCRIPT: Unrecovered TEXT (*partial*): *Life*, II, 209–210.

1409. *To* Eloise E. P. Luquer

Office of The Evening Post,
New York, April 22   1864.

Dear Mrs. Luquer

Enclosed is another letter received today from our attentive correspondent Mr. Perry—Consul General at Tunis.[1]

Truly yours
W   C   BRYANT.

MANUSCRIPT: CU.

1. Probably Amos Perry to Bryant, March 26, 1864 (CU). See 1404.2.

1410. *To* John Frederick Kensett[1]

[New York?] April 24th   1864.—

Mr. Kensett

Please send the picture of Cobden by Fagnani[2] to the office of the Evening Post.

I understand that it is intended to send off the pictures today—but so far as this one is concerned I had as lief receive it tomorrow.

Yours truly
W. C. BRYANT

MANUSCRIPT: Archives of American Art.

1. John Frederick Kensett (1816–1872), a member of the National Academy, was one of the best-known and most successful American landscape painters after the death of Thomas Cole in 1848. See illustration.
2. Giuseppe Fagnani (1819–1873), Italian-born portrait and figure painter, came to the United States in 1849 after working for some years in Europe, and settled in New York City. His portrait of Henry Clay hangs in the National Capitol. *DAA.* For his portrait of Richard Cobden see Letters 1412, 1413.

1411. *To* Frances F. Bryant

Office of The Evening Post,
New York, April 25th   1864.

Dear Frances.

I am glad to hear that your cold is so much better. I send a letter from Henry N. Pierson, having first taken out the Certificate of Deposite and endorsed it, returning it to him.[1]

I think I shall not go to Roslyn until tomorrow and have just finished a letter to Mr. Cline asking him to have a fire in the furnace. I hope you will not fail to come out this week. For my own part I have thoughts of settling myself there.

Yours ever
W C. B.

MANUSCRIPT: NYPL–GR.

1. Pierson is unidentified; his letter is unrecovered.

1412. *To* Morris Ketchum[1]

Office of The Evening Post
New York, April 26　1864

My dear sir.

The purchase of the portrait of Mr. Cobden was credited to me in the morning papers, but I stated in the Evening Post, that it was bought on your account. I wrote immediately to Mr. J. A. Stevens jr.[2] of the Chamber of Commerce, concerning your desire to present the picture to that institution. He was absent, but yesterday on his return and a consultation with the president of the Chamber, he wrote me, that the next and regular annual meeting of the Chamber of Commerce will take place on Thursday the 5th of May, when he adds "the portrait may be presented, and will doubtless be received with grateful thanks." I shall write a letter to accompany it if to be published.

Meantime I directed the picture to be sent to this office, to be kept till the time of presentation.

I am, dear sir,
truly yours
W. C. BRYANT.

MANUSCRIPT: Colby College Library ADDRESS: Morris Ketchum Esq.

1. Morris Ketchum (1796–1880), a widely respected New York banker, was a confidant of Salmon P. Chase and a patron of Frederick L. Olmsted.
2. John A. Stevens (1088.3). Bryant's letter to him is unrecovered.

1413. *To* Abiel Abbott Low[1]

New-York, May 2d, 1864.

My dear sir:

I have been desired by Morris Ketchum, Esq. to act for him, in purchasing the portrait of Mr. Richard Cobden, and to present it, in his name, to the New-York Chamber of Commerce.

In doing this, he has more than one motive. He desires to testify his great respect for your body, and his high appreciation of the skill of the artist who has so happily and worthily employed his pencil; but, above all, he wishes to express the admiration which he feels, and which he is confident that the members of your chamber share with him, for the public course and personal virtues of the illustrious English statesman, the wise legislator, and the enlightened friend of justice, humanity and liberty, who has so boldly and so ably defended the cause of our country in this hour of her calamity, against the calumnies and prejudices of those powerful classes in Europe, who either hate our institutions or are jealous of our greatness.[2]

For this manly and generous conduct, I am sure you will agree with me that Mr. Cobden deserves to be ever held in grateful remembrance by the citizens of the United States; and that the page of history, which records the vindication of our cause by him and a few of his eminent countrymen, can never lose its interest with American readers.

May I, therefore, ask of the Chamber of Commerce, in accepting the gift offered by the liberality of our friend, to give it an honorable place on the walls of the building to which its members assemble.

> I am, sir, with great regard and
> esteem,
> Your obedient servant,
> WM. C. BRYANT.

MANUSCRIPT: Unrecovered TEXT: *New-York Chamber of Commerce Bulletin*, 7 (May 6, 1864), 5.

1. Abiel Abbott Low (1811–1893), then president of the New-York Chamber of Commerce, had been a successful merchant in Canton, China, before establishing the firm of A. A. Low & Brothers in New York, trading in silk and tea with China and Japan. He helped to finance the first Atlantic cable, and the Chesapeake and Ohio Railroad.

2. Cobden was one of the staunchest and most consistent supporters of the northern cause in the British parliament throughout the Civil War. After his speech of April 24, 1863, in the House of Commons on the neutrality laws, John Bigelow wrote in his diary on May 13, "No one attempted to answer it. From that day to this the tone of public sentiment in England has been growing daily more tolerant toward America." Quoted in Nevins, *War for the Union*, III, 503–504. See also *ibid.*, 479, 497; Letter 1090; Cobden to William H. Osborn, July 27, 1862, and January 22, 1864, Bodleian Library.

1414. *To* James T. Fields

> Roslyn   Long Island
> May 9th. 1864.

Dear Mr. Fields.

I send you what you ask—a poem for your July number.[1] The matter for the June number, I dare say is already in hand. The one I now send, you remember is not to be paid for.

> very truly yours
> W. C. BRYANT.

P.S. Please retain the date in printing the poem.[2]

> W. C. B.

MANUSCRIPT: NYPL–Berg ADDRESS: Jas. T. Fields Esq. DOCKETED: From W. C. Bryant / Rec^d. May 11th.

1. Bryant enclosed a seventeen-stanza poem in his holograph, "The Return of the Birds." This appeared in the *Atlantic Monthly*, 81 (July 1864), 37–39. See *Poems* (1876), pp. 439–441.

2. The manuscript is dated March 1864, at a time when the war seemed almost to have reached a stalemate. In these verses Bryant sees the early flight of songbirds northward as an escape from the battlefields of the South:

> ... Stay, then, beneath our ruder sky;
> Heed not the storm-clouds rising black,
> Nor yelling winds that with them fly;
> Nor let them fright you back—

> ... And we will pray that, ere again
> The flowers of autumn bloom and die,
> Our generals and their strong-armed men
> May lay their weapons by.

1415.   *To* Eloise E. P. Luquer

New York   May 18th   1864.

My dear Mrs. Luquer

Our attentive friend Mr. Perry, of Tunis, has written me the letter which I enclose, and which came to me yesterday. . . .[1]

MANUSCRIPT: CU.

1. Probably Amos Perry to Bryant, April 13, 1864; see 1404.2. Bryant's complimentary close and signature are missing.

1416.   *To* Frances F. Bryant

New York   Wednesday Evening
May 25th   1864.

Dear Frances.

I found another travelling bag a leather one in the bedroom closet a little smaller than the one I brought from Roslyn—so I put my things into it, and find that it holds them very well. I had forgotten that I had it.

I have put another thousand to your credit on the books of the Evening Post for I found that you had only five dollars left.

Yours ever
W. C. B.

MANUSCRIPT: NYPL–GR.

1417.   *To* Frances F. Bryant

Princeton   Illinois
May 28th   1864   Saturday morning

Dear Frances.

I do not think that I ever before travelled nine hundred miles in the same space of time as I have just done. At seven o'clock on Thursday morning I left New York and this morning at three o'clock I pulled the bell at John's door. He made his appearance immediately and said that he and his wife had been up at the railway station for me that day, but had not expected me in the night. I learn that the Bryants here are all in their usual health. Only Cyrus and William[1] are the invalids.

After being awhile in the train on Thursday morning I found myself out of order and for the greater part of the day I feared that I should have to stop for the night at Buffalo. To cure myself I went without my dinner. At a place called Hornellsville where we stopped to sup I found a pitcher of excellent milk and a repast of bread and milk set me up so that I concluded to pass the night on the train. So I went on to Cleaveland, where we arrived in time to breakfast. In making my arrangements for the night, I looked into the sleeping car, which is puffed in the advertisements as luxury beyond any thing in the known world, but it looked so close and stifling with its three tiers of beds one over another, that I was driven to take a seat in an ordinary car where I had one to myself. It rained all day on Thursday and all Thursday night. The whole country was profusely steeped with rain to a little distance this side of Toledo, when gradually the region grew drier, and soon after became dusty. All along the region south of the lake and here the season is by no means so forward as with us. I said when I left home that I might be back in ten days, but if I go to Peoria as I somewhat think of doing it will give but little time to look after things here, if I make my arrangements to go so early. It may be that I shall find it better not to set out till the beginning of week after next—that is a week from next Monday, which I may do from Peoria.

I did not finish the story of my journey. We got to Chicago in the train about half past eight in the evening. Here a train was to start for Princeton at a quarter past nine. I felt so much better than I did the evening before, that I thought I would not desert the railroad, and after a pretty comfortable ride of five hours I was set down at Princeton, and there I found an omnibus standing which drove with me to John's door. I went to bed and had a nap of three or four hours, and here I am as fresh as if I had never left Roslyn.

All the family here told me that they would have been more glad to see me if you had been with me. They make many inquiries concerning you and Julia. Elijah was particularly desirous to know why Julia did not come. I shall write again the beginning of the week.

Yours ever

W   C   BRYANT

MANUSCRIPT: NYPL–GR.

1. William Austin Bryant (1826–1865?), Austin Bryant's second son.

1418.   *To* Frances F. Bryant

Princeton, May 30th   1864
Monday morning.

Dear Frances.

I said in my letter of Saturday that I had travelled nine hundred miles to reach this place. I left out the whole distance from Buffalo to Cleaveland, which will make it about eleven hundred miles. Please read my other letter with this correction.

I find every thing going on very well here, generally speaking. The house I am in, Johns is very beautiful, the handsomest I have seen in travelling many miles and quite convenient. I am writing in the north chamber which is assigned to me and it opens into a nice bed room on the west. The ceilings both below and above are quite high, and the piazza surrounding the house on three sides is quite pretty. Arthur is doing very well with his nursery. Peter[1] lives in the back part of John's house and has a nice wife and a little baby. Cyrus's Marcus[2] makes a thriving farmer, and the two girls Julia and Chatty[3] are quite good looking. Chatty is quite grown up and is the taller. As to Cyrus, perhaps his temper has not mellowed much with age and ill health. I have commissioned John to buy a filter for him as he does not do it for himself. John drinks only filtered rain water, the water here being hard and full of a calcarious impregnation; he finds himself the better for it. I am just going off to see Austin and suppose I shall have something of a talk with him. Edward[4] owns an undivided half of the house and farm where Austin lives.

The weather here is exceedingly dry, while to the east and the west rains are abundant. On my way hither I saw many beautiful flowers—Azaleas, very red, the dodecathem, with petals like the cyclamen jauntily turned back, lupines of a soft blue, pink and blue ph[l]oxes and the golden flower of the puccoon or red root. It was quite interesting to make them out as I was whirled by them.

Day after tomorrow we are to have the great meeting, about Lovejoys monument. President Sturtevant will speak and the Rev[d]. Mr. Codding, a minister of the liberal Christians, who is here staying with John, and whom I heard preach yesterday.[5] He came Saturday noon. His congregation yesterday was about three times as large as Mr. Ely's and yet they do not consider themselves able to support a Unitarian minister here. Mr. Codding seems able and earnest—he once preached here for a year.

I have not yet decided when I shall return. Love to all,

Yours ever
W. C. BRYANT.

P.S. I shall write again in a day or two. Every body inquires after you—including some persons whom I do not recollect to have seen before.

W. C. B.

MANUSCRIPT: NYPL–GR.

1. Cyrus Bryant's second son, born in 1837.
2. Cyrus's fourth son (1842–1875?).
3. Julia, born 1845; Charity, born 1848.
4. Edward Raymond Bryant (1823–1881), Austin Bryant's second child and eldest son.
5. Illinois congressman Owen Lovejoy died on March 25, 1864, while visiting friends in Brooklyn. Bryant was a pallbearer at his funeral on March 28 in the Plymouth Church on Hicks Street in that city. On April 12 John Bryant wrote Cullen that Lovejoy's widow, Eunice C. S. D. Lovejoy, wished Bryant to persuade the popular historian James Parton (1822–1891) to write a life of her husband for the benefit of his children —a project which was not realized. MS in Bryant's hand, "Extract of a letter from John H. Bryant of Princeton, Illinois, to W C Bryant," HCL. John and Rev. Ichabod Codding (1811–1866) were the organizers of a successful movement to raise a marble monument over Lovejoy's grave in Princeton. Edward Magdol, *Owen Lovejoy: Abolitionist in Congress* (New Brunswick, New Jersey: Rutgers University Press [1967]), pp. 402–403, 409. Rev. Julian Monson Sturtevant (1805–1886, Yale 1826) was president of Illinois College at Jacksonville, 1844–1876.
At the meeting described in Letter 1419 a letter from Abraham Lincoln to John Bryant, dated at Washington on May 30, was read. In this the President wrote of Lovejoy, "Throughout my heavy and perplexing responsibilities here to the day of his death it would scarcely wrong any other to say he was my most generous friend." Quoted in *EP*, June 16, 1864.

1419. *To* Frances F. Bryant

Princeton   June 2d   1864
Thursday morning

My dear Frances.

Yesterday the meeting was held here for the organization of an Association formed to erect a monument to Owen Lovejoy. Mr. Codding, the minister delivered an address, then President Stur[t]evant of the College at Jacksonville made a speech, and then I was called on to say something. There were two speeches besides—and all of them, if you except mine, were quite clever. The association was organized, and trustees appointed among whom they put me. A considerable subscription of money was made on the spot, and the affair went off very well.

When I came here I found the country beginning to suffer from drought. Sunday and the two following days were hot, with a strong south west wind tearing off the leaves of the trees; the roads were extremely dusty and were quite rough besides with deep ruts and ridges, occasioned by the wet weather of three weeks ago. Accordingly the travelling from place to place was quite disagreeable; but on Tuesday towards night we had a thunder shower followed by rain all night and now every thing is fresh, the air delightfully cool, and the roads much smoother.

I saw Arthur's wife last night; she was exceedingly gracious and smiling.[1] I am to go there today and afterwards to Austin's where Sarah[2] is expected from La Moille. On Saturday I am thinking to go to Peoria, and from Peoria I expect on Monday to set out for home, by Logansport not taking Chicago in my way.

We have had here for a day or two a Unitarian clergyman from the south of Illinois, Egypt as it is called, of a Tennessee family, a zealous anti slavery man, simplehearted, but intelligent, and having all the characteristics of the southern race—the better ones I mean, and the peculiarities of manner. I have been much entertained with him. He left us last evening. Love to Julia and all.

Yours ever
W   C   BRYANT

P.S. I have just got your letter[3] and thank you for it and am glad that you are so well.

W   C   B.

MANUSCRIPT: NYPL–GR.

1. Henrietta B. Plummer Bryant; see Vol. I, 12.
2. Sarah Louisa Bryant (b. 1820), Austin Bryant's eldest child.
3. Unrecovered.

1420.   *To* Stephen C. Massett[1]

New York   June 13th   1864.

My dear sir.

Enclosed are the lines of which you have desired a copy.[2]

The article from an Annual which you were so obliging as to send me I had never seen.[3] It is a very kind estimate of what I have done in the way of poetry, and I thank you for the opportunity you have given me of reading it. I return it with this note.

I am, sir,
very truly yours,
W. C. BRYANT.

MANUSCRIPT: UVa ADDRESS: Stephen Massett Esq.

1. Stephen C. Massett (1820–1898) was a London-born musician and elocutionist then or later employed by the San Francisco *Bulletin*. Longfellow, *Letters*, IV, 107; Massett to Bryant, December 22, 1871, NYPL–GR.
2. Unidentified. Massett's request is unrecovered.
3. Unidentified.

1421.   *To* John Bigelow

Roslyn   June 15   1864.

My dear Mr. Bigelow.

I have consulted with my wife concerning your very kind offer of the Squirrels for another season. She found the residence last summer an exceedingly pleasant and healthful one, and is infinitely obliged to you, as I am also, for the permission you give to occupy that beautiful spot again. But certain arrangements which she has already made, in regard to visiting two or three places in the interior will prevent her from availing herself of it. Nor would it be possible for Mr. Henderson's family to be with us there. One of his daughters is suffering from a disease of the eyes for which a summer residence among the Adirondack Mountains has been prescribed by an eminent oculist, and preparations have been already made for a sojourn in that region.

As to politics you have already seen that Mr. Lincoln is nominated for a second term by the representatives of the great body of the Union Party.[1] It was done, in obedience to the public voice—a powerful *vis a tergo* [force from behind] pushed on the politicians whether willing or unwilling. I do not, for my part, doubt of his reelection, though among those who would have preferred some other candidate, there are many who profess to have their fears. Fremont's nomination does not now look very formidable, and I think will make no very conspicuous figure in the returns of votes unless the democrats take him up which does not seem very likely.[2]

From Grant we, that is the great mass of the friends of the Union, and I among the rest expect more than you seem to do.[3] With such a mighty preponderance of military force as we have, and with military talent on our side apparently quite equal to that on the side of the rebels—for Grant thus far has approved himself fully equal to Lee, and Sherman is an abler commander than any man whom the rebels have in the southwest,[4] we ought certainly to bring the war to an end within this year—at least so far as concerns all great military operations. Fully to compose the rebel region and reduce it to perfect order may take a longer time.

My greatest fears arise from the state of the currency, which has fearfully augmented the expenses of the war and will make the public debt nearly double what it ought to be. I do not, moreover, see any symptoms of alacrity in applying the obvious means of reducing the immense redundancy of our circulating medium. My temper, however, you know is hopeful and I do not despair of seeing the evil corrected. . . .[5]

MANUSCRIPT: NYPL–Bigelow DOCKETED: W^m. C. Bryant / July 1864.

1. At the "Union" (Republican) Party convention at Baltimore on June 8, 1864, Abraham Lincoln had been unanimously renominated for the presidency. Nevins, *War for the Union*, IV, 75. Five days earlier Bryant had written in the *EP* that "the plain people believed Lincoln honest, the rich people believed him safe, the soldiers believed him their friend, the religious people believed him God's choice, and even the scoundrels believed it profitable to use his cloak." *Ibid.*, 14.

2. On May 31, at Cleveland, a radical People's Provisional Committee had nominated the 1856 Republican candidate, John C. Frémont, to oppose Lincoln at the November election. *Ibid.*, 72.

3. In March 1864 Ulysses S. Grant was made a lieutenant general by act of Congress, and appointed to command all Union armies. *Ibid.*, 6–8.

4. Upon Grant's promotion, General William Tecumseh Sherman (1820–1891, United States Military Academy 1840) was put in charge of the armies of the West.

5. Conclusion and signature missing.

1422.   *To* Sarah S. Lewis[1]

Roslyn   June 19   1864

Mrs. Sarah S. Lewis—

So many applications reach me of the same nature with yours, that it is not possible for me to find time to answer them—but there is something in your letter which makes your case an exception.[2]

I am not sure that room could be found in the Evening Post for your poem, were it more perfect in the composition than it is—for a great many verses are sent for insertion, which we are obliged to lay aside, to make room for matter which must be published. Your verses show no want either of imagination or of feeling, but they are carelessly written and the expression is altogether inadequate to the idea. What would be bad prose cannot be good in verse. The defects to which I refer will be seen by you when you become more familiar with good models—and I know of no other way to avoid them than the study of those. If you continue to write verse allow me to recommend that method of self improvement.

W   C   B

MANUSCRIPT: NYPL–GR (draft).

1. Unidentified.
2. Her letter is unrecovered.

1423.   *To* Abraham Lincoln

New York   June 25th   1864.

My dear sir.

Permit me to call your attention to a case of great importance to the individual and of some interest to the public.

Mr. Isaac Henderson, who acts as publisher of the Evening Post, has been summarily dismissed from the office of Navy Agent, which he has held for the last three years, and at the same time, arrested by the officials of your administration, on a charge of fraud supported by the affidavit of a man utterly without character, and himself a prisoner in Fort Lafayette, on the charge of infamous frauds on the government.[1] The effect of these proceedings upon Mr. Henderson's reputation, hitherto spotless, cannot but be very damaging, since they imply that in the view of the government, he is indisputably and grossly guilty. The distress occasioned to Mr. Henderson a sensitive man, now for the first time accused and to his family also, you can easily imagine. If you could suppose yourself removed from the office you hold, under circumstances of like indignity, by some branch of the government invested with the power, you would at once conceive what his feelings must be.

I am satisfied that Mr. Henderson will establish his entire innocence at the examination, and you will allow me frankly, but respectfully to say, that I should not bear towards you the esteem that I do, did I not feel equally confident, that, in that event, your sense of justice will lead you to reinstate him in office without delay. It is the only way of making reparation for the great injury, which he has suffered, and which I believe I know you too well to suppose that you would willingly inflict upon an honest man, and a faithful public servant. It is important too, that men of integrity and capacity should understand that, when they accept posts of trust, they are not to be capriciously turned out, on charges preferred against them by any rogue, who may fancy, that his interest will be promoted by their removal.

I did not wish that Mr. Henderson should take the office of Navy Agent. I advised, I remonstrated against it. He pledged himself to me, that he would not allow his hands to be soiled by any gains indirectly gotten, while he should hold it, and I fully believe, that he has faithfully kept his word. I cannot bear that the least shadow of the suspicion of corrupt or even questionable practices should rest upon any person, in any way connected with the Evening Post.

What makes these severe proceedings still more unkind is, that Mr. Henderson has always zealously supported your administration, that he has used all his influence in its favor, and that he desired and has approved your second nomination. Of course no astonishment that he ever felt could equal his, at being so roughly treated by a government which in his mind had always been associated with the idea of fairness and equity.[2]

I am, sir,

most respectfully and truly yours
W. C. BRYANT.

MANUSCRIPTS: LC (final), NYPL–GR (draft) ADDRESS: To / Mr. Lincoln / President of the United States / Washington / Dist of Columbia.

1. An investigation of alleged widespread frauds in the purchase of supplies for the Navy Department, begun in January 1864 by Secretary Gideon Welles, resulted in June in the removal from office and later the arrest of Isaac Henderson, Navy Agent in New York, following testimony by a Brooklyn hardware merchant, Joseph L. Savage, that Henderson had deducted two thousand dollars in settling Savage's claim of about $17,500. Savage had meanwhile been arrested and imprisoned. Welles, *Diary*, I, 511–515, 540–542; II, 54, 60–61, 78–79; Nevins, *Evening Post*, pp. 427–428.

2. In his reply on June 27, after saying that he had approved Henderson's removal from office upon Welles's assurance of his guilt, Lincoln delivered a firm rebuke. "Whether Mr. Henderson was a supporter of my second nomination," he wrote, "I neither knew, or enquired, or even thought of. I shall be very glad indeed if he shall,

as you anticipate, establish his innocence; or, to state it more strongly and properly, 'if the government shall fail to establish his guilt.' I believe, however, the man who made the affidavit was of as spotles[s] reputation as Mr. Henderson, until he was arrested on what his friends insist was outrageously insufficient evidence. . . .

"While the subject is up may I ask whether the Evening Post has not assailed me for supposed too lenient dealing with persons charged of fraud & crime? And that in cases of which the Post could know but little of the facts? I shall certainly deal as leniently with Mr. Henderson as I have felt it my duty to deal with others, notwithstanding any newspaper assaults." LC.

In the *EP* for June 24 Bryant printed a strong editorial defense of Henderson against Savage's charges, and the same issue carried a letter from Henderson denying any guilt, and asking that no opinion be formed in his case until the charges were made clear.

1424. *To* Gideon Welles

New York   June 25th 1864.

My dear sir.

The sudden dismissal of Mr. Henderson from office under circumstances of great indignity must be my excuse for addressing you. The dismissal was accompanied by his arrest on the affidavit of a man known to be unworthy of belief and himself a prisoner on a charge of infamous frauds. It is understood of course by the public that the government is convinced of the truth of the charge against Mr. Henderson and that this was the cause of his dismissal. His character hitherto has been above suspicion, and I believe for my part that a base and wicked conspiracy has been formed against him. I do not suppose that the least desire to injure him has occasioned these proceedings, but their effect is as injurious as if they had been dictated by the most inveterate malignity. It is certain that the administration has inconsiderately listened to the counsels of those who have sought his ruin.[1]

I am satisfied of Mr. Henderson's perfect innocence and am sure that it will appear in the examination. In that event I hope he will be immediately reinstated in office inasmuch as that will be the only method of making amends for the injury done to the reputation of an honest man and a faithful and diligent public servant. As he is the publisher of the Evening Post, I have some personal interest in the matter, for the unmerited disgrace of one thus connected with it is in some measure reflected on me and becomes a wrong to me also.

I have written the enclosed letter to the President on the subject.[2] I take the liberty of sending it to you with the request that you will do me the personal favor to put it into his hands—for I wish that it may be sure to be read by him. You can read it or not as you please.[3]

I am dear sir
truly yours,
[unsigned]

MANUSCRIPT: NYPL–GR (draft) ADDRESS: To the Hon Gideon Welles / Secretary of the Navy.

1. According to Allan Nevins, "The charges [against Henderson] had their origin in the malice of Thurlow Weed, who, angered by persistent criticism of him in the *Evening Post,* sought out the information which he believed to justify them, and laid them before Welles." *Evening Post,* p. 428.

2. Letter 1423.

3. Welles replied on June 27 (NYPL–GR), "The action on Henderson's case was an inevitable necessity, and while regretting the harshness and severity to him, and to you whom I know better than him, there was no alternative. If the result shall verify all that Mr. Savage has stated you will admit that action was necessary—if more is not proven the counsel who have the matter in charge are inexcusably deceived and in fault." Welles denied Bryant's charge of a conspiracy; nor was any action taken, he wrote, as the result of the " 'counsels of those who sought his ruin.' " Weed could not have known the facts; "his especial friend in the cabinet [Secretary of State Seward] was not aware of them until Sunday last, the day on which the remand was ordered." Welles added, "I need not assure you that the necessity of these proceedings has given me great pain. The reputation of the Evening Post is about as dear to me as to its proprietors, and I know that its enemies will endeavor to pervert this case from Mr. H's connection with the paper, to its injury. Truth however will vindicate itself."

Privately, Welles was more blunt, noting later that evening that he had just written Bryant "disabusing his mind of some of its errors, provided his convictions are open to the truth." *Diary,* II, 161. Subsequent correspondence between John Bigelow and Thurlow Weed sheds further light on the case against Henderson, while it seems to give credence to Bryant's charge of a conspiracy. See Bigelow, *Retrospections,* II, 218, 520, 560.

1425. *To* Gulian C. Verplanck

New York, June 27. 1864.

Dear sir,

A movement has been set on foot in the Century Club for the collection of a Library: and in order to lay an appropriate foundation for it, the members who have written books are requested to contribute copies of them.

Permit us to request that you will honor the Club and adorn its shelves by sending copies of those productions which have linked your name indissolubly with our best American literature, and that you will lend to the volumes the added grace and value of your autograph.

With our best wishes for your continued health through many happy years to come,

We are, Dear Sir,
Your friends,
WM C. BRYANT [and others][1]

MANUSCRIPT: NYPL–Berg ADDRESS: Hon. Gulian C. Verplanck.

1. This letter, not in Bryant's holograph, is signed by him, together with John Van Buren, John F. Kensett, Daniel Huntington, Joseph B. Varnum, Jr., Dudley B. Fuller, George Bancroft, George William Curtis, Bayard Taylor, Edward A. Stansbury, A.

Vanderpool, and August R. Macdonough. Early in 1864 Verplanck had retired, under pressure, from the presidency of the Century Club, because of his "lack of sympathy for the Union cause." Robert W. July, *The Essential New Yorker: Gulian Crommelin Verplanck* (Durham, North Carolina: Duke University Press, 1951), p. 265.

1426.   To Salmon P. Chase

Office of The Evening Post,
New York, June 28th   1864

My dear sir,

It certainly has never been my intention to allow any thing to appear in the Evening Post, which should seem either unfair or disrespectful towards yourself or the course pursued by you in the administration of your department. I cannot it is true always look at questions of finance through your eyes, and have certain convictions of my own, which are too inveterate to be changed, but I have never knowingly allowed these to interfere, in any manner with the high respect I bear you both as a private and as a public man. If any thing which has appeared in this journal has seemed to you otherwise than this, I am exceedingly sorry for any unskilfulness committed in the expression of what should have been but a deferential dissent.

Mr. Godwin desires me to say that he has hitherto been withheld by a press of occupation from answering your letter,[1] which he designs to do, as I understand him, somewhat at large. I have spoken to him of your wish to know who is the author of the communication entitled "public service," which was handed to him with the name of the writer, and desired him to answer you on that point. The communication was already answered, and with no little ability in the Evening Post, before your letter reached me.[2]

I am, dear sir.

very truly yours,
W. C. BRYANT.

MANUSCRIPT: HSPa ADDRESS: Hon   S. P   Chase.

1. Unrecovered.
2. Letter unrecovered. On June 24 the *EP* had printed a letter from "Public Service," identified as a "loyal private banker" deploring the "official incapacity, wasted resources, and abused opportunities" in Chase's administration of the Treasury. On the 28th the paper carried a letter from "Veritas and Justitia" defending Chase's actions.
Replying to Bryant's letter, Chase wrote on June 30, "Your good opinion has always been one of my chief treasures, because it is the honest opinion of a candid and just observer." Quoted in Jacob W. Schuckers, *The Life and Public Services of Salmon Portland Chase* (New York, 1874), p. 405.

1427.   To Abraham Lincoln

New York   June 30th   1864.—

My dear sir.

I thank you for the attention you have given to my letter.[1] It confirms my convictions of your equity and love of justice.

You speak of having been assailed in the Evening Post. I greatly regret that any thing said of your public conduct in that journal should seem to you like an assault, or in any way the indication of hostility. It was not intended to proceed beyond the bounds of respectful criticism, such as the Evening Post, ever since I have had any thing to do with it, has always permitted itself to use tow[ard] every successive administration of the government. Nor have I done you the wrong of supposing that any freedom of remark would make you forget what was due to justice and right.

In regard to another point mentioned in your letter, allow me to say that I do not know what the standing of Mr. Henderson's accuser may be in Washington, but here it is bad enough.

I am, sir,
very respectfully and truly yours,
W. C. Bryant

Manuscript: LC address: To Mr. Lincoln / President of the United States.

1. See 1423.2.

1428.   *To* Robert C. Waterston

Roslyn   L. I. July 7th   1864.

My dear Mr. Waterston.

Your letter did not reach me until the event, to which it alluded as probably near, had actually taken place. I was about to call it a sad event, but it is so only in a limited sense—sad to those who survive and who shall see his venerable form and hear his wise and kindly words no more, but, otherwise, no more sad than the close of a well-spent day, or the satisfactory completion of any task which has long occupied our attention. Mr. Quincy, in laying aside the dull weeds of mortality,[1] has with them put off old age with all its infirmities, and (passing to a nobler stage of existence) enters again upon the activity of youth with more exalted powers and more perfect organs. Instead of lamenting his departure at a time of life considerably beyond the common age of man, the generation which now inhabits the earth should give thanks that he has lived so long, and should speak of the blessing of being allowed for so many years to have before them such an illustrious example. I hope that Mrs. Waterston bears the loss with Christian resignation, as an event in the order of nature, yet mercifully postponed for many years.

I was in town yesterday and the day previous where my presence was required in the examination of Mr. Henderson's case, but on Tuesday I found time to write a short article on Mr. Quincy's death for the E. P.— The history of his life I was obliged for want of time, to leave to other hands, without the opportunity of revising it before it went to press. It was not done exactly as I should have done it, but I hope it does Mr. Quincy no essential injustice.

Mr. Henderson will turn the tables on his accusers and will be triumphantly vindicated at their expense.[2] I shall expect that he be reinstated but I would not have him retain the office longer than might be necessary just to show that the government completely exonerates him and desires to make some reparation for the wrong done him. Then I would have him go out. He took the office against my wish and advice.

Now that you have thought of coming to New York I hope you will come soon and so arrange your stay that you can make a visit to this place. My wife and I talk often of the pleasant visit we had from you and Mrs. Waterston last year. She and Julia desire me to say how much they sympathize with you both. Say as much for me to Mrs. Waterston.

I am, dear sir,

very cordially yours.

W. C. BRYANT.

MANUSCRIPT: UVa (final), NYPL–GR (draft dated July 8) ADDRESS: Rev^d. Robt. C. Waterston. PUBLISHED (*in part*): *Life*, II, 210 (there dated July 12).

1. Josiah Quincy (1069.1) had died a few days earlier in Boston, at the age of ninety-two. Waterston's letter reporting his death is unrecovered.

2. In May 1865 Isaac Henderson was acquitted by a jury in the federal court in New York City. *EP*, May 26, 1865; Nevins, *Evening Post*, p. 428.

1429. *To* the Trustees of Madison University[1]

New York   July 8th   1864.—

Gentlemen.

I am glad to hear of the suggestion that Mr. George W. Curtis should receive the degree of Doctor of Laws from your institution. I sincerely hope it will be carried into effect both on account of his merits as a scholar and writer and as a gentleman and citizen.[2]

I am, most respectfully yours.

WM C. BRYANT.

MANUSCRIPT: Boston Public Library ADDRESS: To the Trustees of the Madison University.

1. From 1846 to 1890 Colgate University, at Hamilton, New York, was known as "Madison University."

2. At the annual commencement in 1864, George William Curtis was awarded an honorary LL.D. degree by Madison University. *A General Catalogue of Colgate University Issued in October MCMXIX at Hamilton New York* [Hamilton: Colgate University, 1919], p. 376.

1430. *To* Hiram Barney

The Evening Post, New York, July 15th   1864

My dear sir.

Joshua L. Pell Esq. long an officer in the New York Custom House, laborious, diligent, honest, and in every respect faithful, has I learn applied to have his salary raised from eleven hundred to eighteen hundred dollars.[1] Mr. Pell's experience and accuracy in the drawing up of legal documents for the transaction of the business of the Custom House make his services peculiarly valuable and I sincerely hope that his application, which considering the depreciation of the currency is reasonable will be readily granted.

I am, sir,
truly yours
W   C   BRYANT

MANUSCRIPT: HEHL ADDRESS: H. Barney Esq / Collector &c &c.

1. See Letter 1343.

1431.   To John Howard Bryant

Office of The Evening Post,
New York, July 15, 1864

Dear Brother

I got a letter from you yesterday and today another,[1] besides finding the photographs lying on my table.[2] As for the money, you can do as you please about buying land with it or paying it to me. I can invest it in government securities, and so can Fanny, I suppose if you prefer paying her.

Yours affectionately
W. C. BRYANT

MANUSCRIPT: BCHS TEXT: "Bryant and Illinois," 646 ADDRESS: Jn. H. Bryant Esq.

1. Neither letter has been recovered.
2. Apparently those of the five Bryant brothers; see illustration.

1432.   To Charlotte E. Field

Roslyn, July 20th [1864]

. . . I am glad, and so is Frances, to see that your feelings are with our country in this calamitous war. You have seen, I suppose, enough to convince you that our Government and people are resolved that it shall end in but one way—the absolute submission of those who are in arms against them. We think we see this conclusion of the war at no very great distance. The news of our country, when circulated in England, is, in many instances, much discolored by passing through unfriendly channels. One of the worst consequences of this distortion of facts, and of the hostile comments so often made by your press upon almost every event of our war, is a growing animosity toward Great Britain. Some of us take great pains to distinguish the British nation, so far as relates to this matter, from the British government, and the British aristocracy from the British people; but it is not the great majority of newspaper readers who will attend to these distinctions.

Meanwhile, we are here at Roslyn, in a place where we know little of the war save by rumor, and where the world goes on, or almost stands still, just as it did when you were last here. Birds sing, and the cicada sounds his shrill note from the neighboring tree, and grapes swell, and pears ripen, just as they did then, and children are born, and old people and the sick die in their beds, just as if there were no war. I wish you were here a little while to see how peaceful the place is, and how much pleasanter we have made it, and to join in our prayers that every part of our country may soon be as tranquil. . . .

MANUSCRIPT: Unrecovered TEXT (*partial*): *Life*, II, 210–211.

1433.   *To* Anna Q. Waterston

[Roslyn] July 21, 1864

My dear Mrs. Waterston

The other day as my wife was getting ready to go to the Adirondack Mountains she began a letter to you with which she was not quite satisfied and which she intended to look over and add something concerning Mr. Quincys death. By some misunderstanding Julia got hold of it and sent it of[f] much to her mother's chagrin. To console her I promised to write to you and make every apology.

There was a certain ring which I hope you have by this time in your possession. She found a little forget-me-not a cameo in *pietra dura* [hard stone], which though a mere trifle and not a costly gift by any means she thought you might be willing to have as a memento and bought it for that purpose—not that she supposed you would wear it—but thinking that you might keep it in some drawer where it would occasionally meet your eye and remind you of her. She lost it at one time, and altogether, the sending off the unsatisfactory letter includ[ing that?] had a good deal of vexation with it. I hope it will be all right now.

She has gone to Elizabethtown in Essex County in this state—a little valley in the lap of the Adirondacks, to which if you would be so obliging as to address her a letter with a kind word or two in it it would I know do her a great deal of good. I shall go for her in about a fortnight.

We have a fearful drought. The fields in some places are of the color of toasted bread. We keep the grass about our house from drying up and the flowers alive by water from our reservoir on the hill. Today the air is dark with smoke blown it is said from the burning woods of Maine. We have had this year no cherries ordinarily so abundant, few strawberries and scarce any raspberries. The robins and black thrushes urged by famine steal every berry from Downings mulberry tree as fast as it turns color.

W   C   B.

MANUSCRIPT: NYPL–GR (draft).

1434. *To* Frances F. Bryant

Roslyn   Long Island
Saturday   July 24th. 1864.

Dear Frances.

We have had various experiences since you left us—though none of them very important. Julia brought Miss Sands on Thursday evening. The same evening a seamstress, engaged by Julia for Fanny who was to come by the Arrowsmith, came out by rail— She was too late for the boat, and, for a wonder, was sagacious enough to take the train, buy a ticket to Roslyn, and get to Fanny's, without any instructions except what she picked up by herself. The same day, Willy Cline[1] was ill with first a chill and then a fever, but he is better now. All day Mr. Cline was complaining of pain in his limbs, and on Thursday night had a violent fever, and the next morning kept his bed. He is now up, watering the garden. Henry is better, but still quite lame. Friday morning I went to town and Thomas with me, taking a check for his sister's baggage at Castle Garden. In the course of the morning he came to me, saying that the Superintendent at Castle Garden would not allow him to take his sister's effects—so I wrote a line in his favor and then he got them.[2] Yesterday morning began quite cool—then it grew very cold, and Julia had a fire in the parlor, and I wondered whether you had clothing enough at hand to keep you warm on the journey. At night, after I got home we had another fire in the parlor.

Mrs. Losee on Thursday, was buried at Hempstead.[3] Our horses went, and carried only Mr. Ely, through clouds of dust. Mr. Ely preached a funeral sermon, one of his best. The church was full or nearly so, the assembly being more than three quarters women. Some of the neighbors, however, were not there, Mrs. Cairns among the rest, who had returned from West Point but said she was not well enough to attend.

This morning we all think of going to the Luquers —Fanny and Godwin among the rest—she in our carriage and he on horseback. Annie and others of the children are talking of a blackberry gathering today, in a field beyond the toll gate near the cemetery.

We get no rain yet, and the fields are growing redder and redder in the constant sunshine, which, however, is tempered by the strange smokiness of the air.

I wrote to Mrs. Waterston the day you left us.

The new cook appears to do quite well.

I hope you contrive to keep yourself warm where you are. I shall expect with impatience the news of how you get on in your journey, and how you find yourself in your new quarters. Regards to Mrs. Henderson and her family. Write immediately if you have not written already.

"Your loving husband,"
W. C. BRYANT.

P.S. I have promised Dr. Alden to go to his place on Tuesday.

W. C. B.

MANUSCRIPT: NYPL–GR.

1. William Bryant Cline, son of Bryant's Roslyn superintendent, George Cline.

2. Castle Garden on the Battery at the foot of Manhattan, formerly Fort Clinton, served from 1855 to 1892 as a United States immigration station.

3. Mrs. James Losee; see Letter 1268.

1435.   *To* Frances F. Bryant

New York   July 26   1864
Tuesday morning.

Dear Frances.

Julia got a letter from Mrs. Henderson at Roslyn yesterday morning. We were very glad to learn that you bore your journey with so little fatigue, and hope that a nights rest dissipated all that you had.

We got the enclosed letter from Mrs. Waterston last evening.

Yesterday morning we had several hours of rain, and every thing is now fresh, and the air cool and pleasant. Miss Sands came in with me this morning. The boat last night brought out Miss Patterson, a seamstress for Julia. I saw Miss Jenny Hopkins yesterday afternoon. She is much better. This afternoon I shall go to Dr. Alden's and return tomorrow morning.

You see we have good news from the Southwest. The taking of Atlanta puts every body in spirits.[1]

Yours ever
W. C. BRYANT.

P.S. All well at Roslyn.

MANUSCRIPT: NYPL–GR.

1. On July 22, 1864, Confederate forces under General John Bell Hood (1831–1879, United States Military Academy 1853) were defeated at the Battle of Atlanta by General William T. Sherman's Union army. The city of Atlanta, however, was not evacuated by southern troops until September 2.

1436.   *To* Frances F. Bryant

Roslyn   Long Island
July 28th. 1864   Thursday—

Dear Frances.

I went day before yesterday to Dr. Alden's at a place called B[oi?]ling Spring a little this side of Aquackneck [New Jersey] on the Passaic. Dr.

Alden came himself for me, between one and two o'clock and we reached the place about two. He has a nice comfortable house, comfortably furnished, but there is a very unfinished look about the grounds, and the out buildings are old and ugly. He has, however, planted five acres of his twenty nine with vines, pear trees and strawberry plants, and leaves the ornamental part to be attended to hereafter. Mrs. Alden received me very kindly and appeared in quite a new character—to me at least—that of a rather chatty, conversable person. When I have seen her before she has always seemed rather reserved. With her was her mother Mrs. Livingston, quite an old lady but intellectually well preserved, and an elegant young woman, a Miss Agnes McClure, the affiance of Dr. Alden's son, who is to marry her when he is able to support a wife. She seems to be permanently domesticated in the family, and calls the Doctor and his wife Pa and Mamma.

I had a nice visit and a good sleep, a breakfast the next morning a little before seven, and prayers and a rapid journey to New York, reaching the office about nine o'clock. The ladies inquired about you and Julia.

Yesterday Julia had a letter from Miss Miller, which spoke of you as quite recovered from your fatigue, which I was very glad to hear. Her account of the place was only moderately attractive. I hope however, the change of air, and the absence of care and the novelty of the scenery will do you good.

There is nothing new here except that the Doyenne d'Eté pears [Summer Dean][1] in the garden have ripened. Yesterday the Sunday School Pic Nic took place. Julia at the special request of Mr. Ely attended. The little ones filled themselves with cake and lemonade and were satisfied. The Willis children were not there.

We are sighing again for rain, though the late shower did much good. Kind regards to all.

Yours ever,
W. C. BRYANT.

MANUSCRIPT: NYPL–GR ADDRESS: Mrs. F. F. Bryant.

1. These brackets are Bryant's.

1437.   *To* Frances F. Bryant

Roslyn   July 30   1864
Saturday.

My dear Frances.

On Thursday I got a letter from you[1] at our Roslyn post-office, after my third to you was already written—this is the fourth. I am sorry to learn that the season had made the region so unpleasant to you, but I suppose the drought is over by this time. Here, it is a little mitigated, but there is great want of rain yet—though we hear that it is a great deal worse a little further to the North.

When you are ready to come away, you will let me know, and I will come after you, but do not expect me to stay more than a day or two. The library of Mr. Bigelow was a great resource to me at West Point, but there can be nothing like it where you are, and I should die of lassitude in a boarding house, if I staid longer than the time I have mentioned, unless I had something special to interest me.

I have had a great deal of trouble with one or two intractable stanzas in my hymns, which are next to ready for the press.[2] Dr. Alden wished to see them before they were printed off. I took them with me to his house, and he made a suggestion or two. I must have the new ones ready by Monday, if possible, for I want to get them off my hands.

Last night, Charles Miller came out to our house, passed the evening at Godwin's, where Miss Wheeler is staying with Minna, and today, at noon, he will go back to New York. Julia has invited Mr. Howland to come out this evening and pass the Sunday.[3]

Fanny is not well this morning, having a nervous headache. A day or two since Mrs. Cline, the elder, took what she calls "a pill," which brought on a severe attack of dysentery—of which she is ill yet. Jenny Hopkins is getting better.— This morning Mary our servant, is vomiting and Ann has to do every thing.

Julia received a letter from Mrs. Henderson yesterday, and another from Mrs. Miller. They both represent your health and strength as greatly improved, and speak of your being in excellent spirits. As long as the improvement goes on I think it would be a pity for you to come away.

I hear nothing from Mr. Field yet, as to the time when he will begin his survey.[4] I shall write to him about it.

Ever yours
W. C. BRYANT.

P.S. Susan Leggett is writing in the Evening Post under the signature of "Female Visitor." She says in it that she has never been an inmate of any lunatic asylum, and to show that she is perfectly sane, reprehends the Evening Post for inserting two *"incoherent communications"* on the subject of mad houses. Probably the story that she has been in one is not true.

W. C. B.

MANUSCRIPT: NYPL–GR.

1. Unrecovered.

2. *Hymns*, by William Cullen Bryant [New York: Privately printed, 1864].

3. For Charles E. Miller, see Letter 1486. Neither Miss Wheeler nor Mr. Howland has been identified.

4. Bryant had apparently engaged a New York engineer named Field to lay out an enlarged family plot in the Roslyn Cemetery which he contemplated buying. See Letters 1334, 1442.

1438.   *To* Frances F. Bryant

Roslyn, Monday,
August 1st. 1864.

My dear Frances.

I am very glad to hear such accounts as we have of your continued improvement in health. On Saturday we had Mrs. Miller's letter to Julia, with a brief note from you in it. I infer that although your accommodations are not the most desirable in the world nor the place the pleasantest, the air of the region is doing you good.

Here we are not quite so healthy. Fanny does not get well of her sore throat which is accompanied with fever and nervous headache. Old Mrs. Cline is in bed yet with the dysentery. Yesterday at church Mr. Ely told me that Mrs. Smith the sexton's wife was ill with dysentery, and he feared the family had not the necessaries of life. I went there in the afternoon, and found her quite sick. She had sent for the doctor and he was giving her opium pills. I stopped the pills and gave her some medicines and a little money. Jenny Hopkins is getting better.

The drought is cruel. Yesterday it was also quite hot and the air very still. This morning between two and three there was thunder and lightning, but in spite of that there is every symptom of a clear day, and we are almost in despair as regards rain. —I hear that the cases of dysentery in the neighborhood are numerous which is probably an effect of the unusual state of the weather.

Enclosed you have a letter from Lizzie Kirkland which came on Saturday.

When you can spare time I hope you will be able to write me a letter of more length and tell me all about the place where you are and what you are doing to pass the time.

I have just been over to Fanny's. She is a little better of the sore throat, but still suffering with headache and from want of sleep. As I was coming out Eliza the nurse came to me to prescribe for Nora, who had scalded both her feet with boiling water falling on them. The injury is not serious. You see I am in full practice.

Kind regards to all. We begin to miss you here very much. If it were not for the hymns which keep me at work, and the sick people who keep me looking into manuals, I do not know what I should do without you.

Yours ever,
W. C. Bryant.

MANUSCRIPT: NYPL–GR ADDRESS: Mrs. F. F. Bryant.

1439. *To* Theseus Apoleon Cheney[1]

Roslyn   Long Island
August 1st. 1864.

Dear Sir.

I receive innumerable requests like those contained in your letter, to write a few original lines for some collection. I have always declined, and you will therefore excuse me, if I think it necessary to do so in your case.

I have, however, copied a poem—a little hymn, already on hand and forming part of a collection, though not included among my published poems. I hope you will find it to answer your purpose.[2]

Meantime, I am glad to learn that you are occupied with matters which have in view the good of society and the diffusion of intelligence.

The present aspect of political matters, is to be sure very different from what I could wish but come what will I think we shall blunder through and come out right.

Yours truly
W C BRYANT.

MANUSCRIPT: Princeton University Library ADDRESS: T. A. Cheney Esq.

1. Theseus Apoleon Cheney (1830–1878) published writings on archaeology and American Indians.
2. No work by Cheney including a hymn by Bryant has been identified. His letter to Bryant is unrecovered.

1440. *To* Frances F. Bryant

Roslyn   Aug. 4th   1864.

My dear Frances.

Fanny is quite better this morning though she thinks she recovers very slowly. The inflammation in her throat has subsided in a great degree, though a little of it remains, with some traces of fever, and headache, and she is still very weak. I think the other symptoms which I have mentioned arose from the swelling in the throat. Mrs. Cline is quite comfortable, and the last I heard from Mrs. Smith she was much better.

Miss [Catharine] Sedgwick stopped her paper the daily Evening Post which she has read for the last sixty three years. She said in a note to me that the war obliged her to give up pleasures and luxuries—so I ordered the "luxury" to be continued at my expense and wrote to her to that effect.

The enclosed letter came in a cover addressed to you, but the address on the cover was in Mrs. Clark's handwriting. It was written I infer to Mrs. Hopkins who sent it to Roslyn, in the hope that it might bring you to Great Barrington.

The drought seems to be over. We had a little shower night before last, and last night and the afternoon previous we had a more copious one, which has put a new face on every thing.

This afternoon being fast day a meeting is appointed at the church at four o'clock. I heard yesterday that Dr. Porter[1] is to preach today in recommendation of charity to the wounded and sick soldiers.

Mr. Terry tells me that the house of James Mott[2] on the hill, in which Mr. Terry now lives, has been sold to a Mr. or Major McNally of Baltimore originally and lately from St. Louis, for eight thousand dollars—a large sum for an inconvenient place.[3]

Mrs. Warner left Mr. Cline's last week— I think I have now given you all the gossip that you will care to hear—except to say that Mr. Howland staid with us till Tuesday morning and that he bathed and smoked, and drove out with Julia, and went to Mr. Ely's church and crossed the harbor in our boat with Julia, and seemed well satisfied with his visit. Probably you do not care to hear that Mrs. Cairns's clothsline has been robbed of a nightgown or so. Kind regards to all.

Yours ever

W   C   BRYANT.

MANUSCRIPT: NYPL–GR ADDRESS: Mrs. F. F. Bryant.

1. See Letters 1129, 1474.
2. James Mott (1788–1868) and his wife Lucretia Coffin Mott (1793–1880), both liberal or Hicksite Quakers, were early Abolitionists and leaders in the women's rights movement. In 1848 Mrs. Mott, along with Elizabeth Cady Stanton (1815–1902), was a principal organizer of the convention at Senaca Falls, New York, presided over by her husband, at which the women's rights movement in the United States was initiated.
3. In 1873 N. M. Terry was living in Roslyn at the corner of what are now Bryant Avenue and the North Hempstead Turnpike. Goddard, *Roslyn Harbor*, p. [104]. Major McNally has not been further identified.

1441.   *To* Frances F. Bryant

Roslyn   Long Island

Sunday Evening   August 7th   1864.

My dear Frances.

This is the seventh of my letters to you since you left Roslyn. I hope the other six all came to hand. Yours, finished last Monday, and mailed on Tuesday the second of this month, only reached me on Friday evening,[1] being sent out from New York. Mr. Henderson I have not yet seen. I was in town on Wednesday, but he did not come.

You ask what news from Barrington? I sent you the other day Edwin's[2] letter to Mina saying that he was about to visit Barrington and would be glad to see you there; beyond this I have heard nothing. From Sheffield I have a letter from Mr. Dewey. He had passed ten days with his sister Mary, at Judge Day's place on Memphremagog[3] a noble lake thirty miles long surrounded by grand forests and mountains and passed them very pleasantly, greatly delighted with his host, a man as old at least and as active as I am and ten times more agreeable.

Here we are getting on very well. My patients are mending as fast as could be expected. Fanny drives out. We have had one or two copious showers and several slighter ones, greatly to the content of the cows and their owners in this region, some of whom had to go two miles for water. Every thing now looks green and fresh, and the melons and apples and pears are taking up the moisture and I can see that they grow larger from day to day. Today is quite hot and damp; the church was uncomfortable, and there are now signs of more showers. Yesterday, Julia had Mrs. Callisen now staying at Glen Cove pass the day with her along with Emma Pollitz. Mrs. Callisen is a very lively person and I was quite amused, at the dinner table to hear her cry up America as the finest country in the world, and repeat what her father, a German often says that those who do not like it and are always grumbling about it ought to go out of it at once. I only wished that Mr. Pollitz had been there instead of his daughter.

I hear nothing from Mr. Field the Engineer. I suppose after what you have written me about the place where you are you will not expect me to come to it, if you find any body to come home with. I confess I have not the least inclination to visit Elizabethtown, but I will conform myself entirely to your convenience and wishes. I wish to see you very much, but I had rather see you here or at some place nearer home than Lake Champlain.

I must make the old apology for writing to you in my shirt sleeves. I have been in the orchard and came back quite warm—my waistcoat is off, as I sit in the library and my shirt almost wringing wet.

The old trees on our lawn produce a good crop of pears this year and I must have the children of the district school here again by and by, for their usual feast of pears. I wish you could be present.

My hymns are all right at last and I shall soon put them to press.

Kind regards to all.

Ever yours
W. C. BRYANT.

MANUSCRIPT: NYPL–GR ADDRESS: Mrs. F. F. Bryant.

1. Letter unrecovered.
2. Probably Frances Bryant's brother Edwin Fairchild (b. 1800).
3. This cousin of Orville Dewey's owned several hundred acres and a mile of shore-line on Lake Memphremagog, which straddles the international boundary between Vermont and Quebec, Canada. Dewey had written Bryant on August 4 (NYPL–BG) that Judge Day was "as lithe & vigorous as you are. . . . He admires you above all our men."

1442. *To* Frances F. Bryant

Roslyn   Wednesday, August 10th   1864.

My dear Frances.

I got your letter of Friday the 5th[1] on Monday, and today Julia received a letter from Rockliffe written on Monday. I am glad to learn that you are doing so well, and that the air of the mountain region though hot agrees with you. You say nothing of the probable time of your return for which reason I suppose you have not yet fixed upon it. I do not yet hear from Mr. Field though I have written to him to inquire when he will be at leisure to attend to laying out the cemetery and I have just engaged Mr. Losee to come and make some alterations in that part of the shed near the barn into which people who call upon us drive their carriages. It is unventilated and hot and does not fully shelter the carriages.

Since the showers we have had exceedingly warm weather—close sultry and sweltering. This is the fourth melting day that we have had in succession. Yet the health of the place I think has improved. At all events, Fanny and Mrs. Cline, and Mrs. Smith and Miss Jenny are better, and I hear of no more dysenteries. Yesterday I went to the funeral of Mr. Witherspoon, who lived in the brown house beyond Peter Bogart's. He died at the age of seventy one, of a disease of the brain, occasioned, it is thought, by an injury which he received about two years since, when he was thrown out of a waggon. The place is quite a pretty one, occupying a part of the picnic ground to which you may remember we went when we first came to Roslyn.

I have just come out of the salt water. The bath is our only refreshment these hot days. I often wish that you are to mitigate the discomfort of the heat which you complain of.

Last night brought me a letter from Miss Sedgwick, who is willing to let me send her the Evening Post, which I am very glad of.[2] Her hand writing gives token of her infirmities. She desires much love to you. She is impatient of the protracted war and intimates that she thinks there is a want of energy at Washington. I find that a great many other people are beginning to talk in that way.

I handed Mrs. Smith some money from you yesterday. She burst into tears and asked me to tell you how thankful she was and how much she loved you.—

When I was gone to town on Monday, Mr. Beekman drove over from Oyster Bay and with him Señor Romero, the Mexican minister.[3] They expressed their disappointment at not finding me at home and said they should come again. Mary did the best she could for them, treating them to sponge cake *bocca de Spagna*[4] and iced water of both which they partook freely—she said.

This morning a great many waggons came thundering by, bringing people from the neighboring country to the steamer Arrowsmith, which has gone on an excursion to Staten Island for the benefit of the sick soldiers. Every person who goes pays a dollar and the proceeds go to the soldiers in the hospitals. I am only sorry that they have so hot a day for their pleasuring. Kind regards to all.

Yours ever.

W C Bryant.

P.S. Thursday morning—in town—another [sweltering?] hot day. Hot nights—no rain—

W C B.

MANUSCRIPT: NYPL–GR ADDRESS: Mrs. F. F. Bryant.

1. Unrecovered.

2. On August 5 Catharine Sedgwick had written Bryant (NYPL–GR) thanking him for his "very kind provision for my future daily bread," adding that it would have been hard to break the habit of sixty-three years. See Letter 1440.

3. The young diplomat Matías Romero (1837–1899) was the Mexican minister to the United States from 1862 to 1867. Bryant's editorial support of his efforts to secure American aid against the French invaders who had ousted President Benito Juarez and in April 1864 installed the puppet Emperor Maximilian fostered a friendship which bore fruit during Bryant's visit to Mexico in 1872. Romero, then minister of finance in the Mexican government, was his host throughout a two-week visit to Mexico City, introducing him to President Juarez and to the several literary and scientific societies which honored him. Before Bryant left the capital, he was praised in a leading newspaper as one who, "without any other stimulant than his sympathies, without anything to move him, but his upright conscience, defended with ardor and in the most frank and spontaneous manner, the cause of Mexico during the time of the French invasion." Van Deusen, *Seward*, pp. 367–368; *Life*, II, 319–322; Bryant to *EP*, March 11, 1872 (*EP*, May 11, 1872); *Domingo*, Mexico City, March 10, 1872.

James William Beekman (1815–1877, Columbia 1834), a New York financier and state senator, was president of the Saint Nicholas Society. In 1873 he and Bryant were together elected vice presidents of the New-York Historical Society. Vail, *Knickerbocker Birthday*, pp. 144–145.

4. The customary phrase in Italian for spongecake is *pan di Spagna*. Perhaps Bryant was repeating a dialectal term used by his servant Mary.

1443.   *To* Mr. and Mrs. Samuel P. Bryant[1]

[Roslyn? cAugust 10, 1864]

Dear sir & Madam.

I am sorry to hear that you are in such a state of destitution. Enclosed are twenty dollars which I hope will in some degree relieve you from the inconveniences of your situation. One of you speaks of having seen me at Mr. Corning's—I do not know any Mr. Corning—nor if I did have I ever been to my knowledge at the house of any such person— Please let me know of the receipt of the money.

I am

Yours truly & sincerely

W C Bryant.

MANUSCRIPT: NYPL–GR (draft) ADDRESS: To Mr. & Mrs. Sam¹ P. Bryant.

    1. Samuel P. Bryant, of Hartford, Connecticut, was Bryant's cousin. See Letter 1445.

1444. *To* Augusta Moore[1]

[New York?] Aug. 10. 1864.—

... I published your poem[2] & send you 5 dollars, though as I think I told you the Evening Post never pays for poetry. If you had taken some pains to collect information concerning the progress of the fire in Maine and written me a circumstantial letter about it it would have been worth twice the money I send.

W C B.—

MANUSCRIPT: NYPL–GR (draft) ADDRESS: Miss Augusta Moore.

    1. Unidentified, but see Letter 1446.
    2. Probably "Bless God for the Blessed Rain," "Rewritten for the *Evening Post* by George W. Bungay." *EP*, August 9, 1864.

1445. *To* Frances F. Bryant

Roslyn, Long Island.
August 12, 1864. Friday morning.

My dear Frances.

    Julia tells me that she wrote to you, yesterday, to say that she and I might come to Elizabethtown the beginning of next week. This is contrary to what I have written to you all along. I only come if it be necessary, for the purpose of bringing you home, and do not expect to come till that time arrives. If you can do without me I had rather not come at all. I hear that you will probably go to the lakes, in which case your stay will be considerably prolonged.

    This morning Julia and Fanny are setting out for Fire Island while I write. I shall expect them back on Monday—Julia at least. The weather is a little cooler this morning. Yesterday was fearfully hot. I was in town—all the women in the steamer by which I went and came were mopping themselves with their handkerchiefs. The drought has returned, but our place looks pretty fresh yet. The little arbor over the front door is quite handsome, with the clematis in bloom, and the large flowered bignonia, and the hydrangeas, on each side of the door step.

    Did I tell you, in my last, that I had a pitiful letter from my cousin Samuel Bryant at Hartford, and another from his wife,[1] describing their destitute situation, he sick, and shoeless and she obliged to take care of him? I sent them something of course.

    When I came home, last night, I found your letter of Tuesday,[2] which did not increase my desire to come to Elizabethtown. You say you hope

Edwin did not come to Roslyn as he thought of doing. If you look at the letter I sent you, you will see that he only hoped to see you at Great Barrington. If you go to Ogdensburg, you will have a very fatiguing journey, and I should somewhat fear the effect of it.

I saw Mr. Spring in town yesterday. He and Mrs. Spring had just returned from New England. Their elder son is devoted to sculpture yet,[3] busies himself with modelling in clay, and will think of nothing else. They have got Mr. Reed, of the Stockbridge school, to come to Eagleswood and take charge of the school there, and they have great hopes of its prosperity under his management.[4]

There is some garden news. A little while ago, Mr. Cline, who is no chemist, set fire to some sulphur in the grape-house, by way of curing the mildew. The acrid fumes acted like fire on the leaves immediately above, and more than a peck of the fruit was destroyed, and some of the vines much disfigured. He is very sorry of course, but if he had read the directions in the books on the raising of grapes he would have avoided the accident. The Cedarmere pears have been gathered. The Hartford Prolific grapes are changing color.

While I write I am reminded of Coleridge's lines:

> "All in a hot and copper sky,
>   The bloody sun, at noon,
> Right up against the mast did stand,
>   No bigger than the moon.["]⁵

Such has been the appearance of the sun for a long time past—the air is dusky with smoke. We all long for showers and transparent air. Kind regards to all.

Yours ever

W. C. Bryant.

P.S. I suppose that Julia will come with Mr. Henderson the latter part of next week.

W. C. B.

MANUSCRIPT: NYPL–GR ADDRESS: Mrs. F. F. Bryant.

1. Neither letter has been recovered.

2. Unrecovered.

3. Marcus and Rebecca Spring's son Edward Adolphus Spring (b. 1837), who opened a sculpture studio at Eagleswood, New Jersey, at about this time, later (1877) established the Eagleswood Art Pottery Company. DAA; see also 921.3.

4. Mr. Reed has not been further identified, but his tenure at Eagleswood must have been brief. A printed prospectus of the "Eagleswood Military Academy" for 1866–1867 lists Marcus Spring as proprietor and Frederick N. Knapp as principal; Reed's name does not appear among those of the faculty. Bryant was one of ten trustees, who included Henry W. Bellows and Frederick L. Olmsted.

5. Ancient Mariner, Pt. ii.

1446. *To* Frances F. Bryant

Roslyn   Long Island
August 13, 1864   Saturday.

My dear Frances.

I wrote you yesterday, but Harold, who went to the post-office, brought back a letter from you, dated Wednesday,[1] in which you ask whether I think you should go to the lakes with the rest of the party. By all means, if you desire to go, and are sure that you will find comfortable quarters. According to your account the air of the region is doing you good, and I do not see why you should be in a hurry to come away. Besides, by going, you will get rid of the noise which incommodes you so much at the Valley House.

It is still quite warm, and the atmosphere full of smoke, though the heat is more tolerable than it has been. The nights are very sultry, and we get no rain yet. A letter which I received last night, from Maine, says that, although they have had rain in that quarter, it has not put out the fires by which the woods have been ravaged. Mr. Ely called on me yesterday, and said that since the last rain, he hears no more of the dysentery in this neighborhood. He came to ask me to send him up to the Branch next Tuesday, with Mrs. Ely, in our big waggon, as he is going to Easthampton, on a visit of two or three weeks.

I shall have five hundred copies of my Hymns printed—which I suppose is as many as I shall give away. I am not sure that they are as good as they ought to be, and shall therefore keep the impression, at present, in my own hands. It will be some days before they can be put in covers, since they dry slowly.

The letter I had from Maine is from Miss Augusta Moore,[2] who [made?] a little poem—a sort of prayer for rain, which appeared, a few days since, in the Evening Post. It was preceded by an extract from a note accompanying it, in which the distress of the inhabitants at the progress of the flames was described, and she casual[l]y said that she had not the means to get away. She writes me in a tone of despair, declaring that she was never so ashamed and mortified in her life—that every body is pitying her and offering her help, till she can bear it no longer, and that I must make some explanation in the Evening Post—which I shall do.

All well here, and doing well—except that all want you back. My kind regards to your party.

Yours, ever,
W   C. BRYANT.

MANUSCRIPT: NYPL–GR ADDRESS: Mrs. F F. Bryant.

1. Unrecovered.
2. In the *EP* of August 15 Bryant caused to be printed " 'The Burning Woods of Maine'—A Note from Miss Moore," and with this her letter dated at Winthrop, August 10, 1864, which included verses, "Thanksgiving by Augusta Moore."

1447. *To* Frances F. Bryant

Roslyn   Long Island, Monday,
August 15th. 1864.

My dear Frances.

I got your letter of Friday,[1] today at noon. I rejoice to learn that the air of Essex County is doing you so much good, and think that you are in the right to make the most of it. I think you should go to the lakes by all means. You say that your strength increases, and that your digestion is improving —the strength, I suppose, comes from the good digestion—and it would be the extreme of folly to interrupt the progress of your recovery by coming back now. I do not accompany you, because I do not like, as you very well know, to travel with a large party. It may do for a day or two, but beyond that it becomes a very hard thing to bear. Nor do I like close quarters in hot weather. Here it is hot enough, but I can go dressed like a savage, and I have the whole house to be cool in, and if that will not do, a plunge in the harbor cools me for hours afterwards.

On Saturday, in the evening and until towards morning, we had a nice rain, which has made every thing grow, though the heat is but slightly abated. The same evening Mr. Butcher came out to Mr. Cline's with his wife a little boy and their baby and nurse, and staid till this morning. They went to Mr. Ely's church yesterday and heard what I must allow was an excellent sermon. I expect Fanny Julia and Minna from Fire Island home tonight. The Dearborn pears are ripe and every day little Walter comes over and asks for a pear. Some of the trees give a good promise of ripe plums in a few days. Mrs. Cairns sends to our garden for beans and cucumbers, her own garden being much dried up. This morning an application of another sort was made. Miss Emma Pollitz called to ask me to contribute something to the purchase of a little organ for their chapel, instead of the melodeon. They want a hundred dollars to make the change.

The funeral of old Mr. Wilkie,[2] who died at eighty two years of age, took place yesterday. I did not hear that he was dead, till I was told that he was buried.

Today is the first day with a transparent atmosphere that I have seen for some time past. It is a delight to look into the blue air and see the great white clouds floating through it. A breeze is sweeping through our hall, where the clock is ticking to the two or three flies that have got inside, and Fa[h]renheit's thermometer, at half past two P. M. marks seventy seven degrees and a half above zero. I often think that you would be more comfortable here than where you are and wish you were with me, but then I reflect that probably you would not be so well, and I revoke the wish.

Tuesday morning. August 16th. Fanny came home last night the better for her visit to Fire Island, which is only a bare sand bar out at sea amidst the fresh salt air. They had a pleasant time. Mr. Cline has heard from David that his health and appearance have prodigiously improved. He has grown stout and strong. I enclose you a letter which came to you since my last.

Yours ever.

W. C. BRYANT.

MANUSCRIPT: NYPL–GR ADDRESS: Mrs. F. F. Bryant.

1. Unrecovered.
2. Unidentified.

1448. *To* Sarah S. Lewis

Roslyn   Aug   16   1864.

Dear Madam.

I read as little manuscript as I can, on account of the state of my eyes— and have therefore put off reading your chapter on [Th?]ungyford[1] from day to day—for a time of leisure when I could read it by instalments—

My opinion on such a matter is not worth more than that of any person tolerably acquainted with English literature with whom you may happen to be acquainted. To such persons, therefore, allow me to counsel you to have recourse hereafter, in case you have occasion for an opinion on the literary merit of any thing you write. The notoriety of an individual adds no weight to his judgment.

There is no want of talent in the little sketch you have sent me. It shows observation and the capacity of combination. It is, however, marked by one characteristic of a first attempt in the walk you have chosen. It is rather too manifestly elaborate and marked by too much appearance of effort. That will pass away with practice and greater facility will be attained.

Whether I would advise you to go on or not is another matter. I never advise any body to pursue a literary career. There are many competitors, the rewards are slender and bitter disappointments are the most frequent lot of those who essay it.

I am   madam &c
W   C   BRYANT

MANUSCRIPT: NYPL–GR (draft) ADDRESS: Miss Sarah S   Lewis.

1. Unidentified.

1449. *To* Frances F. Bryant

Office of The Evening Post,
New York, August 17th   1864.

My dear Frances.

Coming to town this morning, I am met by your letter written to me and Julia, dated "August,"[1] without the day of the month, and the day of the week so obscurely written that I cannot make out whether it is Sunday or Tuesday evening. The letter is addressed to Julia and myself—but the inquiry in it has been answered in my two last letters. I think you had best, by all means, go with the party to the lakes. Julia will come up with Mr. Henderson, leaving here on Friday. As for myself, the more I hear about the matter, the less inclination I have for coming, and I shall therefore remain behind. Besides I expect a carpenter about those days, and before he finishes Mr. Godwin will be on the way to Lake Memphremagog with Fanny. In the last week of the month, while he is absent, the great democratic convention will assemble at Chicago, for the nomination of a democratic candidate for the Presidency, and I ought to be on the ground, to comment upon their doings.[2] This is a matter which cannot well be left to the judgment of any person but the principal editors. So you see, I have business cut out for me which will make it inconvenient for me to come at present.

I shall go to Roslyn this evening, and take with me your letter, for Julia's instruction in regard to her journey. Miss Jenny and her sister want to try the effect of a short residence in the country back of Catskill, upon their throats, which are in a bad way, and Julia has been trying to persuade them to accept the means of doing so, which she did, I believe, with much difficulty. Tomorrow we have the pear-eating party of school children on the green under our trees. The cake has been ordered, and Mr. Cline takes the charge of the entertainment, the school master and school-mistress and Miss Br[uin?] all being absent.

It still continues very warm—the nights are so sultry that I sleep with the south window of the bed chamber wide open, and scarce can bear a linen sheet on me. This morning, however, has been showery, and I landed from the steamboat, in the midst of a driving rain.

The political pot is simmering and walloping, and threatens to boil over. Winter Davis has been here, has gone to Long Branch and is to be here again. He called yesterday with Mr. D. D. Field. He is one of those who want another candidate than Lincoln, and with them is casting about to see what can be done to get one before the people with any chance of success.[3] It is very remarkable to what a degree Mr. Lincoln has lost ground since his nomination. A great many persons now say, that the advice of the Evening Post to postpone the sitting of the nominating convention at Baltimore until September, was wise and judicious.[4] By that time the friends of the Union would probably have made up their minds as to the man whom they preferred.— I wish you a very pleasant visit to the Saranac. The pear-party would be much pleasanter, however if we had you at Roslyn. All are well at Fannys. Kind regards to all.

                                                    Yours ever.
                                                    WM. C. BRYANT

MANUSCRIPT: NYPL–GR ADDRESS: Mrs. F. F. Bryant.

1. Unrecovered.
2. On August 31, 1864, a convention of "Peace" and "War" Democrats combined to nominate General George B. McClellan for President, and Ohio congressman George Hunt Pendleton (1825–1889) for Vice-President, to oppose the Union party candidates nominated earlier, Lincoln and Tennessee governor Andrew Johnson (1808–1875). Bryant's phrase "on the ground" referred to his presence at the *EP*; he did not go to Chicago.
3. Maryland congressman Henry Winter Davis (1817–1865) and New York lawyer David D. Field led a movement to persuade Lincoln to withdraw in favor of a "stronger candidate." Nevins, *War for the Union*, IV, 91.
4. See "The Nomination for the Presidency," *EP*, April 2, 1864, an editorial urging that the later the convention, the better. A week earlier Bryant had joined a number of New York political leaders and legislators in an open newspaper letter to the Union and Republican party executive committees suggesting that the nominating convention be put off until November. And on April 8 an *EP* leader denied a charge in the New York *Times* that the suggested postponement was simply a strategy to prevent Lincoln's nomination.

1450.   *To* Christiana Gibson

Roslyn, August 18th [1864]

. . . I wish I could write you a letter as bright and beautiful as this morning, and as full of freshness and life. A long and severe drought, in which all the vegetable world drooped and languished, has just closed, and the earth has been moistened with abundant showers. For a sultry atmosphere, a blood-red sun, and a sky filled with smoke from our great forests on fire, we have a golden sunshine flowing down through a transparent air, and a grateful breeze from the cool chambers of the northwest. Our usual fruits, meantime, with the exception of the raspberry, have not failed us; we have plenty of excellent pears, and I have just come in from gathering melons in the garden. This afternoon the school-children of the neighborhood are to have their annual feast of cake and pears on the green under the trees by my house, and I am glad they are to have so fine a day for it.

Julia has told you where the mistress of the mansion is at present—in a place where, for her at least,

"—good digestion waits on appetite,"[1]

and some measure of health on both. In September I hope to have her back again, looking and feeling "amaist as weel's the new." From the place where she has already passed several weeks—a sandy vale lying in the lap of the grand Adirondack Mountains, about ten miles west of Lake Champlain—she is seized with an adventurous desire to push her explorations to Saranac and its sister lakes—very picturesque, it is said—and this she will do, I suppose, next week. I do not go, for I am not a gregarious animal. I cannot travel, like the locusts, in clouds, at least with any degree of contentment. Yet, as my wife makes no objection, and reports her health improved, I encourage her to proceed. Meanwhile, I employ myself in reading Taine on "La Littérature Anglaise."[2] M. Taine has studied English literature thoroughly and carefully, and is almost always brilliant, but sometimes too elaborately so. He looks at everything through French spectacles, but his book is none the worse for that. He often exaggerates, but I have been much interested in his work. Look at it if it comes in your way.

How this dreadful Civil War lingers! We are now also making wry faces over the bitter fruits of that great folly against which I protested so vehemently, and most alone as a conductor of the Republican press—of making paper a legal tender.[3] ...

MANUSCRIPT: Unrecovered TEXT (partial): Life, II, 211–212.

1. Macbeth, III.iv.38.
2. Hippolyte Adolphe Taine (1828–1893), Histoire de la littérature anglaise (1864).
3. See, for instance, EP editorials of January 15 and February 14, 1862; July 14, 1863.

1451. To Frances F. Bryant

Roslyn, Thursday Evening
August 18th[1] 1864.

My dear Frances.

As Julia leaves this place tomorrow morning, I cannot let her go without a line to you. We have just had our pear feast for the school children and it went off well. There must have been more than eighty of them, twenty boys and the rest girls. They seemed very glad to get the fruit, and some of them carried off loads of them. We have also both of us written to Miss Christiana Gibson and Julia takes the letter to town tomorrow. I have asked Mr. Nordhoff and his wife to come out on Saturday evening and pass Sunday with us.[2] Mr. Losee is at work at the shed making it more commodious for those who come to call upon us with carriages. He will also put up the little building on the north side of the garden. Mr. Field I expect as early as the beginning of next week at least.

We had a fine rain yesterday and a transparent atmosphere today, although, as the sun is setting it has become somewhat sultry again.

I shall not know how to direct my letters after this, but I suppose you will tell me before you leave Elizabethtown. I should be quite impatient for you to return, if I was not pretty certain that you are getting good from your sojourn. Remember me kindly to all your party.

Ever yours
W. C. BRYANT.

MANUSCRIPT: NYPL–GR ADDRESS: Mrs. F F. Bryant.

1. Bryant mistakenly wrote "17th."
2. In 1861 Charles Nordhoff (1830–1901) had succeeded William Sydney Thayer (924.4) as managing editor of the *EP*. Nevins, *Evening Post*, p. 315.

1452.   *To* Frances F. Bryant

> Roslyn   Long Island
> August 23d   1864.
> Tuesday morning.

My dear Frances.

Yesterdays mail brought to this place your letter of Friday,[1] giving an account of the adventures of Josey, John Weir and Guy.[2] I hope the troubles of all three are over before this time, and that they will have no consequences unfavorable to the plans which your party have formed for amusing themselves.

I was in town yesterday, and came out in the afternoon with Mr. Field, who is now engaged in laying out the Cemetery. He will probably finish it tomorrow. The carpenters have made the alteration in the shed, which is a considerable improvement, and we are now at work on the little building north of the garden. We had another nice rain yesterday—which, in addition to one that fell on Saturday night, has made the country as green as in spring. Mr. Field says that this neighborhood seems to have suffered much less from the drought than that where he lives. We have now plenty of nice ripe pears. In town is a great abundance of peaches, which are cheaper than usual. The grapes are beginning to turn, and by the time you are back, I think we shall have ripe ones in the grapery.

Mrs. Vandeventer is quite sick; on Friday night she had a still born child. Fanny is quite well again, and the rest of her family are in their usual health. They had Mr. Howland there to pass last Sunday. Mr. Nordhoff and his wife, whom I had invited, did not come. Today the Miss Hopkinses were to set out for Kiskytom, back of Catskill. I believe I did not tell you— I could not for I have not written since—that on Friday I went with Mr. Cline to Jericho, for the purpose of getting some strawberry plants—Wilson's Albany—that we took the carriage, and took in four ladies from Mr. Condon's—Julia having desired that something like this should be done. Mrs. Condon was of the number—a very grave personage. They call her Madam—that, I am told, is the style in which her husband addresses her, which you must allow is very respectful.[3]

I have a letter from the Reverend Horatio[4] N. Powers, of Davenport in Iowa, who, in his flowery youth, used to write poetry for the Evening Post. It relates principally to the crops, which are abundant out in the northwest, but he takes occasion to overwhelm me with compliments, having read my last volume of poems. Most of those whom his imagination, when he was young, placed in the rank of heroes, are now degraded to the ranks, but he lets me stand where he put me then—perhaps a few inches higher. It is a comfort to learn that people, as they grow better able to judge, do not think worse of one than they did when their judgment was less sure.

I have a letter for you from Cordelia Kirkland,[5] which I would enclose, only I suppose it possible that this may not reach you, and I know you would be sorry to lose hers. It is dated at *Tilton*—a name which they have been obliged to substitute for that of *Bryant*—there being another post-office of the name of Bryant in Illinois previously established.

This place is now exceedingly beautiful, but you remember Campbell's lines—

"The world was sad, the garden was a wild,
And man the hermit sighed" &c.[6]

Next week I go to work in town, if Godwin goes to the lake with the long name. Kind regards to all.

Yours ever.

W C. BRYANT.

MANUSCRIPT: NYPL–GR ADDRESS: Mrs. F. F. Bryant.

1. Unrecovered.
2. The young artist John Ferguson Weir (1841–1926), a son of Robert W. Weir, was later the first director of the Yale School of Fine Arts. Josey was perhaps Julia Bryant's friend Leonice Josephine (Moulton) Stewart. Guy is unidentified.
3. The Condons, who apparently ran a Roslyn boardinghouse, have not been further identified.
4. Bryant mistakenly wrote "Hiram."
5. Cordelia (b. 1835) was the third daughter of Caroline Kirkland.
6. Thomas Campbell, *The Pleasures of Hope* (1799), Pt. I. Bryant's ampersand stands for "—Till Woman smiled."

1453. *To* Frances F. Bryant

Roslyn   August 25, 1864.
Thursday morning.

My dear Frances.

Now that I am assured that my letters to you, addressed as formerly, will reach you, I send you Cordelia Kirkland's letter, and one from Mrs. Bigelow written from Bonn, on the Rhine, which has just come to hand.

I have scarce any thing to tell you, except that I lead the life of a perfect hermit here! Your letter of Monday the 22d. I received yesterday[1]—Wednesday at noon—and am glad to be able to infer from it that you continue well and stronger than when you were here. On Tuesday the Miss Hopkinses set out for Kiskytom—they passed the night at Fannys house, intending to continue their journey in the morning, but something had been forgotten, and Louise came back for it, which caused a day's delay. Whether Fanny goes to Lake Memphramagog or not, seems to be a little uncertain. I shall try to persuade her. I suppose that a little persuasion in a tangible shape would effect the *object*.

I have just done it. The objection was the enormous expense at the hotels. I removed the objection, which, I knew, you would be *glad to* have done.

Last evening I got an invitation to the funeral of Daniel Stanton[2]— which took place yesterday at Dr. Bellows's church; I had not heard of his death—but I had heard some weeks since of his illness.

The something which the Miss Hopkinses forgot, I have just learned, was their money. They went off without a penny.

Since the late showers, the weather is more temperate—not cool, but, on the whole, agreeable. The nights are yet so warm that a single linen sheet suffices for covering.

As to my coming to Elizabethtown, if you come back with the rest of your party, there will be no necessity of my coming, and, in that case, I will meet you at New York, if I learn when you are expected.

Yours ever.
W. C. BRYANT

MANUSCRIPT: NYPL–GR ADDRESS: Mrs. F. F. Bryant.

1. Unrecovered.

2. In 1842 Daniel Stanton, a New York merchant, had preceded Bryant as president of the Apollo Association, forerunner of the American Art-Union. Henry W. Bellows was minister of the Unitarian Church of All Souls at Fourth Avenue and Twentieth Street, New York, where, in 1878, he conducted Bryant's funeral service.

1454.   *To* John Howard Bryant

Office of The Evening Post,
New York, August 25th   1864

Dear Brother.

I got your letter of the 20th yesterday.[1] What Mr. Ames asks I will do.[2] As to Mrs. Stowe I have heard nothing. You told me she lived at Hartford and I wrote to her there.[3] If she had received the letter she would have answered it and my conclusion is that she is not there. I will try to find out where she is and write again.

Sometime since you talked of paying me some money. If you do not intend to do it I should like to know. The opportunity to invest in the new government loan will perhaps be gone soon.

We have now very fine weather. The drought seems to be at an end, and the country has been made beautifully green with showers. I am here quite alone—that is quite alone at Roslyn. Frances has been absent for some weeks at Elizabethtown among the Adirondack mountains, where she writes the air is doing her good, and last week Julia went also. I watch the pears and the grapes—the first ripening—one sort after another, and the grapes beginning to change color. The Hartford Prolific grapes are already almost black. Of pears I have a pretty good supply.

You do not say whether you will come eastward or not.

Kind regards to all.

Yours affectionately
W. C. BRYANT.

MANUSCRIPT: NYPL–BFP ADDRESS: John H. Bryant, Esq.

1. Unrecovered.

2. On the next day, August 26, the EP noted that among public lecturers for the coming season was the Rev. C. G. Ames of Albany, and quoted praise for his wit and brilliancy from "one who knows him well"—probably John Bryant.

3. A few years after her great success with Uncle Tom's Cabin (1852), the novelist Harriet Beecher Stowe (1811–1896) had settled on Farmington Avenue in Hartford, Connecticut, where, in 1871, Mark Twain became her next-door neighbor. Bryant's letter to Mrs. Stowe is unrecovered.

1455. To Frances F. Bryant

Office of The Evening Post
New York, August 26 1864
Friday morning.

My dear Frances.

I write this, as you see, from town—not that I have any thing very particular to say, but I suppose you would like to hear that, as the Spaniards express it, *no hay novidad* [I have no news].

We had a fine dash of rain yesterday, and the shores of the Sound are now as green as the fields of Ireland. The melons—and very good ones—have been tumbling in upon me from the garden, in basketsful, and, if I were to go to the Adirondacks, who would there be to eat them? I have sent the superfluous ones to Fanny's, but as I came to town this morning, in passing out at the door, I met Thomas with a dozen or more, and bid him carry one to Mrs. Vandeventer, who I am glad to say is better. I have distributed pears among the families of the neighborhood—Cedarmeres, Dearborn's Seedlings, and Bartlett's, and perhaps have made myself popular with those who are fond of them. The tomatoes are coming in very plentifully, and I may have to do the same thing with them, as I hear they are quite scarce. Mrs. Cairns had none.

Mr. Cline has one of Mr. Butcher's children, a boy, boarding with him. Bryant Godwin came home yesterday, bringing with him another youth, Prescott Butler. Bryant is a strapping lad; he has grown considerably during the summer.

I had a letter from my brother John yesterday. He does not say that the

Bryants are not all well there, but he complains of the drought, which has been hard upon Princeton, while there have been showers upon all the surrounding country.

It is probable that I shall go up with Mr. Pell to pass the Sunday at West Point. Fanny and Godwin will not leave this [place][1] for the Lake until the middle of the week. You cannot, I think, have more than a fortnight more of warm weather in the region where you are. With the second week in September will come chilly nights, and perhaps you will then begin to think of coming a little nearer to your old friend, the sun.

My Hymns are with the binder, who is slow in finishing his work. Mr. Manly, the foreman in the [EP] Job Office, tells me that the binder is taking more than common pains with the book, and that I must wait a few days yet.[2] I have also, at John's request, directed fifty copies of his poems to be put in covers.

Kind regards to all of your party. Tell Julia I wish she would write to me.

Yours ever,
W. C. BRYANT.

MANUSCRIPT: NYPL–GR ADDRESS: Mrs. F. F. Bryant.

1. Word omitted.
2. Bryant was evidently printing his *Hymns* on the *EP* press.

1456. *To* Ellen S. Mitchell

Office of The Evening Post,
New York, August 30, 1864

My dear Niece.

I have just received a letter from my wife who is off among the Adirondack Mountains and is I learn the better for her sojourn there. She wishes me to invite you and one of your daughters to make a visit to Roslyn while I am living there alone, as I do now, and ask your husband to bring you. A visit of a few days to this place might do him good and a longer stay might be beneficial to yourself. We shall begin to have grapes by the time you are here and I hope the nice pears will not be all gone. The summer also lasts longer here than with you, and you will have a soft air here when it has begun to be a little sharp at Dalton. Fanny desires that when you come, if you should stop in New York, you come directly to her house No. 19 East Thirty Seventh Street, where there is a woman, having the care of the house, who will have directions to attend to you. Let me know, as soon as you receive this, whether you will come, and if you answer in the affirmative, I will send you a little money to pay your expenses hither and back. The sooner you come the better, since the sea bathing is now good.

Please let me know as soon as may be whether you will come and when. My best regards to the two Mr. Mitchell's and your children.

If it should be inconvenient for your husband to come perhaps your father-in-law would escort you. We, that is I—for the family is now reduced to myself only—should be very glad to welcome him to this part of Long Island.

Yours affectionately,
W. C. BRYANT.

MANUSCRIPT: Weston Family Papers.

1457.   *To* Frances F. Bryant

Roslyn   Long Island
August 30, 1864.   Tuesday morning.

My dear Frances

On Friday I was in town and wrote to you thence. That afternoon I went to West Point, and passed Saturday and Sunday at Mr. Pells, among his pears and peaches. On Saturday we crossed the river and drove to Governor Fish's—a place which he has very much beautified, though you remember it was always beautiful. The Osborns were not at home.[1] West Point is now quite revived by the late showers, and the country is as beautiful as a new verdure can make it. I came back on Monday morning, and reaching this place in the evening, I find your letter of Thursday the 25th.[2] I am glad that the climate continues to agree with you. I am sorry that Mr. Henderson has to undergo the suffering of another boil of the malignant kind and Josephine I am sure must be exceedingly disappointed at losing the amusement of camping out. So far as I can understand the condition of your party, I do not see much to recommend it save the fine air, and the pleasure of being able to say that you have been among the Adirondacks.

Coming home last evening I heard two pieces of news. One that Mrs. Dr. Warner is again a mother and doing well. The other, that the mosquitoes have come like a cloud over Roslyn and the neighboring country. Nobody has ever seen them here in such numbers before. They come into Fanny's house, but the fly-screens keep them out of ours. Fanny and her children are quite well. She and Godwin do not go on their journey until Friday.

Another piece of news of much greater importance I learned from Gen[1]. Wetmore[3] in coming out. A Commissioner from the state of Georgia, with credentials from the rebel Governor Brown, and with the concurrence of Mr. Toombs the great secessionist, and Alexander H. Stephens, the Vice-President of the rebel government, has arrived with proposals of submission and reconciliation. This step is taken independently of Jeff Davis and his government, and it is added by the Commissioner that if any negociation with that government is set on foot he will withdraw the proposals of Georgia. Georgia is willing to give up slavery, but desires that a little time may be taken for its extinction. Wetmore and another gentleman accompanied the Commissioner to Washington, where he was well received.[4] The rebel league is crumbling to pieces. Georgia is the most important of the Gulf states.

I send a copy of my Hymns. Kind regards to all. I have written to Ellen.

Yours affectionately
W. C. BRYANT.

MANUSCRIPT: NYPL–GR ADDRESS: Mrs. F. F. Bryant

1. Hamilton Fish and William H. Osborn had established summer homes at Garrison's Landing, opposite West Point, in 1861 and 1855, respectively.
2. Unrecovered.
3. Prosper M. Wetmore (227.1, 523.1).
4. Joseph Emerson Brown (1821–1894), Democratic governor of Georgia, 1857–1865, became an active Republican a year after the war ended. Robert Augustus Toombs (1810–1885), United States senator from Georgia, 1853–1861, served briefly as Confederate secretary of state before his opposition to the policies of President Jefferson Davis (1808–1889) led him to resign his post and take a military command. Alexander Hamilton Stephens (1812–1883, Georgia 1832), a former United States congressman from Georgia who served as Confederate vice president from 1861 to 1865, was also dissatisfied with Davis' handling of the war. Their peace overtures were unsuccessful, as was an abortive effort at about the same time by New York *Tribune* editor Horace Greeley to negotiate with Confederate agents. Van Deusen, *Seward*, p. 425; Thomas and Hyman, *Stanton*, p. 323.

1458. *To* Abraham Lincoln

Office of The Evening Post
New York, August 30, 1864

My dear sir.

It has been suggested to me that I ought to write to you on a subject which greatly concerns the interests both of the country and your administration. It relates to the Navy Department.

The transactions of that Department, have become vast, numerous, and immensely complicated. Mr. Welles its head is a man of strict honesty and great good sense. He cannot, however, do every thing, and he has for his Assistant Secretary an active and stirring man, Mr. Fox by whom all that may be called the outdoor business of the department is transacted.[1]

The distrust of this man's capacity and integrity is wide spread and vehement. It is complained that vast sums are expended without any adequate results, that there is not only extreme wastefulness but gross corruption, that those who desire to obstruct the progress of the war have profited by this extravagance, and [been][2] supplied with the means by which they seek to overthrow the Union Party, and that finally to this man's management is owing the destruction which has befallen our commerce at sea.

It is not the object of this letter to express any opinion in regard to these complaints.[3] It is enough for me to state the existence of that impatience and dissatisfaction which universally prevails in regard to the class of transactions of which I have spoken. The remedy, if there be any, and whatever it be, remains with the Executive.

I am sir,

very respectfully and

truly yours

W. C. BRYANT.[4]

MANUSCRIPTS: LC (final); NYPL–GR (draft) ADDRESS: Mr. Lincoln / President of the United States.

1. Gustavus Vasa Fox (1821–1883), a former naval officer, was assistant secretary of the navy from 1861 to 1866. A rather arrogant official who overstepped his authority at times, he was on the whole an able aide to navy secretary Gideon Welles. Comments on Fox's strengths and weaknesses may be found in Welles's *Diary*, I, 401, and II, 232–233.

2. Word omitted.

3. Although Fox had antagonized a number of congressmen, as well as naval officers—Welles described him as "sometimes rough and sailor-like in manner, which gives offense" (*ibid.*, II, 247)—there seems no substantiation of Bryant's charges, which he is careful not to make his own. His bias may, however, be traceable to Fox's zeal in gathering evidence of fraud on the part of Isaac Henderson, as well as other navy agents. Early in the investigation of their acts, Welles commented, "Fox is so greedy to get hold of the fellows that I fear he does not sufficiently respect private rights." *Ibid.*, I, 539.

4. Lincoln's reply to this letter, if he wrote one, is unrecovered.

1459.   *To* Frances F. Bryant

Roslyn   August 31st   1864.

My dear Frances.

I neglected yesterday to attend to your request to send you something in my hand writing to give to those who ask it. I do it now.

The weather is delightful, and the country covered with a lively verdure, but the mosquitoes are a perfect pest. Nobody remembers any thing like it here. The wind won't blow to drive them off. When I go to a little distance from the house, I must run in coming back, or they follow me in a cloud, and some of them get within the wire doors in spite of me. Those, however, that do get in I murder without remorse and defy their comrades without, who have no power to revenge their death.

I see nothing in the newspapers yet about the Commissioner from Georgia, but it is a true thing and will come out soon, to the confusion of the wise men of the democratic party assembled at Chicago. It will turn their plans topsy turvy.

Yesterday I sent you by mail, a copy of the Hymns.

Last night was so cool, that it occurred to me that in the latitude where you are the coolness of the air might be greater than was agreeable to you, and that you might by and by think of coming back. We must have the Deweys here you know and I want them to come while the weather is mild. Yet not before the mosquitoes are gone, and if what I was told the other day is true, that their life is but nine days, they must be gone by the end of the week. Love to Julia and kind regards to all.

Yours ever
W. C. BRYANT.

MANUSCRIPT: NYPL–GR ADDRESS: Mrs. F. F. Bryant.

1460. *To* Frances F. Bryant

Office of The Evening Post,
New York, September 2d. 1864

My dear Frances.

I heard your letter of the twenty eighth of August to Fanny read by her and am glad to hear that you continue so well. The weather here is so fine that it almost seems as if nobody could be otherwise than well. The mosquitoes, however, have not gone from Roslyn, which they still infest though there are scarce any in town, as I hear. Almost every body else is gone—Mr. Ely with his wife to Easthampton, Eastman with his wife to I do not know where, the Miss Hopkinses to Kiskytom back of Catskill; Mrs. Moulton with David to Baltimore; Mrs. Cairns with [Robert?] Stuarts body to Detroit Mrs. Vandeventer to her bed and Mrs. Losee and Mr. Wilkie to the other world. But there is one arrival, a governess for the Willis children engaged for two months and Mr. Cline's two boys are expected home tomorrow.

The Copperheads are making a great fuss about McClellan's nomination, as if that secured them the victory. The Peace men as I always foresaw support him as heartily as the other wing of the party; indeed one wing is as much made up of peace men as the other, the resolutions which they have adopted insist that the country shall back out of the war and try to patch up some agreement with the rebels. The rejoicing of the Copperheads comes I suppose from this—that the two factions have agreed upon the same man and the same policy in regard to the war. I hear, however, that many of the war democrats are exceedingly disgusted with the platform laid down in the resolutions.

The new tool house in the garden is finished, and with stout trunks of cedars at the corners supporting the roof does not look badly. The change in the shed is a decided change for the better.

Tell Julia that I have received her two letters,[1] the last written on Wednesday, and am much obliged to her for them. She gives me so good an account of your health and the kindly influences of the air of the Adirondacks that I hope you will be in no hurry to leave them. When you come back I expect to see you strong enough to run up the hill east of the house with a hop skip and jump.

Meantime do not trouble yourself about my solitude. It is not absolute. Mrs. Pollitz, going to Mrs. Vandeventer's called yesterday with a bunch of her beautiful German asters and I gave her in return a bouquet of roses and verbenas from our garden with other flowers. I go no where, except to look at the garden the pond and the pears on the hill, only when I am quite tired of solitude I come to town to meet the beggars.

So, keep yourself assured of my contentment, so far as I can be contented without you. I should mention that I am again writing something which keeps me a little interested.[2]

Love to Julia. Kind regards to all your party.

Yours ever,
W   C   BRYANT

MANUSCRIPT: NYPL–GR ADDRESS: Mrs. F. F. Bryant.

1. Neither recovered.
2. It is not clearly evident what Bryant was writing just then.

1461.   *To* Frances F. Bryant

New York   Sept. 6, 1864   Tuesday—

My dear Frances

This is our third rainy day and last night was almost cool enough for a fire—so cool that I frequently thought of you shivering among your northern mountains and wishing yourself at Roslyn, where I also wished you quite as heartily. I dined on Sunday at Mr. Ely's and this morning I heard from Thomas that he has since been very ill, with cholera morbus, I believe. The doctor was with him all night last night—and I was told that they hardly thought he would live till morning. The morning, however, found him better. I hope it was not a congestion occasioned by not getting off a sermon as usual on Sunday; for a Mr. Tuttle, a relative of Mr. T[e?]rry, settled at Pontiac in Michigan preached for him[1]—and very well too.

I have had a letter from Miss Jenny Hopkins,[2] who is boarding at the house of the Rev^d. Mr. Rockwell of Kiskytom back of Catskill. She is not much better. The substance of her letter is this. A jolly host, an obliging and intelligent hostess, pleasant fellow boarders—ladies—a flat country, so low, around them, that it has to be trenched in order to be cultivated, picturesque cliffs of rock near them, which they would visit with more pleasure were they not attacked by hosts of mosquitoes.

Fanny is at home, confined by the rain and Nora, who is so much ailing, with a febrile attack, that Fanny does not think it prudent to leave her.

Godwin says he thinks he shall take Minna and go off somewhere— So I suppose that Fanny has given up her journey for the present.

The mosquitoes at Roslyn were not quite so numerous on Saturday as they had been, and we are in hopes that the cold drenching which they got from the clouds yesterday and last night, finished them, not to reappear, I hope, for some years to come.

Every body was rejoicing yesterday on account of the capture of Atlanta. Today there is additional rejoicing at the defeat of Morgan's gang of guerillas whose chief was killed in the combat.[3] There is great effervescence among the political elements of the Union Party. Lincoln will not stand out of the way and now he has been plied with importunities to reform his cabinet which are constant and vehement and which it is said have at last shaken his determination.[4]

Mr. Willis,—R.S.—has written to me to ask Mrs. Cairns to let him take his children to Detroit on the first of October.[5] I have referred him to her as she is at Detroit. Love to Julia and kind regards to all.

Yours ever,
W. C. BRYANT.

MANUSCRIPT: NYPL–GR ADDRESS: Mrs. F. F. Bryant.

1. Tuttle and Terry have not been further identified.
2. Unrecovered.
3. The Confederate cavalry raider General John Hunt Morgan (1825–1864), who had escaped from a federal prison after his capture in 1863, was killed early in September 1864 at Greeneville, Tennessee, by Union soldiers who had penetrated southern lines.
4. A movement in August 1864 among Republican politicians led by New Yorkers David D. Field and George Opdyke to persuade Lincoln to withdraw from his candidacy for re-election quickly lost momentum on the report of stirring Union victories at Atlanta and Mobile Bay. Nevins, *War for the Union*, IV, 91–98; Hendrick, *Lincoln's War Cabinet*, pp. 531–534.
5. For the conflict between Richard S. Willis and his mother-in-law, Ann E. Cairns, see Letters 1167, 1341.

1462. *To* Robert C. Waterston

New York, September 6th, 1864.—
My dear Mr. Waterston,

You will receive by mail a little collection of hymns of my writing which I have lately occupied myself in putting together, the three last of them recently written. One of them you will recognize as having been composed at your request.[1]

As I am sure you will get them by the mail, and as I am not sure that they are as good as they ought to be, I would rather that you should not write to say that the little volume has reached you.

Mrs. Bryant is among the Adirondack mountains still—much strengthened as I hear by the air of that region, and for the last fortnight Julia has been with her. They make excursions to places almost as remarkable as those seen among the Pyrenees or in Switzerland.

Make my best regards to Mrs. Waterston and believe me,

very cordially yours,
WM C   BRYANT.

MANUSCRIPT: NYPL–Berg ADDRESS: Rev^d. R. C. Waterston.

1. Perhaps this was the "Communion Hymn" on pp. [37]–38 of Bryant's *Hymns* (1864).

1463.   *To* Frances F. Bryant

Roslyn   L. I.   September 7th   1864.

My dear Frances.

Returning last night from town, I found your letter of Friday.[1] I am sorry that Mr. Henderson has so much trouble with his foot. If the boil were anywhere else, I suppose he might join the rest of the party in executing their plans, but having only one leg to go upon, he is poorly fitted for wandering in the woods and scrambling up mountains. I hope to hear, in my next letter from you or Julia, that he is able to walk again.

This morning is beautiful, but so cool that I keep the doors and windows shut, and am reminded at every moment, that autumn is come. The Isabella grapes on the kitchen wall—the outside, I mean, have taken a deep purple tinge, and yesterday Mr. Cline gathered the Roslyn pears—a part of them only. You must be back to try them. I hope that, by this time, you begin to think seriously of coming back. Now that the temperate weather has returned, and that you are well braced up for the rest of the season by a two months sojourn among the mountains I do not think there is much danger of a relapse to the former state of debility. We are to have the Deweys here, you know, and I want them to come in the season of grapes and pears, and while the weather is agreeable. From Ellen Mitchell I have not heard, though I have written more than once. Nora still continues ailing, and Fanny, though she does not seem to have quite given up the plan of a journey to the North, postpones it for the present.

Yesterday, I heard a good deal of political news which I cannot put into this letter. I wrote a protest against treating with the rebel government which you will have seen in the paper—that of Tuesday the 6th. instant.[2] I was told from the best authority that Mr. Lincoln was considering whether he should not appoint Commissioners for the purpose, and I afterwards heard that Raymond, of the Times, had been to Washington to persuade Mr. Lincoln to take that step, and was willing himself to be one of the Commissioners.[3] Mr. Forbes of Boston desired me to write to the President on the subject—but after I learned that he had appointed Simeon Draper, the old pipe-layer, Collector at New York, instead of Barney—and appointed him for the reason that he was an active electioneerer, I would not write the letter.[4] Kind regards to all—

Yours ever
W. C. BRYANT.

MANUSCRIPT: NYPL–GR ADDRESS: Mrs. F. F. Bryant.

1. Unrecovered.
2. "No Negotiations with the Rebel Government," *EP*, September 6, 1864.
3. This "preposterous suggestion" by Henry J. Raymond (805.1) that Lincoln offer peace on the sole condition that the South rejoin the Union under its constitution, with "no stipulation respecting emancipation, was certain not only to dismay Lincoln, but to fill him with mingled chagrin and resentment." Nevins, *War for the Union*, IV, 92–93. Raymond's suggestion was quickly rejected.
4. In late August 1864, largely to placate Thurlow Weed's faction of former New York Whigs, Lincoln replaced Hiram Barney by Simeon Draper (884.3), a politician of the Weed–Seward wing of the Republican Party for which Bryant had little respect. *Ibid.*, 94. According to the editor of John M. Forbes's *Letters and Recollections*, II, 101, in early September 1864 Bryant wrote Forbes of his disgust with the "Seward and Weed faction, which is filling all the offices with its creatures," adding, "I am so utterly disgusted with Lincoln's behavior that I cannot muster respectful terms in which to write to him." This letter is unrecovered.

1464.   *To* Frances F. Bryant

New York   September 9th   1864.
Friday morning.

My dear Frances.

I came to town yesterday morning and so may possibly have missed one of your letters. The day before, I received a letter from Ellen Mitchell[1] letting me know that she would leave Dalton on Thursday morning, and reach here that day. They came, and by Fanny's invitation went to her house. This morning I have sent Susan with them, to see the Central Park, while I was engaged at the office, and this afternoon we go by the Arrowsmith to Roslyn. Neither Ellen nor her daughter are quite well and they hope to derive some benefit from the change of air.

Godwin and Minna went yesterday to Lake Memphramagog. Nora seemed better when I left Roslyn yesterday morning, but her recovery promised to be a slow one and Fanny was considering with herself whether she ought not to give both her and Harold a change of air. Mr. Cline's boys have returned quite hale and strong.

The mosquitoes in the country were put to flight or at least to death by the cold storm and east wind. Yesterday the weather was almost unpleasantly cool, particularly as the evening drew on. Today is milder and softer. I thought last night—the fourth or fifth of a succession of cool nights that you would soon think of turning your face southward.

The democratic party is much puzzled to know what to do with its platform. McClellan's attempt in his letter to give what is called the go by to that part which relates to the immediate cessation of hostilities makes people laugh.[2]

I shall have, I think, a plenty of fruit in my garden. The Hartford Prolific grapes are fully ripe; the Concords beginning to be ripe, the Roslyn pears just coming in, and musk melons plenty. If I could send them to you by wishing you should have them every day. The next best thing, or perhaps the best of all will be for you to come where they are. Love to Julia. Kind regards to all.

Yours ever.
W. C. BRYANT.

MANUSCRIPT: NYPL–GR ADDRESS: Mrs. F. F. Bryant.

1. Unrecovered.
2. The Democratic Party platform of August 1864, written by the "Peace Democrats," termed the war effort "four years of failure," and called for the end of hostilities, "with a view to an ultimate convention." In his letter accepting the nomination for the presidency, while rejecting the assertion that the war was a failure, McClellan declared that "whenever the South showed a disposition to re-enter the Union on any terms, he would negotiate." Nevins, *War for the Union*, IV, 99–100, 102.

1465.   *To* Frances F. Bryant

Roslyn   Sept. 10   1864
Saturday morning

My dear Frances.

I came out last evening with Ellen and her daughter Louisa—a very quiet young lady with a very large forehead and very fond of reading.[1] This beautiful morning I have been showing them the flowers in the garden, and Annie has now come over and taken charge of her young cousin.

I found no letter from you here but I found one from Hannah [Henderson?] to you which I send with this.— Nora, I learn, is mending, but still not well. The body of Stuart did not go on with Mrs. Cairns, but was exhumed after she went and sent on by some New York undertaker. Nothing else worth noting in Roslyn. The Union party is becoming greatly encouraged as to its prospects in the election of President.

Ever yours
W. C. BRYANT.

MANUSCRIPT: NYPL–GR.

1. Bryant's grandniece Sarah Louisa Mitchell (b. 1846) was the daughter of Clark W. and Ellen S. Mitchell.

1466.   *To* Frances F. Bryant

Roslyn   September 12, 1864
Monday morning.

My dear Frances.

I wrote a letter to you on Saturday to go in the same letter with Hannah's, which I enclosed to you. After that was sent off, I found the letter I had written on my table. I had forgotten to put it into the cover. I send it now.[1] —Yesterday we had a pouring rain nearly all day, beginning the night before. We dined at Fanny's—the rain was too violent to go to church. We ran over to Fannys in the rain and at five oclock returned in the sunshine, and in the evening lighted a fire in our parlor, the first of the season. Today it is again chilly with a lowering sky dropping, a thin sprinkle of rain. I am sure that you will be more comfortable here this weather than in any possible place among the Adirondacks.

Louisa Mitchell, having never been from home before further than Pittsfield and Northampton is much interested in what she sees here, but is very quiet. Her mother thinks of making an end of her visit in "about two weeks" from her arrival. Probably her husband will come for her. She desires her love to you and Julia and hopes you will find among the mountains what she is expecting from the air of the seacoast, greater health and new strength.

Yours ever in the hope of
seeing you soon.
W. C. Bryant.

MANUSCRIPT: NYPL–GR ADDRESS: Mrs. F. F. Bryant.

1. Letter 1465.

1467.   *To* Leonice M. S. Moulton

Roslyn   September 14th   1864.

Dear Mrs. Moulton.

I enclose the letter addressed to you the other day by Miss Tillson, together with my answer to the one addressed to me.[1] When you have read my answer will you please at any convenient time, to send it to the post office. I am sorry to be obliged to answer Miss Tillson's request in the negative, but I have no skill nor facility in writing occasional verses and if I were to comply whenever asked I should have no time for any thing else.

I am, madam,
very truly yours,
W. C. Bryant.

MANUSCRIPT: NYPL–Bryant–Moulton Letters ADDRESS: Mrs. L. M S. Moulton. / Roslyn.
ENDORSED: came, with Letter for C   H   Tillson, / September 14, 1864 / W. C. B. / requesting original verses / — / for Christiana— / Nov   1. 1889.

1. Letter 1468.

1468.   *To* Christiana H. Tillson[1]

Roslyn, Long Island,
September 14th   1864.—

Dear Madam.

I am sorry to seem disobliging, but there are various reasons why I cannot comply with the desire expressed in your note.[2]

Ever since the attention of the public was turned to the sufferings of our soldiers, and the duty of relieving them the mails have brought me requests to compose verses, to be sung or printed or sold in manuscript at different fairs in different parts of the country. These applications I have declined partly for want of leisure and partly on other accounts which, I suppose are not so obvious to others as to myself. You will, therefore, I am sure pardon me, if, in your case, I give the same answer that I have done in others.

I am, madam,
very respectfully yours,
W. C. BRYANT.

P.S. I shall certainly take pleasure in commending your charity to the good will of the publishers of my acquaintance.

W. C. B.

MANUSCRIPT: DuU.

1. Unidentified.
2. Unrecovered.

1469.   *To* Frances F. Bryant

New York   September 15   1864
Thursday morning.

My dear Frances.

I got a letter this morning from Julia[1] dated Wednesday evening—yesterday evening—the 14th, and yet it was postmarked the 12th, which must have been a blunder of the postmaster. From it, I learned that you were all to set out for the Lakes, this morning which has opened beautifully and which, I think, will ensure you a delightful excursion. When you get back I hope you will come home the first opportunity. The weather has been quite cold here. The parlour fire has been burning for several days at Roslyn, and if you are going to remain much longer among the mountains, you may as well make your arrangements to pass the winter there. The air here is now as pure as it can well be. The heats of the season are over, the fissures of the earth have been closed by profuse rains, and the pools are filled with fresh cool rain-water, which no temperature that we can now expect, will cause to send up unwholesome vapors. Mrs. Mitchell and her daughter expect to go away next week or the beginning of the week after, and I wish you could see them before they go. I have written to Dr. Dewey reminding him that he and Mrs. Dewey were engaged to make us a visit this month. He answered, that, in plain truth, he could not afford it; the high prices had so diminished his income—or rather the depreciation of the currency had done it. I rejoined that I would bear the expenses if they would come—this was the day before yesterday and so the matter stands.[2]

I have just received a letter from Mr. R. S. Willis.[3] He has communicated with Mrs. Cairns through Mr. Miller his lawyer. He wants his children to visit him. Mrs. Cairns said that this could only be on the penalty of their disinheritance. Mr. Willis has accepted the penalty, and now desires that I or some member of my family should give that message to the children, in such a manner as that it shall not be an unpleasant surprize to them. Mr. Cairns and Mrs. Stuart are at Detroit with the Stuart children.

Mrs. Mitchell and her daughter are very quiet, but Annie stirs up the younger of the two with walks and boating excursions, and now that the sunshine and warmth have returned to the air, will probably have her in the salt water. Ellen is still languid with the effects of her late attack of typhus or typhoid fever.

The Union party here is in better spirits from day to day and confident of success. Love to Julia and kind regards to all.

Yours ever,
W. C. BRYANT.

MANUSCRIPT: NYPL–GR ADDRESS: Mrs. F. F. Bryant.

1. Unrecovered.
2. Neither of Bryant's letters to Dewey has been recovered; Dewey's letter of September 11 is in NYPL–BG.
3. Unrecovered.

1470.   *To* John Howard Bryant

New York   Sept. 15th   1864.

Dear Brother.

The draft for three thousand dollars was regularly received—but I have been unable till now to get the note from Fanny. I shall send it in my next letter, and endorse the remainder of the money on your note to me.

I attended to Mr. Ames immediately, mentioning him as one of the brilliant lecturers, whose talents were at the service of the public. You probably overlooked the article.[1]

The description of the land to be sold, I duly received, but of the name of the person to whom the conveyance is to be made I have not the slightest recollection. Please let me know it and where he lives.[2] I cannot execute the deed until my wife returns. She is now at Elizabethtown or not very far from it, in Essex County among the Adirondack mountains, where I learn her health has improved.

When you say that my friends in Illinois are usually well, you tell me nothing new. I know that they are usually well and only occasionally sick. I should like to know how they are at present. Please let me know when you write again.

Every body here thinks that since the democratic party has shown its hand, at the Chicago Convention, the election of Lincoln is made certain.[3] Kind regards to all.

                                        Yours affectionately
                                        W. C BRYANT.

MANUSCRIPT: WCL ADDRESS: Jno H Bryant Esq.

1. See 1454.2.

2. On October 28, 1864, Bryant sold a parcel of land in Bureau County, Illinois, to one David Warrington for $350. "Bryant: Illinois Landowner," 12. See Letter 1472.

3. In a leading editorial in the *EP* for September 20, 1864, under the heading "A Certain and an Uncertain Policy," Bryant gave full support to Lincoln's candidacy. Decrying the "political jumping-jacks who have constituted themselves leaders of the opposition," he went on, "The policy of Mr. Lincoln is declared and known. He has now guided the ship of state for more than three years; in that time of tremendous difficulty he has perhaps made mistakes, but he has acted throughout conscientiously, honorably, and with an honest and patriotic desire to do right. He has gained wisdom by experience. . . . There is every reason to believe that, while Mr. Lincoln continues in power, this healthy and beneficial state of things will continue."

1471. *To* Julia S. Bryant

                                        Roslyn   September 16th. 1864.
Dear Julia.

I wrote a letter to your mother yesterday, in which I referred to a letter from you, dated Wednesday evening and just then received. It was post-marked September 12th, but within had no date but the one I have mentioned. I supposed it just written, and that you were about to set out on another excursion, but after my letter was sent off Mr. Henderson convinced me that the letter must have been written the week previous, just before you set out on the journey from which he had just returned. Your mother must have been puzzled to know what I was driving at.

I am glad to know that you had so interesting a time on your excursion to the lakes. It was very kind of you all to think of me in the midst of the grand scenery—but I must content myself for the present with looking at it through your eyes. You speak of Mr. Remington, of whom I had not heard before. Was it the little poet Remington of Rhode Island?[1]

Fanny went of[f] yesterday to town with Harold, Nora having preceded her the day before. She thinks of taking them first to Newburgh and after a little stay at the Powelton House, to proceed to Great Barrington and then probably further up the county but her plans are not very definite. Nora was somewhat better.

Every thing goes on very well here. The weather is heavenly, and the grapes are ripe. Tell your mother that we are all ready for her. Last night the moon shone so wonderfully bright in a cloudless sky, that if I had my young eyes back again I could have seen to read by her light—but there was no one to look at her. The sky was of the tenderest blue and the air very mild and not damp. My guests go to roost with the hens. They are up stairs by nine oclock generally.

I was in town yesterday and could not get time to eat a small—very small—luncheon of bread and cheese which I took in my pocket, so beggar ridden and politician ridden was I the whole morning till three o'clock when I ran for the boat which leaves its wharf now at a quarter past three.

Kind regards to all.

Affectionately &c

W. C. BRYANT.

P.S. Mrs. Cline got your letter night before last—but it was late, and she did not look for your things till yesterday. They were sent this morning to town.

W. C. B.—

MANUSCRIPT: BLR ADDRESS: Miss Julia Bryant.

1. Albert Gallatin Remington (1820–1897), whose volume *Prose and Verse* (New York [1856]) was reprinted half a dozen times.

1472.   *To* John Howard Bryant

Office of The Evening Post,

New York, Oct. 5. 1864.

Dear Brother.

I send you Mrs. Godwins note—or yours to Mrs. G.— I have endorsed on your note, as of the 2d of September, $1450.00—on the larger note of $4,480.—

I am ready to make out the deed to Mr. Warrington—but please tell me what was the *consideration*, and *where he lives.*

In haste

yrs truly

W   C   BRYANT.

MANUSCRIPT: WCL.

1473.   *To* W[illiam?] C[ullen?] Bryant[1]

Roslyn   Oct. 7th   1864

My dear sir

I have your letter of the 28th of September[2] giving an account of the part you have borne in the campaigns and battles of the Southwest. I am glad to hear that you have so faithfully served your country, but regret that it has caused you so serious a loss as that of your right arm. With one arm however you may still be a useful citizen of your country in the walks of civil life to which you have returned. You can no longer bear a part in such victories as those you mention beginning with Fort Donelson and ending with the capture of Atlanta, but you may aid in placing worthy men and true patriots in office and may give in y[our] own life the example of un-bl[ame]able conduct and [illegible word] goodness—a merit higher even than that of a brave and faithful soldier—

W   C   B.

MANUSCRIPT: NYPL–GR (draft) ADDRESS: To W   C   Bryant &c.

1. Unidentified.
2. Unrecovered.

1474. *To* G[eorge?] W. Porter

Roslyn, Long Island,
October 10th   1864.—

My dear sir.

I am much flattered by your asking for my hymns, and now that I have your letter[1] asking for them in such obliging terms, I see no occasion to regret that I did not send them to you before. I have put up a copy for you, and if it should happen that there are any persons to whom you might care to give them I will send you more of them.

Such as they are, they were written at various times within the last forty years;—the three that stand last in the collection within the year.

The printed paper you send me is composed in a very bad spirit, but it is a comfort to be confident that neither that nor any thing of the kind can affect the great result of the next election.[2] It appears to me that the success of Lincoln and Johnson is a moral certainty.

With regard to the affair at the Century Club, my knowledge of it is derived from the same source as your own. I have not been consulted in regard to it, nor has any communication concerning it been made to me. I suppose, however, that those who have charge of it will somewhat expect that I shall be present.[3]

My regards to Mrs. Porter. My wife desires hers to you both. I am, dear sir,

truly yours.
W. C. BRYANT.

MANUSCRIPT: YCAL ADDRESS: Rev^d. Dr. G. W. Porter / the Parsonage / Manhasset / Long Island.

1. Unrecovered.
2. This paper has not been identified.
3. See Letter 1480.

1475.   *To* Edwin M. Stanton

Office of The Evening Post,
New York, October 12   1864.

Sir.

I write to you in behalf of Col. Alfred Gibbs whose friends desire to see him promoted to the rank of Brigadier General. In their opinion, there are few who have earned distinction so fully, and they can only ascribe the failure to promote him, in part to the quiet modesty of his character, and in part to the multitude of claims for promotion which are pressed upon the attention of the Executive. Colonel Gibbs has received a thorough military education; he distinguished himself honorably in the war with Mexico and in wars with the Indians. In the present war as commander of the First Regiment of New York Dragoons, one of the best in the service, and afterwards as commander of different brigades, he has been conspicuous for good conduct. His friends confess to some mortification that with all these merits he should have been so far distanced by others in the career of promotion and respectfully ask that he may receive a commission of Brigadier General in the Volunteer Army.[1]

I am, sir,
with great respect &c
W   C   BRYANT.

MANUSCRIPT: University of Iowa Library ADDRESS: To the Hon. Edwin M. Stanton / Secretary of War. ENDORSED: No. 5 / Wm. C. Bryant / New York, Oct   12/64 / Recommending promo- / tion of Col. Alfred Gibbs / G581 C. B. (Al[c?]o) 1864.

1. Alfred Gibbs (1823–1868, United States Military Academy 1846), a native of Long Island, had been cited for gallantry while wounded at Cerro Gordo during the Mexican War, and brevetted first lieutenant in that action, and later captain at Vera Cruz. After frontier duty in New Mexico, where he was again wounded in action, this time against the Apaches, he commanded the Third United States Cavalry in 1861. Captured and paroled in July of that year, he was exchanged in August 1862, and in September 1862 was made colonel of the 130th New York Volunteers, which became the First New York Dragoons in July 1863. Holding brigade command in Virginia until October 1864, he was commissioned a brigadier general of volunteers one week after Bryant's letter to Stanton. In May 1865 Gibbs was brevetted a major general for gallant and meritorious service.

1476.   *To* James T. Fields

Roslyn, Long Island
October 13th. 1864.

My dear Mr. Fields.

I send you a poem for the Atlantic Monthly.[1] Ask me for no more verses. A septuagenarian has past the time when it is becoming for him to occupy himself with,

"The rhymes and rattles of the man and boy."[2]

Pope was twenty years younger than I am, when he said to Bolingbroke

"Why wilt thou break the Sabbath of my days?"

and

["]Public too long, ah, let me hide my age."[3]

Uhland, who died in his seventy sixth year, did not, in the last twenty years of his life,—or twenty four was it?—add a hundred lines to his published verses.[4] Nobody, in the years after seventy, can produce any thing in poetry, save the thick and muddy last runnings of the cask from which all the clear and sprightly liquor has been already drawn.

I can think of no name for the trifle I send you. Can you suggest one? If not, I must leave the name to be added in the proof.

Please leave the date, as it stands at the close of the poem.[5]

Yours truly
W   C   BRYANT

MANUSCRIPT: NYPL–GR ADDRESS: James T. Fields Esq.

1. "My Autumn Walk," published in the *Atlantic Monthly*, 15 (January 1865), 20–21. See *Poems* (1876), pp. 443–445.
2. Pope, *Horace*, Epis. I.i.18.
3. *Ibid.*, 3, 5.
4. Ludwig Uhland (1787–1862), German lyric poet and composer of ballads.
5. "October, 1864." This, the most poignant of Bryant's Civil War poems, contrasts the beauty of autumn with the slaughter of soldiers in Georgia and Virginia, and the grief of their loved ones:

... I look on the beauty round me,
And tears come into my eyes,

For the wind that sweeps the meadows
Blows out of the far Southwest,
Where our gallant men are fighting,
And the gallant dead are at rest.

The golden-rod is leaning,
And the purple aster waves
In a breeze from the land of battle,
A breath from the land of graves.

Replying to this letter on October 17 (NYPL–BG), Fields suggested the poem be titled either "My Walk in Autumn," or "My Autumn Walk."

1477.   To Daniel C. Gilman

Office of The Evening Post
New York, October 13th   1864

Dear sir.

Enclosed are five dollars and a stamp, with the blank receipt for my dues. Please receipt the bill and send it to me by mail, and oblige

Yours truly,
W. C. BRYANT.

MANUSCRIPT: JHUL ADDRESS: D. C. Gilman Esq.

1478. *To* Abraham Lincoln

New York, October 14, 1864.

My dear sir.

The death of Chief Justice Taney has left vacant the highest judicial post in the republic.[1] Men are asking, all over the country, who is to fill his place. Allow me to present myself among those who will address you on a subject in which the country has so deep an interest.

The general wish of the friends of the Union, so far as I have the means and the capacity of judging, points to Mr. Chase as the successor of the late Chief Justice.[2] For such a post, Mr. Chase is admirably fitted, both by his native and his acquired qualities. As an able and accomplished jurist, profoundly versed in international and constitutional law, and familiar with questions arising out of the relations of the states to each other, and to the federal government, I do not know his superior. I need not speak to you, who know him so well, of his powers of discrimination, his calm and solid judgment and dignity of character. His liberal opinions, in regard to the duties of government, are tempered by a moderation which makes it impossible that he should push them to any rash extremes. All these qualities exist in combination with an incorruptible honesty. In the reconstruction of the Union many questions will arise in which the late Chief Justice would, without the least doubt, have been a most unsafe arbiter.[3] In Mr. Chase the friends of the Union recognize one who would decide these questions wisely and with a judicious regard to the welfare and permanence of our system of government.

If he were appointed to the seat on the Supreme Bench left vacant by Chief Justice Taney's death, the anxieties of many, who have looked towards the final settlement of the controversy in which the country is now engaged, with some degree of painful doubt, would be allayed. It is manifest that the Executive in this important work would need the powerful cooperation of the Judiciary, and with Mr. Chase at the head of the Supreme Court, that cooperation would be given most effectually and most satisfactorily to the country.[4]

I am, sir,
with very great respect
Your ob^t. Servant,
WM C. BRYANT

MANUSCRIPTS: LC (final); NYPL–GR (draft) ADDRESS: Mr. Lincoln / President of the United States.

1. Roger Brooke Taney (1777–1864, Dickinson 1795) of Maryland had served on the United States Supreme Court since 1836, during the entire period as Chief Justice. He had died on October 12.

2. Secretary of the Treasury Salmon P. Chase had resigned on June 30, 1864, being succeeded on July 3 by the then Chairman of the Senate Finance Committee, William

P. Fessenden. This letter, written two days after Taney's death, refutes Allan Nevins' statement that Bryant was among those who recommended Montgomery Blair (1813–1883, United States Military Academy 1836), who had resigned as Postmaster General on September 23, as Taney's successor. See Nevins, *War for the Union*, IV, 117–118, 105.

3. A southerner by inheritance and temperament, Taney had opposed both the war and the abolition of slavery.

4. On December 6, 1864, Lincoln's appointment of Chase as Chief Justice was at once confirmed by the Senate. *Ibid.*, 118, 205.

1479.   *To* John M. Forbes

[Roslyn] Oct   15   1864

Dear Mr. Forbes.

I thank you for the haunch of Venison you were so obliging as to send me. It is on the ice and Dr. Dewey is to be present at the carving of it when it is on the table. Professor Smith is then in addition to his other accomplishments a mighty hunter.[1] I have no skill that way. I sometimes hunt down a public rogue or a false opinion and sometimes I put myself on the chase after rhymes.

Dr. Dewey writes me that if he had known of your invitation when he was in Boston last week he would have gone down to Naushon. Cicero and his friends were played over again in the beautiful groves of your Tusculum in the extended autumn weather of our climate. If I had been there, who am stepping out of my seventieth year into the shadow of my seventy first, I might have said a word or two *de Senectute* to that company of sages. Did people grow old earlier in those ancient times than now? Cicero was my junior.[2]

I hope to be more fortunate another time and mean yet to see your island and its kind possessors. If you ever have a little time when at New York, may I not hope to see you at this little home of mine, about which are some rather peculiar aspects of natural beauty—

I am dear sir
truly yrs
W   C   BRYANT

MANUSCRIPT: NYPL–GR (draft).

1. Late in September Forbes had invited Bryant to visit his summer home on Naushon Island on October 8 to meet Goldwin Smith (1823–1910), professor of modern history at Oxford University, who lectured in the United States in 1864, and who returned here four years later to become a professor of English literature and history at Cornell. A liberal democratic journalist and an educational reformer, Smith strongly supported the northern cause in the Civil War, and Forbes wished him to meet men who would give him a true account of northern feeling. Although Bryant had declined regretfully on September 29 (letter unrecovered), Emerson and others attended. An invitation to Orville Dewey failed to reach him in time. Forbes to Bryant, September 30, 1864, NYPL–BG; Forbes, *Letters and Recollections*, II, 108–111. On December 4, 1864,

Bryant apparently dined with Smith at George Bancroft's home. Bancroft to Bryant, November 28, 1864, NYPL–BG; Letter 1498.

2. The orator and rhetorician Marcus Tullius Cicero (106–43 B.C.) had a suburban villa at Tusculum, near Rome. *De Senectute* ("On Old Age") was one of his several writings on moral philosophy.

1480.   *To* George Bancroft

Roslyn, Long Island
October 17th   1864.

My dear Sir.

I thank my excellent friends of the Century Club for the kindness manifested in their design of marking my seventieth birth-day with some expression of their good-will. I hope I shall not be accused of affectation when I say that I sincerely think I have no title to such a testimonial of their regard, and yet I will add that there is no set of men from whom I would accept with less hesitation than from the body over which you preside and with the members of which my relations have always been so delightful. I accept therefore the invitation which you have communicated in such obliging terms.[1]

I am, dear sir,
truly yours
W. C. BRYANT

MANUSCRIPTS: MHS (final); NYPL–GR (draft) ADDRESS: Hon   Geo   Bancroft / President of the / Century Club.

1. The extraordinary celebration of Bryant's seventieth birthday given him by four hundred members of the Century Club and their guests is described in detail in *The Bryant Festival at "The Century," November 5, M.DCCC.LXIV.* (New York: D. Appleton, 1865). Earlier in 1864 Bancroft had succeeded Gulian C. Verplanck, first president of the Century. Nye, *Bancroft*, p. 219.

1481.   *To* Richard H. Dana

Roslyn   Long Island
October 17th. 1864.—

Dear Dana,

Mr. Godwin having answered your inquiries concerning his safety and that of Fanny, I did not think it necessary to write to you immediately. The injury he received was but slight, and he is entirely recovered. Fanny, being badly bruised and sprained, with some cuts about the forehead and elsewhere, will get well more slowly. For sometime she has been unable to move in her bed, without help, but the physician says that there is no permanent injury and that she needs only time to be perfectly healed.[1]

I suppose you have heard that the Century Club have invited the poets to meet me at their rooms in town, on the occasion of my birthday. How little such things are to my taste, I need not say, but it was very kind of them, and I cannot decline. You are invited, and know how glad I shall be to see you, and take you down to this place. But for Fanny's accident I would ask you—and she would be very glad of it—to make her house in Thirty Seventh Street your stopping place in town, but as she is so ill, and not well provided with servants I cannot.[2]

Please overlook my writing on such elegant note paper. It is a present from my bookseller.

Give my best regards to your daughter and sisters. My wife desires hers to all of you. Julia is away, but will soon be back. I am, dear sir,

truly yours,

W. C. BRYANT.

MANUSCRIPTS: NYPL–GR (draft and final) ADDRESS: R. H. Dana Esqre.

1. On October 10, while Fanny and Parke Godwin were traveling with friends from Westport, Connecticut, to New York City on a New Haven Railroad train, the car in which they rode was overturned near Eighty-Fifth Street by the train's derailment. Though painfully cut and bruised, Fanny suffered no broken or dislocated bones. *EP*, October 10, 11, 1864.

2. Dana did not attend the birthday festival on November 5, regretting in a letter to Bancroft that "infirmities" prevented him from honoring his "old friend Bryant." *Bryant Festival*, pp. 15–16.

1482.   *To* Ellen S. Mitchell

Roslyn, Long Island, October 17th, 1864.

My dear Niece.

Fanny is not able to write to you, having been badly hurt by the accident which happened the other day to the train on the New York and New Haven Railroad, when the cars were thrown off the track. My wife cannot write because she is so busy. Fanny however is mending. No bones are broken; but she is so badly bruised and sprained that she must yet keep her bed for some time.

As to Nora and Harold, Harold is here and much better. Nora is now at Great Barrington with her grand aunt and her health is improving. It will not, therefore, be necessary for Fanny to avail herself of your obliging offer.[1]

Mrs. Bryant has recovered from the fatigues of her journey in returning from the mountains. She sends much love to you all. Julia is expected every day from Great Barrington, where she has been ill with a boil in her ear.

We want to hear how you and Louisa find yourselves after a few weeks in Dalton, and whether you can trace any beneficial effect on your health from the short stay you made at Roslyn. The weather has been very changeable since you left us. A few very charming days, some pretty cold ones, and some rainy ones. We have had also several frosty nights but the flowers are yet, for the most part unharmed in our garden, and the roses are in full bloom, nor have the grapes on our cornice been gathered.

Kind regards to all the family,
Yours affectionately,
W. C. BRYANT.

MANUSCRIPTS: Weston Family Papers (final); NYPL–GR (draft).

1. Letter unrecovered.

1483.   *To* Lydia H. H. Sigourney

Roslyn   Long Island,
October 20th. 1864

My dear Mrs. Sigourney,

I give you a thousand thanks for the fine lines you have sent me, and only wish that their subject was more worthy of them. I shall reckon it among the fortunate circumstances of a rather fortunate life, that my entrance on my seventy first year was marked by so kind a testimonial of approbation from such a quarter.[1]

I am, dear madam,
very truly yours,
WM C. BRYANT.

MANUSCRIPTS: ConnHS (final?); Princeton University Library (fair copy?) ADDRESS: Mrs. L. Huntley Sigourney.

1. Mrs. Sigourney's verse tribute, in which she called Bryant "The master of our Western lyre!," was printed in *Bryant Festival*, p. 35.

1484.   *To* Caroline R. Howard[1]

[Roslyn?] Oct. 24. 1864.

Dear Madam

I have read your letter carefully and perfectly understand your situation. I have also looked at the samples of your poetry which you have sent me and find them in thought and execution superior to most of those which are admitted into our periodicals. You ought to succeed in a literary career, but you must be aware that this career is crowded with competitors, and that the growth of a literary reputation, in a large majority of cases is exceedingly slow. That has been in a particular manner my own case—such reputation as I have being the result of an acquaintance of the reading world with my writings lasting through half a century.

You speak of my influence as likely to be of advantage in your literary prospects. If it be influence with the booksellers, that you mean, I can boast but little. I have tried it without success. The booksellers have their own critics, who proceed upon a principle peculiar to themselves. The booksellers do not want to know whether a work is good but whether it will have an immediate sale.

If it be influence with the periodicals, I have as little. The editors judge for themselves. I have sent them articles by my friends which they rejected.

If you publish any thing which I can commend in the Evening Post I shall be glad to do so, or if you can point out any other way in which I can serve you I am ready to do what I can.

Poetry you should know is the slenderest possible dependence for a livelihood. If I had depended on my poetry for a living I should have starved long ago. Literature in any of its departments is a very precarious dependence, and should, I think be combined with some other branch of useful diligence in order to secure those who make it a pursuit from poverty and disappointment.

W   C   B

MANUSCRIPT: NYPL–GR (draft) ADDRESS: To Miss Caroline R   Howard.

1. Bryant's solicitude for Miss Howard suggests that she may have been one of his father's cousins in West Bridgewater. See Letter 37; 473.5.

1485.   *To* James T. Fields

Roslyn   Long Island
October 27th   1864.

Dear Mr. Fields

The check you sent me for the poem "My Autumn Walk"—a name which I accept with all due acknowledgments—reached me duly. You are the most prompt of magazine publishers.

Please give the poem the title I have quoted, and in the last line of, the twelfth stanza I think it is—instead of

"And the banks of the noble James"—

read

"And the wasted banks of the James."[1]

Yours very truly
WM C. BRYANT.

MANUSCRIPT: WCL ADDRESS: Jas. T. Fields Esq.

1. See Letter 1476. This line stands as corrected in *Poems* (1876), p. 444.

1486. *To* August R. Macdonough[1]

New York   Oct. 28th   1864.

My dear sir.

I should be obliged to the Officers of your Club if they would invite
the Rev^d. R. C. Waterston and his lady, of Boston. Mr. Waterston is not unknown as a poet— May I also ask that Mr. H. T. Tuckerman if not a member, be invited and also the following persons,

Chas. E. Miller with ticket for
a lady. 270 Lexington Avenue.
Dr. [Warren?] and lady
43 East Twentieth St.—

Yours truly
W. C. Bryant—

MANUSCRIPT: MHS ADDRESS: A. R. Macdonough Esq.

1. Secretary of the Century Club.

1487. *To* Robert C. Waterston

Roslyn   Long Island
October 31st   1864.

My dear Mr. Waterston

You and Mrs. Waterston are invited to [a] meeting of the Century
Club on Saturday evening the 5th of November, when I am to be congratulated, on what I would willingly put off for ten or twenty years to come—
the completion of my seventieth year. I write this to say how happy we—my
wife and Julia and I—should be to see you both here. It is very pleasant
here yet— the last smiles of autumn are on the landscape; the roses are in
bloom in our garden, and the autumnal dandelions sprinkle the grass, and
the yellow and ruddy trees are reflected in the waters of our harbor, and
something of this beauty will remain to us for a considerable time yet. We
shall go to town on Thursday and remain until Monday, and shall account
it a peculiar good fortune if we can bring you out with us. We cannot ask
you to Fanny's, in town—for her house will be filled to its entire capacity.
She is getting on quite as well as could be expected after the terrible bruises
and sprains which she suffered from the accident on the railroad. All send
their love to you and Mrs. Waterston.[1]

I am, dear sir,
very truly yours
W. C. Bryant.

MANUSCRIPT: Century Association ADDRESS: Rev^d. R. C. Waterston.

1. Apparently the Waterstons did not attend the birthday festival. But see Waterston's memorial *Tribute to William Cullen Bryant at the Meeting of the Massachusetts
Historical Society, June 13, 1878* (Boston: John Wilson & Son, 1878).

1488.   *To* Maria P. Codding[1]

[New York? *ante* November 8, 1864]

. . . I am glad that Mr. Codding is engaged in the political campaign, and am sure that he will do the good cause good service. Please present to him my regards. I have printed—not published—a little collection of hymns of my writing, which I shall send him by mail and hope he will accept.

I am, Madam.

truly yours,

W. C. BRYANT.

MANUSCRIPT (*partial*): Swarthmore College Library ADDRESS: Mrs. Maria P   Codding.

1. Wife of Rev. Ichabod Codding (1418.5). This letter is dated conjecturally, on the assumption that Bryant refers to the campaign of 1864, and because of his reference to his *Hymns* (1864). Codding died on June 17, 1866. Edward Magdol, *Owen Lovejoy: Abolitionist in Congress* (New Brunswick, New Jersey: Rutgers University Press [1967]), p. 409.

1489.   *To* Frank W. Ballard[1]

Office of The Evening Post,

New York, November 10   1864.

My dear sir.

It will be impossible for me to attend the meeting at Cooper Institute tomorrow evening, on account of an earlier engagement.[2] I shall be present, however, in spirit, and take part in the rejoicings inspired by the glorious result of the late election, which should be chronicled among the signal favors shown by Providence to our republic. It will do more to hasten the close of the war than twenty battles.

I am, sir,

truly yours

W. C. BRYANT.

MANUSCRIPT: Brown University Library ADDRESS: Frank W. Ballard Esq. / Secretary of the / Young Mens Republican Union / Gibson's Building / Cor   of Broadway and 13th St. / —New York—. PUBLISHED: *EP*, November 12, 1864.

1. See descriptive note, and Letter 1165.
2. At this "Union Jubilee," celebrating the re-election of Lincoln, this letter from Bryant was read, and the next day printed with an account of the meeting in the *EP*.

1490.   *To* George Bancroft

[New York? *c*November 10, 1864]

Dear Mr. Bancroft.

The accompanying verses of Mrs. Sigourney and Miss Mary Booth,[1] though sent to my address at Roslyn, seem properly to form a part of the papers relating to the affair of last Saturday Evening. Desiring to keep the originals I send you copies of them.

very cordially yours,
W. C. BRYANT.

MANUSCRIPT: MHS ADDRESS: Hon Geo Bancroft.

1. Mary H. C. Booth, of Wisconsin, whose verse tribute to Bryant, accompanied by "a blossom of EDELWEISS, from the Swiss Alps, eleven thousand feet above the level of the sea," was printed in *Bryant Festival*, pp. 32–34.

1491. *To* George Bancroft

Office of The Evening Post,
New York, Nov. 11th 1864.

Dear Bancroft.

I wrote out my speech the next morning while it was fresh in my mind. As yours is to be printed in the E. Post and mine will follow it, I will send it to you in print, if that will answer.[1]

I shall be happy to have my name joined with yours in proposing Mr. Tilden who is a worthy man and a friend of mine, though now we are a little apart in politics.[2]

Truly yours
W. C. BRYANT.

MANUSCRIPT: MHS ADDRESS: Hon Geo. Bancroft.

1. Bryant's response to the introductory tribute at the Century celebration by Bancroft was printed in *Bryant Festival*, pp. 9–13, and Bancroft's speech, on pp. 6–9.

2. Samuel J. Tilden had remained a Democrat, opposing Lincoln's election in 1860 and again in 1864. While he strongly supported the Union cause after initially opposing the war, he warned against the draft, the suppression of habeas corpus, and other acts of arbitrary power by the national administration. John Bigelow, *The Life of Samuel J. Tilden*, 2 vols. (New York: Harper, 1895), I, 153–154, 171–172; Nevins, *War for the Union*, II, 394; III, 168; IV, 98. Tilden was elected to membership in the Century Club.

1492. *To* O. D. Teall[1]

Roslyn Nov 12 1864

Dear sir.

To the questions put in your letter—although of so personal and unusual a nature—I have only an affirmative answer to give—such an answer as would I think occur to any one who had read my published writings. I am glad that you have been called as your letter expresses it, into "the way of holiness," and pray that the satisfaction which arises from the conscious-

ness of this, may not have its foundation in any error as to your own religious character.

Yours &c

W   C   B.

MANUSCRIPT: NYPL–GR (draft).

1. Teall, identifiable only as a young man in Madison, Wisconsin, had written on
November 5 saying that his heart had been "thrilled & exalted" in reading some of
Bryant's "productions," and asking whether their author was a Christian who had
"made his peace with his Maker, through simple faith in the Saviour." NYPL–GR.

1493.   *To* William W. Snell

Roslyn, Long Island
—November 16th. 1864.—

Dear Cousin

It is sometime since we heard from you,—more than a year I think, and
both my wife and I think that we ought to stir up your remembrance of us
a little, and ask you to let us know how you are getting on. I do not see that
you have gone to the war, as so many of your cloth have done; at least, I
have not met with your name in the list of killed and wounded. If you and
your family are in the land of the living I hope you will let us know; if you
are not we will excuse you.

I have lately printed for distribution among my friends a little collection of the hymns which I have written. A copy of it, I send you by mail.

We are all in our usual health, except Mrs. Godwin, who was almost
crushed to death in the disaster on the New York and New Haven Railroad,
about five weeks since. No bones, however, were broken, and she is in a way
of recovery. We are all sad at the prolongation of the war with all its mis-
eries, horror-struck at the iniquities perpetrated around us, but comforted
by the knowledge that great virtues are called forth, rejoicing in the result
of the late elections and confident tha a good Providence will order for the
best even those things which have the most unpromising aspect.

Julia is absent in town, but my wife desires her kind regards to you and
your family.

I am dear sir
very truly yours
W. C. BRYANT.

MANUSCRIPT: Catholic University Library ADDRESS: W^m. W. Snell.

1494.   *To* Julia Ward Howe

Roslyn   Nov. 21, 1864.

Dear Mrs. Howe.

I am sorry that your beautiful verses were so marred in the printing.[1]
If I had been in the office, to look at it before it went to the press, the errors

would not have been allowed to remain. Nobody however will lay it to your charge. I have had a paragraph inserted putting it right.

> I am, dear Madam,
> very truly yours,
> WM. C. BRYANT.

MANUSCRIPT: DuU ADDRESS: Mrs. Julia Ward Howe.

1. Julia Ward Howe (Mrs. Samuel Gridley Howe, 1819–1910), whose "Battle Hymn of the Republic" had been a spectacular success upon its publication in the *Atlantic Monthly* in February 1862, was invited by George Bancroft to offer a verse tribute to Bryant at the Century's festival on November 5. The first—and perhaps the only—woman ever to address the club, she responded with a poem in eleven stanzas, "A Leaf from the Bryant Chaplet," later printed in *Bryant Festival*, pp. 36–38. Years later she remembered the occasion as "the greatest public honor of my life" when she entered the hall on Bryant's arm, and then heard him refer to her in his address as "she who has written the most stirring lyric of the war." Julia Ward Howe, *Reminiscences, 1819–1899* (Boston and New York: Houghton, Mifflin, 1900), pp. 278–279.

Mrs. Howe's verse tribute was printed in the *EP* for November 16, where a misprint in the last stanza substituted "heart" for "breast," destroying the rhyme. This was corrected in the newspaper on the day Bryant wrote this letter.

1495. *To* Lydia H. H. Sigourney

> Roslyn, Long Island, N. Y.—
> —November 28th. 1864.—

My dear Mrs. Sigourney.

I thank you very much for the copy you have sent me of your "Past Meridian." I do not know that you have written anything which more engages the attention of the reader. It almost makes one in love with Old Age. You teach us how to grow old becomingly, wisely, genially, happily. I wonder not that the work has passed through so many editions.[1]

I certainly did not expect to see you at the commemoration of my birth day. The kind words you sent to those who gave out the invitations were more than my due.

I send you a little thing printed for private circulation,[2] which you may perhaps be willing to place in your library.

> I am, dear Madam,
> Cordially yours,
> W. C. BRYANT.

MANUSCRIPTS: ConnHS (final); NYPL–GR (draft) ADDRESS: Mrs. L. H. Sigourney.

1. Mrs. Sigourney's *Past Meridian* (New York and Boston, 1854), a volume of essays on the pleasures of old age, was often reprinted thereafter. With a letter to Bryant dated November 23, regretting that she had not been able to attend his birthday festival at the Century Club, Mrs. Sigourney had sent him a copy of this book. NYPL–GR.

2. Bryant's *Hymns* (1864).

1496.   To Bella Zilfa Spencer[1]

Roslyn, Long Island, N. Y.
November 28th. 1864.

My dear Mrs. Spencer.

I thank you for the good wishes you have so kindly expressed, and assure you, that I reciprocate them most cordially. Long life, if only accompanied with good health and a contented mind, is a great blessing and with these concomitants, I wish it to all my friends. But while I accept your friendly wishes to their fullest extent, I feel that I have no right to all the compliments with which you accompany them.

Your region, you tell me, is bright with the first new-fallen snow, and merry with the sound of sleighbells. Here, we have another sort of beauty—a little lingering green, in the lawn before my door, roses in bloom in my garden, and the *Sweet Alyssum*, blooming on, in spite of the autumnal frosts. If you were here, I could, in return for the imaginary sleigh ride at Watertown, gather you a small bouquet of the latest flowers of the year.

With my thanks to your friends for their kind wishes expressed through you, I am, Madam,

very truly yours,
WM C. BRYANT.

MANUSCRIPT: NYPL–BG ADDRESS: Mrs. Belle Z. Spencer

1. British-born Bella Z. Spencer (1840–1867), wife of the Union cavalry commander Colonel George Eliphaz Spencer (1836–1893), was a writer of popular tales living in Watertown, New York, near the Canadian border. The letter to which Bryant replies here is unrecovered.

1497.   To George Bancroft

Office of The Evening Post,
New York, Nov   29th   1864

Dear Mr. Bancroft.

The manuscript of my speech which you have, is in a very unsightly condition, besides being on paper of a size inconvenient for binding. I send you a better copy with what you wished my signature.[1]

When the proceedings are printed I hope to see a proof, that I may make my part correct.

I am dear sir
Cordially yours
W   C   BRYANT.

MANUSCRIPT: MHS ADDRESS: Hon   Geo. Bancroft.

1. See 1491.1.

1498. *To* Fanny Bryant Godwin

Office of The Evening Post,
New York, Nov. 29th   1864

Dear Fanny.

I want to be in town next Sunday and if it be not inconvenient to you I wish to come to No. 19 East 37th. Street on Saturday night.

Your mother is almost sick with a severe cold, but begins to mend a little—

Yours affectionately
W   C   BRYANT

MANUSCRIPT: NYPL–GR ADDRESS: Mrs. F. B   Godwin.

1499. *To* Richard H. Dana

Roslyn, Long Island   N Y.
November 30, 1864.

Dear Dana.

I did not by any means think you would come to the affair at the Century Club. I know your unwillingness to leave home and your valetudinarian habits, and expected, of course, that you would do in my case as you do in others. Besides, I feel that as one goes down the hill of life, he is less and less inclined to caper out of the trodden path. I find in myself the greatest unwillingness to go to any of our large towns on any public occasion, where I may be made an object of attention.

Your letter was very kind,[1] and was as long as it ought to have been. Short letters on such occasions, have the best luck, are more certain of being read, and if read do not tire the audience. A book is to be made of the proceedings of the evening, and your letter will have a place in it with the rest. Your son, who was so kind as to come, had some friendly words to say, for which I wish you would thank him.[2]

Mrs. Godwin was kept in her bed about [five?] weeks after her accident, the greater part of the time without the power of changing her place, except as she was moved. She now begins to get about her room, lamely of course, but is continually mending.

This is a beautiful day—a soft south west wind, the grass still green about my house, and roses and two other of the very hardy flowers in bloom in my garden, beneath a golden sunshine. But what frightful crimes are committed in the world of mankind! That attempt [to] set the whole city of New York on fire![3] Kind regards to all of your household.

Yours ever
W. C. BRYANT.

MANUSCRIPT: NYPL–GR ADDRESS: R   H. Dana Esq.

1. In his letter to the Century, Dana had written, "It is good for us to give honour where it is due; and it would be cheering to me to pay it to one who has done so much to throw beauty over our common life. As it is, I must be content at home with setting apart the time of your meeting together to thinking upon what you are all enjoying, and to going over by myself the many years to which our friend has added so much to gladden a protracted life." *Bryant Festival*, p. 16.

2. In his own address at the birthday festival, printed in *ibid.*, pp. 66–68, Richard H. Dana, Jr., after recalling that Bryant's "Thanatopsis," published in 1817, had "At once, . . . commanded its own place in the permanent literature of the English tongue," continued, "No poet, Sir, can hope for permanence to his fame unless he connects himself with something permanent in human nature. Mr. Bryant has always been true to Nature and to Freedom. . . . Never did he pervert his sacred trust of divine poetry to the service of fashion, or trade, or party. True to nature, nature was true to him."

3. On November 25 and 26, 1864, eight men sent secretly to New York by Jacob Thompson (1810–1885), former Mississippi congressman and United States secretary of the interior, and in 1864 operating in Canada as a Confederate agent, made largely unsuccessful efforts to burn ten leading hotels, as well as Barnum's Museum and two theaters. *EP*, November 26, 28, 29, 1864; Nevins, *War for the Union*, IV, 138.

1500.   *To* Simeon Draper?[1]

Office of The Evening Post,
New York, Dec 1st   1864.

Prof. J. W. Fowler[2] is an applicant for a place in the Custom House. I have no doubt of his qualifications in respect of either capacity or character. He is in politics zealously loyal, and a friend of the true cause from the beginning. I cannot therefore but wish him success.

W. C. BRYANT.

MANUSCRIPT: UVa.

1. See 1463.4.
2. Unidentified.

1501.   *To* William P. Fessenden

Office of The Evening Post,
New York, Dec. 2d   1864

Sir.

I am informed that the name of S. Bromberg Esq. of this city,[1] has been laid before you as that of a proper person to take charge of the Custom House at Pensacola, in the capacity of Collector. I have been acquainted with Mr. Bromberg for more than thirty years. I think him well fitted for the post he solicits, both by business habits, commercial and custom house experience and personal character, to say nothing of his political views, which have been, from the first, in harmony with those of the administration.

I am, sir,
very respectfully yours,
WM C. BRYANT.

MANUSCRIPT: UVa ADDRESS: To the Hon   Wm P. Fessenden / Secretary of the Treasury.
ENDORSED: Collector — Pensacola. / Florida. / — / S. Bromberg. / of N. Y. / Applicant. / — / Recommended by / Hon. W. C. Bryant / — .

1. Unidentified.

1502. *To* the United States Senate and House of Representatives
[New York? ante December 8, 1864]

The undersigned, citizens of the United States, respectfully represent
that the interest of the country, in their judgment, requires the passage of
a bill appropriating money for the founding and support of a national
home for totally disabled soldiers and sailors of the army and navy of the
United States.

Your memorialists, therefore, respectfully ask Congress to make a
suitable appropriation, or to take such other action in reference to the subject as the representatives of the people and the States shall deem proper
to promote an object of such vast national importance, and so pregnant
with the interests of thousands of citizens of the Union who have given up
all their best energies to their country, and who have been rendered help-
less by such devoted service.

[signed] WM. C. BRYANT [and others][1]

MANUSCRIPT: Unrecovered TEXT: Thirty-Eighth Congress, Second Session, Miscellaneous
Senate Document No. 3.

1. This letter was introduced as "Petition / of / William C. Bryant, Henry W.
Longfellow, Horace / Greeley, John A. Dix, U. S. Grant, and Others, / Citizens of the
United States." In addition to those named, it was signed by 109 persons and organi-
zations, including many prominent in various fields, such as poet and essayist Nathaniel
P. Willis, physicist Joseph Henry, superintendent of Union army nurses Clara Barton,
historian George Bancroft, architect Richard Morris Hunt, publisher George P. Put-
nam, New York *Times* editor Henry J. Raymond, manufacturer Peter Cooper, Texas
Unionist Andrew Jackson Hamilton, Columbia University professor Francis Lieber,
Harvard chemist Wolcott Gibbs, copper merchant William E. Dodge, and showman
Phineas T. Barnum. Attached to the document is an undated and unsigned letter to
the editors of the *EP* reporting the incorporation in New York of a National Literary
Association for the purpose of raising funds to establish and maintain a National Home
for Fatally Disabled Soldiers and Sailors on the east bank of the Hudson River fifteen
miles north of New York.
A United States Naval Home for "disabled and decrepit Navy officers, seamen and
Marines" had been established in Philadelphia in 1831. A National Home for Disabled
Volunteer Soldiers was created by Congress on March 3, 1865—perhaps in response to
this petition—and such institutions were opened soon thereafter at Dayton, Ohio; Mil-
waukee, Wisconsin; and Hampton, Virginia. None, however, seems to have been located
near New York. *Dictionary of American History*, rev. ed. (New York: Scribner's [1976]),
VI, 336–337; letter to the senior editor, dated June 23, 1981, from Colonel Robert N.
Waggoner, Chief, Historical Services Division, Department of the Army, Washington,
D.C.

1503.   *To* Salmon P. Chase

Roslyn, Long Island,
December 10th. 1864.

My dear sir.

I cannot let such an occasion as your appointment to the Office of Chief Justice of the Supreme Court of the Federal Government pass without a word expressive of my extreme satisfaction.[1] I congratulate you personally on bringing to the office all the qualities it requires; I congratulate Mr. Lincoln on having bestowed it so worthily; I congratulate the country on possessing, in its most responsible judicial officer, one to whom it can look for the wise and enlightened adjustment of the many momentous questions which will arise out of the present new order of things and which will render the post you fill, more important to the country, for many years after the war shall have ended, than the Presidency itself.

I am, dear sir,
very truly yours,
W. C. BRYANT.

MANUSCRIPT: HSPa ADDRESS: Hon   S. P. Chase.

1. See 1478.4. Historians generally agree with Allan Nevins that "Chase had such eminent gifts that in due course he took rank among the great American jurists." *War for the Union*, IV, 119.

1504.   *To* Julia S. Bryant

Office of The Evening Post,
New York, Dec 12th   1864
Monday morning.

Dear Julia.

I send with this a basket of grapes for Fanny—and you too if you do not come out this afternoon—which I would advise you to do. On Saturday I got as far as Glen Cove, but the weather was so thick that we put back. Miss Howard[1] was with me, and came in this morning. Miss [Jerusha?] Dewey came a little before eight o'clock.

Mr. Godwin has just told me that you were not well—so I suppose you will not come today. When you come, please bring out Ellen [Mrs. Benham?][2] unless you are dissatisfied with her— Or make an engagement as to wages &c. and let her come out *this afternoon*, as I shall go back today. It is possible that tonight, unless the weather should moderate, that the boat may be frozen in tonight.

I have heard of the invitation to Mr. [Charles?] Butler's but do not find it convenient to come. I write with fingers yet stiff with cold.

I hope you will soon be well again— All goes on well at Roslyn. Your mother agrees to take Ellen.

Yours affectionately
W. C. B.

MANUSCRIPT: NYPL–GR.

1. Possibly Caroline R. Howard; see Letter 1484.
2. Brackets and question mark are Bryant's.

1505. *To* Miss Valentine[1]

New York   Dec   22d   1864.

Dear Madam.

I have not forgotten your request for books to be sent, I think, to one of the Hospitals, that at Willet's Point—for the reading of the Soldiers. In the package accompanying this I send four volumes.

I am, Madam
very respectfully yours
WM C. BRYANT.

MANUSCRIPT: BLR ADDRESS: Miss Valentine.

1. Probably a sister or daughter of James Valentine (1254.1).

1506. *To* Lydia Maria Francis Child[1]

New York   Dec. 26. 1864.

My dear Mrs. Child.

I give you many thanks for the copy of your charming book—"Looking towards Sunset."[2] You are like some artists who excel in sunset views. You give the closing stage of human life an atmosphere of the richest lights and warmest hues, and make its clouds add to its glory. My wife and I have read your book with great delight.

May I ask you to accept a little volume which I have brought out within the year and which you may not have seen. I send it by mail.[3]

I am, madam,
very truly yours.
WM C. BRYANT.

MANUSCRIPT: YCAL ADDRESS: Mrs. L. M. Child. PUBLISHED (*in part*): *Life*, II, 213.

1. Lydia Maria Francis Child (1802–1880) was a popular novelist as well as an Abolitionist editor and writer.
2. *Looking Toward Sunset, From Sources Old and New, Original and Selected* (Boston, 1865).
3. Probably *Thirty Poems* (1864); see 1370.1.

1507.   *To* George Harvey?[1]

Office of The Evening Post,
New York, Dec. 31st. 1864.

My dear sir.

I have both your letters, one of the 2d and the other of the 10th, of December.[2] Leeds & Miner have the reputation of being perfectly responsible persons.[3] They have now the invoice and as I am informed the affidavit and will attend to the sale of your pictures. When it takes place I will see that attention is called to it in the Evening Post. I thank you, by anticipation, for the view you have made of my place at Roslyn. Considerable change has been made in it since you saw it, but your picture will prove a pleasant reminder of its aspect in the days when you gave us the pleasure of your visit. I suppose that Leeds & Miner will send the picture to me as soon as they get it from the Custom House.

I rejoice that you remain so constant and zealous a friend of our country. I could indeed expect nothing else from your past course. I do not think that our differences with the English government will come to an outbreak yet I can see nothing but extreme folly in the contempt it has shown for our goodwill. I do not print your lines on "Progress" not because their satire is [not?][4] understood, but because the severity is greater than is perhaps politic.

I thank you for offering to contribute to the "Portfolio."[5] The size of the pasteboard on which the sketches are fastened is this.

24 inches

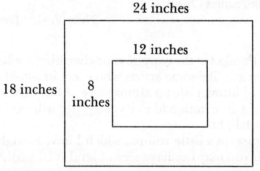

12 inches

18 inches   8
inches

The outer parallelogram gives the dimensions of the entire sheet eighteen inches by twenty four. The inner parallelogram gives the space occupied by the sketch or drawing. If you send the drawing, the board might be procured here and the drawing attached to it.

Before I hear from you again I think the sympathizers with secession in your country will have nearly given up their hopes of the success of the rebellion.

I am, dear sir,
very truly yours
W. C. BRYANT.

MANUSCRIPT: NYHS.

1. The recipient of this letter is identified conjecturally. It is uncertain when Harvey (see Letter 1080), who lived in his native England, last visited the United States. *DAA.*

2. Neither letter has been recovered.

3. Henry H. Leeds (1801–1870) and Allen B. Miner were leading New York art auctioneers, with offices at 8 Wall Street. New York *Times,* March 13, 1870, p. 5.

4. There is no word between "is" and "understood."

5. At the birthday festival on November 5 Bryant had been given a portfolio of sketches by forty-six artist members of the Century Club, who expressed their "consideration of the sympathy you have ever manifested towards the Artists, and the high rank you have ever accorded to art." *Bryant Festival,* pp. 38–42, 87–88. These sketches, which Julia Bryant willed to the club, are described in Charles Downing Lay and Theodore Bolton, *Works of Art Silver and Furniture Belonging to the Century Association* (New York: Century Association, 1943), pp. 43–46. No work by Harvey, however, is listed therein.

1508. *To* Jacob Beakley[1]

[New York?] Dec 1864.

My Dear Sir

Will you oblige me by laying before the proper officers of the New York Homoeopathic Medical College, this letter which I desire may be received as a formal resignation of my office as President of the Council of the College in which I have never felt at my ease.[2] I take this occasion to thank the other officers of the institution particularly the professional ones for the forbearance they have shown towards my deficiencies while I have held the office.

I am sir
very truly yours
W C BRYANT

MANUSCRIPT: NYPL–GR (draft) ADDRESS: Dr. Bleakly [*sic*] ENDORSED: My letter to Dr. Bleakly.

1. See Letter 1174.

2. But, according to the college's historian, Bryant continued to serve as president of the Board of Trustees, or Council, of the New York Medical College until 1872, when he resigned after ten years in that office. Leonard Paul Wershub, *One Hundred Years of Medical Progress: A History of the New York Medical College Flower and Fifth Avenue Hospitals* (Springfield, Illinois: Charles C. Thomas [1967]), p. 45.

1509. *To* William Stoodley Gookin[1]

[1864?]

My dear sir.

I am really obliged to you for the opportunity which you have given me to look over your copy of my poem entitled Thanatopsis which you have so beautifully illuminated. What you tell me of not having models before you increased my admiration. You have shown extraordinary ingenuity in varying the forms of letters and the embellishments you have given them and have shown a very uncommon taste both in outline and color. It makes me quite proud of my verses to know that they have been worthy of so much pains and of being expressed in such beautiful characters.

I found on the inside of the box which contains your superb volume[2] a request that I should send it to Mr. Bailey at A. T. Stewart's warehouse[3] which I have done and am, with my thanks

Your [obliged?] Servant
W   C   BRYANT.

MANUSCRIPT: NYPL–GR (draft) ADDRESS: Gookin.

1. William Stoodley Gookin (1799–post 1872) was a portrait and fancy painter and daguerreotypist based in Dover, New Hampshire. DAA.
2. Although several elaborate editions of Thanatopsis illustrated by other artists appeared during the second half of the nineteenth century, none of those listed in the National Union Catalogue is attributed to Gookin.
3. In 1862 Alexander Turney Stewart (1803–1876) had opened the largest retail store in the world on Broadway at Ninth Street, New York. This was bought in 1896 by John Wanamaker (1838–1922), a Philadelphia merchant. Bailey has not been further identified.

Abbreviations and Short Titles

ACAB. Appleton's Cyclopaedia of American Biography. Edd. James Grant Wilson and John Fiske. 6 vols. New York: D. Appleton, 1900.

BDAC. Biographical Dictionary of the American Congress, 1774–1961. Washington: United States Government Printing Office, 1961.

Bigelow, *Retrospections.* Bigelow, John. *Retrospections of an Active Life.* . . . 5 vols. New York: The Baker & Taylor Co., 1909–1913.

"Bryant and Illinois." "Bryant and Illinois: Further Letters of the Poet's Family." Edd. Keith Huntress and Fred W. Lorch. *New England Quarterly,* 16 (December 1943), 634–647.

Bryant, "Diary, 1857–1858." Manuscript "W. C. Bryant's Diary of Travel Abroad, May 1857–June 1858" in 2 vols. in Goddard–Roslyn Collection, New York Public Library.

Bryant Festival. The Bryant Festival at "The Century," November 5, M.DCCC.LXIV. New York: D. Appleton and Company, . . . 1865.

"Bryant: Illinois Landowner." Baxter, David J. "William Cullen Bryant: Illinois Landowner." *Western Illinois Regional Studies,* 1 (Spring 1978), 1–14.

Bryant, "Irving." Bryant, William Cullen. "Washington Irving, A Discourse on his Life, Character and Genius, Delivered Before the New-York Historical Society, at the Academy of Music, in New York, April 3, 1863," in *Orations and Addresses by William Cullen Bryant.* New York: Putnam's, 1873. Pp. [95]–154.

DAA. Groce, George C., and Wallace, David H. *The New-York Historical Society's Dictionary of Artists in America, 1564–1860.* New Haven and London: Yale University Press [1957].

EP. New York *Evening Post.*

Forbes, *Letters and Recollections. Letters and Recollections of John Murray Forbes.* Ed. Sarah Forbes Hughes. 2 vols. Boston and New York: Houghton, Mifflin, 1899.

Goddard, *Roslyn Harbor.* Goddard, Conrad Godwin. *The Early History of Roslyn Harbor, Long Island.* Printed by the Author [1972].

Hendrick, *Lincoln's War Cabinet.* Hendrick, Burton J. *Lincoln's War Cabinet.* Garden City, New York: Doubleday [1961].

Hoyt, "Bryant Correspondence." Hoyt, William D. Jr., "Some Unpublished Bryant Correspondence (I)," *New York History,* 21 (January 1940), 63–70; "Some Unpublished Bryant Correspondence (II)," *New York History,* 21 (April 1940), 193–204.

Life. Godwin, Parke. *A Biography of William Cullen Bryant, With Extracts from His Private Correspondence.* 2 vols. New York: D. Appleton, 1883.

Longfellow, *Letters. The Letters of Henry Wadsworth Longfellow.* Ed. Andrew Hilen. 4 vols. Cambridge: The Belknap Press of Harvard University Press, 1966–1972.

LT II. *Letters of a Traveller. Second Series.* By William Cullen Bryant. New York: D. Appleton, 1859.

Mott, *American Journalism.* Mott, Frank Luther. *American Journalism: A History of Newspapers in the United States Through 250 Years 1690 to 1940.* New York: Macmillan, 1941.

NAD Exhibition Record. National Academy of Design Exhibition Record, 1826–1860. 2 vols. New York: The New-York Historical Society, 1943.

Nevins, *Emergence of Lincoln.* Nevins, Allan. *The Emergence of Lincoln.* . . . 2 vols. New York and London: Scribner's [1950].

Nevins, *Evening Post.* Nevins, Allan. *The Evening Post: A Century of Journalism.* New York: Boni & Liveright [1922].

Nevins, *Fish.* Nevins, Allan. *Hamilton Fish: The Inner History of the Grant Administration.* . . . 2 vols. New York: Frederick Ungar [1957].

Nevins, *Ordeal.* Nevins, Allan. *Ordeal of the Union.* . . . 2 vols. New York: Scribner's [1947].

Nevins, *War for the Union.* Nevins, Allan. *The War for the Union.* . . . 4 vols. New York: Scribner's [1959–1971].

Nye, *Bancroft.* Nye, Russell B. *George Bancroft: Brahmin Rebel.* New York: Knopf, 1945.

Poems (1876). *Poems by William Cullen Bryant.* Collected and Arranged by the Author. Illustrated by One Hundred Engravings from Drawings by Birket Foster, Harry Fenn, Alfred Fredericks, and Others. New York: D. Appleton [1876].

Spivey, *Bryant Cautions and Counsels Lincoln.* Spivey, Herman E. *Bryant Cautions and Counsels Lincoln.* Reprinted from *Tennessee Studies in Literature* VI. Knoxville: University of Tennessee Press, 1961.

Thirty Poems. Bryant, William Cullen. *Thirty Poems.* New York: D. Appleton. 1864.

Thomas and Hyman, *Stanton.* Thomas, Benjamin P., and Hyman, Harold M. *Stanton: The Life and Times of Lincoln's Secretary of War.* New York: Knopf, 1962.

Vail, *Knickerbocker Birthday.* Vail, R. W. G. *Knickerbocker Birthday: A Sesqui-Centennial History of the New-York Historical Society, 1804–1954.* New York: The New-York Historical Society, 1954.

Van Deusen, *Seward.* Van Deusen, Glydon G. *William Henry Seward.* New York: Oxford University Press, 1967.

War of the Rebellion. The War of the Rebellion. . . . *Official Records of the Union and Confederate Armies.* 128 vols. Washington: United States Government Printing Office, 1880–1901.

Welles, *Diary. Diary of Gideon Welles, Secretary of the Navy Under Lincoln and Johnson.* Edd. Howard K. Beale and Alan W. Brownsword. 3 vols. New York: Norton [1960].

Index of Recipients
Volume IV

References are to Letter numbers.

Alexander, Mrs. L. G., 1381
Allibone, Samuel Austin, 1076, 1147
Appleton, William Henry, 1075
Atlantic Monthly, Editor, 1200

Ballard, Frank W., 1489
Balmanno, Robert, 1221
Bancroft, Elizabeth Davis (Mrs. George Bancroft), 1106, 1108, 1133
Bancroft, George, 1063, 1100, 1105, 1157, 1246, 1480, 1490, 1491, 1497
Barney, Hiram, 1209, 1217, 1222, 1231, 1232, 1261, 1343, 1430
Beakley, Jacob, 1174, 1508
Berrian, Hobart, 1305
Bierstadt, Albert, 1279
Bigelow, John, 1008, 1042, 1044, 1060, 1066, 1077, 1087, 1094, 1120, 1126, 1127, 1132, 1136, 1250, 1309, 1333, 1342, 1421
Bliss, Alexander, 1394
Blood, Benjamin Paul, 1336
Bogart, Daniel, 1277, 1322, 1334, 1349, 1406
Bonner, Robert, 1137, 1153, 1171, 1183, 1187, 1199, 1244
Brown University, President of?, 1097
Bryant, Cullen, 1168, 1249
Bryant, Cyrus, 1078, 1354
Bryant, Frances Fairchild, 1115, 1121, 1143, 1165, 1167, 1186, 1193, 1214, 1215, 1256, 1257, 1273, 1275, 1291, 1292, 1293, 1297, 1298, 1301, 1302, 1320, 1341, 1344, 1345, 1352, 1359, 1364, 1368, 1371, 1380, 1385, 1396, 1411, 1416, 1417, 1418, 1419, 1434, 1435, 1436, 1437, 1438, 1440, 1441, 1442, 1445, 1446, 1447, 1449, 1451, 1452, 1453, 1455, 1457, 1459, 1460, 1461, 1463, 1464, 1465, 1466, 1469
Bryant, John Howard, 1025, 1062, 1079, 1112, 1131, 1139, 1144, 1148, 1155, 1158, 1161, 1169, 1185, 1223, 1228, 1229, 1247, 1248, 1251, 1255, 1355, 1391, 1408, 1431, 1454, 1470, 1472
Bryant, Julia Sands, 1059, 1061, 1073, 1086, 1101, 1103, 1170, 1227, 1240, 1243, 1362, 1363, 1471, 1504

Bryant, Mr. & Mrs. Samuel P., 1443
Bryant, W[illiam?] C[ullen?], 1473
[Bucky?] Mary E., 1402

Chapman, John Gadsby, 1013, 1016, 1068
Chase, Salmon Portland, 1236, 1245, 1313, 1369, 1384, 1426, 1503
Chatelain, Jean-Baptiste François Ernest de, 1393
Cheney, Theseus Apoleon, 1439
Child, Lydia Maria Frances, 1506
Christian Intelligencer (editor Elbert Stothoff Porter?), 1353
Clay, Cassius Marcellus, 1141
Cline, George B., 1357
Codding, Maria P., 1488
Colgate University Trustees ("Madison University"), 1429
Colton, G. L., 1230
Cox, Samuel Hanson, 1306, 1375
Cozzens, Frederick Swartwout, 1056
Cronkhite, James P., 1038

Dana, Charlotte R., 1145, 1194, 1335
Dana, Richard Henry, 1065, 1088, 1107, 1146, 1152, 1172, 1314, 1338, 1387, 1481, 1499
Messrs. Derby & Jackson, 1113
Dewey, Orville, 1028, 1055, 1091, 1098, 1099, 1140, 1151, 1156, 1211, 1242, 1278, 1286, 1339, 1348, 1358, 1366, 1372
Draper, Simeon?, 1500
Durfee, Calvin, 1104

Eben, Charles Theodore, 1388
Edmonds, John Worth, 1128
Emerson, Ralph Waldo, 1403, 1405
Evening Post, 1026, 1040, 1047?, 1053, 1177
Everett, Edward, 1197

Faulkner, A. D., 1164
Fay, Theodore Sedgwick, 1287
Fessenden, William Pitt, 1323, 1501
Field, Alfred, 1017, 1116, 1350

Field, Charlotte Errington (Mrs. Alfred Field), 1017, 1432
Field, Edwin Wilkins, 1051, 1351
Field, Ferdinand Emans, 1057, 1252
Field, Mary Bryan Stone, 1397
Fields, James Thomas, 1175, 1235, 1326, 1379, 1382, 1414, 1476, 1485
Folsom, Charles, 1178
Foote, Andrew Hull, 1303
Forbes, John Murray, 1238, 1239, 1262, 1296, 1479

Gallup, Charles, 1280
Gardner, L. M., 1119
Gibson, Christiana M., 1034, 1058, 1090, 1130, 1159, 1398, 1450
Gilman, Daniel Coit, 1072, 1114, 1329, 1477
Godwin, Fanny Bryant, 1039, 1050, 1226, 1274, 1317, 1365, 1378, 1498
Godwin, Parke, 1361
Goodman, A. T., 1295
Gookin, William Stoodley, 1509
Gourlie, John Hamilton, 1009, 1210
Gray, John Franklin, 1035
Green, William Henry?, 1331
Richard Griffin & Co., 1110

Hall, Samuel Carter, 1052
Hardinge, Emma, 1267
Harris, J. Dennis, 1163
Hart, C[harles?] H[enry?], 1307
Harvey, George, 1080, 1507?
Henderson, Isaac, 1012
Hillhouse, Thomas, 1294
Holmes, Oliver Wendell, 1403
Howard, Caroline R., 1484
Howe, Julia Ward, 1494
Hudson, Henry Norman, 1346
Hull, A. Cooke, 1340
Hyde, Thomas C. P., 1373

Jay, John, 1124
Johnson, Oliver, 1284, 1389
Jônain, Pierre-Abraham, 1310

Kensett, John Frederick, 1410
Ketchum, Morris, 1412
Kingman, Bradford, 1241, 1374
Kirkland, Caroline Matilda Stansbury, 1029, 1370
Kirkland, Elizabeth, 1377

Laun, Adolf, 1282, 1311
Leach Giro, William, 1030
Lee, D. W., 1111
Leupp, Charles Mortimer, 1032
Messrs. Lever & Francis, 1332
Lewis, Sarah S., 1422, 1448

Lincoln, Abraham, 1149, 1162, 1180, 1182, 1188, 1190, 1191, 1192, 1195, 1196, 1201, 1202, 1205, 1207, 1219, 1224, 1233, 1253, 1264, 1269, 1283, 1290, 1299, 1337, 1423, 1427, 1458, 1478
Lincoln, Solomon, Jr., 1218
Messrs. J. B. Lippincott & Co., 1206
Longfellow, Henry Wadsworth, 1383, 1401
Long Island Fair, Committee of the, 1390
Loring, Charles G., 1328
Low, Abiel Abbot, 1413
Lowell, James Russell, 1200, 1403
Luquer, Eloise Elizabeth Payne, 1404, 1409, 1415

Macdonough, August R., 1486
Manning, W. C., 1074
Massett, Stephen C., 1420
Mayer, Brantz, 1125
Mercier, Victor, 1070
Mitchell, Ellen Theresa Shaw, 1037, 1281, 1456, 1482
Moore, Augusta, 1444
Morgan, Edwin Denison, 1123, 1134, 1138, 1276, 1312, 1315, 1319, 1327, 1347, 1376
Morris, George Pope, 1135
Moulton, Joseph White, 1330
Moulton, Leonice Marston Sampson (Mrs. Joseph White Moulton), 1033, 1082, 1220, 1225, 1234, 1254, 1259, 1265, 1268, 1308, 1324, 1467
Munroe, John & Co., 1041

Nelson, Lorenzo, 1118
Newbold, Miss, 1216

Orr, Hector, 1093, 1102
Osgood, Samuel, 1258
Owen, Robert Dale, 1015, 1048, 1285
Owen, Mary Jane Robinson (Mrs. Robert Dale Owen), 1023

Paton, John Brown, 1092
Pease, E. D., 1386
Perkins, F. S., 1122
Pierce, Henry Lillie, 1084
Porter, Elbert Stothoff? (editor, Christian Intelligencer), 1253
Porter, G[eorge?] W., 1129, 1474
Powers, Hiram, 1166
Powers, Horatio Nelson, 1288
Putnam, George Palmer, 1150

Rice, Harvey, 1356
Richards, Edward E., 1204
Rubini, Rocco, 1010

Sedgwick, Charles Frederick, Jr., 1360
Sedgwick, Elizabeth Ellery, 1014

Sedgwick, Henry Dwight, Jr., 1289
Sedgwick, Theodore III, 1117
Seevoss, E. B., 1081
Sherman, C. E. K., 1081
Sigourney, Lydia Howard Huntley, 1367, 1483, 1495
Smith, Buckingham, 1007
Snell, William Wingate, 1260, 1493
Spencer, Bella Zilfa, 1496
Stabler, Frances D., 1085
Stanton, Edwin McMasters, 1304, 1392, 1475
Stillman, Thomas Edgar, 1271
Sumner, Charles, 1043, 1266

Teall, O. D., 1492
Tefft, Israel Keech, 1096
Thompson, Cephas Giovanni, 1011, 1045
Messrs. Ticknor & Fields, 1400
Tilden, Samuel Jones, 1263
Tillson, Christiana H., 1468

Unidentified, 1024, 1067, 1071, 1083, 1181, 1198, 1272, 1316

United States Senate and House of Representatives, 1502
Valentine, Miss (of Roslyn?), 1505
Verplanck, Gulian Crommelin, 1154, 1425
Vinton, Francis, 1399

Walker, James P., 1109
Wallace, A. S., 1300
Ward, Townsend, 1179
Waterston, Anna Cabot Lowell Quincy (Mrs. Robert Cassie Waterston), 1095, 1173, 1176, 1321, 1433
Waterston, Robert Cassie, 1018, 1019, 1020, 1021, 1022, 1031, 1036, 1046, 1049, 1054, 1069, 1089, 1160, 1173, 1184, 1189, 1203, 1318, 1321, 1428, 1462, 1487
Webster, Sarah Morris Fish, 1395
Welles, Gideon, 1212, 1213, 1237, 1270, 1424
Wickham, W. H., 1081
Willis, Richard Storrs, 1027, 1064
Wilson, James Grant, 1142
Winthrop, Robert Charles, 1208
Woods, John H., 1407
Wool, John Ellis, 1325

Index

The numbers refer to pages.
An asterisk marks a page containing principal biographical data.

Abbott, Gorham Dummer 71, 72
Adams, John 165
Adams & Co. 107
Addison, Joseph 161
Adler, George J. 123
Albert Edward, Prince of Wales 174
Alden, Dr. & Mrs. Joseph 329, 330, 374–375, 376
Alden, William Livingston 171
Alexander, Francis 335
Alexander, L. G. (Mrs. Francis Alexander) 334, 335
Allibone, Samuel Austin 95, 157, 158
Ames, C. G. 394, 395*, 407
Andrew, John Albion 229, 230*, 341
Andrews, Amos 283, 284
Ann (Bryant servant) 115, 376
"Anonyma" (Catherine Waters) 291–292
Antoninus Pius 15, 16
Appleton, D., & Co. 44, 45, 79, 333, 334, 354
Appleton, William Henry 94, 130
Ariosto, Ludovico 8, 59, 63*
Arthur, William 257, 258
Attila 60
Avery, John 118

Bailey (of A. T. Stewart's) 432
Baker, George Augustus 306
Ballard, Frank W. 170, 171, 420
Balmanno, Alexander 217
Balmanno, Mr. & Mrs. Robert 217
Bancroft, Elizabeth Davis (Mrs. George Bancroft) 115, 119, 120, 121, 145, 146, 249, 347
Bancroft, George 3, 80, 87, 88, 108, 114, 115, 119, 121, 164, 165, 175, 234, 243, 248, 249, 271, 342, 347, 367, 415, 416, 420, 421, 423, 424, 427
Banks, Nathaniel Prentiss 96, 97*, 99, 100
Barker, Jacob 46, 47
Barney, Hiram 11, 85*, 193, 199, 200, 202, 206, 209, 210, 215, 217, 223, 224, 251, 252, 312, 313, 340, 370, 371, 403
Barney, Mrs. (Hiram?) 327

Barnum, Phineas Taylor 427
Bartholomew, Edward Sheffield 6, 35*
Bartlett (William O.?) 129, 130
Barton, Clara 427
Bates, Edward 139, 140*, 144, 200, 254
Baylies, William 301–302
Beakley, Jacob 176*, 431
Beecher, Henry Ward 91, 143, 175, 341, 348
Beekman (James William?) 381, 382
Bellows, Henry Whitney 153–154, 160, 194, 243, 384, 393
(Benham?) Ellen 428, 429
Bennett, James Gordon 230
Béranger, Pierre Jean de 137, 149
Berrian, Chandler 46
Berrian, Hobart 284, 285
Berrian, William 46, 47*, 285
Bierstadt, Albert 3, 259*, 263
Bigelow, Jane Poultney (Mrs. John Bigelow) 1, 13, 66, 86, 90, 92, 97, 105, 111, 130, 139, 145, 148, 237, 287, 304, 311, 312, 392
Bigelow, John 1, 4, 9, 11, 12, 29, 31, 64, 65, 66, 78–79, 85, 86, 90, 92, 93, 95, 98, 104, 105, 108, 110, 129, 134, 137, 139, 140, 144, 146, 147, 148, 149, 153, 156, 183, 193, 194, 196, 200, 218, 234, 235, 236, 237, 238, 244, 245, 253, 286, 287, 303, 311, 312, 339, 341, 357, 362, 363, 367, 376
Bishop (English doctor in Naples) 20
Bixby (tradesman?) 153
Black & Bachelder 213
Blair, Francis Preston (1791–1876) 144
Blair, Francis Preston (1821–1875) 129, 131*, 144, 189
Blair, Montgomery 414
Blancard (boardinghouse keeper) 131, 273–274
Bleecker, A. Lispenard 217, 218
Bleecker, Anthony J. 217–218
Bliss, Alexander 346, 347
Bliss, Elizabeth Davis (see Bancroft, Elizabeth Davis)
Blood, Benjamin Paul 306, 307
Bogart, Daniel 262*, 297, 305, 316, 353

440 LETTERS OF WILLIAM CULLEN BRYANT

Bogart, Peter 381
Boggs, William G. 299–300
Bolingbroke, Henry St. John, 1st viscount 412
Bonaparte, Louis Napoleon (Napoleon III) 130, 131, 137, 138, 287
Bonner, Robert 3, 79, 149*, 162, 174, 184, 185, 187, 204, 233
Booth, Mary H. C. 420, 421
Borland, Solon 219
Borrow, George 318
Bouterwek, Friedrich 123
Brady, Matthew 80
Brewster, Miss (singer at Naples) 28, 29
Briggs (office applicant) 212
Bright, John 257, 258
Bromberg, S. 426, 427
Brown, George Loring 44, 46
Brown, John (of Osawatomie) 1, 81, 130, 133, 139, 140, 179
Brown, Joseph Emerson 396, 397
Brown (Brooklyn artist?) 350
(Brown University, President of?) 113
Browning, Elizabeth Barrett (Mrs. Robert Browning) 1, 7, 8, 9, 54*, 71
Browning, Robert 1, 7, 8, 9, 54*, 71, 72
Bryant, Arthur 238, 284, 285, 321–322, 323, 360, 361
Bryant, Austin 87, 220, 221, 359, 360, 361
Bryant, Charity ("Chatty") 360, 361
Bryant, Cullen (Cyrus' son) 97, 98*, 134, 172, 173, 195, 236, 245, 324
Bryant, Cyrus 97, 98, 134, 193, 195, 222, 245, 318, 319, 359, 360
Bryant, Edward Raymond (son of Austin Bryant) 360, 361
Bryant, Elijah (son of John Bryant) 31*, 100, 151, 186, 345, 359
Bryant, Frances Fairchild (Mrs. William Cullen Bryant) 1, 3, 4, 5, 6, 7, 8, 9, 10, 12, 13, 16, 17, 18, 19–20, 21, 22, 23, 24, 25, 26, 27, 28, 29–30, 31, 36–37, 38, 40, 41, 43, 44, 45, 46, 47–48, 49–50, 51, 53, 54, 55, 56, 57, 65, 66, 67, 69, 71, 72, 73, 76, 77, 80, 82, 84, 85, 86, 87, 88, 89, 90, 91, 92, 94, 98, 100, 101, 105, 106, 107, 108, 111, 112, 113, 114, 115, 119, 120, 121, 124, 130, 131, 138, 141, 142, 145, 151, 152, 153, 155, 161, 164, 165, 166, 167, 170, 171, 172, 173, 175, 176, 177, 178, 185, 186, 190, 193, 194, 195, 200, 207, 210, 211, 213, 214, 218, 219, 220, 221, 226, 230, 231, 232, 233, 236, 245, 248, 250, 251, 260, 261, 263, 264, 267, 271, 272, 273, 274, 275, 277, 278, 280, 282, 287, 293–294, 296, 303, 304, 309, 310, 311, 312, 313, 315, 316, 317, 318, 319, 321, 323, 324, 325, 326, 327, 328, 333, 334, 337, 339, 340, 341, 347, 355, 358, 360, 361, 362–363, 370, 372, 373, 374, 375, 377, 378, 379,

380, 381, 382, 383, 385, 386, 387, 389, 390, 391, 392, 393, 394, 395, 396, 398, 399, 400, 401–402, 403, 404, 405, 406, 407–408, 410, 416, 419, 422, 425, 429
Bryant, Harriett Wiswall (Mrs. John Howard Bryant) 31, 87, 98, 100, 142, 151, 186, 220, 221, 345
Bryant, Henrietta B. Plummer (Mrs. Arthur Bryant) 361, 362
Bryant, John Howard 3, 29, 31, 78, 87, 99, 122, 123, 134, 135, 142, 150, 151, 154, 158, 162, 163, 165, 168, 169, 173, 183, 186, 195, 218, 220, 221, 222, 226, 235, 236, 238, 247, 248, 319, 345, 354, 359, 360, 361, 371, 393, 394–395, 407, 408, 409
Bryant, Julia (Cyrus' daughter) 360, 361
Bryant, Julia Everett (Mrs. Cyrus Bryant) 195, 222
Bryant, Julia Sands 3, 5, 10, 13, 16, 23, 24, 25, 26, 27, 28, 31, 36, 37, 40, 41, 42, 44, 48, 53, 54, 56, 66, 69, 76, 77, 82, 84, 85, 86, 88, 91, 92, 94, 98, 103, 105, 107, 109, 111, 112, 113, 114, 115, 116, 119, 120, 121, 126, 130, 131, 141, 142, 145, 155, 164, 166, 167, 170, 171, 173, 174, 175, 177, 178, 185, 186, 190, 211, 213, 216, 220, 221, 226, 230, 232, 233, 236, 248, 249, 250, 251, 261, 263, 264, 273, 274, 277, 278, 282, 287, 294–295, 296, 303, 304, 312, 313, 317, 319, 323, 324, 325, 328, 338?, 342, 352, 359, 362, 370, 372, 373, 374, 375, 376, 379, 380, 381, 383, 384, 386, 387, 388, 389, 390, 391, 394, 395, 399–400, 401, 402, 404, 405, 406, 407, 408, 416, 419, 422, 428, 431
Bryant, Julian Edward (son of Cyrus Bryant) 31*, 243, 284*, 322
Bryant, Marcus (son of Cyrus Bryant) 361, 362
Bryant, Dr. & Mrs. Peter 132, 133, 147, 231, 331, 418
Bryant, Peter (son of Cyrus Bryant) 360, 361
Bryant, Dr. Philip 331
Bryant, Mr. & Mrs. Samuel P. 382, 383
Bryant, Sarah Louisa (daughter of Austin Bryant) 361, 362
Bryant, William Austin (son of Austin Bryant) 359
Bryant, W[illiam?] C[ullen?] (soldier) 409, 410
Bryant, Wm C., & Co. 29, 79, 113, 148, 218, 248, 334
Buchanan, James 13, 14*, 31, 66, 69, 70, 78, 86, 96, 97, 99, 101, 174, 183, 197, 201, 202, 229, 230
Buck, Dr. & Mrs. Edward 109, 110
[Bucky?] Mary E. 351
Buffon, George Louis Le clerc, comte de 137, 149

Bulwer-Lytton, Edward George Earle Lytton, first Baron Lytton 7
Bungay, George W. 383
Burdell, Harvey 97
Burgoyne, John 240
Burnside, Ambrose Everett 255*, 279, 290, 291
Burt, T. M. 215
Busteed, Richard 265, 266
Butcher, John 262, 289*, 386?, 394?
Butler, Andrew Jackson 295
Butler, Benjamin Franklin (1795–1858) 85
Butler, Benjamin Franklin (1818–1893) 243, 295*
Butler, Charles 154, 428?
Butler, Prescott 394
Butler, William Allen 348
Butterfield, Daniel 243
Byron, Anna Isabella Milbanke (Lady Byron) 7, 65

Caesar, Julius 38, 43
Cairns, Ann Eliza (Mrs. William F. Cairns) 172, 250, 251, 257, 278, 282, 311, 373, 379, 386, 394, 399, 401, 404, 407
Cairns, William F. 171, 172, 226
Callison, Mrs. (daughter of O. W. Pollitz) 380
Cameron, Simon 189, 192, 193, 197*, 198, 199, 200, 201, 202, 226, 228, 229, 241, 254, 272
Campagna, Marquis of 7, 37*, 39*, 43, 48
Campbell, Thomas 392
Cannon (furnace man) 124, 131
Canova, Antonio 58, 63*
Carlyle, Thomas 10
Carpenter, Francis Bicknell 298
Carpenter, William Benjamin 9, 72*
Carpenter, Willie 171
Carpenter, Mrs. (friend of Catharine Sedgwick) 154
Carrington, Henry Beebee 243
Cary, Alice 174
Caspari, Carl Gottlob 280
Cass, Lewis 65, 66
Catherine de Médicis, Queen of France 60
Cavour, Camillo 131
Chalmers, Thomas 109, 110
Chambers, Messrs. W. & R. 208
Chandler, Joseph Ripley 69, 70
Chandler, Zacariah 341
Chapman, Mr. & Mrs. John Gadsby 3, 7, 15, 16, 17, 18, 19, 21, 22, 30, 44, 46, 55, 91, 124
Chapman, Maria Weston 249
Chappel, Alonzo 80
Charles Albert, King of Savoy 63
Charles V, of Holy Roman Empire (Charles I of Spain) 58, 63
Charley (Roslyn servant) 115
Charlotte (Roslyn servant) 282

Chase, Salmon Portland 3, 78, 99, 100, 135, 184, 189, 192, 193, 199, 200, 201, 202, 212, 227, 230, 233, 234, 241, 248, 249, 253, 256, 290, 298, 299, 307, 327, 328, 336, 356, 368, 413, 414, 428
Chatelain, Jean-Baptiste François de 147, 148*, 328, 346
Chaucer, Geoffrey 147, 149
Cheney, Theseus Apoleon 378
Child, Lydia Maria Frances 429
Cicero, Marcus Tullius 7, 414
Clark, Alonzo 327
Clark, Jonas Gilman 107
Clark, Lewis Gaylord 214
Clark, Mrs. (of Great Barrington?) 325, 378
Clay, Cassius Marcellus 152, 153*, 202, 203, 272
Clay, Henry 133, 355
Cline, David 387, 399, 403
Cline, Mr. & Mrs. George B. 1, 71, 72, 99, 127, 128, 244–245, 249, 257, 274, 282, 295, 305, 319, 355, 373, 384, 386, 388, 391, 394, 499, 402, 409
Cline, William Bryant 373, 374*, 399, 403
Cline, Mrs. (mother of George B. Cline) 376, 377, 378, 381
Cobb, Howell 201, 202
Cobden, Richard 1, 80, 108, 138, 139, 355, 356, 357
Cockle, John 136, 234, 336*
Codding, Ichabod 360, 361*, 429
Codding, Maria P. (Mrs. Ichabod Codding) 420
Cole, Thomas 71, 80, 134, 355
Coleridge, Samuel Taylor 35, 384
Colton, G. L. 222
Condon, Mr. & Mrs. (Roslyn boardinghouse keepers?) 391, 392
Conway, T. W. 234–235
Cookson, Henry Wilkinson 9, 72*
Cooper, James Fenimore 54, 106, 107, 134, 194, 200
Cooper, Peter 91, 427
Cornelius, Peter von 34–35
Corning (of Hartford, Connecticut?) 382
Coronado, Caroline (Mrs. Horatio J. Perry) 79, 149
Cowper, William 308, 309
Cox, Samuel Hanson 285*, 325, 326, 332
Coxetter, Louis Mitchell 230
Cozzens, Frederick Swartwout 83
Cranch, Mr. & Mrs. Christopher Pearse 9, 68, 69*
Cronkhite, James P. 1, 55
Cropsey, Mr. & Mrs. Jaspar Francis 9–10, 71, 72*

Cunningham, Emma Augustus 97
Curtis, George William 151, 193, 282, 367, 370

Dana, Charles Anderson 130
Dana, Charlotte 89, 90, 106, 120, 155–156, 175, 200, 291, 305, 308, 416
Dana, Edmund Trowbridge (1818–1869) 290, 291, 309
Dana, Richard Henry 3, 4, 80, 89, 90, 106, 120, 134, 155, 156, 161, 162, 175, 193, 211, 213, 214, 290, 305, 306, 308, 338, 339, 415, 416, 425, 426
Dana, Richard Henry, Jr. 120, 156–157, 291, 292, 426
Dante Alighieri 8
Davis, Henry Winter 388, 389
Davis, Jefferson 396, 397
Day, Judge (Orville Dewey's cousin) 380
Dee (of Princeton, Illinois?) 158, 218
Defoe, Daniel 152
Demosthenes 37, 43
Dentzel, Mary J. 283
Derby & Jackson 123
Dewey, Charles 315
Dewey, Chester 117
Dewey, Jerusha 37, 132, 260, 293, 428
Dewey, Louisa Farnham (Mrs. Orville Dewey) 27, 82, 108, 151, 152, 160, 161, 164, 167, 193, 210, 211, 213, 232, 263, 325, 329, 330, 399, 402, 407
Dewey, Mary 380
Dewey, Mary E. 37, 82, 232, 233
Dewey, Orville 3, 4, 10, 36, 80, 82, 83, 106, 108, 114, 151, 152, 160, 161, 163, 164, 167, 193, 210, 211, 213, 232, 233, 249, 262, 263, 268, 309–310, 315, 321, 325, 327, 329, 330, 339, 380, 399, 402, 407, 414
Dickens, Charles 9, 351
Dithmar, Henry 104, 105*, 145, 304
Dix, John Adams 201, 202, 240, 427
Dix [John Homer?] 155, 156
Dodge, Robert 335
Dodge, William Earl 271, 427*
Douglas, Stephen A. 1, 13, 14*, 78*, 96, 99*, 139–140*, 266
Douglass, Frederick 344
Downing, Obadiah J. 275–276*, 292*
Doyle, Richard 9, 72*
Draper, Simeon 340, 403, 426
Drouyn de Lhuys, Eduard 286, 287
Duggan, Paul Peter 9, 71, 72*
Durand, Asher Brown 16, 80, 90, 91, 102, 331
Durand, John 16, 44, 80, 91, 102, 285, 331
Durand, Mary Frank (Mrs. Asher Brown Durand) 16
Durfee, Calvin 117, 118

Eastman, Henry W. 297*, 399
Eben, Charles Theodore 343
Eckel, Christian G. 144, 145
Edmonds, John Worth 140
Edward I of England 10
Effingham, Mrs. (London landlady) 9, 71
Elliott, Charles Loring 305, 306
Ellsworth, Elmer Ephraim 220, 221
Ely, Samuel R. 152, 160, 164, 167, 170, 171*, 172, 208, 282, 284, 305, 324, 360, 373, 375, 377, 379, 385, 386, 399, 400
Ely, William 273
Emerson, Ralph Waldo 3, 10, 69, 339, 342, 351, 353, 414
Emerson family (of Princeton, Illinois?) 313
Ericsson, John 195, 260*
Esperanza (Godwin servant?) 333
Espy, James Pollard 163, 164
Everett, Edward 101, 102, 148, 175, 203, 222

Fagnani, Giuseppe 355
Fairchild, Edwin 379, 380*, 384
Fairchild, Mr. & Mrs. Egbert Nelson 79, 85, 107, 108, 248–249, 278, 327, 341, 343, 344
Fairchild, Sarah 85
Fairfield, Sumner Lincoln 350
Faulkner, A. D. 170
Faulkner, Mrs. (New York boardinghouse keeper?) 154
Fauriel, Claude Charles 123
Faustina the Elder (consort of Emperor Antoninus) 15, 16
Fay, Theodore Sedgwick 269, 270
Ferdinand II of the Two Sicilies 26
Fessenden, William Pitt 3, 244, 297, 298*, 299, 413–414, 426, 427
Field, Alfred 10, 11, 23, 24, 82, 83, 124, 316, 317
Field, Charlotte Errington (Mrs. Alfred Field) 11, 23, 24, 82, 126, 371
Field, Cyrus West 166, 315
Field, David Dudley 133, 154, 184, 216, 254, 268, 269, 284, 388, 389, 401
Field, Edwin Wilkins 9, 10, 71, 72, 82, 300, 301, 317
Field, Ferdinand Emans 10, 24, 71, 72, 77, 82, 84, 85, 98, 238
Field, Mary Bryan Stone (Mrs. Cyrus West Field) 329, 348
Field (engineer for Roslyn cemetery) 376, 380, 381, 390, 391
Fields, James Thomas 3, 176, 177, 196, 205, 226, 300, 333, 334, 335, 357, 411, 412, 418
Figanière, Frederico Francisco de la 204–205
Figanière, Joaquin de la, 204
Fillmore, Millard 100
Fish, Elisha 319

Fish, Hamilton 6, 21, 22, 133, 347, 396, 397
Fish, Julia Kean (Mrs. Hamilton Fish) 6, 347
Fitch, Ebenezer 117, 118
Flanders, Benjamin Franklin 295
Flower, Charles Edward 10, 83*
Flower, Mr. & Mrs. Edward Fordham 10, 11, 76, 77*, 82, 83
Flower, Richard 83
Folsom, Mr. & Mrs. Charles 181, 182
Fontana, Giuseppe 7, 29*
Foote, Andrew Hull 283, 284
Forbes, John Murray 4, 80, 135, 228–229*, 230, 241, 246, 252, 276, 340, 341, 402, 403, 414
Forrest, Catherine Norton Sinclair (Mrs. Edwin Forrest) 104, 105
Forrest, Edwin 104, 105
Foster (publisher) 345
Fowler, J. W. 426
Fox, Gustavus 341, 397, 398*
Franklin, Benjamin 102
Frederick (Bryant coachman) 171, 274
Freiligrath, Ferdinand 204
Frémont, John Charles 96, 97, 99, 159, 195, 363
Freneau, Philip 343
Fuller, Dudley B. 367
Fuller, Thomas 300*, 318
Furness, William Henry 244

Gallup, Charles 264
Gardner, L. M. 128
Garibaldi, Giuseppe 175
Garrick, David 11
Garrison, William Lloyd 249, 267*
Gell, William 32
Gibbs, Alfred 411
Gibbs, Wolcott 427
Gibson, Christiana M. 3, 47, 49, 85, 107, 113, 121, 142, 165, 295, 310–311, 317, 349, 389, 390
Gibson, John (Liverpool sculptor) 43, 44, 45
Gifford, Sanford Robinson 80
Gillilan (of Newport, Rhode Island?) 174
Gilman, Daniel Coit 93, 124, 301, 412
[Giulay?] General (Austrian governor of Sardinia) 60, 63
Godwin, Alfred 1, 133, 141*, 156, 161
Godwin, Annie 170, 171, 261, 273, 281, 282, 373, 407
Godwin, Fanny (1854–1923; Mrs. Alfred White) 278
Godwin, Fanny Bryant (Mrs. Parke Godwin) 1, 3, 11, 36, 48, 56, 57, 70, 84, 98, 99, 107, 113, 138, 142, 158, 166, 171, 172, 177, 210, 211, 219, 220, 226, 231, 236, 245, 248, 261, 273, 274, 277, 278, 287, 293, 295, 317, 323, 324, 325, 333, 341, 371, 373, 376, 377, 378, 380, 381, 383, 386, 388, 391, 392, 393, 394,

395, 396, 399, 400, 401, 402, 403, 405, 407, 408, 409, 415, 416, 419, 422, 425, 428
Godwin, Harold 138, 248*, 277, 278, 325, 385, 403, 408, 416
Godwin, Martha Parke (Mrs. Abraham Godwin) 138, 139
Godwin, Minna 170, 171, 226, 261, 273, 274, 278, 323, 376, 386, 401, 403
Godwin, Nora 323, 377, 400, 402, 403, 404, 408, 409, 416
Godwin, Parke 1, 45, 71, 79, 98, 116, 126, 138, 142, 149, 150–151, 166, 193, 194, 200, 218, 220, 235, 236, 248, 275, 278, 282, 295, 314, 317, 318, 320, 322, 323, 341, 345, 368, 373, 376, 388, 392, 395, 396, 400, 403, 415, 416, 428
Godwin, Walter 236*, 273, 386
Godwin, William Bryant ("Willie") 11, 166, 170–171, 277, 278, 320, 324, 394
Goethe, Ottilie von 7
Goodall, Walter 9, 72*
Goodman, A[lfred?] T. 276
Gookin, William Stoodly 431, 432
Gordon, Miss (Godwin nursemaid) 170, 171
Gourlie, John Hamilton 13, 14, 16, 91, 124, 153, 210
Graham, John A. 178
Grant, Ulysses Simpson 1, 243, 246, 276–277*, 339, 340, 341, 363, 364, 427
Gray, Asa 213, 214
Gray, John Alexander Clinton 258
Gray, John Franklin 49, 50, 86, 91, 124, 310
Gray (newspaper writer) 252
Greeley, Horace 91, 150, 183, 244, 340, 397, 427
[Green, William Henry?] ("Professor Greene") 302
Green & Nelson 67
Greene, George Washington 148, 149
Greenough, Richard Saltonstall 9
Griffin, Richard, & Co. 121, 122
Griswold, Rufus 106
Gurney, J., & Son 274, 275
Guy (Adirondack traveler) 391

Haggerty, Ogden 224
Hahnemann, Samuel 280
Hall, Anna Maria Fielding (Mrs. Samuel Carter Hall) 73
Hall, Samuel Carter 73
Halleck, Fitz-Greene 94, 148–149
Halleck, Henry Wager 269*, 290, 291
Halpine, Charles Graham ("Miles O'Reilly") 314
Hamilton, Andrew Jackson 427
Hamilton (Roslyn schoolteacher) 324
Hamlin, Hannibal 180, 181*, 183
Hammond, Jabez D. 126

Hammond, James Henry 99, 100
Hammond, J. H. 227
Hanscom (*Evening Post* correspondent) 96, 97
Hardinge, Emma 256, 257
Harper, Joseph Wesley 11, 85*
Harris, J. Dennis 169
Harris, Thomas Lake 140–141
Hart, C[harles?] H[enry?] 285, 286
Hart (china merchant) 170
Harvey, George 3, 100, 101, 430, 431
Hatfield, Julia 323
Havemeyer, William Frederick 129–130, 131
Hawthorne, Nathaniel 1, 7, 8, 41, 42, 43, 54
Hawthorne, Sophia Peabody (Mrs. Nathaniel Hawthorne) 7, 8, 41, 43, 54
Hays (Cleveland, Ohio, doctor) 220, 221
Heath, Mrs. (New York boardinghouse keeper) 273
Heenan, John Carmel ("The Bernica Boy") 292
Helper, Hinton Rowan 81
Hemans, Felicia Dorothea Browne 326
Henderson, Esther Fairchild (Mrs. Allen Henderson) 172, 278
Henderson, Hannah 172
Henderson, Isaac 1, 9, 11, 18, 19, 29, 65, 66, 79, 93, 95, 96, 104, 111, 142, 144, 145, 148, 218, 237, 248, 272, 275, 294, 320, 326, 340, 363, 364, 366, 367, 369–370, 379, 384, 388, 396, 398, 402, 408
Henderson, Mrs. Isaac 248, 272, 273, 274, 373, 374, 376
Henry, Joseph 427
Henry IV of France 309, 310
Henry (Roslyn laborer) 295, 373
Hepp, Julie 283
Herbert, Lady (at Florence) 8
Hering, Constantin 280
Hicks, Thomas 80
Hildreth, Richard 124, 126
Hillhouse, Thomas 275
Hills, Alfred C. 97
Hitchcock, Ethan Allen 243, 268, 269*
Hoe, Robert, & Co. 104, 105
Hoffman, Michael 234*, 336
Hogeboom, John T. 199, 200
Holmes, Oliver Wendell 339, 342, 352
Holt, Joseph 228, 229
Holte, Thomas 83
Home, Daniel Dunglas 7
Homer 245, 302–303, 308–309
Hood, John Bell 374
Hooker, Joseph 307
Hopkins, Charles W. 261, 333
Hopkins, Jenny 170, 171, 274, 374, 376, 377, 381, 388, 391, 392, 393, 399, 400
Hopkins, Louise 274, 388, 391, 392, 393, 399

Hopkins, Mina (Mrs. Charles W. Hopkins) 172, 278, 325, 378, 379
Horace 47, 251
Hosmer, Harriet Goodhue 41, 43
Hovey, Charles Edward 284
Howard, Caroline R. 417, 418*, 428?, 429
Howard, Oliver Otis 307
Howe, Julia Ward 3, 422, 423*
Howe, Samuel 213
Howe, Sarah Lydia Robbins (Mrs. Samuel Howe) 213, 249
Howells, William Dean 196
Howland (Godwin guest) 376, 379, 391
Hows, John Augustus 189, 190*, 293, 294
[Hubbard?] Frederick G. 332
Hubbard, Henry 332
Hudson, Henry Norman 314
Hulbert, Charles Augustus 71, 72
Hull, A. Cooke 310
Hunt, Richard Morris 427
Hunt, Wilson G. 116
Hunter, David 314
Huntington, Daniel 9, 71, 72, 306, 342, 367
Hyde, Thomas C. P. 330, 331

Iggulden *et Cie.* 42
Ingham, Charles Cromwell 80
Irvin, Professor (at Roslyn convention) 170
Irving, Washington 1, 11, 80, 83, 107, 128, 133, 134, 146, 148, 149, 152, 155, 156, 157, 158, 160, 162, 164, 167, 189, 190, 206, 209, 214, 351
Irving (New York boarder) 272
Isaac (Godwin servant?) 273
Ives, Estelle (Mrs. John Milton Mackie) 5, 8, 9, 12, 19, 23, 24, 25, 26, 27, 28, 36, 40, 41, 42, 44, 48, 52, 53, 56, 67, 69, 85, 91, 109, 115*, 168
Ives, Pamela Bushnell (Mrs. David Ives) 115, 328

Jackson, Andrew 197
Jacob (Roslyn laborer) 320, 321
James, Henry 139
Jameson, Anna Brownell 7, 9, 64, 65*
Jay, John (1817–1894), 133, 136, 249
Jefferson, Thomas 102–103
Jenkins, Charles 118, 119
John (Roslyn laborer) 320, 321
Johnson, Andrew 339, 389*
Johnson, Oliver 266, 267*, 343
Johnson, Samuel 11, 83, 161, 162, 291, 292
Jônain, Pierre-Abraham 288, 289
Jones, Alfred 91, 92
Juárez, Benito Pablo 382

Kaye (of Evesham, England) 84
Kemble, Fanny 7, 65
Kennedy, John Pendleton 6, 347
Kensett, John Frederick 3, 351, 355, 367
Ketchum, Morris 356
Key, Philip Barton 104, 105
Kilborn (Jersey City, New Jersey, poet) 281
King, Charles 268, 269
King, John Alsop 292
King, Preston 78, 134, 183
King, Rufus 292
Kingman, Bradford 231, 232*, 331
Kinne, Asa 137
Kinne, Eveneline J. 137
Kirby, J. M. 305
Kirkland, Caroline Matilda Stansbury 3, 38, 131, 211, 326, 327, 328, 329, 330, 333, 339, 392
Kirkland, Cordelia 392
Kirkland, Elizabeth ("Lizzie") 332, 333*, 377*
Knapp, Frederick N. 384
Kolisch (Bigelow's steward) 303, 311, 312

Lamb, Charles 92
Landa, Juan Trabado de 41
Lander, Frederick West 259
Lardner, Rev. & Mrs. Dionysius 5, 112
Larned, Sylvester 118, 119
Laun, Adolf 264, 265*, 288, 289
Laurence, Samuel 45
Lawrence (friend of John H. Gourlie) 15
Leach Giro, William 40
Le Clerc, Miss (schoolteacher) 48
Ledyard, Mrs. (Bryant friend in New York) 278
Ledyard (West Point cadet) 278
Leavenworth, Elias 187
Lee, D. W. 122
Lee, Robert Edward 81, 244, 291*, 339, 340, 363
Lee, Mrs. Gideon 44, 45
Leeds, Henry H. 431
Leeds & Miner 430, 431
Leggett, Augustus W. 297
Leggett, Susan 376
Leggett, William 80
Leslie, Charles Robert 207
L'Estrange, Sir Roger 152
Leupp, Charles Mortimer 1, 14, 16, 43, 80, 91, 108, 122, 133
Lever, Charles James 8, 54*
Lever & Francis 303
Lewis, Sarah S. 364, 387
Lewis, William David 85
Lieber, Francis 271, 427
Lincoln, Abraham 1, 3, 4, 11, 72, 78, 93, 133–134, 135, 140, 142, 143, 149, 159, 160, 169, 173, 180, 182, 183, 184, 186, 187, 188, 189, 192, 193, 195, 196, 197, 198, 199, 200, 201, 202, 203, 205, 206, 208, 209, 211, 212, 215, 216, 218, 220, 224, 228, 229, 234, 239, 240, 241, 242, 243, 253, 254, 255, 258, 265, 266, 268, 269, 270, 271, 272, 278, 279, 287, 296, 297, 298, 299, 307, 314, 320, 339, 340, 341, 361, 363, 364, 365–366, 368, 369, 388, 389, 397, 398, 401, 402, 403, 408, 413, 414, 420, 421, 428
Lincoln, Solomon, Jr. 215
Lindley, John 108, 109
Lippincott, J. B., & Co. 208
Livingston, Mrs. (mother of Mrs. Joseph Alden) 375
Lockwood (of Roslyn) 257
Longfellow, Henry Wadsworth 3, 134, 146, 175, 193, 204, 213, 335, 337, 339, 342, 344, 347, 350, 351, 427
Loop, Henry Augustus 8, 9, 67*
Lord [John?] 102
Loring, Charles Greely 300, 301*, 317
Losee, Mr. & Mrs. James 257*, 373, 374, 381, 390, 399
Loudon, John Claudius 108, 109
Lovejoy, Elijah 242
Lovejoy, Eunice C. S. D. (Mrs. Owen Lovejoy) 361
Lovejoy, Owen 1, 135, 183, 242, 341, 360, 361
Low, Abiel Abbott 356, 357
Low, A. A., & Bros. 357
Lowell, James Russell 3, 177, 204, 205, 342, 343, 352
Luquer, Eloise Elizabeth Payne 352*, 353, 355, 358, 373

MacDonough, August R. 368, 419*
McClellan, George Brinton 242, 243, 244, 255*, 268, 269, 279, 339, 341, 389, 399, 404
McClure, Agnes 375
McCormick, Richard Cunningham 170?, 202, 203*
McDowell, Irvin 255
McKibbin (boardinghouse agent) 131
McNally, Mr./Major (of Roslyn) 379

Mackie, John Milton 115*, 231
Mackie, Estelle Ives (see Ives, Estelle)
Mahan, Dennis 243
Manly (foreman, Evening Post printing office) 395
Manning, W. C. 94
Maqua[y?] (at Florence) 50
Marble, Manton Malone 93*, 243
Marcy, Erastus Edgerton 327
Marcy, William L. 13, 14
Margarita (Roslyn servant) 142, 313, 318

Maria (Roslyn servant) 274
Mario, Jessie White 111, 112
Marius, Caius 38
Marsden, Mrs. (Naples acquaintance) 28, 29, 69
Marsh, Alfred J. 97
Marsh, George Perkins 259
Marshall, D. T. 150
Mary (Roslyn servant) 376, 381, 382
Mason, James Murray 196, 236, 237*
Mason, John Young 14
Massett, Stephen C. 362
Mather (of Princeton, Illinois) 221, 222
Mathews, William T. 80
Mathews (owner of Leasowe's) 82
Mayer, Brantz 137
Maximilian, Archduke Ferdinand, Emperor of Mexico 382
Meade, George Gordon 244
Mercier, Victor 92
Michelangelo (Michelangelo Buonarroti) 35
Miller, Mr. & Mrs. [Charles E.?] 248?, 375, 376, 377, 419
Miller (attorney) 407
Milne, Alexander, first baronet, and Lady Milne 329
Milton, John 63, 161
Miner, Allen B. 431
Mitchell, Clark Ward 54, 395–396, 404, 405
Mitchell, Elisha 54*, 396
Mitchell, Ellen Theresa Shaw (Mrs. Clark Ward Mitchell) 53, 264, 319, 322, 395, 397, 402, 403, 404, 405, 406, 407, 416
Mitchell, Frances Bryant 54
Mitchell, Sarah Louisa 403, 404*, 405, 406, 407, 416
Montfort, Simon de, Earl of Leicester 10
Moore, Augusta 383, 385
Morgan, Edwin Denison 3, 136, 144, 146, 147, 150, 262, 289, 292, 294, 300, 314, 315*, 332
Morgan, John Hunt 401
Morgan, Mr. & Mrs. Junius Spencer 11, 70*, 85
Morrill, Justin Smith 229, 230
Morris, George Pope 147, 174
Morris, Philip Van Ness 118, 119
Morton, Agnes V. 349
Morton, Thomas 142
Mott, James 379
Mott, Lucretia Coffin (Mrs. James Mott) 379
[Moulton?] David 399
Moulton, Joseph White 46, 47, 225, 247, 282, 286, 301, 302
Moulton, Leonice Marston Sampson (Mrs. Joseph White Moulton) 3, 45, 102, 216, 217, 219, 224, 226, 247, 250, 251, 254, 257, 282, 286, 299, 301, 302, 399, 405

Mozier, Joseph 7, 55, 56
Mudge, Amy 274, 277, 348
Mudge, Elizabeth 348
Mulready, William 10, 71, 72*
Munroe, John, & Co. 12, 18, 41, 52, 63, 64, 66, 85, 226
Myers, Mrs. (domestic service agent) 116

Nash, James 233
Nelson, Mr. & Mrs. Lorenzo 127, 128*, 170, 172
Newbold, Miss (autograph collector) 214
Nordhoff, Mr. & Mrs. Charles 1, 194, 390, 391*
Northrop, William 118, 119
Norton, Charles Eliot 244
Nostrand, C. P. 297*, 324
Noyes, William Curtis 216*, 268

Ogden, William Butler 85, 87, 166, 220, 221
Olds, Charity Louisa Bryant (Mrs. Justin H. Olds) 100, 220, 221, 345
Olds, Justin H. 122, 123, 238, 313
Olds, Sarah Snell 100*, 282, 313, 319
Oliphant, Lawrence 141
Olmsted, Frederick Law 1, 79, 99*, 108*, 194, 243, 356, 384
Olmsted, John Hull 108
Olmsted, Mary Cleveland Bryant (Mrs. Frederick Law Olmsted) 108
Opdyke, George 116*, 129, 198, 199, 200, 201, 202, 252, 268, 401
Ordronaux, John 46, 47*, 226
"O'Reilly, Miles" (see Halpine, Charles Graham)
Orr, Hector 110*, 116
Orton, Azariah Giles 118, 119
Osborn, William Henry 80, 121*, 235, 277, 357, 396, 397
Osgood, Samuel 249, 250*, 352, 353
O'Shea & Co. 12
Owen, Mary Jane Robinson (Mrs. Robert Dale Owen) 5, 16, 28, 29, 267
Owen, Robert Dale 5, 6, 7, 16*, 19, 21, 28, 29, 69, 70, 140, 141, 242, 266, 267

Packenham & Hooker 66
Palfrey, John Gorham 213, 214
Parsons, Theophilus 213
Parton, James 361
Paton, John Brown 109, 110
Patterson, Miss (seamstress) 374
Payne, John Howard 352–353*
Payne, Thatcher Taylor 352
Peabody, George 9
Peabody & Co. 70
Pease, E. D. 337, 338
Peel, Robert 108

Pell, Alfred 138, 139, 395, 396
Pell, Joshua L. 312–313*, 370–371
Pendleton, George Hunt 389
Perkins, F. S. 132
Perry, Amos 351, 352*, 353, 355, 358
Phillips, Willard 193, 211, 213, 214
Pickering, Edward 213, 214
Pierce, Henry Lillie 102, 103
Pierson, Henry N. 355, 356
Pius IX 32, 34, 35, 46
Pliny the Elder (Caius Plinius Secundus) 70
Poe, Edgar Allan 343
Polk, James Knox 197
Pollitz, Emma 380, 386
Pollitz, Mr. & Mrs. O. W. 282, 283*, 390, 400
Pompey the Great 38
Pope, Alexander 177, 412
Pope, John 268, 269
Porter, Elbert Stothoff 318
Porter, G[eorge?] W. 141*, 379, 410
Powers, Mr. & Mrs. Hiram 3, 8, 52, 53, 54, 171, 334, 355
Powers, Horatio Nelson 270, 271, 391–392
Prentice, George Dennison 175
Putnam, George Haven 134, 143*
Putnam, George Palmer 143, 156, 160, 427

Quincy, Josiah 92*, 167, 175, 177, 178, 206–208, 369, 370, 372
Quincy [Miss?] (sister of Anna Cabot Lowell Quincy Waterston) 177

Rackemann, Mr. & Mrs. (Sedgwick family friends) 153, 154
Radetzky, Joseph Wenzel, 60, 63
Rankin, Mr. & Mrs. (of Glasgow, Scotland) 48
Raphael (Raffaello Sanzio) 7, 35, 66, 67, 91
Ray, Charles H. 192, 199*
Raymond, Henry Jarvis 279, 340, 402, 403, 427
Reed, James 251–252, 327, 328
Reed (Eagleswood School principal) 384
Remington, Albert Gallatin 408, 409
Reni, Guido 35, 91
Rice, Harvey 320
Richards, Edward E. 207, 208
Ripley, Sophia Dana (Mrs. George Ripley) 155
Ristori, Adelaide 9
Robbins, Eliza 249
Robinson, Henry Crabb 9
Robinson [Edward?] 145
Rockwell, Rev. (of Kiskytom, New York) 400
Rockwood, George Gardner 350–351
Rogers, Charles H. 20, 21
Rogers, Randolph 55, 56
Rogers, Samuel 9

Rogers, Mrs. (of Easthampton, New York) 282
Romano (Neapolitan artist) 25
Romer, Leo 204
Romero, Matías 381, 382
Roscoe, Thomas 123
Rosecrans, William Starke 284
Roskilly, Dr. (Helen Waterston's physician at Naples) 70
[Roth?] Miss (of Cooper Institute) 343
Rothermel, Peter 8
Rubini, Rocco 5, 7, 17*, 20, 21, 23, 28, 30, 38, 49, 50, 51, 70
Russell, A. T. 210
Ruskin, John 9

Sadler, Thomas 9
Sainte-Beuve, Charles Augustin 137, 139, 140
Sands, Julia M. 85, 146, 373, 374
Satterlee, Mrs. (boardinghouse keeper) 267
Savage, Joseph L. 365, 366, 367
Saxe, John Godfrey 174
Sayers, Tom ("The Little Wonder") 292
Schiller, Johann Christoph Friedrich von 2
Schlegel, Friedrich von 94
Schultz, Jackson S. 140
Scott, Leonard 257
Scott, Walter 11
Scott, Winfield 237, 240
Sedgwick, Catharine Maria 80, 132, 153, 154, 164, 339, 379, 381, 382
Sedgwick, Charles Frederick, Jr. 118, 119*, 322
Sedgwick, Elizabeth Ellery (Mrs. Robert Sedgwick) 6, 17, 18, 19, 21, 67, 154, 271
Sedgwick, Grace Ashburner 9, 17, 21, 67*
Sedgwick, Henry Dwight (1785–1831) 271
Sedgwick, Henry Dwight (1824–1903) 153, 271*
Sedgwick, Jane 9, 17, 21, 67*
Sedgwick, Theodore III 1, 80, 125, 127, 133
Seevoss, E. B. 101, 102
Semmes, Raphael 230
Seneca, Lucius Annaeus 37, 43
Seward, William Henry 78, 96, 97, 99, 129, 130, 131, 133, 134, 135, 140, 143, 146, 148, 149, 159, 183, 184, 188–189, 192, 193, 197, 199, 200, 212, 228, 229, 237, 242, 270, 297, 298, 299, 340, 352, 367, 403
Seymour, Horatio 279*, 287
Shakespeare, William 339, 352
Sharpe, Samuel 9, 72*
Shaw, Lemuel 190, 191
Shaw, Samuel 54
Shenstone, William 11, 82, 83*
Sheridan, Philip Henry 341
Sherman, C. E. K. 102
Sherman, John 81, 229, 230*

Sherman, William Tecumseh 246, 341, 363, 364*, 374
Sherwood, William 261, 281
Sibley, Henry Hastings 263
Sickles, Daniel Edgar 104, 105
Sigel, Franz 307, 308
Sigourney, Lydia Howard Huntley 174, 326, 327, 417, 420, 423
Sismonde de Sismondi, J. C. L. 123
Sims, Thomas 301
Sinopoli (Neapolitan doctor) 49, 51
Skillman, Francis 247
Slidell, John 196, 236, 237*
Slosson, John 222
Smith, Buckingham 12
Smith, Caleb Blood 228, 229
Smith, Goldwin 414, 415
Smith, John Somers 12
Smith, Rebecca 170?, 278*
Smith, Stephen 257, 258
Smith, Timothy 250
Smith (East River ferryman) 261
Smith, Mrs. (Roslyn sexton's wife) 377, 378, 381
Snell, Thomas 235, 304
Snell, William Wingate 235*, 251, 422
Snow, Mrs. (William Ely's mother-in-law) 273
Socrates 37
Soulé, Pierre 14
Sparks, Mr. & Mrs. Jared 213
Spence, Mr. & Mrs. Carroll 5, 13, 14*
Spencer, Bella Zilfa (Mrs. George Eliphaz Spencer) 424
Spencer, George Eliphaz 424
Spencer, John Canfield 157, 158
Sperry, Mrs. (New York boardinghouse keeper) 273
Spring, Edward Adolphus 384
Spring, Marcus 40, 384
Spring, Rebecca Buffum (Mrs. Marcus Spring) 40, 384
Stabler, Frances D. 103
Stansbury, Edward A. 39, 205, 367
Stanton, Daniel 393
Stanton, Edwin McMasters 3, 229*, 241, 254, 255, 267, 269, 284, 345, 346, 411
Stanton, Elizabeth Cady 379
Starkweather, H. A. 186
Stasia (Roslyn servant) 115
Stebbins, Emma 55, 56
Stephens, Alexander Hamilton 396, 397
Stevens, John Austin 106*, 356
Stevens, Thaddeus 242
Stevenson, Andrew 65, 66
Stewart, Alexander Turney 271, 432*
Stewart, Leonice Josephine Moulton (Mrs. John Stewart) 216, 217, 299, 323?, 391?, 396?

Stewart, Sara Wool 299
Stillman, Thomas Edgar 259, 260
Story, Emelyn (Mrs. William Wetmore Story) 41, 43
Story, William Wetmore 8, 43
Stowe, Harriet Beecher 3, 393, 394*
Strutt, Edward, first Baron Helper 111, 112
Stuart, Ellen Elizabeth Cairns (Mrs. Robert Stuart) 250, 278, 407
Stuart, Robert 278, 294, 399, 404
Sturges, Jonathan 121
Sturtevant, Julian Monson 360, 361
Sumner, Charles 3, 9, 42, 64, 65, 241, 242, 255, 256, 305
Susan (New York servant?) 403
Syracuse, Prince of 26

Taber, Samuel T. 348
Taine, Hippolyte Adolphe 390
Taney, Roger Brooke 413, 414
Tasso, Torquato 8
Taylor, Bayard 272, 367
Taylor, Jeremy 318
Taylor, Tom 72
Teall, O. D. 421, 422
Tebbetts, Horace B. 314–315
Tefft, Mr. & Mrs. Israel Keech 113
Tefft, Thomas Alexander 71
Tenerani, Pietro 58, 63
Terry, Luther 43, 44, 45, 55
Terry [N. M.?] 379*, 400, 401
Thackeray, William Makepeace 9
Thayer, William Sydney 1, 79, 96, 97, 106, 134, 138, 148, 149, 291
Thomas, George Henry 251
Thomas, Philip Francis 202
Thomas (Roslyn laborer), 320, 321, 373, 394, 400
Thompson, Mr. & Mrs. Cephas Giovanni 3, 7, 17, 18, 66, 67, 351
Thompson, Jacob 426
Thoreau, Henry David 98
Thorn, Henry 225
Tibullus, Albius 321
Ticknor, George 123
Ticknor & Fields 334, 350
Tilden, Samuel Jones 85, 86, 253, 421
Tillson, Christiana H. 405, 406
Tillson, Welcome 132
Titian (Tiziano Vercellio) 91, 334
Titus, Willet 297
Toombs, Robert Augustus 396, 397
Toucey, Isaac 229, 230
Townsend (book publisher) 200
Trumbull, Lyman 189, 193, 199
Tucker, Gideon J. 64
Tuckerman, Henry Theodore 48, 49, 213, 419

Tuttle, Rev. (of Pontiac, Michigan) 400, 401
Twain, Mark (Samuel Langhorne Clemens) 394
Tweedy, Mary Temple (Mrs. Edmund Tweedy) 139
Tweedy, Edmund 138, 139

Valentine, James 247*, 429
Valentine, Miss (of Roslyn) 429
Valerio, Lorenzo 9, 60–62, 63*
Valerio, (of New York) 154
Van Buren, John 367?
Van Buren, John Dash 256
Van Buren, Martin 79, 99, 100
Vanderpool, A. 368
Vanderpool, Barent 240
Vandeventer, Dr. & Mrs. (of Roslyn) 225, 226, 282, 324, 348, 391, 394, 399, 400
Varnum, Joseph B., Jr. 367
Vaux, Calvert 1, 79
Venturi, Carlos 12
Verplanck, Gulian Crommelin 3, 91, 92, 162, 306, 367, 368, 415
Victor Emmanuel II of Italy 131
Victoria, Queen of England 174
Vingut, Francisco Javier 350
Vingut, Gertrude Fairfield (widow of Francisco Javier Vingut) 350
Vinton, Francis 349–350
Virgil (Publius Vergilius Maro) 108, 285

Wade, Benjamin Franklin 129, 131
Wadsworth, James Samuel 243–244, 255, 268, 269, 279*
Walchner, Friedrich August 233
Walker, E., & Sons 211
Walker, Edward 211
Walker, James P. 121
Wallace, A. S. 279–280
Wanamaker, John 432
Ward, Townsend 182
Ward, Mrs. (daughter of Jacob Barker) 46
Ware, Mary Waterhouse (Mrs. William Ware) 213, 233
Ware, William 117
Warner, "Mrs. Dr." (guest of the George Clines) 379, 396
[Warren?] Dr. & Mrs. (guests at Bryant Festival) 419
Warrington, David 408, 409
Washington, George 68, 78, 203, 302
Waters, Catherine (see "Anonyma")
Waterston, Anna Cabot Lowell Quincy (Mrs. Robert Cassie Waterston) 6, 24, 25, 26, 27, 28, 42, 50, 73, 74, 75, 76, 77, 92, 107, 112, 167, 168, 175, 176, 177, 185, 189, 190, 193, 207,

213, 293, 295, 296, 369, 370, 372, 373, 374, 402, 419
Waterston, Helen Ruthven 6, 10, 24, 25*, 26, 27, 28, 41, 42, 50–51, 52, 67–68, 69, 70, 73–75, 76, 112, 166–167
Waterston, Robert Cassie 3, 4, 6, 10, 24, 25, 26, 27, 28, 41, 42, 50, 67, 69, 70, 73, 74, 75, 76, 77, 92, 107, 112, 166, 168, 172, 173, 174, 175, 176, 177–178, 185, 186, 189, 190, 193, 206, 207, 213, 293, 295, 296, 369, 370, 401, 402, 419
Webster, Daniel 65, 106, 133
Webster, Sarah Morris Fish (Mrs. Sidney Webster), 347
Weed, Thurlow 129, 131, 140, 183, 184, 188–189, 192, 193, 199, 212, 230, 340, 367, 403
Weeks (Roslyn shopkeeper) 324
Weir, John Ferguson 391, 392
Weir, Robert Walter 97, 98, 245, 392
Welles, Gideon 3, 184, 189, 192, 193, 198, 199, 200, 211, 212, 227, 229, 253–254, 259, 263, 340, 365, 366, 367, 397, 398
Wenzler, Anthon Henry 80
Wetmore, Prosper Montgomery 396, 397
Wheeler, Miss (companion of Minna Godwin) 376
White, Edwin 9, 68, 69*
White, Judge (of Washington) 297, 298
Whitman, Walt 116
Whitney, Erastus 345, 346
Whitney, Stephen 144, 145
Whittier, John Greenleaf 168, 190, 342
Whittredge, Worthington 351
Whitwell, Sophia L. 344
Wickham, W. H. 102
Wiggins (of Princeton?, Illinois) 345
Wilcox, Carlos 331
Wilder, Alexander 96, 97*, 105
Wilkes, Charles 196
Wilkie, "Old Mr." (of Roslyn) 386, 399
Williams, Fanny 295
Williams, Walter Francis 130, 131*, 169
Williams, Mrs. (boardinghouse keeper) 272, 273
Willis, Annie 36, 52*
Willis, Blanche 36, 52*
Willis, Cornelia Grinnell (Mrs. Nathaniel Parker Willis) 282, 283
Willis, Jessie (Mrs. Richard Storrs Willis) 36, 37, 48, 51–52, 88–89, 172
Willis, Jessie (b. 1858) 52–53*
Willis, Jessie (New York marriage broker) 97
Willis, Nathaniel Parker (104, 147, 174, 264, 282, 283, 427
Willis, Richard Storrs 36, 37, 85, 88, 172, 310, 311, 401, 407
Wilson, James Grant 153

Winans, Ross 178, 181
Winans, Thomas De Kay 178, 181
Winthrop, Robert Charles 134, 190*, 206, 209
Wise, Henry Alexander 138*, 139, 140, 255*
Witherspoon (of Roslyn) 381
Wood, Bradford Ripley 209
Wood, Fernando 129, 131
Wood, George 144, 145
Wood, Samuel J. 218–219
Woods, John H. 354
Wool, Mr. & Mrs. John Ellis 286, 299, 300

Wordsworth, William 72
Worth, William Jenkins 308
Wright, Silas 215
Wynne, James 215–216

Xerxes I of Persia 285

Young (New York artist?) 91

Zollicoffer, Felix Kirk 250, 251

Date Due

NOV 18 1980			
			UML 735